# Records of the Moravians Among the Cherokees

## March to Removal, Part 3

## In Their Own Voice — 'Power to Remove'

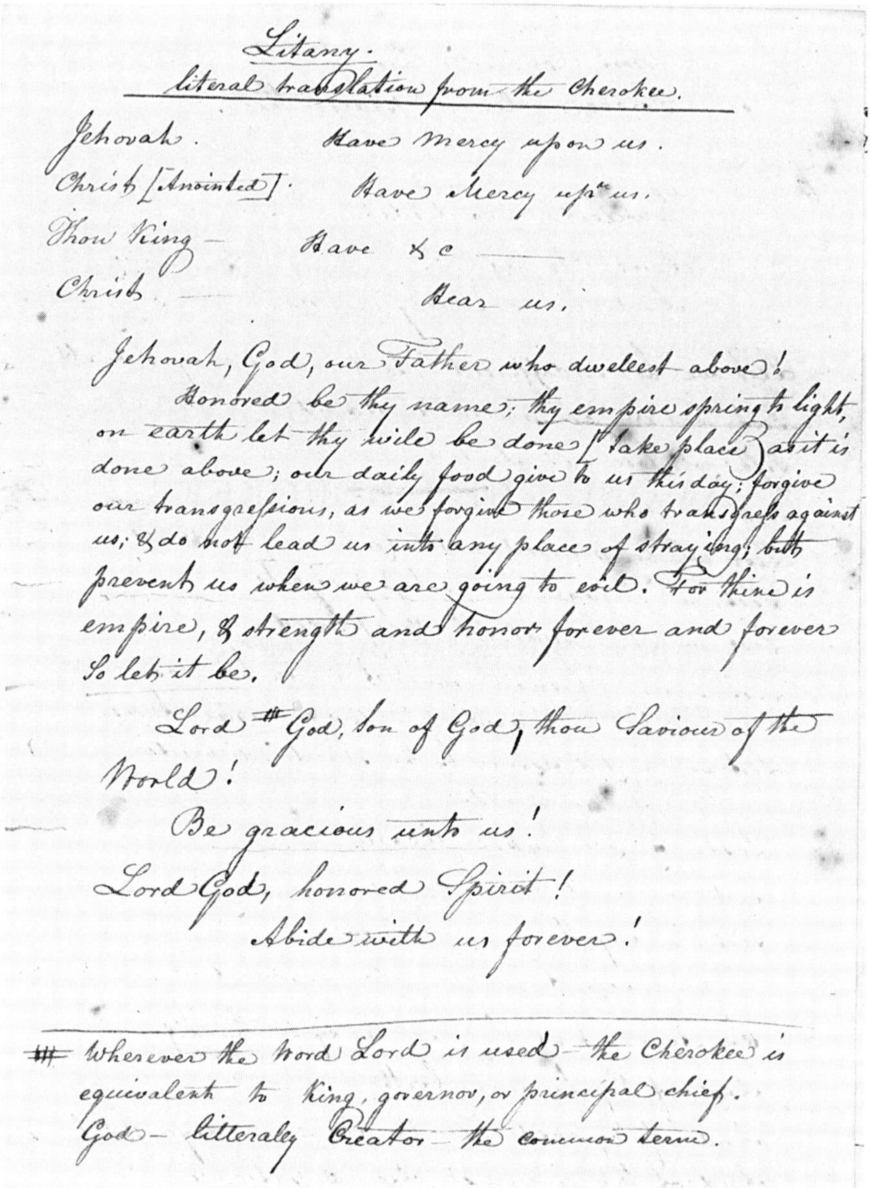

Litany.

literal translation from the Cherokee.

Jehovah. Have Mercy upon us.

Christ [Anointed]. Have Mercy upn us.

Thou King — Have &c —

Christ — Hear us.

Jehovah, God, our Father who dwellest above!

Honored be thy name; thy empire spring to light, on earth let thy will be done [take place] as it is done above; our daily food give to us this day; forgive our transgressions, as we forgive those who transgress against us; & do not lead us into any place of straying; but prevent us when we are going to evil. For thine is empire, & strength and honor forever and forever So let it be.

Lord # God, Son of God, thou Saviour of the World!

Be gracious unto us!

Lord God, honored Spirit!

Abide with us forever!

# Wherever the word Lord is used the Cherokee is equivalent to King, governor, or principal chief. God — litteraley Creator the common term.

*Page one of M 421-B-3, Br. Henry G. Clauder's copy of Samuel A. Worcester's retranslation of the Moravian Church Litany from the Cherokee translation. See the Litany, M 421-A-1, page 4206, and Rev. Worcester's cautionary note, M 411-1-30, page 4248.*

# Records of the Moravians Among the Cherokees

## MARCH TO REMOVAL, PART 3

## IN THEIR OWN VOICE — 'POWER TO REMOVE'

Volume 8

1828 – 1830

Richard W. Starbuck

Editor

Cherokee Heritage Press
Tahlequah
Oklahoma

Published by:
Cherokee Heritage Press, Tahlequah, Oklahoma,
a division of Cherokee National Historical Society, Inc.

Distributed by:
University of Oklahoma Press, Norman, Oklahoma

Funding for this project provided by:
Cherokee Nation
Eastern Band of Cherokee Indians
Cherokee Moravian Historical Association
Wachovia Historical Society
Friends of Moravian Archives

Library of Congress Control Number:
2017964172

ISBN 978-0-9994521-0-3

What the Nation would decide, they [the missionaries] did not know. According to some expressions they do not want to come under Georgia's laws, but neither do they want to migrate, and would rather let themselves be destroyed. They seemed also to want to get the thoughts of the United States Supreme Court concerning the validity of the various treaties which they have had up to now with the General Government, which have all been ratified and paid heed to in the Senate of the United States and by the Presidents up to the present. And if then they must go, they do not want to remain under the protection of the United States Government but to go somewhere else.

Provinzial Helfer Conferenz<br>
Salem, North Carolina<br>
July 30, 1830

Perhaps you think I did this completely without consideration. No! I have certainly considered it thoroughly before the Lord, and He also granted me the assurance that He will continue to help me as He has until now. The thought that I would perhaps separate myself from the Gemeine, in which I have already enjoyed so much good, caused me much concern. Indeed I owe a great debt of gratitude to it. However, I hope and also ask humbly that you not despise me and do not cast me out and that you still consider me a member of it, although I do not know if I will ever move close to a Gemeine.

Maria Rosina Gambold Copeland
Oochgeelogy, Cherokee Nation
to
Theodor Schulz
Salem, North Carolina
July 17, 1828

On the occasion of her marriage to Br. Alex Copeland without approval of the Lot * . She and her husband are buried in the Floyd Cemetery in Shelby County, Indiana, less than 10 miles north of Hope Moravian Church.

# *Contents*

# *Documents, Names, Quotes, etc.*

1828, part 4



1828, part 5



1828, part 6



1828, part 7



1828, part 8

The Jurnel of ower Trip



1829, part 3



1829, part 4



1829, part 5

1829, part 6



1829, part 7



1829, part 8



1830, part 1



1830, part 2

# *Introduction*

Volume 8 of *Records of the Moravians among the Cherokees* continues the ominously named subtitle series *March to Removal* with opposing themes: *In Their Own Voice — 'Power to Remove.'* Though volume 8 covers the shortest time span, 1828 to July 1830, it is the events of these years that seal the fate of the Cherokees east of the Mississippi. And the Moravian missionaries at Springplace and Oochgeelogy faithfully report almost daily as history unfolds before them.

With his syllabary, Sequoyah had devised the means for the Cherokees to write their own language. Now the Cherokees put it to use with a printing press and a newspaper to speak their opinions to one and all, both in their own language and in English. Missionary Gottlieb Byhan is so taken with the *Cherokee Phoenix* that he signs up seven subscriptions (3791) for his fellow Moravians back home in Salem, a church community of only 511 in North Carolina — perhaps the greatest concentration of subscribers outside the Cherokee Nation.

Such response surely must have encouraged editor Elias Boudinot, who as Buck a decade earlier had attended the Springplace mission school (*Records: Cherokees*, v. 4, 5). In only the ninth issue of the *Phoenix*, April 24, 1828, Boudinot publishes the obituary of "Father" John Gambold, who had been instrumental in the success of the Moravians' mission to the Cherokees.

Aside from the *Phoenix*, the press at New Echota published other works in the Cherokee language. First was a hymn booklet; second was the Gospel of Matthew, translated by Presbyterian minister Samuel A. Worcester. The third booklet, also translated by Worcester, was the Moravian Church Litany (4206). Worcester cautions: “A literal translation from English, into Cherokee, or from Cherokee into English, is impossible” (4248).

The Moravians’ Henry Clauder makes a further discovery of the syllabary. Though unable to understand the Cherokee language, all he has to do is learn the pronunciation of the symbols to read a tract to his congregation. “But praise God,” he declares (4166), “I am far enough that I can read intelligibly to the Cherokees.”

One Moravian unable to surmount the language barrier was Franz Eder. He volunteers from Europe to serve in the Cherokee Nation but quickly discovers that English is impossible, let alone Cherokee (3984). However, it is during Br. Eder’s brief tenure at Oochgeelogy that a substitute name for the mission is proposed: Tekoa (3994). But that spell-able name lasts only a little longer than Br. Eder does in the Cherokee Nation.

Personnel turmoil reaches a new low in the Moravian missions when Br. Johann Renatus Schmidt, after eight years of service in Cherokee Nation, falls to the temptation of the communion wine (3800). Despite his pleas of reform, he is recalled to Salem. (Br. Schmidt will return in volume 10 of *Records: Cherokees* when he serves as the Moravians’ senior missionary, “loved and respected by the Cherokee Nation,” along the Trail of Tears.)

But then church authorities in Salem stumble upon the solution to personnel problems: rely on family members. Joining Br. and Sr. Byhan’s children Nathanael and Rachel in Springplace is their cousin, Nancy Becker (3894). At Oochgeelogy Br. Clauder brings his wife Elisabeth Ruede, whom he raced to Salem to marry. No need for the traditional asking the Lord for approval through the Lot * ; they know they are made for each other (4084).

Taking a bold step to assure her future by marriage is Oochgeelogy’s Maria Rosina Gambold, daughter of old Joseph Gambold and niece of Father John Gambold. Sizing up Br. Alexander Copeland’s proposal, after careful consideration and despite his being 10 years her junior, she concludes (3869) “he suited me.” But then she pleads that church authorities “do not cast me out and that you still consider me a member” of her beloved Gemeine, the Moravian Church. She gets her wish in volume 9 of *Records: Cherokees* by joining the newly organized Hope Moravian Church in Indiana.

Family members are a vital part of the entire series *Records of the Moravians among the Cherokees.* In volume 7 the Moravian missionaries recorded 43 baptisms. Volume 8 lists 34, often with parents or other relatives named. To Cherokee genealogists, *Records: Cherokees* is a gold mine of who's who in their ancestral trees.

Gold! The very word sends visions of "strike it rich" through Georgian and Cherokee alike in 1830, especially who owns it all, the Cherokee Nation or the state of Georgia. Both are certain it belongs to them, but the claims of both run far deeper than that. The crux is neatly summarized in the Moravians' *Periodical Accounts* (4073-76) published in London, so that the claims and counter claims have reached international renown. In a nutshell, the United States government, through numerous treaties with the Cherokee Nation and its Compact of 1802 with Georgia has promised the same thing to two diametrically opposed entries — the land where the Cherokees reside.

The opening year of volume 8 *Records: Cherokees*, 1828, sees the election of a brash, determined frontiersman, Andrew Jackson, hero of the Battle of Horseshoe Bend (*Records: Cherokees*, 4:1860) before the Battle of New Orleans, as president of the United States, upsetting the staid politics of the time of Virginia and Massachusetts trading presidencies. This is one president who will cut through the Gordian knot of mutually exclusive promises to the benefit of his fellow frontiersmen.

Events move swiftly following Jackson's inauguration. Br. Henry Clauder reports to Salem June 26, 1829, that Secretary of War, John H. Eaton, has told a delegation of Cherokees that "but two alternatives are offered, either to emigrate or to come under the Georgia Laws June 1830" (4041).

Br. Byhan reports August 29, 1829, that the governor of Tennessee asked to purchase more Cherokee land, whereupon the Cherokees replied, "they had no more land to give away" (4077). Word is, Br. Byhan continues, that the governor "had gotten a completely different understanding of the Indians" since "he had imagined a bunch of wild people, which only, so to say, live in the bush in miserable cabins."

And then, completing the subhead title of volume 8 of *Records: Cherokees*, the solemn news arrives in July 1830, as recorded by church authorities in Salem, that "Congress of the United States at the end of May legally decided, and gave the President power to remove the Cherokees and other Indian Tribes to the west of the Mississippi" (4261).

Br. Byhan reports the reaction in the Cherokee Nation (4257): "I have already attended a number of Councils among the Cherokees, but I must admit not a single one was like this one, where one sees the poor Indians so discouraged, so quiet and serious, and at the same time so composed. When you speak with them they act so loving toward us that we feel deep compassion and regret their current situation. This visit at an Indian Council will always remain in my memory, and the emotions I felt during it actually pressed tears and sighs from me: Dear Savior, have mercy on these poor lost sheep and care for them mercifully!"

*Records of the Moravians among the Cherokees* would not be possible without the generous support of the Moravian Church in America, Southern Province, Wachovia Historical Society, Friends of the Archives, and most especially $25,000 annual grants from the Cherokee Nation and Eastern Band of the Cherokees. Thanks go to Mary Palmer Linnemann and Hargrett Rare Book and Manuscript Library, University of Georgia Libraries for the dust jacket image; C. Daniel Crews for carefully zeroing in on correct translations that translator Julie Tomberlin Weber most often got right in the first place. And lastly many thanks to my wife Susan, who has permitted me to work at all hours day and night during the production of *Records: Cherokees*.

Next up, volume 9. And you thought things were bad in volume 8. Just you wait.

Richard W. Starbuck
Moravian Archives
Winston-Salem, North Carolina
April 2018

# Records of the Moravians Among the Cherokees

## March to Removal, Part 3

## In Their Own Voice — 'Power to Remove'

## *1828, part 1*

[M 414-2-40: Translated by Julie Tomberlin Weber. Br. Gottlieb Byhan continues his Dec. 31, 1827,[1] letter to Br. Theodor Schulz in Salem, North Carolina.]

Jan. 1, 1828 at 10 o'clock in the evening. First of all we wish all of you a friendly glance from our dear Lord as we enter this year. May He shower us all with blessings and help us in this as well through all difficulties and all weaknesses with victories and blessings.

Now, my dear Br., I would like to know your thoughts on our future house construction. I had planned to build a frame house, but after careful consideration I was concerned first that it would cost more than a block house, and then it would be difficult to get so many bricks to lay, when I will perhaps be happy to get enough for the chimneys. A frame house might also cause a stir among the residents here. There are also many things associated with building a frame house which are not associated with a block house, so that I have almost decided just to build a house from blocks, and indeed one about 36 or 40 feet long, about 24 or 26 feet wide, with a hall through the middle, so that on each end of the house there will be a sitting room and bedroom. It will be one and a half stories high so that 2 more bedrooms or rooms can be made above, and the kitchen on the gable end of the house with a sloping roof, something like the mission house in Ochgologee. Be so good and let me know your thoughts about this, really as soon as possible. Mr. Jos. Vann will saw the floorboards for me yet this winter.

---

[1] See *Records: Cherokees*, 7:3726-29.

We currently have 11 scholars, 5 boys and 6 girls. We have made the Claytens' house into a schoolhouse in the interim. Nath. holds school for them. Sometimes Rachel also teaches the girls. Otherwise, Rachel cares for the girls completely. She washes them and cleans them otherwise from bugs when she has noticed such on them. We currently have nothing more to complain about except that I currently labor with sore eyes. They are especially painful in the evening. My dear wife survived the same problem. As you can easily imagine we have much work since the Claytens left, since we have no help and everything falls upon us.

Next Sunday we have the confirmation for Holy Communion of the Indian Brother John Jacob before us. The Savior approved this * in our last Conference on the 30th of this month, during which Br. Shmidt was present, as well as that the single [married] Sr. Rachel, who will also be a confirmand for Holy Communion.

Now, dear Brn., think often of your poor Br. and Sr. here in Springplace before the Savior, because we need His support and assistance in a very powerful way. We ask you to greet all the Brn. and Srs. most sincerely. Please do not neglect our daughter Soph. Dor. Please tell her that she should write to us once. Two post days have already passed without hearing anything from Salem. Put yourselves in our positions. Now, dear Br., another most sincere greeting and kiss from your Br. who loves you sincerely,

Gottlieb Byhan

N.B. The press for printing in Newtown, or Echota, has not yet arrived, but two printers arrived a couple of weeks ago. I subscribed to a newspaper for you.

Now I want to share with you names the Cherokees gave me and by which I am usually called. With Cherokee characters it is written as follows:

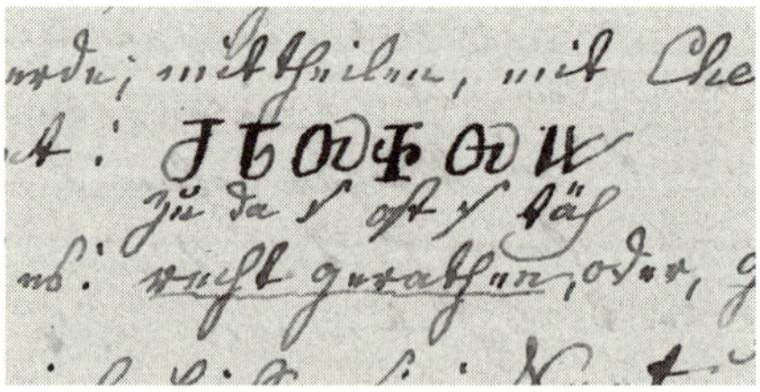

Germanized it means: well done or directly hit. They call Nathaniel Naat, and Rachel Neetchal.

[Springplace (M 407-1) and Oochgeelogy (M 409-1) Diaries. Translated by Julie Tomberlin Weber. Handwritings are Johann Renatus Schmidt's (Ooch.) and Gottlieb Byhan's (Spg.).]

*Jan. 1.* [Spg.] With confidence in our dear Lord that He will guide and direct us in this year, we entered into this new year. We surrendered ourselves once again to His ways and into His blessed care with a thousand joys that He will direct and lead us further as our Head and Shepherd.

Since our neighbor Jos. Vann had arranged a horse race for today in his field close behind our God's Acre, so a crowd of Indians came, and since they had brought a good quantity of brandy wine, as is customary on such occasions, it was pretty loud. So in the evening and night there was fighting among them, and they made noise and rollicked all night. Some drunken Indians also came to our house doors during the night and demanded to be let in, but since our living room serves as a sleeping room for our school girls, we did not let them in. They finally went on into the kitchen, where they got something to eat and then went into the boys' schoolhouse.

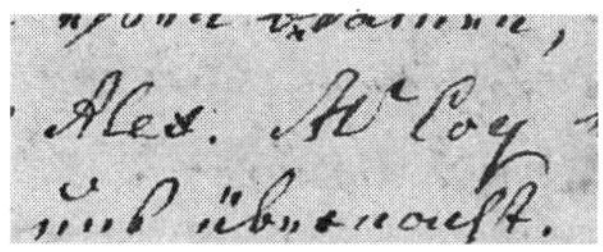

Mr. Alex McCoy from New Echota, who came here today, spent the night with us. This Alex McCoy is clerk in the National Council and a respected man in the Nation.

[B 61-3: Provinzial Helfer Conferenz, meeting in Salem. Translated by C. Daniel Crews.]

*Fri., Jan. 4.* The last minutes of Oct. 16 last year were reviewed. On Nov. 7 in Oochgelogy, four days before the arrival of our Br. and Sr. Byhan in Springplace, it pleased our good Lord to bring to an end the earthly life His faithful servant John Gambold, beloved and respected by us and by the Cherokee Nation, and to take His own to Himself after a long illness. After our Br. and Sr. Byhan had gotten themselves somewhat settled, Br. and

Sr. Schmidt with their children moved to Oochgelogy according to their appointment. They arrived there on Nov. 21. The widowed Sr. Gambold and her niece, the single Sr. Polly Gambold, will remain for the time being to help with material things and with the school. Br. Byhan's written reports about our baptized Cherokees and about their edifying progress were truly uplifting and stirred up thanks to our dear Lord. We were likewise comforted by Br. Byhan's thorough exposition of Br. Clayton's accusations against Br. Schmidt following the inquiry he conducted, and we hope that Br. Schmidt, according to his own contrite written statement will let this serve as a warning to let himself be freed ever more fully from unacknowledged faults. May he through grace be more watchful and faithful in his important post.

According to the last reports of Br. Byhan, it appears that Br. and Sr. Clayton want to leave Springplace soon. In that case, Br. Byhan will be advised to try to get locally what help he needs.

[Springplace (M 407-1) and Oochgeelogy (M 409-1) Diaries.]

*Sun., Jan. 6.* [Ooch.] To celebrate Epiphany we prayed the Church Litany in the first service. Afterward we discussed this day and then read to the Brn. and Srs. about the Wise Men from the East. We knelt in prayer and commended all of our missions and congregations among the heathen, especially the dear Indian congregations in North America, to the Savior's blessing.

At her request, Sr. Sally Copeland, formerly McDonald, was readmitted. Some years ago her way of life was undesirable, but through the Savior's grace and faithfulness as a shepherd she has been found again.

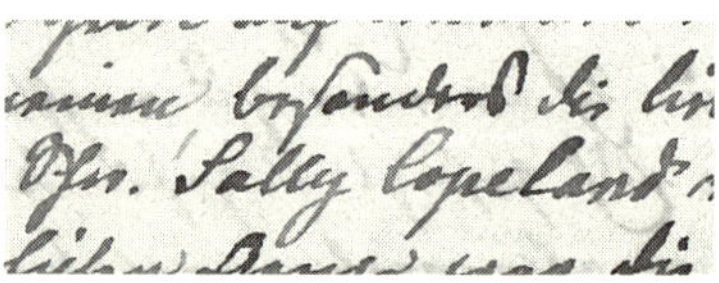

In the afternoon we had the most blessed enjoyment of the body and blood of Jesus in Holy Communion. At the end of this happy day we had another joyful lovefeast with our communicant Brn. and Srs., those who have been baptized, and our candidate for baptism. The dear Savior revealed Himself to us most wonderfully today.

For a long time we have sensed the work of the Holy Spirit in the heart of Alexander Copeland, a young man whom we have hired to do our outside work. The final hours and death of our dear Br. Gambold made a deep impression on his heart. He has made an initial decision to surrender himself to the Savior, and he expressed his desire to receive baptism, a grace in which he did not participate in his childhood. Since baptism also means joining our congregation and he is a white man, we discussed this with Br. W. A. Hicks. He was very pleased about his intention and said: If only all the white people in the country would sincerely convert, we would gladly count them all as part of the congregation here. Today Br. Schmidt had a thorough talk with him and we found no reason at all to be concerned about accepting him as a baptismal candidate. He also received instruction for this.

*Sun., Jan. 6.* [Spg.] Festival of the Heathen. First of all in the morning we prayed the Church Litany, then we read the story of the day, with a talk. Afterward we had a lovefeast with all of our Brethren and Sisters, which made quite a sweet impression on them. During this we explained the reason for this festival to them. In the 4th service there was the confirmation of the Indian Br. John Jacob for his first enjoyment of Holy Communion, which we celebrated immediately thereafter with an indescribably blessed feeling of the presence of our dear Lord. The feeling and the emotion which one feels in such a service of faithful Indians can only be felt and enjoyed; it cannot be described.

Our single Sr. Anna Johanna, our Br. Joshua's daughter, served as translator for us in all of our services. Never before had we seen our Indian Brn. and Srs. so happy as they were today. It was a true day of blessings for us all. The married Sr. Rachel, Br. Samuel's wife, was informed today that she would watch at our next Holy Communion as a confirmand.

The following should also be noted: on Jan. 4th, completely unexpected, a son of John Sneider, brother of Sr. Byhan, arrived at our place and offered to help with our external work. We accepted this offer as from the hand of the Lord, because we were just in need of such help, and we will keep him for an indefinite period of time.

*Jan. 7.* [Spg.] Since David Dazizi has owed the mission $15 for a couple of years already, he brought us three pigs today as payment. We were very happy about this since we are in need of pork. He and his brother spent the night with us.

*Jan. 12.* [Spg.] Br. Byhan visited a Negro named Jonson, who was ill at Jos. Vann's. Since he has been ill for a number of weeks he was asked if he would become healthy again? Said he: he believed not. This caused him to direct him with all of his misery to the Savior, who does not turn away any sinners who want comfort, and he advised him to turn to Him who took our sins upon Himself and paid for them with His bitter sufferings and death in our place.

*Sun., Jan. 13.* [Ooch.] The sermon was on Isaiah 53, and the service that followed was well attended, although we had expected only a few because it rained today. John Fields, husband of the recently baptized Sr. Susanna Elisabeth, sent word through Br. W. A. Hicks that he wants to have his sins washed away through holy baptism. He lives more than 20 miles from here. We will talk with him as soon as he can come here.

*Sun., Jan. 13.* [Spg.] Because of rainy weather today only a few of our Brn. and Srs. came to the services. We prayed the Church Litany and then the reading service was on the new birth of the heart.

*Jan. 14.* [Ooch.] Br. Schmidt visited our Brn. and Srs. in the neighborhood.

*Jan. 14.* [Spg.] Mr. Buttrick and a Presbyterian preacher named Green from Boston came to our place today and spent the night. The latter is on a trip visiting all the mission posts among the Indians. He is planning to go all the way to the other side of the Mississippi to visit the mission posts among the Cherokees there and among the Osage Indians. We had happy conversations together about mission matters.

[M 414-3-1: Translated by Julie Tomberlin Weber. Addressed to: Revd. Theodor Shulz, Salem, Stokes County, North Carolina. Postmark: Springplace, C.N. No date. Free. Gottlieb Byhan, P.M. Received Feb. 11.]

Springplace, Jan. 14, 1828

Dearly beloved Br. Shulz,

We were very happy to receive on the 10th of this month your letter dated Dec. 20 last year with the enclosures of $100, a note to H. Clayten, and a note about our Sophia. I immediately went to Mr. Jos. Vann with the $100 to see if he could perhaps exchange it for me and to pay my debt to him at the same time — or more precisely Br. Schmidt's debt. But he could not change it and told me he would be patient with me. Still it seems I would be viewed somewhat more cordially if I offered money from the State Bank of North Carolina than when I come with Newbern notes. Still they would rather have Georgia notes.

With the last mail I also received my commission as postmaster from Washington, so this matter is now in order. Currently 4 mails arrive at Springplace every Thursday. Since New Year there has also been one between Springplace and Newtown or Echota and Ridge's Ferry.

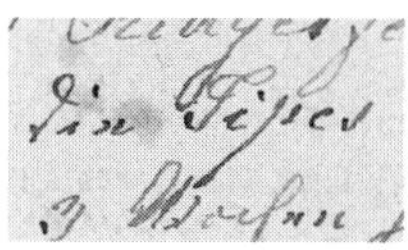

The press in Echota is still not working. They have not yet received the Tipes and the Presses. The printers themselves have already been here for 3 weeks and are waiting the arrival of the press.

On Jan. 6, Epiphany, we had a very happy and blessed day here. First of all we prayed the Church Litany. We then read and discussed the account of the day of the Wise Men from the East. In the third service we had a lovefeast with the communicants and baptized Brethren and Sisters. In the 4th was the confirmation of Br. John Jacob for his first enjoyment of Holy Communion. Then we partook of Jesus' body and blood in Holy Communion, during which Br. John Jacob joined us in partaking for the first time. It was a true day of blessing. We have hardly ever seen our Indians as happy as they were this day. Our Sr. Anna Johanna interpreted faithfully for us. It is really a shame that we cannot always have an interpreter, because when an interpreter is here you can always tell that the Indian Brethren and Sisters are much happier than when nothing is interpreted for them. We are sincerely sorry, but for now we cannot change this.

On Feb. 17 we have another confirmation, that of the married Sr. Rachal, Br. Samuel's wife.

On Jan. 4 a son of John Shneider, Sr. Byhan's brother, arrived at our place from Tenessee completely unexpectedly. He is planning to work here in the country for a while to earn some money. And since we do not have anyone to assist us in our outside work, we hired him to help us. He is about 23 years old. I have not yet made an agreement with him. First I wanted to see how he gets started.

I received the English Daily Texts from Bethlehem 3 weeks ago, as well as 3 German ones 14 days ago. Dear Br. Shaaf's German newspaper, with notes and Christmas hymns, also comes pretty regularly. Extend to him my gratitude and my sincere greetings for the printed hymns. I presume they were printed at the Salem press?

Our school is now in full swing, since they have all returned. Currently we have 14 children in the school, 8 boys and 6 girls. Sometimes singing lessons are held for them, during which the piano is a big help. Sometimes our Rachel holds school for the girls, which they really love. She also often sings with them at the piano. She tells them the hymn line by line and then they sing quite well, accompanied by the piano. Sometimes Nathal. holds a Singstunde for them and Rachel plays, which is very uplifting to hear.

Regarding what Major Ridge owes the Girls School in Salem and that perhaps I get something from him, I must say I do not believe that this will help me very soon, although it would certainly help me, because I really need it, and then I would get money which I could perhaps spend without giving an advance. I will do my best to get something from him, and perhaps it would also be good if Br. Reichel sent me an order for him to pay me something, since then you could pay it to Br. Reichel in

Salem later? But as far as I can tell and can find out, his finances are not such that he could pay many hundreds of dollars at one time. Still perhaps he is better off than people know. In any case it would be good if, when he perhaps wants to bring his daughter home sometime, he had an order to leave some of the money here for me, and I would inform you, dear Br., how much, and you could then pay it to Br. Reichel.

Before you receive this, you will probably already have found out where the Claytens are planning to spend the winter, in Columbus, Tennessee, about 40 miles from Springplace. You write me in your letter that you hope Clayten will give an account of the money he received from Br. Shmidt. Now I do not know what he bought or did with this money, but I deducted it when I paid him the note, so that I paid him only $52.75 in cash for the note. When I get a chance I will send you the slip of paper which you sent him.

Now concerning the management of the physical household here, Mother Byhan and Rachel really have to do almost everything, because Pleasant is too old to do much anymore. If we had not brought our Rachel with us, Mother would not have been able to manage it, so we are very happy that we have Rachel with us. She also does much for the schoolgirls. She can keep them in good order. She also cleans them of vermin which are peculiar to the Indians, and she does not rest until she knows they are completely clean. They children love her and help her in return when they can.

In your letter you write me that if there is a black couple at your place or at our place who could help us, we should act quickly. We hardly know what to say about this matter of having a Negro family here in Springplace. At <u>this</u> time we would not know where we could lodge a Negro family, because our kitchen is too small and we must admit that old Pleasant should actually not be in the kitchen. I do not really need to say why not. Now if we wanted to have another Negro couple sleep in the kitchen, one might completely lose his appetite for eating things from the kitchen. Therefore, we do not believe that at <u>this</u> time it would work to get involved with a Negro couple until we have more room to lodge them, and we must manage as well as we can for now. We also do not like hiring a Negro woman here. We had hired a Negro woman from our neighbor, Jos. Vann's wife, for a couple of days at Christmas. She brought 3 children with her, who were naturally under foot at that time in our small houses. One cannot hire good Negro women, and the other workers little or not at all, especially if they come to our old Pleasant. And so we hardly know what to say about this matter, and yet we really need help.

It seems to us the best thing would be if there were two Married Couples here, as it was while the Claytens were here. N.B.: They would just have to be completely dedicated to the work, or it would not work out again. Now may the Savior guide us and help us!

Now I must share with you an idea we came up with in our last Conference, whether it would work or could be arranged for us or for the Brn. and Srs. in Springplace to have only boys in the school and the Brn. and Srs. in Ochgologe only girls, or vice versa. Since we have only two mission sites in this country, so we thought such an arrangement could be carried out. We would like to learn your thoughts about how to approach this matter and arrange it, and if it would be necessary and would be considered appropriate. It is, however, true and agreed that if each post had only boys or girls, the children first of all would learn more, and the missionaries would have incomparably less trouble and work. One can judge more about the matter here on the spot than can be written.

In answer to the enclosed note in your dear letter about Sophia, we just wanted to say this much. We have no objections if our Sophia leaves the school and goes to Br. and Sr. Shröther, which we also wrote to her. Concerning the *Museum*, which Br. Benzien gets two copies of, it is as I believe I personally told Br. B.: one copy for me, and when the bill comes from Br. J. Jordan it should be debited from me. A large number of things makes everything confused. This is surely also the case with Br. B., so that I do not think badly of him if he can no longer remember that I told him this. Please greet him very sincerely from us. We greet everyone, especially dear Brn. Benade and Shaaf. And you, dear Br., accept another special greeting and kiss from your faithfully obliged Br.,

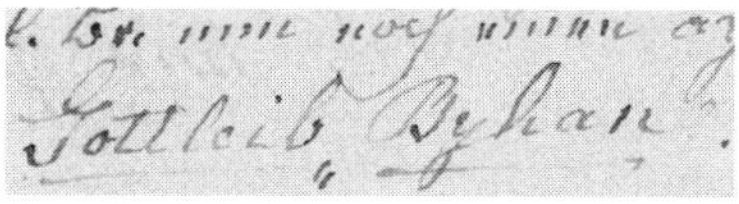

Gottlieb Byhan

([Margin notes:] I have another request for you, dear Br., since our Nathl. wants to have a frock or flyer for summer, and we can get no fabric like cotton. We asked Sophia in her letter to make one, if you would agree to pay for the cotton for this from the missions account.

(In your next letter please let me know how things turned out with the Negro matter in Salem, etc. Did you have a Coll. vote?)

[Springplace (M 407-1) and Oochgeelogy (M 409-1) Diaries.]

*Jan. 16.* [Spg.] Mr. Buttrick came back by here. He had accompanied Mr. Green, the above-mentioned preacher, to Brainerd. David Tazizi also came to our place today and spent the night here.

*Jan. 17.* [Spg.] We received German Daily Texts for this year from Bethlehem.

*Sun., Jan. 20.* [Ooch.] The sermon was on the Watchword, Isa. 43:25. Then there was a service celebrating yesterday's anniversary of the beginning of the mission in Greenland 95 years ago. We read a report about the missions there. To conclude the service the scholars recited the verses they had learned in school.

*Sun., Jan. 20.* [Spg.] The Sunday services were as usual. There were about 50 people present. We had a heart-to-heart and thorough talk today with the Negro Br. Chr. Jacob, our candidate for Holy Communion.

*Jan. 21.* [Ooch.] We slaughtered pigs.

*Jan. 23.* [Ooch.] In the presence of Br. W. A. Hicks we had a thorough and sincere talk with the unfaithful Joseph Crutchfield, unfortunately without success. Br. Gambold wrote him a letter a long time ago, since he was hardly coming to services anymore. He asked him as a faithful father to turn back to the loving Savior and straighten himself out, but also without success. The verse, "He who has searched and found all his sin, finds the path to the wounds is open to him," now seems very foreign to him.

*Jan. 23.* [Spg.] Mr. John Adams from Tenn., who faithfully served the mission here last year and went home on Nov. 18th, returned to us today. Since we are in need of help in our external work and also on the fields and Mr. Adams is a very willing, diligent, and respectable man, we took him back to work.

*Jan. 24.* [Ooch.] Mr. Buttrick from Hightower visited us for several hours.

*Jan. 26.* [Ooch.] It rained the entire day, as it also did on

*Sun., Jan. 27,* [Ooch.] and so only a few people could come to the services. We invited our communicants to partake in Holy Communion next Sunday. We let the elderly mother Hannah know that she can watch this as a confirmand. We were also happy to inform Alex. Copeland that he will be baptized at Easter. He received instruction for this.

*Sun., Jan. 27.* [Spg.] It rained extraordinarily heavily day before yesterday and yesterday, and the streams were very flooded, so no one came to the services today except Br. Josua's family and 3 or 4 Negroes. We prayed the Church Litany and then something was read from the Tracts on the words [2 Cor. 6:2]: Today is the day of salvation. Then there was Bible reading. Toward evening Br. Byhan, Rachel Byhan, and one of our school girls visited at Br. and Sr. Josua's on the Connessaga River about 3 miles from here.

*Jan. 28.* [Spg.] Today we had cause to speak with our schoolboys, and indeed primarily about the loathsomeness of lying, which they had come to deserve. We explained to them that this vice is detestable in God's eyes, and that Satan is the father of lies. We hope this may have a made a good impression on them.

*Jan. 28.* [Ooch.] Br. Schmidt visited Br. and Sr. W. A. Hicks.

[M 414-3-2: Translated by Julie Tomberlin Weber. Addressed to: Revd. Theodor Schulz, Salem, Stokes County, North Carolina. Postmark: New Echota, Ch.N., Feb. 16, 25 (cents). Received Mar. 20.]

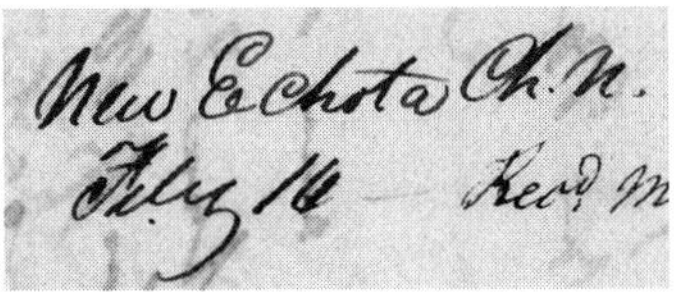


Oochgeelogy, Jan. 28, 1828

My dearly beloved Br. Schulz!

Yesterday evening I received 2 dear letters for me from you, the latter dated Dec. 26. Herewith I want to thank you most obligingly for them, and send sincere greetings from my wife and me.

Praise God, we here in Oochgeelogy are all healthy and well, and God's peace has filled all our hearts until now. The celebration of Christmas Eve, during which our Saal could hardly hold everyone, as well as Christmas were blessed days for us. Likewise the Savior looked upon us in grace on Epiphany. On this day we had the joy of readmitting Sr. Sally Copeland, formerly McDonald. This took place during a lovefeast which we had with our baptized communicant Brethern and Sisters and candidates for baptism. With gratitude to our dear Savior, we recognize that He will not neglect His work of grace here.

The Word of Jesus' patience is most powerfully seen here in the hearts of listeners. Now we have four candidates for baptism who have testified to us that it is their firm decision to become Jesus' property and they have the desire to receive the waters of holy baptism as a seal of their faith:

1. Elex Copeland, the young person whom we currently have as our farmer and who has now behaved as an upright man for more than a year. More than 4 months ago he expressed his desire to belong to our congregation and to be baptized. Since he is a white man, we had first had objections to taking him into our congregation. I spoke with Br. W. A. Hicks about his desire to become Jesus' property, and he showed his sincere joy about this. With the sincere desire that many more white people here in the Nation might become His, he gave his complete support, and that if it could be arranged for him to join our congregation

through baptism, he would be really happy. We laid the question before the Savior whether He approved that Elex Copeland should be baptized, and to our joy received His approval * for this. So we scheduled this celebration for next Easter.

At our next Holy Communion next Sunday, old Mother Hanah will watch as a confirmand.

The second candidate for baptism is Joseph Crutchfield's wife. Her name is Tschinasse. We also had her under consideration, but did not receive the Savior's approval.

The third is Br. W. A. Hicks's daughter, our scholar from Springplace, in whom the work of God's Spirit has been seen for a long time and who has expressed to us her desire for Holy Communion. The Savior also does not approve her at this time.

Fourth is John Fields, the husband of the recently baptized Sr. Sussanna Elisabeth Fields. He also repeatedly let us know of his desire for Jesus' grace. However, since we have not seen him recently, he has not yet come into consideration.

Thus the good Savior continues revealing Himself in our poor service.

The school has also grown. Sr. Polly currently has 13 scholars who bring her joy through their diligence and obedience. Since we have been here Sr. Polly has enjoyed good health. She has had very few of her previous attacks. Br. Joseph is also very well. We are thinking of postponing his little house until next fall. He is also satisfied with this. We will get a fence around our God's Acre as soon as possible. Recently we were very busy slaughtering pigs. We have slaughtered 16 pigs. We are happy and grateful that Mother Anna Maria is with us. She helps us faithfully with everything.

I am almost ashamed of my scrawl. The letter deserves to have been twice as long, but since time and opportunities to send mail here are scarce, please excuse my bad writing. We will see what else the Savior will do for and with us. We trust confidently in Him to carry out His plans for peace with us. The dear letter dated Dec. 26 was very encouraging and uplifting for me. I know I have failed. The Savior alone can comfort me and He also does this and helps me in my weakness. I pray very often with blessed Br. Gregor: "Be my strength in weakness. . . ," and in grace He will consider my poor prayer.

Poor Br. Blum is certainly to be pitied. Thanks be to the Savior, that due to the large water [supply], the area was not in danger.

Now, although not happily, I must add one request, and that is for money. We have only about $20 left in the account, but we owe Elex. Copeland more than $200. Please be good enough to help us as soon as possible. It is always very difficult for a mission to ask for money, but I can do nothing else, and I simply must do it. With God's help, we will try to keep expenditures as low as possible in the future. Still we must live, and you, dear Br., know how it is at a post where you cannot always act as you would like to and as you should. I expect Br. Byhan from Spring Place any day so that we can communicate about this matter.

The weather is currently very pleasant and like it is in Pennsylvania in the spring. I expect Mr. Green, a Presbyterian preacher, any hour. He is visiting the missions here and checked in here yesterday evening. Now, dear Br., accept this scrawling for this time. More soon. I wish I were in a position to send you a thorough Diary of last year, but since our blessed Br. Gambold only wrote down a little, I must just deliver it as well as I can. It will be soon.

Please sincerely greet your dear colleagues, Brn. and Srs. Steiner, Buchholz, Pfohl, Reichel, and M. Reich. My wife joins me in greeting your dear family. In Jesus' loving communion, you are greeted by your faithfully obliged Br.,

Johann Renatus Schmidt

Sr. Gambold urgently asks to send enough money so she can keep her promise to Elex Copeland. Please greet my friend Luis [page torn].

J. R. S.

We have all exerted considerable efforts with poor Joseph Crutchfield. But in vain so far.

[Springplace (M 407-1) and Oochgeelogy (M 409-1) Diaries.]

*Jan. 29.* [Ooch.] Dr. Green from Boston, who is visiting the Presbyterian missions, stopped in to visit for a few minutes and said that he will visit us officially tomorrow. We neither saw him nor heard anything else from him again. The mother of our scholar Squequa and another Indian woman visited us. We extolled the Savior, who came into the world to save sinners, to them as well, since they understood some English.

*Jan. 30.* [Ooch.] We received 2 new scholars, a boy named Dikanesky and his sister named Zikanella. Today we received pleasant letters from Br. Schulz in Salem. We are having rainy weather almost every day now.

*Jan. 31.* [Spg.] Today we were forced to take a girl [Elisabeth Falling] who was brought to the school just 14 days ago back to her friends on the Highwassee River, because without knowing it, she had scabies when she was brought. It seemed that it was getting worse instead of better, and we feared all our children might be infected with it. We were also advised to take her back to her friends when our friends asked us how such children should be treated until she is cured. She no longer has a father, and a completely blind mother.

*Feb. 1.* [Ooch.] Br. Schmidt visited people in the surrounding area.

*Sun., Feb. 3.* [Ooch.] Only a few people could come to the services because of the continuing rains. The sermon was on the Doctrinal Text for today, Mark 1:15. The 3rd service was a Singstunde. The Holy Communion scheduled for today had to be postponed until next Sunday. Sr. Gann was here, and we were touched when she told us that her husband almost lost his life a few days ago while felling a large tree. The tree fell right across his body, but the branches kept the tree from crushing him. Some other people helped rescue him, but he was seriously injured. His young son, a 6-year-old child, was standing there too and was also knocked down and covered by the branches of the tree. But he escaped without injury. We heard that Br. W. A. Hicks was very sick, so Sr. Gambold rode there in the afternoon, despite the rain. She found him suffering from pain in his limbs but improving.

*Sun., Feb. 3.* [Spg.] Because of high streams only a few Brn. and Srs. came to the services today. We prayed the Church Litany and read a sermon on the words [John 1:29]: Behold the Lamb of God, which taketh away the sin of the world. In the afternoon Br. Byhan left Spring Place to go visit in Oochgology, where he was invited to come already last week, but had always been held from going by bad weather. He had ridden hardly 4 miles when he heard that Holly Creek 8 miles from Spring Place had to be swum, and also that the ferryboat across the Coosa River had gotten loose a couple of days earlier and had gone down the river, and that it had not yet been possible to bring it back up, so that the Coosa River had to be swum too. And so Br. Byhan turned back to Spring Place at this news.

*Feb. 4 and 5.* [Spg.] It rained almost continuously. We heard that the streams have all risen to an extraordinary height.

*Feb. 8.* [Ooch.] Br. Schmidt visited Br. Hicks, who is ill. He is recovering. The weather finally cleared up for a while.

*Sun., Feb. 10.* [Ooch.] In the 1st service we read from the booklet, *The Word of the Cross*. The 2nd service was a liturgy. In conclusion the children recited the verses they had learned in school. In the afternoon we partook most blissfully in the body and blood of Jesus in Holy Communion, and the elderly Mother Hannah watched as a confirmand. We had a private talk with Chinassee and instructed her in the truths of salvation. In the evening we had Bible reading. Carrington Hicks returned to our school today. He had accompanied Br. Schmidt to Springplace some time ago and injured his leg there so that he could not return. Squirl, one of our scholars, went home today without our knowledge. We had rain throughout this entire week.

*Sun., Feb. 10.* [Spg.] Today almost all of the Brn. and Srs. who live close to us came, because the streams had receded somewhat. Some of them had already arrived yesterday evening and were here overnight. After the last service today, Br. Samuel gave a talk to the Brethren and Sisters. He had asked Br. Byhan for permission to do this, and it was gladly given him. We later heard that he is supposed to have spoken very beautifully and sincerely. He told us himself that he had often given addresses in his house. However, since no one or only very few came to him, it had not happened for a long time. God's peace and His presence could be felt, especially among our Brn. and Srs. Days like today sweeten the occasional unpleasant things which arise at heathen posts. Finally we also had the joy of a young single Indian dropping in at our place and expressing his wish to us of becoming Jesus' property. Since Br. and Sr. Byhan have been here, he has attended the services regularly and was always extremely friendly toward us, and we could see in him that God's Spirit was busy in his heart. His name is Nic Tiger. Nathanael and Rachel Byhan today went to visit at Mr. McNair's.

*Feb. 14.* [Spg.] With the mail today we received a brief letter from the Secrt. of War in Washington addressed to Br. John Gambold accompanied by 2 printed books containing the travel description of Mr. McKenney and his visit among the northern and southern Indians. Because of a lack of time he was not able to visit the Cherokees here but promised to visit them as soon as possible.

*Sun., Feb. 17.* [Ooch.] We entered into the holy season of Lent with a brief talk, and then we prayed the Litany of the Life, Sufferings, and Death of Jesus. The 2nd service was a sermon on the words of John 1:36: Behold the Lamb of God! After this Br. Schmidt baptized George and Lucy Hicks's baby daughter, granddaughter of Br. W. A. Hicks, into Jesus' death with the name Nancy Elenora. In the evening we had Bible reading. Br. Hicks could not come because he was ill. The Indians do not remember ever having such a mild winter. Although we had a lot of rain, it has always cleared up and gotten warm again.

*Sun., Feb. 17.* [Spg.] In the first service in the morning, for the beginning of Lent, we prayed the Litany of the Life, Sufferings, and Death of our Lord Jesus Christ, along with a brief talk to the Brn. and Srs. In the 2nd service was the confirmation of the married Sr. Rachel, our Br. Samuel's wife. Afterward, accompanied by a blessed feeling of the presence of our dear Lord, we had Holy Communion, during which the married Sr. Rachel joined us in partaking for the first time. Then was the baptism of a little child of Mr. Archibald Fields and Elis. Fields, daughter of our blessed Br. Charles Renat. Hicks, a baby girl, about 3 months old, with the name Martha Ann. The presence of our dear Lord could be felt in all of the services, especially during the enjoyment of Holy Communion. Oh, how such days and hours give us new encouragement, when it makes the difficult things, which do exist, sometimes small, when we see the Indian Brn. and Srs. with happy expressions around us, and see in them that they have really sought and found grace in the Savior. The feelings one experiences here cannot be described. They have to be felt and enjoyed. Oh, may the Savior give us the grace that we at least do not destroy anything in His vineyard, even if we cannot always achieve what many others in our situation might. May He lay His blessing on our weak efforts so that His kingdom may be ever increased.

*Feb. 18.* [Spg.] We heard that last week about 6 or 7 miles from here, on the way to Ochgoloogy, an Indian was murdered when his head was wounded in a horrible way. People suppose that the deed was carried out by white people but do not know anything for sure. Mr. John Shneider from Hamilton County in the state of Tennessee, Sr. Byhan's natural brother, arrived here this evening to visit with us to their mutual joy, since it has been nearly 40 years since they saw each other.

*Feb. 20.* [Ooch.] Br. Schmidt visited Br. and Sr. W. A. Hicks. Br. Hicks is still suffering from pain in his limbs, and he is very weak. An express messenger who was sent from Willsvally to the missionary in Echota, Mr. Winchester, stayed with us. We learned from him that Rev. Ard Hoyt had died the day before yesterday. He was the eldest Presbyterian missionary here in this country. When he went to bed he was still completely healthy and well; around midnight he woke up his wife, and then he died before she got up.

*Feb. 21.* [Ooch.] The children received their religious instruct-tion, which is given every Thursday. During this they recite a verse they have memorized, as they do from the hymnal after the sermon on Sundays.

# *1828, part 2*

[M 414-3-3: Translated by Julie Tomberlin Weber. Addressed to: Revd. Theodor Schulz, Salem, Stokes County, North Carolina. Postmark: Springplace, C.N., Feb. 28. Double, 37½. Received Mar. 12.]

Oochgeelogy, Feb. 21, 1828

My dearly beloved Br. Schulz!

Since I wrote to you just a few weeks ago, I do not have much else to write this time. I just want to send sincere greetings to you and your dear family from my wife, Sr. Gambold, Br. Joseph, and myself. Herewith I am sending you part of our Diary from 1827 until Feb. 21, 1828. The rest I will send to Br. Benade.

We here are all healthy and well. We are really longing for letters and news from the Gemeine. Next Easter I will have the grace of baptizing Elex Copeland into Jesus' death. We have entered into the blessed Lent season with the request to the Savior that He would paint before our eyes this time as well His sufferings and death as a lasting blessing for us and the dear brown flock. The weather this winter was especially mild; however, we have had a lot of rain. With sincere greetings, I remain your faithfully obliged Br.,

J. R. Schmidt

[M 414-3-4: Translated by Julie Tomberlin Weber. No address; no postmark. Sealed with M 414-3-3.]

Oochgeelogy, Feb. 29 [24?], 1828

My dearly beloved Br. Shulz!

Yesterday Br. Byhan delivered your letter of the 31st of last month, which was very painful to me. Oh, dear Br., you and your dear colleagues please be assured that I accepted your faithful warning as it was meant. I regret my mistakes and shortcomings. Through the Savior's grace, I have taken stock of myself, and He will help me to exhibit more faithfulness in the future. Bury the past and accept me, your poor Br., in love again. I thank my dear Byhan for his faithfulness. With sincere greetings, I remain your faithful friend and Br.,

Schmidt

[Springplace (M 407-1) and Oochgeelogy (M 409-1) Diaries. Translated by Julie Tomberlin Weber. Handwritings are Johann Renatus Schmidt's (Ooch.) and Gottlieb Byhan's (Spg.).]

*Feb. 22.* [Spg.] Br. Byhan went to Ochgoloogy. Since the streams were still very high, he had to make a pretty significant detour to get across the Holly Creek. However, since they had not yet been able to bring the ferryboat, as mentioned above, back up the river, since it had gone about 60 miles down the river, this river had to be crossed in a small Indian canoe and the horse swum through it. Toward evening Br. Byhan arrived safely at Br. and Sr. Smidt's in Ochgoloogy, and returned safely from there to Spring Place on the 26th. Last Sunday, the 24th, there were no services in Spring Place.

*Feb. 23.* [Ooch.] We were delighted to receive a visit from Br. Byhan from Spring Place.

*Sun., Feb. 24.* [Ooch.] Despite all the rain yesterday, John Fields, who lives 23 miles from here, came to our place. He had expressed his desire for holy baptism through Br. W. A. Hicks, so we spoke with him about this today. We found his spiritual disposition such that we joyfully accepted him as a candidate for baptism. He is the husband of our Sr. Sussanna Elisabeth, and he has attended our services for a long time. Br. Hicks confirms that he is an orderly man and that the occasional conversations he has had with him leave no doubt in his mind that he is a man awakened by the Spirit of God. In the first service we prayed the Church Litany. In the 2nd service we read from the Gospel of John. In the evening was Bible reading.

*Feb. 26.* [Ooch.] Br. Byhan returned, accompanied by Eli Hicks.

*Feb. 27.* [Ooch.] An Indian named Muskrat came here to work at our place for several days.

[M 414-3-5: Translated by Julie Tomberlin Weber. Addressed to: Revd. Theodor Shulz, Salem, Stokes County, North Carolina. Postmark: Springplace, C.N., Feb. 28. Free. Gottlieb Byhan, P.M. Received Mar. 12. Br. Schulz has written in the address: *Cher. Phoenix* subscribers: Theod. Shulz, A. H. Shulz, John S. Jemison, Abr. Steiner, L. W. Benzien, Sophia Byhan, Tho. Pfohl. At $2.50.]

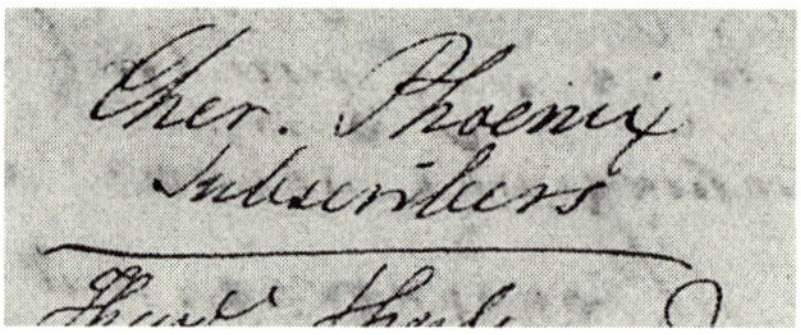


Springplace, Feb. 27, 1828

Dearly beloved Br. Shulz,

On the 21st of this month, I received your dear letter of Jan. 30 and *Wöchentliche* and *Monatliche Nachrichten*, as well as the Protocoll and accounts from the Wachovia Society for the Heathen and the letter to Br. Schmidt in Ochgologee. I was sorry, indeed very sorry, not to find any money in it, and on this occasion I want to ask you urgently to send me some as soon as possible, even if it is North Carolina money, because this works best along with Georgia money. The Creditors are swarming, so that I do not know what to do. They are all J. R. Schmidt's creditors — if they could just be satisfied for once!

Yesterday I returned from Ochgologee, where I had gone to visit. I personally delivered your letter to Br. Shmith. After he had read it, he declared himself to be a debtor and said that he would never let such debts mount again in the future, as he will surely have written to you about this as well. I hope that it may have made a healing impression on him and that in the future he might refrain from such things. Srs. Gambold also tell me that as long as he has been in Ochgologee, they cannot say anything against his behavior.

I also looked through the Ochgologee account books, but as was to be expected I just found confusion, although not as bad as in Spring Place. I balanced the income and expenditures with the cashbox as well, and I gave the books and cashbox to Br. Schmidt. Until now Sr. A. Maria Gambold had control of the cash and had taken care of the income and expenditures. They currently owe their worker about $160 and also wish to get some additional money. Their cashbox consisted of $12.30. Last week another $10 Cape Fear bank note, which Br. Schmidt had spent, was returned, for which I must now give N. Carolina money. This has now happened repeatedly. Now I have this money on hand, and I cannot spend it anymore.

We must be very careful concerning Maj. Ridge's debt to Br. Reichel, because this man is very easily affronted. But we will do everything that we can — as far as we can go — to get some from him. I think in my last letter to you I expressed my views about this request for payment of debt that I believe it will be difficult to get anything without an order or instructions from Br. Reichel. People believe he does not often have hundreds of dollars.

When you receive this letter, the first Cherokee newspapers will also make their appearance in Salem. In accordance with your order, I made and paid for a subscription for 7 newspapers in Salem, for Theod. Shulz, Abr. Steiner, Sr., Wm. L. Benzien, Aug. H. Shulz, John S. Jemison, Saml. Th. Pfohl, and Sophia Dor. Byhan, a total of $17.50, which you need to settle with them. And because I naturally also wish to have one and I am answerable for the above subscribers, I receive my newspaper gratis.

On the 17th of this month, after the confirmation of Sr. Rachel, Br. Samuel's wife, we had a blessed enjoyment of the body and blood of Jesus in Holy Communion. All the communicants were here except for two, one of whom was Clement Vann. A new baptism by the Spirit would be desirable for this Br. Despite the fact that the streams were pretty flooded, Sr. McNair and Sr. Felicitas Hicks were present. A young Indian inquired about Holy Communion, as did an Indian woman. I will write more about this in my next letter.

We currently have 15 scholars boarding, 8 boys and 7 girls. In addition there are 3 who go to Jos. Vann's for room and board. Nathanael completely takes care of the school. We currently have 2 workers, John Adams and William Shneider, who are very busy in the field. Yesterday some of our oats were sown.

I must also inform you that I tried to get the piece of land which Jos. Vann has lying between our fields — I think you will remember where it is — for a fair price. After long negotiations, I asked him to tell me what I would have to pay him to give it to us. Finally he said if I paid him $50 he would release it. It is about 22 acres, almost 40 years in cultivation. This seemed like too much to me and unfair, so I told him that I could not give him this, and we parted in love and peace. Now it is true that this piece of land lies right in the middle, so that we must make a large detour to get to part of our fields, and there are many unpleasantries concerning the fences. Please be so good and let me know in your next letter what your thoughts are about this matter.

Three weeks ago Mr. Nealy, a Methodist preacher and husband of Mr. McNair's daughter, died from consumption, so that Polly is now a widow.

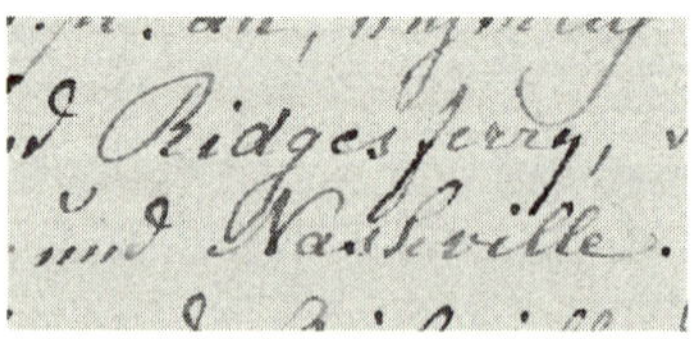


Currently 4 mails arrive at Springplace, 3 on Thursday and 1 on Friday from New Echota and Ridge's Ferry. The 3 on Thursday come from Georgia, Knoxville, and Nashville. If only I had a separate little room for the Post Office so that I did not have to use the church for this.

We are currently all healthy except for Rachel, who is somewhat sickly. Sometimes she is still homesick.

I spoke with Br. Abr. Willm. Hicks about the separation of our boys and girls in Spring Place and Ochgologee. He gladly agreed to this and said that he would announce this among the Indians right away. The question was withheld in my last letter to you because of this. Br. Hicks said that these arrangements should have been made long ago.

Please greet the Brn. of the Prov. Helf. Conf. most sincerely from us, as well as the Aelt. Conf., yes, all friends of mission work. With the most sincere greetings to you and your family from your faithful friend and Br.,

Gottlieb Byhan

Please greet Br. Shaaf especially from us and tell him that the German newspapers arrived here safely. Still I believe that some floated around in the world longer than was necessary, but they eventually do find Springplace.

G. B.

[M 414-2-32: Translated by Julie Tomberlin Weber. No address; no postmark; no date.]

Concerning our household, we have managed without help until now. Mother and Rachel take care of the kitchen — because Pleasant can do nothing anymore — and the milking. We are currently milking 7 cows. Rachel washes for us, and the girls for themselves, and Pleasant for the boys as well as she can. We have everything locked up so that the children cannot go through things as before. The Claytens live in Columbus, where he has been very ill for some weeks, and she has a young son. In the last mail he wrote to me that I should send him $10. But since I am short on money, I could not do this. By the way, we do not regret that the Claytens are gone from here.

If anyone comes this way this spring, be good enough to send me an English chorale book. Please do not forget this. We received German Daily Texts from Bethlehem. Br. Shmidt really regrets that he does not have a German almanac for this year.

What is Br. Henry Blum doing? Is he planning to come here in the spring? We would be able to use him throughout the summer. Our preparation for building is still going very slowly, because I still have no people who can do such work, although I have heard from one carpenter. Jos. Vann promised to saw floorboards for me, but not a foot has been sawed yet! In short, everything here has difficulties associated with it. Your friend,

Br. G. Byhan

[Springplace (M 407-1) and Oochgeelogy (M 409-1) Diaries.]

*Feb. 28.* [Ooch.] The children received their religious instruction.

*Feb. 29.* [Ooch.] Mrs. Hicks came here from New Echota to visit us.

*Feb. 29.* [Spg.] We once again heard that an Indian, about 8 miles from here, was murdered by another one. Brandy wine is usually to blame for such events.

*Sun., Mar. 2.* [Ooch.] Since it rained today only a few people came to the service. We had Bible reading in the evening.

*Sun., Mar. 2.* [Spg.] Only a few Brn. and Srs. were in our services because of the continuing rainy weather. After these we had another conversation with a young Indian — the above-mentioned Nic Tiger — and 3 Indian women who asked for holy baptism. We could feel that it was their honest desire to give themselves to the Savior. With tears they said that they wanted to become Jesus' property and be cleansed from their sins in holy baptism through Jesus' blood. We could do nothing but accept them as baptismal candidates.

*Mar. 3.* [Spg.] In the evening Mr. Worcester from New Echota returned from a journey in Tennessee and spent the night with us.

*Mar. 6.* [Ooch.] The children received their religious instruction. A young man from Tennessee came to our place today to work on our farm for a month.

*Sun., Mar. 9.* [Ooch.] The sermon was on Isa. 53. In the 2nd sermon we read some of David's Psalms. In the evening we had

Bible reading. Today we heard that Edmund Crutchfield died suddenly yesterday evening, and that he was buried very early this morning.

*Sun., Mar. 9.* [Spg.] Our church was pretty full of listeners, as well as on. . . .

*Mar. 10.* [Ooch.] We began working in our garden today. Srs. Gambold visited Sr. Hannah, who is sick.

*Mar. 12.* [Ooch.] Br. Schmidt visited Br. and Sr. Hicks.

[B 61-3: Provinzial Helfer Conferenz, meeting in Salem. Translated by C. Daniel Crews.]

*Mar. 14.* We felt somewhat better about the occurrences with Br. Schmidt, partly because of Br. Byhan's information which he sent at the time, and partly because of Br. Schmidt's contrite statement written in his own hand (see minutes 4 Jan.). Then we got the information Br. Byhan sent on 29 Jan.[1] about Br. Schmidt's conduct in regard to his too great use of strong drink, and his attitude toward finances and his handling of them, which Br. Byhan had found out after his earlier report and for which he had admonished him out of devotion to the work of the Lord, and for which he could not fail to notify us.

This caused us sorrow and embarrassment and moved us to write to him very earnestly once again to bring everything up to him and to give him to understand that without a complete change, it is impossible for him to remain in the service to which he has been appointed.

Following this, yesterday there arrived the answer both from Br. Byhan and also from Br. Schmidt.[2] The former indicates that our earlier admonitions and reprimands had a good effect on Br. Schmidt — according to close and rigorous observation on the

---

[1] Br. Byhan's Dec. 31, 1827, letter received by PHC Jan. 29, 1828. See M 414-2-40, *Records: Cherokees*, 7:3726.

[2] Br. Byhan's Feb. 27 letter and Br. Schmidt's Feb. 29 [24?] note, both received by PHC March 12. See M 414-3-5, page 3790, and M 414-3-4, page 3789, above.

spot by our widowed Sr. Gambold. Br. Schmidt's behavior since then has been just as we desired, and we trustingly expect his complete change for the better, and may our last earnest letter work favorably for this.

However, nothing is known or noted about his work among the Indians.

Br. Schmidt declares himself very humble and penitent for all his transgressions. He asks for patience and promises in the future to show more faithfulness by grace in God's work. He begs for forgiving and forgetting of the old things, and that we further receive him in love. The P.H.C. can do nothing else than to grant this in the hope that he will keep his promise and keep himself in the future from such aberrations.

To our pleasure we learned from the letter which arrived here yesterday from our dear Br. Christlieb Reichel, dated 14 Dec. last year, that our measures for the staffing of the Cherokee Mission through Br. and Sr. Byhan and our arrangement for the temporary service of the congregation in Bethabara through Br. and Sr. Jacobson from Bethania have the agreement of the U.A.C. They have also succeeded in finding a missionary assistant for the Cherokee Mission: the single Br. Franz Eder in Niesky. He has accepted this call. We will receive him with our whole heart, and wish that our dear Lord will be favorable to him and bring him here safe and sound. Br. Schulz was commissioned in the meantime to write to our friend Mr. Fr. Graf in Baltimore about his arrival here and also about the forwarding of his things, as the Brethren of the U.A.C. are planning to send him by the first available ship.

Br. Byhan asked the P.H.C. for permission to try to get possession of Joseph Van's field which lies between their fields for the asking price of $50.

There has been the suggestion, which has now been renewed, to have only girls at one of our mission posts, and only boys at the other. The P.H.C. earlier communicated our thoughts about this suggestion, and doubts that it can be workable. We also think that the costs of our mission posts would likely be increased by this, since parents who live in the vicinity of these posts send their children of both sexes to the day school, and they can feed and clothe them without our missionaries being burdened with this. If the latter [separate schools] should be the case, however, where they would send one or more of their children 30 or more miles away, many would be disinclined to send their children so far, and would rather not send them to school at all. However, the P.H.C. gives permission to our missionaries to make a try of it.

[Springplace (M 407-1) and Oochgeelogy (M 409-1) Diaries.]

*Sun., Mar. 16.* [Ooch.] We prayed the Church Litany in the first service. After the sermon, 2 of our Sr. Sarah Copeland's baby girls were baptized; a 2-year-old daughter received the name Sarah Jane and a 4-week-old baby girl received the name Ruth Elisabeth. We had a long talk today with George Hicks, eldest son of our Br. William Abr. Hicks. In the presence of his father, he expressed his desire for holy baptism. We were pleased at his statements, and we found him to be a man awakened by God's Spirit. He is sincerely concerned about belonging body and soul to the Savior, who purchased him with His blood. He was accepted as a candidate for baptism and received instruction in the Christian truths of salvation for this.

. . . *Sun., Mar. 16,* [Spg.] despite the unfriendly and raw weather. Until now it has been the custom in Springplace during Passion Week to read the story of Jesus' Passion every evening during the week, as in the settlement congregations. But many Brn. and Srs. live so far from here that they cannot be at home the entire week if they want to attend the evening services, and have to stay with us or our closest Brn. and Srs. So the Brn. and Srs. were asked today if it would be all right with them if we read the Passion story of our Lord perhaps the Sunday before up to the story of Good Friday, and then on Good Friday finish the story, or if we should leave it in the old way, that the Brn. and Srs. come every day of the week to hear the Passion story of our Lord. All of them voted for the former, and we could see in them that they really like the arrangement.

*Mar. 17.* [Ooch.] Br. Nickolaus Ignatius and Mr. Adams came here from Springplace by wagon this evening to get some household necessities. Today Br. Schmidt went to visit George Hicks. He was delighted to learn that he would be baptized during the next Easter festival. Sr. Anne Maria Gambold traveled with the Spring Place wagon to visit there on the 18th.

*Mar. 17.* [Spg.] Today our workman John Adams traveled by wagon to Ochgoloogy accompanied by our boy Niclaus Ignatius.

*Mar. 19.* [Ooch.] We were very hurt to learn that some of our scholars have been letting things happen for a good while that we cannot allow in our school. We spoke seriously and lovingly with them. One boy was so upset by this that he immediately ran home; 3 others informed us that they wanted to go home and that if we didn't allow them to do this, they would run away too. And so we sent for our Br. W. A. Hicks, who spoke very seriously with all of our scholars and explained to them that running away was a punishable act of disobedience against their parents and us. This was enough to calm the boys down until Br. Hicks could send word to their parents to come and take them home, which they did.

*Mar. 20.* [Ooch.] David Taucheechy visited us.

*Sun., Mar. 23.* [Ooch.] We discussed the words from the Gospel of John 19[:5]: Behold the man. There was an unusually large number of listeners today. In the 2nd service a Negro child, the baby boy of Michael, son of the old Negro woman Pleasant in Spring Place, was baptized into Jesus' death with the name Salomo Michael. We took this opportunity to have a loving talk with the child's father as well. He was also baptized as a child by our Brn. and Srs. in Springplace. It turns out that the good impression of the Savior that he received as a child has not been lost. He wants to belong to the Savior completely again, and it is his desire to become more closely associated with us.

*Sun., Mar. 23.* [Spg.] Many attentive listeners were in our Sunday services once again. Today the Brn. and Srs. were informed that next Sunday, Palm Sunday, we would begin reading the Passion story of Jesus, and they were asked not to miss the services except in extreme circumstances.

[M 414-3-6: Translated by Julie Tomberlin Weber. Addressed to: Revd. Theodor Shulz, Salem, Stokes County, North Carolina. Postmark: Springplace, C.N., March 27. Free. Gottlieb Byhan, P.M. Received Apr. 8.]

Springplace, March 24, 1828

Dearly beloved Br. Shulz,

I was joyful to receive your letter of Feb. 28 with the $100 N.C. bank note with the last post on the 20th of this month, and I thank you very sincerely for this. I also received your note to me dated Feb. 15, as well as the *Museum*. Please greet Br. Benzien very cordially from us and tell him that he should be good enough to report to Br. Jordan in Philadelphia that he should discountinue my copy of the *Museum* at the close of the year. First of all, I can save the money, and secondly, I really do not have time to read, because reading the *Museums* in my current situation is of no use to me.

Now to come back to your letter, I want to answer it point by point. I have already informed you that I received your letter of Jan. 30 with the note to Br. Shmidt, and that I delivered this to him, and he once again declared himself a debtor. However, I cannot keep things from you dear Brn., and I cannot do this with a good conscience, and I think I owe it to you and to my dear Savior not to hold anything back where I think the Savior's work, either now or in time, could suffer from this. Therefore, I must admit to you that we are not completely comforted by Br. Shmidt's general living habits, and we do not know what to think about this. It is also impossible for me to put everything down on paper about his living habits and behavior.

Sr. Gambold, who certainly is faithful to the Savior and His work, is currently on a visit in Springplace, and so much has been revealed to us which was shocking. Just to report a few things, because as said, to put everything on paper is impossible for me, for example, in October last year, before we arrived, the accounts show that he had 8 gallons of wine sent by a certain Lavender from Augusta, but if we had not brought wine from Knoxville, we would have had no wine for our first communion in Springplace. Now when he came to Ochgologee and there was supposed to be the first Holy Communion there, there was no wine there. Instead Sr. Gambold had to offer some of her own for this, and then he said to Sr. Gambold that he usually mixes the communion wine with water. What should we think about this?? I do not know. I have never heard such things before.

Now there is the question of what happened to the 8 gallons of wine? Sr. Gambold has to offer her own wine for Holy Communion now, which I do not consider fair. I am considering giving her some of our wine, so that they have some for Holy Communion, but Sr. Gambold should keep it in her care.

Further, in the October accounts one finds that he got 3 gallons of Jamaica rum. We also do not know where he got this. There are signs, though, that he split this with the Claytens. But how much he gave him we do not know, because when we arrived here he assured us that there was neither wine nor spirits in Springplace, until I found otherwise when I became more acquainted with things.

This leads me to the next point I wanted to make, that his words cannot be believed, and I would almost like to say he deals in untruths. And what is to be done with a person who means something different from what he says and twists or misinterprets what you say to him? Oh, I sincerely wish I could speak with you in person. I could tell you much. You cannot believe how we feel under such difficult circumstances. I cannot describe it to you. We wish Br. Shulz could visit here again now.

I cannot keep from making one more comment concerning Br. Smith, about which I have already thought a great deal. Indeed I must say I have already worried that we accept too hastily, but also that we not be negligent when God's Spirit touches a heart and makes it clear to him that he will certainly be lost in his natural condition if he does not allow himself to be cleansed from his sins by the blood of Jesus Christ. I think that we should also not let them wait too long, so that they do not lose courage.

I do not know if what I really mean here will be understood, because I believe that it is not good in any case if people just basically persuade people, if I can express myself this way, to let themselves be baptized when they do not feel any true need in their hearts. I am not saying that this was the case with Br. Shmidt, that I could point to obvious examples, but I see traces — and Sr. Gambold supports me in this — that in this respect a little more caution is lacking in him, and this important matter should be handled with a little more care.

It is true that grace and wisdom from above are needed for this and that we must pray for this. A little gathering of souls who have sincerely converted is better in my eyes than a large crowd of those who just follow along. I do not want people to understand that the latter was the case. No, I must say we have Brn. and Srs. who know what they have in the Savior, admittedly some more and some less, just like everywhere. I have felt moved to tell you dear Brn. my thoughts about this matter because, as said, I have noted traces that this important matter should be treated with more respect, with much care, and as though before God's eyes.

I hope you will not think badly of me for having reported the above about Br. Smith, but since it is expected of me and I am in debt in this matter, I could not neglect it. I would much, much have preferred it if I could not have written such things. I would still like to add that I personally do not know what Br. Shmidt has for principles and cannot quite understand what he thinks about how things should be done in the long term. May the Savior help us!

You write to me that you cannot get any Georgia notes there. That is all right, just send me North Carolina money quickly. This still works best, as do South Carolina notes. I do not like to remind you of money all the time, but I must admit that I will soon need a lot of money, especially when we finally get around to building. Currently I still have to pay a lot of the debts made by Br. Shmidt, and I am not yet finished with this. And so I really must ask you to remember me diligently in this respect. I also wanted to add here that you should not think badly of me for asking for more money. Surely at the end of the year I will not be able to say, as Br. Smith did, that he made a surplus of $124 since he spent $124 more than he actually had in cash, as his accounts show ____________.

I sent Br. Reichel's letter straight on to Major Ridge with the mail. Time will tell what good it will do. I hope it will be of use. As you write, my post duties indeed seem to increase, because Thursdays we get 3 mails and on Friday one, from Ridge's Ferry and New Echota. But I must say, it is a pleasure for me to take care of the mail, and then we at least get some advantage from this even if not a large income.

I cannot tell you anything certain about Br. Smidt's post accounts, because they are in the same shape as the rest of his accounts. I have begun anew with this account, and I have started a separate account in my book, so that at the end of the year I can show whether the post affair brings a loss or profit. Then I will also have collected more of the old debts, which are written down very negligently.

Currently there is a very contagious illness raging among the Negroes in our neighborhood and especially among Jos. Vann's Negroes — they call it Head Pleurasy. A number of them have already died from it. Once 2 of them died in one night. Eight days ago today one of our schoolboys became ill. People believed this was the same illness. The rest of the scholars were very upset about it and said right away they would go home and return in a couple of weeks. So they all gradually went home except for one girl, our Br. Boas' daughter. At first this did not make any sense to us and we were not at all happy to see all of our scholars go home except for one. But we were comforted for the most part when our neighbors and friends assured us that if it really had been the above illness, we could have done nothing better than let the children go home, and that it would not be good if so many people were together where this illness was, because people believe it is contagious.

The Claytens are still living in Columbus in Tenn. They had a young son, and he has already been ill for a long time. People say he had hypochondria. He had word sent to us he would visit us soon. We are not concerned about his visit. Some time ago he asked us through the postmaster in Columbus to advance him $10, but since I was still in financial trouble myself, I thought it best not to grant his request. Besides, he still owes me $6.

If this man was not openly mischievous, then no one has ever been. We already believed he would offer to move back to our place, but although we are really in need of help with the household, as all the household work has fallen on my wife and Rachel and we could not manage at all without the latter, and we really want help, still we could not agree to hire the Claytens again.

Time will tell how things concerning the household will go this summer during the construction when we will have many workers. My wife will not be able to endure this long, because it seems almost too hard for her. One must really include Pleasant in the expenditures, because she can no longer do much. Also we cannot hire a Negro woman, and even if there were one to hire, she would bring a group of children along with her who would also have to be cared for. Now God will perhaps look into this and provide assistance in His time! We must just look around a little and see if we cannot help ourselves in one way or another.

I currently have two workers who are making shingles, so that we have at least begun preparations for construction. God knows, however, when this will take place. Before Christmas I ordered floorboards from Jos. Vann, and till today he has not sawed a single foot of it. Now I have ordered boards at 3 sawmills. I do not know how soon I will get any. I have hired a worker who is supposed to help me frame the house when I finally get the materials together. His name is Brock. But he does not work for less than $1.50 a day. He was recommended to me as a diligent and upstanding person. He is currently working in New Echota for the printer Elias Boudinot. This is how things go in this country.

Everything has difficulties associated with it. First you can hardly get the materials, and when you finally get them you have to pay unheard of prices for work done.

Concerning the arrangements to separate our scholars, probably nothing will come of this at this time. We will at least have to have some more thorough conversations with our Brethren and Sisters here as well as in Ochgologee. I think I already reported to you that I have spoken with Br. Willm. Abr. Hicks about this and that it seemed very reasonable to him and he really hoped this arrangement might be undertaken. He promised to make it known right away among the Brn. and Srs. in Ochgelogee. However, as I now hear, they were not inclined to this. On the other hand, when I told our Brn. and Srs. in Springplace our thoughts, they gave their agreement with no hesitation. That is how things are now, and probably nothing will be done about this matter until I have spoken with Br. Willm. Abr. Hicks about it in detail again. Then we will know if it is advisable to take the matter further or to leave it as it was.

It is clear to us that it would be good if the boys and girls were separated. However, we do not want to carry anything too far, and if we note the least dissatisfaction about this among the Brn. and Srs., then we will gladly refrain from this and not disturb the peace. After all, it seems that the parents have something to say about this as well.

I must also inform you that the Brn. and Srs. in Ochgologee owe their worker $100 to now and have no money to pay him. Please keep this in mind. I also wanted to answer the question from your last letter about where I am thinking of building my house. I cannot find a more suitable place for this than the one which you recommended to me when I was still in Salem, that is, the one between the house where we now live and the shop but a little farther to the right toward the lane. Then I thought when things get this far I would push the shop back a little to the fens above the church so that the yard becomes a nice square. Those are my thoughts.

In recent times we had good hopes that at Easter we would be able to count some more Indians, who asked for holy baptism some time ago, among the congregation of believers through this means. We personally had no reservations about laying the question before the Savior in our Conference whether He would approve that they be baptized. However, the answer was no. It was 4 persons. The Savior only approved that Sr. Ruth watch as a candidate at our next Holy Communion, which we are planning to celebrate on Easter. It was quite disappointing to us, but we remembered that the Savior knows best what is in people's hearts.

I must also inform you that we will not hold the Passion Week services as Br. Smith did. He had services every evening, to which only a few Brn. and Srs. came. Those who live farthest away could not come at all, and those who farm either had to be on the road day and night or not be at home all week. I discussed this with our Brn. and Srs. in a separate meeting and asked them if they would like a change, because the most distant Brn. and Srs. would have to spend the entire week either in Spring Place or with Br. and Sr. Josua, which is naturally burdensome for them. The Brn. were all for beginning the reading of the Passion Week story on Palm Sunday, and specifically on that day in different services, and then the rest of it on Good Friday.

Br. Smith assured me that the services in the evening were well attended. However, we heard the opposite from reliable people. The arrangement here then is just like the country congregations around Salem. In our view, this arrangement is the best. At least it is the best where the Brn. and Srs. are so scattered. Please let us know your thoughts about this.

Sr. Anna Maria Gambold asks me to report to you that the blessed Br. John Gambold's estate owes the Missions Diaconie $38, for which Br. John Gambold bought wine, rum, and other private items for himself. Please debit the $38 from Br. Gambold's account with you and credit it to the Missions Diaconie. Along with a sincere greeting from her, she also said that she will stay with Br. and Sr. Smidt a while longer, as long as it is possible for her. However, when she can no longer tolerate it, then she will come to us at Spring Place.

Now this epistle has grown long, and so I want to close. Greet all from us, even if I do not list the names. And please accept a special greeting and kiss from your familiar friend and Br.,

Gottlieb Byhan

N.B. I will send this letter by way of Knoxville to see if it arrives in Salem any earlier.

G. B.

[Springplace (M 407-1) and Oochgeelogy (M 409-1) Diaries.]

*Mar. 26.* [Spg.] One of our neighbor Jos. Vann's Negroes died, again from an illness which has been raging among them this spring. This is already the 3rd one he has lost in this way. The doctors here call the illness head pleurisy.

*Mar. 29.* [Ooch.] Sr. Gambold returned from her visit in Springplace. The Older Girl Rachel Byhan also came along to visit us.

*Sun., Mar. 30.* [Ooch.] Palm Sunday. After a brief talk, we prayed the Litany of the Life, Sufferings, and Death of Jesus. Then we began reading the story of Passion Week in 3 sessions. We spoke individually with our Brn. and Srs. today. Old Mother Hannah received instruction for her coming confirmation. Sr. Sussana Elisabeth Fields, who will observe the next Holy Communion as a candidate, was also present during this instruction. We had a very good crowd of listeners today.

*Sun., Mar. 30.* [Spg.] It was Palm Sunday, and the Brn. and Srs. came in great numbers. In the first service we pleaded with the Savior in a prayer on our knees to bless us anew in the hearing of the story of His passion and death, and in the consideration of His sufferings and His love for us unto death to bring our hearts to life anew and to inspire us to bring our hearts to Him as a return sacrifice for all He has done in and for us. Then in 3 sessions we read the first part of the story of Passion Week. All who were present were very attentive to what was read.

*Mar. 31.* [Ooch.] Toward evening Br. Nathl. Byhan came here from Springplace. We are very busy now in the gardens and fields. Yesterday and today we planted potatoes, sweet potatoes, and some Indian corn. During the night between Mar. 31 and Apr. 1 we had a hard frost that destroyed our hopes of having fruit.

*Apr. 1.* [Ooch.] We had services this evening, Wednesday, and Thursday of this week to hear the story of Jesus' passion. A few of our Brn. and Srs. attended each of these, as did our scholars.

*Apr. 3.* [Spg.] In the evening Dav. Taziz came to us to serve us as interpreter at Easter. We were very happy about this.

*Apr. 4.* [Ooch.] Good Friday. In the first service we prayed the Litany of the Life, Sufferings, and Death of Jesus, and then in 4 sessions we read the story of the events leading up to Jesus' death and about His death on Golgotha. At the words, Jesus bowed his head and died, we fell on our knees and surrendered ourselves to be His eternally, for His great love for us even until death. Many Brn. and Srs. from Springplace attended the services today. We had a thorough talk today with Chinasse, Joseph Crutchfield's wife, whom we have accepted as a candidate for baptism. Sr. Anna Johanna Tusawallety from Springplace was our interpreter. We were pleased with Chinasse's spiritual state. Her husband, who left our fellowship some years ago and joined the Methodists, is not trying to hinder his wife, and he is happy that she wants to belong to Jesus.

*Apr. 4.* [Spg.] Good Friday. We read and encouraged ourselves with the last part of the Passion Week story. The Savior's suffering on the Mount of Olives and His death on the cross, and at the words, He bowed his head and died, we joined our dear brown people in falling on our knees and gave Him our hearts anew as a payment for His pains, and asked Him to have mercy on this Nation, so that many more of them might convert and experience that He also shed His blood for them for the forgiveness of sins. Great emotion in the hearts of those present could be felt.

*Apr. 5.* [Ooch.] Great Sabbath. In the evening we sang a liturgy in adoration of Jesus' body.

*Apr. 5.* [Spg.] Since we have realized for a long time already that the wife of our baptized Br. Boas, who has not yet been baptized, has begun reflecting on the state of her heart, and we could clearly see that the Spirit of God is working in her heart, today we gave her a chance to talk with us about the state of her heart. However, she did not appear in response to this invitation. We then spoke with her husband Br. Boas about her. He told us she often says to him that she feels that she should convert, but still feels too bad for this. We encouraged him and asked him to tell her that precisely this kind of person, who feels himself to be bad and unworthy, is most pleasing to the Savior, and that He shed His blood for the greatest sinner, etc. He promised to do so.

*Sun., Apr. 6.* [Ooch.] Easter. We joined our Brn. and Srs. and about 100 people who had gathered to pray the Easter Litany, partly in the Saal and partly at the grave of our Br. John Gambold, who died in blessing last year. The entire proceeding made a sweet impression on all those present. Then we had the festival sermon, after which Br. Schmidt baptized both of our baptismal candidates, Alexander Copeland and George Hicks, into Jesus' death. During this we experienced a powerful feeling of the close presence of the Holy Trinity. The former received the name Alexander James and the latter was named George Augustus.

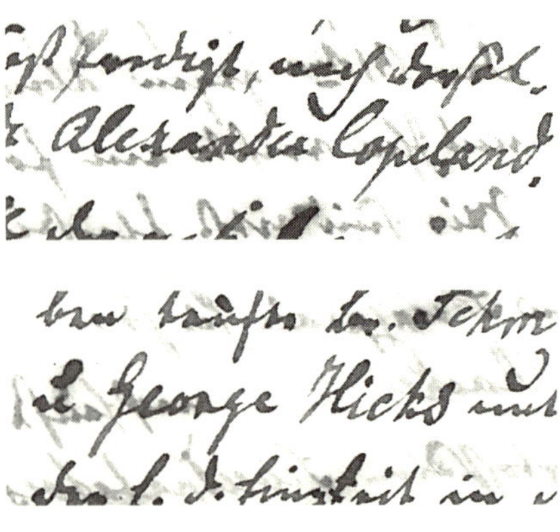

During the service that followed Br. Schmidt baptized the newborn baby daughter of our Sr. Sussanna Elisabeth Fields into Jesus' death; she received the name Rachel. Then we experienced the most blessed enjoyment of the body and blood of Jesus in Holy Communion. The elderly Sr. Hannah was also present for the first time and participated as a candidate for confirmation. During the final service the Indian Br. Samuel from Spring Place also delivered a touching talk to our Brn. and Srs. He encouraged them to remain faithful to the Savior and asked them to pay attention always to the voice of the Holy Spirit and never to forget that the Savior had achieved our eternal salvation through His bitter sufferings, bloodshed, death, and resurrection. Today we spoke with Queti, grandchild of our Sr. Hannah. This was a day the Lord made for us. Toward evening some of the Springplace Brethren and Sisters returned home. The rest followed them in the morning on the 7th. We had cold weather this week and heavy frosts at night.

*Sun., Apr. 6.* [Spg.] Easter. Because of the unusually cold and rainy weather, only a few of our Brn. and Srs. could come here. There were also very few friends here. In the first service in the morning, after the call to the congregation, The Lord is risen, the Lord is risen indeed! we prayed the Easter Litany in the Saal. After this was a talk to the congregation on the purpose and usefulness of the sufferings, death, and resurrection of our dear Lord, which Dav. Tazizi interpreted into Indian sentence by sentence. In the second service was the baptism of the baby boy born 7 weeks ago in Columbus to Henry and Mary Clayton, who had come here on a visit, with the name John Chitty. In the third service, we had with our communicant Brn. and Srs. — during which Dav. Tazizi and Young Wolf, who goes to Holy Communion in the Methodist faith, were present as guests — the sacramental enjoyment of the body and blood of Jesus in Holy Communion, during which the married Sr. Ruth watched as a candidate. Few eyes remained dry during this Holy Communion, and everyone was very touched.

# *1828, part 3*

[M 414-3-7: Translated by Julie Tomberlin Weber. Addressed to: Revd. Theodor Schulz, Salem, Stokes County, North Carolina. Postmark: Springplace, C.N, Apr. 17, 37½. Received May 1.]

Oochgeelogy, Apr. 8, 1828

My dearly beloved Br. Schulz!

With these lines accept my sincerest greetings. I should have written to you again a long time ago, but various things have prevented me from doing so.

Praise God, we here are all healthy and well. Passion Week and Easter were very blessed for us and our Brethren and Sisters. On Easter I once again had the grace of baptizing two persons into Jesus' death, George Hicks, a married man and eldest son of our dear Br. W. Abr. Hicks, who received the name George Augustus in holy baptism, and Alex Copeland, a young white man who has taken care of our farm in past years. In holy baptism he received the name Alexander James. Both of them are persons full of hope whose desire it is to become and to remain the Savior's complete property. George Augustus Hicks was the first Indian boy who came to the school in Spring Place during Br. and Sr. Wolfahrt's time. His wife belongs to the Methodists. His 3 children were baptized by the Brn.

At Easter more than 100 people arrived at our place, and many were very touched, so that we have hope that many took a deep and lasting impression home with them. For Holy Communion old Mother Hannah Qualiyuka was confirmed and participated for the first time. On the same day, I also baptized a baby daughter of our Sr. Sussanna Fields with the name Rachel. We also spoke with both of our other candidates for baptism, John Fields and Chinasse, Joseph Crutchfield's wife. They are both in a pleasing spiritual condition.

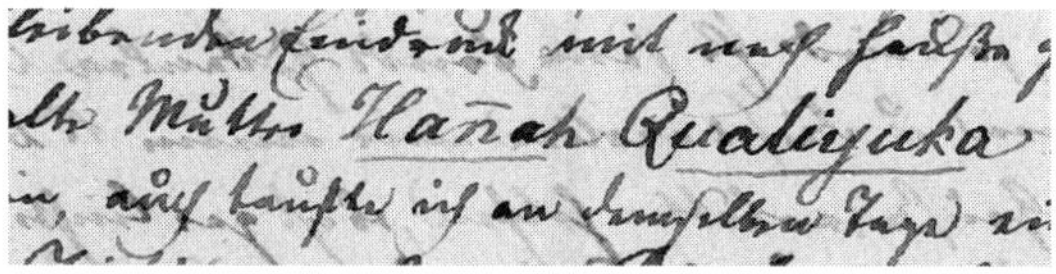

However, recently there has been much among our scholars about which we are sorrowful, since the boys and girls allowed things with each other which we cannot and may not permit. Luckily we found out about it in time. When the boys wanted to be stubborn and contrary and threatened to run home, we sent for Br. W. A. Hicks to come. He spoke very seriously with them. Through him we also had word sent to the parents to pick up their children (that is the boys), which then took place in a few days.

We are in agreement with Br. Hicks that it would be better if the boys were in the school in Springplace and the girls were here, especially since Sr. P. Gambold currently has to take care of the school. Since Br. Byhan shared this suggestion with the P.H. Conf., we are now waiting for their decision. In the meantime, Br. Byhan and I have spoken provisionally with many of the parents. There will not be a lack of difficulties, since parents do not want their children to go far from home. In all respects, and especially because of the frequent visits home, this would be very advantageous for their children. However, Br. Hicks thinks that we should not let ourselves be prevented, since keeping the sexes apart is very difficult but now all the more necessary. The Lord will also guide us in this respect.

For some weeks we have had especially raw weather and frost every night, which is very bad for the things in our garden. In the area around Springplace there is much illness, especially among the Negroes. Just last week Joseph Vann lost 2 more Negro women to death. So far everyone is healthy here in our area.

Accept the most obliging thanks for your last dear letter, which indeed hurt me deeply but also through God's grace led to contrite effort. I hope my dear Brethren will bury everything and not think about the old things any more. May the Savior keep me in His hand and give me, His weak child, grace, and keep me walking before Him in poverty, humility, and lowliness. In this way He will still be able to carry out His plans of peace in me. I ask my dear Brn. in the P.H. Conf., whom I herewith greet most sincerely, to help me pray for this. It is very easy to fall, but grace to find yourself again and to find all debts in yourself and lay them at the feet of a merciful Savior. I make this confession with tears, and now I want to extend to you and your dear family very sincere greetings from my wife and me.

Accept especially a very sincere greeting from your humble Brother, faithfully bound in Jesus' loving fellowship,

Johann Renatus Schmidt

Sr. Gambold, Sr. Polly, and Br. Joseph send sincere greetings.

[Springplace (M 407-1) and Oochgeelogy (M 409-1) Diaries. Translated by Julie Tomberlin Weber. Handwritings are Johann Renatus Schmidt's (Ooch.) and Gottlieb Byhan's (Spg.).]

*Apr. 8.* [Ooch.] David Steiner Taucheechy visited us and spent the night. We set the dry grass around us in the bush on fire to improve the pasture for the cattle. Today we had beautiful warm weather all day.

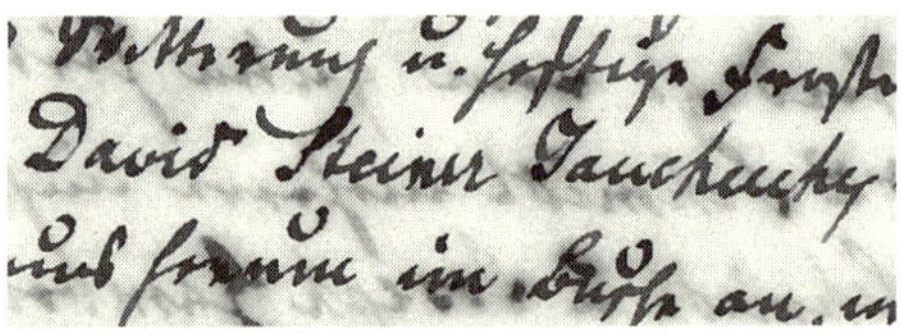

*Apr. 9.* [Ooch.] Once again D. S. Taucheechy visited us.

*Apr. 9.* [Spg.] Mr. McNair and Mr. McCoy from Newtown visited us. Since they had business at Mr. Jos. Vann's, they did not stay long at our place.

[M 414-3-8: Translated by Julie Tomberlin Weber. Addressed to: Revd. Theodor Shulz, Salem, Stokes County, North Carolina. Postmark: Springplace, C.N., Apr. 10. Free. Gottlieb Byhan, P.M. Received Apr. 24.]

Springplace, Apr. 9, 1828

My dearly beloved Br. Shulz,

I just want to inform you hastily with this post, which leaves here this morning, that I received your dear letter of March 17, and to answer your letter with all possible brevity because my time is running out. I cannot write any more in the evenings — at least not at this time — because my eyes are still not in very good shape.

But how surprised we were at the news in your letter that a single Br. has finally been found who is willing to serve the Savior among the heathen. I cannot describe to you how we felt at this news. We were beside ourselves with joy. Thanks and praise to God! So there are still Brn. in the Gemeine who are willing to do something for His work. I have not yet had the opportunity to share this news with the Brn. and Srs. in Ochgologee. But God willing, I will pay a visit there myself day after tomorrow, and with the next post, which leaves here on the 17th, I will be able to answer you in detail everything you asked about in your last letter, that is, about whether both Srs. Gambolds are coming or remaining.

But my dear Br., what will you say about my last letter and its contents? I can do nothing else, and I will not stand for more of it. As you can believe, I am really fed up with such, but I also cannot watch it silently when the things which should be treated with reverence and respect are carried out with apathy, and I would like to say, are done sloppily in haste. If I could only speak with you in person for 2 hours sometime __________.

I wrote to the Editor, Elias Boudinott, about the first issue of the Cherokee newspaper. However, when I go to Ochgologee I will speak to him myself

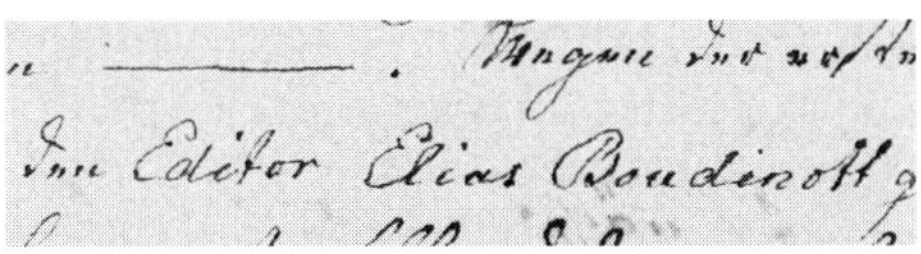
Editor Elias Boudinott

about this. The newspapers must have been stolen in the mail. It really is a shame that when the newspapers get to my Post Office, they have to lie around for a whole week or 6 days before I can send them on, because the posts from Georgia, Tennessee, and Alabama arrive here together on Thursday, and the New Echota mail comes on Friday. And so the newspapers must lie around in Springplace until the next Thursday, when they can be sent on. The G. Postmaster has been written about this matter, but an answer has not yet come.

Concerning Vann's field, you write that the Conf. advises us to do everything to get it for the mission, and that he perhaps would go down from $50. I do not believe that Jos. Vann will give up anything. However, I will do what I can to get it as cheaply as possible. I would ask the Conf. to tell me for sure if I should refrain from getting it if he will not negotiate, or if I should give him $50 to get it. He has now sowed it with oats. Today another of his Negroes died from the illness which has been raging among them, so that he has lost 6 Negroes from this illness now.

Our construction is going as usual for here — slowly. I have not yet gotten a floorboard sawed, although I ordered boards from Jos. Vann at the beginning of December. Now George Harlen has promised to saw some for me. Time will tell when and if I will get some from him. About 1,500 shingles have been made.

Nothing has yet been done in the matter concerning separating the boys and girls. We find we must be somewhat cautious about getting it to work. In my last letter to you I wrote that most of the scholars went home. Now most of them have returned. Nathanael completely takes care of the school. Confidentially, I wanted to inform you of this much: It has been more difficult for our Nathl. to get used to things here, and we do not believe he will stay here longer than next fall. He also says openly that he only wants to stay until a new house is built, then he will return to Salem, so that it will be good if the H. Conf. is also prepared for this case. If you ever have anything to note about this issue, please enclose it in your letter on a separate sheet of paper, so that we can keep it between us.

Last week the Claytens visited us and spent Easter with us. On Easter Sunday I baptized their child with the name John Chitty. They are in bad circumstances. He wanted to borrow money from me, which I had to flatly refuse. As far as we noticed, they would not have had anything against it if we had offered them a chance to stay with us. But we must admit that we are happy that we currently do not have them here. They have admitted openly it is their own fault. I believe they also realize this. On this occasion I would also like to remind you that my wife cannot endure it long without help, so it will be good if you remember this matter as well.

The Georgia post will be here any time, so I must close. Praise God, we are currently all healthy, and we greet everyone. Farewell. Your friend and Br.,

Gottlieb Byhan

I just received H. Blum's letter of March 23, for which we express our gratitude. I will answer him another time and send him greetings.

G. B.

[Springplace (M 407-1) and Oochgeelogy (M 409-1) Diaries.]

*Apr. 11.* [Spg.] Mr. Buttrick visited us and spent the night.

*Apr. 12.* [Spg.] Br. Byhan went to Ochgeloogy today on business. With him went Mr. Buttrick to Newtown.

*Apr. 12.* [Ooch.] Br. Byhan visited us from Spring Place. We learned from a letter from Br. Theodor Schulz that the single Br. Franz Eder in Niesky has received a call to serve the Cherokee mission, and he has accepted it. We were joyful and excited about this. May the Savior accompany this Br. on land and sea with His protection and sweet presence, so that we will soon have the pleasure of welcoming him among us.

*Sun., Apr. 13.* [Ooch.] During the first service, Br. Byhan prayed the Church Litany. During the 2nd service we continued reading the story of Jesus' resurrection. In the afternoon we had a strong storm with hail and hurricane-like wind. This did considerable damage to our roofs and fences, although the damage we suffered is nothing compared to what many of our poor neighbors endured.

*Sun., Apr. 13.* [Spg.] There were no services in Spring Place, which was announced to the Brn. and Srs. last Sunday, because Br. Byhan would be absent.

*Apr. 14.* [Ooch.] Br. Byhan returned in the morning. Today we heard from many of our Brethren and Sisters and neighbors how they had been in real danger of losing their lives. The roof was torn off our neighbor Austin Copeland's house, as well as all of his other buildings. They had to hide in their cellar with their children to be safe from the rain, hail, and shingles that were flying around. Sister Lydia Chisolm was in the bush more than a mile from home when the bad weather hit. She had a grandchild with her who was carried more than 50 feet by the wind. The largest trees around her were uprooted. We have not yet heard of anyone being killed by this storm, but the destruction it caused is amazing. More than 50 huge oaks and pine trees that were uprooted by the wind are lying all around us. Other trees lost their highest branches, which were carried a long way by the wind.

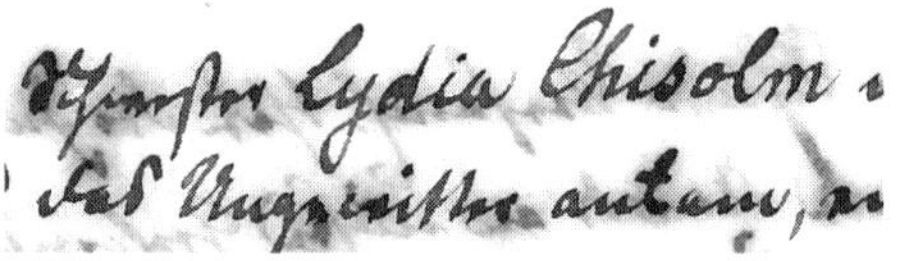

*Apr. 14.* [Spg.] Br. Byhan returned from Ochgeloogy. With him came Sr. Polly Gambold to visit for some days at Spring Place.

*Apr. 15.* [Spg.] Dav. Tazizi, who had stayed in our area for several days because of his cattle and was usually at our place at night, returned home today. Because Tazizi's cattle usually stay close to us and usually with our cattle, we have the freedom of keeping his cows which have calves and using the milk.

[M 414-3-9: Translated by Julie Tomberlin Weber. Addressed to: Revd. Theodor Shulz, Salem, Stokes County, North Carolina. Postmark: Springplace, C.N., Apr. 17. Free. Gottlieb Byhan, P.M. Received Apr. 30.]

Springplace, April 16, 1828

My dearly beloved Br. Shulz,

In the last post I already informed you of the receipt of your dear letter dated March 17, which contained the happy news that the single Br. Franz Eder in Nisky had received and accepted a call to serve the mission among the Cherokees.

At the beginning of this week I was in Ochgologee and shared the contents of your letter concerning this Br. with the Brethren and Sisters there. Br. Shmidt seemed to be pretty satisfied with this. However, Sr. Shmidt did not seem to want to understand it, instead of being happy as she should have been. In keeping with your request, I spoke with both Sisters Gambold about whether they will remain here or return to Salem. The widowed Sister Gambold said that she will stay in Ochgologee no longer than the arrival of the Brother — or Br. and Sr. — Eder. Either she will return to Salem, or she will be willing to serve the mission <u>in Springplace</u> further in the taking care of the household. She will no longer stay in Ochgologee. Sr. Polly Gambold is planning to return to Salem with this opportunity.

But old Br. Joseph Gambold felt a little bit as if no one was thinking about <u>him</u> with a single syllable, and asks what should become of him? He himself has not told me what he is planning to do, but Polly G. tells me that <u>she</u> believes if <u>she</u> left he would also go, so it would be possible for him to come to Salem with his daughter. He also does not want to stay in Ochgologee, and there really is no room for him in Springplace. He is old and weak and is also afflicted with certain problems which require that he should stay in a house by himself, which we do not have in Springplace. In brief, we presume that he will probably return to Salem with his daughter. With my encouragement, he promised to write you himself or through his daughter.

But, dear Br., on this occasion I also cannot neglect laying our situation in external matters on your heart. My wife is no longer young and has no help with the household except for Rachel. Sometimes this is just too much for her, and it is no wonder when there are about 20 people at the table at every meal. She also takes care of the milking, because Pleasant can no longer take a step outside of the kitchen without a cane, so that my wife naturally must take care of everything. We are currently milking 13 cows, 9 of our own, and David Tazizi has 4 here. To describe all the external work that falls on the Sisters would be too rambling. Remember us in love, we really ask you.

The housemother just told me that she could send you a quantity of butter with the wagon. The price of butter here is 12½ cents. We have already sold a little.

To say another word about help in our household, if we still have a word to say we just want to say this much. We would be very happy if Sr. A. M. Gambold could help out in our household for a while until further help comes. We are convinced that we would get along together quite well in external matters. Now the Savior will provide guidance and assistance in His time! Sr. Polly Gambold is currently visiting here in Springplace. Her illness still overtakes her often, but it usually does not last long.

At Easter we had very cold weather here. All the fruit was frozen, even our peas in the garden, which were a foot tall, froze to the ground, as well as our early potatoes, which had already sprouted. We celebrated the Easter festival in blessing. The Easter Litany could not be prayed on God's Acre because of the cold weather.

With tomorrow's mail, with which this letter should go, I am sending the *Phoenix*, that is, 2 of the first issue which had not yet found its way to Salem. Day before yesterday I was in New Echota myself at the press at Mr. Boudinott's. He was immediately willing to have the first issues follow for you and Br. Steiner, along with sincere greetings to both of you.

But tell me what has become of the Anderses? We hope they have not had an accident. Now perhaps they will arrive soon. It seems Th. Wohlfarth is still his old self and still has not improved!

When will he ever convert and look inside himself? May the Savior have mercy on him!

The construction of my house is going very slowly, as is usual here in this country. I have spoken with a carpenter named Brock about framing the house. He asks for $1.50 a day. Such a high price! Should I give it to him or not? Perhaps I can negotiate him down somewhat or find someone cheaper. I will do my best. Dear Br., just send me money again. South Carolina or North Carolina — the former is better than the latter. The debt which Br. Shmidt made with a certain Lavender at the end of Oct. last year amounts to $192 and is still not yet paid, and I also cannot pay it, although Lavender reminds me of it again and again. In the bill which Lavender gave Br. Shmidt it says among other things: "For Commission and so forth for the above Sum 25 pro Cent — $38 — as per Agreement." As a result Br. Schmidt got the value of only $154 from him. This debt is oppressive and concerns me greatly. Perhaps Major Ridge will pay something soon. We will hope for the best.

But poor Br. Chr. Blum — what can be said that such things should happen to him? If we could help him to some degree, but how? The Savior will not leave him. He knows ways and means to help His children. He will also do this here in His time. Greet him and Sr. Blum from us. The housemother here asks me to inform you that the dried peaches we left behind should not be sold, but should be sent with the next opportunity, because there are none here this year.

Praise God, we are currently all healthy and greet everyone sincerely. And you, dear Br., accept the warmest greeting and kiss from your friend and Br.

Gottlieb Byhan

[Springplace (M 407-1) and Oochgeelogy (M 409-1) Diaries.]

*Apr. 20.* [Ooch.] The sermon was on the Good Shepherd. In the afternoon Srs. Gambold and Schmidt visited many of our Brn. and Srs. in the neighborhood.

*Sun., Apr. 20.* [Spg.] The Brn. and Srs. came in good numbers again. After the services the Indian Brn. and Srs. asked for permission to sing their spiritual hymns, of which they have a good number, which we gladly gave them. It was quite pleasant to listen and to see how they sit and sing so intensely and reverently together. Their melodies have much monotone about them; still they are quite pleasant to listen to. We could not get the contents of the hymns translated.

*Apr. 21.* [Ooch.] Brn. Schmidt and Joseph Gambold went to Joseph Crutchfield's to visit. They went to inform his wife Chinasse that she has been approved to receive holy baptism next Pentecost, May 25. Joseph Crutchfield lives on the river about 9 miles from here. We left here right after breakfast. None of us has ever been to his place, and unfortunately we got lost and did not arrive at the Crutchfields' until almost sunset. After we had roamed around in the woods about 30 miles today, the family received us with much love and hospitality. Br. Schmidt had a very pleasant talk with him until after midnight. He recently joined the Methodist Society and every Sunday he holds a school in his neighborhood; about 20 scholars attend this.

*Apr. 22.* [Ooch.] Br. Schmidt returned, accompanied by Mr. Crutchfield. Br. Joseph Gambold was very exhausted from yesterday's journey, and so he stayed there to rest for one day and did not return until the 23rd.

*Apr. 22.* [Spg.] Today we received a pleasant visit from the Chief of the Nation, our Br. Willm. Abr. Hicks, and Mr. John Ridge and his wife. They were returning from the Agency where they had been invited by the Agent, Mr. Montgomery, to a conversation about their Constitution. It was a shame that our Br. Hicks was not doing well this evening, and had to go to bed early, after we had given him something to strengthen him. His visit would have been even more interesting to us and would have given rise to many pleasant conversations. One can see in this Br. what the power of God's blood can do in the hearts of humans. What they say applies to him: The wolf is made into a lamb. We can see in him that he has sought and found grace in Jesus' blood. May the Savior keep him by Him until the end of his days.

[M 414-3-10: Translated by Julie Tomberlin Weber. Addressed to: Revd. Theodor Schulz, Salem, Stokes County, North Carolina. Postmark: Springplace, C.N., Apr. 24, 1828. Free. Gottlieb Byhan, P.M. Received May 8.]

Springplace, Apr. 22, 1828

My dear Br. Shulz,

Since I wrote to you just 8 days ago, dear Br., I do not have anything special to report today, but just want to send you greetings from everyone. Praise God, we are all healthy.

Actually, one thing occurs to me which I would like to have advice on. Mr. Boudinott, editor of the *Phoenix* in New Echota, has already asked me repeatedly if I would not like to have something put in the *Phoenix* in memory and honor of blessed Br. John Gambold as missionary, either his Lebenslauf or something else about his character among the Indians, and that I should deliver this to him. You can believe that I do not know what to do in this matter. I could not agree to print the entire Lebenslauf — as you recently sent it to me — in the newspaper without first learning your opinion about it. So please be so good and let me know your thoughts about it as soon as possible. To be free of him — Mr. Boudinott — for the most part, I thought I would allow him to include in his newspaper a kind of Obituary, that is, his death and the last sentence in the Lebenslauf, which then will appear in the *Phönix* dated March [April] 24, as I presume.

Last month I received from the Secretary of War 3 copies of Mr. McKenny's *Tour to the Lakes* and to the northern Indians, with engravings, as well as his negotiations among the southern Indians last fall, among others with the Creeks. Two copies were addressed to Revd. John Gambold "for the use of the School at Springplace." This gave me reason to write to the Secretary of War to report to him the receipt of the books and to express my gratitude to him for this, and also to report Br. Gambold's death and to commend the mission here

to his further remembrance. I will share with you here verbatim the answer I received with the last post.

[Br. Byhan copies Col. McKenney's letter in English:]

Department of War
Off: Ind: Affairs
25th March 1828

To Revd. Gottlieb Byhan, Springplace, C.N., &c
Dear Sir

Your Letter to the Secretary of War, of the 6th Inst. is received. The Secretary and all who had hitherto enjoyed the pleasure of the late Revd. Mr. Gambold's correspondence, and who knew and appreciated his worth and services, deplore his death. But thus it hath pleased God.

You are recognized as his Successor, and the best wishes of the Department will attend upon your labours.

The fruits of Mr. Gambold's instructions will no doubt encourage his successors to imitate so virtuous an example.

Such aid as can be furnished from the Civilization fund will be continued to you.

With my best wishes, yours Respectfully,

Tho. L. McKenney

[Br. Byhan concludes his letter to Br. Schulz in German:]

Yesterday we had a visit from our Chief, Br. Willm. Abr. Hicks, and Mr. John Ridge and Lady. They returned from the Agency. They had been invited for a conversation with Mr. Montgomery about the Cherokee Constitution. I could not learn anything about their negotiations. However, they told me that the whole proceeding would appear in the *Phoenix* dated Apr. 23. Since Br. Willm. Abr. Hicks was not well, I could not speak with him much, and besides they were also in a great hurry to get home, because they had already been held up almost 3 days by high streams. They spent the night here. I am planning to visit Mr. Montgomery if I can ever get away, but I cannot yet say when this can happen.

On this occasion I must add that in our current economic situation we absolutely cannot think about visiting our Brethren and Sisters. These visits were strongly recommended to us, and we also agree that it is very necessary for such house visits to be made. If the Claytens had stayed here and had had more heart for the work here, then we could have made such visits. However, as our situation is now, we cannot consider any visits. And so it is extremely necessary and very desirable if another Brother and Sister could be found who were willing to help the Savior gather in His reward for suffering, in whatever manner. Because I maintain that each person at a post among the heathen, whether he is hired to do the external or the spiritual work, is viewed in the Savior's eyes as if it were being done to Him — if it is done faithfully. But not like the Claytens, who according to his statements viewed the whole matter as deception. May the Savior allow a Br. and Sr. to be found soon to help serve the Savior here sincerely!

The illness among Jos. Vann's Negroes has still not subsided. He has now lost 6 already, and it almost seems as if he would lose another soon, his sawmill worker. I do not yet know when I am going to get boards and such sawed. At times I almost lose the courage to build. In the meantime, I will not give up yet.

I keep forgetting to report to you about the fat-belly horse we were given. I can say this much: It is a really good horse on the farm. I could not wish for a better one. It looks completely different now than it did when it came to Salem from the Quarter, also much better than it was after it had been fed in Salem for 6 weeks. I would not take $75 for it now. It would bring even more here, if we wanted to, and could sell it. I sold the old mare and her foals which were here for $55. The mare was very lame. But I did not get money for this, but work, so my cashbox did not get anything. Please send me some more money. Please greet everyone from us, including Br. and Sr. Chr. Blum. We certainly have much sympathy for their fate. I remain your abiding friend and Br.,

Gottlieb Byhan

[Springplace (M 407-1) and Oochgeelogy (M 409-1) Diaries.]

*Apr. 23.* [Ooch.] Sr. Polly Gambold returned here; she had been visiting at Springplace. In the following days Br. Schmidt visited with Br. and Sr. W. A. Hicks and with our other Brn. and Srs. and neighbors who live close by.

*Apr. 24.* [Ooch.] Another young girl, who is 7 years old, was brought to us as a boarding student in the school. Her parents belong to the Presbyterian congregation in Turnip Mountain. The father is an exhorter in that congregation. Mr. Buttrick advised the parents to put their child in our care.

*Sun., Apr. 27.* [Ooch.] The sermon was on John 20:26-29. During the 2nd service we sang a liturgy. We wanted to speak with our baptismal candidate Chinasse, who was still here today, but Br. W. A. Hicks was sick and could not be here, so we did not have an interpreter and could not do this. In the evening we had Bible reading.

*Sun., Apr. 27.* [Spg.] Once again only a few Brn. and Srs. came to the services, because the streams were very swollen by the frequent and heavy rain showers. Also even Br. and Sr. Josua and the Brn. and Srs. who live in the area were not here, because last night a small child from Br. Josua's circle of friends had died and was buried today. In the night from the 29th to the 30th we had strong storms again with heavy rain showers, mixed in with hail, which, however, did no damage. The streams around us rose very strongly again.

*Apr. 28.* [Ooch.] We started school again which we had canceled for several months. Today we received pleasant letters from Salem.

*Sun., May 4.* [Ooch.] We prayed the Church Litany during the first service. During the 2nd service we read from the booklet *The Word of the Cross* instead of having a sermon. In the evening we had Bible reading.

*Sun., May 4.* [Spg.] The Sunday services were as usual, but no Negroes were here today, because yesterday a grown Negro who belonged to our neighbor Jos. Vann died again as a result of the epidemic which has prevailed among them this spring. This is the 7th Negro whom Mr. Jos. Vann has lost to this illness. David Vann, who stayed close to here last week, visited us today and was present in our services. In the evening Mr. James McNair and his sister Mrs. Nealy came to us and spent the night. Mr. Dav. Vann also came this evening to our place on a visit, but returned to Mr. Jos. Vann, where he spent the night.

*May 5.* [Spg.] This morning Mr. James McNair went, and with him Mr. Jos. Vann and Dav. Vann, to the District Court which will be held in Coosawatee this week. The latter stopped in at our place. Early today we also saw that last night an attempt had been made to steal corn from our corncrib, when an opening was made in the roof to climb into it. Apparently, however, their plan was disturbed when Br. and Sr. Byhan heard a noise at midnight, and Br. Byhan went out to see what was happening, and they ran away. We did not discover the intended robbery, however, until morning. Still we saw that they had pulled out a small quantity of corn through a slit between the blocks.

[*Cherokee Phoenix*, April 24, 1828, p. 3, col. 5.]

OBITUARY

We were in hopes of obtaining, for the columns of our paper, a biographical notice of the late Rev. John Gambold, one of the first Missinaries to this Nation. At present, we merely give a Notice of his death, sent to us by a bereaved fellow labourer. We take pleasure in inserting it, though at this late hour.

Departed from this life, November 7th 1827, at the Moravian Missionary station at Ochgelogy among the Cherokees, the Rev. JOHN GAMBOLD, aged 67 years, 4 months, and 21 days, of a pectoral dropsy.

His faithfulness, humility, and zeal for the missionary cause, in behalf of which he sacrificed every thing, his childlike confidence in the heavenly Father, which was never shaken, even in the most difficult and pressing circumstances, his philanthropic, collected, and highly circumspect behavior in word and deed, which was so peculiarly adapted to the character of the nation, among which he preached the Gospel, and by which he was esteemed and loved as a Father — all these qualities will insure to the dear deceased, a grateful and glorious tribute in the ranks of departed, and illustrious missionaries.

## *1828, part 4*

[M 414-3-11: Translated by Julie Tomberlin Weber and C. Daniel Crews. Addressed to: Revd. Theodor Shulz, Salem, Stokes County, North Carolina. Postmark: Springplace, C.N., May 8. Free. Gottlieb Byhan, P.M. Received May 24.]

Springplace, May 7, 1828

My dear Br. Shulz,

We were delighted to receive your dear letter of April 17 with *Wöchentliche Nachrichten, Missy. Intelligencier*, etc., on May 1. I will get right to answering your dear letter.

Major Ridge has paid me nothing yet, and I fear if his prospects are the way we hear they are then it may be a long time yet before I get anything from him. He received Br. Reichel's letter. Since then I have only heard that he was very surprised that he is supposed to owe Br. Reichel so much. When his son John Ridge visited Spring Place recently, he spoke in a rambling manner as if he wanted to visit his sister in Salem this summer or fall. But probably nothing will come of this.

I had completely forgotten that I subscribed to the *History of S. America*. But I did finally remember it. Send it to me when you get a chance.

We cannot yet speak of improvement concerning the health of our neighbors, specifically among our Jos. Vann's Negroes. Last Saturday George, the old cripple Jacob's son, who worked at his sawmill, died, so now 7 of them have died of the same illness. There are some who are still sick, but currently not seriously. Mr. Jos. Vann is in fact very badly off. He cannot continue his fieldwork, because his best hands have either died already or are not healthy. He is really to be pitied. The inexplicable thing about this illness is that it is just among Jos. Vann's Negroes, for whatever reason.

I have spoken again with the carpenter who is supposed to frame the house for me, and I have explained to him that $1.50 a day would be a salary exceeding all limits, and I personally could not give him this without first getting the thoughts of the Directors of our Missionary Society. I was worried he would say: The agreement has been made; I must have this salary. But instead he said he would not insist on having $1.50, if I thought this was too much, he would work for somewhat less. I told him that I could not make a firm agreement with him until I had an answer from the Directors. This is how the matter still stands. He currently works in New Echota. He is supposed to be a good workman.

But when I may come so far as to need a carpenter, I just do not know. For no one can have any idea how slowly building goes here in the Land. Before Christmas I ordered the flooring boards from Jos. Vann, and to this day not one foot of them has been sawn! I have turned to George Harlen and McNair, both of whom have sawmills. With McNair the stream was either too high or too low, and in the meantime he had to saw either for himself or for other people what he had already promised to saw last year. Harlen had 300 feet of floor boards for me last Saturday, and about 1,000 feet of smaller boards, and that is all that has been sawn for the house.

This spring I gave Jos. Vann what one calls a "wood ticket," but he has sawn little or nothing, and now the one who runs his sawmill has died, and so nothing at all will come of that. He is indeed talking of getting a white man to saw for him. Perhaps it would have been better if I had gotten just one of them to saw for me, since Jos. Vann, as I heard, said when he first heard that

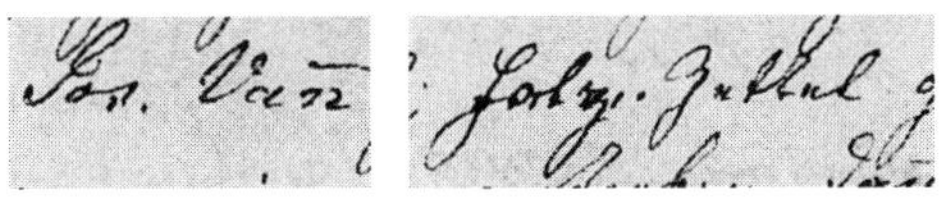

I was wanting to build, that as he is also our neighbor, I was obliged to give the sawing to him. We are afraid that we will have to pass one more winter in our little house. It appears that this year only preparations for building will be made. Add to this the fact that the wood will have to be cut while it is still running with sap, for I cannot have the logs for the house cut and dressed until I also have all the other materials together on the place, for it occurs to me that getting the logs is the least of my worries. And so I really cannot say how things can go, only that it will sometimes be even more difficult. We trust that the Savior will undergird us in this matter also. Oh, how I wish I could just talk with you for a couple of hours!

As to what you, dear Br., now report about Br. Eder's living accommodations, and whether he comes to us or to Ochgeloogy, my suggestions about his or their dwelling are these: As soon as Br. Eder, or Br. and Sr. Eder, arrive in Ochgoloogy the room where the Sisters Gambold are presently living will become empty, for as I already reported to you, the two Sisters will remain there no longer than the Eders' arrival in Ochgoloogy. The widow Gambold will, or wants, as she says, to come back to Salem or to us in Springplace, and it appears she would rather do the latter than the first, because she believes she owes it to the Mission to serve longer. What a notion! And Sr. Polly Gambold has decided to come back to Salem, and so the new arrivals can live in the Sisters' dwelling.

But what will become of Br. Joseph Gambold? It seems that he does not want to stay in Ochgoloogy longer either. In fact we really have no room for him in Spring Place until we have built. I am inclined to believe that he will come back to Salem, but he has not yet stated what he is planning to do.

Concerning the construction of a new church in Ochgoloogy, I must just say this much. This will require thorough consideration, as you write, and whether such construction could be undertaken as long as Br. Shmidt is there. Br. Eder would have to carry out the whole undertaking. When the wagon which brings out Br. or Br. and Sr. Eder is returned again, I will send you Br. Shmidt's income and expenditures, as he has written them down.

In response to your question about whether we asked for the approval of each of the 4 baptismal candidates <u>individually</u>, the answer is <u>yes</u>.

I have not yet been able to do anything about the Cherokee Alphabet, but I will try to make the comparison as soon as possible. I do not know whether this

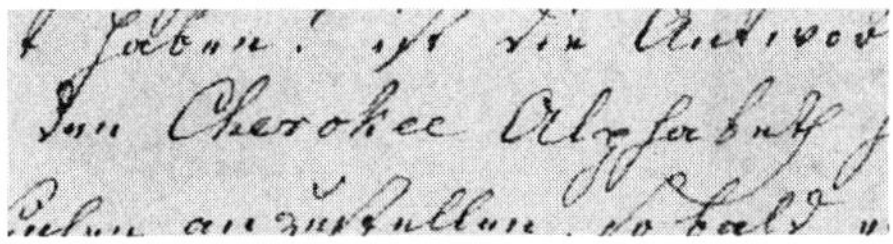

can take place in Mr. Boudinott's presence, because when I visit him in New Echota he will hardly be able to take the time to go through the Alphabet with us because he is buried under with work, and people say that in his current situation he will not be to endure it much longer, but will die under this load. And then

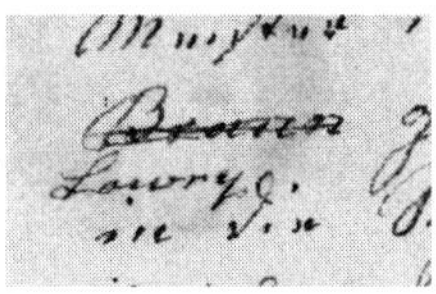

I have also heard that he is no master in the pronunciation of the Charackters, because a certain ~~Brown~~ Lowry apparently said that he would advise Mr. Boudinott to go to school a while longer to pronounce the Characters better and to learn to print them. But perhaps on occasion I can find someone with whom I can go through the Alphabet. There are many Indians who can read the printed Cherokee well. I will do my best to fulfill your wish.

<u>All</u> contained in your dear letter we were very glad to hear. <u>All</u> that seems insignificant to you is interesting to us so far away.

Praise God, we are currently pretty healthy. Still, strangely enough, we all have felt a certain pressure in our stomachs for the last 14 days, some more and some less. We do not know if it is the water or something else causing this, because recently, since the weather is getting warmer, we have drunk more water, and we thought this might be the cause of it. Primarily because of all the work, we have discontinued vespers and drink our coffee with the evening meal. Otherwise, we need help in the household. I sincerely wish and hope the Negro help you have planned succeeds, and also that we might have it soon. My dear wife most sincerely returns greetings to your dear family. Please accept a separate greeting and kiss from your friend and Br.,

Gottlieb Byhan

Charles R. Hicks's heirs will send the packet of *Missionary Intel.* when they can. This week the Court is in Goosawatty, about 16 miles from here, which usually lasts 5 days. Perhaps something about the proceedings will be put in the *Phönix.*

G. B.

[Springplace (M 407-1) and Oochgeelogy (M 409-1) Diaries. Translated by Julie Tomberlin Weber. Handwritings are Johann Renatus Schmidt's (Ooch.) and Gottlieb Byhan's (Spg.).]

*May 8.* [Ooch.] The children received their instruction.

*Sun., May 11.* [Ooch.] The first service was the Litany. David Steiner Taucheechy, who was visiting us today, interpreted the sermon. Old Fire and the father of the Christian Indian John Arch, who died several years ago in Brainerd, were among the Indians here. We spoke with Chinasse and instructed her in the truths of salvation of the Christian religion. In the evening we had Bible reading. An Indian woman who lives in Ustenaly and is married to a white man sent word that she is very ill and wanted us to visit her, so we decided that Sr. Gambold and Sr. Sally Hicks should visit her tomorrow. But heavy rains that began during the night and continued the following day prevented the visit. After some time, this person recovered and was able to visit us herself, and we took the opportunity to talk with her thoroughly about her spiritual state.

*Sun., May 11.* [Spg.] Many Brn. and Srs. and neighbors came to the Sunday services. After these Br. Samuel held a talk to the Brn. and Srs. in which he advised them to come very regularly to the services in Springplace and not, as some had often done, to go to the Methodists or Baptist services, because they could hear the word of God here as well as there, and should hold fast together as Brn. and Srs. and also love each other well, etc. The Brn. and Srs. departed very happily, only Sr. Rebecca, who felt spoken to by Br. Samuel's address with reference to visiting services in other places, said farewell with tears in her eyes. Through Polly Vann, Sr. Byhan encouraged her and consoled her that she should not take Br. Samuel's words so hard. We were convinced that she would not leave the congregation in Spring Place. She seemed to be comforted for the most part about this.

Afterward we had the pleasure of being able to inform three Indians, an elderly Indian woman, our Sr. Deborah's mother, our Br. James's wife, and a young single Indian, that at their repeated request they would receive holy baptism. We spoke with them thoroughly about the purpose of baptism and about what is important when a person has a desire to be cleansed from sins through Jesus Christ's blood in holy baptism. They expressed themselves to our satisfaction and testified that they recognized themselves as poor sinners and were convinced that they needed a Savior who would help them and could cleanse them of their sins through His blood. Then they were told that on Trinity Sunday they would receive the waters of holy baptism and be cleansed and washed of their sins through the blood of Jesus Christ. They were very happy about this.

[M 414-3-12: Translated by Julie Tomberlin Weber. Addressed to: Revd. Theodor Schulz, Salem, Stokes County, North Carolina. Postmark: Springplace, C.N., May 15, 37½.]

Oochgeelogy, May 11, 1828

My dearly beloved Br. Schulz,

I received your dear letter of March 24 by way of New Echota on the 27th the next month, and with these lines I want to send sincere greetings as well as obliging thanks for this.

I had already learned with pleasure from your dear letter to Br. Byhan that Br. Franz Eder has received a call to the

Cherokee Mission and that he will probably be assigned here in Oochgeelogy. In response to your letter, we have also discussed the home for this Br. among ourselves, and we are completely in agreement (and Br. W. A. Hicks also agrees to this) that for now, whether he comes single or married, there will be sufficient room here and that we do not need to undertake construction of a new house, especially since Br. Joseph Gambold has definitely stated that he is planning to return to Salem with his daughter. And if this should not work out we can always have him a small house built with little cost. Currently we have only one boy here. The rest of the scholars are all girls. If we ever lack living space, we could hold school in the Saal for a time as has also been done in Springplace. In the summer it is feasible to have it on the upper gallery, where there is room for 14-20 scholars. It would be a shame to build a new house with many expenses now, since we cannot know whether in some time the Saal could become too small after all, especially for fest days, and then it would seem necessary to build a new church. The room where the Srs. Gambold live in the schoolhouse is almost as large as ours. However, a chamber is missing, which would be easy to add on. On the other side is the same space for the boys and dayworkers, and why couldn't school be held in this without problems. If Br. Joseph should stay here, which we encourage and have promised to take good care of him, then a house should be built for him. It seems he would rather live in Spring Place with Br. and Sr. Byhan. But how could this dear Br. and Sr. take care of an old man, since they are going to build and there is really no place there, at least not for now. Without a doubt he himself will write, as will Sr. Polly, whom we are really sorry to lose, because she loves the Indians here, and she takes care of the school so faithfully. Everyone also loves her in return.

We are all healthy and well. I already wrote you about the blessed celebration of Easter and the baptism of Alex James Copeland and George Augustus Hicks in my last letter to you. John Fields is an Indian husband of our Sr. Sussanna Elisabeth. For Pentecost the dear Savior has planned another blessing for us. On this day Chinassee, Joseph Crutchfield's wife, is supposed to be baptized. John Fields was omitted for this time. I still have hope of winning poor Crutchfield, and I visited him with Br. Joseph Gambold 14 days ago. This visit was very costly to us, though. He lives about 8 miles from here on the river. We departed here early in the morning after breakfast but got lost in the bush and had to wander around the whole day in swamps and woods, and we did not arrive at Crutchfield's until sundown. We probably went over 30 miles. On the following day I went home with Joseph Crutchfield, but Br. Joseph was so exhausted that he had to rest there for a day.

We have spoken with Major Ridge about money, but have little hope for now. I do not understand why absolutely no money is coming from the Secy. of War. Things are going very well with Br. Alex Copeland's tilling our farm. We just wish that we could pay him one way or another since we owe him over $200. Would it not be good to give him a note with interest, since it has been so long since he got his salary? I hope he will stay with us a long time yet. It seems this is also his intention. He is still young, understands the Cherokee language, although just minimally, but still in time he could also be helpful to us in this way.

From the Echota newspaper you will have seen that another murder has taken place in the Nation. We are now having very pleasant weather and hopefully the night frosts will let up now. I am taking care of the garden here, my favorite secondary occupation. All is growing well. If you should write to our dear Br. Hüffel, greet him very sincerely from me. I recently received a letter from Br. Wolle. He reports the death of God's servant Joseph Eastburn in Philadelphia, whom I knew well. The epidemic at Springplace among Vann's Negroes appears to be subsiding.

Br. W. A. Hicks and his family send sincerest greetings to you. Your visit is still well remembered by the Brn. and Srs. This afternoon I had a thorough conversation with Br. Joseph about his staying here, especially because if he stays various articles of clothing will have to be sent. But he is firmly set on returning to the Gemeine. Would it not be possible to find a little place for him to retire in Bethlehem? It is really hard for an older Br. if he so much wants to spend his last days in the Gemeine, and this cannot be granted him. I see well that this would not happen in Salem. My wife and I also want to take this opportunity to ask for articles of clothing for us and our children, as well as some articles for the post here such as a cover for the Saal table and a half dozen walkway lights like Br. and Sr. Byhan brought for Springplace. Also I will enclose a list of this. Mother Gambold cannot write anything until things are decided concerning her further stay in the Cherokee Mission. Shoes are an article which is hardly available in Oochgeelogy.

Please greet your dear colleagues most sincerely from us, as well as Br. and Sr. Steiner and Buchholz and M. Reich. My wife joins me in greeting your dear family. You are especially greeted by your faithfully obliged Br.,

Johann R. Schmidt

P.S. Concerning my suggestion to give Br. Alex Copeland a note with interest, Sr. Gambold thinks that he would get the interest generously through this since his clothing until now has been made and mended for him at no cost. Still the suggestion should be considered, especially since it is so difficult to send money. I have not yet had an opportunity to discuss this matter with Br. Byhan.

J. R. S.

[Springplace (M 407-1) Diary.]

*May 13.* [Spg.] A drunken Indian came and went straight into the schoolhouse, where Br. Nathl. Byhan was holding school, and tried to give the Indian children good advice. But it did not go well. Afterward he began to sing with them. After they had sung a while he went on, as he said, "to get a little whiskey." We later heard that he used to go to the school here. His name is Murphy.

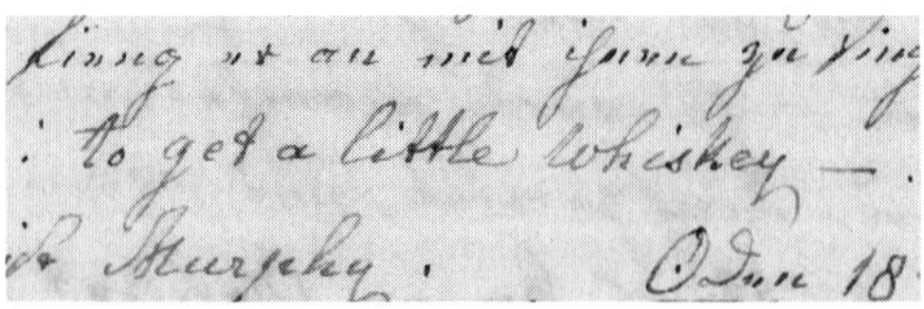

[M 414-3-13: Translated by Julie Tomberlin Weber. Addressed to: Revd. Theodor Schulz, Salem, Stokes County, North Carolina. Postmark: Springplace, C.N., May 15. Free. Gottlieb Byhan, P.M.]

Springplace, May 14, 1828

My dear Br. Shulz,

Since I just wrote to you with the last post on May 7, I do not have much special to report to you today concerning the external situation. But concerning the internal life of our dear Brn. and Srs. in Springplace, we must say, to the glory of the Savior, that this is definitely pleasing, at least this is to be concluded from their statements and behavior, and we often see clear signs of a true life from God among them. May the Savior keep them by Him and bring them ever closer to Him and ground them ever more in His merits!

We must admit that we are very happy among them. Last Sunday our Indian Br. Samuel held another talk for the Brn. and Srs. after the regular services. In this he warned them to remain with the Savior and with the Gemeine. If we ourselves could understand him, then we could tell you more about the contents of it. The talk was pretty long. Oh, if we just had more help here, so that we could do more with the Brethen and Sisters and visit them besides on Sundays!

We sit here and see our Brn. and Srs. only on Sundays. It is not possible for me to go out during the week and leave the whole work to my dear wife and Rachel. I must help out. Otherwise, we will not manage, because the household is large, and Pleasant is no help. The livestock especially takes much work and time.

I must also share with you another happy circumstance. First the Negro Br. Christian Jacob will observe Holy Communion as a confirmand for the last time on Pentecost. And secondly, God willing, we will have the baptism of three adult Indians on Trinity Sunday: a young Indian named Nic Tiger and our communicant Br. James' wife, and then a somewhat elderly Indian woman, our Sr. Sarah Deborah's mother. May the Savior reveal Himself graciously during this holy proceeding and let those newly baptized feel Him quite close and also support me, His poor tool, with grace and power so that, not only during this solemn event but at all times, I might do for Him that for which he has made me worthy and has sent me. Our concern is always that we at least do not ruin anything in His work as long as we are here. May He protect us for this!

Enclosed you will receive the printed Cherokee Alphabet,[1] which will meet your expectations. It is all pronounced as in German, for example,  like the German a, [characters],

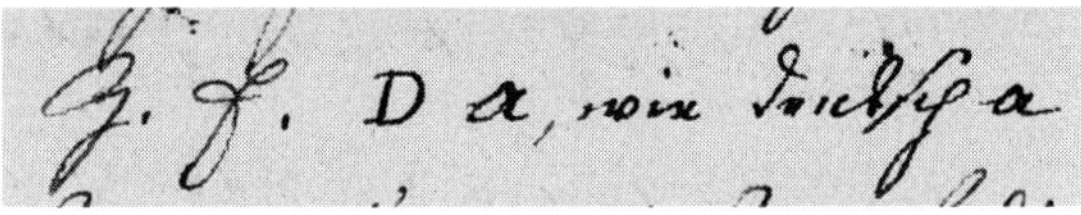

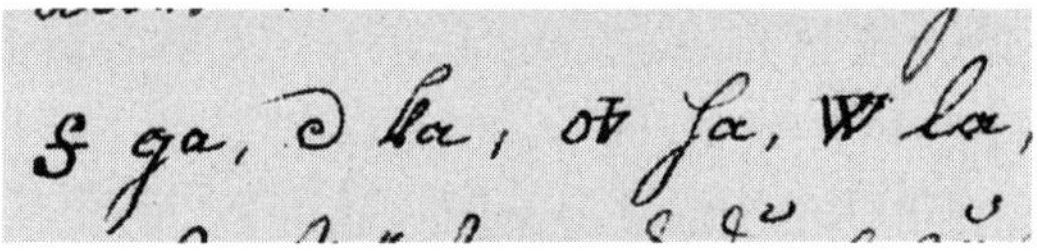

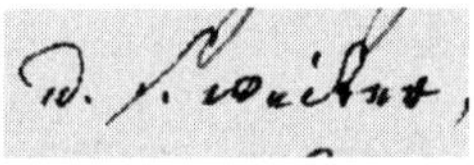

and so forth, although in the end one does not know what it means in English or German until one can speak the language itself. See what you can do with it. Let me know.

Praise God, we are currently all healthy, and everyone sends most sincere greetings. I expect something from you in the mail again tomorrow, and perhaps then again — money! The miserable Major Ridge has not yet paid me a cent, and I must admit I do not expect anything. In the meantime we want to hope for the best, if I could just finally get rid of Shmidt's old debts!!

Please greet Br. and Sr. Schaaf most sincerely from us, and tell them that his German newspapers arrive safely from time to time. What are the poor Christian Blums doing? We feel sorrowful compassion for their misfortune. Please greet them very sincerely from us. Also greet Br. and Sr. Clauder from us when you

---

[1] This document is not found.

get a chance. I have often thought about writing them a couple of lines, but because of the pressing circumstances this has never happened. But I will do it sometime. If Mamy Clauder could just get around better, we would almost wish they were here with us.

Accept, then, the most sincere greetings and a kiss in the spirit from your constantly loving friend and Br.,

Gottlieb Byhan

N.B. Please diligently remember your poor Byhans concerning external help and also internal matters.

Written in haste. With our post you will receive a number of letters from Ochgoloogy. As far as I know, they are well there.

G. B.

[Springplace (M 407-1) and Oochgeelogy (M 409-1) Diaries.]

*Sun., May 18.* [Ooch.] We observed Ascension Day with the usual services. We talked with our baptismal candidate Chinassee and instructed her.

*Sun., May 18.* [Spg.] We observed the festival of our dear Lord's Ascension after the fact with a talk and prayer on our knees asked our risen [Lord] to give us a part in this blessing as well which He gave his disciples at his ascension, to let us be aware of His dear presence daily, and we read the Ascension story. Afterward was another Bible reading. Then was the instruction for baptismal candidates, 3 of them, who will receive the waters of holy baptism on June 1.

*May 22.* [Spg.] Mr. Buttrick and his wife came to our place on their way to Brainerd, spent the night, and went on farther on the 23rd.

*Sun., May 25.* [Ooch.] About 90 persons gathered with us here for Pentecost. In the first service we sang the Liturgy to the Holy Spirit. Then we read the story for today from Acts 2. David S. Taucheechy served as interpreter. In the 2nd service Br. Schmidt baptized our baptismal candidate Chinasee into Jesus' death and gave her the name Maria Rosina. She is Joseph Crutchfield's wife. Her husband was also present and seemed to be very touched.

In the afternoon we had a blessed Holy Communion with our communicants. The married Sister Sussanna Elisabeth Fields observed as a confirmand. Taucheechy attended as a guest. Today we also had the opportunity to talk to 8[?] new people in whose hearts we could see the work of the Holy Spirit.

*Sun., May 25.* [Spg.] Pentecost. In the morning in the first service was a talk and prayer on our knees. In the afternoon we had Holy Communion, accompanied by a blessed feeling of the presence of our dear Lord, during which the Negro Br. Christian Jacob watched as a confirmand and Sr. Esther as a candidate. Afterward was another conversation with the baptismal candidates.

*May 26.* [Ooch.] Srs. Gambold and Schmidt visited Br. and Sr. Hicks. Late in the day David Taucheechy came for a brief visit.

There is such a shortage of corn this year that people are coming to us from far and wide to buy some. We have more than we need, so we are letting them buy it for a low price.

*May 26.* [Ooch.] The Sisters Gambold visited people in the neighborhood.

*May 27.* [Ooch.] Br. Schmidt went to see Br. and Sr. Hicks. Their son Jay, previously our scholar in Springplace, was enduring a lot of pain from colic. In the following days Br. Schmidt visited a number of our Brethren and Sisteers and neighbors; he was well received everywhere.

Lucy Hicks, wife of our Br. George Augustus Hicks, expressed her desire to join our community. We had made her acquaintance in Spring Place, where her heart was blessed by attending our services. But she moved completely out of this neighborhood some years ago and later joined the Methodist congregation and was baptized by them. She then married Br. Hicks a number of years ago and moved to our area. Since then she has been attending our services and had us baptize her three children. She is an individual who has been thoroughly awakened by God's Spirit. We do not want to draw people from other confessions, but we could not deny her request, especially since her husband belongs to us and all of her children were baptized by us. We advised her to discuss her circumstances directly and openly with the pastor of her church and to ask him to give us a certificate. Br. W. A. Hicks volunteered to take care of this matter, which he considers appropriate in all respects, and to discuss it with Mr. Henderson, the Methodist preacher here.

[M 414-3-14: Translated by Julie Tomberlin Weber. Addressed to: Revd. Theodor Shulz, Salem, Stokes County, North Carolina. Postmark: Springplace, C.N., May 29. Free. Gottlieb Byhan, P.M. Received June 12.]

Springplace, May 27, 1828

Dearly beloved Br. Shulz,

I received your dear letter of May 3 on the 15th, for which I thank you sincerely. Praise God, we are currently pretty well. The last couple of weeks have admittedly provided us various things to complain about, but things are going well again. It was mostly headaches that bothered almost all of us more or less, with pain in our limbs. This morning one of our scholars — Alexander — suddenly was overcome with a headache. He had to lie down right away and said it seemed as if everything went black before his eyes. We hope that he is well soon.

Now I want to answer your dear letter. Concerning the thoughts of both Sisters Gambold in Ochgolgoogy, they will surely have written to you themselves. Perhaps Br. Joseph G. has also done so now. During my visit in Ochgoloogy he was not yet sure what he would do. We also have no room for him in Spring Place at this time. It could be that there is a little place for him in Spring Place when we have built, but certainly nothing before then. Concerning his living in Ochgoloogy, you thought the small supply house could and should be prepared for him. There was talk about this on my visit there, but Br. Smith told me that Joseph apparently said it would not be necessary to get the house ready for him. He would continue to stay in his old house. Perhaps he will also not live too much longer. As a result, the little house was not fixed up. I do not know what he is planning now, whether he will stay or go. In my previous letter to you, I wrote about my thoughts concerning the home of Br. Eder — or Br. and Sr. I would also like to add that I will not persuade Br. Joseph to stay here. He is old and weak and sometimes somewhat untrusting.

Now concerning our house construction, things are going very slowly, as is usual here in this country. As far as I know, not a footboard has been sawed yet for this. I believe that really nothing or very little will be done on the construction of this house this year, and it can hardly be otherwise at this point, because nothing moves ahead. And besides I have the following to do before next winter: the floor in our children's house must be laid again, and a couple of blocks [beams] have to be put up on this, because one can no longer stand upright in it anymore. Besides, the floor that we laid in it 26 years ago is still in it, and at that time they were old boards. Then the chimney in my house must be taken down and rebuilt, because every time there is a strong wind I am afraid it will fall in, and then there could be a bad accident. Then the doors, door jams, and rotting thresholds must be re-made, because we must get the house in shape for its future use. Then there is the kitchen floor, and the roof of it is in a pitiful condition, so it must also be repaired. Most especially then, some kind of threshing floor must be laid in the barn, because otherwise it is of no use when one plants grain, and many other small details which really have to be done before winter.

It is a shame that nothing at all of this nature has been done the last 7 years, so that this year will really only be a year of preparation for the house construction. At least I no longer see how it could still be built this year, because there is too much other work.

I am very glad you want to have the sashes for the windows for the new house made in Salem. So I will tell you my thoughts about this. For the 2 rooms and 2 chambers, I thought it would require 10 windows, and I would like to have these with 15 panes because the porches will darken the rooms somewhat. Otherwise, 12 pane windows would be big enough. Now, as you know, we brought along 2 boxes of glass, 8 by 10, which is enough for the windows in the rooms and chambers, that is, for 15-pane windows. I counted the panes in the boxes, so if you send sashes for 10 windows — 15 panes, the lower wing 6 and the upper 9 panes, for glass 10 by 8, I would be very glad about this. But now we lack 3 windows for the kitchen and at least 2 for the gable end of the house, which could be just 12 panes. I have no glass for these 5 windows. But I thought glass 10 by 8 would be also be big enough if you could send me glass and frames for these windows. I will leave it up to you what kind of glass you want to send for the 5 last mentioned windows.

I hope you can understand what I mean: If you send me ten 15-pane windows without glass and five 12-pane sashes with glass, it will be right, along with cement for all the windows. I will enclose here a kind of sketch,[1] so that you can see approximately what I am planning to build. I have calculated 8 feet to an inch. It will surely not meet your precise measurements, because I had to use our iron ruler to prepare this. I hope you will not take it too precisely. You will still be able to see approximately what is intended.

I will try then to get the well-known Vann field, but nothing will come of this before winter. Will the Cherokees then be able to keep their land here? This is a difficult question, considering the house construction and purchase of the field.

We were very interested in hearing your water news and thank you for the thorough description of this.

These then were the main things in answer to your dear letter. What is Br. Chr. Blum doing? Please greet both of them very well from us. Now we are already looking forward to the printed *Gem. Nachr.*, which will come with Br. Eder. How are things going for Br. Shulz? Is it then not customary for Br. Smith to be sent the Salem Diary from time to time? At least I saw some here in the Archive under the church steps. If this took place previously, we really wish it would also be continued, and even if it is only extracts from it. Our Diary will also follow in its time.

---

[1] This sketch is not found.

My time is always so short that I have not yet gotten around to copying it, but I will try to send it with the transportation which will be here on Br. Eder's arrival.

Enclosed I send a list of things we would like to receive at the next opportunity. When we moved into the house after Br. and Sr. Shmith's departure it was literally empty. It looked as if no one had lived here for the last 10 years. But that's all the same. We don't want to tarry on old matters anymore. It only wastes time.

Next Sunday we have a baptism of 3 adult Indians and a child of our Br. and Sr. Israel and ~~Rebecca~~ Ester. May the Savior support me with His blessing and His power, and let us be very aware of His dear presence. The 3 baptismal candidates received the appropriate instruction, with the help of Polly Vann, various Sundays in the past, and it seems, according to their statements, that they are convinced that in their current condition they would have to be lost if they were not cleansed of their sins through the blood of Jesus Christ and washed in holy baptism as a seal on the forgiveness of their sins, and they themselves be forgiven. I wish you could visit here a few hours next Sunday. We greet everyone sincerely. My wife especially greets your family. You, dear Br., accept the sincerest greeting and kiss from your familiar friend and Brother,

Gottlieb Byhan

Please enclose some money for me again. Excuse my mistakes in writing!

[Springplace (M 407-1) and Oochgeelogy (M 409-1) Diaries.]

*May 30.* [Ooch.] Br. Joseph Gambold went to Spring Place for a visit. We received a letter from our Brn. and Srs. in Spring Place with the news that 3 more persons will be added to Christ's flock through holy baptism on June 1. We were very happy and excited about this.

*May 31.* [Spg.] Old Br. Joseph Gambold came from Oochgo-loogy to visit us.

*Sun., June 1.* [Spg.] Festival of the Trinity. In the early service we considered the words of our Gospel lesson for today [John 3:3]: Verily, verily, I say unto thee, except a man be born again, he cannot see the kingdom of God. Then was the baptism of three adult Indians: the young Indian Nick Tiger with the name Nicolaus Solomon; also the mother of our Sr. Sarah Deborah, To,tlo,tle,na, with the name Hannah; and the wife of our Br. James, Tsau-a-ju-ga, with the name Anna Rosina, accompanied by a transporting feeling of God's peace. The feelings which we enjoy from the presence of our dear Lord on such occasions cannot be described. They must be experienced. Then one can pray from the bottom of his heart, if all of humanity would surrender itself to Jesus, then the pierced hand would surely bring it to eternal life! [Br. Byhan inserts a hymn verse into the Diary.] More than 100 people were present for this solemn proceeding. In the 2nd service was the baptism of 2 children, the baby daughter of our Indian Br. and Sr. Israel and Esther with the name Lucy, and the baby girl born to our neighbor Joseph and Jenny Vann with the name Jane Elisabeth.

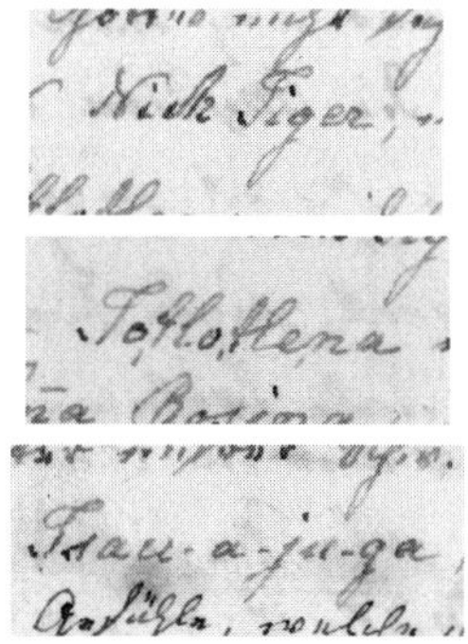


*Sun., June 1.* [Ooch.] In the first service we prayed the Church Litany. Then we considered the Gospel lesson for today. There was no service in the evening.

*June 2.* [Spg.] Dav. Abr. Dazizi came to our place on his way home from a visit in the area of Oochgoloogy and spent the night here. He told us that the Presbyterian missionaries at Turnip Mountain and the area there also have had the joy of baptizing some Indians, which is a blessing for us to do. It seemed to please him a lot that the word of God is finding entry not just in one confession, but at all mission posts in this country.

*June 3.* [Spg.] Early in the day he went on home from here.

*June 3.* [Ooch.] We discovered a 5-foot-long chicken snake under the schoolhouse, and we were able to kill it. When we cut it open we discovered 2 young chickens and 4 whole eggs inside of it.

The heat was oppressive throughout this week.

Sr. Hicks visited us and we enjoyed pleasant conversations with her. Our elderly Brn. and Srs. still think fondly of our blessed Sr. Anna Rosina Gambold, and they honor and respect her as the Lord's faithful servant. Quite frequently our Brn. and Srs. mention how she warmly extolled to them the Savior's suffering, and they say this was an unforgettable blessing for their hearts that prompted them to seek their earthly and eternal well-being. When we had heart-to-heart talks with our Brn. and Srs. it was rare that they did not remember her tenderly and console themselves with the hope of meeting her again before the Savior's throne. She was a true friend of the poor and despised Indians. Sr. Hicks said, God will reward her for this. A text with the title *Traits of the Aborigines of America*, a poem by Lydia Huntley Sigourney describes our blessed Sr. Anna Rosina Gambold thus:

Thou mild Moravian Sister! Thou wert deck'd
with what the giddy, unreflecting world
Might call accomplishment, but thou didst own
A pearl it could not purchase. Thou didst cleanse
Thy knowledge in the fount of Jesus Christ
And pour it to the poor even as the hand
Of the blest angel mov'd Siloam's pool
To heal the impotent. And thou didst die
Even as thou liv'dst unmurmuring, pure, serene
And ardent in thy faith. — Thou hast obtain'd
Eternal gain from sublunary loss
And tribulaton; for thy robes are white
in the atoning blood. Say, shall we shed
The tear for thee, blest Sister! when thy lot
Is better far than ours?

# *1828, part 5*

[M 414-3-15: Translated by Julie Tomberlin Weber. Addressed to: Revd. Theodor Schulz, Salem, Stokes County, North Carolina. Postmark: New Echota, Ch. Na., June 12, 25. Received July 3. Br. Schulz writes in the address: A legal copy of J. G. last will lawfully proved.]

Oochgeelogy, June 5, 1828

My dearly beloved Br. Schulz!

With these few lines, we here greet you most sincerely. Praise God, we are all healthy and well.

On Pentecost, the 25th of last month, the Savior prepared a special day of blessing for us. More than 80 attentive listeners gathered for the baptism of Chinasse, Joseph Crutchfield's wife, who received the name Maria Rosina. Many took home with them a deep impression from this proceeding. On the same day we also had the enjoyment of Holy Communion, during which the married Sr. Sussana Elisabeth observed as a candidate. David Taucheechy, our interpreter, was present as a guest during this. We also had the opportunity of speaking individually with 4 new people who gave us hope for their conversion (all females).

Lucy Hicks, wife of the recently baptized Br. George Augustus Hicks, with whom we had already become acquainted 5 years ago in Springplace and of whom we had hope at that time that we would receive her as our Sr. (In the previous Diary from Springplace she is known by the name of Lucy Fields.) But she moved away from our area and was baptized by the Methodists some years ago. She told us of her deep desire to become a member of our congregation, and we sincerely gave her our hand, if she gets a certificate from her preacher, whom she should tell very directly, so that the Methodists might not get the idea that we want to draw members of their congregation to us. Br. W. A. Hicks himself will speak with the Methodist preacher, Mr. Henderson, who lives about 4 miles from here. I am not at all acquainted with him, however.

From Br. Byhan's last letter of May 23, we see your thoughts about the return of Srs. Gambold and Br. Joseph. The Brn. will know what is best, whether A. M. Gambold should return or stay in the country longer. She seems to me to be completely committed to doing what the Brn. of the P.H.C. suggest. Probably both Sr. Polly and presumably her father will return. For the latter, it would be best if he could decide to spend his last days here, but I ask the dear Brn. just help us to get free of him if he insists on staying. Otherwise, we will have a difficult life with him. We would be happiest if he could be lodged with M. Reich.

It has occurred to us that we could get 2 or 3 bushels of apple cuttings from Salem with the next opportunity. This year we are not getting any fruit. Our peach trees would have many blooms if the frost had not come. But there has been no thought of apples here in 4-5 years. Our Brn. and Srs. in Springplace will probably get some fruit. But with their large family we cannot ask them to give us any of it. We also wish for one or two grain sacks in case we should plant wheat in the future. I have asked for money from Major Ridge myself and also through Br. Hicks. It seems, though, that there is no hope of this at this time. It is said that Col. McKinny has been named as one of the commissioners to the Cherokees. However, he is a man who has few friends here in the country.

In Springplace last Sunday they had the joy of adding 3 persons to the Gemeine through holy baptism, Nick Tiger, Tsauyuka, and old Sally [To,tlo,tle,na]. They must all be known to you. The latter is Sr. Salome Elisabeth Sanders's [Sarah Deborah's] mother. I have not yet learned her baptismal name.

Since I have to send this letter separately in half an hour, I must send sincere greetings from my wife to you and your dear family. Extend the most sincere greetings to your dear colleagues and Father Steiner, Brn. and Srs. Buchholz and Pfohl. I greet you especially, your faithfully obliged Brother,

Johann R. Schmidt

P.S. Our old friend Br. Will. Abr. Hicks, whom I visit once a week, greets you most sincerely. He is very healthy. I always give him news from the *W. Nachr.* of the U.A.C. and from the Bethlehem *Monats Blattes* about our mission. He is very interested in this. His house is always full of visiting Indians, and he never neglects to extol to them God's guidance for our salvation. He is a big friend of ancient Jewish history and reads diligently in Josephus, which he compares with the Bible. He finds much similarity between the Jewish and Indian customs.

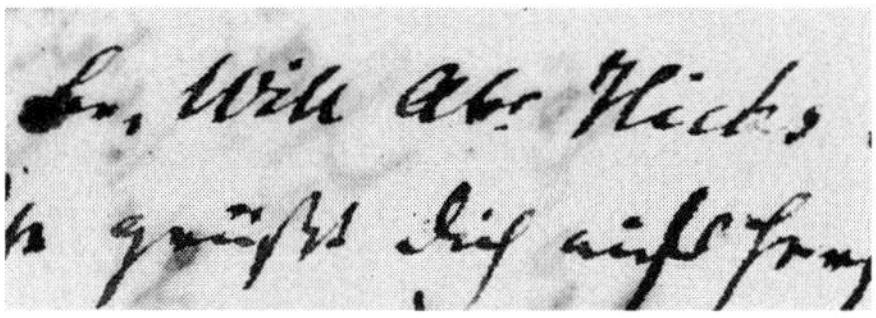

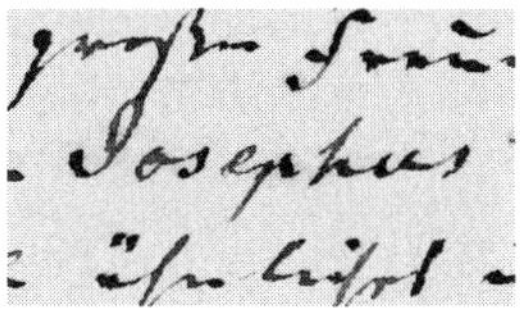

J. R. S.

[M 414-3-16: Translated by Julie Tomberlin Weber. Addressed to: Revd. Theodor Shulz, Salem, N.C. No postmark. Received July 19, 1828.]

Springplace, June 5, 1828

My dear Br. Shulz,

On the last post day, May 29, I received your dear letter of May 5 with the enclosure of $50 for Henry Clayten. I immediately wrote Mr. Clayten a couple of lines and let him know that money for him was here. I expect him here any day now. The receipt will certainly follow. Otherwise, I do not have anything special to report at this time.

Praise God, we are all healthy. Old Br. Joseph G. is now on a visit here in Spring Place. He sends sincere greetings. Since I sent the list of things which should be sent with the next opportunity, the following things have occurred to me:

One good hammer to hammer the scythes,
or to sharpen them.
2 pairs of shoes for me and 2 pairs
for Nathl. from J. Hall.
One straw hat for me in the summer.
My fur is too heavy for me.
One small set of scales with bowls,
so we can weigh pounds and ounces,
and also weights, if possible.
Cream of Tartar pills like the ones Sophia currently
needs, preservative for stomach problems.
2 good German grass scythes, one half-bushel measure.
Some chalk, several ink glasses, a couple of strong
ropes, tape, white — earthen pipes — some
snuff.

Perhaps some more things will occur to me if there is still time to get it.

Last Sunday 3 adult Indians were baptized: a young Indian Nick Tiger with the name Nicolaus Solomon, our Sr. Sarah Debora's mother Totlotlena with the name Hanna, and our Br. James' wife — Tsauanuga — with the name Anna Rosina. Afterward was the baptism of 2 children, a baby daughter born to our Br. and Sr. Israel and Ester with the name Lucy and our neighbor Joseph Vann's baby daughter with the name Elisabeth Jane. It was an extraordinary day of blessing. On such occasions one can feel the Savior's friendliness and closeness in a special way. Oh, if only many had experienced this with us!

The short time does not allow me to write more at this time. I must therefore close. Along with sincere greetings from all of us to all of you, accept the most tender greeting for you from your friend and Br.

Gottlieb Byhan

N.B. Our Rachel is halfway thinking of returning to Salem with this opportunity, if we can spare her from the work. However, it is not yet certain.

[Springplace (M 407-1) and Oochgeelogy (M 409-1) Diaries. Translated by Julie Tomberlin Weber. Handwritings are Johann Renatus Schmidt's (Ooch.) and Gottlieb Byhan's (Spg.).]

*Sun., June 8.* [Ooch.] In the first service we prayed the Church Litany. The sermon that followed was on the New Testament benediction. More than 40 people were present today. We were delighted by a letter from our dear Br. Theodor Schulz this evening.

*Sun., June 8.* [Spg.] In the first service we prayed the Church Litany and read a tract about our eternal well-being. In the second service was the baptism of our Indian Br. and Sr. Joshua and Anna Ajosta's baby boy with the name Abijah Cornelius.

*June 9.* [Spg.] Since there has been a lack for a long time of cedar wood to make pails, containers, etc., for the household, Br. Nathl. Byhan, Willm. Sneider and some schoolboys went into the bush with the wagon today to fetch some. They had the luck about 8 miles from here on a creek called Colleholly, about 5 miles on the other side of the Conossauga River, of finding a nice quantity of good wood, and in the evening they returned safely home generously laden with it.

*June 10.* [Ooch.] We had a big storm with hail as large as a pigeon's egg.

*June 11.* [Ooch.] In the morning we had another intense storm. It has been extremely hot in recent days. Many of our neighbors began cutting their wheat this week. It turned out quite well despite the heavy frost in the spring.

[M 414-3-17: Translated by Julie Tomberlin Weber. Addressed to: Revd. Theodor Shulz, Salem, Stokes County, North Carolina. Postmark: Springplace, C.N., June 12. Free. Gottlieb Byhan, P.M. Received June 26.]

Springplace, June 12, 1828

My dear Br. Shulz,

Time doesn't allow me to write you at length today or this time. I only want to report a few things to you briefly.

On the 5th of this month I received your dear letter of May 19 with the $100, along with the list of books for me. I am especially grateful for this, especially for the bank notes, but I do not know yet what I will do with the $50 from the Newbern Bank. I fear I will have to pay a large discount to get them exchanged. I will try to do the best I can with them. I have sent you our views concerning our construction in one of my previous letters.

It will not be easy for me to make excerpts from blessed Br. Gambold's Lebenslauf and send them out to the public, but when I finally get a little time I will see what I can do.

It seems it will always be difficult for us to get help in the domestic area, and I fear we will just have to learn to be patient. This much is certain, however, that my wife will not endure many years with as much work as she has now. Last week she was pretty ill, but there was no way to think of taking it easy. She had to, and wanted to, continue as well as she could. She is somewhat better now. I was just about ready to fetch Sr. A. M. Gambold from Ochgoloogy to help in our household, and she would have done this, if my dear wife had agreed, because she believes that she will soon get better. May the Savior help us!

If I get some time I will share with you <u>my</u> views about the future situation with the external work in Ochgoloogy, but not until Br. Eder has arrived in Salem and you have informed me whether Br. Eder can also work in the domestic area.

The detailed news of your new water pipes or waterworks was very interesting to us, and we thank you for this. Praise God that you now have enough water in town! Br. Clauder will certainly also be very happy — or will the old water pipe be kept up?

Be so good and send me the package of books that came for me at the next opportunity. I have already written to Br. Benzien about how things are to be done with the payment. If you report anything to me about my account and books, please be so good and do it on a separate sheet of paper.

Beside the mother, we are all pretty well, although this or that person sometimes — like everywhere — has something to complain about. Our Pleasant is the same, old, unable to do anything, and gets more so every day.

My dear wife longs for a letter from Mother Shulz every post day. She sends her sincere greetings. Now, dear Br., greet everyone from us and remember us very often before our dear Savior, that He might strengthen us inwardly and outwardly. And you, dear Br., accept the most sincere greetings and kiss from your poor Br.,

Gottlieb Byhan

N.B. Last Sunday I baptized ~~2~~ 1 child~~ren~~ again into Jesus' death, a baby boy of our Br. and Sr. Josua with the name Abijah Cornelius — ~~and a baby daughter of our Br. and Sr. Israel with the name Lucy~~. Otherwise the Savior is with us.

Written in haste.

When I had folded this letter and was just getting ready to seal it, I received a couple of lines from Mr. Hugh Montgomery, Agent for the Cherokees, in which he writes to me to come to his place next Monday and get $150 which is still due our Establishment from the third and fourth quarters of 1827. Beloved God! I will travel there if nothing comes up. This is very welcome to me! The dear God continues to help after all.

G. Byhan

[Springplace (M 407-1) and Oochgeelogy (M 409-1) Diaries.]

*Sun., June 15.* [Ooch.] We had the Church Litany. Then we read from the booklet *The Word of the Cross*. In the 2nd service we read the text for today from Luke 7:38. In the evening we had Bible reading. We informed our communicant Brn. and Srs. that we would have Holy Communion next Sunday.

*Sun., June 15.* [Spg.] After the usual Sunday services our Br. and Sr. William Henry and Martha's baby son was baptized into Jesus' death with the name Archibald. Afterward Br. and Sr. Byhan left from here on horse to go to the Agency, where Br. Byhan was invited by the Agent, Mr. Hugh Montgomery, to pick up part of the assistance designated by the government of the United States for the mission posts at Springplace and Ochgoloogy. In the evening they arrived at our friend Capt. Dav. McNair's and spent the night there.

*June 16.* [Spg.] Br. Byhan went on to the Agency, where he arrived in the afternoon. He found in Mr. Montgomery a very friendly, religious man who wishes our missions well. A number of matters concerning our mission here among the Cherokees as well as everywhere were discussed, and he seemed very supportive of our work.

*June 16.* [Ooch.] In the evening we had a heavy storm.

*June 18.* [Spg.] In the afternoon Br. and Sr. Byhan arrived back in Spring Place.

*June 19.* [Spg.] Mr. John Schneider, Sr. Byhan's brother, returned home. He lives in Hamilton County, Tennessee. He provided us with various services during his stay with us, primarily in pine carving, since we were really lacking wooden utensils. This lack was for the most part taken care of by him.

*June 21.* [Spg.] Since we heard some time ago that a certain McDonald, who lives 5 miles from here, was using two of our milk cows with calves, we sent our schoolboy Niclaus Ignatius there today to see if this were really true. In fact he found the cows and calves in his cow pen. He brought them safely home. This McDonald is considered a trained thief in the whole country and has already had to pay for such deeds with 300 strokes on his bare back on 3 different occasions. The last time he was close to being shot but was saved by intercession. He was told, however, that if he was guilty of robbery again the latter would be carried out on him. This bad behavior seems inborn in him and he continues secretly in it, but with much care and cleverness. As we hear, the mission in Spring Place has already lost a number of heads of cattle through him. Even Mr. Montgomery, the Agent, told Br. Byhan that McDonald lives much too close to us with respect to our cattle. Dav. Abr. Dazizi also came to our place this evening to stay with us a number of days in our area because of his cattle.

*Sun., June 22.* [Ooch.] The sermon was not well attended today because of the rain. Our communicants could not come either, and since we heard that many of them are sick we postponed Holy Communion till Sunday week. We had a thorough discussion with Nancy, one of old Mother Hannah's grandchildren, in the presence of Br. W. A. Hicks. She has been attending our services regularly and expressed her deep desire for holy baptism. We accepted her as a baptismal candidate.

*Sun., June 22.* [Spg.] Since Dav. Abraham Tazizi was here, he was willing to interpret in our Sunday services. Because of strong storms this morning not many people could come to our services. Only about 10 or 12 present could not understand English.

*June 23.* [Ooch.] Br. Schmidt went to visit Br. and Sr. Hicks.

*June 24.* [Ooch.] Mr. Gann, a white man who is our Sister Caty Maria's husband, was very sick. Sisters Gambold went today to visit him. They found him recovering.

[M 414-3-18: Translated by Julie Tomberlin Weber. Addressed to: Revd. Theodor Shulz, Salem, Stokes County, North Carolina. Postmark: Spring Place, C.N., June 26. Free. Gottlieb Byhan, P.M. Received July 17.]

Springplace, June 24, 1828

My dear Br. Shulz,

Despite the fact that time hardly allows me to write you with this post, I still cannot neglect to report our well-being to you. My housemother has recovered from her sickliness again and is now busy with her usual work.

Since my last letter to you dated the 12th of this month, I was also at the Cherokee Agency and made the acquaintance of the gentleman Hugh Montgomery. He is an honest man, but an extremely stiff Presbyterian. There is much praying in his house

— and sighing. The latter is especially the case with Mrs. Montgomery. Whether it is always like this or whether it was just like this during my presence, I cannot say. I could not investigate his views about the Cherokees' removal or staying, and I also did not want to ask him about this directly. Still if I follow my feelings, I believe that he will not put in many good words for their staying. He and she are somewhat elderly people already, about in their 60's. He was extremely friendly toward me and seemed to wish everything well for our work. But if I compare this to the statements he made previously, and presumably not very long ago, as Dav. Abr. Tazizi told us just day before yesterday, then I do not know how I can make sense of this: That the Moravians received too much annually from government, because they did little or nothing. Also on his visit in Springplace last year he spoke much about the fact that we live too well and waste much too much. Now concerning this I must say he proved it to me and provided an example of how we should live because during my visit with him, breakfast consisted of coffee and very hard baked biscuits which I could not bite and butter, so that he himself said to me while eating it was pitiful to see me eating because of my bad teeth. By the way, he was born and raised in South Carolina, lived in Georgia last, was a member in the Senate in the State of Georgia for a while and is not at all related to the Montgomerys in North Carolina. Otherwise, he paid me $150 for the last two quarters of the year 1827 and indeed everything in silver money.

Please do not publish the above. He, or both of them, treated me very cordially and invited me sincerely to visit him again soon with my wife. My little mother was getting ready to visit the Agency with me this time, and on Sunday after the services we left on horse from Spring Place and arrived safely at our friends the McNairs in the evening. But my dear wife found it impossible to ride on, was able to stay and remain with Sr. Delila McNair, and I rode on to the Agency on the 16th, about 22 miles from the McNairs. I returned to the McNairs on the 17th, and on the 18th both of us returned safely to Spring Place.

I reported in my last letter that I received the $100 sent to me in various notes, but dear Br., what should I do with the $50 in Newbern notes? No one will take them from me. They are thus absolutely useless. Yesterday I had to pay 7 percent on North Carolina notes. I had paid $30 to a certain Henry, who took them along to Augusta, where they charged him 7%, which I had to repay him. Now they say the N.C. notes are 8% below par. What will happen now I do not know. Time will tell. But no one here takes the Newbern and Cape Fear notes. What should I do? Now I have $60 of such notes on hand, and I cannot pay what I owe, or more precisely the debts remaining to Br. Smith. Especially the debt he made with Lavender should be paid, because otherwise I am worried he will send the constable after me. Ridge also does not pay anything. I hear nothing about whether he is intending to pay or not. In brief, financial matters are truly miserable. The debt with Lavender, from Br. Smith, is $192. I am really somewhat concerned about this debt. If Ridge would just pay something — it seems that orders and everything do not help at all.

Now to get to something else. Last Sunday was the baptism of our Br. and Sr. William Henry and Martha's baby boy with the name Archibald. We currently are having very hot weather. The Thermometer is up to 98° every day. June 6 was the hottest day. The thermometer was 99½. On the $4^{th}$ and $5^{th}$ it was 99°, the $7^{th}$ also 99°. It was almost hot enough to suffocate. Currently Br. Jos. Gambold is visiting at the McNairs. He stayed with us for 3 weeks. I believe he is sincerely fed up with things in Ochgoloogy. Has Br. Eder not yet arrived?

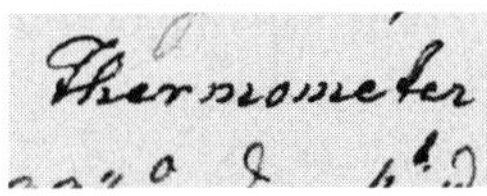


With joy we learned that Br. Heinrich G. Clauder is willing to serve the Savior among the heathen. The harvest is great. There is much to do, and the workers are few. It is delightful when young Brn. are willing to serve the Lord in the vineyard! Perhaps Br. Clauder will be my successor.

Please greet him very well from me and us.

Last week another of Jos. Vann's Negro women died again from the illness raging among them. Today Jos. Vann told me that he has now begun to saw the wood for our construction. Time will tell how long it will take now until everything is sawed.

I have heard nothing else from Ochgeloogy for several weeks now. I have made an attempt to write to Br. Smith with the post because my letters go free as far as New Echota. But when I write, my letters lie for weeks in New Echota. No one picks them up, and they are also not sent to him. It just occurred to me: In Ochgology they owe their worker Alex Copland about $150 to $180 for work. I do not know how this debt should be paid, but I hear from Joseph Gambold that they have sold sweet potatoes, fodder, corn, etc., this spring and summer, so perhaps they could have some to pay out. Even so, they must be short on money, because day before yesterday I just received an order to me from Br. Smith of $20 paid to Mr. Henry. As a result I cannot say how things look in their cashbox. As soon as I have some more time I will visit there.

Enclosed is the receipt from Henry Clayton.

Please greet everyone very well from us. Do not forget our Sophia. Remember us sometimes in love, and the work here. Then you, dear Br., accept a special greeting and kiss from your friend and Brother,

Gottlieb Byhan

N.B. Be so good and send the mission in Springplace a mirror. It seems to me it would not be superfluous. Further, 1 or 2 reaping hooks and some scythe whetstones. If I have named some articles twice, it does no harm. You just need to send them once. Since I did not keep a list for myself of the articles ordered, I just write it how and when it occurs to me. Perhaps something will occur to you that we should have and that we have not thought of. Just send it. Everything is welcome!

G. Byhan

[Springplace (M 407-1) and Oochgeelogy (M 409-1) Diaries.]

*June 25.* [Spg.] In the evening Mr. Buttrick and Mr. Walker from Marysville came to our place and spent the night. We had a Singstunde this evening, accompanied by the Fortepiano.

*June 26.* [Spg.] After breakfast they traveled on to Carmel, one of their mission places about 30 miles from here.

*June 28.* [Spg.] Dav. Abr. Tazizi returned home after spending 6 days with us and in the neighborhood. Throughout this week, we had very hot weather. The thermometer often climbed up to 99° in the shade. It is also so dry that field and garden crops are suffering greatly.

*Sun., June 29.* [Ooch.] Only a few people came to hear the sermon today.

*Sun., June 29.* [Spg.] Our Brethren and Sisters came for the services in large numbers again. We commend ourselves to your loving remembrance before our dear Lord. Your faithfully bound Br. and Sr., Gottl. and Dor. Byhan

*July 1.* [Ooch.] Br. Schmidt and Sr. Anna Maria Gambold traveled to Springplace for a visit and returned on the 3rd.

*July 1.* [Spg.] Br. Smith and Sr. A. M. Gambold from Ochgeelogy came to us for a visit.

*July 2.* [Spg.] We had a communal conversation concerning our schools, since we realize more and more and have noticed that that it would be better if the Indian boys were alone and did not go to school at the same mission site as the Indian girls. Either the boys should receive instruction in Spring Place and the girls in Ochgeelogy or vice versa, and especially since our Br. Willm. Abr. Hicks is of the same opinion. Also the Agent of the Cherokees, Mr. Hugh Montgomery give his agreement to this arrangement and told Br. Byhan when he visited the Agency that we should carry out this arrangement since it would be a great relief for the missionaries, and has noted this in other schools in this country. Since most of our Brethren and Sisters who have children in our schools also gave their agreement, we agreed that now as soon as possible we will take only boys for instruction in Spring Place and only girls in Ochgeloogy.

*July 3.* [Spg.] Br. Smith and Anna M. Gambold returned to Ochgoloogy, and with them old Br. Jos. Gambold, who stayed with us and in the neighborhood here for several weeks.

# *1828, part 6*

[M 414-3-19: Translated by Julie Tomberlin Weber. Addressed to: Revd. Theodor Schulz, Salem, Stokes County, North Carolina. Postmark: Springplace, C.N., July 3. Free. Gottlieb Byhan, P.M. Received July 17.]

Springplace, July 3, 1828

My dear Br. Shulz,

Since I still have a quarter of an hour before the mail arrives, I wanted to share with you quickly a situation which will surprise and amaze you, as it has us. Day before yesterday Br. Smith and Sr. A. Maria Gambold came from Ochgoloogy by wagon for a visit at our place. Alex. Copland was the driver. The former brought us the news: that Alexander Copland and Sr. Polly Gambold are planning to get married ——— ! What do you think about that?

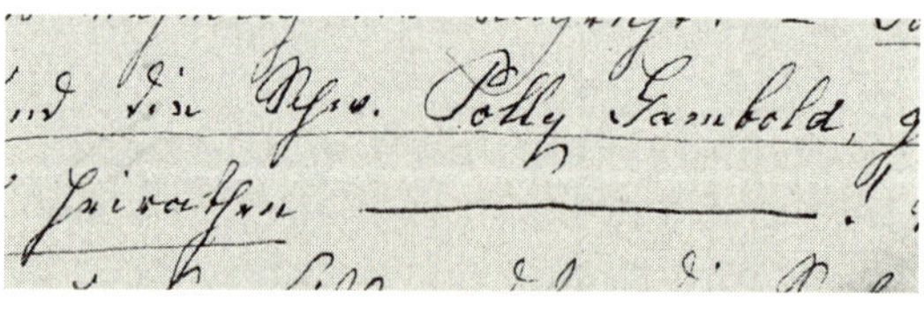

We personally discussed the matter in our Conference and did not find it advisable to object, because we feared that it might have a bad effect on Sr. Polly Gambold. They will supposedly be wed on July 13. Old Joseph gives his approval for this and is planning to stay here now. More with the next post.

Praise God, we are currently all healthy and have much work. I must close; the mail is coming.

Please greet all most cordially from us. Your friend and Brother,
Gottlieb Byhan

Alex. Copeland is the one who was recently baptized in Ochgoloogy, and has faithfully worked for the missionaries there for a couple of years.

[B 61-3: Provinzial Helfer Conferenz, meeting in Salem. Translated by C. Daniel Crews.]

*Fri., July 4.* On 23 June the single Br. Franz Eder, who is appointed to the Cherokee Mission, arrived safe and sound, for which we are heartily thankful, the more so since he recommends himself through his faithful attitude and loving nature. The Conferenz thought that he might suitably remain here until later in the year to learn as much as possible of the English language. The best opportunity for this would be with the boys in the Boarding School, and he has already begun to take advantage of this. We also thought to see about getting him married for his call. To save on expenses at the two mission posts, which are caused by the necessary assistance with farming, etc., Br. Schulz was commissioned to buy two Negro women, who are presently at a cheap price, since those who are now on the Administration farm would not be useful for this, since they have children and cannot be separated from their men.

[Springplace (M 407-1) and Oochgeelogy (M 409-1) Diaries. Translated by Julie Tomberlin Weber. Handwritings are Johann Renatus Schmidt's (Ooch.) and Gottlieb Byhan's (Spg.).]

*Sun., July 6.* [Ooch.] The sermon was well attended. In the 2nd service we read several chapters from the Gospel of Luke. In the afternoon we had the most blessed enjoyment of the body and blood of Jesus in Holy Communion. Sr. Sussanna Elisabeth Fields was confirmed after receiving more instruction, and she participated for the first time. The Indian woman Quaeti expressed her desire to be baptized. She is a granddaughter of our elderly Sister Hannah.

*July 7.* [Ooch.] Mr. Henderson, a Methodist preacher here, visited us. He is a nice man and we really enjoyed his visit.

*Sun., July 6.* [Spg.] Only a few Brn. and Srs. were here for the services. Since everyone is very busy planting corn now and the Brn. and Srs. accordingly are using their horses every day, they like to let them rest on Sunday. Since they do not have much strength left to go on foot 10, 12, 14 to 16 miles without them, it is somewhat far to go here and back, so that one cannot hold it against those who live such distances from Spring Place if they cannot come every Sunday. Still one must be amazed that they come as often as they really can. Most of those who were here today live 7 to 9 miles from here, and most of them came on foot. Last week we had unusually cold weather. The Fahr. Therm. was at 53° some mornings. The weather is also very dry, and we really are wanting a merciful rain.

[M 414-3-20: Translated by Julie Tomberlin Weber. Addressed to: Revd. Theodor Shulz, Salem, Stokes County, North Carolina. Postmark: Springplace, C.N., July 10. Free. Gottlieb Byhan, P.M. Received July 23. Handwriting is Gottlieb Byhan's.]

Springplace, July 9, 1828

My dear Br. Shulz,

Last week I informed you of receipt of your dear letter dated June 12 with the enclosure of letters and money for Br. Smith and me. Herewith I thank you for this. In accordance with your wish, I offered my $100. But he said that for now they could manage with $100. And so I kept it.

It seems that Major Ridge is not planning to pay anything for his daughter in Salem. It is generally the opinion here that he probably will not pay anything. I also hear nothing anymore about the $20 he owes Br. Abr. Steiner for the house locks. I sent him the bill.

With the next mail I will write to the Secr. of War, or Kenney, when I will mention our intended house construction. Just between us, Mr. McKenny is not so highly esteemed among the Cherokees. Perhaps you will find something in the *Phönix* in Mr. John Ridge's essay. Perhaps they are not fair to the man. I cannot judge.

I have already written you in my last letter about our construction and that nothing will come of it this year because of the lack of materials, and when I reflect on the circumstances of this poor Nation, I sometimes do not know what to say about the construction of a house in the current situation. The Cherokees, at least the Chiefs, claim they absolutely will not leave. Nonetheless, we do not know how things can work out. We want to leave it up to Him who governs everything and has everything in His hands!

On the 20th of this month we will have the baptism of another adult Indian woman. She goes by the name of Sally, and expressed her desire long ago to become the property of Jesus and to be cleansed of her sins through Jesus' blood in holy baptism. These are encouraging times, when we see that the Word of the Cross enters into one soul or another from time to time. May the Savior grant us more and more courage and strength to carry out His work here, and to awaken more and more Brn. and Sisters who are willing to work in His vineyard, so that His reward for suffering will continue to be increased. In <u>this</u> Nation there is still much to do, so <u>we</u> want to do what we can as long as we can endure as far as the Savior provides us grace and strength. Admittedly there should be young, energetic champions and witnesses <u>here</u>, so that His kingdom will be extended more and more through them and His reward for suffering might be ever increased!

We really are longing to hear something about Br. Eder's arrival. Please greet him very well from us when he has finally arrived. It just occurred to me, and I have often wanted to mention this, that if Br. Math. Reich is willing to drive Br. Eder, etc., to Spring

Place, then take him up on it. He is a good driver. By the way, just do not keep Br. Eder in Salem too long.

I do not know what to say about your report in your last letter, as well as in previous letters, about the purchase of a couple of Negro women. Sometimes we have worrisome thoughts about this. There would be much to say in favor of this and even more against sending these Negroes. But I do not want to write this in a letter. If things get this far and you get a couple, we sincerely wish that the results might be good. Please do not think badly of me for making this statement. It would be the right time for you to make a visit here now. Much would become clear to you which remained dark on your previous visit, and you would learn much that cannot be shared in letters.

I will try to send the Diary from time to time.

On my visit at Cherokee Agent Montgomery, conversation turned to our school. I shared with him our thoughts about planning to accept just boys into the school in Springplace and girls in Ochgoloogy. He completely approved this suggestion and said he believed that this arrangement would be a great advantage for both schools. So we will put this plan into action as soon as possible if the Prov. Helf. Conf. has nothing against it.

Now I come to the matter I reported to you in my last letter of the 3rd of this month, that Alex. Copeland and Sr. Polly Gambold want to get married. It would have been in vain to try to prevent or reverse this matter, and so we had to allow it to happen. Next Sunday the 13th is supposed to be the wedding. I have been asked by Alex. Copeland to come there and marry them, because, as he said, if I may use his words here: Mr. Smith is a strange man. And he has no confidence in him, and one time he says one thing and the next time something else. I cannot yet say for sure if I will go there and marry them. I prefer not to go.

This situation now gives a turn to the mission work in Ochgoloogy which I cannot predict. For eight days I have heard nothing more about it. Br. Jos. Gambold will probably stay here now and is planning to spend the rest of his days with his daughter. But now the question is, where should they live? And where should Br. and Sr. Eder live in case Br. Eder comes married? We must admit we see no prospects of how we can continue. Now sometimes if I consider the matter, the future looks so dark to me that I cannot see anything ahead of me, and my mind stands still — until the dear Brn. of the Helf. Conf. in Salem come with their guidance and assistance.

Also Copeland has not yet stated where he wants to live, whether he will remain in Ochgoloogy and work for the mission as previously for salary or whether he will stay and work for the mission as the Claytens did in Springplace. Since I am still expecting news from Ochgoloogy today, perhaps I can report more about the Copelands' home or what he is planning to do before I send this letter tomorrow. It seems that going home [to Salem] is just a rumor.

One more thing. If Br. Eder comes now and brings a wife along, then naturally Sr. A. M. Gambold will not remain in Ochgoloogy. She stated this. Then Br. and Sr. Smith will be alone, and if Br. Eder cannot be courageous, then the mission work there will be of no substance. Do not think badly of me for expressing my thoughts so freely. If they were not too rambling here, I would prove it. Perhaps there will be an opportunity for this soon.

Since I have been given the assignment of keeping an eye on Br. Smith with the help of the rest of the Brn. and Srs. in Ochgoloogy, I just wanted to mention a circumstance which Br. Jos. G. told me. When he visits his neighbors and comes to them in their houses, he asks for something to drink. And he has his neighbor Aust. Copeland, Alex. Copeland's brother, accustomed to putting the bottle of brandy on the table right away when Br. Smith comes to visit him. What kind of name will the Moravian missionaries get here? Nothing is more repulsive to me than having to say and write such things about a colleague. But I cannot remain quiet, because my conscience, God, and His work here demand it. Speaking with him is of no purpose, because he twists one's words.

So now he says I had already told him that he could keep drinking as much brandy as he wanted — which I truly did not say. In this way he also twisted your words, when he said you had said that he did not need to be thrifty, because the Missions Diacony is rich enough, since it gets so much from Br. Hagen's inheritance. It is the same with me. I do not like, as you dear Brn. can believe, to keep stirring up this matter, and I will still be the cause that he has to be called away perhaps, which I think about with horror. However, I can do nothing else. As soon as I am told that I should not report anything more about him, then I will be quiet.

Currently we are all healthy except for our Rachel who has a very bad cold and has recently been plagued with headaches and toothaches. Otherwise, we continue in weakness, as well as we can. There is a lot of work, but we manage by hiring from time to time. Please greet our Sophia from us and tell her that we have received her letter dated June 14, and that I will answer her with the next mail. Br. Benzien's letter also arrived, and I will also answer it in time. Please greet him. Also Br. Steiner, please greet him as well. Now our dear Br. Benade will be among you again? Greet him well from us.

July 10th. Yesterday evening I received a little note from Br. Smith in Ochgoloogy, in which he informs me that they are all healthy and that the engagement of the previously mentioned couple was supposed to begin. We commend ourselves to your prayer before our dear Lord and greet you all most sincerely. Your faithfully obliged Br. and Sr.,

Gottlieb and Dorothea Byhan

[Springplace (M 407-1) and Oochgeelogy (M 409-1) Diaries.]

*July 10.* [Ooch.] In the evening we celebrated the engagement of the single Br. Alexander James Copeland and the single Sr. Maria R. Gambold. Both are members of the Brüder Gemeine.

*July 10.* [Spg.] With the mail today, along with many letters, we also received a letter from Br. Theod. Shulz in Salem with the happy news that Br. Franz Eder, who has received a call to service at the mission in Oochgeelogy, has arrived in Salem, and we sincerely wish to welcome him here among us, the sooner the better.

We are very happy that the Savior still knows how to find souls willing to help gather his preciously paid reward for suffering. There is a large field open here, where there is still much to do.

*Sun., July 13.* [Ooch.] In the first service we prayed the Church Litany. The sermon was on the Gospel lesson for Sunday, and more than 60 people came for this. In the third service we celebrated the wedding of the single Br. Alexander James Copeland and the single Sr. Maria Rosina Gambold. In the evening we had a Singstunde.

*Sun., July 13.* [Spg.] After the usual service, the Brn. and Srs. were informed that we will have Holy Communion and the baptism of an adult person next Sunday. The communicant members were especially invited to the enjoyment of this. They expressed their joy at this with a loud Indian Yes! and seemed unusually happy about this. Overall today an especially blessed feeling could be felt among our Brn. and Srs. If we could only speak with them in their language, it would be much easier for us. We spoke carefully today with the Negro Br. Christian Jacob, who will be confirmed next Sunday and approach the Lord's Table with us for the first time, and we found him in a happy and blessed spiritual disposition.

[M 414-3-21: Translated by Julie Tomberlin Weber. Addressed to: Revd. Theodor Schulz, Salem, Stokes County, North Carolina. Postmark: New Echota, Ch.N., July 15, 1828, 25. Received July 31.]

Oochgeelogy, July 14, 1828

My dearly beloved Br. Schulz!

I received your dear letter dated May 15, as well as the enclosure in Br. Byhan's letter. Please accept our most obliging thanks for this, as well as sincere greetings. We are all healthy and well, praise God.

Last week I visited our dear ones in Spring Place. Br. Byhan will surely have told you the reason for this in the last mail, that Br. Alex. James Copeland and Sr. Polly Gambold have promised themselves in marriage. Their wedding then took place yesterday after a public sermon by me. God bless them! They had their minds set on it, and our objections, if we had made any, would not have borne any fruit. We were very glad to hear that the Savior brought our dear Br. Eder safely to you in Salem. I am already looking forward to welcoming this dear Br. here soon. May He who gave him the mind to serve the Savior among the heathen successfully carry out His thoughts for peace in him. I have spoken with Br. W. A. Hicks again recently concerning our suggestions about dividing the school, and this has his full approval. Also the parents here have no objections to this. Br. Hicks will soon take both of his sons to Spring Place, and the girls from there should soon move here.

Time will tell how things will turn out with old Br. Joseph, since his children absolutely do not want to stay here, as it seems, and are intending to begin something for themselves in Tennessee. Personally I wish that if it were possible to lodge him in Salem this would be done. In any case he must give me a list (which should have been done a long time ago) of items he needs, so that if time allows these things can be gotten for him.

I have spoken much with Br. Byhan about the suggestion to send a Negro woman to help us. There are certainly many objections to be made against this. On the other hand, this suggestion also has its good aspects, and it is impossible for me to see how my wife will manage without such help if Sr. Anna Maria Gambold should return, which in my opinion would be the most advisable. Even if Br. Eder came here married, which will presumably be the case, you dear Brn. will act according to your best knowledge, and the help which you send us will be welcome.

We wondered if on this occasion we might be able to get a couple of butcher knives for chopping sausage meat. Until now we have had to chop our meat with the ax. Also some bellows.

Now to get to our calling, to the glory of the Savior we can write that His work still continues, gradually but in blessing. In my last letter I wrote to you about the desire of Lucy Hicks, who belongs to the Methodists, and besides her we have 3 more candidates for baptism, Nancy and Quaty, both grandchildren of old

Mother Hanna, and John Fields. At our last Holy Communion Sr. Sussanna Fields was confirmed and was a participant for the first time.

Our corn and other field and garden crops are doing excellently and promise a rich harvest. We are not getting any fruit. Good health prevails in our neighborhood. As soon as possible I will make a visit in the company of Br. W. A. Hicks to Chatogatee at the request of Br. Samuel and the residents, to bring them the happy news that they also have a Savior. Samuel was already expecting us on May 1 and the whole town had gathered. I was sorry that it could not take place, since Br. Hicks could not get away. Drowning Bear, the Chief, let me know that my visit would be pleasing to him and that he and his wife would come to the service.

Accept my most obliging thanks for the $100. For now there is nothing to get at Major Ridge's. Still I will not neglect to knock on his door from time to time. But what will happen with Sr. Polly Copeland's things? Is it possible for her bed, etc., to be sent with the wagon that is coming? She really wants this. She will probably write you a few lines herself today.

Since you get the Echota newspaper, I will not report all the news to you. I am happy that you addressed the letters for us to Echota. Postage is not higher, and we get them sooner, since they could lie in Spring Place 3 or 4 days.

This summer we have had extremely hot weather. Still there has always been sufficient rain, so that the field and garden crops are not in trouble. Sr. Anna Maria will look through Br. Joseph's clothing today, and then we will be in a position to say what he needs in any case.

If they do not find more subscribers for the Echota newspaper (they have only about 250), then they will probably have to give it up, since this does not cover the costs. Elias Boudinot receives $300 as editor and the printer $350.

We made the pleasant acquaintance of Mr. Henderson, Methodist preacher in this area, who visited us last week. He is a pleasant, moderate man. I have probably already informed you that Joseph Crutchfield joined the Methodists. He has also begun a Sunday school in this neighborhood now. Sometimes he has 20-30 scholars. It is just a shame that they go to the school and through this are prevented from going to worship service. But who can stop this. The services at our place are quite passably attended. I recently spoke individually with Br. and Sr. Hicks's children. Even if they do not yet have the whole mind to convert, there is still good reason to hope. Please greet your dear colleagues sincerely. My wife joins me in greeting your dear family. I am and remain your faithfully obliged Br.,

Johann Renatus Schmidt

P.S. In your letter of May 15 you commented on the children of our Brn. and Srs. When I came here they were not yet entered into the Gemein Catalog. But I have entered all the children under 12 of our Brn. and Srs. as well as all who are still under the guidance of their parents into the Gemein Catalog, directly according to the schema you left behind. We count all the children who have been baptized by us, even if only one [parent] belongs to our Gemeine. However, if both parts do not belong to us, then they are just written into the general church book. My arrangement is in complete agreement with your schematic, so that I need to make only a change in the Gemein Catalog. I sent your letter to Br. Byhan. He will also arrange everything according to this in the Catalog of Springplace.

Yesterday and today we dug up our potatoes, which I had planted on 2 squares of our garden, and we got about 30 bushels. We still have a large number in the field to harvest.

J. R. S.

[Oochgeelogy (M 409-1).]

*July 17.* [Ooch.] Br. Schmidt visited Br. and Sr. Hicks. There he saw Major Armstrong, whom Congress appointed to travel around the country and talk with the head Chiefs of the Nation to discuss the planned Cannal.

[M 414-3-22: Translated by Julie Tomberlin Weber. Addressed to: Revd. Theodor Schulz, Salem, Stokes County, North Carolina. No postmark. Received Aug. 8.]

Oochgeelogy, July 17, 1828

My much beloved Br. and Sr. Schulz,

Although I almost feel too silly to write you at this time, I know it is my duty to do so, and I want to ask you to accept it with love from me. Without a doubt, before this reaches you you will have learned from Brn. Byhan's and Schmidt's letters that on the 13th of this month I was married to the young Brother Alex. Copeland, who recently joined our Gemeine. I can imagine that this seems impossible to you, as well as to all who know my situation and me. However, it is true.

I think you know his character through letters, since he has already lived here for 2 years, and I can say nothing except that I have always respected him, because he was so faithful to my people. However, I can truthfully say that it never occurred to me that he would ever propose to me, because he is a good bit younger than I am, and for another thing he has never in the least given any indication that he had something like this in mind until about 4 weeks ago. I milled about for a while, but could think nothing other than that he suited me.

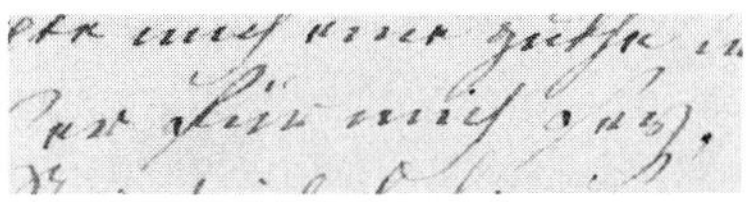

Perhaps you think I did this completely without consideration. No! I have certainly considered it thoroughly before the Lord, and He also granted me the assurance that He will continue to help me as He has until now. The thought that I would perhaps separate myself from the Gemeine, in which I have already enjoyed so much good, caused me much concern. Indeed I owe a great debt of gratitude to it. However, I hope and also ask humbly that you not despise me and do not cast me out and that you still consider me a member of it, although I do not know if I will ever move close to a Gemeine. Still one can never know. For now, we will stay here until this year is over. Then he is planning to rent a

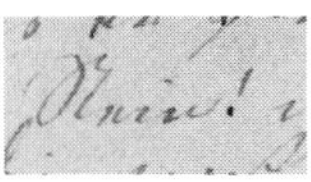

place in Tennessee. I will also take care of the school as I have until now.

Now I have written to you straightforwardly how things came about and how I feel. I know I would have said it just the same if I had been able to speak with you in person, because I also consider you like parents, and I also have confidence that you will accept this as from your child.

Now I must also ask you to be so good and if possible to send me my things with the wagon which brings Br. Eder out. I would be very glad if I could also get my commode. It occurred to me that you could pack part of the bed in the top part. I would also be very happy if I could get my two spinning wheels. But if it is not possible, I must ask you to sell them as well as my bedstead and two chairs, if someone can be found to buy them.

Be so good and also greet Srs. D. Warner and C. Stauber sincerely from me, and please ask them to help with my things. Caty knows where they are, and if I have time I will also write her a couple of lines. I also have an old chest there, but I will leave this. If my father should come to Salem, he will take it and leave his for me here. I will send back the suitcases I brought with the wagon.

Now I must ask Br. Schulz one more thing. Please also send me my money (Sr. Warner has the note). But first deduct the payment for the transportation. We are all pretty healthy, except my father is sometimes pitiful. He is completely satisfied with my marriage, and he and my dear aunt also want me to send you their best greetings. Now I also ask you to greet the children and generally good friends sincerely from me. I remain your faithful friend,

M. R. Copeland

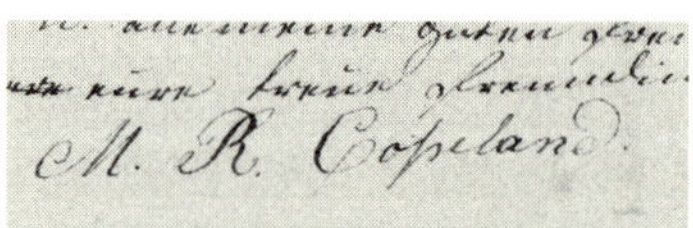
M. R. Copeland

# *1828, part 7*

[Springplace (M 407-1) and Oochgeelogy (M 409-1) Diaries. Translated by Julie Tomberlin Weber. Handwritings are Johann Renatus Schmidt's (Ooch.) and Gottlieb Byhan's (Spg.).]

*July 18.* [Ooch.] Sr. Schmidt suffered attacks of fever that got worse each day. She had to stay in bed for a whole week.

*July 18.* [Spg.] The baptismal candidate Sally, who is supposed to receive holy baptism next Sunday, came to our place to prepare herself for next Sunday. She was very happy at the grace which awaits her in holy baptism. She went on to our Br. and Sr. Joshua's this evening, to receive further instruction from our Sr. Anna Johanna, daughter of our Br. and Sr. Joshua, who always take special interest in our baptismal candidates.

*July 20.* [Ooch.] Only a few people came for the sermon. We had only one service today.

*Sun., July 20.* [Spg.] Today almost all of our Brn. and Srs. came to Spring Place, and all seemed to be especially happy and cheerful. In the first service after a talk accompanied by a transporting feeling of the close presence of the Savior, the Indian woman Sally was baptized with the name Sally Ann. Most all of those who were present — there were about 100 of them — had to give free reign to their tears. The Savior could be felt in our midst. After the baptism all the Brn. and Srs. came individually into our house to shake hands with the newly baptized woman. No eye remained dry during this. In the 2nd service there was first the confirmation of the Negro Br. Christian Jacob, and then we enjoyed the body and blood of our Lord in Holy Communion, during which the Savior let us be comforted by an awareness of his dear presence. Sr. Felicitas Hicks, our communicant Sr., had also come this time for the enjoyment of this, although she lives about 20 miles from Spring Place. She returned home again today, but wanted to go only as far as her daughter Elisabeth Fields's, because she is ill and she wanted to spend the night there. Sr. Delila McNair spent the night with us and on

*July 21* [Spg.] went back home with both of her daughters Martha and Elisabeth Bean, who had come along for a visit.

[M 414-3-23: Translated by Julie Tomberlin Weber. Addressed to: Revd. Theodor Shulz, Salem, Stokes County, North Carolina. Postmark: Springplace, C.N., July 24. Free. Gottlieb Byhan, P.M. Received Aug. 8.]

Springplace, July 23, 1828

My dear Br. Shulz,

I received your dear letter of June 24 on July 10. From this we were delighted to learn that the Savior has brought our dear Br. Eder safe and sound into your midst. We also welcome him sincerely. We hope to welcome him soon to Springplace. In the meantime we ask you to greet him very sincerely from us.

Since the marriage of Br. and Sr. Copland in Ochgoloogy, we have not heard anything from there. Copland asked me to go there and wed them, but a couple of days before this I became so ill and so weak that I was not able to go and at times had to stay in bed. However, praise God, I am now well, as we all are except Rachel, who has had to endure headaches and toothaches for a long time now.

Last Sunday, the 20th of this month, we had a true day of grace and blessing. In the first service was the baptism of the Indian woman Sally with the name Sally Ann. Everyone melted in tears so that the singing was almost interrupted, especially when the woman being baptized lay on her face and prayed, while some of the Sisters, including our communicant Sister Felicitas Hicks, widow of Charles R. Hicks, knelt on the white cloth around the baptized one. The close presence of our dear Lord could be felt. There were more than 100 people present. In the second service was the confirmation of our Negro Br. Chr. Jacob for his first enjoyment of Holy Communion, which we then celebrated immediately thereafter. The Savior let us feel His peace in a powerful manner in this service as well. Days like this one encourage the heart, mind, and body to do everything to help gather in the Savior's reward for suffering, and to wager all for Him.

Would it not be possible to get a white person instead of a Negro woman to help in the household? At least for a short while? We must admit and say that things will not work out well here with a Negro woman. Admittedly we already had sweet visions that if Sr. A. M. Gambold comes to us from Ochgeloogy, we would be helped, but it seems you would rather have her in Salem. Now we do not want to worry unnecessarily. The Savior will help us manage as long as we should still serve here. He has always found ways and means to help us through all difficulties, and He will also do so here.

I just received your dear letter of July 7 with the Salem Diary, for which I sincerely thank you. With the next post I will answer it. Your Br.,

Gottlieb Byhan

[M 414-3-24b: Translated by Julie Tomberlin Weber. No address; no postmark; no date.]

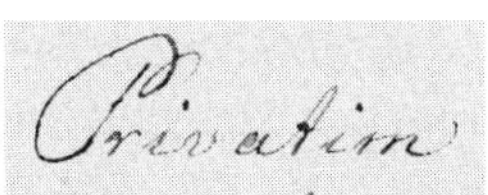


Private:

In answer to the private question regarding our Nathanael, I have this to report to you: His mother and I have spoken with him thoroughly about his presence here, but we have not been able to get anything more out of him except that, as he says, he is planning to continue as before, that is, to take care of the school. We do not believe that he currently has a mind to serve as a missionary. We have already gone through much with him, and occasionally through difficult times.

For the time being he does not seem able to decide on anything or to want to. Presumably he has written you himself. Oh, may he surrender his whole heart to the Savior. Then things would be easier for you and for us as well.

This brooding over many matters, which the young Brn. in the Gemeinen currently lose themselves in, would subside and they would have a happy life. But they reflect on why this or that in the Gemeine is the way it is, what this or that word which was said — particularly about ministers — might mean, etc. In this way they make their lives difficult and waste their time with this instead of surrendering themselves completely to the Savior and submitting themselves to His care and letting themselves do what pleases Him. We have gone over this again and again with our Nathanael, and we have discussed it all.

Now from this I think you can conclude how he is doing. It took much persuasion to get him to write you. Your Br.,

G. Byhan

[B 61-3: Provinzial Helfer Conferenz, meeting in Salem. Translated by C. Daniel Crews.]

*Thurs., July 24.* From the letter of Br. Gb. Byhan, which arrived here yesterday, we learn to our joy that they are all doing well, and that on the 20th they were planning to have the baptism of an adult person at Springplace. Several points and remarks contained therein were the subjects for our present discussions. The remarks concerning Br. Schmidt's methods in Oochgelogy were disturbing to us, but since Br. Byhan writes that he will soon have opportunity to explain these more closely, Br. Schulz will ask him to apprise us of everything pertaining to this and to communicate to us as soon as possible thorough and definite reports which tell the absolute truth.

As for the establishment of their schools there, so that in

Springplace there will be only boys and in Oochgelogy only girls, the only objection we have is that this should not be set up before the arrival of Br. Eder.

As for what concerns the single Sr. Polly Gambold, who wants to marry the white man Alexdr. Copeland, who belongs to the Oochgelogy Congregation, and who up to now has been in charge of the fieldwork there on a daily wage basis, the Conferenz thought that we ought not to get ourselves into any obligations to continue to provide their dwelling. Br. Schulz will report this to them.

[Springplace (M 407-1) and Oochgeelogy (M 409-1) Diaries.]

*July 24.* [Spg.] In the evening Mr. Walker and another gentleman from Carmel stopped in at our place on their way to Brainerd, where next Monday the 28th school exam will be, and spent the night. The former, Mr. Walker, is a missionary in Carmel.

*July 26.* [Spg.] Br. Nathl. Byhan went today to Brainerd on a visit to attend the above-mentioned school exam.

*Sun., July 27.* [Ooch.] After praying the Church Litany we had the sermon. In the 2nd service we read a sermon. Then we had to have a serious talk with Sr. Lydia about some problems in her house. It was extremely hot today.

*Sun., July 27.* [Spg.] Today only a few Brn. and Srs. were here for the services. First of all was the reading service, and afterward was a Singstunde. Yesterday and today we had extraordinarily hot weather, and it is so dry that the field and garden crops are suffering a great deal. The Fahr. Therm. yesterday was 103° and today 102°.

*July 28.* [Ooch.] Today we talked with the Indian woman Nancy, who has expressed her desire to be baptized. Many of our Brn. and Srs. and neighbors are sick with the influenza and fever that are raging, so this week Br. Schmidt visited all the houses in the neighborhood. The soil is thirsty for rain, the crops are starting to die, and the heat is almost unbearable.

*July 29.* [Spg.] Br. Nathl. Byhan returned from Brainerd today.

[M 414-3-24a: Translated by Julie Tomberlin Weber. Addressed to: Revd. Theodor Shulz, Salem, North Carolina. Postmark: Springplace, C.N., July 31. Free. Gottlieb Byhan, P.M.]

Springplace, July 30, 1828

My dear Br. Shulz,

As I have already informed you, your dear letter of July 7 arrived here along with the Salem Diary, etc., on the 24th. Thank you very much for this. Now I will see what I find to answer in your dear letter.

It is now certain that nothing can come of construction on our house this year. And who knows if perhaps it is better if we wait and see a little where things will go with the Cherokees here. By October it will surely be somewhat clear what will happen.

Everyone here is very curious to know who the Commissioners who are supposed to negotiate with the Cherokees will be. You wish further that I might inform the War Secretary about our planned construction in our next report. But I might ask you, dear Br., to make or draft an essay for me so that it will be somewhat similar, because I hardly trust myself to author such a report that is appropriate concerning the house construction. You, dear Br., are very well acquainted with our situation and what the reasons are for our construction of a house.

Enclosed I am sending our Diary until the end of last year, and if it is possible I will send a folio full every week, so that I think everything will arrive before Oct. I see further from your letter that my list of things arrived too late. It was a comfort to us that you had hope of getting the things we ordered in Salem, so that you will not have to write express to Philadelphia on account of our things. We were worried that our list might be too long. However, I might almost conclude that Br. Smidt's list must have been somewhat longer. You write me that something about the ordered tin dishes was not clear. Presumably you mean the metal bowls, about like hand bowls, smaller and larger, because I cannot remember having written for tin dishes.

Now I come to the Negro matter. We see from your letter that it has been entered that <u>one</u> Negro woman should be go to Spring Place to help Mother Byhan and <u>one</u> for Ochgoloogy. Please do not take this badly if we openly share our thoughts about this matter. We are sorry that we did not do so right away when we saw from your older letters that we might be helped in this way. We must admit honestly and say that Mother Byhan cannot expect <u>any</u> help from a Negro woman, and she also will not have this. The help she actually would need, that is, with cooking, baking, milking, taking care of the milk, and many other things too various to mention here, she will not get from a Negro woman. We also do not wish that we must suffer anew with a Negro woman just to have trouble, because what else does one have when one must have Negroes around? And then on top of that, with our old Pleasant, the best Negro woman would be ruined by her, and who can prevent this? We therefore wish and ask, as long as we are still here, to spare us from Negroes. It is a shame that Nancy Becker could not be taken in for a while. Then Mother Byhan would have real help!

On their last visit here Br. Smidt and Sr. A. M. Gambold also said: Just not a Negro, because we get no help from them here in this country. Perhaps Br. Smidt himself wrote something of this nature.

We are currently all healthy, except for Rachel, who for some time has had to endure bad headaches and even more toothaches. We are having extremely dry weather — everything is ready to die. Because he is very sickly, Jos. Vann is currently using the health spring in Sumack Town. We greet everyone most sincerely. Accept a special greeting from your friend and Br.,

Gottlieb Byhan

[Springplace (M 407-1) and Oochgeelogy (M 409-1) Diaries.]

*Aug. 2.* [Ooch.] We received a letter from our dear Br. Schulz in Salem.

*Sun., Aug. 3.* [Ooch.] The sermon on the Gospel lesson for this Sunday was delivered to a large number of listeners. Then another Indian, appointed by the Presbyterian Church to travel around in the country and preach, gave a talk for those gathered. He concluded with a prayer and singing. Many of our children are currently sick with the influenza that is raging. This evening a rain refreshed the thirsty earth and cooled the air nicely. From the comments above, our dear Brthren and Sisters and friends can see that God's work in Oochgeelogy is proceeding somewhat slowly, but there is still hope that a nice little gathering will come together here to be a light in the darkness. And so we ask our dear Brn. and Srs. and friends to remember us often before the throne of grace. We pray that the Savior will use the power of His blood and accomplish thousands of good things physically and spiritually. We need it and He does it.

*Sun., Aug. 3.* [Spg.] After the usual Sunday services was the baptism into Jesus' death of our Br. and Sr. Samuel and Rachel's baby boy with the name Samuel Lewattee. Toward evening we had a strong storm accompanied by wind and rain. We were very thankful for the rain, since everything in both our fields and in the gardens has begun dying. The leaves on the trees at our height became yellow and fell off like autumn, so that it looks very gloomy. Our corn also suffered a great deal, since its leaves were yellow to the stalks. The heat was so extremely high that we hardly knew what to do. Yesterday the Fahr. Therm. was at 104½°.

*Aug. 4.* [Spg.] We had a nice rain again, which somewhat refreshed the ground and plants with a soaking. We brought praise and thanksgiving for this to our Father, who does not forget His children when their need is the greatest.

*Aug. 9.* [Ooch.] Brother and Sister Samuel Canaquiaka and Br. Israel visited us. The former brought both of their twin daughters, Gatheja and Gathege, to our school. This evening we had a Singstunde with the Brn. and Srs. who were present.

*Sun., Aug. 10.* [Ooch.] We began reading Jesus' Passion story in 2 sessions. We will continue doing this every Sunday. Brn. William Abr. Hicks and Samuel Canaquiaka each gave a very touching talk for those present. In the afternoon the Brethren and Sister from Spring Place traveled back home. This evening it rained a little. We had a sincere talk with the Negro Michael. The Brethren baptized him as a child, because he belonged to the Mission in Springplace. It seems that the things he learned in school there during his childhood and what he heard about the Savior have not been erased from his heart.

*Sun., Aug. 10.* [Spg.] Only a few of our Brn. and Srs. were in the services, partly because it looked as if it would be a rainy day, and partly because the Negroes in our neighborhood had requested a Methodist preacher who was supposed to hold a sermon for them. This also took place by a Negro who often gives talks among the Negroes. Toward evening an extremely strong storm moved past us. Close to us there was one strike after another. But as soon as it came into sight above us, it began to rain heavily and the strong thunder suddenly subsided. We were grateful to the Savior that He protected us from harm. Today we also received a boy [Archibald] into our school, the foster child of the Indian Connondoha and our Sr. Hannah. The boy's father lives in Tennessee and promised to provide the boy with clothing if he were sent to our school. Our school boy Ignatius also went home again today on a visit. We learned in the last few days that our neighbor Mr. Jos. Vann was elected as a member of the National Committee at the last election on the 4th of this month.

*Aug. 11.* [Ooch.] Rain made the heat a little more bearable.

*Aug. 12.* [Ooch.] Br. Schmidt visited Br. and Sr. Hicks and others in their area. The decision made last week by the Council and Committee does not reflect the wishes of most of the residents. This has caused much unrest among people, as have the 2 commissioners from the Arkansaw Cherokees who have been ordered by the government of the United States to try to find emigrants from this area.

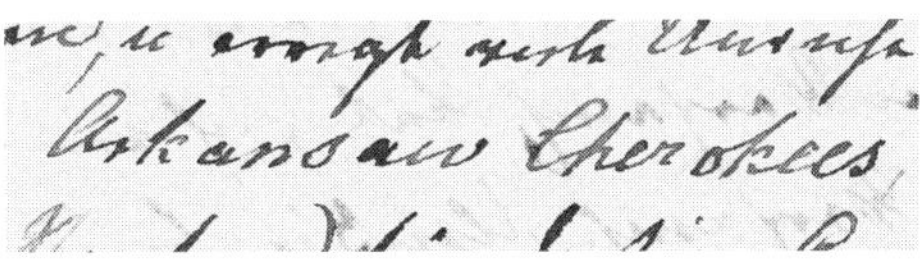


Our plea to the Lord is that His work among them will not suffer because of this. Br. Hicks, whose house is always full of visitors these days, is doing his best to calm people's spirits and to offer each person good advice.

[M 414-3-25: Translated by Julie Tomberlin Weber. Addressed to: Revd. Theodor Shulz, Salem, Stokes County, North Carolina. Postmark: Springplace, C.N., Aug. 14. Free. Gottlieb Byhan, P.M. Received Aug. 28.]

Springplace, Aug. 13, 1828

My dear Br. Shulz,

Enclosed I am sending another part of our Diary. I should have sent it eight days ago, but I did not have the time to copy it. If possible, I will try to continue. This time I have nothing more to report other than that we are all healthy except for Mother, who has been overcome by a weakness so that at times she has to stay in bed. May God provide that she improve soon, because we cannot do without her in our household. Praise God that we have our Rachel with us in such situations.

On the last post day we received nothing from you dear ones in Salem, and we hope that tomorrow we will receive all the more. I have heard nothing from Ochgoloogy. Tomorrow I expect an answer to my little letter to you dated July 3. It just occurs to me, on the last post day I received a note from Br. Shaaf which just contained the question about <u>when</u> I received the German newspaper of July 3 and <u>when</u> I received the one from July 10, the former by way of Knoxville and the latter by way of Augusta. This serves as an answer to this: I received them both on Aug. 7, and indeed in the <u>same</u> hour. Please pass this on to Br. Shaaf along with sincere greetings.

The following items have also occurred to me which I would like to request you send me with Br. and Sr. Eder: An almanac for 1829 if they are available by then. Snuff from Br. Fries, not from Br. Hulthin. The latter's tobacco is not so good. A quantity of flintstones, mostly of the small and medium variety. One pound of lime. If I have already written for these articles, which I do not know because out of negligence I have not kept a list of things I have ordered, then no harm is done.

After almost 4 weeks of drought we now have beautiful, fruitful weather. But it came too late for our Indian corn. This was extra-ordinarily beautiful at first and then was almost burned up in the great drought and heat, so that we can expect only a mediocre harvest. And now the crows and squirrels and woodpeckers are so thick on it that we will lose another large part of it through these vermin. Our oat harvest has turned out very plentiful. Last week we sowed approximately 1½ acres with turnips, which are already sprouting.

Last week we also finally rebuilt our chimney, which should have been done a long time ago, and now we are in the process of repairing the southern door to our house. It was always nailed closed by Br. and Sr. Schmidt, because it needed to be repaired and the threshold was rotten, so that only the door on the northern side of the house could be opened, which was really not very pleasant in the winter. Next week we will repair the barn floor if nothing else comes up, which is often the case here. Then we will repair the springhouse, then the schoolhouse, and kitchen roof — everywhere you look there is something to be repaired and fixed, so that sometimes you hardly know what should be done first.

And things are just the same for our Sisters in the household. Milking, washing, cooking, baking, especially the washing for the children, is a lot of work for them, because sometimes they must do mending for them 2 days, and everything else that there is to do in a household, because our Plesant is an absolute zero. She cannot be counted at all anymore, so it is necessary for good help to be sent, or the Sisters will not make it under the load.

There would be much more to say also regarding the things I should really take care of, or someone else besides me. It was recommended to me, or to us, that we should visit the Brn. and Srs. from time to time and become acquainted with them in this manner. I have done nothing about this, and I also cannot do so until help comes. It has often worried us that we cannot attend to our real call appropriately. Now, I will be silent. The Savior knows His time, when and how to provide guidance.

We greet everyone most sincerely, and you, please accept a special greeting from your faithfully obliged Br.,

Gottlieb Byhan

Please greet dear Br. Eder most sincerely from us and tell him that he should write us a couple of lines. He could enclose it in your letter.

Aug. 14. I also just wanted to report that I gave Br. Smith $100 last week to pay off as much as possible the debt he made with Lavender. So now I have only the $50 Newbern note, which I cannot use at all, because no one will take it from me and change it. Be so good, then, and send me something again. I do not know what to do with the mentioned $50. It is of no use to me. Your

Gottl. Byhan

[Springplace (M 407-1) and Oochgeelogy (M 409-1) Diaries.]

*Aug. 15.* [Spg.] There was a ballplay close to us, and it was actually for Indian women who play themselves. Later we heard that things apparently were not very decent during this.

*Aug. 16.* [Ooch.] We received a visit from Br. and Sr. Byhan in Spring Place. With the mail we received a pleasant letter from Br. Mortimer in New York.

*Aug. 16.* [Spg.] Br. and Sr. Byhan today went to Ochgoloogy on business. They returned from there on the 18th.

*Sun., Aug. 17.* [Ooch.] After praying the Church Litany, we read from Jesus' Passion story in 2 sessions.

*Sun., Aug. 17.* [Spg.] In the absence of Br. and Sr. Byhan, Br. Nathanael Byhan today led the services in Spring Place.

*Aug. 18.* [Ooch.] Br. Schmidt visited Sister Sussanna at Oaty's, 12 miles from here. She was very happy about the visit, especially since she has been quite ill and cannot attend services here as often as she would like. Br. Schmidt also saw her brother Charles Rees there, a nice man we knew in Springplace. He is a member of the Presbyterian Church and serves as interpreter in Brainerd. From him we heard that the well-known Mohak Chief John Norton from Canada, who was an envoy of the Mohack Nation here in this country

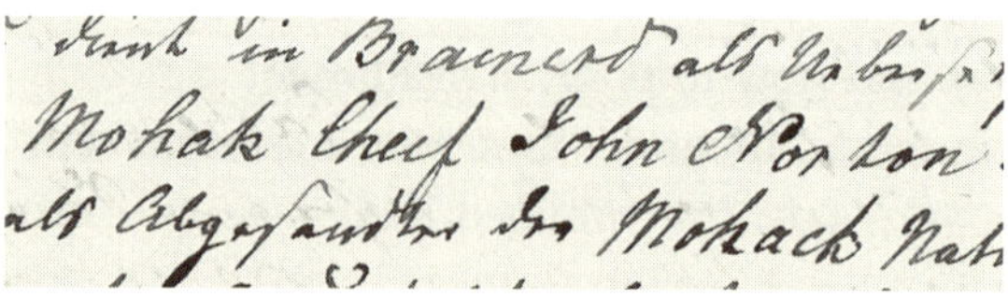
Mohak Chief John Norton

many years ago, visited the Cherokees in Arkansaw last year to renew the old friendship between the northern Indians and the Cherokees, and he died there. His mother was a Cherokee Indian and his father was from Scotland.[1] Br. Schmidt had a pleasant talk with Oaty that lasted several hours, and he heard his whole life's story through an interpreter. He learned to read Cherokee translations in his old age and apparently the translations from the New Testament led him to much reflection. Br. Schmidt also stopped in at Br. W. A. Hicks and met 6 Chiefs from the Vally-towns there on business.

[M 414-3-26: Translated by Julie Tomberlin Weber. Addressed to: Revd. Theodor Shulz, Salem, Stokes County, North Carolina. Postmarks: New Echota, Ch.N., Aug. 20, 25; Springplace, C.N., forwarded Aug. 21. Received Sept. 8.]

Oochgeelogy, Aug. 19, 1828

My dearly beloved Br. Schulz!

I greet you most sincerely with these lines. Praise God, we are all healthy again. Finally our dear Br. W. A. Hicks enabled me to arrange for Major Ridge to pay us $200, which he borrowed and on which he must pay interest.

Some days ago we had a visit from our Br. and Sr. Byhan in Springplace. On this occasion he shared your last letter with us. When Sr. Polly Copeland informed us of her plan to marry Br. Alex, I said right away that the matter should be reported to Salem first. However, Sr. Anna Maria said the matter could not be delayed. And so I immediately suggested that we had to speak with the Brn. and Srs. in Springplace, which then was done 2 days later when I traveled there with Anna Maria. They [said] that we could make no objection to the marriage, and that I should carry it out as soon as possible. Br. Byhan was assigned to inform the Brn. of the P.H. Conf. in Salem along with all the

---

[1] But see *Records: Cherokees*, 3:1322.

[circumstances] with the next post. This was why I believed that I personally did not need to write. They never said anything definite to my wife or me about what they wanted to do now. When Br. Byhan asked them if they were willing to serve the mission as the Claytons did in Spring Place without a salary, their answer at first was under certain conditions, and then they declared that they did not want to stay here in Oochgeelogy with us. We also do not want this for the following reasons:

1. Where should they have a place to live? It would have to be built right away, and the difficulties of construction are clear enough in Springplace, where they cannot get the work done.

2. This would be 3 families at one post, and 2 of them just married. Think about the fact that these families could increase soon, and perhaps both at the same time, and what kind of situation would it be with the mission family in a country where you cannot get help or care? And if Br. Joseph stayed here, he will also soon have to be taken care of completely.

3. Br. Alex Copeland has already worked here for many years for $12 per month. Will he not open himself to much strange talk here among his relatives and acquaintances since the people are completely unacquainted with our customs?

4. We do not know how things will continue with Sr. Polly Copeland's ailments.

5. If Sr. Anna Maria also stays here and if they stayed here, the Indians might think we might soon want to make a fort if they see such an increase in the number of white people here.

6. Would Alex Copeland's parents and numerous relatives not expect certain rights if he is related to us in this way? Most of them are carelessly inclined, and already there is no end to the borrowing and begging.

7. Where so many people live together at a post, the peace is very easily disturbed. If Alex had remained single, we could not have had any better help. He is a diligent and faithful young man, but in his current circumstances he will perhaps be more harmful than useful.

I have written the above since Br. Byhan asked me to write our thoughts. Still if the dear Brn. of the P.H.C. believe it would work, then we are satisfied. We are willing to do what they find best, and completely submit ourselves to their recommendation about this matter regardless of our own choice.

I have answered dear Br. Mortimer's letter thoroughly. He writes that Mr. Samuel Hubberd would always be willing to pay $20 for a child. I wrote him that I would answer him about this as soon as we had corresponded with the Brn. in Salem about this. The matter entails difficulties, but one cannot brush off such an honorable man as Mr. Hubberd. Should we take another child on this condition?

I will try to get Br. John Gambold's papers and related artifacts as soon as possible. (I cannot do this before the first of Sept.) For this we must travel to the court in Coosawattee, which will be held at the beginning of Sept. To save money, Sr. Anna Maria wants to have it postponed until the Council, which will not be held until the middle of Oct. We cannot wait that long.

We are looking forward to seeing Br. Eder, whom we ask you to greet sincerely. Hopefully he has recovered from his fever. As soon as we have received [page torn: money] from Major Ridge, I will let you know. Mr. Lavender is supposed to have been paid for the [page torn: money in] Springplace. Br. Byhan sent me another $100. If the Alex Copelands leave, I hear they want to look for a place in Tennessee. We will also have to satisfy him. We still owe him salary from 2 years. We will be short of money again. Currently I have $200 dollars in the cash box. We are still in debt about $60. We have $38 in outstanding debts. There is still the $100 for the doctor in Tennessee for Br. Gambold. I hope my Diary arrives safely. My wife joins me in greeting your dear ones.

I send sincere greetings, and I am and remain your faithful Br.,

Johann Renatus Schmidt

Please greet your dear colleagues most sincerely.

[M 414-3-27: Translated by Julie Tomberlin Weber. Addressed to: Revd. Theodor Shulz, Salem, Stokes County, North Carolina. Postmark: Springplace, C.N., Aug. 21. Free. Gottlieb Byhan, P.M. Received Sept. 3.]

Springplace, Aug. 19, 1828

Dearly beloved Br. Shulz,

I received your dear letter of July 28 on the 14th of this month, for which I thank you sincerely. Praise God, we are currently healthy and well except that Nathl. is suffering from a sore on his leg. Mother has also recovered, which is cause for gratitude, because nothing works well when she cannot keep going.

Now to get to you dear letter, I must admit I am afraid and concerned, because in this you ask for an open and direct explanation of how things are with Br. Smidt in Ochgoloogy. I will try to do this here as well as can be done on paper. Of course I could tell and explain this better and more thoroughly in person. However, since that cannot be done now, I will do it here. You can believe that it is not easy for me to write things of <u>this</u> nature about a colleague, as I will now have to do, because I want to write openly and directly according to the truth, because you asked me to do this in your last letter, and because I personally am convinced that everything should be stopped which might in time hurt the Savior's affairs and work here.

In your letter you asked me to add more definite news about Br. Jos.'s statement about Br. Smidt, whether it was really true. I have now done so, as follows! When I read your dear letter I agreed immediately that it would be necessary to visit Ochgoloogy right away because of Br. Jos.'s statement, and also concerning Br. and Sr. Copeland's and Sr. A. M. Gambold's staying there, and concerning Br. and Sr. Eder's home. My dear wife and I set out on horse last Saturday the 16th of this month and arrived safely in Ochgoloogy toward evening.

I found Br. Smidt sitting in a chair as usual and smoking his pipe. I went out right away to investigate whether he had often gone to Mr. Copeland either to have his bottle filled or only, as people say, to drink a dram. I personally went to Mr. Copeland's — he lives about ½ mile from Ochgoloogy. He is a brother of Alex. Copeland — and I asked him if this was really the case. He really did not want to say anything, but he finally admitted it and said it had been the case that he had come, admittedly when the brandy had been on the table, because he had workers, so of course he had to offer him a dram, and he had only come a couple of times with his bottle and gotten it filled, as he said.

Sr. A. M. Gambold, as well as Alex Copland, says that he went there almost every day. Sr. A. M. G. told me that there had been talk about brandy at the table once — Sr. G. had the brandy under her protection — and Br. Smidt said that it would be good if some brandy was bought for the house again, because sometimes people need it. To which Sr. G. answered: You have gotten some from Mr. Copeland, and indeed several bottles full. Sr. Smidt then said: Ey, Papy. Did you get brandy from Copeland? To which he replied no in front of everyone at the table.

When I asked him about this matter, he admitted it to me right away and said he had gotten it because his wife had been ill — and yet at the table she knew nothing about it. So it is true that he got it there and drank there often, because Copeland admitted this to me and previously also to Sr. Gambold, as Br. Smidt also admitted to me that it is the truth. Sr. G. and we sometimes cannot help wondering whether Sr. Smidt is also not completely free of it sometimes, whether she might not perhaps drink a little of it sometimes as well. Sr. G. believes to have signs of this. Recently when Mr. Henry, a trader from Tenn. who sells brandy, also came to their house, she told Sr. G. that she did not get brandy from anyone as good as from this Henry. As she says, one could drink it quite "reverend." Sr. G. herself has seen that she made warm "dram," as people say, for herself and her children and presumably also for him in the mornings, and if any was left over, it was poured out. And so we believe if Sr. Smidt was completely free of it, she could do much for her poor husband,

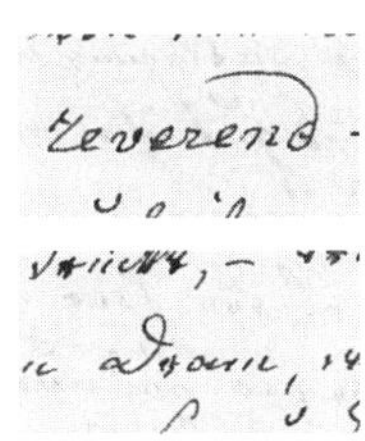

so that he would finally give up his miserable boozing. I must call it this, since naturally she knows about everything that has already been said and written about him.*

Now to come to the conclusion of this account, when I confronted him with his behavior and told him that it is my duty to report all of this to Salem, he once again said for sure: He would not drink another drop of brandy or wine from now on. I told him that he would have to ask for grace and strength from the Savior to carry out this resolution, because otherwise his resolution would not help him, and thus I left him.

In addition, Sr. G. and everyone assure us that he does nothing the whole day long, sits in the grandfather chair by the black fireplace and smokes tobacco constantly and says that he wants to do absolutely nothing. For what should he sacrifice and torture himself. The Missions Diacony is rich enough. Br. Hagen [Haga] willed them enough.

Is it right for a missionary to think like this? He also said that I would completely ruin my character, because I run around with tattered sleeves and barefoot and work — which he would surely not do. He did not want to ruin his character like this. As said, he sits in the living room the whole day, does not have any idea how everything at the site looks, does not know if this or that should be done or repaired, does not concern himself with anything or ask how various things are. When he has something to pay or gets money and wants to write it down, then he immediately calls Sr. G. to tell him how he should do it and write it down, like someone who just began to do such things yesterday. In short, he cannot do anything — or does not want to do anything unless Sr. G. is present. In short he is a childish and — lazy man. This is the truth. I do not want to say anything further about Sr. Smidt except what I said above, except that she has a high degree of complacency.

I also have the following to report about Br. and Sr. Copeland, Sr. Gambold, and Joseph G. They have all decided to stay with Br. and Sr. Smidt no longer than the fall. This is their firm decision, and they have given me the job of reporting this to you as well as sending you sincere greetings. I also informed Br. and Sr. Smidt that none of them want to stay with them any longer. I thought it would be better if I told them right away here, so that they do not learn this from you first, and you dear ones have a freer hand to act.

Now each of them explained the following about his particular situation. The Copelands will move to Tennessee. They say, however, that if they did not have to be with Br. and Sr. Smidt, they would serve the mission for one more year for wages, as previously. They could not agree to work as the Claytens served in Spring Place, without pay. In no case would they stay with Br. and Sr. Smidt's longer than the fall.

Sr. A. M. Gambold says that she will not stay with the Smidts longer than Br. and Sr. Eder's arrival here, if she can endure it that long. She is willing to move where it is considered to be good, whether to Spring Place or back to Salem. As she says, she will now wait eagerly for an answer to this letter.

Joseph Gambold has decided to return to Salem, because he absolutely will not stay any longer at the Smidts's, and he also does not want to move with his children. And so, as he says, he will return to Salem or come to Spring Place.

I just thought of one more thing concerning Br. Smidt. Does he sometimes receive money from you or from Pennsylvania? Because he can always lend money to the mission. When he moved away from Spring Place, the mission owed him $50. Now the mission in Ochgoloogy owes him $30. Sr. Smidt apparently said there are a couple of percents of interest after all. It is bad that the mission here has to pay interest. Without this there is enough. But perhaps he or she brought it along so that they could serve the mission in this way. I also wanted to add that Br. and Sr. Copeland cannot settle down on a separate little site in the Nation. They have to live either in Ochgoloogy or in Springplace and serve the mission, or they would not be allowed to live in this country. And so your suggestion that they could settle close to Ochgoology and perhaps he would continue to work for the mission in Ochgoology as before cannot be followed. And even if this could be done, Br. Copeland told me when I discussed the matter with him that he did not want to work for Br. Smidt any longer.

Now, dear Br., I hope the above will be sufficient to provide you dear Brn. with an important and thorough consideration in your honorable Conf. As far as I have learned, his behavior is not yet known among the Brn. and Srs., praise God! They must keep it very secret. However, it is in fact time that he change. It is at the height with him. If his way of acting comes out as it really is, then there would be horrible damage for the whole mission work here, not only in Ochgoloogy but also in Spring Place. May the Savior help and advise you and allow you to recognize His will so that the beautiful work here will not suffer harm through our fault.

Aug. 20. Now I will still try to answer various things from your dear letter. Sr. Delila McNair can only, or until now has only been able to, come to Spring Place for holy days and communions. We are on a friendly footing with her and also with Mr. McNair. I would be very glad if you could send me some money before Br. Eder's arrival, because last week I sent Br. Smidt the last $100 note, since Lavender was after him for his payment again — that is $192. But now I hear that Major Ridge is making noises about paying something, which will become clear in a couple of weeks. I also hear that John Ridge is planning to visit Salem next Christmas to pick his sister Sally up from there. Time will tell whether anything will come of this. I will let you know as soon as Major Ridge pays and I have a receipt from Lavender.

We sincerely wish that we would find ourselves in our new house soon, but that is still a long way off. Everything of this kind here is associated with hundreds of difficulties, and we must simply practice patience. At the next Council of the Cherokees in Oct. perhaps many things will develop of which we do not yet know. Certainly Mr. McKenny has lost his credit here. One is hardly allowed to mention him. It has almost hurt Nathanael that he has not received an answer to his letter. However, he is very calm now and diligently continues leading the school. The honorable Prov.H. Conf. advised us to wait with the arrangement of our schools until Br. Eder is here, but that cannot be done now. The arrangement has already been partially made, so to speak, because our Brn. and Srs. have already taken girls from here to Ochgoloogy, and others are also planning to take theirs there shortly. Br. Wm. Abr. Hicks told me last Sunday that he will arrive in Spring Place very soon with 3 or 4 boys. And so I do not believe it would be good if we stopped this matter now.

I received the enclosure from Br. Mortimer concerning the Cherokee child taken in by Lady Hubbard, and Br. Smidt received the letter from Br. Mortimer, from which the copy I received was made. Br. Smidt will write to Br. Mortimer himself in detail concerning this. I find in the Spring Place catalogues that this child taken in was a certain Delila Adair. She came to the school here Apr. 21, 1824, and it was noted that she left the school on June 5, 1825. In my opinion Br. Smidt should have informed Lady Hubbard after she had left the school. Then perhaps the Lady could have decided how to proceed, whether to take in another child in her place or not.

Br. and Sr. Smidt say things did not work well with such adopted children, because it always seemed as if such children had a certain advantage over others and caused disunity among the children. If we are supposed to say what we think, we would surely also admit that we are also somewhat concerned about an adopted child. Will such a child not want to have better clothing than all the other children when he knows that we are paid? And as Br. and Sr. Smidt say, the former child Delila Adair demanded that she wanted to walk in Morocco shoes.

We would always have to be worried that the child did not receive the appropriate care and attention in the eyes of other people, and perhaps we might even be reproached by the child himself that we were not doing well enough by him for the payment. And would this not cause bad rumors among the neighbors if they knew that we are paid for him and believed that we did not do enough for him? And what is $20, especially here in this country where everything is so expensive? You cannot buy many special things here before $20 is gone. Not that we consider the gift too little. Not at all. It is just that here it is little to maintain a child for a whole year in better clothing than the others, because they were requested for the $20.

Therefore, our main concern is that by accepting a child in this manner we might bring difficulties upon ourselves and that we might not be able to use this gift in a satisfactory way. In the meantime, we will not hesitate to try it. We currently have a suitable subject in the school. She is a Falling. Her father is dead but she still has a completely blind mother. The girl is about 8 or 9 years old and is a very good natured and honest girl. But in our opinion she should <u>not</u> be allowed to know that someone is paying for her.

Still we do not want to do this hastily, because we do not yet know for sure whether we will be allowed to keep the child or not. This will become clear in a few weeks.

I would also like to pose the question of what is really intended with such a child? Is the intention that such a child must stay in the school here until she is grown, or if she is taken home again in a quarter year or half year that another be taken in in her place? Or what should be done about this? What happens to the clothing such a child has received, that is for or from the $20? If she leaves the school is she allowed to take it home with her? Or does she have to leave it behind so that the next child taken in can use it? All of this should be clarified and explained.

Last Sunday when I was absent and in Ochgeloogy, Nathanael held the services for the few Brn. and Srs. who were here. In the first one he prayed the Church Litany and in the second one was Bible reading.

All the rest of the news in your last letter was very interesting and noteworthy to us.

Yesterday an unusually high number of Indians passed very quietly through our lane and all of them cleanly and nicely dressed. We saw women and children ride by on horses, all of them cleanly dressed. We did not know what to think of this. Finally upon questioning, we learned yesterday evening that the women had

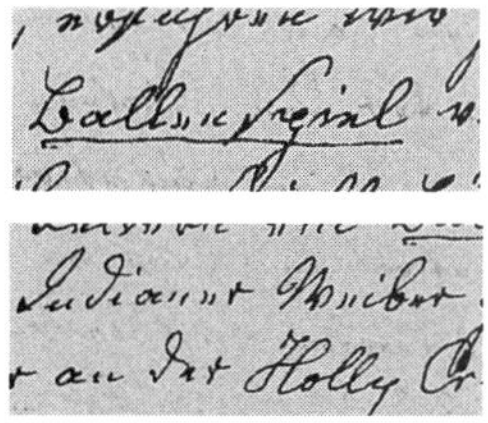

planned a ballplay behind Jos. Vann's fields, where no one had played besides the Indian women————. Next Friday the women will have another ballplay at Holly Creek about 7 miles from here.

Did our Sophia pay you for the *Cherokee Phoenix*? I enclosed the money for it. Perhaps she has paid. Did you pay for my *Western Carolina* at Br. Shober's at the beginning of June? It is paid in advance. I receive it correctly. I would cancel it, because it is almost overwhelmingly for Jackson, but because it is printed near Salem it is important to me.

Aug. 21. Late yesterday evening Major Ridge arrived at our place and spent the night here. I was already happy and looking forward to the money he would pay me, especially when I found that his saddlebag was heavy. However, I found myself deceived. I received not a cent. Since I heard that he had promised to take over the debt with Lavender, I did not want to say anything about it, and he also did not say anything about it. We simply have to wait for it. I also talked with him about our planned construction, which he really approved. He also invited us to visit him sometime soon. This morning he traveled on home.

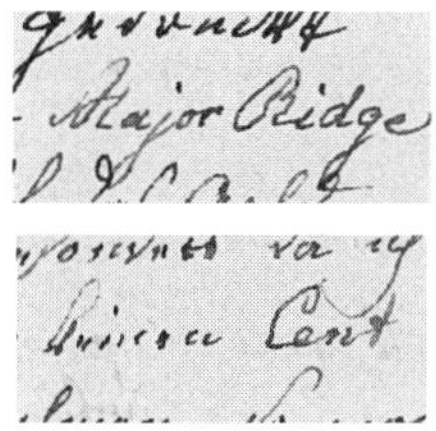


We greet all most sincerely. Do not forget our Br. Eder and our Sophia. And you, accept the most sincere, special greeting from your honest friend and Br.,

Gottlieb Byhan

* Sr. A. M. Gambold told us that since Br. and Sr. Smidt have been in Ochgoloogy 32 gallons of brandy were bought, of which old Br. Joseph has received 6 black bottles full; 8 or 10 gallons might still be on hand. The Alex. Copelands do not drink any brandy. Because of the lack of time, I cannot send any Diary this week.

[B 61-3: Provinzial Helfer Conferenz, meeting in Salem.]

*Thurs., Aug. 21.* After Br. Franz Eder found himself willing and inclined in accord with the decision of the P.H.C. to be married for entering into service in the Cherokee Mission if a Sr. was approved * by the Savior, we now entered into a deliberation of the matter and were completely agreed to suggest the single Sr. Salome Spach of this place for this. Having posed the question * , we received the following directive:

The Savior approves that we undertake that the single Br. Franz Eder marry the single Sr. Salome Spach * .

Br. Benade will now communicate this to him for consideration.

*Mon., Aug. 25.* Br. Franz Eder accepted the proposal to marry the single Sr. Salome Spach, but the latter declined the proposal to marry Br. Franz Eder. Whereupon this Br. asked the Conferenz not to proceed further in this deliberation in that for the present he would much rather go as a single person to the Cherokee Mission. We agreed with him to let the matter lie for the present until we receive a more detailed answer from Br. Byhan concerning the minutes of 24 July in regard to Br. Schmidt.

Since Br. Byhan in his last letter firmly forbade the sending of a Negro woman to assist at Springplace, and since on the other hand the single Sr. Nancy Becker, a relative of Sr. Byhan, suggests that she is willing to go there as their household assistant, we will try to discover the conditions under which she wishes to do this. In this case, however, it is advisable for Br. and Sr. Byhan that their daughter Rahel come back from there. Br. Schulz then will try to buy a Negro woman for Oochgelogy.

[Springplace (M 407-1) and Oochgeelogy (M 409-1) Diaries.]

*Aug. 22.* [Spg.] There was a ballplay close to us again.

*Sun., Aug. 24.* [Ooch.] The service was well attended. After praying the Church Litany we continued reading from the Passion story in 2 sessions. A white neighbor who regularly attends our services with his family, but who is a Methodist, asked for a copy of this story after the service; it seemed to make a deep impression on his heart. Mr. Hollars from Spring Place came here this evening to work at our place for a while. Today we informed our communicants that we would have Holy Communion next Sunday.

*Sun., Aug. 24.* [Spg.] There were many listeners in our services again, and especially Negroes. The Brn. and Srs. were informed of the coming Holy Communion on Sept. 7. Today 3 children also came back to the school. They had been at home on a visit. It is a shame that the children are taken out of school to go home so often, where they usually forget everything they have learned, so that they make only very slow progress in learning. We hope that the agreement that in Spring Place only boys will be in the school will bring about a change in this part, because then some of them will be so far from home here that the visits will not be made so easily and often.

Br. and Sr. Samuel, who had business close to us, spent the night here. Br. Samuel noted and expressed to us that it was regrettable that we so seldom have an interpreter here, that since the Brn. and Srs. do not understand what is said or read in our services, we should try to get Mr. Tazizi more often. We agree from the bottom of our hearts with this desire to have a translator here, but at this time we cannot help ourselves. First of all, Tazizi lives about 18 miles from here, and then he is seldom home on Sundays, because he is often employed by the missionaries in Brainerd and thus cannot come to us, even if he wanted to. And when he is sometimes free from them, then he has business to do for himself. Thus we do not see how we can help ourselves at this time, although we are certainly sorry for our Brn. and Srs. that they understand so little in the services.

Even so, one must be amazed at the faithfulness of the Brn. and Srs. that they are so dedicated to regularly attending the services. Especially Br. Samuel does this faithfully, only he is sometimes a little too ambitious in this, since the Brn. and Srs. who live far from us cannot come as often as those who live close to us, so that the former sometimes become impatient with Br. Samuel's reminders.

And yet love and peace prevail consistently among them, and we can do nothing but testify that they walk in a way which honors the Gospel. If a mistake occasionally comes up among them, they allow themselves to be corrected in love.

*Aug. 25.* [Ooch.] We began drying the corn feed. The Indian Skitihee came here today to work for us.

*Aug. 29.* [Spg.] We began making our corn feed.

*Aug. 30.* [Spg.] Today many Indians went past here, because they have a ballplay again about 8 miles from here, and everyone, men, women and children, has to go and attend this entertainment. In the evening James Foster and his wife came from Coosawattee to our place and spent the night here. He told us that in 7 or 8 days he will bring one of his sons to the school here.

*Sun., Aug. 31.* [Ooch.] In 2 sessions we reflected on the Savior's suffering on the Mount of Olives and on Golgotha. The services were very well attended, especially by Indians. Major Ridge and Cabin Smith were present. A number of baptized Indians from Turnip Mountain, 12 miles below Ridge's Ferry, were also here.

*Sun., Aug. 31.* [Spg.] Only a few Brn. and Srs. were in our services, because they are so busy at the moment making corn feed, and the weather does not look very favorable for such work; and since it mostly seemed today as if the sun wanted to shine, they were all the busier in their fields. After the services we spoke sincerely with our Br. Boas, a candidate for Holy Communion, and with the baptized single Br. Solomon, especially with the latter, who was advised not to forget what he promised the Savior in holy baptism and accordingly to walk worthily. He promised to remember this and to ask the Savior for the necessary grace and strength for this. Sr. Sally Hicks, Br. Wilm. Abr. Hicks's wife, visited us today from Ochgoloogy, with her young child. She had been visiting at her relatives about 15 miles from here. She spent all day Sunday here.

*Sept. 1.* [Spg.] She went on to New Echota. This last week we had such cool weather that we could stand a fire in the fireplace.

*Sept. 1.* [Ooch.] Br. Hicks left on business for the Nation. He will be gone 14 days.

[M 414-3-28: Translated by Julie Tomberlin Weber. Addressed to: Revd. Theodor Schulz, Salem, Stokes County, North Carolina. Postmark: New Echota, Ch.N., Sept 3, 25. Received Sept. 18.]

Oochgeelogy, Sept. 1, 1828

My dearly beloved Br. Schulz,

I greet you sincerely from all of us with these few lines. Praise God, we are all healthy and well. I have finally been lucky enough to get $163 for the Spring Place account from Major Ridge, and I want to ask you to be good enough to pay this amount to Br. Reichel. I have given Major Ridge a receipt for this from my hand. He and his wife Sr. Sussanna were here yesterday. They are both healthy and well and asked me to greet their daughter in the best manner through you and to tell her that one of them will come to visit in Salem at Christmas. Her aunt Sussana Fields also sends her sincere greetings. All of her relatives who often remember her with love are currently doing well. If Sally Ridge needs clothes for Christmas or for the winter, her father asks you through me to have Br. Reichel, whom he greets sincerely, get them for her on his account. When one of them comes to Salem it will be paid.

These past Sundays we have once again considered the story of Jesus' sufferings to the blessing of our hearts. Yesterday many listeners were here, most of them Indians. We reflected on Jesus' death on Golgotha. Br. Hicks was interpreter. In the afternoon we had a blessed and comforting Holy Communion. Both George Augustus Hicks and Alex James Copeland observed during this as candidates.

Today Br. Hicks is leaving on a trip visiting through the whole country, which will probably take him 14 days. The reason for this is that the Agent for the Nation has received the assignment from the President of the U.S. to visit in the company of both Arkansas Delegates to promote the emigration to Arkansas. He writes each family down and estimates its Improvement, which is supposed to be purchased by the government. They are supposed to try to dispose of their horses and cattle themselves in the settlement. To simplify this matter now (since not a word about this matter has reached the head Chiefs from the government of the U.S.), and everything just came to light coincidentally, Br. Hicks and John Ross are also traveling through the Nation along with some head Chiefs. How the Cherokees have been treated in <u>this</u> respect! They are in a very critical situation. Our dear Br. Hicks is very discouraged. Still he relies on the One who has all power in heaven and on earth. May God help. He can and will help, when His hour strikes.

I am supposed to greet you most sincerely, along with all the dear Brn. of the P.H. Conf. from Br. Hicks and his family. Please greet your dear colleagues from my wife and me. I greet you especially, your faithfully obliged Br.,

Johann R. Schmidt

P.S. Our garden is divided into 6 squares. I planted two of them with potatoes, and I got more than 30 bushels of the biggest and most beautiful potatoes.

J. R. S.

[M 414-3-29: Translated by Julie Tomberlin Weber. Addressed to: Revd. Theodore Shulz, Salem, Stokes County, North Carolina. Postmark illegible. Received Sept. 18. Handwriting is Gottlieb Byhan's.]

Springplace, Sept. 4, 1828

My dear Br. Shulz,

I received your dear lines of Aug. 12 on the 28th of that month, along with the Salem Memorabilia for the year 1827, for which I thank you sincerely. Praise God, we are all healthy. Enclosed I am sending some months of the Spring Place Diary again. Time will tell if I can send a couple more months before the first Thursday in Oct. There is much work! I also wanted to send the income and expenditures through the end of August, but I do not yet know if this will be possible or not.

Our current house is such that we think we can spend one more winter in it. We also laid a threshing floor in the barn, which was very necessary. Now we are driving wood and boards from the mill for the new house construction, as long as our little wagon holds up. The cost for transportation is twice as expensive here in this country as it is where you are, so it is cheaper if we can drive the wood ourselves. We are currently making corn feed. Our corn did not turn out as well as we were expecting due to the extreme drought. I have not heard anything recently from Ochgoloogy.

We almost counted on Sr. Polly Steiner for the school in Ochgoloogy but were deceived. We join you in thanking God that your long suit has finally been decided in your favor. Do not let yourself be concerned about the school in Ochgoloogy and about Elijah Hicks's writing in the *Phönix*. Everyone here knows it was Elijah Hicks. I hope it will not have any consequences.

Farewell! And accept the most sincere greetings from your Br. and Sr.,

Gottlieb and Dor. Byhan

P.S. It also occurred to us that a visit from Br. Theod. Shulz and Sr. Shulz in the current situation here would be of the greatest use and advantage. This visit could be undertaken with Br. and Sr. Eder and would be very pleasant for us.

Byhans

[B 61-3: Provinzial Helfer Conferenz, meeting in Salem.]

*Wed., Sept. 3.* The expected answering letter from Br. Byhan (see minutes of 24 July and 25 Aug.) arrived today and states to our sorrow that our poor Br. Schmidt not only continues the misuse of strong drink, but also tries to drink it at neighbors' houses and in addition evidences no faithfulness in taking care of household, economic, and money matters, and wastes his time in careless idleness. Therefore, nothing remains for us to do but to recall this Br. and Sr. to avoid additional harm and loss to the Mission. If they return in the wagon which is going there we thought it to be for the best provisionally to assign them to Bethabara as a place to live. Br. Schulz will report this to them and also ask the widowed Sr. Gambold to remain longer in Oochgelogy as assistant and counselor. It seemed all the more important to the Conferenz at the time of this change that we undertake the marriage of Br. Franz Eder. Br. Benade will talk with him about this.

Because Br. Gottlieb Clauder has a faithful mind for mission service and has indicated an inclination to go among the Cherokees, the Conferenz decided that he should go with Br. Eder as assistant at the mission in Oochgelogy. This is the more so, since he has been of great help to Br. Eder in learning the English language and in many respects can also be of great use in regard to the school and in learning the Cherokee language. Br. Benade will propose this to him.

Concerning the intended establishment of the schools where only boys in Springplace and only girls in Oochgelogy will receive instruction, the view of the P.H.C. will be communicated to them by Br. Schulz, which is that the establishment of these schools should be postponed until after the arrival of Br. Eder because the practicality of this will become more evident then.

*Mon., Sept. 8.* In accord with the previous minutes Br. Benade had a talk with Br. Franz Eder concerning his undertaking marriage so that the latter was convinced of the necessity of his going to mission service in Oochgelogy with a helpmeet. For this purpose he suggested the single Sr. Carolina Friderica Eberhard, who is a teacher in our Girls School. As this Sister, as did he, indicated her willingness for this if the Lord allowed, therefore in today's Conferenz we asked this question in the Lot, and we received the Lord's approval:

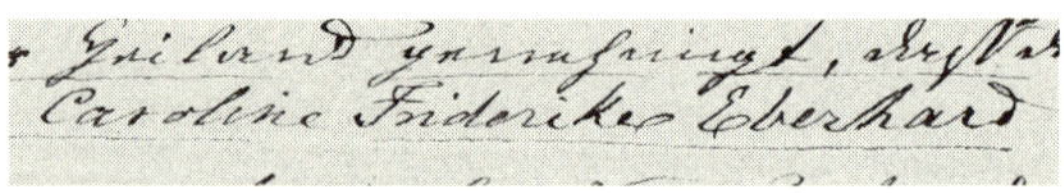
Caroline Friderike Eberhard

The Savior approves that Br. Franz Eder marry the Sister Caroline Friderike Eberhard * .

Br. Gottlb. H. Clauder accepted gladly and willingly the proposal to go as assistant to the Mission among the Cherokees. He will also work at his profession as tinsmith.

# *1828, part 8*

[Springplace (M 407-1) and Oochgeelogy (M 409-1) Diaries. Translated by Julie Tomberlin Weber. Handwritings are Johann Renatus Schmidt's (Ooch.) and Gottlieb Byhan's (Spg.).]

*Sept. 5.* [Ooch.] The Methodists' camp meeting began 4 miles from here.

*Sept. 6.* [Ooch.] The Methodist preacher invited Br. Schmidt to attend the camp meeting, and he had the opportunity to make the pleasant acquaintance of 8 preachers there. They remembered the friendship Mr. Wesley had with the Brethren in London and Georgia, particularly Brethren Peter Boehler and Schulius, and how he experienced his true understanding of the Gospel through these Brn. Today there were 3 sermons. Turtle Fields, one of their baptized preachers, fervently shared a sermon in the Indian language on Jesus' words on the Mount of Olives [Matt. 26:38]: My soul is sorrowful, even unto death. He is a gifted speaker and has the character of a true child of God. During the service everything was orderly and quiet.

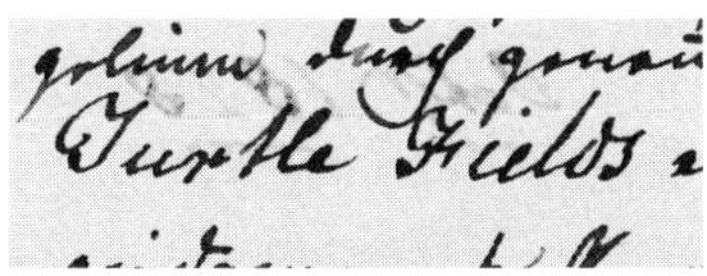


*Sun., Sept. 7.* [Ooch.] Many people went to the camp meeting, so only about 20 people came to the service. Sr. Gambold and Alex. Copeland attended the camp meeting and spent the night there. Apparently things were very loud and noisy today. The weather has been especially dry and cool recently.

*Sun., Sept. 7.* [Spg.] We joined ourselves in spirit to the Married Choirs in the Gemeinen which are celebrating their Choir festival today. The Savior did not leave us without blessing, especially during Holy Communion, which we enjoyed today with our Brn. and Srs. During this was the confirmation of the married Sr. Ruth, wife of our Br. John Jacob, for her first enjoyment of Holy Communion. The single Br. Niclaus Ignatius watched as a confirmand as did the married Sr. Esther, Br. Israel's wife, and as a candidate, the boy Alexander Benjamin. Our Sr. Felicitas Hicks was also able to come this time. Since an insignificant matter prevented our Negro Br. Christian Jacob from the enjoyment of Holy Communion, and he then visited us after this, we spoke seriously with him and warned him against apathy and lukewarmness. He asked to be forgiven for it this time. He was told that he should ask the Savior to keep him by Him so that the enemy, who is always trying to lead souls away from Him, will not get power over him again. At both his baptism and his confirmation he promised the Savior to be completely His, and to live only for Him, and that he should ask the Savior to grant him grace and power so that he would be able to keep his promises, etc.

*Sept. 8.* [Spg.] Today we finished making corn feed. We have had dry weather the whole time since we began this work, so we got a relatively large quantity of feed. But our corn harvest will not turn out as plentiful as it seemed at the beginning of the summer, first of all because it was unusually dry, and now there are so many ravens, squirrels, and woodpeckers that it looks as if little corn will be left.

*Sept. 11.* [Ooch.] Capt. McNair and his son visited us. The children had their lessons.

*Sept. 13.* [Ooch.] John Hollars, who has been working for us for a while, went home today. We heard the sad news today that the Indian Sope murdered another Indian with his knife. Before he escaped, he threatened to kill 3 more, since he would have to die anyway. Some traces have been found of him. This sad tale took place just a few miles from here.

*Sept. 13.* [Spg.] Br. Nathl. Byhan today went to visit Mr. McNair, who stopped in at our place day before yesterday and today, while he had been in the area of Oochgelogy on business.

*Sun., Sept. 14.* [Ooch.] It rained hard all day, so only 5 people came to the service. On *the 15th* we received a letter from Br. Schulz in Salem. Br. Hicks returned home recently from his business travels around the country.

*Sun., Sept. 14.* [Spg.] Since there was rainy weather today, only our baptized Br. Solomon came to the services. In the afternoon Br. and Sr. Samuel came from 9 miles away, unexpected and completely soaked. Since Br. Samuel had business in our neighborhood, he spent the night with us.

*Sept. 15.* [Spg.] We received a cordial visit from the missionary at Candys Creek, Mr. John Holland, with his wife and 2 children and an Indian woman. We spent the evening very happily with them, partly in conversations about the promotion of God's Kingdom in this Nation, and about the Indians in general, and partly singing at the piano. Both Mr. John Holland and Mrs. Holland are true children of God, and helping to promote the Savior's matter among <u>this</u> Nation is an essential thing for them.

*Sept. 16.* [Spg.] After breakfast they went on to Mr. McNair's. The mission site, Candies Creek, is about 35 miles away from Spring Place, 4 or 5 miles from the Highwassee River, and 6 or 7 miles from the Cherokee Agency.

[M 414-3-30: Translated by Julie Tomberlin Weber. Addressed to: Revd. Theod. Schulz, Salem, Stokes County, North Carolina. Postmark: Springplace, C.N., Sept. 18, 1828. Free. Gottlieb Byhan, P.M. Received Oct. 1.]

Springplace, C.N., Sept. 17, 1828

Dear Br. Shulz,

I received your dear letter of Aug. 26 with *Monatliche Nachr.* for May and June on the 11th this month, for which I sincerely thank you. Praise God, we are currently all very healthy. We saw from your letter that you will try to engage Nancy Becker and send her to Spring Place to help, which we were very happy to hear. But we cannot agree with the Prov. Helf. Conf.'s belief that it would be advisable for our Rachel to return then. Mother would then have no more help, and Rachel says that as long as Mother stays here, she will not think about returning. We are sorry that Br. Eder's marriage [proposal] is not going well. Perhaps something will work out. He must simply have courage. Greet him very sincerely from us. If only we could soon hear and learn when he will leave from Salem.

The news about the changes in Salem was very interesting to us. It seems that the Boys School has finally folded; we are sorry that it could not be continued. Major Ridge finally paid Br. Smith in Ochgoloogy $163, about which he himself will tell you more. And so the debt made with Lavender last year, which consisted of $192.75, has also been paid with our help. We want to be cautious in the future with Lavender, however, because I do not like to pay 25 percent commission, which was paid to him in this bill according to agreement, as he himself writes.

Enclosed I am sending a receipt from Henry Clayten for $25 which he received. They are still living in Columbus, and will probably stay there a while longer.

We have finally been able to get wood and boards here from the mill, so it looks as if there might be some construction after all. However, I must admit I do not yet know, and I am not yet decided, whether I want a frame house or a block house. Some advise me to do a frame house, but none to do a block house. Be so good as to advise me.

We greet all most sincerely. Your faithfully obliged Br.,

Gottlieb Byhan

In haste. Nath. Hicks does not want the *Missionary Intel.* sent to him anymore.

[Springplace (M 407-1) and Oochgeelogy (M 409-1) Diaries.]

*Sept. 19.* [Spg.] In Bible instruction today for our children, a special attentiveness to what they were told could be felt, so that we can really tell that the Spirit of God is working in their tender hearts.

*Sun., Sept. 21.* [Ooch.] The sermon was on Rom. 5:8-13. In the 2nd service we read Chapters 5 and 6 of Paul's Letter to the Romans. Among the listeners was a Baptist preacher who is currently staying in Echota. We hear that many of our friends in Echota are ill with fever.

*Sun., Sept. 21.* [Spg.] Today a relatively large number of listeners were in our Sunday services again, Indians as well as Negroes. They were all very attentive.

*Sept. 23.* [Spg.] Today Lewis, one of our schoolchildren, left here without our knowledge and went home. This boy has not seemed to be very happy recently, and went home often and missed school for months at a time. He has been in the school since Feb. 4, 1821, so we did not really have anything against having a place open for another child, since there are enough requests to take in new children.

*Sept. 25.* [Spg.] With the mail today we received a letter from Br. Theod. Shulz in Salem, with the announcement that the Helf. Conf. in Salem has decided to recall Br. and Sr. Smith in Ochgoloogy from their posts and for Br. and Sr. Eder and the single Br. Henry G. Clauder to come in their place to serve the little congregation there.

*Sept. 26.* [Spg.] Today Br. Byhan traveled to Ochgoloogy on business, partly to inform Br. and Sr. Smith of their recall, and also to arrange some matters of the dwellings for the Brn. and Srs. who are coming.

*Sept. 26.* [Ooch.] Br. Byhan visited from Spring Place and brought us letters from Salem; from these we learned that dear Br. Gottlieb Clauder has received and accepted a call to the Cherokee Mission, and that Br. and Sr. Schmidt have been called to Salem from their previous service among the Cherokees.

[M 414-3-31: Translated by Julie Tomberlin Weber. Addressed to: Revd. Theodor Schulz, Salem, Stokes County, North Carolina. Postmark: Springplace, C.N., Oct. 2, 18¾. Received Oct. 22.]

Oochgeelogy, Sept. 27, 1828

My dearly beloved Br. Schulz,

I received your dear letter dated the 3rd this month yesterday evening through our dear Br. Byhan. It hurts us deeply that we, through my habits and behavior, have caused our dear Brn. in the P.H.C. in Salem to call us away from our post here. It is, however, also comforting to me as a poor sinner that I have learned to see my mistakes and have received grace and forgiveness and comfort at the Savior's feet. He also showed me the priceless grace of freeing me some time ago from the ruinous enjoyment of strong drinks in answer to the prayers of my dear wife and me. I no longer drink a drop, and I do not have the slightest desire or appetite for it, and through His grace I will be able to keep my resolution not to drink any wine or other strong drinks. Oh, if I had only done this when I was warned about this the first time. Then I allowed myself a little bit still, and the little bit turned into excess again. I will thank the Savior into eternity if He helps me, through His grace.

Despite all the calmness I received from the Savior over my mistakes, it was clear that we would not be able to stay here. And so our recall was not surprising, despite all the pain. I am certain that it is wise guidance by the Lord. It hurts us greatly to leave our Indians whom we love tenderly, as they do us. We comfort ourselves that the Savior will bless our dear successors, and we wish them a thousand good things and the powerful and strengthening help of the Lord.

It will be very refreshing for me to talk with my dear Brn. in the P.H. Conferenz about my entire service here. You, dear Brn., always treated us faithfully and honestly as before the countenance of the Savior, and our trust in you is unbounded. Ask the Savior to bring us safely to you. How happy I will be to delight in the bosom of the Gemeine after 13 years and to enjoy the beautiful worship services. Greet your dear wife from us, as well as your dear colleagues. Your poor, sorrowful Br.,

J. R. Schmidt

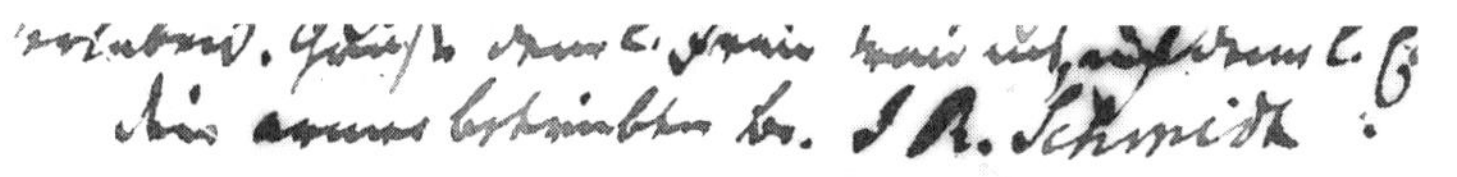

[B 61-3: Provinzial Helfer Conferenz, meeting in Salem. Translated by C. Daniel Crews.]

*Tues., Sept. 23.* Since Br. Schaaf is going to Bethabara next Friday, he was commissioned to have the preliminary discussion with the Committee there concerning Br. and Sr. Schmidt, that they will stay in the future in the presently unoccupied Gemeinhaus, and Br. Schmidt will take care of the school.

We decided that Br. Eder should be ordained as a deacon of the Brethren's Church, and asked Br. Benade to take care of the ordination, which will take place next Tuesday the 30th in the evening.

On the 30th Sr. Carola. Eder and the single Br. Gb. Clauder will be received as acoluths in the morning.

*Tues., Sept. 30.* Today the P.H.C. had a lengthy discussion about its work with our Br. and Sr. Eder and the single Br. Gottlieb Clauder, who according to their call will leave next Monday for Oochgelogy among the Cherokees. Since Br. and Sr. Schmidt will travel back here soon after their arrival there, Br. Eder will take over leadership of this mission post, and Br. Clauder will assist by taking care of the school and in other ways. There was impressed upon their hearts the faithful care of the school as well as diligent visiting among the Brn. and Srs. and anywhere there is a door open to them for the proclamation of the Gospel. After we had had a thorough discussion with them about the Mission in general and about its finances in particular, we wished them God's blessing and assured them of our constant love and intercession for them, Sr. C. F. Eder and Br. Gb. Clauder were received as acoluths.

[Oochgeelogy Diary (M 409-1).]

*Sun., Sept. 28.* [Ooch.] The sermon was on Isaiah 53. In the 2nd service we sang a liturgy.

*Sept. 29.* [Ooch.] Br. Schmidt visited with Br. and Sr. George Augustus Hicks. Sr. Sarah Hicks visited here.

*Oct. 1.* [Ooch.] Br. Schmidt visited at Br. and Sr. Hicks's.

[M 414-3-32: Translated by Julie Tomberlin Weber. Addressed to: Revd. Theodor Schulz, Salem, Stokes County, North Carolina. Postmark: Springplace, C.N., Oct. 2. Free. Gottlieb Byhan, P.M. Received Oct. 22.]

Springplace, Oct. 1, 1828

Dearly beloved Br. Shulz,

On Sept. 25 I was joyful to receive your two dear letters of Aug. 28 and Sept. 8 and 11. Everything enclosed in them was very interesting and important to us, especially the recall of Br. and Sr. Smith from their post. This news was not unexpected to us, because things could not have gone on too much longer with him if he had not changed, since his irresponsible inactivity is in fact great.

Last Friday I visited there and delivered Br. Smith the letter from you containing his recall. When I had dismounted, he came flying out of the house with a long Flyer on and the 5-foot long tobacco pipe in his hand, but before I had unsaddled my horse he was already back in his grandfather chair, and the pipe was lit. He assured me that he had not done the least thing during the last five weeks since I visited there. I must say, I have never seen such f____t [laziness] with any human. It is time that he had to move a little bit.

As soon as he read your letter he said that he had not drunk a drop of brandy since my last visit there 5 weeks ago, which was also confirmed by the other Brn. and Srs. He also does not look as red anymore as he had been. They seem to be satisfied about their recall. He told me that he was happy that he would finally be able to talk about the entire matter with the Brn. in Salem.

Br. and Sr. Copeland are planning to move to Tennessee. He is now on a journey there to look for a site in the area of Columbus on the Highwassee. Br. Joseph Gambold is planning to return to the Gemeine, if his health allows. He is often plagued with weakness in the head, but otherwise he is very energetic. Sr. A. M. Gambold is willing to assist the newcomers in the household for a while.

Concerning the homes, we have come to the following conclusion. Br. and Sr. Eder, naturally, will move into Br. and Sr. Smith's house, and Sr. Gambold will make her bed in a corner of the living room in the mission house for the winter. That is, if Br. and Sr. Eder do not have any objections to this. In the spring we will then see how things should be done. Br. Clauder is moving into the schoolhouse where the Copelands now live, and the room where Jos. Gambold lives would be the room where the school would be held in the winter. In the summer this will be held in the Saal. The Negro woman must live and sleep in a little room over the schoolroom.

Sr. Smith and Sr. Polly Copeland have exchanged commodes or chests of drawers, and Sr. Polly must pay Sr. Smith $2. Sr. Copeland asked me to inform you and to ask you to sell the attachment to her commode and to pay Sr. Smith $2 from the money gotten by this. I also spoke with Br. Willm. Abr. Hicks about the change in Ochgoloogy. He does not have anything against it if Br. G. Clauder carries out his trade. He believes rather that this would be useful for the neighborhood. When I informed him of the change of Br. and Sr. Smith, he said after a silence: "We cannot always live together, & must part once, sometimes even with our best Friends, till we meet once again in Heaven."[1] Br. Hicks is a true child of God, which his words and actions testify.

We are eagerly awaiting the arrival of the whole Cherokee company. We will and want to welcome and accept in love <u>all</u> the visitors as well as those who are staying. We want to make

---

[1] The quote is in English in the original German manuscript.

your dear son's stay with us as pleasant as possible. Nathl. is planning to travel to Columbus on the Highwassee River to meet them. I thank you very sincerely for the $100 you sent. It came at just the right time and as if sent from God, because 10 minutes after I had received it, the Georgia postrider presented me with a draft from the General Postmaster, which as you know has to be paid at sight. And the postrider was able to exchange your note for me, so I could pay the draft right away. I would not have been able to pay it without this note, since I had no money except the $50 Newbern note.

I will wait to send the reports to the Sect. of War until we see and hear what will come of the coming Council, according to your faithful advice. It can already be noted, however, that the Cherokees will not be persuaded in any manner to move. As they say, they will sit quietly and see what the Government will do with them further. I think the plan is good. The more calmly they act, the better it is for them. Time will tell how things can and should go. God rules over all. He can guide the hearts of humans.

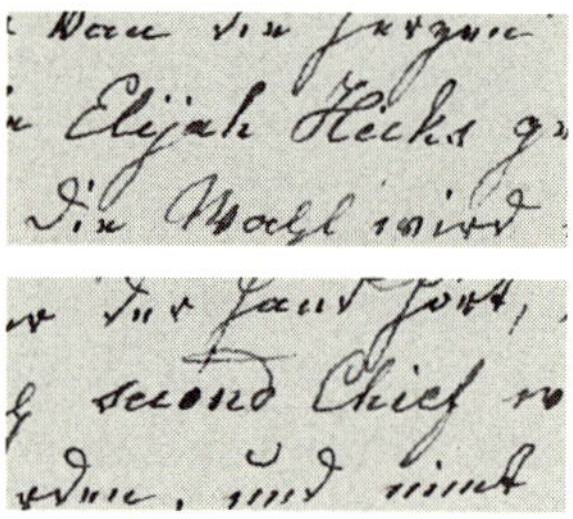


As we hear confidentially, Elijah Hicks wants to become second Chief if not Principal Chief. The election will be held at the next Council, which begins Oct. 13. People believe it will last about 6 weeks this time, so the Cherokee company will arrive here during the session of the Council. I thank you very sincerely for the instructions for the Sect. of War regarding construction of the new house.

I was not able to do the accounts in Ochgoloogy on my last visit last week, because they still had all sorts of things to pay as well as various things to request. So when I get time I must visit there once again to get these in order. I fear they will be just as confused as the ones in Springplace were, where after all, as he said, he made a profit of $100 — after he had paid out $100 more than he really had in cash. When the company returns, I will send you his income and expenditures as he wrote them.

We are very glad that Nancy Becker is coming along to assist in our household. My dear wife and Rachel really do need help, since they have to be on their legs from early in the morning until evening in the large household, and in the evening they still have to do mending for our scholars and repair their old clothes. Our old Pleasant can no longer be counted.

The Methodists are now holding many Camp meetings around here in this country. Fourteen days ago there was one about 5 miles from Ochgoloogy, during which things were supposed to be pretty wild, especially during the night. Last week there was one on this side of the McNairs'. We heard that 15 preachers were there together.

Praise God, we are currently all healthy and well. In general we hear little about illness among people. Our neighbor Jos. Vann was sickly the entire summer, however. He also used the health spring in Sumak. However, it seems that all this did not help, so that sometimes we must believe that the man will not live to be old. If only he would convert!

Now we sincerely greet everyone, and you, along with Br. Benade and Br. Shaaf, accept another special greeting from your Br. and Sr., bound to you in Jesus' death,

Gottl. and Dor. Byhan

P.S. Since it is known that Br. and Sr. Smith have been replaced, more is heard about his behavior in Springplace, so that we really must be ashamed, and it is a shame he was not called away from this post long ago. A true shame for the Savior's work here, and for us!

G. B.

[Springplace (M 407-1) and Oochgeelogy (M 409-1) Diaries.]

*Sun., Oct. 5.* [Ooch.] The sermon was on Luke 19:10: the Son of man is come to seek and to save that which was lost. In the afternoon we had a very blessed Holy Communion, during which the married Br. George Augustus Hicks watched as a confirmand.

*Sun., Oct. 5.* [Spg.] Despite the fact that it rained heavily this morning, some Brethren and Sisters still came for the services. We also heard from our Br. Joshua that the communicant Sister Deborah was bitten on the hand by a poisonous snake yesterday, and that her whole arm up to her shoulder is very swollen, and she seemed to be very ill. We hope that she will recover, although her situation seems to be very serious. Today we also asked our Brn. and Srs. about our runaway boy Lewis. We found that he is telling all sorts of untruths to excuse his running away. Among other things he is supposed to have said it is not worth his efforts to go to school here anymore since learning would not get him into heaven.

*Oct. 6.* [Ooch.] Br. Schmidt visited Brn. and Srs. in their homes. Most of our scholars were taken home for a while to visit their families. In recent days Sr. Schmidt has visited Br. and Sr. W. A. Hicks. Two of her children were seriously ill. The youngest had a swollen throat.

*Oct. 8.* [Ooch.] Alex Copeland, who had been in East Tennessee on business, returned home. Many of our Brn. and Srs. and friends came and visited us before our departure for Salem. We had a pleasant visit from old Chief Chuleoa or Gentleman Tom. He stayed at our place overnight.

*Oct. 8.* [Spg.] Br. Byhan received a letter from Mr. McNair in which he was asked to go there tomorrow to marry Mr. David Vann and his daughter Martha. Br. Byhan set out for there on the 9th and in the evening performed the wedding. A relatively large number of people had come for this.

*Oct. 11.* [Spg.] Today Mr. David Vann and his wife and Polly Nealy stopped in at our place on their way to New Echota. After they had eaten lunch with us they went on to New Echota, although it was already late in the day.

*Sun., Oct. 12.* [Ooch.] The sermon was on Ezek. 33:11. Rev. Kendrick, a Methodist bishop, preached in our neighborhood and had a large crowd.

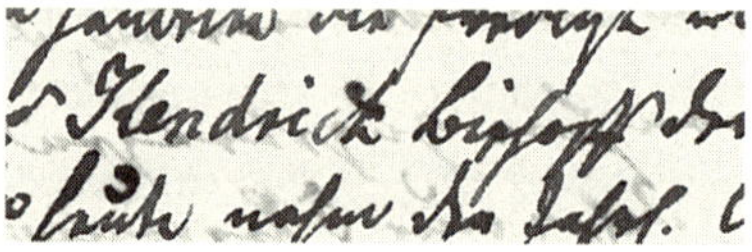

*Sun., Oct. 12.* [Spg.] The Sunday services today were attended as usual.

*Oct. 13.* [Ooch.] Today the annual Council of the Nation opened. Br. Hicks and most of our Brn. and Srs. from here went there on business. All of our scholars except two were taken home for visits. The number of scholars at our school is currently 16, including 4 boys and 12 girls.

*Oct. 16.* [Ooch.] Br. Schmidt went to the Council on business.

*Sun., Oct. 19.* [Ooch.] Services as usual. The sermon was on Matt. 24:13. Pleasant, the elderly Negro woman from Springplace, came here to visit Br. and Sr. Schmidt once again before their departure.

*Sun., Oct. 19.* [Spg.] Because of the National Council, which is now sitting in New Echota, there were only a few Brn. and Srs. here today. First, we held a reading service, and then Br. Nathl. Byhan led a Singstunde. Many Indians and white people passed by here in these days to attend the Council. Today we also heard that day before yesterday Mr. John Ross was elected first Chief in the Nation.

*Oct. 23.* [Ooch.] Br. Schmidt went to Echota once again where he ran into many friends and acquaintances. He said farewell to them before his coming departure.

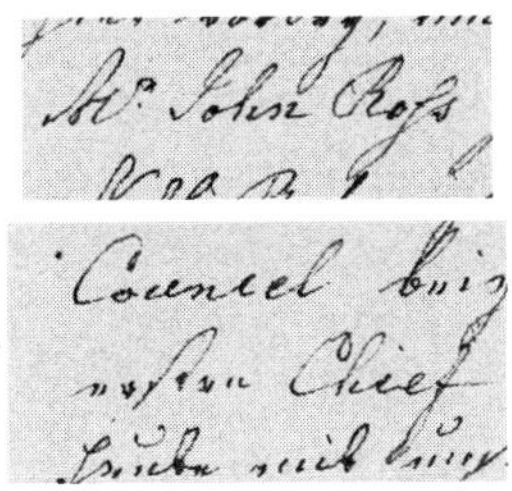


The Cherokee Gemeinlein in Oochgeelogy currently consists of 15 baptized adults, of whom 12 are communicants, 2 noncommunicants, one woman not yet accepted, and one baptismal candidate. Total: 16 people. In addition are their 23 children. Grand total: 39 people.

The mission family (except for Alex Copeland) is not included in that number.

*Oct. 23.* [Spg.] Br. Nathl. Byhan today drove with our small stage wagon to meet Br. and Sr. Eder and party from Salem who are expected soon, and he actually planned to go to Columbus to buy necessities for our household at the same time.

*Sun., Oct. 26.* [Ooch.] In the first service we prayed the Church Litany. Then Br. Schmidt delivered a farewell sermon on Rom. 5:1-5. In conclusion he baptized into Jesus' death the baby daughter born several days ago to our Sr. Maria Rosina Crutchfield; she received the name Sussanna.

*Sun., Oct. 26.* [Spg.] The services were as usual, and a nice number of listeners came for them. During the first service, in which a talk was held for the Brn. and Srs., which was interpreted by Dav. Steiner Tazizi, we had the joy of seeing our dear Br. and Sr. Eder and dear Br. Henry G. Clauder and other traveling companions, the single Brn. Aug. H. Shulz and Lewis Eberhard, the married Br. Chr. Grabs of Bethania, Br. Math. Reich as driver, and the single Sr. Anna Marg. Becker of Friedland for help in the household in Spring Place. After the service we greeted them most sincerely. The joy on both sides was great, and we joined them in thanking our dear Lord for bringing them to us so quickly, safely, and without any harm. With them we received also a beautiful supply of *Gemein Nachr.* and letters, as well as various things which we needed in our household from our dear Brn. and Srs. in Salem, for which we thank them with our whole hearts. In the evening we had a happy Singstunde with our dear traveling company, in which we brought our dear Lord thanks for bringing the traveling company safely to us here. Br. Aug. Henry Shulz played the piano during this. Due to a number of circumstances which came together, we decided that Br. and Sr. Eder and the single Br. Henry G. Clauder, who is designated for service at the mission in Ochgoloogee, will stay with us in Spring Place until Nov. 3.

*Oct. 28.* [Ooch.] Through Brn. Christian Grabs and Luis Eberhard, who arrived at our place this evening, we learned that Br. and Sr. Eder and their party have arrived safely in Spring Place, and they are planning to come here next week.

*Oct. 28.* [Spg.] Brn. Nathl. Byhan and Aug. H. Shulz went to Brainerd today on a visit. Brn. Grabs and Lewis Eberhard also went on a visit to Ochgoloogee, the former primarily to visit his sister, our Sr. Anna Maria Gambold.

*Oct. 31.* [Spg.] Both companies returned. Sr. Anna Maria Gambold came for a visit with the Brn. from Ochgoloogee.

*Nov. 1.* [Ooch.] We received a friendly visit from Capt. McNair. He stayed with us until the following day.

*Sun., Nov. 2.* [Ooch.] The services were held in the usual order. Today we said an emotional farewell to many of our friends and Brn. and Srs.

*Sun., Nov. 2.* [Spg.] Today almost all of our Indian Brn. and Srs. arrived here for the services, so that it was pretty lively here today. In the first service there was the Litany and a talk on the Daily Text for today [Matt. 24:42]: Watch therefore; for ye know not what hour your Lord doth come. In the second service we had the blessed enjoyment of the body and blood of Jesus in Holy Communion. Before this the single Brother Niclaus Ignatius and the married Sr. Esther received the confirmation blessing for their first enjoyment of this. The Savior allowed us to be deeply aware of His dear presence in a transporting way.

*Nov. 3.* [Spg.] Br. and Sr. Eder and the single Br. H. G. Clauder, accompanied by Br. Byhan, traveled from here to Ochgoloogee in accordance with their assignment. Br. Byhan arrived back at Spring Place on Nov. 5th.

[The handwriting of the Oochgeelogy Diary changes from Br. Johann Renatus Schmidt's to Br. Franz Eder's.]

Report of the Mission in the Cherokee Indians in Oochgeelogy from Nov. 1828 to the end of Apr. 1829.

*Nov. 3.* [Ooch.] Br. and Sr. Eder arrived here in Oochgeelogy, and the rest of the travelers arrived on

*Nov. 4.* [Ooch.] They were filled with praise and thanks to our dear merciful God and Savior, who so graciously protected us from all physical and spiritual harm throughout the difficult journey.

[M 414-3-33: Translated by Julie Tomberlin Weber. Addressed to: The dear Brother Theodor Schulz in Salem. No postmark. Received Nov. 18, 1828.]

To the dear Brother Schulz!

With the most sincere thanks, I am answering in all haste your letter which was so dear to me. I was delighted to receive it on Oct. 30 through our dear Br. Byhan, and I can immediately inform you of our safe arrival of which you will surely already have learned. Praise and thanks be to the Savior, we are all healthy and well and rejoice as children in your love, concern, and prayer. God willing, we are planning to begin our journey to Oochgelogy tomorrow, accompanied by dear Br. Byhan, and to complete it on the $4^{th}$ of this month, so that I can write from here and not from Oochgelogy. I would really have preferred to do this, because we hear from dear Sr. Gambold, who is here visiting, that Br. and Sr. Schmidt have been ready to travel for several days already. They are planning to stay only one more night after our arrival, so I cannot expect that there will be much time left for writing. Our [illegible] not much until then. Br. and Sr. Byhan feel unusually happy [illegible] accepted [page torn].

We ask you to greet our parents. Please forward the enclosed letters on to Germany when you get a chance. Finally we commend ourselves to your love and prayer before the throne of grace. Your faithfully obliged Br. and Sr.,

F. Eder

Springplace, Nov. 2, 1828

N.B. I want to greet you at least from here even if it is only with a couple of lines. I am delighted with my whole heart to greet you today, even if in haste, from Ochgelogy already, my dear Br. Schulz! Br. Byhan, his daughter, Sr. Gambold, and my wife and I separated ourselves yesterday from the above company with the intention of reaching Ochgeelogy and were fortunate enough to be here at 6 o'clock in the evening despite the bad road. In silence we all thanked our dear Savior, who so mercifully protected us from all physical and spiritual harm. It is very natural that everyone is still very excited with all the packing and unpacking today on the $4^{th}$. This must also have its time, after all. It is only very natural to me that a somewhat awkward feeling prevails between Schmidt and Br. Byhan. The Smiths are planning to leave tomorrow. I do not yet know how the accounts match up. Br. Byhan is worried. Once again greetings from your loving Brother,

Franz Eder

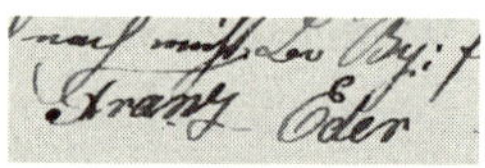

Please give Br. Benzien along with D. Welfare greetings in this letter from Oochgelogy, Nov. 4, 1828.

[Springplace (M 407-1) and Oochgeelogy (M 409-1) Diaries.]

*Nov. 5.* [Ooch.] We said farewell to Br. and Sr. Schmidt and Br. J. Gambold, who were returning to Salem in accordance with their call. Our best wishes for blessings accompanied them on their pilgrimage.

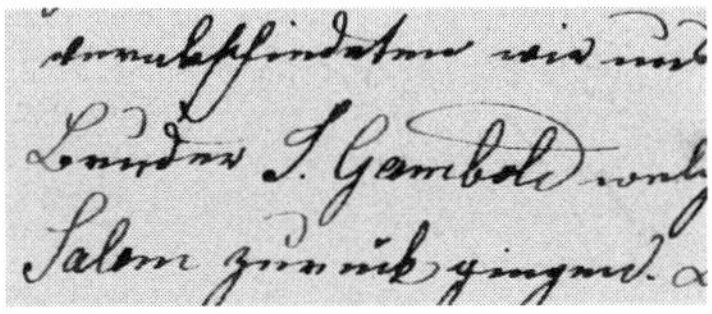

*Nov. 6.* [Spg.] Br. and Sr. Smith arrived here with Br. Math. Reich's wagon. Br. and Sr. Smith, who had received a recall from the Prov. H. Conf. in Salem from our mission post in Ochgoloogee, began their farther journey from here to Salem on

*Nov. 7* [Spg.] accompanied by our wishes for blessings.

## *1828, part 9*

[M 414-3-34: Translated by Julie Tomberlin Weber. Addressed to: Revd. Theodor Shulz, Salem, Stokes County, North Carolina. Postmark: Favored by Br. A. H. Schulz. Received Nov. 18.]

Springplace, Nov. 7, 1828

My dear Br. Shulz,

Since my time is so very short and I sometimes hardly know what I should do first, I hope you will not think badly of me if I express myself very briefly this time and just report the main things to you, and since my letters go free with the mail anyway, I must make up the rest in time.

On Oct. 26 we had the joy of welcoming Br. and Sr. Eder, Br. Clauder, and company to Springplace. The company stayed with us until Nov. 3 when we all moved to Ochgoloogy together, except for Sr. Byhan and Nancy Becker. We stayed there until the 5th of this month, when we began our return journey to Springplace, and we all arrived here again yesterday on the 6th. Early today Br. and Sr. Smith and company began the journey from here to Salem.

During my stay in Ochgoloogy, I took up Br. Smith's accounting for last year, but found the same confusion I found last year in the one at Spring Place. And so I will have to do as you advised with the one in Springplace and begin a new one. According to the income and expenditures he had written, he should have about $100 in the cashbox there, but he could produce only $5 and a few cents. Since I am planning to go back to Ochgoloogy tomorrow, perhaps I can give you more information about this matter in my next letter.

Now I just want to bring the following to your attention.

1) Br. Smith advanced the mission in Ochgoloogy $30, which you will probably have to pay him in Salem.

2) Further, the Smiths left a large Roseblanket which they were given as a gift or to take along here. I do not know if it belonged to the mission or to them. They would need to be compensated in Salem for this as well if it was their own.

3) Further, they left an old spinning wheel in Springplace, which is their own. They also wanted to be paid for this or to receive another one in its place.

4) As you will know without a doubt, Lewis Eberhard brought out a new rifle with him, and since the Brn. in Ochgoloogy want to have a weapon there, we dared to keep this rifle for Ochgoloogy, for which Br. Lewis Eberhard will need to be paid $18.

5) Then Sr. Smith left 4 pairs of teacups in Ochgoloogy, for which she is to be paid 50 cents.

I gave Br. M. Reich and Chr. Grabs $60 for the return journey, which I hope they will perhaps bring to Salem. If there is not enough, the above-named Brn. will help from their own resources, since I did not want to give them more money than was absolutely necessary in any case, since it is very difficult to get here. On this occasion already I must lay it on the hearts of you dear Brn. again not to forget me in this respect, because I will now be thinking seriously about my construction. And then the mission in Ochgoloogy is pretty deeply in debt. Doct. Four has also sent someone knocking again for his $100 and asked that he not be forgotten. And then they owe Copeland over $100 along with other smaller debts, so that contributions are always welcome here.

I wish we were out of debt once and for all, especially in Ochgoloogy. Perhaps things are going better, or will go better soon.

The visit by your dear son A. Henry was exceptionally pleasant to us. He will surely tell you himself how he was treated. We greet all of you most sincerely. More another time. I will close now. I remain your faithfully obliged Br.,

Gottlieb Byhan

Br. Lewis Eberhard will deliver to you the letters and *Gem. Nachr.* along with a specimen from Br. Smith in the years 1826 and 1827.

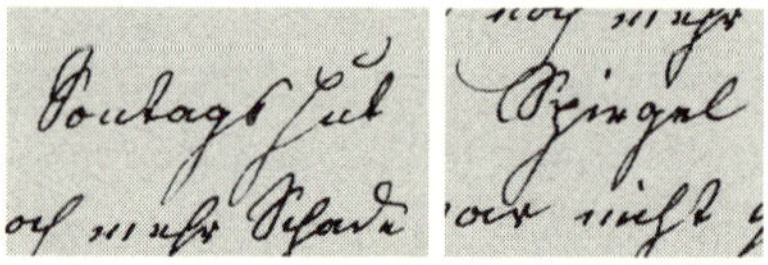

It is a shame that I did not receive a Sunday hat. And it is even more of a shame that the beautiful mirror was in a thousand pieces. It was not packed well.

[Springplace (M 407-1) and Oochgeelogy (M 409-1) Diaries. Translated by Julie Tomberlin Weber. Handwritings are Franz Eder's (Ooch.) and Gottlieb Byhan's (Spg.).]

*Nov. 8.* [Ooch.] Brn. Clauder and Eder, accompanied by Sister Gambold, visited our Brn. and Srs. who live nearby. Wm. A. Hicks welcomed us warmly. In the evening Br. G. Byhan from Springplace delighted us with a pleasant visit.

*Nov. 8.* [Spg.] Br. Byhan today went to Ochgoloogee from where he returned to Spring Place on *Nov. 10.* He had left the Brn. and Srs. there strong and of good courage.

*Nov. 9* [Ooch.] A small number of listeners came for the service. Br. Clauder first prayed the Church Litany and then delivered a sincere talk to explain why we have come here. In the evening we had House Gonference, in which we discussed the school. Following the wishes of the P.H.C., the girls will be there in the future, so we decided that every morning Br. Clauder will teach (and Br. Eder will support him as much as possible until his English is good enough), and Sr. Eder will provide instruction in female handwork in the afternoons. Sr. Gambold is also willing to continue assisting us with everything, as she has previously done.

*Nov. 10.* [Ooch.] After a very short but pleasant visit Br. Byhan returned to Spring Place.

*Nov. 11.* [Spg.] Toward evening our friend Capt. Dav. McNair stopped in on his way home from the Council for a brief time.

After he had eaten something and warmed himself he went on, so that he could get home this evening, since his eldest son James is seriously ill.

[M 414-3-35: Translated by Julie Tomberlin Weber. Addressed to: Revd. Theodore Schulz, Salem, Stokes County, North Carolina. Postmark: New Echota, Nov. 12, 25. Received Dec. 4.]

Dearly beloved Brother Schulz!

For the second time now I have the joy of greeting you all in writing in the name of the house congregation here in Oochgelogy and assuring you all of our well being. Surely you know that we arrived here safely on the 3rd of this month and both of our wagons on the 4th of this month. (I have just remembered that I wrote you this myself in a couple of lines.) Also Br. and Sr. Schmidt's departure on the 5th of this month. Br. Byhan, who accompanied us here and returned to Spring Place with Br. and Sr. Schmidt, promised to come back on Saturday. During this time we had so many things to get in order.

Our dear Br. Clauder especially found much to do in organizing Br. Schmidt's somewhat difficult accounts. However, until now he has not been able to clear them up.

Our dear Br. Byhan came faithfully Saturday in order to introduce the little congregation to us three, at their request, but we were all sorry this could not take place. At least Br. Byhan did not find it appropriate, and we agreed, because of all those present perhaps 30 were Methodists and only 3-4 souls from our congregation. And so before the worship service Br. Byhan suggested that the people might rather designate one day during the week after the Council had ended to meet here for a small lovefeast to welcome and to covenant with us during the enjoyment of Holy Communion, since some of our people, especially Srs., were busy cooking there. We left it like this. Br. Byhan prayed the Church Litany and a while afterward Br. Clauder gave the listeners a very sincere talk and prayer to acquaint people with the reason for our coming and staying here, and so this worship service was concluded after we sang. If time and circumstances allow, Br. Byhan will be here on the appointed day.

In the evening after a small House Conference in which we spoke seriously about the school to be held here, we decided that Br. Clauder would hold school every morning until I am far enough along to support him as well as possible. Further, since our Mother Gambold is sincerely willing to support us in everything and to be active in the future as previously, my dear wife will instruct them in the afternoon in female handwork. She will also have an hour of religious instruction each week. Currently only one girl is here. We are expecting them all, as we hear 12, 15, 17, after the end of the Council.

We must also ask a question of the dear Brn. of the P.H.C. and ask for a decision. Since it has never come up in Spring Place, our dear Br. Byhan could not reassure us about it and so directed us to you dear Brn. The wife of George Hicks, our candidate for communion, is a member of the Methodist congregation and wishes to be accepted into our congregation. What we know about this woman, through our M. Gambold, is that she attends our services here regularly with her husband our Br. Hicks, and otherwise leads a quiet and blameless life, which naturally pleases us. In order not to cause any offense or irritation to these Methodists, we wondered if it might not be good if this woman brought us a letter from her preacher to avoid any unpleasantness and also to avoid the appearance that we want to draw members from their congregation to ours. We hear from M. Gambold, however, that her father-in-law, our Br. W. Hicks, has spoken himself with her preacher Mr. Handerson, who told him that he had no objections. This statement indeed removed the first difficulty, but we still wanted to hear your thoughts.

There is then also the question of how we should register it — as a member by acceptance into the congregation and at the same time communicant (she is also a communicant with the Methodists) or according to the old manner of the Brethren, first acceptance into the congregation and then later as a communicant? If the first should be the case in your opinion, then there is the question of whether we accept her into the congregation with the kiss of peace?

We ask to hear your opinion about all of this soon if possible.

Further, we ask you, dear Br. Schulz, to provide us soon with more than a little money, because we found a burden of debt here of about $320 and have only the $100 which I received from you, because Br. Schmidt took the rest from Br. Clauder and also some from Br. Byhan as well for the trip. We still owe Br. and Sr. Cobland, who will leave here tomorrow, $124. Further, [we owe] the honorable Doctor Fore, who served blessed Br. Gambold, $100. His time is up and we expect him any day.

If you do not mind, dear Br., we thought maybe you could send letters which contain money to and for us to Br. Byhan, because first of all they would go that far for free, and we could perhaps be easier about their getting lost. Since we will try to engage in regular communication with Spring Place, we will always receive it pretty soon. However, if you do not find this possible, we would not want to make any demands. Br. and Sr. Cobland will take this letter with them to Spring Place today.

We ask you to greet our dear parents and to tell them that we are healthy and well. We would like to have written them but have no more time. I will write them in the future. If letters have come for me from Germany, I ask you to have them sent to me as soon as possible. In the name of the whole house congregation, I greet you in sincere joy and love as your faithfully bound Brother,

Franz Eder

Oochgelogy, Nov. 11, 1828

Br. Clauder greets his dear parents a thousand times. He is healthy and happy. Please greet Br. and Sr. Benzien and D. Welfare.

[Springplace (M 407-1) and Oochgeelogy (M 409-1) Diaries.]

*Nov. 12.* [Spg.] Br. Byhan visited our sick Sr. Anna Ajosta, Br. Joshua's wife, today. She has already been sick for 2 weeks. Praise God, she is now recovering.

*Nov. 13.* [Spg.] Today Br. and Sr. Copeland from Ochgoloogee stopped in on their way to Tennessee. They are moving to the area of Columbus on the Highwassee River, about 45 miles from here, and are planning to attend the service in Spring Place from time to time, although it is pretty far and will be difficult. Since it seemed as if rainy weather would come, they traveled on today to cross the dangerous streams before it and are planning to spend the night at Capt. McNair's.

*Nov. 15.* [Spg.] Our Indian Sr. Anna Ajosta, whom Br. Byhan visited once again today, had recovered again enough that she could be out of bed again.

*Sun., Nov. 16.* [Spg.] Only a few of our Brn. and Srs. came to the Sunday services today.

*Nov. 16.* [Ooch.] After praying the Church Litany, Br. Clauder preached on the Gospel lesson for Sunday. There were just a few Indians here. Br. Wm. Ab. Hicks interpreted what was said.

[M 414-3-37: Translated by Julie Tomberlin Weber. Addressed to: Revd. Theodor Schulz, Salem, Stokes County, North Carolina. Postmark: Springplace, C.N., Nov. 20. Free. Gottlieb Byhan, P.M. Received Dec. 3.]

Springplace, Nov. 19, 1828

My dearly beloved Br. Schulz,

On the 13th of this month I received your dear letter of Oct. 27. I had also already received all your previous ones, that is of the 2nd, 6th, and 16th. We thank you very sincerely for all of them. We here, and as far as we know also the Brn. and Srs. in Ochgoloogy, are currently all healthy, praise God.

As is commonly known and as you will already know, our dear travelers arrived here in Spring Place on the 26th of last month, happy and healthy. They stayed with us until Nov. 3rd, after they had enjoyed Holy Communion with us on Nov. 2nd and had attended the confirmation of two members, that is, of the single Br. Niclaus Ignatius and the married Sr. Esther, during which we were powerfully aware of the Savior's presence.

On the 3rd the party then continued. Our Rachel and I went along from here. On the 5th I returned to Spring Place, and on the 6th Br. and Sr. Smith and company also arrived here and spent the night. On the 7th they then continued their journey to Salem, accompanied by our wishes for blessings. At the same time Br. A. H. Schulz, accompanied by Br. N. Byhan, also left from here for Salem. Nathl. B. went with them as far as Knoxville. On the 16th the latter arrived here at Springplace again.

On the 8th I went to Ochgoloogy to introduce Br. and Sr. Eder and Br. G. Clauder to the Brn. and Srs. there, in accordance with your wishes, but only one single Sr. came to the service, so the introduction could not take place. Time will tell when it can take place now. However, I must confess to you that the circumstance that no one except this one Sr. came to the service awakened various thoughts in us, among others whether Br. and Sr. Smith sowed tares [Matt. 13:25], as Br. Eder expressed it, before their departure. In brief, whatever the case may be, it was and is not quite right. Since I have heard nothing from there since I was there, if last Sunday there also turned out so empty, I am very anxious to learn how things went and will continue to go. Perhaps Br. Eder or Br. Clauder will also write you.

The Council is still sitting. However, people say it will conclude this week. Without a doubt you have seen in the *Phoenix* that the Council passed a law that a Committee has been named that will visit the schools in the Nation once annually and make a report to the Council about the progress the children are making in learning. From this you can see that it is important to them that the schools in the country are maintained — and not, as someone in the Council asked, for what the purpose the schools and the missionaries were actually in the country.

And at the same time there is now the matter about which we, that is here and in Ochgoloogy, do not really know what to do. It is this: Our children are taken home so often and then stay out of school for perhaps a half, whole, or several months and longer. Then when they return they have forgotten almost everything, I must say have become wild, until they finally have learned something again with great effort. Then they go home again for a while and forget it again. This continues with repeated learning and forgetting and in the end they learn nothing.

I must confess that I believe we will fare badly upon the visitation of our school. It will be said that one child or another has already been here in the school for five or six years and still cannot read appropriately. They, the Committee, will therefore conclude that the children are not learning anything in our school, since they have spent half of the time at home with their parents or relatives when it is properly investigated. Now it will surely be said: You should not have let them go home so often; this is your own fault. And so we are assigned all the blame.

Now how can this matter be taken care of? I ask for your thoughts. The Brn. in Ochgoloogy and I have discussed this matter together, and we agreed that we will have to do what is done in the school in Brainerd. After their school exams, which they have every year, the children will be allowed to go home for 4 weeks. As soon as the 4 weeks, or even 5 with some, have passed, then they return to the school and are not allowed to leave the school and go home again until after the next annual exams. Those who go home in between or just miss school for a brief time will be struck from the list — except in the cases of illness when exceptions will obviously be made. We had wondered if we should not tell the parents when they bring their children back now, that we would be required by the law of the country to insist that they no longer take their children home except for once each year, which could perhaps be during the Council. Still we would not want to be too strict, so that if a child were just taken home for 8 days we would allow this. But if he stayed away longer than 8 days without being able to present a sufficient reason why he stayed away longer, then we would strike him from the school roll. Please, let us know your thoughts about this matter.

Our neighbor Jos. Vann lost his big suit with our friend McNair. If McNair had lost, it would have seemed like just envy. If Vann's oft-mentioned field can be obtained for $50 do you have any objections if I take it?? It is very much in our way as things are now. It seems our dried peaches could not be sent along. Sell them and have the money gotten from them given to our Sophia.

Today the man who is supposed to prepare the wood for the new house came to us. His name is Dav. Schneider, son of John Schneider, brother of Mother Byhan. Last week we broke stones. They are somewhat far from here, but very nice. I have probably already informed you that I have found an old wagon here on which the wood was broken and rotten. I had it repaired, and we will be able to drive the wood, stones, etc., on it ourselves, because I had it made very strong. Thus we can save some of the horribly expensive transportation costs here. I paid $42 for it. The whole wagon is now worth at least $80.

For everything sent to us with the dear Brethren and Sisters and with the wagons, we sincerely thank you. There was probably a misunderstanding concerning my hat, because I expected a fur hat instead of a wool hat. But it doesn't matter. I can also wear the wool hat for a change. It is just a little too heavy in the summer. It is a shame that I cannot get a straw hat.

Nancy Becker has settled in and is very busy. She really likes it here. I just wanted to add that there is now a completely different atmosphere among the dear Brn. and Srs. in Ochgoloogy than there was before.

Another most sincere greeting from all of us and a special, sincere greeting to you from your familiar friend and Br.,

Gottl. Byhan

[*Records: N.C.*, 8:3851: Aeltesten Conferenz, meeting in Salem. Translated by Douglas L. Rights.]

*Nov. 19.* Br. A. H. Schulz returned yesterday from his visit to the Cherokee mission. Now he and Br. Josua Boner will conduct the town school according to plan. The travellers reached Springplace on Oct. 26, after a pleasant journey of twenty and a half days.

[Springplace (M 407-1) and Oochgeelogy (M 409-1) Diaries.]

*Nov. 20.* [Ooch.] Last night we had a very strong storm.

*Nov. 21.* [Ooch.] Chief Tulira, an elderly Indian, and his wife and two daughters visited us. He was coming from the Council and told us it was over. We were very sorry that we could not tell this man who shares our redemption a single word about our crucified Savior's love that redeems everyone, because they did not understand or speak a word of English. Br. and Sr. Eder and Sr. Gambold visited our Br. and Sr. W. A. Hicks, and the visit was mutually enjoyable.

*Nov. 21.* [Spg.] We finished harvesting our corn. Because of the long drought last August, the harvest was not as plentiful as we had expected, so that we fear that we will have to buy some next summer. Because of our house construction, we began preparing wood for our new house today.

*Sun., Nov. 23.* [Spg.] The first service — which was not very well attended, as there was the burial in our neighborhood of Willm. Thomson, a white man who had literally drunk himself to death and supposedly had not been sober for five weeks, so everyone went there to attend it — was led by Br. Byhan, and the Singstunde afterward was led by Br. Nathl. Byhan.

*Nov. 23.* [Ooch.] Only a few people came for the service, in which we read aloud from the *Idea Fidei Fratrum.*

*Nov. 25.* [Ooch.] Brn. Clauder and Eder visited our Br. and Sr. George Hicks. We were delighted by the heartfelt words of this Br. who was recently baptized. We asked him to continue allowing the Holy Spirit to instruct him and to accept this, so that he could become and remain the Savior's own and would bring Him joy. His wife, who was baptized by the Methodists 8 years ago, has asked repeatedly to be accepted into our congregation. It is against our principles to accept members from other confessions, but since has she asked on several occasions, we will ask the P.H.C. in Salem for advice in this matter. We were even happier about this request, because we know her to be a very quiet and orderly person. Her life, which is consistent with the Gospel, reveals the One in whom she believes.

*Nov. 26.* [Ooch.] Br. Clauder went to Springplace to invite dear Br. and Sr. Byhan to the next Holy Communion, during which we will be introduced to the Gemeinlein here. At noon today a Cherokee came with a rifle on his shoulder, as is typical. After he had eaten something he asked Br. Eder to go with him. He repeatedly asked him where or how far it was or what the reason was. He did not speak or understand English and could not clarify but just indicated 2; we did not know if it was two items or two miles. We did not suspect anything bad about this man, and Br. Eder and Sr. Gambold went with him to see what he wanted. After we had gone about 1½ miles, we got worried the man would lead us very far, and then we would not know the way home in the dark. And so we asked him how much farther it was and explained our concern to him as clearly as we could. Then the honest man replied to us through gestures that he would go back to Oochgeelogy with us; we should not worry. Our curiosity about where this man was leading us and what we would find or do there grew with every minute. Finally, after we had gone another 1½ miles, we reached the site and found two large deer and our curiosity was satisfied. Now it was time to skin and gut them. Br. Eder and Sr. Gambold helped the poor Cherokee, although neither had skinned one before, and it went better and more quickly than expected since we could not communicate verbally with this upstanding man. Each of us took as much as we could carry and returned home safely before night. We were even more grateful for this venison, because we were completely out of meat, and we could not find our livestock in the bush to slaughter them.

*Nov. 26.* [Spg.] Today we received a very pleasant visit from Br. H. G. Clauder, and [who] invited Br. and Sr. Byhan to come to Ochgoloogee next Tuesday, Dec. 2, to attend the welcome lovefeast for Br. and Sr. Eder and Br. Clauder, which they have planned, as well as a confirmation and Holy Communion, which they are planning for this day.

*Nov. 28.* [Spg.] Br. Clauder returned to Ochgology today. In the last days we have been busy repairing the little house where our scholars sleep, since it has looked more like a stall than a house. We tore it apart down to the foundation and put it more in a row with the other houses, so that we finally have our courtyard in a square. Our boys stayed in the church during these repairs, because it has a fireplace.

*Nov. 30.* [Ooch.] Br. Clauder preached to a good number of attentive listeners on the words of Matt. 6:24: No man can serve two masters, etc. Through an interpreter we also had the opportunity to speak with our Sr. M. Ros. Crutchfield, who has endured many difficulties with her husband. It is very unfortunate that we cannot speak with these people without an interpreter; actually it is difficult to learn much even through an interpreter since they are very reserved by nature.

*Sun., Nov.* 30. [Spg.] On the first Sunday in Advent, in the morning we prayed the Litany of the Life, Sufferings, and Death of Jesus Christ. Afterward a talk was held about the purpose and intent of God's Son's appearance in the flesh. Today the single Br. Nicl. Ignatius returned to the school after an absence of 16 weeks, as did his sister Ekey, who had also been at home for a long time. We are frequently sorry that the children are taken out of school so often by their parents, and that they keep them at home for so long. However, we do not know how we can improve this situation without offending the parents, because they usually present reasons which make it seem really necessary to us as well for them to go home. And yet on the other hand it is really true that the children, when they go home so often and stay away for so long, cannot make any progress in their learning, because every time they forget what they had learned here before they went home. We must, so to speak, start again from the beginning with them, which is very difficult for those who have to take care of the school.

*Dec. 1.* [Spg.] Br. and Sr. Byhan today went to Oochgoloogy on business, and returned to Spring Place on Dec. 3.

*Dec. 1.* [Ooch.] Dear Br. and Sr. Byhan from Spring Place delighted us with a pleasant visit. In a Conference this evening we discussed issues that concern both posts. We had already asked our Cherokee Brn. and Srs. 8 days ago to gather here on

*Dec. 2* [Ooch.] to covenant with us to be the faithful followers of Christ through partaking of the most holy body and blood of Jesus in Holy Communion, but only a few of them came. Br. Byhan first confirmed our Br. George Hicks, and then he joined the congregation in this high good for the first time. Although the number of those present was small, we were still very comforted by the blessed presence of our dear Lord. We also experienced what our dear Savior once stated [Matt. 18:20]: Where two or three are gathered together in my name, there am I in the midst of them.

*Dec. 3.* [Ooch.] Br. and Sr. Byhan returned to Springplace after a short but very pleasant visit.

*Dec. 4.* [Spg.] With the mail today we received a letter from Mr. Hugh Montgomery, Agent for the Cherokees, in which he informed us that once again a small amount of assistance from the government for the support of our mission was lying ready at his place, for the first two quarters of 1828, and asked us to pick it up from him.

*Dec. 5.* [Spg.] In the evening there was a Singstunde.

*Dec. 7.* [Ooch.] Only a very few people came for the service, and instead of the sermon we read aloud a couple of chapters from the New Testament. Today we had a very pleasant conversation with our Br. George Hicks. When we asked him what he felt when he partook of Holy Communion, he replied that he felt the peace of God in his innermost being as he had never experienced it before in his life, etc. On the whole, this man brings us much joy, and as far as we have gotten to know him thus far, he has given us much hope that he will become very useful and helpful to his fellow Brn.

*Sun., Dec.* 7. [Spg.] Because of heavy rains today only a few of the Brn. and Srs. came to the services. During the day we had only one service, and in the evening a Singstunde.

*Dec.* 8. [Spg.] Br. Nathl. Byhan went to the Agency today to pick up the above-mentioned assistance from the Government for our schools. On [see next Diary entry]. . . .

[B 61-3: Provinzial Helfer Conferenz, meeting in Salem. Translated by C. Daniel Crews.]

*Dec. 5.* Brn. Schaaf and Schulz had a conversation today with Br. John Renatus Schmidt about his former service among the Cherokees, from where he with his wife and two children returned on 30 Nov. Since it is not to be mistaken that Br. and Sr. Schmidt during their service in this Mission enjoyed the blessing of the Savior as well as the love and trust of the Cherokees, this made it the more sad for the P.H.C. that because of the circumstances cited above (see minutes of 3 Sept.) we were forced to recall them. Br. Schmidt declared himself contrite over these events and assured us that the Savior in grace had assured him of His forgiveness, and that it was up to him in the future to guard himself against such aberrations.

[M 414-3-38: Translated by Julie Tomberlin Weber. Addressed to: Revd. Theodor Schulz, Salem, Stokes County, North Carolina. Postmark: Springplace, C.N., Dec. 11. Free. Gottlieb Byhan, P.M. Received Dec. 24.]

Springplace, Dec. 9, 1828

Dearly beloved Br. Schulz,

Your dear letter of Nov. 20 and some *Wöchentliche Nachrichten* arrived here on the 4th of this month. We thank you sincerely for this. From these we saw with pleasure that your dear son, Br. Aug. Heinrich, reached you safely again on Nov. 18. We certainly join you in thanking our dear Lord for bringing him safely back to you! Please, greet him very sincerely from us. Almost every evening we think about his pleasant visit with us and about how happy we were together.

You asked in your letter if I was able to convince myself in the confused accounts of Br. Smith in Ochgoloogy that Br. S. advanced the mission there $30. To this I answer, No! Personally I do not believe it until I am convinced of something better. He did not advance the mission the money. He will therefore have no blessing from it, and he has it on his conscience. I could also not learn anything from the rest of the accounts, and I gave them to Br. Clauder, since Br. S. left them behind, to go through them with Sr. A. M. Gambold when she has time for this to see if sense can really be made of them. On my last visit there, however, Br. Clauder told me that nothing could be done with the accounts, and Br. Clauder therefore had to follow the advice which you gave me a year ago concerning the Springplace accounts: Begin a new one! Because according to his income and expenditures, as Br. S. had written it down, he should have about $100 in the cash box, and yet he turned over only between $6-7 to Br. Clauder.

By the way we are very grateful to the Savior that things went as they did, because we could not have tolerated it much longer as things went throughout last year, because one cannot live where people use untruths and twist words. But now there is a completely different atmosphere in Ochgoloogy. Everyone walks in love and friendliness. People share joy and sorrow with each other and encourage each other to do everything to further the Savior's work. And this is how it should be at a heathen post. Otherwise, nothing is done for the cause.

You also write me that you have received one part of the *Gem. Nachr.* with your dear son Henry. I sent all the *Nachr.* that I had in Spring Place. When I came to Ochgoloogy I asked Br. S. if perhaps some *Gem. Nachr.* were still there which should be sent on to Salem. I received the answer that no more were there. And then when Br. and Sr. Eder cleaned up in Ochgoloogy, because all the books and papers were thrown together in a chest, they found a packet of *Gem. Nachr.* that should have been sent to Salem. Now they are in Spring Place and will probably have to wait for transportation, or should I send them with the mail? We would be extremely happy if the *Gem. Nachr.* written for us could be sent with the mail. But if this will not work, we will just wait patiently until they can be sent with a wagon.

Our dear Br. and Sr. Benade have a strange way of acting. Now the Savior will certainly make everything work out for the best. He surely has His good and wise purposes for this. We sincerely thank you for everything else shared in your dear letter! We confess some of it amazed and shocked us, especially concerning the Christmans.

In your dear letter which I received with Br. Eder, I was given the assignment of introducing Br. and Sr. Eder and Br. Clauder to the Gemeinlein in Ochgoloogy as their future workers. Accordingly I went to Ochgoloogy on Nov. 8 to introduce the said Brn. and Sr. to the congregation on the 9th, but unfortunately only one Sr. came to the services. And so the introduction could not take place on that Sunday. Otherwise, there were a good many friends in the services. We decided afterward in a Conference which we had together that we would call the Brn. and Srs. together one day during the week so that we would not be disturbed. In addition to this we wanted to hold Holy Communion and a confirmation, so this seemed very appropriate to us since we could celebrate them without being disturbed.

It was left up to the Brn. and Srs. in Ochgoloogy to set the day and to inform me of this afterward. On the 19th Br. Clauder visited here in Spring Place and informed us that they had set Nov. 25 for this and that the Indian Brn. and Srs. would come on that day. Mother Byhan and I therefore set out to go there on the 24th and found Br. and Sr. Eder and Br. Clauder happy and well. On the 25th most of the Indian Brn. and Srs. came, except for a few who live very far away. In the first service we had a lovefeast with the Brn. and Srs., in which I introduced to them the now arriving Brn. and Sr. as their future workers, and commended them to their love and remembrance. In the second service first of all there was the confirmation of Br. George Hicks, son of our Br. Willm. Abr. Hicks, and then Holy Communion. The Savior made us powerfully aware of His dear presence. The Indian Brn. and Srs. were really very happy and blessed. On the 26th we returned to Spring Place.[1]

I sent off the Report[2] to the Secretary of War two weeks ago, because according to your advice I was supposed to wait until

---

[1] Br. Byhan is a week off on his dates. See the Diaries, pages 3929 and 3930-31.

[2] Br. Byhan's report and Col. Thomas L. McKenney's reply are on pages 3960-62.

the Council was over to see first how things would work out concerning the Cherokees remaining here. However, it seems that things will stay as they were for now.

On the last post day I received a letter from the Agent, Hugh Montgomery, in which he informs me that I could pick up our Allowance from the Govenment for the first two quarters of this year. He did not say how much this was. Since I did not have time to go to the Agency this time, I sent my Nathanael there, and I expect him back day after tomorrow.

It seems your dear son Henry was not able to get rid of the $50 in Newbern money I gave him to exchange? Presumably he turned it back in to you, so I will debit it for you in the book. I will soon need a lot of money again, because the wood for the new house is now being felled and prepared. However, I fear things will be a nuisance concerning the boards, because Jos. Vann does not have anyone running the sawmill, and even if he hired someone at the sawmill for a couple of weeks, still he and the sawmill are not much use. I have also had stones broken now and really quite nice ones. They are just a little far to pick up because none can be gotten close to here. Last week our so-called children's house, which, however, would more easily be called a stall, was broken up, or actually picked up and put in a line with the kitchen so that in time the yard will make a Square. The house was so bad and dilapidated that we would really be ashamed if strangers came and saw how and in what kind of a hole we lodged our children.

Also last week I received a letter — the letter was actually addressed to Br. Smid, but since I noted that it was money to pay again I opened it — from Gales & Seaton, Editors of *National Intelligencier*, with a bill for newspapers from Apr. 6, 1825, to Apr. 6, 1829, for $24. They urgently request, yes, they almost demand, that the money be sent immediately. What should I do? I cannot possibly send that much money to Washington, because I am too poor for this. If I remember correctly, I once heard you, dear Br., say in Salem that you had paid Gales & Seaton for the Spring Place newspaper and indeed through the newspaper printer in Raleigh? Please arrange it so that I at least do not need to send money to Washington. I will at least wait for your answer first before I do the least thing in this matter. Now I will close for today. It is 12 o'clock midnight.

The 10th, about 9 in the evening. Half an hour ago our Nathl. returned unexpectedly from the Agency and brought along $100. According to this our Allowance has been reduced to $200 a year, which I had also presumed, because when I was at the Agency last June, I saw a list of all the mission sites in Indian country, along with the amount of money which each post was supposed to receive annually, and I saw then that only $200 was designated for Springplace, and Mr. Montgomery was surprised already then that he had orders to pay me $150 for the half year in 1827. Now, it would surely be nice if we received more, but we want to be thankful for what we do receive.

I wanted to report one more matter to you. I had wondered if it would not be of great use for our Cherokee Brn. and Srs. — and we believe it can be of great use — if our Church Litany were translated into the Indian language and some copies printed to distribute them among our Brn. and Srs., because most of them can read the Indian language now. And we realize more and more that it would certainly be very appropriate if our Indian Brn. and Srs. could also read such things in their language or also hymns and songs which they hear sung. It is really regrettable if the Brn. and Srs. are in our services on Sundays and hear us singing, reading, and talking, and they cannot understand a word of it, since it is really rare that we have an interpreter. Things are better in this respect in Ochgoloogy, because Br. Willm. Abr. Hicks is always at their service in this way. In Spring Place on the contrary we have no one like this.

For the publication, Mr. Elias Boudinott is willing to translate for us at no cost. Of course we would have to pay for the printing. Please let us know your thoughts about this matter as soon as possible.

Praise God, we are currently all healthy except for our Rachel, who is bothered a great deal with headaches and sometimes with toothaches. She is also overcome sometimes recently with a certain weakness during which, as she says, she almost cannot walk or stand. However, when she feels healthy she works harder than she should, so that we sometimes really have to remind her that she should be a little easier on herself and take a little more time for her work. Nancy is well, healthy and very diligent. We greet all of you. And you, dear Br., accept a special greeting from your,

Byhan

[Springplace (M 407-1) and Oochgeelogy (M 409-1) Diaries.]

. . .*Dec. 10* [Spg.] he returned here. Yesterday we had to take our Niclaus Ignatius home again with our small wagon, because he eye was so painful that he could see almost nothing.

*Dec. 12.* [Spg.] In the evening was a Singstunde. Today we also finished harvesting our turnips, which produced exceedingly well this year. We got between 175 and 200 bushels of them, and they were so big that most of them weighed 6, 7, 8 to 10 pounds. The biggest we could find weighed 11 pounds.

*Dec. 13.* [Ooch.] Br. Nathl. Byhan delighted us with a pleasant visit. At the same time we were all delighted to receive letters.

*Dec. 13.* [Spg.] Since some letters for the Brn. and Srs. in Ochgoloogy had arrived here on the last mail day, Br. Nathl. Byhan went there today to deliver it. In the evening we had a heavy storm with strong downpours of rain. Because of this the streams in our area became very swollen again. We were more than a little concerned about Br. Nathl. Byhan's return, because Holly Creek, about 8 miles from here, usually gets so swollen during moderate rains that it cannot be crossed without swimming it, and since the creek comes from very far away, it ususally takes a number of days before it recedes so it can be crossed. Sometimes we are cut off from our Brn. and Srs. in Ochgoloogy for weeks, even months, in the winter.

*Dec. 14.* [Ooch.] Br. Clauder preached on the words from Luke 14:11: For whosoever exalteth himself shall be abased, etc.

*Sun., Dec. 14.* [Spg.] There were more Brn. and Srs. in the services today, despite the fact that we heard from them that the streams are very swollen. We announced to them today that on the coming Christmas Day we will have Holy Communion, and they were very happy about this. To our sorrow Mrs. Polly Vann, who only lives about ¾ of a mile from here and visits us often and mostly on Sundays, moved to a place last week which is 3 miles from here. This made us more than a little concerned about how we will be able to communicate with our Brn. and Srs. in the future, since our Sr. Anna Johanna, Br. Joshua's daughter, who also understands English well, cannot come so often. She also is not as free and brave in interpreting, and holds back more what the Brn. and Srs. say than Mrs. Vann did. Jenny Vann, Mr. Jos. Vann's other wife, who lives with him in his house, also visits most of the Sunday services. But we have not yet had such confidence in her with spiritual matters to speak through her with the Brn. and Srs. So in this respect we are in bad shape here in Spring Place. We want to look to the Savior also in this respect. Also in this matter He will show us the way in His time.

*Dec. 16.* [Ooch.] Br. Nathl. Byhan returned to Spring Place after a visit which lasted for 2 days.

*Dec. 16.* [Spg.] Today Br. Nathl. Byhan returned from Ochgoloogy. He had to stay there a day longer, because the streams between here and there were so flooded from the heavy rains.

*Dec. 19.* [Ooch.] The howling of some wolves that came close to our fences disturbed our evening devotions, which we usually hold with our scholars each day. We followed them intending to kill one, but this was in vain.

*Sun., Dec. 21.* [Spg.] Since it continued raining last night and the entire day today, no one came to the services today. In the evening we had a Singstunde. In these days we heard that our baptized Sr. Sally had been hit by a stroke-like attack which left her lame on one side.

*Dec. 22.* [Ooch.] Because of extremely bad weather we didn't expect anyone, or at least very few people, to attend the service. Instead of having a sermon, we read several chapters of the Bible to these few souls.

*Dec. 22.* [Spg.] The Indian Deer in Water, who has three children in our school, came and brought them articles of clothing, which they really needed. Otherwise, the rainy weather continued today, so that we had to fear that our Brn. and Srs. would not be able to come to the Christmas celebration because of the streams and bad roads.

*Dec. 24.* [Ooch.] Last night we had the first heavy frost of this year, but the sky was bright and clear, so we hoped that at least our closest neighbors who were already familiar with our usual Christmas Eve celebrations would attend. We could hardly expect this of those who live far away, first because there were no visitors here last Sunday to whom we could appropriately announce it, and also the other two churches nearby, which are pretty large, the Presbyterians and Methodists, do not celebrate or mention Christmas Eve. However, contrary to our expectations, more and more people came toward evening, so that when we rang the bell for the service, we counted about 150 souls. Br. Clauder opened the service with some hymns and a sincere address for the listeners. He explained the purpose of this celebration as well and as clearly as he could, particularly for the youth, and read the story of the day. And then by the manger in spirit we worshipped and adored the incarnate Son of God and surrendered our hearts to be His eternal property. During the entire service everyone was very attentive and quiet, and we hoped that what was said made a lasting impression on many.

*Dec. 24.* [Spg.] In the afternoon Mr. Tazizi came to us, completely unexpected, to celebrate the Christmas festival with us. The Indian Young Wolf, who belongs to the Methodists, also came to interpret for us if requested. In the evening most of our Brn. and Srs. arrived here for the celebration of Christmas Eve, as did many strangers. At 7 o'clock in the evening we gathered in our Saal for the celebration of Christmas Eve, which those present could hardly comprehend, and we worshipped our incarnate God in the manger on our knees after we had read the story of Jesus' birth. We asked Him that many more from this Nation might bend their knee before Him, the God and Savior who was born for us, and accept Him as their Savior and Redeemer. A powerful feeling of the close presence of our dear Lord prevailed. Afterward we had a lovefeast, during which burning wax candles were given out to our children. Since our houses were all full of people, many had to sleep in the barn and the feed house in relatively cold weather.

We must also mention that just as the Christmas Eve service was supposed to begin, the chimney where Br. Nathl. Byhan sleeps caught on fire. Since it was discovered early and extinguished, there was no great damage. But if it had not been discovered and we had been gathered in the Saal, then the greatest misfortune could have happened. We were grateful to the Savior for protecting us against this greater misfortune.

*Dec. 25.* [Ooch.] Br. Clauder preached to a large crowd on the words of Luke 2:10: Behold, I bring you good tidings of great joy, which shall be to all people, etc. We were even more delighted that for those Cherokee who do not understand English we had Mr. Budinot, a native who could interpret word for word.

*Dec. 25.* [Spg.] For the Christmas sermon many listeners came again, so that the Saal was completely full. Dav. Steiner Tazizi, who had interpreted yesterday evening word for word, did the same in the sermon. This was very pleasant for our Brn. and Srs. After the sermon, Young Wolf led a talk and prayer, and afterward there was singing in the Cherokee language. In the afternoon we had Holy Communion, during which the married Br. Alex. Copeland joined as a participant for the first time after he had received the confirmation blessing. The single Srs. Anna Rachel Byhan and Anna Margarethe Becker and the Indian Br. Boas watched as confirmands. Br. Israel and Sr. Hanna watched as candidates for the first time. During this Holy Communion the Savior's walk among us could be felt.

*Sun., Dec.* 28. [Spg.] Since only a few Brn. and Srs. came today, a reading service was held in the morning, and in the evening Br. Nathl. Byhan led the Singstunde.

*Dec. 28.* [Ooch.] Br. Clauder preached to a small but very attentive number of listeners on the words of John 14:15: If ye love me, keep my commandments, etc. Recently we also had the opportunity to speak with one of our baptismal candidates [John Fields] who seems to be somewhat lukewarm. We asked him, unfortunately through an interpreter again, why he attends services so rarely, and he first explained how far away he lived, and also how poor he was, and that he had no horse to bring him the 20 miles to our place as often as he would like to come, and other such things. Furthermore, he feels that since he has not come here so often he has had to endure numerous temptations to sin. However, the Savior has mercifully protected him from these. He asked anew for holy baptism because it was his earnest desire (as he said) to live only for the Savior and to become His complete property. We lovingly advised him to be patient and told him we would remember him before the Savior in prayer. Excuses like this are unfortunately too well founded to deny them. On the other hand, it is just as true that they like to make excuses to hide their idleness and negligence.

*Dec. 31.* [Ooch.] We joined with our Cherokee Brn. and Srs. in partaking of Jesus' body and blood in Holy Communion, which was a blessing for our needy hearts. Then we concluded the year 1828 with praise and thanks to our faithful, merciful Lord and Savior for all the proofs of His love and faithfulness and great forgiveness He has shown us this year. We asked Him to continue His faithfulness in the New Year and lead us and guide us with His shepherd's crook even when it does not always seem gentle to us, and we who are weak will follow Him like obedient little sheep. We particularly laid before His faithful heart the mission work among this Nation. In the evening we received another pleasant visit from Mr. Jos. [David] Vann and his wife. She was very happy to find here Sr. Eder, one of her former teachers from the Salem Girls School. She is the daughter of our friend McNair.

*Dec. 31.* [Spg.] In silence we made a contrite conclusion to this year now ending, asked our dear Lord for the forgiveness of our many mistakes and shortcomings, and asked him to give us the grace, strength, and power to become more diligent and faithful in our calling. We then entered into the year 1829 with the peaceful confidence that He will also be our comfort, advisor and helper in the future year.

At the conclusion of the year 1828, the Gemeinlein in Springplace consists of 30 adult baptized Brn. and Srs. of whom 23 are communicants, 25 baptized and unbaptized children. Total: 55 people. In addition, there are two couples of white Brn. and Srs. and the missionaries with their children and other family, 9 people. The grand total of all those associated with Springplace is 64 people.

We commend ourselves further to all the Brn. and Srs. in the congregations, along with our faithful little crowd, to their remembrance and prayer before our dear Lord.

Gottlieb and Dorothea Byhan and Nathl. Byhan

[M 414-3-39: Translated by Julie Tomberlin Weber. Addressed to: Revd. Theodor Schulz, Salem, Stokes County, North Carolina. Postmark: Springplace, C.N., Jan. 1. Free. Gottlieb Byhan, P.M. Received Jan. 14.]

Springplace, Dec. 31, 1828

Dearly beloved Br. Schulz,

Your dear letter of the 6th of this month, along with the letters to Br. Willm. Hicks, further written *Nachrichten*, and $80 in cash reached my hands on Christmas Day the 25th between the first and second services.

What should I answer in reply to your letter now? We really had not expected anything like this. It surprised and amazed us. After we had recovered a little bit — I would almost say from shock — it became clear to us that we should conclude under the circumstances that the whole matter is godless slander to bring down the honest and faithful old soul, Sr. A. M. Gambold. If we all, ourselves not excepted, and particularly Br. and Sr. Smidt, had acted as faithfully in external as well as in internal things as faithfully and honestly, then they surely would not have been called away. Upon her departure from here Sr. Smith told Mrs. Vann that everything which is currently still dark will come into the light and be clear on the Day of Judgment. I fear however, through this circumstance, Br. and Sr. Smith and her way of acting and his behavior will come to light before that, and indeed so clearly that they will be amazed and will wish that they had not accused Sr. Gambold of matters in which she is completely innocent. But it will come to light now.

Br. Smith drank too much brandy, and instead of trying to keep him from drinking so much, which was in her power, she supported him in this and assisted him in this.

This time I will not write any more about this matter, because our emotions are still too high and also because the Brn. in Ochgologee still know nothing of this matter, and I will not deliver them the news about this until Jan. 2, 1829. This will surely not be a happy way to enter into the New Year. I will also deliver your letter to Br. Wilm. Hicks in accordance with your wishes. I just wanted to mention that it would be irresponsible if Smith did not have to learn how it feels when someone has to earn his money, as I also learned when I returned from Springplace in 1812.

According to the last news from Ochgologee, the Brn. and Srs. there were all well and very happy, and I am sorry that I must disturb them again with unpleasant things.

We here in Springplace celebrated a very happy and blessed Christmas festival. For the celebration of Christmas Eve and on Christmas Day, our church was packed full of people, and we hope that many took home with them a lasting blessing. In the second service on Christmas Day we enjoyed Jesus' body and blood in Holy Communion, during which Br. Alex. Copeland from Tennessee, who had come here with his wife, joined us for the first time as a communicant after he had first received the confirmation blessing. Our Anna Rachel, Nancy Becker, and the Indian Br. Boas watched as confirmands during this. The Indian Br. Israel and the Indian Sr. Hannah also watched as candidates.

To our joy we had two interpreters here, Tazizi and Young Wolf. The former interpreted in all of our services, and the latter gave a talk and a prayer in Cherokee. The Savior let us feel His dear presence in a comforting way. Such times are especially well-suited to provide us courage to do everything to help extend His reward for suffering. The way you feel then, when you see eager and attentive listeners before you who grasp every word you say to them about the Savior and His Redemption, it seems that sometimes you have to be silent on account of blessed emotions and dry your tears———.

We greet everyone most sincerely, and ask you to accept a separate greeting from your poor Br. who loves you,

Gottlieb Byhan

[*Records: N.C.*, 8:3832: Salem Memorabilia of 1828. Translated by Douglas L. Rights.]

Often we have been edified together, especially by the reading of the *Gemein Nachrichten*, the memoirs of members who have gone home, and by the encouraging reports from the spread of the kingdom of God, showing the blessing attached to the progress of the mission work in general, and especially of the missions of the Unity of Brethren. It has given particular joy that from this congregation, and from the Female Missionary Society, there have been those who were willing to enter mission service. In answer to a call, the Single Brother Franz Eder arrived from Niesky on the 23rd of June; he remained for some months to learn the English language. He married the Single Sister Carolina Friederica Eberhard; and on September 30 he was ordained a deacon of the Unity of Brethren by our Br. Benade. Her reception as an akolouthe followed; and then in October they left for their post in Oo-yu-ge-lo-gee, to take the place of Br. and Sr. Schmidt. The Single Brother Heinrich Gottlieb Clauder, formerly teacher in the boys school, received a call to go with them, to help in the mission and teach the school, and he was received as an akolouthe. They left on October 6th with the Brn. Matthaeus Reich and Christian Grabs, accompanied by the Brn. Aug. Henry Schulz and Lewis Eberhard. They had unusually fine weather, and reached Springplace on October 26, where they made a pleasant stop and could rejoice over the work of grace in the hearts of the Indian members. Then Br. and Sr. Eder and Br. Clauder went to their post in Oo-yu-ge-lo-gee, where Br. and Sr. Schmidt took an affectionate leave and returned to Salem, accompanied by Br. Joseph Gambold.

# *1829, part 1*

[Springplace (M 407-1) and Oochgeelogy (M 409-1) Diaries. Translated by Julie Tomberlin Weber. Handwritings are Franz Eder's (Ooch.) and Gottlieb Byhan's (Spg.).]

*Jan. 1.* [Spg.] Br. Byhan went to Ochgelogy on business today.

*Jan. 1.* [Ooch.] We had the pleasure of welcoming our Br. G. Byhan from Springplace.

*Jan. 4.* [Ooch.] Br. Clauder preached on the words of John 6:35: I am the bread of life, etc., to a small number of listeners. Since it was the first Sunday in 1829, we then urgently commended to our dear Lord this place where the word of His redemption is proclaimed, and with a feeling of great weakness and insufficiency we prayed it might bless each heart where it is proclaimed among Christians and heathens. We also prayed He would equip us, His weak tools, with new power daily through grace and wisdom.

*Sun., Jan. 4.* [Spg.] In Br. Byhan's absence, Br. Nathl. Byhan led the Sunday services.

[M 414-4-1: Translated by Julie Tomberlin Weber. Addressed to: Revd. Theodore Schulz, Salem, Stokes County, North Carolina. Postmark: Springplace, C.N., Jan. 8, 18¾. Received Jan. 28.]

My dear Brother Schulz!

I was very delighted to receive your two kind letters, dated 27 Nov. and 15 Dec., with the enclosure of $80, and I thank you for them. Our dear Br. Byhan came from Springplace to deliver them personally, along with a letter to the Conference here.

We were very curious, although not worried, about the contents of this since Br. Byhan had sent us several lines 8 days earlier saying that he would visit us about a certain situation. But oh! When we read it we were saddened by the shameful, extremely unfair, and unscrupulous accusations and slander against our good Mother Gambold. At first we worried about whether we should share the entire contents of the letter with her or not. But since we have always read such things and she has always expected such things, we agreed to read to her every word in order to avoid even the slightest appearance of suspicion this could have caused toward Br. and Sr. Byhan or us.

We shared all of our genuine compassion for the hurt that such shameful and really unfair accusations and slander must have caused her, despite the conscientiousness and faithfulness she has so actively revealed during her service at the mission here, in internal and external matters. But we were all surprised and even happier that she listened to everything with true Christian peace and calm, as only people with a good conscience can do. Her comfort amidst these false accusations is this: The Lord knows His people, and so also her and her faithfulness. We can bear witness for Mother Gambold that our mission work and especially the internal and external matters here are close to her heart, and she certainly lifts it fervently and frequently before the Lord in prayer. It would be a great loss to this mission if she were called away because of illness or even if the Lord called her home.

We defend her so strongly not because she has in truth acted as a mother to us all since we have been here, but because we consider it our duty to defend innocence and truth as it defends itself, in a case like this one, to help defend it in the eyes of the world as well.

We consider the complaints that she wants to control everything just as false and deceitful as those about her miserliness. She lovingly carries out and manages all her work here like a reasonable and experienced woman, and anyone who deals with her and wants to say the truth will bear this witness about her. Further, as long as we have known her, she has been economical and thrifty without being miserly. Admittedly, in her own work, she considers nothing more hateful than waste, especially in or with things that are not her own, which she, unfortunately, has experienced for ages.

Concerning her unkindness toward visiting Brn. and Srs. or friends, we find this as untrue as everything else. As proof, we continue to have many visitors, just as we did previously. She is further accused of dealing with debts or money matters before or after the services, and this happened once, as she says, with Reich. This actually was done at Br. Schmidt's request when Br. Reichel in Salem requested this.

Br. and Sr. Schmidt's accusations reveal to all of us here and in Spring Place mean, hurtful slander. They even knew how to confuse old Father Gambold and win him for themselves. Mother [Gambold] did not deserve for him to speak so harshly and unkindly about her. We could not even believe that either of the letters[1] from A. Wm. Hicks and Reich was based in fact. Well, we will see and hear when Br. A. Wm. Hicks visits us tomorrow and has a friendly discussion in Mother Gambold's presence.

So that is enough about this matter for now.

For Christmas Eve on Dec. 24th we had so many visitors that we actually ran out of room and had to make a fire in the courtyard; we also baked as many cakes as we do every year, but there weren't nearly enough. There may have been 150 souls here. We were so happy to see John Fields among the visitors. He is a baptismal candidate who hadn't been seen for a long time, and his words were quite comforting to us. We followed your rules precisely in accepting Lucy Hicks.

We are glad to hear that you are planning to send us money soon, because we had to pay A. Copland at least $40 from the $80, because they really need it under the current circumstances. Furthermore, Mr. Henry is coming next Feb. and bringing flour and sugar for which we will have to pay him, along with the $40

---

[1] These letters are not found.

we still owe him from a year ago, if we don't want to be ashamed. And then we do not have anything for the hired workers. We could get some things 2 or 3 percent cheaper if we have cash. And so we ask you to send more just as soon as you can so that we can get out of our old debts for once.

We were very poorly advised about our Negro woman, and now we find it is necessary to sell her to the first best buyer. We hope that you will have nothing against this, although I at least cannot see how the two Sisters should or can ever finish the excessive amount of work they have. In addition to the other work and the school, they also have to cook, wash, and mend for 14 children. The Negro woman with her sickliness, which is perhaps feigned, we don't know for sure, has been little or almost no help so far. She is, as people say, lazy and very undependable, and as many old Negro women tend to be, she is very slow. That may be so, but if only she were not horribly stubborn and head-strong, so much so that often one cannot point her in the right direction with either goodness or with beating, which was tried once in one small attempt. In addition, we must have good reason to fear that with her Negro foolishness she will impose on these 14 children several bad things instead of good things, for which we will have to share responsibility in the end. The final and by far the worst problem we have to fear is if she gets a husband and children, then everyone might say that we are her Negro. And so we want to ask you to send us the bill of sale with the next letter, so that if we find a buyer for her we can deliver it to him.

Regarding the unfriendly and unkind treatment of Br. and Sr. Gambold toward Gaenppnell and Tatzizi, I would like to add that they would like to have kept them, although Br. Gambold was deathly ill, but they could not keep their horses because of a lack of space, which they also realized. (The corn was lying completely open all around the courtyard.) She says now she had a friendly talk with the latter about this and now everything has been put aside, if there ever was anything.

On Dec. 31 we blissfully partook of the body and blood of Jesus with our Gemeinlein in Holy Communion. We felt our unseen Friend's presence in a very blessed manner. Afterward we concluded the year 1828 at our Savior's feet with praise and thanksgiving and the most urgent plea that He would take us anew in Jesus' faithful and strong hand and guide us into the new year we have just entered, through all the difficulties and also through all infirmities, and that he would help us through. He will certainly add His yes and Amen.

I must ask you to excuse me for leaving almost until the end what I should have written first: We are obliged to all of you in Salem [torn page] our best and most heartfelt wishes for blessings. Things are still going very slowly with my English, and I have reason to fear that since I have little opportunity here to learn it I will not be able to have it at all despite all my efforts, which strengthens my feeling that I cannot and will not be here long. I secretly worry that I cannot support dear Br. Clauder much more with all his work, and this really weighs me down and disheartens me. I will tell you more about this later.

Tomorrow Br. Wm. Hicks will come, and then I will be able to say more about Mother Gambold.

Jan. 4th. Today we had the opportunity to speak with Br. A. Wm. Hicks in everyone's presence, and it turned out that he had gotten everything he wrote to Salem accusing Mother Gambold — how she wanted to control everything, was miserly, unfriendly, and unkind toward all the visitors, etc., — from Br. and Sr. Schmidt. (Every time he or anyone else wanted to ask, have, or buy anything else, they always replied: We are not in charge here. We are not allowed to do as we please; Ms. Gambold is.) They even claimed Sr. Gambold alone was responsible for saying the Cherokees who visit on Sundays should not be fed anymore. In brief, they acted shamefully. However, they alone are completely responsible for this. We carefully described only particular characteristics of the Schmidts, but he seemed to have completely enough and asked us to forget everything and left us very cordially. Br. Byhan will explain the entire matter more thoroughly, since he is already better acquainted with such problems. I am really fed up with it since it has disturbed us the entire time. We greet you and your beloved ones in the name of the entire little house congregation.

In sincere Brotherly love, your faithfully obliged Brother,

Franz Eder

Oochgelogyy, Jan. 4, 1829

It would encourage Mother Gambold greatly if she received a letter from you dear Brn. that confirmed her [illegible] from your side about our statements. Those are just my thoughts.

Eder

Jan 5, 1829

We sincerely ask you to greet our dear parents and ask them to write us soon. We also ask you to extend our warm greetings to father Steiner, Bagge, Petersen, Burghard especially Benzien, and D. Welfare. Don't forget Civily. I also hope that letters from Germany are there for me as well.

[Springplace (M 407-1) and Oochgeelogy (M 409-1) Diaries.]

*Jan. 5.* [Ooch.] Br. Byhan returned to Springplace.

*Jan. 5.* [Spg.] Br. Byhan returned from his visit in Oochgology.

*Jan. 8.* [Spg.] In the evening Mr. Elijah Hicks stopped in at our place and spent the night here.

*Jan. 9 and 10.* [Ooch.] We had extremely cold weather, and we always pity our poor scholars with their bad clothing during such cold weather. As much as we would have liked to help them, even with the best intentions we couldn't manage, because there are so many, and they all are in need.

[M 414-4-2: Transcribed by Grace S. Robinson. Addressed to: Rev. Theodore Shulz, Salem, North Carolina. Postmark: New Echota, Ch.N., Jan. 21, 25.]

Ochgelogy C.N., Jan. 9, 1829

Dear Father Shulz,

I have to acknowledge the receipt of your favour of Dec. 15th which came to hand on the 1st inst. much to my encouragement & satisfaction. The very disagreeable representation which Br.

Smith rendered concerning Mrs. Gambold, has upon close examination, proved false, as you will find more particularly in Br. Eder's letter. Br. William Hicks has promised to exert his influence in restoring the Love & confidence of Mrs Ridge, who it appears wrote an epistle to her daughter at Salem, bestowing the severest censure upon poor Mrs. G. — we are lead to believe under the influence of Mrs. Smith. In reliance upon Him who is the friend of Widows & the enemy of Hypocrites who will sooner or later bring to light their hidden deeds, we are ennabled to bear up cheerfully under every cross & amidst shame & reproach.

I find it impossible, under present circumstances, to commence the study of the Cherokee language, first, for want of time, secondly for want of an Instructor, but I am convinced that it can be easily acquired, if these requisites are attainable. With reference to the school at this place, our hopes are the best, we have 13 scholars, all females, who are all in a progressive way, and if the Methodists, who have a school 2 miles from here do not persuade them away, as they have two, we are of the belief that we can satisfy all parties. What will Congress do with these poor Cherokees? I have seen rather ominous words in the President's Message & Secrety of War's report. I expect the question will be decided before March.

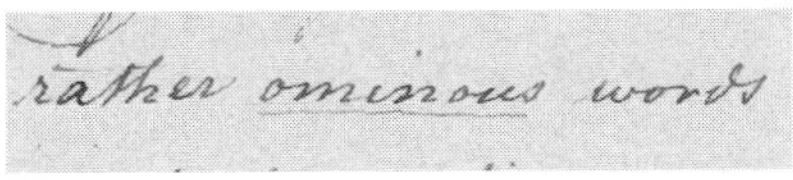
rather ominous words

Annexed you will find an account of contingent expenses during Br Smith's, (or rather Mrs Gambold's) stewardhip. The plan upon which books have been kept here is neither single nor double entry, in short I can't understand it.

I have been sadly disappointed by not receiving a Letter from my friend Henry A. Give him my best respects — also my dear parents; we are in good health & sincerely wish the same to all our Salem Friends.

Excuse faults & brevity & believe me to be sincerely your devoted friend & Brother,

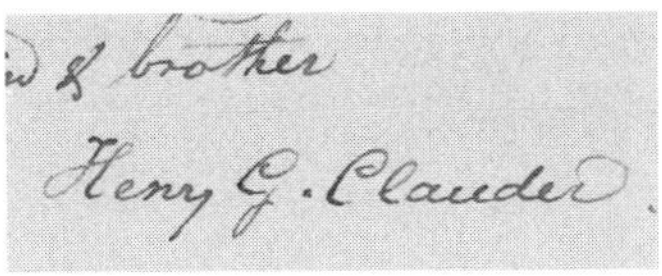
& brother
Henry G. Clauder

Henry G. Clauder

Revd T. Shulz

[Br. Clauder's annexed account]

Cash receipts

| 1828 | | |
|---|---|---|
| Feb. 26 | Amt in Treasury this day (recd. of Mrs. Gamd., who had to keep the Accounts until this day) | 13.20 |
| Feb. 27 | Recd. of Br. Byhan $2.00; for 4 B. oats sold $2.00; for cabbage 0.50 | 4.50 |
| Feb. 29 | Recd. for wool $1.00; oats $1.00; Mrs. Gamb. for knitting $1.25 | 3.25 |
| Mar. 13 | Recd. of McCoy for cabbage $1.00; for oats $1.50 | 2.50 |
| Mar. 21 | Recd. for 1½ B. corn 0.75; for 1½ doz blades fodder $1.12!!! | 1.87 |
| | Recd. for 4½ B. oats $2.25; for 4½ B. sweet potatoes $2.25 | 4.50 |
| May 21 | Recd. for eggs 0.50; for 8 B. corn; $4.00; postage for Springplace 0.25 | 4.75 |
| May 29 | Recd. for 1 B. potatoes 0.50; corn 0.50; for 9 B. potatoes 4.50 | 5.50 |
| June 13 | Recd. for 21 B. corn $10.50; for 4 doz eggs 0.50; ½ B. potatoes 0.25 | 11.25 |
| June 21 | Recd. from Mr. Smith in advance $30.00; July 3 from H[enry] S[hulz] $100 | 130.00 |
| July 3 | Recd. from E. Boudinot 0.75; from Sr. P. Copeland $3.50 | 4.25 |
| Aug. 3 | Recd. from Br. Byhan $100; for oats $4.00 | 104.00 |
| Sept 18 | Recd. for lard 0.12½. soap 0.50; for a steer in exchange for sugar $15.00 | 15.62½ |
| | | $305.19½ |

From the time of Br. Smith's arrival at Oochgelogy until Feb. 26th the Treasury was in the hands of Mother Gambold, notwithstanding her unremittent calls upon him to take the Accts & everything connected therewith into his care — Br Byhan at length prevailed, or rather compelled him to attend thereto, with what accuracy, the above will show, being a true transcript of the original.

## Cash Expenditures

1827
Dec. 7 Pd. A. Copeland for 1000 Brick 5.00;
for Br. Gambold's coffin $4.00 .................................9.00
Jan. 17 Pd. for powder & lead 0.87½; for hunting hogs 0.25;
for 3 days work $1.50 ............................................2.62½
Feb. 4 Pd. Mr. Ware for an old debt $2.50;
Jos. Crutchfield for timber $76.91½ .......................79.41½
Pd. for nails $2.22; for 2 cows $21.00;
for weatherboard $1.00 .........................................24.22
Pd. balance of Crutchfield acct. .......................................17.55½
Feb. 27 Pd. Eli Hicks for Br Byhan $1.20;
pd for threshing oats 0.50 .......................................1.70
Mar. 1 Pd. an Indian for work $2; 1 mo. salary to Masey $12.00 . 14.00
May 5 Pd. for hauling 1 barrel flower from Spring Pl. $1.00..........1.00
May 26 Pd. for shoes for Br. Smith $2.50; for combs $2.25;
buttons 0.50 ..........................................................5.25
Pd. for silk 0.50; for coopers's work $2.12½;
hauling brick 0.87½................................................3.50
May 31 Pd. for leather $2.50; 8 lbs. coffee $2.25;
sugar $1.40; molasses $3.50..................................9.65
June 7 Pd. for tinware $1.62½; Eli Hicks for service
at Br. Gamb. funeral $1.50 .....................................3.12½
July 23 Pd. for timber to the graveyard fence $8;
palings for $27.71 ...................................................35.71
Pd. J. Copeland for 7days work $3.50;
for a vial British Oil 0.37½ .......................................3.87½
Aug. Pd. for a fanner 0.25; wages to two Indians
in making fodder $4.25 ..........................................4.50
Oct. 6 for 90 lbs. sugar recd. in barter for a steer.......................15.00
Pd. Alex. Copeland for work on acct.................................55.00
Oct. 22 Pd. for 2 pairs shoes for Smith $5
(discount on $100 N.C. money $10).......................15.00
Paid Mr. Henry for the following (not entered
by Smith but by Br. Byhan):
32 gal. whisky $16.00; 2 barr. salt $26.00.... $42.00
5 yds. homespun $2.87½;
2 pr. shoes $4.00; lead 1.50 .................. 8.37½
36 yds. linen $9; 4 b. flower $30.50;
16 lbs. iron $2.60................................ 42.10
100 lbs. coffee $25; 100 lbs. sugar $16.50;
yarn $1.50 ........................................... 43.00
Cloth 6.12½; shirting $1;
2 pair fire hounds $8.00...................... 15.12½
1 barrel flower $6.50; for feathers
& iron pots, etc. 14.66½...................... 21.16½
for Copeland
Henry pd. Lavender for Smith........................ 33.62½ ...205.39
$505.51½

[Springplace (M 407-1) and Oochgeelogy (M 409-1) Diaries.]

*Jan. 11.* [Ooch.] Br. Clauder preached on the words of Luke 18:1-8. Only a few people were here.

*Sun., Jan. 11.* [Spg.] Because of very cold weather, very few Brn. and Srs. were in our services. In the evening Br. Nathl. Byhan led the Singstunde. Today two of our schoolchildren also returned to the school. They had been at their parents' home for several months. We really regret that it is so common here for parents to take their children home for such a long time, since they then usually forget most of what they have learned. However, in this matter we can do little or nothing because we realize that the parents take it hard if we want to keep them from taking their children home so often.

*Jan. 13.* [Spg.] Br. Gottl. Clauder visited us from Ochgology. We went over the accounts with him for the missions in Ochgology and Spring Place.

*Jan. 16.* [Spg.] Br. Gottl. Clauder returned to Oochgology today.

[M 414-4-3: Translated by Julie Tomberlin Weber. No address; no postmark; no date.]

Springplace, Jan. 12, 1829

Dearly beloved Shulz,

On the last mail day, the 8th, I received your kind words dated Dec. 15 of last year, as well as a letter to Br. Eder with $80, *Gem. Nachr.*, and German and English Daily Texts, for which we sincerely thank you all. The Brn. and Srs. in Ochgeelogy were very happy about the $80 and are really pleased that you will continue sending money.

In answer to your letter of Dec. 15, I have the following comments: You write that it might not be bad if the construction

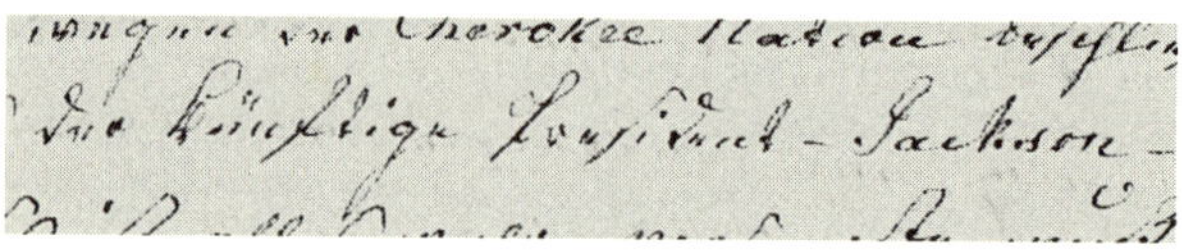

of our house were postponed. Who knows what

the current Congress might decide about the Cherokee Nation, and we also do not know much about what the future President — Jackson — will say to the entire matter. While this is all true, I must continue for now, because I have already gone too far with the preparations for building. Soon all the wood will be sawed and transported and the house beams/logs have already been hewn, except for a few, although they have not yet been transported, but this will be done soon, and we really must build the house next summer, so that we do not have to spend another winter in our old houses. It is almost intolerable when the therm. is 7° Fahrenheit, as was the case yesterday. If the Indians actually have to move, we will be paid for the house either by the Government or by those who take possession of it after us.

Those are my thoughts.

In addition, something Br. Willm. Abr. Hicks said in a conversation I had with him about this matter 8 days ago yesterday really pleased me and encouraged me. He said he would never move across the Mississippi with the Indians but would rather be buried in the Settlement or stay where he is. It occurred to me that since this Br. is indeed a man with great influence on his countrymen, perhaps our Brn. and Srs. will be persuaded to stay here even if everyone moves away, and this will draw us closer together and form us into a settlement congregation.

The Lord knows what will happen. We will cast our troubles on Him. He will arrange everything for the best. I sent the report to the Secrt. of War, and I will send you a copy of it. I also received an answer to it, which I will enclose with this letter.

Now in response to your letter of Dec. 6, concerning the letter from Br. Willm. Abr. Hicks to you, I have the following comments. First, we had certainly hoped and believed that we were finally through with Smidt's problems, but as you see, here comes the final blow, which has caused us much trouble and worry. Indeed, Smidt bears the brunt of this last blow, because now the Indian Brn. and Srs. will know what kind of people the Schmids were, since Br. Willm. Hicks will now present your letter to the Brn. and Srs. here. Br. Willm. Hicks had eagerly waited for an answer to his letter to you. When I personally delivered the letter of

Jan. 1 to Ochgoloogy, Brn. Eder, Clauder, and I had a Conference in which we read your letter to me and the one to Br. Hicks. Should we tell Sr. Gambold about the entire matter, or not? We feared that if we kept the matter from her, she would find out eventually, and then she might reproach us for not being honest with her and for being against her, which would cause distrust between us. And so we decided to acquaint her with the entire story, and not to withhold anything. We read her the letter written to me and the one from you to Br. Hicks, after we had first told her what it said and prepared her to hear it. She listened with amazing composure to the accusations made in it, and she was even able to laugh sincerely at it. She said she had always expected something like this from Smidt's disregard and that it did not surprise her at all.

However, since Br. Willm. Hicks was not at home, I could not give him the letter until Sunday, Jan. 4. Then we all went to the meeting Saal, because Br. Hicks had asked Br. Clauder to read your letter to him. After we read it, we had a Brotherly and thorough conversation with him, and it became clear that the Smidts had also blamed everything that had happened on Sr. Gambold, saying that the Smidts were not allowed to do or choose to do anything if they did not have Sr. Gambold's approval, and that she was the reason guests were no longer fed on Sundays after the services — this last matter really bothered Sr. Gambold somewhat, because the food for the visitors on Sunday had already been stopped during Br. John Gambold's lifetime. In brief, Smidt blamed everything that happened on her.

Smidt was also responsible for asking for money on Sunday, because when Major Ridge visited in Ochgeelogy on Sundays, Br. Smith followed every step Sr. Gambold took and did not give her any peace and nagged her — because Mr. Ridge was there now — to ask him for the money he owed Br. Reichel, until she finally did it, but only at Smith's insistence. Now this was indeed Smith's work, and he really should be ashamed for saying that it was Sr. Gambold who drove the Brn. and Srs. and other people away on Sunday by asking for money.

It would take too long to explain everything here. In our conversation, Sr. Gambold talked openly and frankly, without holding anything back. I did the same, until finally Br. Hicks seemed to be convinced that both of the Smiths drank too much, at least she supported his excessive drinking. Otherwise she would have been able to save him from falling. Br. Hicks accepted everything lovingly and said he would inform the Brn. and Srs. of the entire situation; he sincerely hoped these circumstances would not disturb the love people have for each another and that we would think and act as if nothing had happened. We gladly promised him this on our parts.

Praise God, another of the Smiths' messes has hopefully been put aside. May God grant that this is the last one. This much is certain now, that the Smiths' character has now been openly revealed among the Ochgoloogy Brethren and Sisters, because Br. Hicks will and must explain it to the Brn. and Srs., since they have asked to know why the Smiths were called away.

However, it is sinful and irresponsible of the Smiths to make faithful old Mother Gambold look bad; we did not expect that a Br. and Sr., especially those who are supposed to preach the Gospel, could slander their Brn. and Srs. in this manner. Sr. Gambold uprightly managed the external economy in Ochgoloogy, because he was not able to. He was either too ignorant or too lazy for this. The latter was probably the case, and that was the reason, according to his own admission, that he became such a drunkard.

Now perhaps that is enough about this matter. We are grateful to the Savior that everything could be resolved in love and peace. In the meantime, Br. and Sr. Eder, Br. Clauder, and we are very happy that Mother Gambold has expressed her willingness to continue helping in the household there, despite everything. However, she asked me to inform you that she would be prepared to go back home as soon as the Brn. in the H. Conf. find it appropriate to call her back.

Br. Eder also asked me to report that the Brn. and Srs. in Ochgoloogy do not believe that things can continue much longer with their Negro woman, first because she is ignorant, and one must conclude from her behavior that she doesn't have all of her senses about her, and then she is lazy beyond measure. In addition they still believe that she is pregnant. If this is true, then they really would be in a bad situation, because where should they put her when she delivers? The only thing they could do is put her in the storehouse that was intended for Jos. Gambold. The Brn. and Srs. also say that she is harmful to the schoolchildren there because she discusses bad things with them, etc., so that I believe things are more difficult with her. Br. Eder himself will probably have written to you about her.

I forgot to mention above that the Indian Brn. and Srs. in Ochgoloogy generally are extremely friendly and kind to the missionaries there now, which is a great encouragement to the Brn. and Srs. there. We here in Spring Place are all doing well, praise God! Greet all of our friends most sincerely.

Now I also want to inform you that I have done something for which I perhaps deserve to be scolded by the H. Conf. I gave Mr. Boudinott our English Church Litany, as well as the story of our dear Lord's birth as it is written in the Gospel

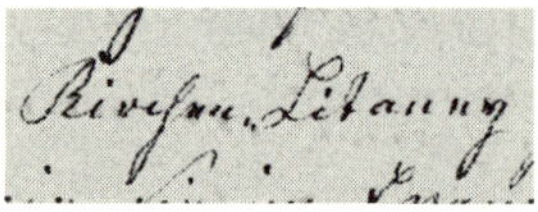

of Luke, to translate into Indian. We believed it could really help our Indian Brn. and Srs. if they could read this themselves, since most of them can read Indian. Admittedly it will cost something, but it cannot possibly be much, and if it accomplishes anything for the Savior's work, then it is not a loss. If this does not meet your approval, just let me know. Perhaps I can get it back.

Could you send us 2 German almanacs? One for Spring Place and one for Ochgoloogy. It would be especially helpful to the Sisters.

I wish there were a man in your area who could frame in a house, and who was willing to come here in the summer or even in the spring to frame the new house. I have to admit that I am afraid of the carpenters here, because they really do not know what they should ask. I have enough offers, but they are excessively expensive. I do have one advantage here: In order to get a job they become somewhat less expensive, one after the other, and in the end I will have one to hire. Still the least expensive is always expensive enough.

You probably have not been able to do anything about my note to the late David Schneider yet?

How do things stand, or what will happen, with the subscription for the *Cherokee Phönix* next year? Should they all be paid in advance again, or are some stopping? Please be so kind and let me know who wants to continue receiving the newspaper. How are things with John Jemeson's newspaper? Presumably someone else is taking charge of it since he is away. Our Sophia wants to give it up, if I understood correctly. Since the Brn. and Srs. in Ochgoloogy would like to have one, I'll take hers for them.

You have probably paid for the newspaper from Gales & Seaton for Spring Place. Through Apr. it was $24. If you have not taken care of this please do. Otherwise, he will write me another letter.

Perhaps it would be good if I informed Mr. McKenney or the Secrt. of War again that the Smiths have left Ochgoloogy and other missionaries are there? And that we will begin our new construction now? Or should we wait and watch to see what Congress will do with the Cherokees? You have surely heard that the Cherokee Council has sent a Deputation to the Congress in Washington? Everyone here is very anxious and waiting to see how and what Congress will decide about this people and country, and there is such a strange quiet in the country that it is amazing.

I also wanted to ask if Nancy Becker began her salary on the day she left Salem and started traveling, as I presume? She and our Rachel are very happy together. Nothing is too much for Nancy. She undertakes everything, even men's work if it is necessary, and is very happy to be here. Rachel has also become more active because of her, so that we, or the Mother, has real help in her. We are sincerely happy and grateful for the written *Nachrichten* you sent us. Reading it is true nourishment for our hearts, and we usually do this in the evening.

Now, dear Br., we send everyone our sincere greetings. Don't forget our Sophia. Also dear Br. Abr. Steiner, Sr.; please tell him not to be unhappy with me for not answering his letter, since my hands are very full right now. I will write him at the next opportunity. Dear Br., please accept the most sincere greetings from your friend and Br.,

Gottlieb Byhan

[M 414-3-36: Transcribed by Grace S. Robinson. No address. Handwriting is Gottlieb Byhan's. Br. Schulz writes in Salem: Received Jan. 28, 1829.]

Copy of the Report to the Secrt. of War, dated Nov. 15, 1828

Springplace, Nov. 15, 1828

To the Honbl. the Secrty. of War

Sir:

In Conformity to the Regulations of Government, respecting Schools for the Instruction of Indian Youth I have the Honor to Report: That the School for the Youth of the Cherokee Nation established in this Place, continues to afford prospects of Usefulness.

The School has been continued on the same Plan as persued hitherto, that is to say: The Scholars have been instructed in spelling, reading, writing, arithmetic, Bible history, & the Elements of Geography, in all of which they have made Considerable Progress. Some of them read intelligible & write a legible hand. The most essential points of our holy Religion have likewise been inculcated, & most of them have committed to Memory some of the Scriptural Texts, & also some Hymns. The Boys have as heretofore been occasionally employed in the Labours of the Field, & the Girls in sewing, knitting & other domestic Avocations. The above can [also] be said of our School at Ochgeelogy.

The persons employed at Springplace are: Revd. Gottlieb Byhan & his Wife, his son Nathanael Byhan, as Teacher, his daughter Anna Rachel Byhan, & a single Woman Nancy Becker, the two last to assist in housekeeping, also one old Negroe Woman, & 2 hired Men to cultivate the field.

The Persons employed at Ochgeelogy are: The Revd. John R. Smith & his Wife; Mr. Joseph Gambold, Mrs. Anna R. [M.] Gambold — widow of the late Revd. John Gambold — & Mrs. Mary

Copeland, who assist the Revd. John R. Smith in teaching School, and one hired Man to cultivate the field.

The Deficiency of Expences in the Exhibit of Springplace of $683.60 have been defrayed by the Agents of the United Brethren's Missions at Salem, N.C.

For the Kind Assistance by Government in receiving last June, by the hands of the honbl. Hugh Montgomory $150 for the last two quarters for the Year 1827, we make our grateful acknowledgements.

Finally, I beg leave, to state the following circumstances & intention: Our two old log dwelling houses, which were erected 27 Years ago, being too small for the present location & in a rapid state of decay, it was our intention some Years ago to erect, with the advice of our Directory in Salem, N.C., a new and larger Building, suitable to our Object in View. The execution of it was, however, always delayed on Account of the unstable state of the Cherok. Nation. But as the necessity of obtaining a safe domicile becomes more & more urgent, we are obliged, to execute the said design next Year, in Order to prosecute our Missionary & School plan with more vigour & to a greater extent.

We trust it will have the cordial approbation of the President of the U.S., and every assistance to the erection of said Building will be gratefully acknowledged by us, and by the Board of Directors of the United Brn.'s Mission at Salem, N.C., who have until the present date defrayed the greatest part of the usual & extraordinary expenses.

This new dwelling house is to be erected near our present houses, which will be repaired for the use of the School & board of the Scholars. It will be built of logs 40 feet by 28, One Story high, containing on each Gable End, South & Northward a Room & a Chamber, & a passage in the Middle of said Rooms, with porches on both front sides East & West. The whole Cost of the House will probably amount to $900 or $1,000.

That our feeble Efforts to do some good to the Cherokee Nation, may prove beneficial to them & to the United States is the Wish & Aim of your humble Servt.,

G. Byhan

Copy of the Answer to the above

Department of War Off: Ind: Affair
13th December 1828

D[ear] Sir:

Your Annual report of the State of the two Schools at Springplace & Ochgeelogy is received. But like too many others, too late for one of the objects for which they are required, viz: to furnish means of reporting, thro' this office, to the President of the United States for the information of the Congress. It is hoped this delay may not occur again.

Your Report is very satisfactory. In regard to your purpose of erecting a new building, there can be no objection to it — and if the fund will authorize it, some aid may be afforded during the next Year. Springplace is venerable, no less on account of its late venerable and pious inmates, Mr. & Mrs. Gambold, than as the place whence the light first went forth, with effect, among those people, and where the Alter was first built on which the fire that has not yet gone out, was kindled.

With best wishes for your individual prosperity, and the further Success of your undertaking, I am, Revd. Sir., Yr. Obt. Servt.,

Tho. L. McKenney

[Oochgeelogy (M 409-1) Diary.]

*Jan. 18.* [Ooch.] We had constant cold weather the entire week, so few people came to visit today. We read aloud from the *Idea Fidei Fratrum* for these few. After this our Sr. Lucy Hicks, wife of our Br. George Hicks, was accepted into the congregation.

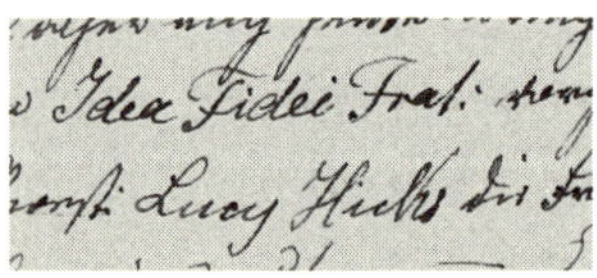

[M 414-4-4: Translated by Julie Tomberlin Weber. Addressed to: Revd. Theod. Shulz, Salem, Stokes County, North Carolina. No postmark. Received Feb. 6.]

Springplace, Jan. 22, 1829

Dearly beloved Br. Shulz,

With these few lines I want to thank you very sincerely for your kind letter of Dec. 29 last year along with $200 cash, and the German Daily Texts which I reported a week earlier. You wrote me that I could perhaps give all of the $200 to Br. Eder. However, in my current situation I cannot do this very well, because I have hired people who are preparing for the construction, and I always have to pay people cash when they work here. This is also good, because then the debts do not mount up so much. Yesterday evening Br. Clauder arrived completely unexpectedly from Ochgoloogy for a visit here in Spring Place. He told me they can manage for now with $100, so I gave him $100 for Ochgoloogy.

My construction is progressing slowly, but still moving forward. The wood has almost all been hewn now, and God willing, it will be brought here next week. Some stones have already been transported. The worst thing is how slowly the boards and other wood are being sawed at Vann's mill. The shingles were already made last fall. The most difficult thing now is getting the bricks for the chimneys, but since our neighbor Jos. Vann is planning to build a brick kitchen, and he will have to make bricks, there is some hope that I can talk him into making them, or get them by the thousand from him. I will see what I can do.

Things are hardly working out with our old Pleasant any more. We had a little falling-out with her yesterday, because she was spreading lies about us to other people. She is also harmful to our children, and everything our Rachel and Nancy Becker do in the kitchen is wrong, and they are scolded for it. She also talks pretty harshly about my wife behind her back. Some time ago she threatened to leave us and go somewhere else, because she was tired of living in this old kitchen. We told her that she could go if she wanted to, but we would not send her away, so that she could not say we had gotten rid of her. Yesterday she actually went over to Jos. Vann's Negroes and has not returned. The main reason for her dissatisfaction is that she does not get as much brandy as she used to before our time. Perhaps more about this matter in the future.

Since we have been here, we have had to struggle with all sorts of problems. Things must have been bad here before. There was no thought of order, and it irritates the old Negro woman now that everything should have its appointed time.

Praise God, we are all well. Greet everyone most sincerely, including our Sophia. Accept another special greeting from your loving Br.,

Gottlieb Byhan

[Springplace (M 407-1) and Oochgeelogy (M 409-1) Diaries.]

*Jan. 23.* [Spg.] We had a brief visit from Mr. and Mrs. Chamberlain. They were on their journey to Carmel, but they stayed with us only about an hour, because they had to be in Carmel tomorrow evening.

*Sun., Jan. 25.* [Spg.] Since the weather in recent days has been somewhat milder, a good number of Brn. and Srs. came to the services once again today. Br. Nathl. Byhan led the first one, and Br. Byhan the second one.

*Jan. 25.* [Ooch.] Once again there were just a few people for the service. The reason was that a Cherokee was preaching nearby. Naturally they always like to go since they can understand better. The sermon here was on the words of Matt. 5:20: For I tell you, unless your righteousness exceeds, etc., and we emphatically laid on the listeners' hearts the righteousness that comes to us through Christ's merits and which alone will enable us one day to stand before God.

*Jan. 26.* [Spg.] Today Mr. Dav. Steiner Tazizi brought us some pigs we had bought from him. Today we also began driving the timber from the bush for building our new dwelling house. We had most of the iron items needed for a wagon, rings, bands, and everything, scattered around, some in the barn, some in the field, so we had a new wooden wagon body made in the hope that we could drive in our lumber ourselves with our two horses, which was successful. Drivers from Tennessee had offered to drive in our wood if we would pay them $2 a day and provide food for two people and feed their horses. This would have been a lot higher than if we drove it in ourselves with our horses. And then their horses would also have eaten up our horse feed, which we then might have had to buy and pay dearly for.

*Jan. 29.* [Ooch.] We have had continuous rainy weather for a number of days. It rained constantly the past two nights, so we could hardly believe our eyes this morning when we saw Mr. Chamberlin arrive at our place with his wife and two small children. We were even more amazed when they told us that they had gotten lost in the bush the previous evening and had spent the entire long night outside with their children without a fire or tent. We were as happy as children to show our love and compassion to this fellow worker in the Lord's vineyard. (He is a Presbyterian missionary.)

*Jan. 31.* [Ooch.] These dear people left us, happy and grateful for the very open love and friendship, as they expressed it.

*Feb. 1.* [Ooch.] Despite the bad weather, a small gathering came for the service today, which we did not expect. Among these was our Br. Samuel from Springplace; he has two girls in our school, and he visited them. After the service this Br. gave a talk for all of our children. We are always happy when this happens, since most of them do not understand English and so we cannot always speak with them as we would like to.

*Feb. 1.* [Spg.] Because of rainy weather today, only a few Brn. and Srs. were in our services.

*Feb. 2.* [Spg.] There was a horse race in our neighborhood again, which our neighbor Jos. Vann had arranged. However, this time it took place without brandy wine being consumed, which made us very happy.

*Feb. 3.* [Ooch.] An Indian and his wife visited us. They seemed concerned about the salvation of their eternal souls. We were sincerely delighted to have an opportunity of this kind, but it is very unfortunate that even with an interpreter we cannot talk much with these poor people. We tried our best to explain to him about the love of our crucified Savior, and we told him to visit us as often as possible, since we could talk with him more with a proper translator. He promised to do this.

*Feb. 5.* [Spg.] Last night the eldest Negro who belongs to Mr. Vann, named July, died. He had already been bedridden for a long time, weakened by old age, and we had visited him a num-

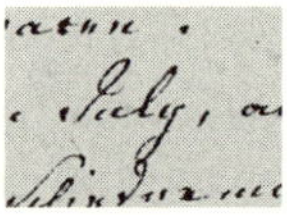


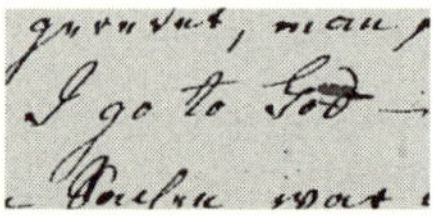


ber of times and offered him refreshment. We also talked with him about his spiritual condition. But we did not find much entry with him. Still he expressed himself a number of times in this way: "Me know, I go to God——." But then he immediately began begging, because begging for clothing, tobacco, and other things seemed inborn in him, and he could not be talked to without his begging. People believed he was well over 100 years old.

*Feb. 7.* [Spg.] In the evening Mr. Dav. Steiner Tazizi came to our place on his way from New Echota, and stayed with us.

*Feb. 8.* [Spg.] A certain Charles Buttler, who is staying about 7 miles from here, today told Br. Byhan of his desire to become the property of Jesus. We spoke thoroughly with him and told him what everything depends on, and what would be required if a person wants to become a child of God and become part of our congregation. However, we have noticed for a long time that he often visits our Indian Sr. Anna Johanna, and also noticed and heard that Sr. Anna Johanna does not like his visits at all but actually tries to avoid him. We were thus assured for the most part but sometimes overcome by the thought that perhaps other intentions might lie at the bottom of his desire to belong to our congregation than his concern to be saved, as he said. And so we told him to be patient, and if it is the Savior's will for him to belong to our congregation, He will find the ways and means for this, and he was especially told with clear words what becoming the property of Jesus depends on.

*Feb. 8.* [Ooch.] The sermon, which Br. Clauder held, was on Isa. 45:22: Look unto me, and be ye saved, all the ends of the earth, etc. Afterward, the newborn daughter of our Sr. Cath. Gann was baptized into Jesus' death with the name Ruth Gambold. After this proceeding, which Br. Eder had the grace of leading for the first time, a traveling preacher from the Presbyterian Church, a Cherokee, gave our children a talk and a prayer on his knees in their language.

*Feb. 9.* [Spg.] In the presence of the parents and relatives of our single Sr. Anna Johanna was the wedding of the single Charles Buttler and our single Sr. Anna Johanna. This was more than a little unexpected to us, but since the parents of Sr. Anna Johanna requested it we had to allow it to happen to prevent annoyance.

*Feb. 10.* [Ooch.] Brn. Clauder and Eder visited our Br. and Sr. Wm. Ab. Hicks to their mutual pleasure.

*Feb. 10.* [Spg.] An Indian woman [Peggy] from the Chickamaga area brought her 13-year-old son into our care and instruction.

[M 414-4-5: Translated by Julie Tomberlin Weber. Addressed to: Revd. Theodor Shulz, Salem, Stokes County, North Carolina. Postmark: Springplace, C.N., Feb. 12. Free. Gottlieb Byhan, P.M. Received Feb. 25.]

Springplace, Feb. 10, 1829

My dear Br. Shulz,

I received your letter of Jan. 20th on Feb. 5th, along with *Monatl.* and *Wöchentliche Nachrichten* and the *Missionary Intel.* Many thanks for this. Everything reported in your letter, sent previously or earlier, arrived here safely, as well as the $80 and also the $200 to me. I will send our Diary as soon I can copy it. I currently have my hands so full with work because of the house construction that I can hardly get anything else done.

We are very busy now transporting the wood for construction here and are almost finished with that, except for some sleepers and collar beams. Then there are some stones to transport, and then we want to try to raise the house. I also have most of the boards together, but they are not yet dried. Currently I have five workers, all from Tennessee. Sometimes I have only 2, sometimes

3 or 4, once I had 6 for a short time. One must be tenacious if planning construction. But amazingly enough, we made progress this winter, although admittedly we ourselves had to be there for everything. Otherwise, either nothing would get done, or things would be done backward.

From all of this you see now that I will need a nice sum of money to continue the construction. Until now I've just barely had enough to pay the necessities, and then there were also the expenditures in the household. I ask you not to leave me waiting too long before you see that my account has something in it again. I also had to buy pork this winter because of the construction, which I would not have had to do otherwise, because I will have to have meat for the workers this summer. From the last $200 you sent me, I shared $100 with the Brn. in Ochgoloogy.

I haven't heard anything from our Brn. and Srs. in Ochgoloogy for several weeks. We here in Springplace are pretty well, praise God, except for Nancy Becker, who has a very bad so-called cold, and our Rachel has been suffering a lot from headaches. On the 22nd our Rachel and Nancy Becker and the Indian Br. Boas were approved in their baptismal covenant and confirmed for their first partaking of Holy Communion.

Today our school received another addition of one Indian boy, Young Deer — he is about 13 or 14 years old, from the area of Chickamaga.

Last week the old Negro July died. He belonged to Jos. Vann and people thought that he was about 110 years old. Br. Steiner, Sr., probably also knew him well. We visited him occasionally in his last days, and we sometimes tried to say a few words to touch his heart, but we did not find him especially interested in listening. Still, he once said, "Me know, me go to God." Otherwise, he was a relentless beggar, primarily for articles of clothing.

Now I must also inform you about the very embarrassing situation we found ourselves in yesterday. A certain young person, named Charles Butler, a quarter-Indian whose father is a half-Indian and whose mother was a white woman, was staying with a certain Adair about 7 miles from here. This person often came to our services on Sundays. We did not believe he came to hear something for his heart, but just to see our single Indian Sr. Anna Johanna, as we heard and as it really turned out. After the services he usually went home with Br. Josua, Anna Johanna's father. We also heard a number of times that Anna Johanna did not like these visits at all and that she tried to avoid this person as much as possible. This young man left Mr. Adair's 8 days ago and visited his father who lives on the Highwassee River, and he returned to Mr. McNair's last Saturday evening and spent the night there.

On Sunday morning he set out very early, went past Mr. Adair's, and came directly to our place. It was not really remarkable that he came to see us, but he came very early from Mr. McNair's, walked directly into our house, and sat down at the fire — which he had never done before — and this was somewhat uncomfortable for us, and we did not know what to make of it. After the services he wanted to talk to me alone, and I immediately gave him the opportunity to do so. Then he told me he would like to hurry and be saved and one day get to heaven, as he said, and he wanted to join our society. I clearly explained what was involved in becoming a child of God and that one must feel the conviction in his heart that he is a sinner worthy of curse and damnation, and then turn with all his sinfulness to the Friend of Sinners, who had redeemed our sins on the cross. He forgives us our sins and cleanses us with the blood He shed for us and accepts us as his children, etc.

Then I asked him if there might be other reasons underlying his desire to come to us and join our community, because I was not really very easy about the whole matter. He assured me that he had no other intentions besides being saved and becoming a child of God. I let him go then with the comfort that, if it was his true desire to convert and if he sincerely wanted to convert, etc., we would discuss this more another time and talk more about it. He said that he would visit us again next Sunday. This was all very proper, and we were happy that a soul had once again come that is concerned about salvation — although we could not deny that it seemed a little unclear if it was really his true serious desire to convert.

However, yesterday Br. Joshua came with all his friends and

neighbors, and Charles Butler and our Anna Johanna, for me to marry them. At first we were shocked and did not know what to do. They had known this the previous Sunday when they were here at our place but hadn't said anything to us about their plan. We had a serious talk with our Sr. Anna Johanna about it, but she gave us little information. What should I do now? We couldn't refuse to marry her and send them away, because we clearly saw that we would annoy the entire family, and yet the entire matter was against us. I have never wanted your advice more than I did at that hour. After lengthy consideration and thinking this way and that, I married them. Time will tell what kind of marriage it will be. What do you dear Brn. think about this matter? And what should we do in future cases that might come up? One of our communicant Srs. married a man who was not baptized. Is this not questioned if it occurs at other heathen posts?

It has often occurred to me, and I have wished to know, if Br. Math. Reich when he returned to Salem from Spring Place in the fall of 1827 gave you a $5 note, Bank of Cape Fear, which I sent back because it was believed to be counterfeit. Did you receive it, and was it really not good?

From your letters we see that Brn. John Vogler and Van Zevely want to pay a visit in Spring Place and the area this spring, which we were happy to hear. Please greet them from us. Could you please send us some blank books along, perhaps in the format of the cash book of the Gemein Vorsteher. If they come by wagon, I think that should work.

Please accept the most sincere greetings from all of us, and especially from your friend and Br.

Gottlieb Byhan

Please be so kind as to give Br. Martin Hauser the enclosed receipt from Henry Clayton when you have a chance.

[Springplace (M 407-1) and Oochgeelogy (M 409-1) Diaries.]

*Feb. 12.* [Ooch.] Recently we have been busy repairing the chimney in our schoolhouse, which was beginning to show damage.

*Feb. 12.* [Spg.] Today we finished driving in our timber for construction, except for what we still have at the saw mill, like boards, scantlings, etc. Many difficulties are associated with everything required for building here in this country. When one finally has gotten the wood sawed at the mill, then he still has to pick it up himself, and the transporting fee is usually already included, or is added to the price of the wood so that the sawed wood is incomparably more expensive here than in the Settlements.

*Feb. 15.* [Ooch.] Only a few people came to our service. Among these was a woman with three children, two of whom she left in our school. This same woman visited us for the first time 14 days ago, and we spoke with her through an interpreter and made her aware of the salvation of her eternal soul. We also directed her lovingly to the Savior as the Friend of Sinners.

*Sun., Feb. 15.* [Spg.] The services were as usual. After that Br. Samuel gave a talk for our Brn. and Srs. and us, which was partially interpreted for us by our Sr. Anna Johanna.

*Feb. 18.* [Spg.] Today Br. and Sr. Byhan visited Mrs. Vann, Polly, Jos. Van's second wife, who currently lives about 3 miles from here.

*Feb. 19.* [Spg.] Toward evening the Indian Brn. Alexander Sanders, and James, stopped in here at our place on their way to our Br. Joshua's. After they had eaten they went on.

*Feb. 22.* [Ooch.] Br. Clauder spoke on Acts 16:30: What must I do to be saved? Afterward the recently born baby son of our Sr. Sussanna Waity was baptized into Jesus' death and named Charles Edward. Then we joined with some of our Brn. and Srs. for the first time this year and renewed our strength in the highest enjoyment of the body and blood of Jesus in Holy Communion, during which we experienced the Savior's comforting presence in a beneficial way.

*Sun., Feb. 22.* [Spg.] Most of our Brn. and Srs. gathered here for the enjoyment of Holy Communion. For their first enjoyment of this, the following three persons received the confirmation blessing: the married Indian Br. Boas, the single Sr. Anna Marg. Becker, and Anna Rachel Byhan. The Savior's presence could be powerfully felt in this service. After this the Indian Br. James gave an address for our Brn. and Srs., in which he advised them to remain with the Savior and not to leave the Gemeine. One could clearly tell from the tears they shed that he spoke to the Brn. and Srs. in a heartfelt way. He also extended greetings to us from Br. Willm. Abr. Hicks, and to our Brn. and Srs. Afterward our Brn. and Srs. set out on the way home, all of them very happy. Sr. Felicitas Hicks, widow of the blessed Br. Charles Renatus Hicks, and Sr. Delila McNair, were also able to come this time, to our mutual joy.

Days like today serve primarily to encourage us anew to continue applying everything our bodies and souls can to His service, and to help Him who loved us unto death gather in His reward for pain, even if the enemy continues to make efforts to lay obstacles in our way and to turn His away from Him. Still He who is strong and powerful in the weak knows how to keep us with Him and to undermine the enemy's attacks, as we recently clearly experienced when he tried to sow tares among the wheat and to cause impurity in the congregation. Through the Savior's grace, however, this did not succeed.

*Feb. 23.* [Ooch.] We had a pleasant visit from our Br. Nathl. Byhan from Springplace, and on the 25th he went back there.

*Feb. 23.* [Spg.] Br. Nathl. went to Ochgoloogy today on business. When he wanted to return home on the 25th, he found Holly Creek, 8 miles from Spring Place, so flooded that he could not cross it. Since it was already late in the evening and there was no house for 10 miles back toward New Echota, he decided to spend the night at the creek. Late in the evening he had to endure a storm with rain and hail, during which he had no shelter except an umbrella.

*Feb. 26.* [Spg.] In the morning since the creek had not yet receded, he decided to return to Ochgloogy. But when he had ridden ten miles he met the post rider between New Echota and Spring Place, with whom he turned around again. They took another road farther up the creek, and he arrived at Spring Place again at noon. He had gotten pretty cold while camping at the creek, but he recovered from this in several days.

# *1829, part 2*

[M 414-4-6: Translated by Julie Tomberlin Weber. Addressed to: Revd. Theodor Schulz, Salem, Stokes County, North Carolina. Postmark: Springplace, C.N., March 5. Free. Gottlieb Byhan, P.M. Received March 19. Handwriting is Gottlieb Byhan's.]

Springplace, Feb. 24, 1829

Dearly beloved Br. Shulz,

I received your kind letter of Feb. 5, along with *Monatliche* and other *Nachrichten*, as well as the *Missionary Intel.* of 1828. I have already informed you that I received the $200 and *Nachrichten* you sent me in a letter dated Dec. 16.

Now I want to try to explain to you the situation in which we currently find ourselves, as well as can be done on paper. It seems that we are meant to be tortured by Smith and his stories as long as we are here, and it seems almost inevitable that Smith is still trying to cause unrest among our Brethren and Sisters in an underhanded manner, because we can't help but believe that Smith is writing letters to his supposed friends to provoke us. Now to the heart of the matter.

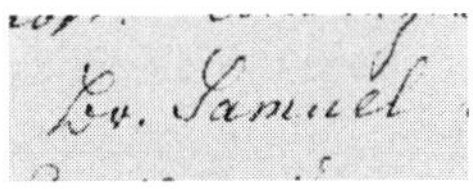


Last Sunday, eight days ago, the 15th of this month, Br. Samuel called all the Brethren and Sisters to gather in Springplace. Almost all of them, at least almost all of them from the area around Sumak, were here. We had heard the previous week that they had been called to come, but we did not know why or what the reason was.

When the first service on the said Sunday was over and we were getting ready to go our separate ways, Br. Samuel stood up and called all of us back, because he had something to say. We were happy, because we thought he would perhaps admonish our Brethren and Sisters in Indian, and we sat down again. Br. Samuel then began and said in a quite irritated tone that he had recently been in Ochgeelogy and had visited Br. Willm. Hicks, who told him that the Brn. and Srs. in Springplace were responsible for having Br. and Sr. Smith called away, and that I must have reported this to the Directors.

This news shocked us more than a little, and we could not grasp how Br. Wilm. Hicks could conclude anything like this from the letter he had received from you! In brief, we did not know what we should think about being accused of this now. And since we could not believe that Br. Willm. Hicks could have based this accusation on your letter, we must believe that Smidt, as stated above, is corresponding with his supposed friends. We know what kind of friends these are, those who say nice things to his face and then say terrible things about him behind his back.

If it really is true that Br. W. Hicks told Br. Samuel such things without being led to do this by Smidt, then we do not know what to think about the entire matter, and it really worries and troubles us. I must also add that Br. Samuel said that Br. Hicks told him to tell the entire Springplace congregation. And he did so faithfully, to our great humiliation, because not only were our Brn. and Srs. present but also our children and some Negroes. Those of the latter group who understand Indian left when they saw and heard that we were being accused of such things, and our explanations made no difference.

As you can imagine, it was difficult for us to have to listen to these accusations before the entire congregation and the children and Negroes. We did not receive any satisfactory responses to our explanations, because Br. Samuel lost his temper, and we have reason to believe, and actually heard from others, that our Sr. Anna Johanna did not interpret faithfully. So we left each other feeling badly. Some Brn. and Srs. came along to our house where we sat around the fire. Among them was also Br. Samuel's wife.

Now we believed we had to tell this company the real reason he was called away. We did this and told them the honest truth. It seems we will have no peace until Smidt's character is known to all the people here. We had to reveal him, because otherwise people say we or other innocent people are responsible for having him called back and must feel the pressure.

Afterward I announced to the Brn. and Srs. that we will have Holy Communion in eight days and invited them to it with the request that they forget all that had happened and surrender it to the Savior. It seemed that everyone except Br. Samuel was satisfied with this. But Br. Samuel said quite curtly that he did not know if he would come, and in fact he did not come last Sunday. This is how the entire matter stood as everyone went home.

We had a difficult week and did not know what to make of the entire matter. I often wished that we had never gotten involved with the miserable Smidts and thus had been spared this. No one can believe what we have had to endure the past year because of the miserable Smith, and we do not want to endure anything else like this. The whole story repulses us, and we are truly tired of it.

The 25th. Last Sunday the 22nd we had Holy Communion and most of our Brn. and Srs. gathered for this. Srs. Felicitas Hicks and Delila McNair also came. Br. Boas and Srs. Anna Margareth Becker and Anna Rachel Byhan were confirmed and joined us in partaking of this high good for the first time. We could feel the Savior in our midst. Before Communion Br. James told us that he wanted to say a few words to the Brn. and Srs. after Holy Communion, if he was permitted. He said that the words he wanted to say were good, so I told him we would be very happy if he wanted to say a word of admonition to the Brn. and Srs. After communion I gave him the opportunity to present his matter. He told the Brn. and Srs. that he had also visited Br. W. Hicks in Ochgoloogy last week. He had told him to greet our Brn. and

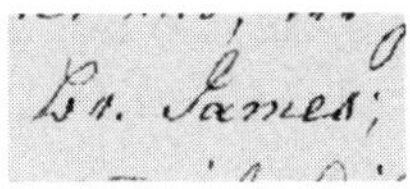

Srs. and also us by name, and to encourage the Brn. and Srs. and admonish them to remain with the Savior and the Gemeine and not to let anything turn them away from the Savior, etc. As he spoke many tears were shed, from which we could see that he must have spoken very sincerely.

Everyone was very satisfied when parting ways and going home. This Sunday encouraged us to continue helping to spread His kingdom, even in great weakness. We are convinced that other Brn. and Srs. could do much more for the Savior's work here than we can, and we ask the dear Brn. to please consider that we are here only on an interim basis, so that His work here does not suffer. We can assure you that we have had unpleasant matters and difficult times since we have been here and long for good times soon. Now the Savior will help us manage as long as we are here and will not let us be defeated.

But what are we supposed to think about all these issues? Through Br. Samuel, Br. Hicks sent us the unpleasant news and accusations above, which naturally had to cause difficulties for us and our Brn. and Srs. And then again through Br. James we are sent such a friendly and loving admonition. We do not know what to think about this and how to interpret the entire matter.

Br. Samuel feels attacked and unhappy, but we do not know why. As far as I can remember, we have never said anything in words or in letters to suggest that the Springplace Brn. and Srs. were responsible for Smidt's recall. We do not know where he got this idea. I said above that we can only believe Smidt must have secretly written letters to people here to free himself of the accusations, but we do not know to whom. If he really is doing this, he will not only fail to free himself from these, but will just add to them and cause us to reveal even more about the entire matter.

Since our Nathl. went to Ochgoloogy yesterday and is expected back here today, I will not close this letter until he returns. Perhaps the matter will be cleared up somewhat.

March 2. Our Nathl., as I mentioned above, set out from Ochgoloogy on the 25th of Feb. and returned to Spring Place on the same day. However, since it had rained the preceding day and night, the creek 8 miles from here was so swollen that he could not cross it and so had to spend the night alone in the bush and endure a strong storm and hail. In the morning of the 26th the creek was even less passable, so he went back toward New Echota and Ochgoloogy but met the post rider from New Echota who knew a detour where the creek can be crossed on a bridge, and so he reached Springplace on that day. With him I received the following lines from Br. Clauder of Feb. 24:

"The unexpected visit last Friday of Brn. Josua and James from Springplace was somewhat remarkable, and what I heard from Br. Willm. Hicks yesterday (who had asked me last Sunday to visit him yesterday) also explained the purpose of their special visit. In the letter that Br. Shulz wrote Br. Wm. Hicks, with the reasons Br. and Sr. Smidt were called away from here, Br. Shulz said among other things that certain Cherokee friends knew of Br. Smidt's behavior and had also reported it.

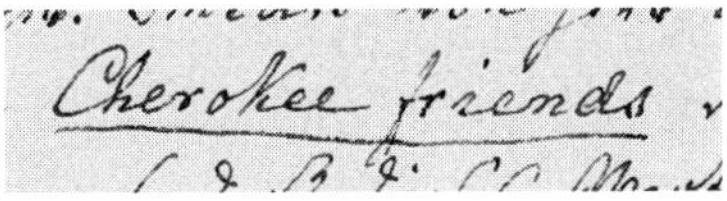
Cherokee friends

"(You will surely remember that these words, Cherokee friends, were used in pretty much the same sense in Br. Shulz's letter to Br. Hicks.)

"According to this the Cherokee friends (whether Brethren and Sisters or other friends is not clear) had given their own reason for the eternally regrettable recall of Brother and Sister Schmidt. Br. Hicks said that should now be investigated in order to reveal the reason for their accusations against Br. and Sr. Smidt to the Cherokee friends about whom Br. Shulz writes, and to avoid the appearance of the lack of gratitude toward the departed teachers. Br. Hicks also said that Br. Samuel acted imprudently, in his usual overzealous quest for the truth, in an address (about which you write in your dear letter), which you said also offended you, and that a misunderstanding arising from this was probably the reason Br. Samuel was not present for Holy Communion. Br. Hicks will pay a visit to our Brethren and Sisters as soon as his horses return from Augusta, to put aside this extremely unpleasant matter in love with the Lord's guidance."

That is what Br. Clauder wrote. This has given us information and clarity about the matter, and this is also what occurred to us more and more, and it was also that which should have been interpreted for us when Br. Samuel presented the matter publicly and not as was interpreted for us, that I accused our Brn. and Srs. of being responsible for Br. and Sr. Smidt's recall, which has occurred to us more and more, and that I had written this to the Directors. If it had not taken place in a public meeting in front of friends, children, and Negroes in a quite aggressive manner, it would not have bothered us so much. However, as things stand now, some of our Brn. and Srs. have now been taken in by this and think it might be true that we placed the responsibility on them. We saw that they are not served by our humiliation and excuses and explanations or, as it seemed, these did not make any impact on them. This causes us great worry now day and night, so that sometimes we hardly know what we should think or do. May the Savior help us!

In my answer to your letters of Dec. 6 last year and Jan. 13 this year, I wrote to you that after my conversation with Br. Wm. Hicks and after reading your answer to his letter to you — that everything was settled in love, or would be dismissed again — we allowed ourselves to hope that this immeasurably unpleasant and irritating story would be put aside now and we can once again enjoy our life, but unfortunately we really deceived ourselves.

It is just now reaching its full force, so that we hardly know what to do anymore. As said, now the worry is gnawing at us day and night and our courage is fading — and we must wish that we had never accepted the call to serve here or that we had never seen Br. and Sr. Schmidt. Anyone who feels as we now feel will not think badly of us for saying this, and we really wish that a couple of other Br. and Sr. might be found who are more skillful than we at helping to extend the Savior's work here and who are willing to take our place and let us go.

Now we are expecting a visit or visitation from Br. William Hicks concerning the sinful matters of Br. and Sr. Smidt; time will tell how the matter ends. We simply cannot say that we are very afraid or worried about it, because the Lord is in charge and we trust that He will arrange everything for the best. However, the truth must be revealed and it will remain.

We have always tried to keep Br. Smidt's behavior hidden from our Brn. and Srs., but it seems they now have a great desire to know and there is nothing to do but present them with the truth. If Br. Smidt were sincerely concerned about the Savior's work here as well as his own honor, the only possibility would be for him to write a letter to the Cherokee Brn. and Srs. both here in Spring Place and in Ochgoolgy, in which he explained himself as a sinner, if he believes that he is a sinner and acted irresponsibly, and expresses his remorse at his mistakes and negligence and explained to them that he alone bears the responsibility for being called away. Admittedly this will be difficult for a man as arrogant as Br. Smidt was here. Then the eyes of the people would be opened, and they would be quieted.

God willing, we will finally be released from this mess with the Smidts. As it is, we have already been preoccupied with this affair of the Smidts for a year. I do not know any more what I should call it, and still see no end to it. Help us pray that the Savior will soon help us out of this confusion, so that once again we can live our days happily. And if you can advise us or otherwise help us, we beg you to do so, because soon we will not know what to do or where to turn. We are so sincerely weary of the Smidts' affair that it really disgusts us. Now we will see what happens, and I will not fail to inform the dear Brn. in detail about everything.

We are busy with our construction now. We have begun raising the house. It is going slowly however, as this kind of work typically does in this country. With the last post, the 26th of last month, we received the German calender, with written *Gem. Nachr.*, for which we thank you sincerely. I thought I would find more enclosed, but this time did not find anything. We are currently, praise God, all healthy except for our Rachel, who has a bad cold and suffers a lot from headaches. Yet she is still busily helping us. Otherwise, the Nation is beginning to get uneasy about moving away. They continue to understand more and more that they will have to give in eventually, because otherwise they will have no peace.

Everyone, accept the sincere greetings from your poor

Byhans

Please give our Soph. greetings from us and tell her that we received her dear letter and will answer soon.

B.

[Springplace (M 407-1) and Oochgeelogy (M 409-1) Diaries. Translated by Julie Tomberlin Weber. Handwritings are Franz Eder's (Ooch.) and Gottlieb Byhan's (Spg.).]

*Mar. 1.* [Ooch.] As we entered into this blessed Passion season, we prayed the Litany of the Life, Sufferings, and Death of Jesus. Then we pleaded with the Savior to make our hearts especially aware during this time that His meritorious sufferings and death, endured for us, are the only reason for our salvation. During this we felt His merciful Yes and Amen.

*Sun., Mar. 1.* [Spg.] Because of the cold weather, no one came to the services today.

*Mar. 2.* [Spg.] We began putting up our new house.

*Mar. 3.* [Spg.] We began sowing our oats, since we had not been able to do this earlier because of cold weather.

*Mar. 7.* [Spg.] Our Br. Joshua came to our place and told us that his eldest son Archibald had died the day before yesterday as the result of a fall from a horse during a race. He asked for a hammer and some nails to make a casket for him. Since he was supposed to be buried today, Nathl. and Rachel Byhan and Nancy Becker went there this afternoon to attend the burial. However, when they were making the grave they hit water, and they had to start a second grave, which kept them from having the burial today. We would hope that this occurrence might be a warning for the Indians, since horse racing has recently been carried out

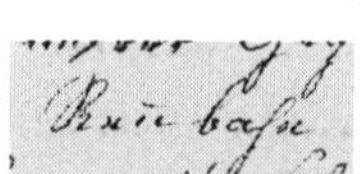

a lot in our area. Our neighbor Jos. Vann has also contributed a great deal to this, because he himself has set up a race track in his field.

It is actually right behind our God's Acre, so that we have had quite enough of this bad thing. However, we are happy each time it takes place without drinking and fighting.

*Mar. 8.* [Ooch.] Br. Clauder preached on Isa. 49:14-15. After the sermon we had a pleasant conversation, with the help of an interpreter, with a young widow who gives us hope that she will become part of our gathering of the faithful. At least we could tell from what she said that she is concerned about her spiritual salvation, or at least is beginning to think about this. Oh, we are always so happy when we occasionally find a soul who is at least beginning to wonder: <u>What must I do to be saved</u>! We rejoiced especially over her since two of her sisters already belong to our little congregation. In the past few days two of our new scholars have caused us more than a little distress. Without the slightest reason they left us and ran home, a distance of about 12 miles. We didn't learn about this until they were several hours away. The only thing we could do was inform our Br. Wm. A. Hicks about it that same evening. He reassured us and said that there was no doubt the children were at home. This was indeed the case. The third day the parents of both brought them back. Usually we do not take back children like these who have already tried this several times, but since the parents seemed to think it was very important for them to be here, we told them that they should make it very clear to the children, and we told them (the parents) and the young ones, that if they tried to run away one more time we could not take them in again, etc. They replied that they had already done this, and they would do so one more time in our presence.

*Sun., Mar. 8.* [Spg.] There was the burial of the above-mentioned son of our Br. Joshua, for which Br. Samuel gave an address to the gathered Indians and they sang in their language. Our Br. Solomon was the lead singer. Our Sunday services were held in the usual order.

*Mar. 9.* [Spg.] Our friend Dav. Steiner Tazizi came to our place for a visit. He told us that he was now planning to begin his own household 40 miles from Spring Place. We really regret this, since there is now little hope that we can later have him as interpreter in our services any more. In this concern we will now have to help ourselves as well as we can in the future. Today our neighbor Mrs. Vann also visited us. She told us that Mr. Vann is planning to give us the field between our fields for $50. This consists of approximately 18 to 20 acres. Since this field is right between the Spring Place fields, we believed we would give him this sum for the improvement of it, because by owning it, we will no longer be surrounded by Vann's fields and are no longer so penned in. Our fields are also no longer separated, but now adjoin each other.

*Mar. 10.* [Spg.] Once again we received an Indian boy [Hunter] into our school from the area of Chickamaga, about 18 or 20 miles from here. Mr. Dav. Steiner Tazizi returned home from here today.

[M 414-4-7: Translated by Julie Tomberlin Weber. Addressed to: Revd. Theodor Schulz, Salem, Stokes County, North Carolina. No postmark; no date.]

Springplace, March 11, 1829

Dearly beloved Br. Schulz,

With these few lines I just want to inform you that on the 5th of this month I received the second German almanac, along with the written *Nachrichten*. I will send this almanac on to Ochgoloogy. We thank you very sincerely for it. I was expecting a letter from you in answer to mine about Br. Wm. Hicks's letter, but it did not come. I almost believe that a letter from you must have gotten lost, because the answer concerning Hicks's letter has not come for so long, or mine — dated Jan. 13th [Jan. 12] — must have gotten lost. Something must have gone wrong somewhere, because with the last post on the 5th I received a letter from Br. Shaaf dated Feb. 3, which took four weeks to deliver. It is impossible to know where something went wrong. I hope my letter to you dated March 4th [Feb. 24, postmarked March 5] does not take so long to reach you.

Praise God, we are all pretty healthy, except for insignificant bouts of illness and so-called colds. Our Rachel has had a very bad cold, but now seems to be improving.

Our construction is proceeding slowly. We are currently raising the house and might finish that this week, because we have a good carpenter, so we help him put up the beams and then go about our other work until he needs more beams. Then we help him again. However, I must ask you not to forget me in terms of my account, because I currently need a lot of money. Just the day before yesterday our neighbor Jos. Vann came and completely unexpectedly managed to take $60 from my wallet. I have now obtained the field which belongs to Jos. Vann, or which used to be his, and lies between our fields, for $50. Accept these few lines for now, because my time is very short right now, and my eyes hardly allow me to write in the evening, and during the day I cannot think about writing at all now, because first I have to do something here and then something there.

I also want to inform you that last week our Br. Joshua's eldest son fell off his horse at a horserace, or jumped, and he died after two days. Accept the sincerest greetings from all of us, and you, dear Br. especially from me, your Br. in Jesus' death,

Gottlieb Byhan

March 12, 1829. This very hour I received your dear letter from Feb. 8th, with the enclosure of $44, for which I thank you sincerely. I will answer your kind letter another time.

G. Byhan

[M 414-4-8: Translated by Julie Tomberlin Weber. Addressed to: Revd. Theodor Shulz, Salem, Stokes County, North Carolina. Postmark: New Echota, C.N., Mar. 11, double: 50. Received Mar. 25.]

Oochgeelogy, March 12, 1829

My dear Brother Schulz!

We all thank you sincerely for your kind letter of Feb.9th, which we received on Saturday the 28th. We were especially happy that Mother Gambold received one of her own, which really pleased her. She sends her gratitude, especially for the signs of your love and confidence in her, and she seems willing again to serve here as long as it pleases the Lord. The Smiths' inhumane actions seem to have been completely forgotten, at least among our Brn. and Srs. here. However, we do not know what things are like in Springplace right now.

On Jan. 18th Sr. Lucy Hicks was accepted into the Gemeine. Feb. 8th We shared in the grace of baptizing a little baby into Jesus' death for the first time, and then again on Feb. 22nd. The mothers of both children belong to the Gemeine. After the baptism we enjoyed the body and blood of Jesus in Holy Communion for the first time this year, although only with some of our Brn. and Srs. It was a blessing for our needy hearts. Our Sr. Maria Rossina Crutchfield is supposed to be confirmed for the next Holy Communion. Unfortunately, we cannot say much about our baptismal candidate John Fields except that he seems to be quite apathetic. He has not visited us since Christmas, although we have sent word to him several times.

Thanks be to the Savior, everything else is going as it should. Br. Clauder is holding school every morning without exception for the 16 children we now have, and when we have had our evening devotions with them he has sung some verses with them in Cherokee almost every evening. My dear wife holds school with them every afternoon except for wash days. Sr. Gambold is always untiringly busy as well, and I also do what I can, since there is plenty of work everywhere. Things are currently not going very well with the Negro woman.

My dear Brother Schulz, I thank you for your loving encouragement of my attempts to learn the English language, which I unfortunately really need. At times I have completely lost heart, as I believe many in my situation and circumstances would surely have done. That is also why I ask you, dear Brn. of the P.H.C., to accept my request, which I also ask you to send on to the Brn. of the U.A.C. in Germany in the enclosed letter. Surely this will seem premature and surprising to you, dear Brethren, but there is nothing else I can do, and I consider it your duty toward me to do this as well as for the work for which I speak. I am truly sorry to have to inform you so soon that I am so utterly miserable here, and therefore I cannot remain here long. I also ask you very sincerely to do what you can to help me be placed at any other mission post.

I would not have had to bother you with this concern, which may seem laughable to you at first, if I thought that you would make this decision or carry it out on your own. However, you will surely report this to the Brn.'s U.A.C., and I myself would like to inform them of my thoughts about my presence here and also ask them for a change. And so I believe it will be a while before this can be decided and a place found for us.

One reason I will never be satisfied here and never be peaceful is first: despite the small size of the gathering of believers here, I do not feel skilled and capable enough to serve them with word and sacrament. Second: the bleak prospect, or better said, the complete impossibility, of learning English. It is well-known that practice is necessary for anyone, and there is, so to speak, no mingling with English speakers here. I believe there is proof of this in Brn. Burghard and Petersen, who have been there for 10 years now and how far are they??

How depressing and discouraging it is for me from my perspective (except I only know what I have already gone through) to have to think: I am here, and I should serve the work here no matter how small it is. But I must leave absolutely everything up to my dear faithful colleague Br. Clauder. So far it has been absolutely impossible for me, and things could continue like this for years. From a different perspective, how depressing and discouraging it is for Br. Clauder, as well, to have to watch this and to realize that he must do everything except some things that would naturally bring him pleasure, but he is not allowed to do and must stand behind me in my wretchedness. He is not allowed to distribute the sacraments or bless them. And so, dear Brn., please believe that I have compassion for Br. Clauder, whom God has given such special gifts and knowledge, when he must see himself held back like this or feel this.

Furthermore, one cannot possibly expect it to last long when one places Brn. and Srs. together in this way, which is just the case here. Can a man like Br. Clauder be expected to remain in these circumstances or situation? I often silently feel sorry for him, because he gets no understanding or encouragement from any side. I cannot do this despite my best intentions, because my ever-increasing pain, worry, and disheartened spirit or mind speaks and shows itself in all my actions, and there is no one else here. I now feel too clearly that I am not at all by nature what I should be for Br. Clauder, and my weak wife is just as unable to assist good Mother Gambold with this large household. I have it from pretty reliable sources that Br. Nathl. Byhan is going to Salem this school year because of his marriage, so I ask in a very childlike manner: Could this not also be done for our Br. Clauder, who has such a sincerely lively interest in mission work, particularly here?

And furthermore, assuming that a place could be found at any other mission station, except Canada, couldn't this same wagon take us the 200 mi. from here to Auguste? If not, we can get a very good wagon here to take us there???

You will surely and with good reason say: The good Br. thinks too far in advance. There will be time for that if things get to that point, etc. Once and for all, since I cannot remain here, I would rather earn my bread anywhere through the work of my hands, if this is necessary, until something else is found for us. I certainly believe that the mission here will or would only be provided with a skilled worker, effective in every respect, through Br. Clauder's marriage. Not everyone has been given the beautiful and certainly blessed interest, as this Br. has, in both internal and external work. This is necessary at this post where the external work is the main thing, at least for now.

Furthermore, we have already mentioned that I experience more proof each day that despite her best intentions my dear wife, who is known to be weakly, is absolutely not the person on or for this post, where there is such a large household with no help, especially for mission work. Thus it is natural that we both feel very pressured. I can [page torn] and my wife as little Mother Gambold. All of this [page torn] gives me hope that that you will join me in realizing that I can never be happy here.

I very sincerely hope that after considering this you will help bring about a change, because I know my fellow Brn. also would like me to be satisfied with my life, and I cannot be so here. Furthermore, your thoughts will accompany my letter to the U.A.C. It is probably not necessary to ask you to keep all of this to yourselves until something has been determined. I hope that even Br. and Sr. Byhan will not hear anything about this, because with the best intentions they would certainly share it with Mother Gambold and Br. Clauder. This could easily and incurably damage the current good relationship and trust which thus far, praise God, has existed between us and which has also eased my situation somewhat. I have also considered the costs this would mean for the Missions Diaconie, but I was led to conclude that our Savior wants his servants to serve with a willing heart, as weak and powerless as they feel, and to be happy with their lives. I cannot do either here.

Now my dear Brn., in the happy hope that you will consider and deliberate about what is best for everyone, please accept our sincere, Brotherly and Sisterly love, Your Br. and Sr., faithfully bound through our Savior's glance,

Caroline and Franz Eder

I really would like to know if this letter will go here in America for postage due. In order to save on postage I will send the Diary with Brn. Vogler and Civily when they come.

Eder

([Margin note:] On March 1. we prayerfully and pleadingly entered the season of Lent, which is so full of blessings for us. Please sincerely greet our dear parents.)

[Springplace (M 407-1) and Oochgeelogy (M 409-1) Diaries.]

*Mar. 15.* [Ooch.] Br. Clauder preached to a small but attentive number of listeners on the words of Mark: 12:34: Thou art not far from the kingdom of God, etc. Every evening recently we have heard wolves howling close to us because of our livestock; our sheep were particularly upset. We also found two of our sheep torn apart by these animals very close to our house, and we couldn't find a number of young lambs.

*Mar. 16.* [Ooch.] Br. and Sr. Eder visited our Br. and Sr. George Hicks and our Sr. Copland, and both really enjoyed it.

*Mar. 16.* [Spg.] Today we finished putting up our new house, without needing the help of the neighborhood. Our schoolchildren helped us faithfully with this. We were grateful to our dear Lord for protecting us from all harm up to that point during this construction. In the evening we had a storm with heavy rains.

*Mar. 22.* [Ooch.] Br. Clauder preached on the words of Matt. 26:38: My soul is exceeding sorrowful, even unto death, etc. There were just a few listeners.

*Sun., Mar. 22.* [Spg.] Today there were only a few Brn. and Srs. in our services because of the cold, stormy, and unfriendly weather which we had today and the whole last week. Everything in our fields and in the gardens is unusually far behind in growth, so that the residents here are saying that they have never experienced such a late spring here.

*Mar. 24.* [Spg.] We began working in our garden for the first time this spring, because the raw weather has not allowed this until now.

[B 61-3: Provinzial Helfer Conferenz, meeting in Salem. Translated by C. Daniel Crews.]

*Thurs., Mar. 26.* In a letter received yesterday of our Br. Franz Eder dated 12 March, he reports that for the first time he has had the grace to baptize a child and that on 22 Feb. they had the first Communion with their little flock to the blessing of their hearts. He also reports, however, that he is ever more convinced that he will not learn the English language there and will never become proficient enough to serve the little congregation there properly. It fills him with sadness, grief, despondency that most of the work falls to Br. Clauder, to whom he cannot be as he should be. He expresses himself very positively that it is impossible for him to remain there even if he has to get his bread with the labor of his own hands, and he asks that the P.H.C. obtain from the

U.A.C. a transfer to any other post — Canada excepted — so that he may be happy in his life as he cannot be there.

This request of our dear Br. Eder came to us totally unexpected and too soon, and places us in great embarrassment, since we learn that Br. Clauder is in good spirits and feels validated and blessed in his service in the school and in other material work in other aspects of the mission. Also the widowed Sr. Gambold is willing and glad to help faithfully in the mission at Oochgelogy in any way she can.

First off, we held it to be our duty as well as we can to advise our Br. Eder, who presumably is very homesick (which evidenced itself here too), to think this step over very carefully and to see that it is too hasty. He should do this before we notify the U.A.C. and forward the letter to Br. Hüffel which he included in his letter to us. We decided that each of us will write him lovingly to encourage him to rely more on the Savior's help and support, since the Brethren Vogler and Zevely are going on the 30th for a friendly visit with our Brn. and Srs. there.

[Springplace (M 407-1) and Oochgeelogy (M 409-1) Diaries.]

*Mar. 26.* [Spg.] We planted the first potatoes.

*Mar. 27.* [Spg.] Mr. Dav. Steiner Tazizi visited us once again this evening. He is now getting his cattle together, which are with our cattle in our area, to drive them to the new place he is establishing.

*Mar. 29.* [Ooch.] The sermon was on the words of Malachi 3:14: Ye have said, It is vain to serve God, etc. There was a pretty good little gathering of attentive listeners. After Br. Clauder's sermon, we read some mission reports, which seemed to interest the listeners.

*Sun., Mar. 29.* [Spg.] Today our Brn. and Srs. came in large numbers to the Sunday services again, because the weather was warm and pleasant again. In the second service was the baptism into Jesus' death of the baby boy born to our Br. and Sr. Richard

Daniel Sanders, approximately three weeks old, with the name John. In the services today our friend Dav. Steiner Tazizi served faithfully as interpreter. We could feel the Savior's dear presence in all of our services today, and the Brn. and Srs. were especially touched. After the last service they were told that 14 days from today is Palm Sunday, and that on this day we would begin reading the Passion story of our dear Lord, and that we would finish this on the Friday after this. On this day we also wanted to solemnly consider the sufferings and death of Jesus. Furthermore, that on Easter Sunday, 3 weeks from today, we would solemnly celebrate the resurrection of our dear Lord. Also that on the last-mentioned day we also have before us the enjoyment of the body and blood of our Jesus in Holy Communion. They were all sincerely happy about this, which one could clearly see in their expressions.

*Mar. 30.* [Spg.] Mr. Dav. Steiner Tazizi today went back home from here. He promised to serve us as interpreter for the coming holy days.

*Mar. 31.* [Spg.] Mr. Worcester from New Echota stopped in at our place on his trip to Tennessee. Recently he received the office of postmaster in Mr. Elijah Hicks's place in New Echota. Through him we learned that our Brn. and Srs. in Ochgeloogy, from whom we have heard nothing for a long time now, are healthy and well. In the evening we had a storm with wind and heavy downpours of rain.

*Apr. 3.* [Spg.] Br. and Sr. Byhan today went to Mr. Dav. McNair on a visit and returned from there on the 4th.

*Apr. 5.* [Ooch.] Br. Clauder preached on the Gospel lesson concerning Jesus' temptation, Matt. 4:1-11. There were only a few listeners. The Cherokees have been very upset and unsettled about their Emigration for several months now. We don't know what we should say about this, and we often feel a little disheartened about or because of this matter. Under the leadership of the single Br. G. H. Clauder, the school is doing well and we are all pleased by the students' attention and progress in learning. We were especially happy when we saw these dear young ones gathered around us in the evening and heard their small voices singing praise to their Creator. No one can deny that God's Spirit has begun His work in some of them. May He also accomplish the salvation of their immortal souls, gloriously and victoriously. That is our sincere desire and prayer for them!

*Sun., Apr. 5.* [Spg.] The Sunday services were held as usual. After these our Indian Brn. and Srs. and schoolchildren sang some hymns in the Indian language, during which the single Indian Br. Solomon was lead singer. Afterward Br. Samuel offered a prayer on his knees in the Indian language. Mrs. Polly Vann, who was also present, told us later that he had offered a sincere prayer and that he especially asked for the strengthening of our faith in Jesus. The way we feel on such occasions, when we see an Indian lying on his knees and praying very fervently to the Savior, and the kind of feeling that prevails throughout, must be experienced. It cannot be described. Everyone then went happily home.

[M 414-4-9: Translated by Julie Tomberlin Weber. Addressed to: Revd. Theodor Shulz, Salem, Stokes County, North Carolina. Postmark: Springplace, C.N., Apr. 9. Free. Gottlieb Byhan, P.M. Received Apr. 22.]

Springplace, Apr. 7, 1829

My dear Br. Shulz,

On Apr. 2 I received your kind letter dated March 17, and I sincerely thank you for this. We were very interested in everything in it and happy to hear it, including answers to my questions about the marriage of our Indian Sr. Anna Johanna, as well as the other news. A note from Br. Shaaf, dated March 23, reached our hands on Apr. 2 after it had been under way for only 10 days, and from this we were very touched to learn about the homegoing of our dear Sr. Reichel on the 22nd [18th]. May the Savior comfort our dear Br. Reichel for his loss. He alone can ease the pain that such a wound causes. Praise God, we are all healthy and well in Spring Place right now, and as far as we know everyone in Ochgeloogy is healthy too.

You will surely have received my letter of March 4th [Feb. 24, postmarked March 5] a long time ago, and we are eagerly awaiting an answer to this. Last Sunday Br. Samuel was here again for services, for the first time since that remarkable Sunday in Feb. He was friendly and seemed to have forgotten what happened, because after our usual services our school children sang and the Indian Brn. and Srs. sang in Indian from a little hymnal with hymns printed in the Indian language, recently published by Revd. Saml. Worcester. During this the single Indian Br. Solomon was the chorister. After the singing, we all fell on our knees and Br. Samuel led a prayer which, as Polly Vann later told us, was exceptionally beautiful. Primarily, she said, he prayed that our faith in the Savior would be strengthened.

It is impossible to describe how we felt seeing an Indian on his knees, singing, and his pouring out his heart with tears before his Savior. You have to witness this and hear it for yourself! I have never seen such quiet and reverence among the Indian Brn. and Srs. as during this prayer. This prayer and this occasion encouraged us anew to continuing carrying out His work with good courage, even when the enemy sometimes threatens to divert hearts from our Lord and tries to cause disturbances in the congregation. We see again that the impression of Jesus' death and sufferings is there in the hearts of the Brn. and Srs., and that they know to whom they belong.

Now we have holy Passion Week and Easter before us, and our hope is surely that hearing about the Savior's suffering unto death will once again awaken in all of our hearts the decision to live only for Him in this world and to completely surrender our hearts to him as payment for His pain. Mr. Tazizi promised he would interpret for us during these holy days, which certainly pleases us, and this will be more of a blessing for the Indian Brn. and Srs. On Easter we are planning to have Holy Communion, during which the boy Alexander Sanders and the married Sr. Hanna will receive the confirmation blessing for their first enjoyment of this. Now may the Savior make this holy day a blessing for all of us.

Brn. John Vogler and Van Zevely will presumably be on the way to visit us. We would be happy if we could find out before they arrive here what day they left Salem and also how they are coming, on horse or by wagon.

For now, be happy with these lines. My time is very limited. We all greet you all most sincerely. Accept a special greeting from your loving Br.,

Gottlieb Byhan

Please greet our Sophia from us.

[Springplace (M 407-1) and Oochgeelogy (M 409-1) Diaries.]

*Apr. 11.* [Ooch.] Today we were inexpressibly happy to welcome Brn. J. Vogler and Wmn. Zivily from Salem, two true followers of Jesus and friends of the mission here. The joy on both sides was so great that we had to let tears speak instead of words. In addition, these dear Brn. delighted us with wonderful letters from all our dear ones in Salem. It was a day of true blessing.

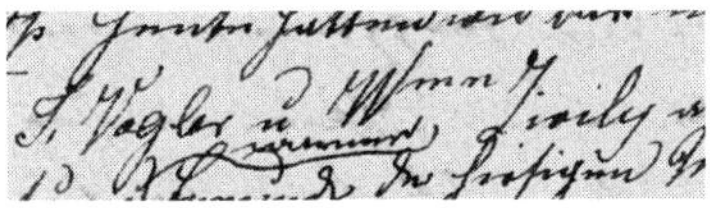

*Apr. 12.* [Ooch.] There was no sermon. Instead we offered a sincere prayer in which our dear Lord blessed us; then for the beginning of the very sacred Passion Week we read two passages about Jesus' story of suffering. This seemed to make a blessed impression on the listeners. Among the few brown listeners present, we rejoiced to have one who seemed to be seriously concerned about the salvation of his immortal soul. We became completely convinced of this in the conversation we had with him afterward. He spoke very sincerely about his sinfulness and the ruin of his heart and about his uneasiness about this, etc. We lovingly directed him to the Savior as the Friend of Sinners, and commended him to the further guidance of the Holy Spirit, as well as we could through an interpreter. We are always as happy as children when we can have even the slightest hope from time to time, when someone is led to consider: What must I do to be saved? etc.

*Sun., Apr. 12.* [Spg.] Palm Sunday. Today most of our Brn. and Srs. came for the services. Today we began reading the Passion story of our dear Lord, with fervent pleas to our dear Lord to bless us anew as we once again hear this, and once again to give us the intention to live only for Him in this world, because He won us so bitterly with His sufferings and death.

[M 411-1-22: Translated by Elizabeth Marx. Addressed to: Revd. Theodor Shulz, Salem, Stokes County, North Carolina. Postmark: New Echota, C.N., Apr. 15, 50. Received May 7.]

My dear Brother Schulz,

[Translator's summary: He reports the joyful and entirely unexpected arrival of the Brn. V. & Z. They are all well with the exception of himself who has had such a severe rheumatism for two weeks that he can hardly sit or stand. The Negro woman has been sold for $300. Please let us have a bill of sale for Mr. Samuel Henry as soon as possible. He is disappointed that his last letter has not been forwarded to the U.A.C. The rest of the letter is a plea for an answer to the request he has made. He writes

that he has no joy in the work, cannot learn the language, and finds himself inadequate.]

Franz and C. Eder

Tekoa, Apr. 12, 1829

[M 411-1-23: Translated by Elizabeth Marx. Addressed to: Revd. Theodore Shulz, Salem, Stokes County, North Carolina. Postmark: Favor of Br. Vogler. Received May 4.]

Tekoa, C.N., Apr. 13, 1829

Dear Brother,

[Translator's summary: The first half of the letter has to do with the sad state of Br. Eder, who is not suited to the work, either by disposition or capability. He has trouble with English and is not able to learn the Cherokee language, and is depressed most of the time. Sr. Eder has no inclination for the work either but does what her strength allows.]

[Translation in full:]

You should have been informed before this that we have sold the worthless Negro woman Cathy, and in fact to Mr. Samuel Henry, who has been supplying this place as well as the Spring Place mission with flour, sugar, etc., for several years, and will continue to do so. The price of $300 was received for her on the following terms: We are in debt to Mr. Henry for the sum of $60 and the Spring Place debts for Br. Byhan are also canceled with her, and for the balance Mr. Henry pledges to supply Spring Place and us with everything which we have been buying from him and for which he received money (when we had it!). The reasons that caused us to sell her were as follows: She couldn't be made to work with requests or with blows. Her constant unavoidable contact with the children was of the greatest harm to the latter. For instance, she instructed and enticed them to all kinds of bad language, to stealing, and to lying, etc. This moved all of us unanimously to press for her early sale. The purchaser, Samuel Henry of Blount County, Tennesse, demands a bill of sale, which we are requesting. If I had a copy of it, that could be handed over to him.

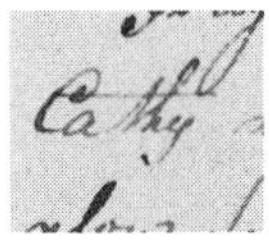

What else concerns the school: At present it is made up of 16 little Cherokee girls who are all very dear to all of us. Most of them are making good progress in learning, even though I am able to fulfill my responsibilities to them only in part. The singing in their language provides all of us joy and encouragement.

Sr. Gambold asks me to report to you the following in reply to your question in regard to the support of her daughter Dorothea; she is completely convinced that her daughter must be helped and in fact from her own interest, until she acquires the necessary ability to maintain herself with the work of her own hands. And so Sr. Gambold requests that you let her daughter have all necessary help.

Dear Br., I am in a special situation in which the Lord is strengthening me very specially and has granted me health, courage, and strength thus far to use my small talents for His glory. Think of us in your prayer that the Lord would grant new love and strength for His work to those whose courage has failed and that He would continue to send faithful laborers into His harvest. In particular I commend myself to your prayers. United with you through Jesus' death, your friend and Brother,

H. G. Clauder

[Springplace (M 407-1) and Oochgeelogy (M 409-1) Diaries.]

*Apr. 13.* [Ooch.] Br. and Sr. Eder arrived at our Br. and Sr. Wm. Abr. Hicks's accompanied by the visiting Br. J. Vogler. Everyone enjoyed the visit.

*Apr. 14.* [Ooch.] Br. Clauder, accompanied by Brn. Wn. Zivily and Vogler, visited Brn. and Srs. and friends who live close to us. This was a great pleasure for both Brn., who made many pleasant acquaintances in our neighborhood.

*Apr. 15.* [Spg.] Mr. Worcester stopped in at our place on his return journey from Tennessee. After he had had breakfast, he went on to New Echota.

*Apr. 16.* [Ooch.] Maundy Thursday. We felt the heart-warming presence of our dear Savior while partaking of His body and bread in Holy Communion. Everyone shed tears of contrition and love. On this occasion one of our Srs. was confirmed and blessed and dedicated in her baptismal covenant. Praise and honor to the Savior for this! It was a day of rich blessing!

*Apr. 16.* [Spg.] With the mail today we received a letter from Br. Eder in Ochgeloogy from which we learned that the Brn. and Srs. there are doing well, except for Br. Eder, who has been suffering from attacks of rheumatism. But when the letter was sent he was recovering. At the same time we also received a letter from Br. John Vogler, dated Ochgeloogy, in which he reports to us that tomorrow or on Great Sabbath he and Br. Van Zevilly will arrive in Spring Place for a visit.

[*Records: N.C.*, 8:3883: Bethabara Diary. Translated by Douglas L. Rights.]

*Apr. 16.* Br. Johannes R. Schmidt, of Salem, recently returned from the Cherokee Mission, held service.

[M 411-1-25: Translated by Elizabeth Marx. Addressed to: The dear Brother Theodor Schulz. Received May 4.]

My dear Brother Schulz!

With somewhat more calm in respect to my condition, I am able to answer your kind letter, which indeed did not have anything encouraging for me. In the first place, I could conclude that you don't sympathize with me, that I am not granted credence nor a hearing, either personally or in any other way. If you had only sent the letters on to Germany for some relief. But I hope to God that you will not contribute your part [to my unhappiness] but will sympathize with me and thus [help] for some relief, which consists in this: that a change take place and that soon. I can assure you, beloved Brethren, that all the feelings with which I was overwhelmed in Salem, and which I often expressed before you with the bitterest tears — I call on God the righteous to be my witness — through which I begged you for a turning away, which could only have taken place if I had not had to come here after I had seen the whole situation somewhat more closely and had learned to know it in quite another light, and therefore all my joy fell away. In reality all our suffering here is no longer a golden shining principle; now it goes on a much higher level daily, nay hourly, so that I simply have to succumb. Who feels the pressure with us? At least up to now no feeling heart: But God the Almighty, He surely still counts our tears and gathers them in His little pitcher.

Believe me, dear Brethren, that I am not writing so much and so urgently [for myself]. No, it is for the sake of the cause, which clearly suffers very much under [this] and from every point of view, under which I — the Lord knows it — since I cannot be so energetic as I should like, I suffer twice as much and finally in an irreparable way. And in the end, I am afraid our dear Brother Clauder, if he shall continue in such circumstances, he will also lose all courage, and so this Mission will lose a Brother [the like of] whom it will — I will not say will never find again, for the Lord has and knows His servants — but according to human insight, it will not find such a one again.

Furthermore, what I have already mentioned to you before: Sr. Gambold and my wife at her side, both will have to succumb in the end. As has already been said, as I experience more every day, that my dear wife, much as she would like, because of her frailty and experience is not at all suited for this position any more than I am. Imagine, every day to cook for 22-24 people, also to take care of the washing and the school. She finally has to succumb with Sr. Gambold, and to what troubles can this not lead as time goes on. We are human beings. How must I feel in view of that — put yourselves in my place. To have to see all that all of us suffer for one and so we feel ourselves pressured twice. For that reason, dear Brethren, do what you can so that a change takes place. It is impossible that I remain here longer than to the late fall; should I use up the little that I still have with you? Should it [last] until some little spot is found for me in any of our mission stations?

But enough of that, now just the request: Dear Brethren, please do what you can, not alone for me personally but for the sake of the cause, which as already said, suffers under it. With every day I experience more and more that this place is not for me, chiefly because of the language, where there is no time or opportunity to [learn it].

Yesterday, the 16th, with some Brn. and Srs. and the visiting Brethren we celebrated a very blessed Holy Communion at which Sr. Crutchfield was confirmed.

The Negro woman was sold on March 14th to Mr. Samuel Henry in Tennessee for $300, for which we request that you send us the bill of sale. I could hardly continue with her. I steered against it [resisted the sale] as long as I possibly could, but finally had to give in because of the many unpleasant things which happened for all of us in every way.

I really don't know whether I included the place, day, and year of my birth. At all events I will do again what was already done for Br. Benade in Salem. In fact, I am the sixth child of my now departed parents. They were Mathias Eder and my mother Theresa Eder m.n. Hadinger. I was born on Apr. 26, ~~182~~ 1798, in Wolfsegg near Linz in Austria.

The baptism of J. Fiels was scheduled for the first Sunday after Easter, but since a relative of his was found who was concerned about the salvation of his immortal soul, he requested to wait until that one should be baptized also, although the former had visited us for the first time just the Sunday before Easter. We could not do otherwise than to concede to this extraordinary and quite unexpected request. We do not — at least I don't — know what to think of this strange person who has been a candidate for such a long time and has put himself back so long through his own indifference, and when the question was finally put [to the Lot] and the Savior allowed it, he put it off again. We cannot now do [otherwise] — if it should take as long as with the latter — than to wait until Fiels himself asks about it again. At least I have no joy in pressing baptism on him, when he has no longing for it.

I must ask my dear Brethren for forgiveness for my bad and disjointed writing. For just as my spirit is distraught and depressed, thus also my letters. Here I have lost courage for everything. I thank dear Br. Schaaf once again for his kind letter with the promise to answer him next; no matter how gladly I would do it, I have countless letters with the Brethren.

In addition to the most cordial greetings, I commend myself to your prayer and intercession before the Throne of Grace, as your very much depressed Brother,

Franz Eder

Tekoa, Apr. 17, 1829. [In Salem, Br. Schulz has penciled in: Tekoa?]

[Springplace (M 407-1) and Oochgeelogy (M 409-1) Diaries.]

*Apr. 17.* [Ooch.] We joined with a small gathering of attentive listeners for the reading of the story for today, and in spirit we were with our dying Redeemer at Golgotha. We brought Him our humble gratitude for the inexpressibly great work of redemption which He, our loving Lord and Savior, took on and so gloriously carried out for our eternal redemption. During both services a loving feeling of God's presence prevailed. Our Br. Gorge Hicks interpreted what was read into Cherokee.

In the evening we held our evening devotion as usual and commended the dear Brn. J. Vogler and Wn. Zivily, who wanted to set out from here to Spring Place the next morning, to the merciful protection and guidance of the Lord on their long and dangerous journey. We commend ourselves to the faithful intercession of all our Brn. and Srs. and friends, your

Br. and Sr. Franz Eder
the Single Br. H. Gottl. Clauder
the widowed Sr. A. M. Gambold

*Apr. 17.* [Spg.] Good Friday. All of our Brn. and Srs. came to listen to the story of Jesus' sufferings. We were sorry that our interpreter Tazizi had not yet come as he had promised, but he arrived toward evening. Circumstances had prevented him from coming earlier. Despite this, however, we could clearly tell that the consideration of the Savior's sufferings and death made a blessed impression on the hearts of the Brethren and Sisters because everyone seemed to be very touched and moved.

*Apr. 18.* [Spg.] Great Sabbath. In the afternoon we had the joy of welcoming Brn. John Vogler and Van Zevely from Salem among us for a visit. They had stayed with our Brn. and Srs. in Ochgeloogy since the 11th of this month and had celebrated the blessed Passion Week with our Brn. and Srs. there.

*Sun., Apr. 19.* [Ooch.] The number of visitors today was far too small, so we read the story of Jesus' resurrection instead of having a sermon. Our Br. Gorge Hicks interpreted this into Cherokee as he had done for the school children in recent days.

*Apr. 19.* [Spg.] Easter Sunday. Since it rained very heavily this morning, we could not pray the Easter Litany on God's Acre as we are accustomed to doing. Nonetheless, we gathered in our Saal to pray it. Afterward was the sermon. After this, in the third service, was the baptism into Jesus' death of the baby girl born to our Br. and Sr. John Jacob, with the name Elisabeth. Afterward we had the most blessed enjoyment of the body and blood of Jesus in Holy Communion. The Indian Sr. Hannah joined us in her first enjoyment of Holy Communion, following her confirmation in her baptismal covenant. The Savior could be felt in our midst. The many tears which were shed often testified to this. Afterward Brn. Zevely and Vogler gave another address and admonition to the Indian Brethren and Sisters, in which they encouraged the Brn. and Srs. to remain with the Savior and to set a good example for their countrymen in word as well as in deed, showing how they have sought and found grace in the Savior so that many more from their Nation might also turn to the Savior and believe in him. This made a sweet impression on the Brn. and Srs.

[Inserted from the April 30 entry of the Springplace Diary:]

The following belongs to April 19. Whether it should be included in its rightful place I will leave up to the Brn. in Salem.

Yet one troublesome circumstance must be mentioned here which wants to dampen our joy and our blessedness. The married communicant Br. Clement Vann apparently drank too much brandy wine this morning, as

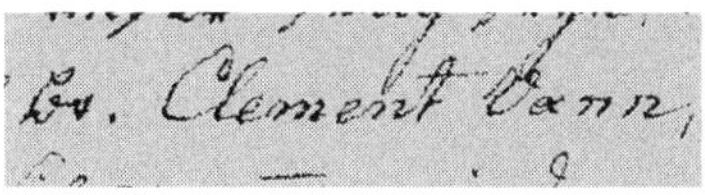
Br. Clement Vann,

he was causing disturbances already in the first service and caused offense during the sermon when he began talking loudly about things which one does not like to discuss with Brn. and Srs. on Sundays outside of the church, much less in the church, during worship service. We were worried about whether we should let him go to Holy Communion under these circumstances. We were of the opinion that if he did not change his behavior, we would turn him away this time, to prevent more offense and annoyance. However, we were happy when we saw that he did not seem to notice when the Brn. and Srs. gathered for the enjoyment of Holy Communion. He sat in the yard on the timber lying there. We let him sit undisturbed thus, and we were happy to be spared the unpleasantness of turning him away. In the state he was in, we would have had no joy in letting him in, because without a doubt he would have caused more disturbances. He also talked between the services about nothing but horse racing, etc. Among other things he insisted that the roof of the new house is too steep.

[Br. Byhan's April 30 addition to April 19 ends.]

*Apr. 20.* [Spg.] Our Indian Br. Israel was not here yesterday and had killed a large deer last week. Since he had heard that a couple of Brn. from Salem were visiting in Spring Place, he set out late yesterday evening on the way to our place with a couple of cuts of venison. He arrived with them here at midnight and slept in our barn until he could give them to us this morning. We gave him powder for these.

Since we had not been able to do anything on our new house for a long time, we were happy that two carpenters who came a couple of days ago began working on it today, so hopefully we will be able to move into it before next winter.

[M 414-4-10: Translated by Julie Tomberlin Weber. Addressed to: Revd. Theodor Shulz, Salem, Stokes County, North Carolina. Postmark: Favored by Mr. John Vogler. Received May 4.]

Springplace, Apr. 21, 1829

My dearly beloved Br. Shulz,

First I want to inform you that we joyfully welcomed our dear Brn. John Vogler and Van Zevely to Spring Place about 3 in the afternoon on Great Sabbath. They can tell you personally about their stay here and how they liked it. Their visit was a great encouragement for us to continue working and acquainting the heathen with the Redeemer of our sins and to help extend His kingdom. Our Easter festal days were blessed, and we hope that the word of Jesus' suffering left a deep impression in the hearts of listeners. Mr. Tazizi was our interpreter at Easter. On Easter we enjoyed Jesus' body and blood in Holy Communion. The married Sr. Hannah joined us in partaking for the first time after the preceding confirmation. Br. Vogler will be able to tell you about everything else that happened here.

Please do not think badly of me for keeping my letter brief this time, because my time is really short. I have hired 2 carpenters to help finish our house. As I have already informed you, I have to pay one of them $1.50 a day, and the other, his brother who is also a mason, $1, so that I have to pay two dollars and a half every day. I know you will say that is really too much, but it is impossible to find inexpensive workers or carpenters here in this country. I spent a long time looking for reasonable ones, but in vain. Some even asked me for $2-2½ per day. This man I have now has worked a lot for the missionaries in Brainerd, Wills Valley, Carmel, etc., where he received the same wages. He began working here yesterday and although one cannot really say anything yet, it seems he is a diligent man and the work flows from his hand. His brother is expected any day.

Concerning the miserable Smidt affair, not much of significance has happened since my letter to you dated March 5, at least in Spring Place. The Brn. and Srs. seem to be content; only Br. Samuel could not get over the misunderstandings, because he has been to Spring Place only once since the beginning of March or the end of Feb. I believe he would be satisfied if we could discuss the entire matter with him once, through a good interpreter. From Ochgeloogy I hear that the Brn. and Srs. there want to forget the matter completely and, as Br. W. Abr. Hicks said, to <u>bury</u> it.

We still need to do this with our Br. Samuel, and we hope that he will allow himself to be brought on the right track, with God's help.

I received your dear letter of March 23 on April 9, and dear Br. Shaaf's 2 notes of March 30 and Apr. 2 on Apr. 16th. Please tell Br. Shaaf thank you very much for <u>everything</u>. We received everything in your kind letter of March 27th, which I received through Brn. Vogler and Zevely, along with the packages, money, *Nachrichten*, calenders, etc., sent earlier. We cannot adequately express our gratitude that we have been lucky enough that everything sent to us has arrived as it should; some time ago $200, which was mailed in my Post Office, was lost between Spring Place and Nashville and never reached the intended destination. The money belonged to the contractor for the mail route between Spring Place and Athens, Ga. I am very obliged for the increase in my account these 2 kind letters made.

Br. John Vogler had some money with him and did not think he would need it on his return journey, so I asked him to leave some of it for me since money always has to be sent to me and this is somewhat risky, and I told him that you would repay him for this in Salem. He was very willing to leave me $100, say, One Hundred Dollars, so please pay Br. John Vogler $100 in Salem. I hope you approve of this? The money he paid me was $80 United States notes and $20 South Carolina notes.

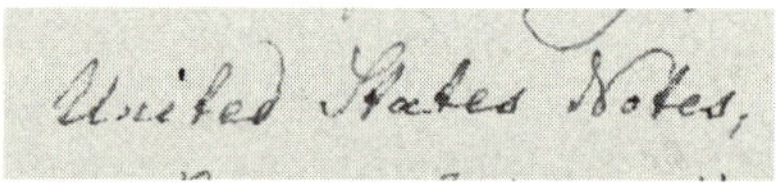


Br. J. Vogler will be able to give you detailed news in person about my construction and how far I have gotten with this.

Enclosed I also send you the remaining written *Nachrichten* and 3 months of the Spring Place Diary from the beginning of July until the end of Sept. 1828. More will follow with the next opportunity. Be patient with me.

With the most sincere greetings from all of us, I remain your faithfully obliged Br.,

Gottlieb Byhan

[In English:] This is to Certify that I received of Mr. John Vogler $100 for the Use of the Mission at Springplace, which Sum is to be paid him again by Revd. Theodore Shulz at Salem.

Gottlieb Byhan

Springplace, C.N., Apr. 22, 1829

[Springplace (M 407-1) and Oochgeelogy (M 409-1) Diaries.]

*Apr. 23.* [Spg. Inserted from the April 30 entry.] After a sincere farewell from our dear visitors, Br. Van Zevely and John Vogler, these two Brn. began their return journey to Salem after a very happy visit in Ochgoloogy and Spring Place, accompanied by our most sincere wishes for blessings. In the afternoon we had a strong storm with unusually strong downpours of rain, which washed out much of the corn we had planted and washed it away and did much damage otherwise. The streams then rose to a great height, which made us worry about our dear travelers since they will have to cross two dangerous streams tomorrow, the Conaussaga and Maoi.

*Apr. 23.* [Ooch.] This morning our friend and neighbor Mr. Copland came and told us that he had just shot a wolf about ¾ of a mile from our house. Br. Clauder immediately went with him to the place and brought it back here. It was probably young, but still quite large. We were very happy to have killed at least one of these dangerous animals; they have made the entire area unsafe for some time now.

*Sun. Apr. 26.* [Spg.] Today only a few Brn. and Srs. were present in our services. Last night it was so cold here that most of our fruit froze, and it did much damage to the potatoes, beans, and such in the gardens. All the corn, which had already come up, also froze completely.

*Sun., Apr. 26.* [Ooch.] The sermon was on the words of John 20:19, Peace be with you. Only a few listeners were here, but they seemed to be very attentive. Last night we had a heavy frost which was very bad for our garden and orchard, especially for the peaches. Br. Clauder has been visiting at Springplace.

*Sun., May 3.* [Ooch.] There was a small number of listeners present. Instead of having a sermon we read them a couple of chapters from St. Paul's letter to the Romans and then a short tract. Today Br. William Abraham Hicks told us very sadly that three more Cherokee families emigrated just yesterday and that many more would follow soon; this always upsets him.

*Apr. 29.* [Spg.] We received a pleasant visit from Br. H. G. Clauder from Ochgeloogy. The Brn. and Srs. were all well, except for Br. Eder, who was not yet recovered. On this occasion we should add that we have decided that the mission place in Ochgeloogy should no longer be called Ochgeloogy but in the future

Tekoah. This is partly because the area there is called Ochgeloogy and it has sometimes happened that letters sent to our Brn. and Srs. there have gone all over the area before they reached our Brn. and Srs.

*Apr. 30.* [Spg.] Br. G. Clauder went back to Tekoa today.

We commend ourselves most fervently to the congregation for their remembrance and prayer before our dear Lord,

Gottl. and Doroth. Byhan.

[Br. Byhan wrote his addition to April 19 and the April 23 entry here.]

*Sun., May 3.* [Spg.] After our usual Sunday services, Br. Samuel gave a talk to the Brn. and Srs. in which he advised them to remain with the Savior and not to become lukewarm in their love for Him and among themselves, etc. Afterward he had his son Flea interpret for us what he had said to the Brn. and Srs. Some misunderstandings which have been prevalent among our Brn. and Srs. for some time were thoroughly put aside today. We promised each other we would forget everything and forgive each other and love each other sincerely as members of one body, and would prove ourselves children of God and show that we have sought and found the forgiveness of our sins with the Savior. God's peace could be felt powerfully in our midst during this conversation. All the Brn. and Srs. then went home very happily. On this occasion we could clearly see that our Indian Brn. and Srs. have received a deep impression of Jesus' death and sufferings in their hearts, and that through the work of the Holy Spirit they are convinced that he also shed his blood for them and that they also, through faith in Him, can be made righteous and saved. Sr. Nancy Becker also got a fever today after she had been feeling sickly for several days. Since then all the household work, of which there is currently a lot in all respects, falls completely on Sr. Byhan and her daughter Rachel, so that sometimes they hardly see how to get through it and take care of it. In addition there is the fact that the Negro woman Pleasant went to visit her son Michael in Ochgeloogy, although we really have little or almost no help in her anymore, and when she is not home we can live in more peace and quiet.

[M 414-4-11: Translated by Julie Tomberlin Weber. Addressed to: Revd. Theodor Shulz, Salem, Stokes County, North Carolina. Postmark: Springplace, C.N., May 3. Free. Gottlieb Byhan, P.M. Received May 25. Handwriting is Gottlieb Byhan's.]

Springplace, May 3, 1829

My dear Br. Shulz,

Since the post from Georgia arrives here on Sunday now, according to a new arrangement, and I have a quarter of an hour before it comes and the services begin, I will write you a few more lines to tell you how we are doing. When this reaches you, Brn. J. Vogler and v. Zevely will probably already have given you the report about their visit in Indian country.

Since the Brn. left us, our Nancy Becker has had a fever. Today she has one again. Since it is still so early in the year we are afraid that she will have it for a long time. We will hope for the best, though, that she soon overcomes it. Otherwise, I broke my glasses since the Brn. left. I would like to ask you to buy me another pair from Br. Vogler and send them to me with Mr. John Ridge. Br. Vogler knows what kind fit me. My eyes are not as good as they were when I left Salem, because they suffered a good deal last winter. Otherwise, Mother would like to have a couple of thimbles for children. Please send some that are closed on one end. Also, some blue thread. Mr. Ridge will be happy to bring all this along for us.

Last week we had a pleasant visit from Br. Clauder. They were all well in Tekoah, except that Br. Eder was suffering from rheumatism. The Brn. and Srs. in Ochgeloogy decided not to call the mission site there Ochgeloogy anymore, but rather Tekoah, because the entire area around there is called Ochgoloogy. Brn. Eder and Clauder will probably already have reported this to you.

Your kind letter of March 31 reached me on Apr. 30th. We will do what we can about the Tracts. Mr. Boudinott is currently not home. However, I will have an appropriate talk with him as soon as he returns home, and I will send you a report about this. The post has just arrived so I must close.

We remain your loving Br. and Sr.,

Gottlieb and Dorothea Byhan

N.B. Please extend our best greetings to our Sophia. Most of our fruit has frozen.

[B 61-3: Provinzial Helfer Conferenz, meeting in Salem.]

*Tues., May 5.* Yesterday our Brn. John Vogler and Vanem. Zevely returned safe and sound from their visit to the Cherokee Land. They were very happy for the grace and blessing which prevails among our brown members in Springplace and Oochgelogy. They left all our dear Brn. and Srs. in good health, and assured us that they had seen and felt more than they expected, and praised the Brn. and Srs. who were deemed worthy to serve in this work of God.

They were made very happy that Br. Eder has entered into the English language above their expectations when they attended a confirmation and Holy Communion which Br. Eder conducted. They brought us letters from our dear Brn. and Srs., and from Br. Eder, who, however, remains firm in his decision and appears to be discouraged (as Br. Clauder writes too). He maintains that he cannot stay there longer than the end of this year, and so we are forced to lay his request before the U.A.C. and forward his letter to Br. Hüffel.

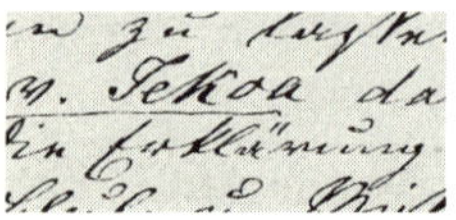


Since the letters of our Brethren were dated <u>Tekoa</u>, we received from Br. Vogler the explanation that, because another school and mission has been established by the Methodists on Oochgelogy Creek the Brn. Eder and Clauder have given their mission post this name to prevent confusion in correspondence. They have done this without consultation with us, and for this they will be corrected.

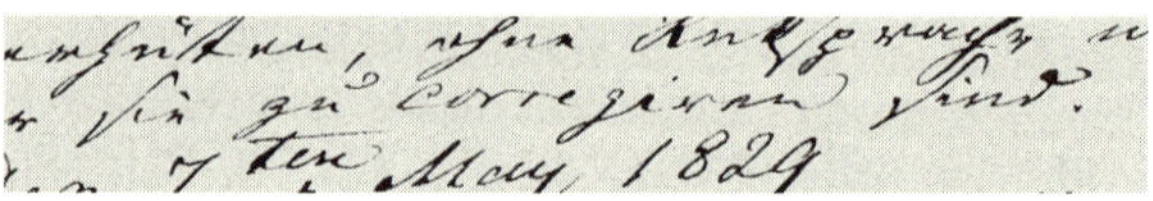

# *The Jurnel of ower Trip to Springplace & Tekoa*[1]

[M 407-9: Transcribed by Grace S. Robinson. Handwriting is John Vogler's.]

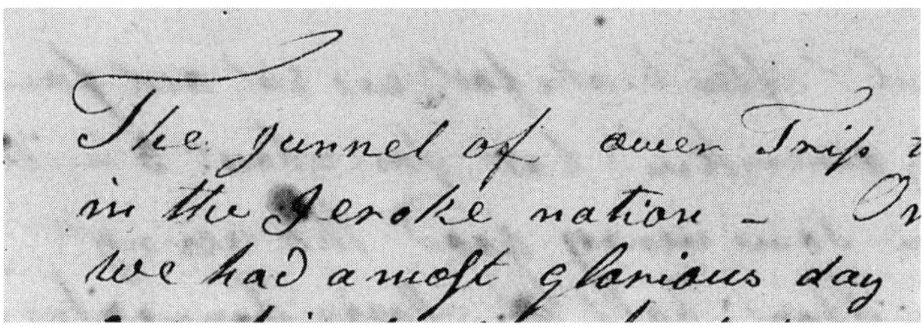
The Jurnel of ower Trip
in the Jeroke nation –
we had a most glorious day

The Jurnel of ower Trip to Springplace & Tekoa in the Jeroke nation

[That is how Br. John Vogler began the diary of his and Br. Vaniman Zevely's journey from Salem to Springplace in 1829. The travel portions of the diary, March 30-Apr. 11 and Apr. 23-May 4, are published in *Records: N.C.*, 8:3902-9. The portion omitted in *Records: N.C.*, their visit in the Cherokee Nation, Apr. 12-23, is published here. Br. Vogler's completely phonetic style of spelling has been modified.]

[*Sun., Apr. 12.*] . . .Br. Clauder opened meeting with a short address & prayer & commenced reading the history of the last days of our blessed Lord & Saviour. Br. Zevely was asked & kept

---

1 Penciled in: Uchgologe.

the second meeting. Afterward Br. Clauder spoke much with an Indian who is concerned about the salvation of his soul & wishes to be baptized. The nature of the spiritual & visible baptism was explained to him, & he [was] directed to the Saviour who turns not away any truly penitent sinner who pleads for pardon. It appeared to give much pleasure to our Indian Brothers & Sisters to hear of 4 or 5 more who are also under conviction, & they have hopes that they will soon see them come in & join their little flock. This is all in puplick, & you may now & then see the Indian take hold of part of his garment & wipe off his tears. This was a find day for us, & we could not have had a faint idea of what was yet in store for us.

Monday, Tuesday & Wednesday [*Apr. 13-15.*] was spent in visiting Newtown & this neighborhood & found many dear & gentle people. On Wednesday my beast was lame on account of the abuse it had received from my friends during the night, which compelled me to stay at home. And well enough it was, for this gave an opportunity to repair Brn. Eder's & Clauder's watches. Brn. Clauder & Zevely continued their visits in company with

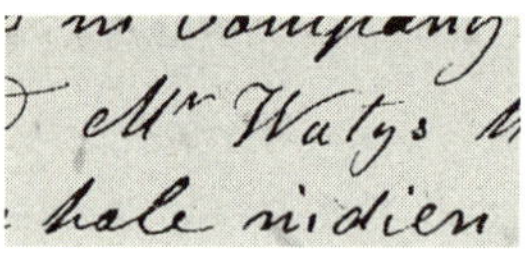
in company
Mr Watys
hole indien

Br. Wm. Hix. This day they visited Mr. Waty's, the parents of our known Budenott, who is a whole Indian & an as intelligent & gentle a man as can be found, no nation excepted. His lady is white & very fair. These are members of the Presbyterian Church & live in the greatest harmony with the Reverend Mr. Wuster & family. These are also dear people, have quite fine 2 story buildings here at Newtown, a fine printing establishment, & this bids fair to becme a large town in time, a large & boatable stream running close by & a fine level country.

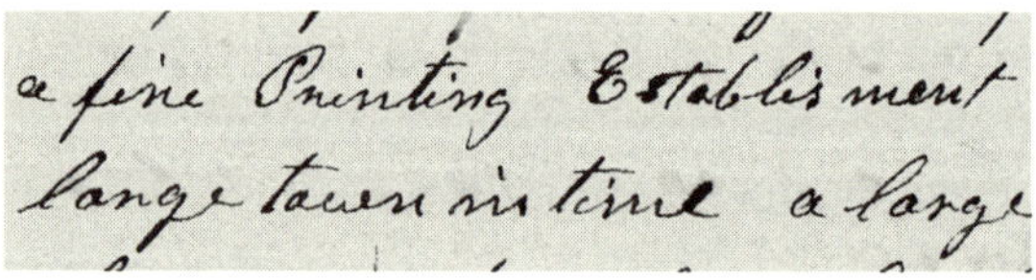
a fine Printing Establisment
large town in time a large

Thursday, [*Apr.*] *16.* According to invitation the communicants came in, eight in number. So there was 14 of us who after 2 more meetings besides a confirmation drew nigh to the Lord's Table & partook of the Lord's Supper. This was a day never to be forgotten by us. The divine presence & the love which seemed to bind us together with our dear red Brothers & Sisters would let us not separate until toward evening. Br. Eder, who kept this meeting in the English language, immediately returned, & here we were seated in a group. Tears covered the cheeks of white & brown, & I trust you will pardon me if I tell you I had to give vent to my feelings in speaking to all, by the way of encouragement. After a while, one after the other silently moved downstairs, & there we all were seated in the same way, wiping tears with what was most convenient. Br. Zevely could no longer keep in, spoke very appropriate, & thus we passed this glorious day, & parted toward evening. One of these old Sisters is a great grandmother, about 80 years of age, came 8 miles on foot, & her daughter the mother of Eleven Children, with her daughter[1] came ten miles carrying her small child, & they were this glorious day richly rewarded for their walk. They all went off into the neighborhood, & after supper 4 of these dear Souls came in again not satisfied yet. Br. Clauder soon had his school seated, & he at the head of the table with his violin sung hymns in the Indian language, &

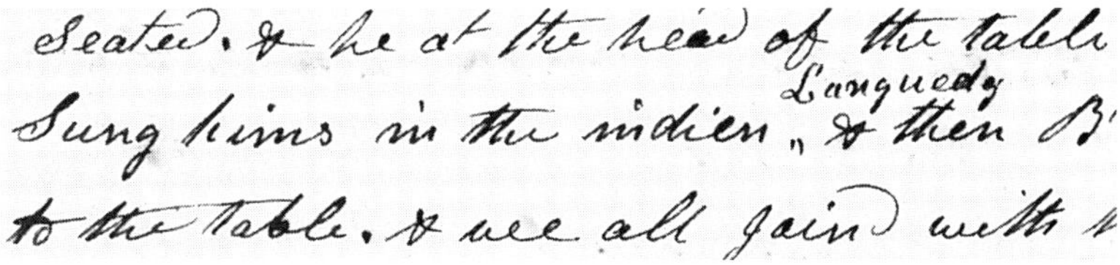
Seated. & he at the head of the table
Sung hims in the indien Languedg " & then B'
to the table. & wee all jain with &

then Br. Zevely was asked to the table, & we all joined with them in the English & closed this glorious day with fervent prayer, as we did all while we were here (tho' once not in publick).

Good Friday [*Apr. 17*] was another day which the Lord had made for enjoyment. About 50 white, brown, & black came in to meeting. We had also some Methodist friends who had real enjoyment with us.

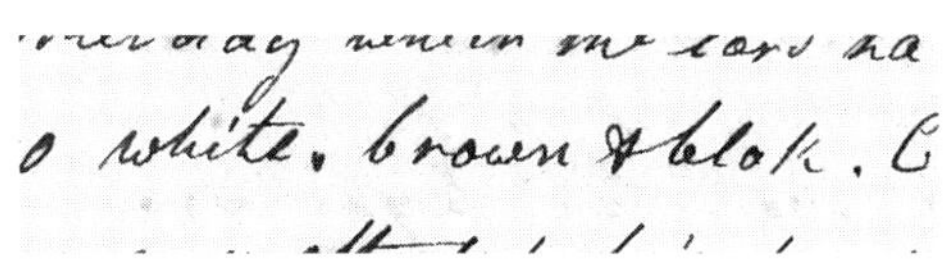
o white, brown & blok. C

But now came on the parting with these friends, & it was a

[1] Old Sr. Hannah, her daughter Sr. Lydia (Zauejuka) Chisholm, and granddaughter Sr. Caharina Maria (Caty) Gann, mother of 11 children.

parting with tears on both sides, some of them asking us to continue to pray for them, we admonishing them to be faithful & press forward & take others by the hand and also lead them to the Saviour, & in heaven we had hopes to meet again, never, never more to part.

This evening Br. Clauder recommended us this great work & themselves that laboured in it to the further protection of the great Head of the Church, who so kindly condescended to be with us in such a special manor in these past days.

Saturday [*Apr. 18*] after breakfast we parted with our dear friends here at Tekoa. Hardly was an eye without tears, even of our Indian girls. Mounted our horses away we went, richly rewarded for our four hundred miles ride, passed on cheerfully & and in passing through Newtown we again spoke with friend Budenot & Wuster about the translation & printing of some tracts in the Chereke language. Crossed Kusa River, a fine stream, passed through very muddy roads, particularly at the Holly Creek, the worst mud I ever seen. And in the afternoon we had the pleasure to meet Br. Byhan coming to meet us.

After the welcome I asked him to ride, & I walked on to Springplace where everything was prepared to receive us. And we were joyfully received by all & felt ourselves happy in their midst &

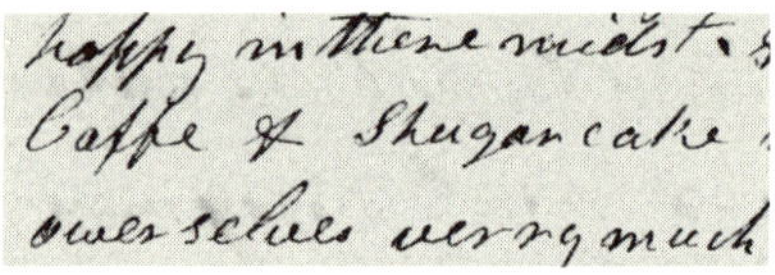


quite like at home. An excellent coffee & sugar cake was soon placed before us. And we enjoyed ourselves very much with this dear old pair & with all around them. Soon after us arrived old Sr. McNair with part of her family for the Easter festival.

Next day [*Sun., Apr. 19, Easter*] it rained very brisk this morning so that Br. & Sr. Byhan feared that few would come in to meeting, but about 50 gathered in meeting, were called by ringing of the bell, & we all attended, white, brown, & black. Br. Byhan preached a sermon which was interpreted by David Steiner, formerly called Dawtsetse, after which we attended a confirmation & a baptism & then again partook of the Lord's Supper with these dear people. Here also, like at Tekoa, was the divine Spirit manifested amongst us, & we had great enjoyment.

After these meetings Br. Byhan rung the bell again & gave Br. Zevely & myself an opportunity to speak with this congregation, which we cheerfully did, & afterward parted with many who were in tears. These were times which will ever be dear in our memory.

This dear Springplace will, after the large house which is now building is finished, be a beautiful little square, surrounded with many excellent fruit trees, & as I told Br. Byhan after, all this feel[s] beauty like a paradise, & at present all carried on very nice. Here is peace & plenty, combined with frugality. And our prayer is that the Lord may strengthen these good old people to continue in this station where they bear their burden with contentment.

On Monday [*Apr. 20*] morning when I went out to the barn an Indian [Br. Israel] got up out of the straw, showed me his venison hams, tho' we could not understand one another. After David Steiner came out he told us that he had understood last night by some who came home from meeting that some of Br. Byhan's friends were at Springplace on a visit. He took his venison hams, which he had just killed that afternoon, rode 10 miles that night, and crossed a river near shining [sunrise] to bring them to Br. Byhan's to treat their friends with fresh venison. I wished to shoot with him. He signified that powder was scarce, & he got some for his hams, & we added some more to it, & he left us after breakfast well pleased.

One of these days that we stayed here we walked with N. Byhan & the Indian boys about 3 miles & went into a cave & came home very tired. The last evening we were here we had a fine evening meeting.

# *1829, part 3*

[*Records: N.C.*, 8:3870-71: Salem Diary. Translated by Douglas L. Rights.]

*May 4.* The Brethren John Vogler and Zevely returned from their visit to Springplace and Oochgeelogy. They brought good reports of the progress of the work in both these Indian congregations.

[M 411-1-24: Translated by Elizabeth Marx. Addressed to: Revd. Theodor Shulz, Salem, Stokes County, North Carolina. Postmark: Favored by Mrs. Ridge. Received May 17.]

Tekoa, May 3, 1829

My dear Brother Schulz!

Just now we learned through our Br. Wm. A. Hicks that this evening he is expecting at his house Maj. Ridge and his wife who are on the point of getting their daughter from Salem, with which we again have an opportunity to greet you most cordially with a few lines, and to thank in particular for your kind letter as well as for the forwarding of the [letter] from our dear Br. G. Hüffel, which I received to my great joy this last Friday, the 1st of this month. When you receive this letter, the two Brn. will probably, God willing, have arrived safe and sound among their own, and thus you will not only have received the letters but also have heard many things.

Our condition since the Brn. left, except for Br. Clauder, is not anything extra. For some time already Mother Gambold has been complaining about headache and weakness, etc., especially in the morning. Whether the incidents are more frequent in the spring than in other seasons of the year I do not know. At all events, I believe that she must begin gradually to feel that her youth — or her best years — are gone. I would not wish that her children, in order not to disturb her unnecessarily, might sense something of that. My dear wife also complains frequently, especially about weakness which I attribute to the great exertion, in view of her particular frailty and her unfamiliarity [with conditions here]. My rheumatic pain has now moved into the feet, so that I sometimes am hardly in condition to walk. Br. Clauder, who is always very active and takes care of the school in particular with great concern and faithfulness, was in Springplace this past week for several days to visit Br. and Sr. Byhan.

The number of children is still the same. During this past winter, which was so notably cold, not only I but several others, including also the two visiting Brn., felt the urgency and need that a fireplace should be built in the bedroom, the only place of refuge which we especially have during the winter. Since this would entail an expense, according to our calculation of about $60-70, we wanted to hear first your concurrence and get your permission before we do anything in the matter. I personally do not insist on it at all, since we hope to God that hopefully we shall no longer be here the next winter! But we will gladly yield and let it happen so that others may have it to enjoy. And so we ask you to share your opinion with us quickly, so we can begin with it as soon as possible, because everything goes exceedingly slow here and is also coupled with many difficulties, because before it takes place or is completed autumn will probably be here.

There is nothing at all to be reported about the mission. I have no knowledge at all about the farm, what it really is. I do know this much, that the corn has been almost all planted, the oats have come up and are growing very nicely. We have 8 fine calves running around in the yard. The wolves have done a lot of damage to our sheep and young pigs. During the last 14 days through the wolves we have lost 10 young pigs which we had in the pen. Never before were these monsters supposed to have been as bad as they have been this year. About a week ago, our neighbor Mr. Copland shot a wolf about ¾ mile from our house. On Apr. 25 and 26 we had such severe frost here during the night that very little fruit has been left; at least the peaches seem all to have frozen. What a pity!

If Dr. Kühln could send me something for my rheumatism with this opportunity, I would be very grateful. I should be happy to know what you might have said about the sale of the Negro woman. I sincerely hope and trust that you will have forwarded my letter to Europe. You will conclude from this that I have not been able to say "yea and amen" to your letters, which are in other respects so loving and Brotherly. And I shall never be able to do it!

As we hear here, the financial situation of Maj. Ridge is supposed to be very uncertain, so it will not go well with his paying Br. Reichel. And so for their reassurance and ours, Br. Wm. A. Hicks wrote to Br. Reichel in this matter, namely that Ridge would pay the balance of the account, which will probably be somewhat large, gradually to us, and it could then be canceled by you with Br. Reichel. Nevertheless, this mission is not guaranteeing it with Br. Reichel but will only transfer whatever we receive from him through you to Br. Reichel.

In sincere love you are greeted by all of us and in particular by your faithful Brother and Sister,

F. Eder

Br. Wm. A. Hicks tells us today to his sorrow that yesterday again three Cherokee families emigrated and more will soon follow these.

[M 419-B-7a: Transcribed by Richard W. Starbuck. Addressed to: Revd. Theodore Shulz, Salem, North Carolina. Postmark: New Echota, Ga., May 6, single 25. Received June 4.]

Tekoah, May 5, 1829

Beloved Br.,

Annexed you will receive an account of receipts and expenditures in and from our Treasury for the two quarters expiring this day. I have endeavoured to render the statement comprehensive and hope you will find it so. In consequences of the debts due from this establishment to sundry individuals, some of which have been paid in full, the expenditures have amounted to a larger sum than otherwise would have been the case. Br. Alexander Copeland, who laboured here so faithfully for two years, still remains our chief and most patient creditor. Besides the ballance of $189 due him for labour, he assumed and has actually paid the debt of $100 due to Doct. Fore for medical assistance on Father Gambold, so that the whole amount due to A. Copeland was $289, toward which you will perceive from the annexed account he has received $165, leaving a balance of $124 still due him. Our present hireling, Mr. Gann, has likewise been paid to April, and it is our desire to pay punctually every person employed by us monthly or the moment the work has been rendered, if in our power, in order to avoid large debts for the future.

Last week two of our scholars eloped and returned home, a circumstance not to be regretted, as they were bad children and unwilling to submit to the rules. Since then their places have been filled by two new scholars. One of them is a grandchild of Sr. McNair. The number of children under our care at present amounts to 16, as many as we can under present circumstances attend to.

We are quite encompassed by labour in the farm, which compels us to employ another hireling for a few months, and thus with our own individual assistance we hope to get through. We are all in perfect health, which is one among the innumerable subjects of our highest praises to our blessed Savior.

The emigration of the Cherokees still continues, though slowly. Last Saturday three families passed through the neighborhood on their way to the region beyond the Mississippi. The subject is high in agitation among the Indians, and the Lord only knows what the final result will be. I am certain that more than a thousand eyes are watching the conduct of Br. Wm. Hicks with regard to emigration. He is one of the principal props to the tottering Nation, and if he gives way (which, however, is not to be feared) I do not know what can sustain the Nation here.

That the Lord may grant him and us wisdom, patience, and perseverance in these trying times, this is our fervent and constant prayer. And to your further prayers and intercessions we all consign ourselves, and in particular your unworthy friend and Brother,

H. G. Clauder

Cash Account of the United Brethren's Mission at Tekoah (formerly Oyugillogy) from Nov. 6, 1828, to May 5, 1829, inclusive

| | | |
|---|---|---|
| 1828 | Dr. | |
| Nov. 6 | Balance in Treasury | 5.61¾ |
| | Missions Diaconie recd. of Br. Shulz in Salem | 200.00 |
| Nov. 10 | George Hicks cash recd. on his acct | 17.00 |
| | Elijah Hicks ditto ditto | 2.00 |
| | Expenses recd. of 4 lbs. lard | 0.50 |
| Nov. 29 | George Hicks cash recd. in full | 14.50 |
| Dec. 23 | Expenses recd. for cabbage: 0.75 | 0.75 |
| 1829 | | |
| Jan. 5 | Missions Diaconie recd. of Br. Shulz per mail | 80.00 |
| Jan. 19 | A. McCoy recd. on acct. | 1.25 |
| Jan. 23 | Spring Place recd. of Br. Byhan | 100.00 |
| Mar. 19 | Recd. S. A. Worcester cash in full | 1.25 |
| | Elias Boudinot recd. on acct. | 2.25 |
| Mar. 25 | A. McCoy recd. on acct. | 1.00 |
| | Expenses recd. for butter: 0.25; potatoes: 0.25 | 0.50 |
| | | $426.61¾ |

| | | |
|---|---|---|
| 1828 | Cr. | |
| Nov. 6 | Pd. for a knife 0.25; Saml. Copeland for 8 days work | 3.75 |
| | Profit & loss: counterfeit Augusta note returned | 5.00 |
| Nov. 10 | Alexander Copeland: paid him on acct. | 75.00 |
| | Pd. for a hog $2.50; for a basket 0.50 | 3.00 |
| Nov. 26 | Pd. John Hollers for work 1.50; for venison 1.25 | 2.75 |

| | | | |
|---|---|---|---|
| | Pd. ferriage at Echota sundry times | | 0.56¼ |
| | Saml. Henry: pd. him on his act. | | 30.00 |
| | Amt. pd. on the journey from Salem to Spg. Pl. | | 55.00 |
| | Missions Diaconie: pd. Br. Byhan for Smiths' journey | | 42.00 |
| 1829 | | | |
| Jan. 5 | Alex Copeland: pd. him on his acct. 90.00 | | 90.00 |
| Jan. 8 | Pd. for 173 ft oak plank (for a barn floor) | 2.60 | |
| | Ferriage Holly Creek 0.25; pd. G. Hicks for 4 hogs 14.00 | 14.25 | |
| Feb. 7 | Pd. Agnew for a desk in the chapel 1.25 | 1.25 | |
| | Pd. A. Miller for 4 days work 2.00; potters ware 1.00 | 3.00 | 21.10 |
| | Oliver Gann: pd. him for work 7.00; Mar. 16: ditto for 5 months' labour at $10 per month 50.00 | | 57.00 |
| Mar. | Aust. Copeland: pd. postage of a letter for him | | 0.10 |
| | Pd. for a basket 0.55; for 7 lbs. maple sugar 1.00 | 1.55 | |
| Apr. | Pd. for shoes for Sr. Gambold, lace, knives & forks | 4.50 | |
| | Pd. an Indian for venison 1.00; postage 0.37½ | 1.37½ | |
| | Pd. for a pocket hymnbook 0.37½; ferriage 0.31¼ | 0.68¾ | |
| May 5 | Pd. Agnew for a bread tray | 1.00 | 9.11¼ |
| | Balance in Treasury | | 32.24¼ |
| | | | $425.61¾ |

[Springplace (M 407-1) and Oochgeelogy (M 409-1) Diaries. Translated by Julie Tomberlin Weber. Handwritings are Franz Eder's (Ooch.) and Gottlieb Byhan's (Spg.).]

*May 5.* [Spg.] Today we had to hire a Negro woman from Mr. Jos. Vann, because our Sisters really needed help with the household. Admittedly if we were not in the middle of construction, it would be easier to see how to get through the household work. But since this is the case, the work is multiplied considerably through the workers.

*May 9.* [Ooch.] Br. Clauder visited in our neighborhood and everyone enjoyed this.

*Sun., May 10.* [Ooch.] Only 5 or 6 souls came for the service. Br. Clauder spoke to these few on the Doctrinal Text for today: "Let him that thinketh he standeth take heed lest he fall," 1 Cor. 10:12. This very sparse attendance at services, which has been the case for several weeks, sometimes discourages us. We do everything we can for these people, internally and externally, but it seems in vain or fruitless. It is very difficult for the Brethren and Sisters who serve here, where there is no internal or external encouragement!!

*Sun., May 10.* [Spg.] Most of our Brn. and Srs. were here for the services. After these they sang in Indian again.

*May 17.* [Ooch.] The sermon today was on the words of Matt. 18:3-4: "Verily I say unto you, except ye be converted, and become as little children, ye shall not enter into the kingdom of heaven," etc. We used [these words] to stress seriously and emphatically to the hearts of those present the [need for] rebirth or change. They were urged not to postpone conversion, especially until they were old or in their sick beds. After the sermon we strengthened ourselves physically and spiritually in the great act of partaking of Jesus' body and blood in Holy Communion. During this we felt comforted by the forgiveness and blessing presence of our dear Savior.

*Sun., May 17.* [Spg.] Today only a few people came to the services, so only one service was held. Last week we finished planting corn.

[M 414-4-12: Translated by Julie Tomberlin Weber. Addressed to: Revd. Theodor Shulz, Salem, Stokes County, North Carolina. Postmark: Springplace, C.N., May 24. Free. Gottlieb Byhan, P.M.]

Springplace, May 22, 1829

My dearly beloved Br. Shulz,

Your kind letters of Apr. 24th and 30th arrived here on the 17th, and we sincerely thank you for these. From these we learned that everyone is doing well, and we join you in thanking the Savior that your dear wife has almost recovered from her cold. We are currently all healthy enough that we can continue working on our construction, which is almost too much. Nancy Becker has also recovered from her attack of fever or cold. But our Rachel is often weak and among other things has to endure lots of headaches. If she were easier on herself when she feels well, she would not have to suffer so much. But all the talking doesn't help at all, and she doesn't take care of herself until she has to spend another day in bed or at least has to rest. It is not much better for N. Becker, but she can tolerate the hard work better. Amazingly, Mother remains healthy and well so that she is always able to continue helping with the current difficult housekeeping, although occasionally she hardly knows what to do in the evenings she is so tired. The Savior helps from day to day, for which we cannot thank Him enough.

May 23rd. I am happy I can finally report to you that the miserable Smith affair has been resolved and ended for now, with God's help, and we have made a mutual promise with our Brn. and Srs. in Spring Place that we will not think about this matter any more and will bury it. Our Br. Samuel did not come here for the Easter holy days, but visited in Ochgeloogy instead, and he wasn't seen here at our place for 5 or 6 weeks.

On May 3 he finally came again, and we could immediately see that he was quite happy. Smith's story was not mentioned, however, until before the last service, when he asked me if he could speak a few words after the service, actually to the Brn. and Srs. gathered in the church. I immediately agreed, but I prepared myself to confront him if he brought up anything new about the miserable story once again, and to be able to tell him the truth and what we thought about his behavior, etc. However, he had not been talking for long when we saw that the Brn. and Srs. there were very touched and some were crying. He spoke for a pretty long time, and we really wished we had an interpreter who could have translated this for us. Everyone left very happily. Then Br. Samuel came into our house with some other Brn. and Srs. and called his son Flea, one of our scholars who can speak English, and Br. Samuel addressed us through him with these words:

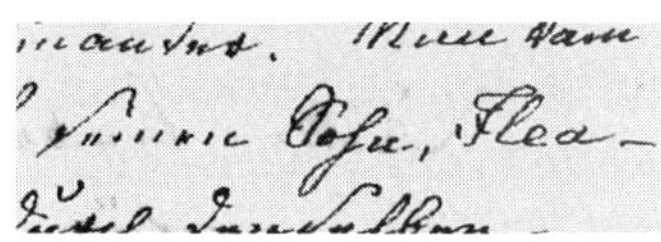

Presumably we would like to know what he said to the Brn. and Srs. in the church, and we confirmed this. He then said that he told them we should love the Savior and each other, and that he hoped the events that had recently taken place among us would not be remembered anymore, but forgotten and buried, and that he had misunderstood the matter — that is, Smith's story, etc.

We no longer considered it good or advisable to confront him now about his aggressive manner of acting, because we saw that he himself realizes that he had gone too far in his zeal for S. Who knows if the matter would not have opened up again, and God knows we are truly fed up and weary of it. But we took the opportunity to have a heart-to-heart talk with him and the others present, and to warn them not to pay too much attention to others and to stand their own ground and consider how our own hearts stand with the Savior, Who has done so much, if we love Him above everything else. He forgave our sins in holy baptism and washed and cleansed us of these with His blood. If we do this diligently, we will find enough on our own to drive us to ask the Savior daily for new forgiveness of our sins and misdeeds, because we are all weak and sinful beings, etc. Br. Samuel expressed his complete agreement.

Now we believe and hope that the wretched S.'s story has finally reached its end. May God grant that nothing else comes up about it in the future!

You told me in your dear letter that Br. Samuel should really publicly renounce what he said about us publicly. This would surely be no more than fair, but it is also true, as you write, this would be a difficult matter for an Indian. We are just happy that he actually realizes that he went too far. We are therefore glad to forgive him for this and to forget it. Presumably Br. W. Abr. Hicks talked to him about this on his last visit there and helped him out of his confusion.

Things are still progressing very slowly with the construction of our house. More than half of the house and the porches are covered, but I discovered I did not have nearly enough shingles. At just the right time, as if sent by God, an old German man from Tennessee came here. He was on his way to New Echota to work for Boudinott, but since the latter was not ready for him, he was happy to work for me. He made shingles for me and will be finished with this in a couple of days. I am also short on various kinds of nails, for which I have sent to Tennessee.

But dear Br., what will all this cost before the house is finished? I do not want to think about it. As you know, I have had two carpenters working since Easter, who are paid $2.50 a day. Just imagine what it will cost before the house is finished. And so, dear Br., you will have to send money faithfully. We have tried, Brn. Zevely and Vogler and I, to appeal to the carpenters' conscience about their wages, but nothing can be done with them. They are unwavering and even say they are working for little.

Day before yesterday our neighbor Jos. Vann visited us. He told me that he was thinking about making bricks as soon as his corn had been put up, and that I could get some for our chimney from him then. He has a mulatto who knows a lot about brickmaking.

Please extend my sincere greetings to Br. Shaaf, and tell him that on the 21st I received his note or enclosure dated May 5th, with the news that Brn. Vogler and Zevely returned safely to their homes on the 4th of this month. I also ask you to give dear old Br. Steiner our best greetings and tell him that his dear letter to me dated Apr. 25 arrived here in Springplace on May 10th. Give him my sincere thanks as well. I will answer them as soon as possible.

We seldom hear anything from our dear ones in Ochgeloogy, or Tekoah as it is now called, so I cannot tell you anything about them. However, I assume they often write to you in Salem and send the letters through the post in New Echota. Sometimes I almost believe you might know more about them than we here in Spring Place do. I have been trying to plan a visit there and with our friends in N. Echota for a long time, especially concerning the Tracts and such, but it has not worked out yet since no horses can be spared from the fieldwork right now and I cannot really be away from home because of the construction. I do not dare to make the journey on foot.

Currently we are having very favorable weather. The field and garden crops look very nice. The last frost in Apr. left us some peaches after all, although not enough to dry, still at least enough to eat. There are lots of apples and also cherries. Not so many pears, but still some. Otherwise, we have a Lokus year here, as irritating as it was in Salem some years ago. I forgot to say that the new kitchen on the north end of the new house, like the one in Tekoah, is also standing.

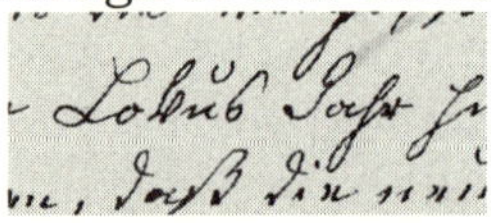

We are very sorry about our dear Br. Reichel's sad circumstances and wish him generous amounts of the Savior's comfort in his difficult situation. Please give him our best regards.

All here send their most sincere greetings to you and everyone. Please accept another special greeting for yourself from your poor Br.,

Gottlieb Byhan

Please give our Sophia our best greetings.

<u>Private</u>

Springplace, May 23, 1829

Dear Br. Shulz,

I believe it my duty and responsibility to report to you all the circumstances here concerning the work of our mission or things that could perhaps have a negative effect on it in the short term or long term.

The issue is this: About 4 or 5 weeks ago Br. Clauder visited us in order to recover and regain his strength a little, as he said. He then told us a number of things about Br. and Sr. Eder and others. The most important thing was that Br. Eder has completely lost his desire to serve here, both to serve and to learn English, and he — Br. Clauder — told us that he has already written to the U.A. Conf. asking to be released from this post and given a call to another post, as he believes, perhaps with the approval of the Prov. H. Conf. in Salem, although he did not know for sure. Sr. Eder is also supposed to have said that she did not come here to work. And Mother Gambold is supposed to have said that if Br. Clauder left, she would not stay in Tekoah another day.

From this it is clear that things there are not as they should be. Br. Clauder certainly has a difficult post. He is completely dedicated to the work, preaches the Gospel every Sunday in church and elsewhere when he has the opportunity. In brief, he is a complete missionary and servant of the Lord, and I must truthfully say he absolutely shames me. At the same time, however, I must see if his fellow Br. will lose all courage or has already lost it, so that Br. Clauder, as he himself says, sometimes is worried that he might lose courage as well.

The reason Br. Eder has lost his courage is probably this: He sees that he cannot help and support Br. Clauder as he would like to, because he is not progressing in English. Therefore, he is ashamed and worried that Br. Clauder might perhaps lose his courage and tell him: I am tired of this; you are the first man here; figure out how you can work things out.

Br. Eder has such unnecessary thoughts. Br. Clauder has often assured him that through God's grace this will not happen, but he will not be convinced of anything, and my words and those of Br. Clauder do not help. Br. Clauder told us that he is also indifferent about learning English except for what he has to say to people and the Brn. and Srs. Br. Clauder, on the other hand, does all that he can to encourage him and to guide him to the One who is strong in weakness, but it has no effect on him. His courage has sunk and no talking will help.

I am planning to visit Tekoah soon, and I will see how things currently stand with them. And so I ask you not to make use of these few lines yet, until I write more about this matter. Personally, I do not know what to think about this matter. They love the Indians, and they are loved by them in return. I do not know why Br. Eder cannot be content! When I can finally visit there, I will perhaps be able to write you more. I ask you once again to keep the above matter to yourself for now, because I would not like to have it said yet that I interfered in their matters. Your poor Br.,

Gottlieb Byhan

May 24th. This minute I received your letter dated the 12th. But I cannot read it until after the services. Thank you!

[Springplace (M 407-1) and Oochgeelogy (M 409-1) Diaries.]

*Sun., May 24.* [Spg.] It rained a lot last night and in general last week, and it seems as if the rainy weather would continue. This may well be the reason that only a few people came to the services again today, except for those who live close to us. Still our baptized Indian woman Sally, who lives about 14 miles from here, came. With her came another Indian woman with her child. We took the opportunity to have a heart-to-heart talk with this Indian woman through our schoolboy Flea. She may well have considered this, because we could see that she could not keep the tears back. She promised to visit us again. With the mail today we received the happy news from Salem that Brn. J. Vogler and Van. Zevely arrived safe and sound back with their families after their visit in Cherokee country. We joined them in bringing our dear Lord thanks for this. Mr. Dav. Vann from Ridge's Ferry also stopped in at our place today on his way to his parents-in-law, David McNair's. After he had taken some refreshment, he traveled on. Since he had been with our Brn. and Srs. in Tekoah overnight, we were overjoyed to hear from him that the Brn. and Srs. there are all healthy and well. This was all the dearer to us since we had heard nothing from them for a long time.

*May 24.* [Ooch.] Only 7 or 8 souls came here, and because of this extremely small number we did not have a sermon. We read a Lebenslauf, and Br. Clauder gave a brief and fitting talk about God's wonderful leading and guidance, which often seem so dark to us, which enable each and every heart that has surrendered to Him to rest, even in the most difficult circumstances, as a small child rests in its mother's arms. In the past few days we have been busy improving our God's Acre. It is 50 feet long and 60 wide; although this is really somewhat small, it will be large enough for many years for the small and very scattered little congregation here, where some of the corpses cannot be brought the great distance in warm weather.

*May 31.* [Ooch.] Br. Clauder preached on the words: God has gone up with a shout, the LORD with the sound of a trumpet

Psalm 47:6[:5]. We were very happy about the relatively large gathering of attentive listeners who came here today. They renewed and strengthened our wavering courage.

*Sun., May 31.* [Spg.] A nice number of our Brn. and Srs. came for the services. In the first service there was a talk and prayer. Since last Thursday was Ascension Day, we celebrated it today. In the second service, the Indian Br. Samuel held a talk for the Brn. and Srs. in which he encouraged them to remain with the Savior and to love Him because He shed His blood for us and redeemed us from sins and from the evil enemy. Afterward he offered a prayer on his knees, during which most of the Brn. and Srs. shed tears. Everyone seemed to be very touched and departed happily. We could feel the Savior's dear presence in all of our services today in a powerful way. After the services the Brn. and Srs. were informed of the Holy Communion to be held on June 14th, about which they were very happy. It was remarkable how their look — which showed what they had just enjoyed for their hearts in the services — changed, how it changed into a respectful and reverent one. We can do nothing but testify that our Brn. and Srs. — at least many of them — know what they have in the Savior, and what He has done for them. Although the enemy is doing his best to bring impurity and discord among them, still we experience again and again that He has the strength for us and destroys the enemy's attacks.

*June 2.* [Spg.] Today a horribly big snake was killed in our yard. It was just in the act of catching young chickens when it was discovered. Our people said that they had never seen such a big one. It was one of the so-called Copperbellys snakes.

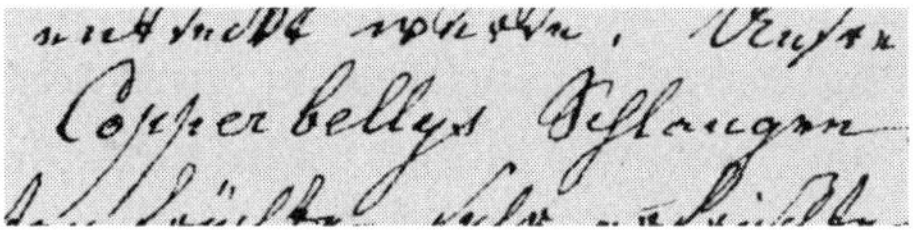
Copperbellys Schlangen

*June 3.* [Spg.] We had a nice soaking rainstorm, which really refreshed field and garden crops. Also today Mr. John Martin, our District Judge, visited us on Post Office business. He had given a letter of considerable worth to the post office here to be forwarded. However, it was sent to

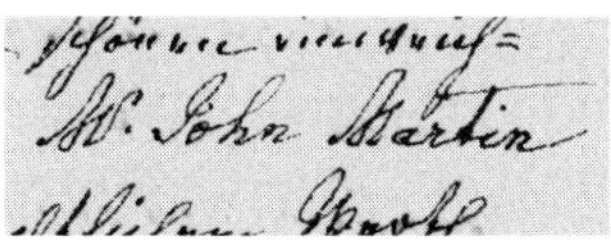
Mr. John Martin

the General Post Office as a dead letter and now had been sent back to the Post Office there to find out who the writer was. Since he — that is Judge Martin — is the writer of it, he took it back from the Post Office here.

*June 4.* [Ooch.] A very old Cherokee who is almost completely blind visited us. He is known throughout this area as a sorcerer and so-called rainmaker, and it is incredible when people say they [pity] the life of this man with these lies of his and his family, which is indeed very needy. He told me through an interpreter that he was also a doctor and was in fact on his way to visit a poor sick man and [to cure him]. I asked him if he really believed he could heal this man, and he answered yes. I continued by asking him why he doesn't heal his own eyes, with which he can no longer see, or bring back his sight, if he really was so skilled in helping others, making it rain, etc. He said that he could not.

In the same way, I said, he could not help other people through his falsehood, and it was sinful, indeed almost unforgivable, that he thus robbed God of the honor, etc. However, he stuck to his opinions although we tried to convince him that everything, even the smallest good deed, came from God, and especially the rain and sunshine that he pretended to cause, and he himself certainly knew that it was a lie. We read in the Bible, which is God's word, that He, dear God, allows his sun to rise over good and evil and lets it rain on the righteous and the unrighteous, etc., and I just had to tell him I didn't believe in his sorcery at all. He couldn't do this any more than I could.

I also asked him to stop doing this and to join us in worshipping the great God who created heaven and earth and everything and to believe in His son Jesus Christ, whom He sent to earth for our redemption; this all seemed to be completely new to him. The poor man seemed to have heard enough for today, because he said a friendly farewell and promised to visit us again soon to discuss this matter more.

*June 4.* [Spg.] Br. Byhan today went to Tekoah on business, and Rachel Byhan accompanied him there. Br. Byhan returned to Spring Place on the 6th. Rachel Byhan stayed in Tekoah a number of days longer to rest, because she was not used to traveling the long and bad road two times right after each other without having a rest in between.

*June 5.* [Ooch.] Br. G. Byhan from Springplace delighted us with a pleasant visit. In the evening we had a Conference about Br. and Sr. A. Copland, who have expressed their willingness to continue serving at the mission here, Br. A. Copland in the economy and Sr. Copland in the school. The mission families here and at Springplace agreed to this. Br. G. Byhan returned to Springplace on the 7th.

*June 7.* [Ooch.] Pentecost. Br. Clauder preached on Acts 2:1-12, explaining God's work of grace in human hearts, and we laid this on their hearts. After the sermon our Br. George Hicks interpreted this in Cherokee as well as he could. This man and his wife bring us much joy through their very Gospel-like way of life, and we are hopeful they will become very useful for their countrymen.

*Sun., June 7.* [Spg.] Pentecost. We brought God the worthy Holy Spirit thanks and adoration for His faithful efforts to make people of God out of us. In the first service we read the story of the day. Then was the sermon on Acts 2:36-39, with a prayer on our knees. In the second service we sang a Pentecostal liturgy. Today we also spoke with Charles Buttler, our Sr. Anna Johanna's husband, about the well-being of his soul, and advised him to consider what will serve his peace. When asked if he did not wish to become the property of Jesus and to have himself cleansed of his sins through Jesus' blood, he answered with tears: Yes. He seemed to be very beaten down and did not say anything further about his spiritual condition, so that for now we did not know what to make of him. Afterward we heard that last Sunday he was at a ballplay and had behaved pretty badly, from which we could conclude that at this time he is not yet serious about surrendering himself to the Savior.

*June 8.* [Ooch.] Br. Clauder visited our Br. and Sr. A. Copland in Tennessee.

*June 8.* [Spg.] Today Br. Clauder came from Tekoah to visit at our place. With him Rachel Byhan returned from there. Br. Clauder traveled farther on to Tennessee on business, to Mr. Alex. Copeland. Currently we are having a lot of rainy weather, so that little or nothing can be done in the gardens and fields. It is especially a pity for our grass, which cannot be made into hay, because it has rained more or less every day the last two weeks.

*June 10.* [Spg.] Mr. Jos. Vann visited us. He told us that as soon as his corn is put up he would make bricks, which we could then get from him for our chimney. We were very happy about this, because otherwise we would have to have several more workers to make them for us.

*June 11.* [Spg.] Our workers finished putting the roof on our new house. We are happy that it is finally under roof. Also Mr. Elijah Hicks came to our place for a brief visit today. Mrs. Bean, David McNair's daughter, also stopped in at our place on her way to Tekoah, where she has her daughter in the school.

*June 12.* [Spg.] Early today we had a heavy rain, so that the workers could not do anything in the field again.

*June 13.* [Spg.] Br. H. G. Clauder returned to our place from his business trip in Tennessee. He brought us letters and *Nachrichten* from Salem, which Mr. John Ridge, who picked up his sister at the Girls School in Salem, had left at David McNair's, for which we were very grateful.

*June 13.* [Ooch.] We had a pleasant visit from Doctor Bean's wife, who recently brought her 8-year-old daughter to our school.

*Sun., June 14.* [Ooch.] Not many listeners were here. Among the few present were some Christian friends from New Town in our neighborhood. Br. Eder prayed the Church Litany in the first service and read a couple chapters from the Gospel of John. In the second service the talk was on Matt. 16:26. After this the recently born baby son of our Br. and Sr. Abr. Wm. Hicks was baptized with the name John Benjamin.

*Sun., June 14.* [Spg.] Br. Clauder gave the sermon in the morning here in Spring Place. In the afternoon, with a blessed feeling of the presence of our dear Lord, we had the enjoyment of Holy Communion. During this the boy Alex. Benj. Sanders, one of our school children, received the confirmation blessing for his first enjoyment of this. Afterward Br. Samuel gave another address to the Brn. and Srs., during which they seemed to be very touched. Otherwise, we currently are able to rejoice over the walk of our Brn. and Srs., because we can see from them that they have surrendered their hearts to the Savior and that true Brotherly love prevails among them.

*June 15.* [Spg.] This morning Br. H. G. Clauder returned to his post in Tekoah. Yesterday was once again the first day for almost three weeks that no rain has fallen at our place. Because of this the fieldwork has multiplied so much that we hardly know where to begin. Our corn and other field crops are looking extremely good, however, so that it seems that we can hope for a plentiful harvest if the heavenly Father protects us from bad weather. In the evening Mrs. Bean and her young child came back from Tekoah, where she had gone on a visit some days ago, and she spent the night with us.

*June 15.* [Ooch.] Br. Clauder returned healthy and well from his visit with our Br. and Sr. A. Copland in Tennessee. He was full of praise and thanksgiving toward our dear Lord for the merciful protection of his body and soul during his trip. He found the said Br. and Sr. healthy and well and very eager for contact or fellowship with Brn. and Srs. or other children of God, which, as they said, they had had to forego almost entirely since they left here. Br. Clauder also found them very willing to return completely to mission work, as we had already learned from letters from our dear Br. Th. Schulz, if he, Br. A. Copland, could take care of the economy and his wife could take care of the school.

[M 414-4-13: Translated by Julie Tomberlin Weber. Addressed to: Revd. Theodor Shulz, Salem, Stokes County, North Carolina. Postmark: Springplace, C.N., June 21. Free. Gottlieb Byhan, P.M. Received July 13.]

Springplace, June 17, 1829

My dear Br. Shulz,

Hopefully by now you have received my letter to you dated May 24th, in which I informed you of the conclusion of the wretched

Smidt affair, and you can surely join us in celebrating this. Now I have two letters from your worthy hand before me which I have not yet answered. I received the first on May 24th and the latter with Mr. J. Ridge, which he had deposited with Mr. McNair. He thinks it is good not to come past Springplace, so he gave it to Br. H. G. Clauder, who was visiting Br. and Sr. Copeland.

I sincerely thank you for the enclosure of $125, because my account seemed to have gotten consumption again. Oh dear God! Where will it finally end? I do not believe you will be able to get together enough money before my construction is finished. Since the Brn. and Srs. in Tekoah needed some money, Br. Clauder took $25 of it right away. You will see this in the account, since I am planning to close the account from here on June 30 and send it to you so that you will have it on hand on the first Thursday in Oct. Have a little more patience with me about the Diary. I will send it soon, when I have a little more time to copy it. My eyes do not allow me to write in the evening, and during the day I hardly have an hour of undisturbed peace. I know it should have been sent a long time ago, but since then I really have not been able to find time to copy it. Have a little more patience!

Now I want to reply to your dear letters. We were happy to learn that dear Brn. Vogler and Zevely arrived safely at your place and theirs again. This visit was a great encouragement for us and without doubt also for them. I was also surprised that Ocholoogy was changed into Tekoah. It is true that either it or the area should have been named something different a long time ago, but if I had had anything to say about it, or had even known anything about the site getting another new name, I would have suggested a different one. But the name has been given, and it is all the same now.

Concerning Br. Copeland providing help with external work for Tekoah, I was in Tekoah on a visit about two weeks ago, and we had a joint Conference. All the Brn. and Srs. favored taking in Br. and Sr. Copeland again, if they were willing to do this. Br. Clauder visited them about this last week, and they are happy and grateful to have another opportunity to live with the Brn. and

Srs. and to be able to attend services. They also want to serve without a salary. As they expressed it, they will gladly work for food and clothing as long as they have a pasture for their hearts again. So this has now been confirmed.

However, we could not reach a decision in our Conference about a place for Br. and Sr. Copeland to live. We could not resolve to build at this time, and we did not see an opportunity to fix up the house intended for Jos. Gambold for them, because it is really too bad and not worth repairing. Also they would have no supply house then, which they really cannot do without. In the end we believed it would be best for now if we do not change any house for them or designate one, because it is very likely that there will be a change next fall with the Brn. and Srs. in Tekoah.

Br. and Sr. Eder claim they cannot stay any longer than the fall. Overall, we do not really know where we stand. Br. and Sr. Eder do not <u>want</u> to stay, and <u>if</u> they stay, good Br. Clauder claims that he cannot stand being with them — and <u>I</u> believe him too. Anyone who is thoroughly acquainted with the current circumstances there and with Br. Eder's stubbornness and dejection will not think badly of Br. Clauder if he cannot stand it. I must admit I have never known anyone who will not allow himself to be encouraged or persuaded in the least to pray for grace and contentment, faithfulness in the Lord's will, and courage and happiness from the <u>One</u> who is powerful in weakness.

Nothing helps with him. It is like talking to a wall. He insists he has lost courage and is not at all up to the work here, and they should not have married him right away and made him first man, in his opinion. And so nothing can be done with him. He has gotten it firmly in his head that he is not staying <u>here</u>, and in his opinion there is no other way. I wish him luck. However, I believed he was firmer and more solid than he actually turns out to be. Br. Clauder says the same, and that he would not be in a position to get to know him thoroughly.

Now concerning the Tracts, Br. Clauder has spoken with Mr. Boudinott and Mr. Worcester. The former is willing to print the Tracts, but the latter is causing some difficulties. Since Mr. Worcester is personally acquainted with the Secretary of the Tract Society he wrote him about this matter, and he does not want to do anything more until he has an answer from him.

Things are moving forward slowly with our construction. The roof has been on for 2 weeks now, and we will start laying the floorboards next week.

What will you, or what will all of you, say when you read this week's *Phönix,* dated the 17th? It will soon be reported what will happen with the poor Cherokees. It seems they really cannot stay longer in their current situation. They must either move or

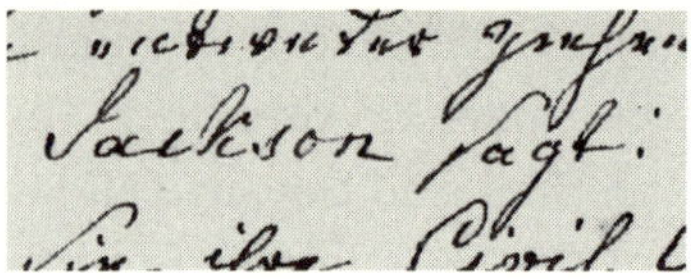


submit to the laws of the United States. Jackson says: that the state of Georgia cannot be restrained if it extends its civil laws beyond its state. But what should we do in these circumstances? Certainly we submit this matter to our highest Ruler, who can arrange everything for the best, and we continue our work as before without allowing ourselves to get involved in political matters at all. It seems to me, or really to us, we should quietly prepare for both cases, which surely will be discussed and considered in your worthy Helf. Conf. One does not hear the Indians saying much about it yet. But it could be that this will arouse a sensation once the matter is well known and they consider it thoroughly.

And now what about our new house? I have to admit I have often wished we hadn't built, but who can know everything in advance? Now we want to surrender this to the Savior. He knows what is good and beneficial!

Mother Byhan and Rachel are thinking about visiting and using the health springs, about 9 or 10 miles from here, with Mr. Jos. Vann's family next Monday and staying there for a number of days. The water is supposed to be extremely restorative and good for all sorts of things.

May 20. ([penciled in:] June) I just received a letter from Br. Clauder in Tekoah, in which he reports that the Brn. and Srs. there are well. Among other things he writes: "Concerns go on as usual with my poor Companion. I wish he were released from his situation."

Otherwise, our Brn. and Srs. here in Springplace are in a nice rhythm, so that every Sunday we are encouraged anew to continue doing what is within our powers to help extend His kingdom. Love and peace prevail among them now. May the Savior keep them with Him and with His wounds! Otherwise, we are all pretty healthy right now, at least enough that we can all still work. Please greet everyone most sincerely from us. We commend ourselves to your further remembrance and prayer before our dear Lord. And you, dear Br., please accept the most sincere greeting from your humble Br.,

Gottlieb Byhan

N.B. Please give our best greetings to our daughter Sophia.

The 21st. The Georgia mail has just arrived, but again there is no letter from Salem except for a small note from Br. Shaaf, from which we read about Br. Math. Reich's homegoing.

G. B.

# *1829, part 4*

[Springplace (M 407-1) and Oochgeelogy (M 409-1) Diaries. Translated by Julie Tomberlin Weber. Handwritings are Franz Eder's (Ooch.) and Gottlieb Byhan's (Spg.).]

*June 18.* [Ooch.] Br. Clauder visited our Br. and Sr. G. Hicks and friends in New Echota, and everyone enjoyed the visit.

*June 18.* [Spg.] Today Mr. and Mrs. Vann visited us. This was all the more remarkable to us because such visits occur so seldom, although Mrs. Vann usually comes to our services every Sunday. Mr. Vann today came primarily to eat cherries, which we have in great plenty this year.

*Sun., June 21.* [Ooch.] The sermon was on Jesus' words from John 14:6: I am the way, the truth, and the life, etc. Then we refreshed our thirsty hearts with the most sacred enjoyment of the body and blood of Jesus in Holy Communion. We should mention that, to the glory of our good, merciful Lord and Savior, we experienced an extremely blessed feeling of joy during this, and we all felt the Savior's forgiveness in a very humbling and comforting manner. All shed tears of love and contrition and each person pleaded that the Lord would always let it be like this for us and would allow us to be and remain His own. With heart and hand we surrendered ourselves to Him and promised Him anew childlike faithfulness and obedience. It was a day which the Lord made.

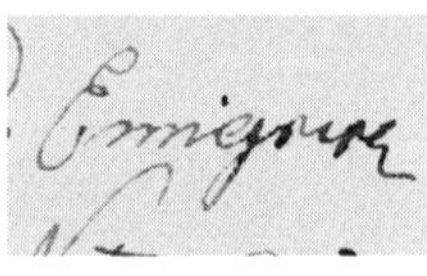

In the past several days our poor Cherokees have been very upset and uneasy about their Emigation since a certain Ross,

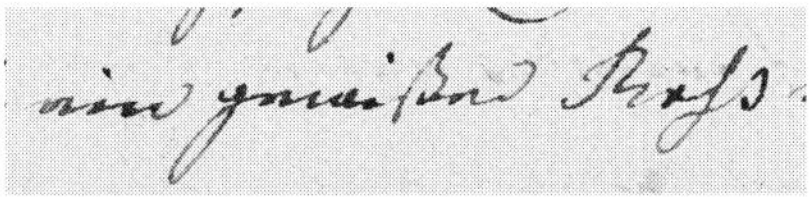

a Chief of the Nation, returned from Washington. A meeting on this matter has been going on in his house with the rest of the Chiefs and head people of the Nation for two days.

*Sun., June 21.* [Spg.] Today only a few Brn. and Srs. were in our services.

*June 22.* [Spg.] This morning Sr. Byhan, Nathanael, and Rachel Byhan drove to the therapeutic spring, about nine or ten miles from here. Sr. Byhan is planning to use the waters for a number of days to see if they might be of any use against certain weakness, which overcomes her frequently. Sr. Rachel Byhan will stay with Mother Byhan at the spring, but Nathanael Byhan will return today. Mr. Jos. Vann also went today to the same spring with his whole family to use the waters there for some time. Mr. Vann claims that if he had not used these waters last year, he would no longer be alive. This much is certain, however, that this water is supposed to have helped many people with certain internal complaints and illnesses, so that the spring can be of great benefit.

This week the Chiefs and the other Headmen met about 60 miles from here for a Council to consider what the best thing to do is in the current desperate situation of the Nation in response to the comments made by the President of the United States

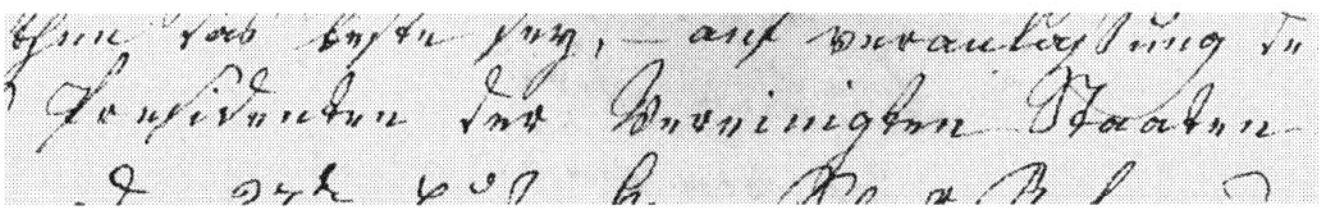

made known in public newspapers concerning the Cherokees who live in the State of Georgia.

*June 24.* [Ooch.] Today Sister Gambold visited our Br. and Sr. Wm. A. Hicks and found our Sr. Sally Hicks very sad and disheartened because of this unrest. Still we were happy she has completely submitted to Savior's will in this and trusts in His omnipotent guidance.

[M 411-1-26: Translated by Elizabeth Marx. No address; no post-mark.]

Tekoa, June 23, 1829

My dear Brother Shulz!

[Contents summarized; translated parts are in quotations.]

[Br. Eder starts the letter by thanking Br. Schulz for his May 29 letter and for letters from Europe. He is happy that his letters have brought the desired result, and hopes that now the Lord will provide another little place where they can serve. He hopes too that this place will be better served than it has been by him. The rest of the first page is devoted to long and repeated expressions of regret and asking for forgiveness for the way in which he wrote his letters and that he offended the Brethren of PHC.]

[There was a misunderstanding in regard to changing the name of the place, for which he was not responsible, but he does not think it is that important, and it could continue to be known by its former name until a suitable one is found. He says that mistakes like that occur when inexperienced and unskilled boys like himself are put into the work. They should be stationed first with understanding and skilled older persons, and he hopes that the Lord will make it like that for him. They were all heartened to learn what the Brethren Vogler and Zevilly had reported about their visit. The Holy Communion celebrated with these Brethren was a real blessing as was the one they just had when all the members were present except Sr. Lassly.]

[He mentions Br. Byhan's visit, for which all of them were happy. Br. Byhan acted offended since he had not been let in on Eder's request for re-assignment, which he felt should not have been concealed from him since he is the senior missionary. The whole matter was talked out, and Eder asked for forgiveness. He continues writing about his situation and the reasons for his desire to be moved, what Br. Byhan might think or report, and that his request was not motivated by a desire for his own advantage. He continues saying that God guides and will do what is right for His kingdom and will surely find some little spot where they, the Eders, can be of service, but he is sure that this is not the place where they are to continue to be active.]

[Their candidate for baptism, Joh. Fiels, lets himself be seen only seldom, so there is nothing much to report. Br. Eder fears that he will go over to the Methodists as his sister-in-law has done. But if they will only grow for the Savior, they can belong to any church fellowship.]

"Our field and garden crops are growing well, and up to now everything promises an abundant harvest. I recently heard from Br. Clauder that the new fireplace for our house would probably not happen this fall, but with the help of Br. A. Copland, perhaps it can be done next year. This summer our house will be plastered with lime outside. That should keep the cold out a little!

"About the present unrest of the Cherokees because of their emigration I am not able to say much, except that many and particularly Bodinout in New Echota are again very much disturbed, since a certain Chief of the Nation, Ross, returned from Washington. Br. Wm. Ab. Hicks told us yesterday that today there is to be a big gathering at Ross's house. A true [account] will probably be seen in the newspapers.

"My rheumatism has fortunately disappeared completely. The number of our children at the present time is 12. We are waiting for one little girl shortly. It is such a misfortune that with as few girls as we have at the time, there are only 2 who can speak English with whom we are able to do anything or talk. Br. G. Byhan has doubtlessly written to you that Br. and Sr. A. Copland will be here soon after the harvest and probably also that Br. Clauder visited them. It will probably be only late in the year that we will hear anything definite about the Cherokees."

[The letter closes with the customary greetings.]

Franz Eder

[M 411:1:27: Transcribed by Grace S. Robinson. Addressed to: Rev. Theodore Shulz, Salem, North Carolina. Post stamped: New-Echota, Cher. Na. July 9, 18¾. Received July 30. Lightly edited.]

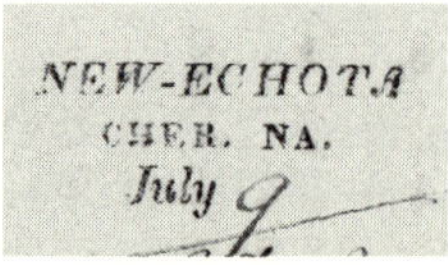


Tekoa, C.N., June 26, 1829

Dear Brother,

Your very dear favour of May 10th came to hand on the 29th quite unexpectedly & I hasten to render my sincerest thanks to you for the paternal Love & advice therin contained. My d.b. [dearly beloved], excuse me for writing these few lines in the Engl. Language. My situation has had this effect, that my mother tongue has become, in a manner, unpractical to me.

The contents of your favour were of the most encouraging nature, & happy should I be were it my power to communicate favourable & joyful news to you. I rejoice to perceive an increased interest toward these dear people in the hearts of the Brethren of the congregation, which I assign chiefly to the visit of the Brethren Vogler & Zevely. But I cannot forbear remarking, that the impression which they received here & at Spr. Pl. is almost too favourable, so that the good anticipations with which they left us, may possibly degenerate into painful disappointments, particularly since the unhappy political condition of this beloved nation is increasing, and affairs, as you may have learned from the *Phoenix*, are rapidly approaching to a crisis.

The consequences therof will be undoubtedly of, the most calamitous nature, & I expect to be, should I remain here, an eye-witness to heartrending Misery on the part of the poor Cherokees. There is at this time a universal excitement throughout the Nation & a fearful looking for the things to come. Under such circumstances my heart is frequently dejected & cast down, but I never shall be able to thank the good Shepherd of my Soul sufficiently for the aid He has so far extended to me, & I entertain the joyful hope that He will still further strengthen & support me.

Our dear Cherokee Brn. & Srs. need consolation in their distress, & our prayer is that God may strengthen their faith in the trying hour that they may be reconciled to the wonderful ways of His providence. I fear, however, the dispersion of our dear little flock. Some talk of remaining, others of removing to some of the states, & others of emigrating to Arkansas.

This week the heads of Nation had a convention at Chief Ross's, since which the excitement is, if possible, still greater, as his communications to the people were in supportf of the Message received by the Delegation from the Secty. of War in which but two alternatives are offered, either to emigrate or to come under

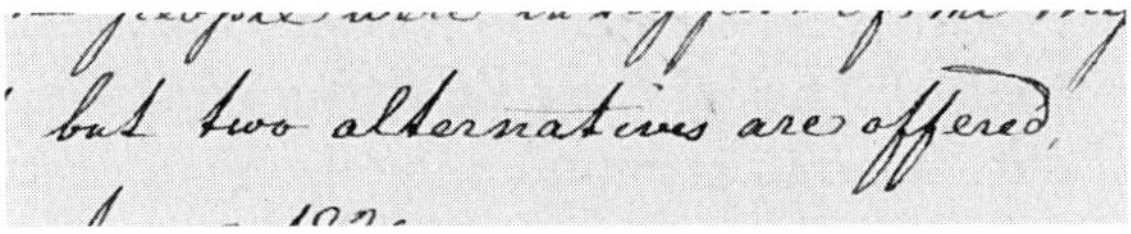
but two alternatives are offered,

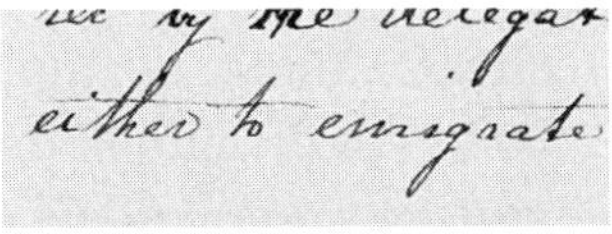
either to emigrate

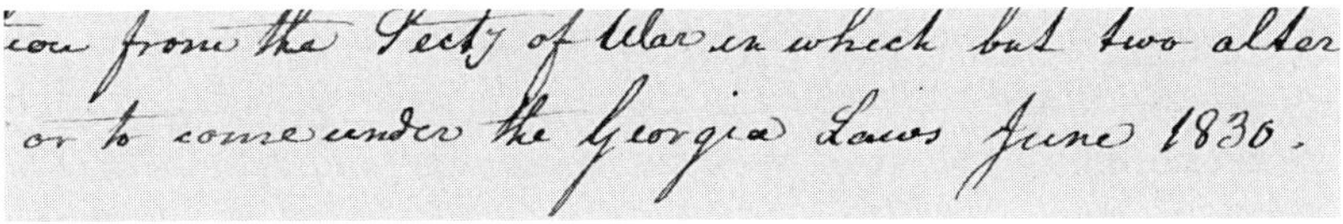
from the Secty of War in which but two alter
or to come under the Georgia Laws June 1830.

the Georgia Laws June 1830.

With regard to the internal affairs of our household I can only say for my own self that I receive daily new proofs of the Love & Grace of my Saviour whereby I am ennabled to press forward though all difficulties & discouragements so plentifully to be met with in this wicked world. Notwithstanding this, it must needs be an object of concern to you to perceive the affairs of this Mission in hands which are partly quite discouraged & unwilling (I will not say unable) to act or at best resting upon inexperienced & weak powers, which nothing but Divine strength can, according to their slender capacities, sustain. Should it be found necessary still further to supply this station with Teachers, I hope and pray that competent instruments may be found, better ones than I know myself to be. My companion, who craves my deepest sympathy, entertains high & almost certain expectations of a removal from this place next fall. Should he be disappointed I have a fearful foreboding of sad consequences, & yet I can not see the probability of his hopes becoming realized unless the total suspension of this Station should follow as a consequence to the removal of the Cherokees, which I most certainly expect.

There are at present 10 scholars here whom I instruct in Spelling, reading, and writing as time allows, but I find it impossible to observe regularity, because my circumstances are too unfavourable. However, this difficulty will be obviated when Br. Copeland returns hither next fall. I must not forget to mention (but Br. Byhan has probably done so before) that Copeland is willing to enter the service here as formerly, on the Missionary plan. He craves no other remuneration than his support & the privilege of remaining in communion with the church. I visited them lately & esteem him as a real friend of that which is good.

We had, until lately, two hirelings in employ, & I fear our Crop of Corn, containing 25 acres, will compel us to procure another assistant to the one we have at present. We have had a fine season, & our fields, as well as those of our neighbours, look promising — all calculated to render the Country endearing & the thought of exchanging it for an Arkansas prairie still more painful. This week we are engaged in harvesting our Oat crop, & I laboured yesterday for the best part of the day in the field until a violent headache compelled me to desist. But fortunately an Indian came here at the same time whose services we engaged for a few days.

I have not yet received an account of the receipt of my Letter to you of May 5 containing our Accounts Current for the last 6 Months, but can't doubt its arrival. I hope it proved satisfactory.

I should be very glad to receive the sanction of the dear Brethren of Conference to my plan of visiting my dear Parents during the approaching session of Council when my absence from this place would be immaterial. I have a variety of reasons which, in my opinion, render it highly necessary that I should visit my native place, and as they are principally of a private nature no expenses shall accrue to the Missions Diacony. In fact I can not believe that the Brethren could give me a denial, considering my circumstances, yet I do not consider myself at liberty to absent myself from this place without their sanction. Should that, however, not be the case & my situation remain as at present, I do not know to what I may be urged.

Dear Brother, I wish I could pour out my overflowing heart to you as a child to its parent, but this cannot be done through the Medium of a Letter. My only hope & consolation is that I have One above who can & will help me in my situation as long as my faith remains unwavering. But then alas, there is my complaint so often — my faith. The only support under trials is tottering & not unfrequently entirely prostrate.

But enough for the present; more, I hope, verbally. Please let me hear your views of this subject speedily. In the meantime & forever, may the Lord grant us more Faith & heavenly wisdom & hearts filled with Love toward our neighbours as to ourselves, pressing toward the mark for the prize of the high calling of God in Christ Jesus.

I remain, in fellowship with the church militant, your unworthy young friend & brother.

H. G. Clauder

Revd. Th. Shulz

[Springplace (M 407-1) and Oochgeelogy (M 409-1) Diaries.]

*June 27.* [Spg.] Today Sr. Byhan and Rachel Byhan returned from the therapeutic spring. The use of this has had a good effect on their health. It was just a shame that they could not use it longer, because there was not enough time. The spring is already heavily visited, although it is actually still too early in the year. Currently 4 families are there, and many more are expected. Otherwise, we had much rain again throughout this week, so that the necessary fieldwork again could not be done as it should be. The wet weather was especially disadvantageous for our wheat, because it is ripe and could not yet be cut. Otherwise, the wheat turned out very well, and if the wet weather continues for a while, then we can expect a plentiful corn harvest.

*Sun., June 28.* [Spg.] We were recently sent a printed circular by a society in the Nation which attacks the use of strong drink and calls for this evil to be controlled. It asks those who have decided themselves not to drink any more brandy wine to sign their names under this resolution. So this circular was presented and read aloud to our Brn. and Srs. after the Sunday services, because it was printed in English and the Cherokee language. Afterward all of them signed in Cherokee letters, and those who could not do so had their names written for them and they put their sign next to them.

*Sun., June 28.* [Ooch.] The sermon was on the words: There remaineth therefore a rest to the people of God, Heb. 4:9. Even though the weather was very nice, we had only a few listeners here. Generally it is very regrettable that the services are so empty, and the Cherokees particularly hardly attend them. They do not seem to recognize their current time of grace, even though they are so frequently and urgently asked to turn to the Friend of Sinners. This is so often the case with humans, until it is too late for them!!

*July 3.* [Ooch.] Br. and Sr. Eder visited Br. and Sr. Wm. Ab. Hicks and everyone enjoyed it.

[M 414-4-14: Translated by Julie Tomberlin Weber. Addressed to: Revd. Theodor Shulz, Salem, Stokes County, North Carolina. Postmark: Springplace, C.N., July 5. Free. Gottl. Byhan, P.M. Received July 17.]

Springplace, July 4, 1829

My dear Br. Shulz,

I am hurrying to inform you that on the 2nd of this month I received your letter of June 16 with the enclosure of $200 along with *Wöchentliche Nachr.* from the Prov. H. Conf. Many thanks are due to you, dear Br., for remembering my account so nicely. And we want to thank God for bringing everything of this nature so safely to Spring Place!

It is completely right, as you think, to send all the money for both sites to me. It is possible for letters to the Brn. and Srs. in Tekoa to lie around in the New Echota Post Office for one week, perhaps 2 weeks or even longer. It has happened that letters I had written to the Brn. and Srs. there stayed there about 4 weeks before they were picked up. From this you can also see that there is little correspondence between Spring Place and Tekoa. Everything has to be done in person. Br. Clauder does not always have time to go to N. Echota to pick up letters, and Br. Eder does not trust himself to converse with English people as much as this requires.

Now to return to your letter. What will become of our poor Cherokees now? It really seems as if their stay here will not last much longer, and it seems there is no more mercy for them. Perhaps God is still awakening hearts among the white people, or in the government, who will act as their friends. Humans make plans; God makes things happen! In any case, things look very sad in the Nation. It seems to us that they are not discussing this among themselves as much as we would expect. There is currently a certain quietness among them, so that one does not hear them say what will happen and what they are planning to do. Presumably their Council will meet in Oct. and the next Congress will resolve the matter. We would like to know what our Cherokee Brn. and Srs. here think about this and what they will do if it reaches that point. We do not trust ourselves to question them at this time and to discuss this matter with them unless we happen to have a very good interpreter. We have not yet heard a word from Mr. John Ross and the rest of the Delegates who were in Washington. Otherwise, we do not know any more than what we see in the newspapers.

Following your advice, I will now do just the most necessary things in the construction of my house, but enough that we can move into it before winter. I have also changed my plans about the fireplaces on the chimneys, so that I will be finished with it earlier. Also regarding the rooms upstairs in the house, I will now have one less made and otherwise cut things as much as possible, because I agree with your belief that the Government will repay us little or nothing. If it really becomes necessary to move, there will be all kinds of things to consider concerning Spring Place and Tekoa, but it is too early for this now. As soon as I hear more definite plans from the Indians, I will let you know right away. I just hope the Georgians do not come with force, because then it would be very bad, and we could be in an awkward situation. May God in His grace prevent this!

A couple of weeks ago some of the Chiefs and most respected men gathered to consider what they should do in their current very difficult circumstances. I have not yet heard the least about their considerations. If I get time next week I will visit the Brn. and Srs. in Tekoa and share with them the most essential things from your dear letters, primarily about the construction of their chimney, as well as about our Br. and Sr. Copeland's acceptance. I have not heard anything from our Brn. and Srs. there for a long time now. In my opinion it would be useless to call Br. and Sr. Eder away from there next fall, until it is clear what the outcome with the poor Cherokees will be. He can, by the way, last fine for one more year. Perhaps his stubbornness will be broken somewhat. I have nothing to say to this, but his entire story seems absurd to me.

There is nothing to say yet about whether our young Brn. should go along if our Indians go west. Br. Clauder actually told me some time ago that if our Brn. and Srs. went west, he would go with them. I have not yet heard any statement from our Nathanael, and so I cannot say anything about him. These decisions cannot be made until it is certain whether they are going or not.

Now we want to lay this matter diligently on His faithful heart. He knows best what is best for this poor oppressed Nation. He will look upon them in grace and will not leave them, especially our poor Brn. and Srs. He still sits on His throne and guides everything. He will not leave this poor people and will certainly care for them.

July 5th. Once again we had a nice soaking rain last night, so that the field and garden crops look unusually good and promise a plentiful harvest. Otherwise, we are all well except for Rachel, who is never completely healthy and almost always complains of headache, stomachache, toothache, and cramps in her limbs. We have often been quite concerned about her and sometimes have wished we had a doctor to consult. But perhaps things will go better for her when she has finally finished growing, because she is getting so tall and has outgrown both of us.

Please greet Br. and Sr. Bechler from us. We wish them the powerful assistance of our dear Lord and much grace and many blessings in their new calling in Wachovia. We feel much compassion for Br. Reichel's situation. Please extend our best greetings to him and tell him he should pay a visit to Spring Place and Tekoa. Please be satisfied with these few lines for this time. More soon. We greet all of you most sincerely. Please accept the most sincere greetings from your lowly but loving Br.,

Gottl. Byhan

N.B. Please give our Sophia our best greetings and tell her we have been waiting eagerly for a letter from her for a long time; we are surprised she has not written us for so long. Please extend our greetings to dear Br. Shaaf and tell him that the German newspapers with notes arrive regularly, and we are very grateful for them. Otherwise, dear Br., I believe it doesn't matter which post you use to send your letters to me, through Augusta or through Knoxville. They get here just as quickly with one post as with the other. The Georgia post arrives here on Sundays now, and the rest, through Knoxville, Nashville, and New Echota, on Thursday. Farewell!

G. B.

July 5. I just received Sophia's letter to us dated June 11.

[Springplace (M 407-1) and Oochgeelogy (M 409-1) Diaries.]

*Sun., July 5.* [Ooch.] Once again very few people came to the service, so there was no sermon, but Brother [*sic*] read a little tract and offered a sincere prayer on his knees and then held another brief address for the few listeners. Attendance at services continues to be very sparse, and we try to calm people about each small circumstance or incident that happens around us. For example, yesterday and today there were services in the Methodist churches in our neighborhood. These are always better attended than ours.

*Sun., July 5.* [Spg.] Because of continuing rainy weather only a few Brn. and Srs. came here to the services.

*July 11.* [Spg.] Today one of our carpenters, who had worked on our house over 2 months, left us because he had to be told that he had not done what he owed in proportion to his high wage.

*Sun., July 12.* [Ooch.] The sermon was on Jesus' words in Luke 15:1-10 and the attentive listeners were directed to Jesus' special shepherd-like faithfulness, which He our Savior shows to all who confess and follow Him and shows to each and every individual heart. We tried to impress this on their hearts. During this they were urged not to waste any time — at least not from now on — by neglecting the gentle voice of the Good Shepherd which has blessed, peaceful intentions for each of us, and to listen to it and follow it. We were sorry to hear today that many of our neighbors, including some of our Brn. and Srs., are sick or not well. We attribute this to the damp weather we have had the last 3-4 weeks.

*Sun., July 12.* [Spg.] Early today Br. and Sr. Copeland from Tennessee came on a visit to our place. With them came Br. H. Clayton, who is planning to work here for some time and help us with our house construction or in the agricultural work. Since the two workers who had been taking care of the agricultural work until now are planning to leave us, we took him in to work for an indefinite period of time. Today a nice number of listeners also came to our services. After the sermon Br. Samuel held a long talk to those present and afterward offered a prayer on his knees in the Cherokee language, during which the listeners were very touched. Br. Samuel and Br. Israel had already arrived here yesterday evening and spent the night.

*July 13.* [Ooch.] Br. and Sr. Eder visited our Br. and Sr. Gorge Hicks, where our Sr. Lucy Hicks has been quite unwell for a number of weeks. Although she was still very weak, it seems that she is on the road to recovery now. In the evening Br. and Sr. A. Copland delighted us with a pleasant visit from Tennessee, where they have lived since last fall. In the following days we (Br. and Sr. Eder) joined them in visiting Brn. and Srs. and friends in our neighborhood, where they were very warmly received everywhere.

*July 13.* [Spg.] Today one of our workers once again left here and went to New Echota, because he had long ago promised to work for Mr. Boudinott and Mr. Worcester. So we currently have only one worker who is working on the new house. We should also add that Mr. George Harlen visited us yesterday and told us that he is planning to travel west next fall to look at the landscape there to which the Indians here are supposed to move, so that he would know if the land was really as good as it is described.

*July 15.* [Spg.] Rachel Byhan and Nancy Becker visited Polly Vann 2 miles from here, who is seriously ill. They found her very weak, so they hardly believed she would recover.

*July 16.* [Spg.] At 2 o'clock in the afternoon a cloud gathered above Spring Place. When it was almost directly above us it produced lightning and thunder so hard 4 times that it made us more than a little worried. But the Lord kept all harm and misfortune from us. The cloud moved away all of a sudden again, so that we could hear no more thunder.

[Attached to the end of the 1828 Springplace Diary:]

Springplace, July 16, 1829

My dear Br. Schulz,

If I am not mistaken, I have already informed you that the $200 you sent me arrived safely in my hands. Praise God, we are currently all relatively healthy except for Nancy Becker, who recently complained of stomach pains. But she seems to be better today.

Things are progressing slowly with our construction, since we currently have only one carpenter, whom I pay 25 cents less salary a day. The other carpenter, this one's brother, left me completely because I also wanted to pay him lower day wages. But he would not work for less than one dollar a day. The one whom I still have works now for $1.25 a day instead of $1.50 as I informed you. Currently Henry Clayton is here and is underpinning the porch. He is planning to work a while here for $10 a week. This week we began making bricks, which Mr. Jos. Vann is also having made. He is planning to build a brick springhouse.

We currently hear little or nothing concerning the Cherokees' move to the west. I should think Br. Eder or Br. Clauder could write you more about this matter than we, because they actually live closer to the place where the matters are really discussed, and Br. Abr. W. Hicks can inform them about everything. Br. and Sr. Alex. Copeland are visiting in Takoa this week, and we expect them back at Spring Place this week. They are willing to serve the mission in Tekoa for board and clothing.

Apropos, have you canceled my *Western Carolinian*, as I asked Br. John Vogler to tell you to do? Previously I always paid for it at Br. G. Shober's in advance, at the beginning of July. Everyone sends sincere greetings. Accept a very special greeting from your Br. whom you know and who loves you,

Gottlieb Byhan

*Sun., July 19.* [Ooch.] Br. Clauder preached to a pretty large gathering of listeners on Luke 16:1-9.

*Sun., July 19.* [Spg.] In the morning was the sermon on 2 Cor. 6:2: Behold, now is the accepted time; behold, now is the day of salvation. Afterward was Bible reading. Toward evening we had a strong storm again with a heavy downpour of rain.

*July 20.* [Ooch.] Our Br. and Sr. A. Copland returned to Tennessee by way of Spring Place after a pleasant visit here of 8 days. Before they left we had a thorough discussion with them about living with us in the future. Br. and Sr. Eder accompanied them to New Echota. On this occasion we were able to visit our Christian friends and neighbors there, which we all enjoyed.

*July 20.* [Spg.] Today our neighbor Jos. Vann visited us on business and stayed here a number of hours. Toward evening Br. and Sr. Copeland, who had been visiting in Tekoah, stopped in at our place again on their way home and spent the night. Otherwise today, after the heat had risen to 100 degrees Fahr. we had another strong storm, but which passed over with no rain.

*July 21.* [Spg.] Br. and Sr. Copeland today traveled on and are planning to reach their home tomorrow. Mr. Jos. Vann visited us once again today on business.

*July 24.* [Ooch.] In recent days we have been busy harvesting our hay, which turned out better than expected, praise be to our dear Lord. Our dear Br. Clauder complained a lot with a sore throat today, and this made talking very difficult for him. In the following days this pain developed into a full-blown throat infection and caused him a great deal of suffering for several days. We were beginning to worry about him since he could not eat anything except some clear soup, and even more since we were not able to get any medical assistance because of the great distance. But we were joyful and grateful that the best Doctor of body and soul blessed the measures we used and provided him great relief, and a few days later he was healthy and well.

*Sun., July 26.* [Ooch.] Once again there was only a very small gathering of listeners here for the service. We prayed the Church Litany and then read a couple of chapters from the Gospel of St. John and held a sermon for these few. We are hurt and sorry that attendance at services by Christian and heathen Cherokees is so low or so infrequent, and even if one or several of them are occasionally present, it is extremely rare that one can get around to a discussion of religious matters with them. Even though both of our Brn. Hickses, who speak both languages, have thus far graciously provided us with translation assistance, one can often hardly get a yes or no from them. It has often happened that when they have attended services several times, we have taken the opportunity to speak with them and tell them they should seek the salvation of their immortal souls soon and attend services often. They agree, but then they never come back. From all of this it seems clear to us that there is no hunger or thirst among them for the Word of Life or need for a Savior, and their hour of grace is not yet here. On the whole, we are somewhat comforted (which admittedly should not be the case) when we look at the work and few successes of missionaries from other confessions such as the Methodists, of whom there are many among this Nation, and see they have just as little success. Although it is sad, it must be said there is no foundation at all of Christian truths or instruction in the truths of salvation; they aim for numbers.

*Sun., July 26.* [Spg.] Today none of our Brn. and Srs. was in our services except for Br. Boas. In the afternoon we had a hard rainstorm again.

*July 27.* [Ooch.] In the evening, Br. G. Byhan delighted us with a visit.

*July 28.* [Ooch.] Br. Clauder had very bad colic pains.

*July 29.* [Ooch.] Br. Gottlieb returned to Springplace, accompanied by Br. Clauder.

*July 27.* [Spg.] Br. Byhan today went to Tekoah on business and returned from there on

*July 29* [Spg.] with Br. Clauder, who has been unwell for some time. Since Br. Clauder's illness seemed to become more and more serious, on

*July 31* [Spg.] he went to Doct. Bean, about 9 miles from here, with Br. Nathl. Byhan in our small stage wagon, to get some advice from him.

This Doct. Bean is a white man and lives in Sumak town. He

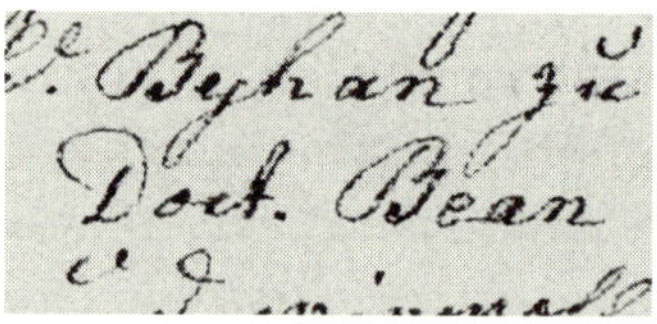

is used pretty often as a doctor, and although he actually keeps little medicine and has only worked his way into the art of healing by himself, he still usually has success and in praxis sometimes really cures, which make him famous as a doctor here in this country. He sometimes visits us, and he told us just recently that he wanted to serve us Germans for free at all times, if we need his help.

In the evening Brn. Clauder and Nathl. Byhan returned from Doct. Bean's. This evening Br. Clauder seemed to be noticeably better, so that on

*Aug. 1* [Spg.] he was able to leave here and go to Tekoah. An Indian woman came today and wanted to take two of our schoolchildren [Young Deer and Hunter] home with her. We told her, however, that we could not allow this unless the mother of the children [Peggy from Chickamauga], who had brought them here, came. Then we would let them go, although not gladly, because in a short time they would forget the little that they had learned.

# *1829, part 5*

[M 414-4-15: Translated by Julie Tomberlin Weber. No address; no postmark. Received Aug. 17.]

Springplace, July 31, 1829

My dear Br. Shulz,

I believe I already informed you that on July 2 I received your kind letter of June 16 along with $200, and expressed my sincere gratitude for this. Of the $200, Br. Clauder shared $80, so now I have only $29 in my account. However, at this time I do not owe anything to the workers on my house or in the field, or very little.

The two carpenters who were working here until last week have gone. I let one of them go 3 weeks ago, because he, in <u>my</u> opinion, did not work enough or diligently enough for his high wages. The other, his brother, stayed until last Friday after I paid him 25 cents less per day for the last 3 or 4 weeks. No one is working on the new house currently, but one man from Tennessee offered to finish the house for me for $1 a day — the carpentry work — which might be about 3 or 4 weeks of work. If he does come, I will probably hire him. The floors are all laid except one porch. The doors and windows are all trimmed, and the doors and window shutters have been made. The stairs are also finished and both wooden walls between the main rooms and bedrooms are partly done. Most of the bricks for the chimney have been made and will probably be used within 2 weeks. I have also hired a mason to brick in the chimney. So the house will finally be finished after we have practiced untold patience and had many irritations, and this will surely be the last one which I will undertake to build, as long as the circumstances in this country remain as they currently are. It will cost a lot, but I cannot help it since workers here in this country believe that missionaries find money on the streets. They have no mercy on them. It is just the same for the missionaries in Brainerd and other mission sites.

This week I finally paid another visit to our dear Brn. and Srs. in Tekoah where, I must say, the situation and circumstances really are quite confused. The Brn. and Srs. there are actually all to be pitied. They make things extremely difficult for each other. Good Br. H. G. Clauder deserves the most compassion, because he feels very pressured and is suffering spiritually and physically. He has decided to journey to Salem at the beginning of Sept. to explain personally to the Conferenz the entire situation and circumstances of the mission there, and I must say I approve this plan, because the way things are in Tekoah right now, it is extremely difficult for Br. Clauder, and he would not be able to endure it for long.

It seems to me there is too much distrust among the Brn. and Srs. there, and everyone thinks he must do the most, and everyone sees himself as a Negro to the others. It is not good, and it is very difficult if an idea like this and an attitude like this get established at a mission post, as you perhaps, dear Br., will already know from experience, and in this matter Br. Eder is confused, because he sees himself — as he himself said in our Conference — as a Negro, because he has to work the entire day from early until late at night.

The situation is this: He gives himself much too much to do and becomes a burden for others with his unceasing busy-ness, since the other Brn. and Srs. would much rather see him practicing to learn the English language, while he says that he has no time for this. Otherwise, he has completely lost the desire and the joy of serving this mission further, and he says that he is not up to the work and could not manage what would be expected from him as the head man, because he has not mastered the English language. And yet amazingly enough, when in the Conference I indicated my wish that Br. Clauder should once again come back to his post he jumped up and said that he should not return for his sake, which he repeated two or three times. I was shocked, because he had just said that he was not good for the work here since he could not speak English, and through this he showed indeed that he dares to manage alone. I do not know what to think of him. Br. Clauder also says he could not get to know him well either. In brief, I am confused about him. I do not know what he wants.

Aug. 1st. In your dear letter of June 16th you made the following comment about Br. Eder: "However, if, as you write, they think and do not want to work at all," etc. — here I must have been misunderstood. The situation concerning the outside work is as I noted above. Eder is on his legs and busy the entire day. However, concerning the work of winning souls for the Savior and relating to the people, etc., he holds back too much in this. It is also said that Br. and Sr. Eder mostly stay in their rooms on Sundays instead of talking to the visitors. In brief, you will learn about everything in detail from Br. Clauder. I wanted to share one more thought: If it is possible to find other help, it would perhaps be good if Sr. Gambold could be spared there.

I must also refer to Br. Clauder here. Br. Clauder has been very poorly for several weeks and last Wednesday came to Spring Place with me for a visit and, as he said, to recover. His body and mind have been very affected by the current circumstances and relationships in Tekoah. This morning he went back to his post. He asks you to greet his parents warmly. When he left here this morning he was very energetic again, so that he will surely recover. A visit in Spring Place always provides him, as he says, with great encouragement.

I shared with the Brn. and Srs. in Tekoah what you wrote me in your letter about the construction of a chimney there, and this displeased them. It is a shame that our house construction cannot be undone. I would gladly stay in our hut until we see where things will end with the Cherokees. During my visit in Tekoah, I also visited Br. Abr. Wm. Hicks, and on his own he began to talk about the current difficult situation of the Cherokees. The

Indians themselves do not know what will become of them. They are very divided in their opinions. Some take their circumstances lightly; some claim they would not go west; and some others do not seem to have much against it if they must move. Otherwise, they are generally somewhat dissatisfied with, indeed almost suspicious of, the Delegation that was in Washington last winter, because they have not yet made any public announcement about their negotiations there, as you will have seen from the *Phönix* dated July 29th.

It is possible that our Nathanael will come to Salem with Br. Clauder to visit. If it should come to this, I will explain it in more detail in my next letter. Even Rachel really wants to come, because she has so many cramps in her legs and primarily suffers from headaches, so that she cannot get around as she would like to. But her coming is very uncertain.

In your letter to me you write: "Accepting the Copelands or not will now also depend on the situation of the Cherokee Nation." We cannot retract this acceptance, because Br. and Sr. Copeland immediately and happily accepted the offer to serve at the mission again, whether in Tekoah, Spring Place, or in Arkansas. If we do not accept them now because of the situation of the Cherokee Nation, it would make people wonder if perhaps we didn't know anything certain about the fate of the Cherokee Nation, so that we might be viewed with suspicion. People in the country here, and the Indians especially, have very watchful eyes on us, especially now, to see if we will perhaps indicate anything that could make them think we knew more about their relationships and circumstances than they do. And so it is especially necessary that we be very careful not to give any signs or indications that we thought we would not be staying here and wanted to stop doing this or that or planning things this way or that. We must thus always show in our actions as well as in our words that we think we will always stay here, because it is currently a special time of trial concerning the thoughts and opinions here in this country.

Now we want to carry this matter to the Lord diligently and lay it on His faithful heart. He will make all turn out for the best.

Please greet Br. Shaaf sincerely from us and tell him that his announcement about Br. Rüde's homegoing arrived here on July 30th. We are very grateful for his weekly announcements. Otherwise, I wanted to add that it really does not matter whether you send your letters to us via Augusta, Ga., or via Abingdon, Va., because they get here as quickly one way as the other.

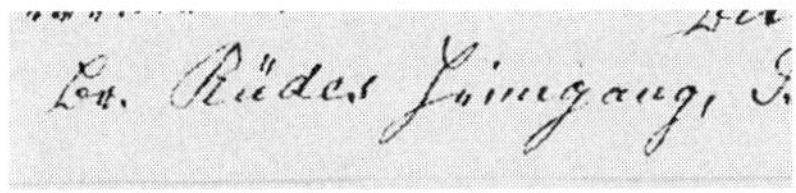
Br. Rüdes Heimgang,

It seems Br. Reichel and Br. Shulz are not able to reach Spring Place, although we have really looked forward to this visit. Br. Reichel is presumably too weak to come to our place. Please greet him from all of us, as well as Br. and Sr. Bechler. Next week Mother Byhan and Rachel are planning to go to the health springs again, not far from Capt. McNair's, in the hope that using it will help their weak conditions. Sr. Delila McNair will visit the same spring at the same time; she is also often sickly.

Concerning the printing of the Tracts in Cherokee, I have spoken with Mr. Worcester in New Echota. He told me that he has corresponded with Mr. Hollock, Secretary of the Am. Tract Society, who informed him that there are now more difficulties printing the tracts in the Cherokee language than they originally expected, especially because the Cherokees' stay is so uncertain. But as I understand it, he has suggested that if a Society is formed here which could send them money, they in return would send the tracts. Mr. Worcester then wrote down a kind of constitution where members of this society will contribute something to get the tracts for this, which could then be translated into the Cherokee language and printed. Br. Clauder will also be able to tell you about everything in detail.

With this mail I am now finally sending our Diary from the last quarter of 1828; the rest will follow soon.

Accept the warmest greetings from all of us and a special greeting from your poor Br.,

Gottlieb Byhan

[Springplace (M 407-1) and Oochgeelogy (M 409-1) Diaries. Translated by Julie Tomberlin Weber. Handwritings are Franz Eder's (Ooch.) and Gottlieb Byhan's (Spg.).]

*Aug. 1.* [Ooch.] Br. Clauder returned from Springplace, where he had another bout of colic.

*Sun., Aug. 2.* [Ooch.] Br. Clauder held a sincere talk for the few listeners present on today's Doctrinal Text from 1 Cor. 13:1 and then we read a couple of chapters from that Epistle and concluded the service at this time.

*Sun., Aug. 2.* [Spg.] After the Sunday services today, the Holy Communion, which will be held in 14 days, was announced to our Brn. and Srs. Sr. Byhan and Rachel Byhan today drove to the therapeutic spring not far from Dav. McNair's. They are planning to use this for a while. Our Sr. Delila McNair will also use it, because she suffers from rheumatism pains. Sr. Byhan wants to use them primarily because of her weakness, and Rachel Byhan because of rheumatic pains in her limbs. We wish and hope that the use of the waters might be beneficial for all of them. Toward evening we had another strong storm with heavy rains.

*Aug. 3.* [Spg.] Today many Indians came past here to attend a Green Corn Dance, which will be held in the Cahoty Mountains.

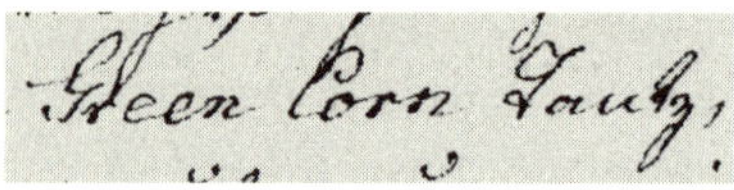

*Aug. 5.* [Ooch.] Brother and Sister Eder visited our Sister Watie at Br. and Sr. Wm. Ab. Hicks's, and other of our Christian friends in our neighborhood to the joy of all.

*Aug. 8.* [Spg.] Today Mr. Niclaus McNair stopped in at our place on his way to New Echota and Ridge's Ferry. From him we heard that the company at the therapeutic spring is doing pretty well.

*Sun., Aug. 9.* [Ooch.] Br. Clauder preached on Jesus' words in Matt. 26:20-28. Afterward we were very blessed as we refreshed our hearts with the most sacred enjoyment of the body and blood of Jesus in Holy Communion. We were very comforted by a feeling of the Savior's loving and blessing presence and forgiveness.

*Sun., Aug. 9.* [Spg.] Because only a few Brn. and Srs. were here today only one service was held.

*Aug. 10.* [Spg.] Today Mr. Parker from Brainerd and his daughter stopped in at our place on a brief visit. They had been visiting in New Echota and Tekoah. After they had eaten lunch they went on farther.

*Aug. 11.* [Spg.] Toward evening Mr. Dav. Steiner Tazizi came to our place to find and bring together his cattle which are partially with our cattle and partially in the bush close to us.

*Aug. 13.* [Spg.] He went home again without his cattle, which he really wanted to find.

[M 414-4-17: Translated by Julie Tomberlin Weber. Addressed to: Revd. Theodor Schulz, Salem, Stokes County, North Carolina. Postmark: Springplace, C.N., Aug. 13. Free. Gottlieb Byhan, P.M. Received Aug. 24.]

Springplace, Aug. 12, 1829

Dearly beloved Br. Shulz,

Your kind letter dated July 20 along with the *Miss. Intel.* reached my hands on the 6th of this month, and I sincerely thank you for this. I do not need to assure you that we are very touched by the loss of your only dear brother; we know from experience that it cuts deeply to lose a brother or a child through death, but it is a great comfort to know that they have left all the problems of this earth and will see Him in whom they believed here and will praise and glorify Him with His wounds through eternity. Oh! What a thought to know that this joy also awaits us! In the meantime, we want to remain faithful in our appointed calling and business, so that this call might also be granted to us one day: Well done, thou good and faithful servant: thou hast been faithful over a few things. I will make thee ruler over many things: enter thou into the joy of thy Lord [Matt. 26:21].

<u>That</u> part of our house family which is currently living in Spring Place is healthy and well. The other part, Mother Byhan

and Rachel, who have been at the health spring not far from Capt. McNair's since the 3rd of this month, were also well according to news that arrived day before yesterday. Tomorrow I am planning to go and bring them home.

You will have seen from Nathl.'s letter to you and from my comments in his letter that he has decided to come to Salem with Br. G. Clauder. They are planning to set out from here on Sept. 7. In my future letters I will write you more details about Nathanael's visit. Br. Gott. Clauder has not been well for some time already, but he is still able to carry out his business as needed. His spirit has been very affected and primarily over Br. Eder's affair. I should not get involved in writing on his account, because it would only be somewhat incomplete, since Br. Clauder can tell you everything thoroughly.

With these few lines I send you 2 more months of Diary, Jan. and Feb. of this year. Our construction is proceeding slowly. Currently I have only one carpenter working on it. The bricks for the chimney are now being baked and will be finished in a couple of days. I also have several people now who are busy burning chalk, but it is somewhat difficult because it is between 2 and 3 miles to the place where you get the stones to burn chalk. Br. H. Clayton is one of them [page torn] my workers, for $10 a month. I must pay the carpenter I now have $1 a day.

I will try to make the report to the War Secret. early and send it in, although I believe writing reports will not be of any more use, because everyone, one might almost believe, is against the poor Indians.

All is quiet in the Nation as far as we know. Yesterday I heard from our friend Dav. Steiner Tazizi that the Georgians had dispersed, and that the Cherokees, Creeks, Choctaws wanted to set out to oppose the Georgians with united force. But as Tazizi told me, this would be denied in the *Phönix*. It seems it was just stirred up to make the Indians look bad. God knows best how things will go. We must commend the matter to Him alone. He knows how to arrange everything for the best. The next Council and the Congress will surely clear up the matter.

The weather throughout this summer was tolerable. Only once

was the Therm. 101°. Otherwise, it has always between 95° and 98°, but unusually fruitful weather. Praise God, we have an overabundance of everything, so to speak.

Please give our best greetings to all the ministers and Brn. and Srs. Please also greet our Sophia nicely from us. And you, dear Br., accept the most sincere greeting from your loving, lowly Br.,

Gottlieb Byhan

[Springplace (M 407-1) and Oochgeelogy (M 409-1) Diaries.]

*Aug. 12.* [Ooch.] Br. and Sr. Eder paid a pleasant visit at our Br. and Sr. Byhan's in Springplace. They found them and their dear children healthy and well. After a pleasant stay of two days, they returned healthy and well here in Tekoa.

*Aug. 14.* [Spg.] Today Sr. Byhan and Rachel Byhan returned home from the mineral spring not far from Capt. Dav. McNair's. The former was very weak, and Rachel had also not gotten much benefit from the use of the waters. Thus it seemed that it had not had the desired effect on them, which was also the case with Sr. Delila McNair. She had also not been able to recover from her illness.

*Aug. 15.* [Spg.] Toward evening a certain Mr. Rodgers stopped in at our place with his wife, David McNair's daughter, the widowed Nealy. They live on the border of Georgia. They spent the night here. Already by this evening some of our Brn. and Srs. had arrived here for the services tomorrow, and they spent the night.

*Sun., Aug. 16.* [Ooch.] There was no sermon again today because of the extremely low attendance. We read several chapters from *Idea Fidea Fratrum* for the few who were present, then concluded the service with a sincere prayer on our knees. We were also very sorry to hear today that our baptismal candidate [John Fields], the only one we have, had participated in a heathen game, the so-called ballplay, where things are usually very wild and heathen. We were sadder to hear this about this man since we have already talked with him repeatedly about how rarely he attends services. He always excuses himself with the great distance and lack of time. This seems to be another sign that he is not serious about his conversion, as seems to be the case with most of the Cherokees.

Sometimes this completely discourages us, especially when we consider the very low attendance of Cherokees or brown people, sometimes none at all, which makes our presence here seem to be completely in vain. For example, even among the youth in the school, which is a real burden for the missions here, because one must always feed the children, wash for them, and often even clothe them, they can do whatever they want. The main problem is that they do not understand English, so studying and lessons are extremely difficult for them. Naturally it takes a long time before they can understand anything. Experience has shown that when one works with them a long time and has a little hope, they suddenly lose their small desire to learn. They run away, and they don't come back. The parents seem to have no control over their children, or they don't want to use it. We have found this true even among some of our Brn. and Srs.

*Sun., Aug. 16.* [Spg.] In the morning at 11 o'clock was the first Sunday service. We prayed the Church Litany and after this there was a talk on the Daily Text for today, 1 John 2:1,2. In the second service we had a blessed enjoyment of the body and blood of Jesus in Holy Communion. The married Br. Israel and the married Sr. Rosina watched as confirmands during this. During the preceding speaking with Br. Israel and Sr. Rosina both expressed themselves very contritely and in a pleasing manner and expressed their honest intention and desire to become and remain the property of Jesus. Some of our communicant Brn. and Srs. could not come this time because of illnesses. We felt particular compassion for the situation of our Br. Samuel, who was thrown by his horse yesterday evening when he was getting ready to set out on the road to our place. His horse shied at another horse, and he sprained his elbow. We sent him some medicine to ease his pain. His son Flea, our schoolchild, asked with tears in his eyes for permission to be allowed to go home to see his father. We could not prevent this, because he will presumably also need help on the farm.

[*Records: N.C.*, 8:3872-73: Salem Diary. Translated by Douglas L. Rights.]

*Aug. 16.* At the request of Br. Abraham Steiner the Br. Johannes Renatus Schmidt became his assistant with the Negro congregation, by appointment of the Provincial Elders Conference.

[Springplace Diary (M 407-1).]

*Aug. 17.* [Spg.] Early in the morning two of our schoolchildren left our place without our knowledge. They were two blood brothers [Young Deer and Hunter]. Their father is running around in the country, and since their mother [Peggy from Chickamauga] could not feed them, she brought them here to the school. Since the older of them has been talked to a number of times about his wild and even unmerciful disposition, this seemed, as we now hear from the other children, to be the cause of his running away. Br. Nathl. Byhan and a dayworker went after them to bring them back. They got them about 5 miles from here and brought them back. The younger one was happy to come back to us again and to get out of the control of his older brother. When he saw Br. N. Byhan, he ran to him with outstretched arms and was happy that he would be brought back. The older one was not so willing, but still went along when he saw that his brother was out of his control.

[M 414-4-16a: Translated by Julie Tomberlin Weber. Addressed to: Revd. Theodor Shulz, Salem, Stokes County, North Carolina. Postmark: Springplace, C.N., Aug. 20. Free. Gottl. Byhan, P.M. Received Sept. 7. Handwriting is Gottlieb Byhan's.]

Springplace, Aug. 19, 1829

Dearly beloved Br. Shulz,

With this opportunity I am once again sending 2 months of the Diary, from March and Apr. When this arrives, the Diary of

Jan. and Feb., which I sent last week, will already have arrived.

In my last letter I informed you that Mother Byhan and Rachel had gone to the mineral spring near Capt. Dav. McNair's to take the waters there, in the hope that it would be beneficial for them. Last Friday they returned from there. But taking the waters from this spring did not noticeably improve their health. Mother returned home very weak, and she has gotten weaker each day, so that she often has to lie down due to weakness. We hope that she might recover soon. She has also been sick with a dysentery-like diarrhea that has been raging in the area around here and in Tennessee, and this has really weakened her.

Last week we had a visit from Br. and Sr. Eder. This was the first time he has visited us. They were all quite well in Tekoah. Br. Clauder has also recovered pretty well from his illness. I think I already informed you that Brn. Clauder and Nathl. are thinking of setting out from here for Salem in our stage wagon on Sept. 7.

Concerning the critical situation of the Cherokees, I can tell you nothing new. They are quite quiet and composed at this time, but Mr. Dav. Vann, who lives in the area near the Ridges, wrote to his parents-in-law, Dav. McNair, that they — the Indians — most of those from his neighborhood — will move next fall and that he himself — Dav. Vann — did not want to move with them, but will move to our area here. Probably nothing else significant will happen until the Council has gathered in Oct. Various things will probably be cleared up then. At least around here, people smile when they talk about the Georgians wanting to have the land. They remain quiet in their daily routine and business, and no one indicates that they are in danger of surrendering house and garden to the Georgians. In New Echota people are building as before, and those whose houses were not finished are completing construction this year, such as Mr. Worcester, Boudinott, and others, so that we see that at this time they are not yet thinking about moving away.

Certainly the poor Cherokees face a change ahead of them, which can be concluded from the situation in which they currently find themselves with Georgia and the Government. But only time will tell how things will change for them and how things will turn out. The Council and Congress will surely decide. As soon as we hear anything new here we will report it to you as quickly as possible.

Presumably rumors concerning the Cherokees are circulating in your area and cause you to worry about us. We can assure you that <u>for now</u> there is no danger. As soon as there are signs of danger I will report this.

<u>All</u> of us greet you and your dear colleagues most sincerely. Accept the warmest greetings from your lowly Br. and Sr.,

Gottl. and Dorothea Byhan

[Springplace (M 407-1) and Oochgeelogy (M 409-1) Diaries.]

*Aug. 21.* [Spg.] Mr. Edward Hicks came to our place from New Echota and spent the night. He told us that the Governor of Tennessee, Col. Carroll, had stayed in New Echota for 2 days this week to learn the thoughts of the Nation or the Chiefs about a negotiation concerning the land which lies in the State of Tennessee, and that he now also wants to visit the Creek Indians on the same business. On his return journey he wanted to visit the Chief of this Nation, Mr. John Ross, to discuss this matter with him as well. Thus the poor Cherokees are besieged and troubled from all sides. Time will tell what they finally decide to do.

*Sun., Aug. 23.* [Ooch. Handwriting is now Henry G. Clauder's.] Br. Clauder preached, the last time for now, on the Doctrinal Text for today: We preach Christ crucified, etc., 1 Cor. 1:23,24, and with sincere admonitions he laid the need for conversion to this same crucified Christ on the hearts of the few listeners. He asked them not to waste an hour before surrendering their hearts to Christ. It was our deepest desire that this sincere admonition might make a blessed and lasting impression on everyone and especially on the youth.

*Sun., Aug. 23.* [Spg.] In the first service was a talk on the Daily Text, and in the second a Bible reading. Only a few of our Brn. and Srs. were present.

[M 411-1-28: Translated by Elizabeth Marx. Addressed to: Dear Brother Theodore Schulz, Salem. Postmark: Fvd. By Mr. Clauder. Received Sept. 11.]

Tekoa, Aug. 23, 1829

Dearly beloved Brother Shulz!

[Contents summarized; translated parts are in quotations.]

[Br. Eder expresses the joy of all of them over the letter of the 16th of the month and their gratitude to the Lord that all there are well. The mission work and the school, consisting of 12 little ones, continues in its usual course without anything particularly pleasing or depressing. There is nothing to be said at the present time about our only candidate for baptism, J. Fiels; he comes very seldom to us, so that we don't know what to expect.] "I must confess that my assurance in respect to this individual has vanished almost completely. Not only my own weak opinion, but a surer sign of his indifference is his own postponing of holy baptism. But on top of that we heard the other day that last Sunday he took part in a pagan merry-making, a so-called ballplay, where, so to speak, things usually are done in a very heathen way, so that we can apply the Word, as David already said: 'Let no man lose heart, God can again turn his heart to guide him to the straight way and narrow gate; he leads hearts like streams of water.'

"At present nothing is heard about the moving of the Nation. I believe the Cherokees know as little about that as we do."

[He says that Br. Clauder is taking this letter, and goes on to explain that they do not know why Br. Clauder suddenly decided to make the trip to Salem now, when it had been planned for the beginning of October. He has noticed that Br. Clauder seems to have lost his enthusiasm and is depressed, but he, Eder, is not in a position to try to cheer him up. He advances several theories as to why this change in a very energetic Brother. Perhaps because the results of the work are turning out to be just the opposite of what he must have anticipated. For one thing, the attendance at their services is very poor. They are surrounded, not by brown people as is the mission in Spring Place, but by white people, most of whom are Methodists. He hopes that Br. Clauder's visit to his parents will cheer him up and that when he returns he should not come back as a single person. His own experience tells him that this is not the place for a young single Brother, nor for a person who does not speak English well, because there is no time to study the language.

[He hopes that by the time this letter reaches Salem, they might have received some word from the U.A.C. about their new appointment and that Br. Schulz will forward it as quickly as possible by whoever comes to Tekoa, so that their relief might not be delayed too long. His wife at present is four months into her pregnancy and would not be able to make such a long and perilous journey later in the year, although they would not be able to accept the call until the spring of next year.]

[In case Br. Clauder would want to return single, we would have some problem in regard to his living accommdations. Br. Schulz knows our situation. Where will Br. Clauder be housed, especially in the winter? The confinements of Eder's wife and of Sister Copeland are only one or several weeks apart, and if no other housing situation is available and they must journey in mid-winter, then where to put Br. Clauder? Perhaps Br. Eder's worrying is unnecessary, or perhaps Br. Schulz might suggest to take over for the time being the room in the schoolhouse where the children sleep. But against that Br. Eder makes an objection arising out of recent experience. When Br. and Sr. A. Copeland recently visited Tekoa the children frightened the Eders with screaming, romping, bursts of laughter, so that both Eders were sick the following day and were not able to do anything. It could be that as a result of such a fright a women in child-bed could suffer an injury that would last a lifetime.]

"In addition, my dear Br. Schulz! you will find a couple of letters to Germany which I ask you to forward to avoid extra expense as opportunity presents itself for ships' sailing, etc.

"Sr. Gambold, though she has illnesses from time to time, sends hearty greetings to all and commends herself to your prayer and intercession. We send greetings to dear Br. and Sr. Bechler, and we, my dear wife and I, commend ourselves to you and wish and emplore your heartfelt love and sympathetic interest, and from our dear Savior we ask His mighty assistance and support for their new undertakings. You, my dear Br. Schulz! and your dear family, and dear Brother and Sister Schaff, please receive the most heartfelt greetings from those who are faithfully bound to you,

"Brother and Sister Franz Eder"

[M 414-4-16b: Translated by Julie Tomberlin Weber. Br. Eder adds a note:]

P.S. Since we certainly believe that Br. Nathl. Byhan at least will return, we would sincerely ask you to send us the following items: for Sr. Gambold and the entire household flaxen linen for shirts, also for Sr. Gambold 1 pair of high and 1 pair of low shoes. For my wife 1 pair of weekday high shoes made somewhat full. For me, one pair of high shoes. Also some gray and white flaxen

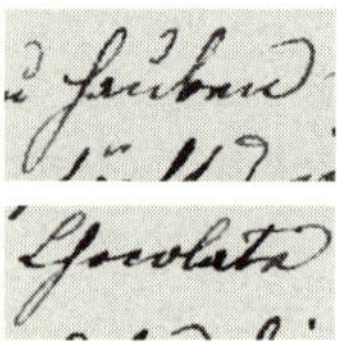

yarn on a spool. White ribbon or tape for Haubes or other uses of every kind. One pair of piece goods further dyed to put in clothing, and some flannel. Some cinnamon and chocolate and two good butcher knives and perhaps some sewing needles. The children use so many.

Also some money because we would like to be free of all old debts for once.

Eder

In addition, we would like a so-called ladle, made of iron, and if possible a tea kettle. The one here is hardly usable anymore. And if I could ask you to send some shoe polish, not to shine but just to preserve the shoes, which completely lose the black from constant damp, heat, and mud, and also some blacking.

Eder

[Springplace (M 407-1) and Oochgeelogy (M 409-1) Diaries.]

*Aug. 24.* [Ooch.] We bid a very emotional farewell to Br. Clauder and sent our best wishes for blessing to accompany him on his long and difficult journey to Salem, where he is planning to visit his dear parents. Sr. Gambold accompanied him to Spring Place, and she returned healthy and well from there on the 26th. A bad eye disease is raging among children and adults in our neighborhood. So far we have been spared as have our schoolchildren. We are all the more grateful for this because it takes 4 or 5 weeks for the eyes to heal, and we would not know what to do with so many children for such a long time. We can't send them home, because there are few opportunities to do this.

*Aug. 24.* [Spg.] We received a pleasant visit from Br. H. G. Clauder and Sr. A. M. Gambold from Tekoah. Br. Clauder is getting ready to go to Salem on a visit, and Br. Nathl. Byhan will accompany him there.

At the end of this Diary, if we want to offer a glance into the inner working of the Gemeine in Spring Place at all, then we admittedly must be ashamed before our dear Lord that we have not come further in grace, in love for Him and among ourselves, and we have much cause to plead with Him for forgiveness. However, we also cannot deny, and to the honor of our dear Lord we can say, that we have Brn. and Srs. in our Gemeine who have sought and found grace, mercy, and forgiveness of their sins in Jesus' blood. This is especially to be seen in adult baptisms, confirmations, and Holy Communions, upon which occasions we always receive courage and happiness anew from Him who is powerful in weakness. And He who set us, His poor servants, here will continue to stand by us, to support us further with his grace as long as He has us here, so that we at least will not ruin anything in His vineyard. We commend ourselves and our dear Cherokee Gemeinlein to your loving remembrance and prayer before our dear Lord.

Gottl. and Dorothea Byhan

*Aug. 26.* [Spg.] Sr. A. M. Gambold today returned to Ochgoloogy. In the evening Mr. Dav. Steiner Tazizi came to our place and spent the night.

*Aug. 27.* [Spg.] Early in the day Mr. D. A. Tazizi went on to Hightower to bring home his brother who goes to the school there, and returned with him in the evening on

*Aug. 28* [Spg.] and spent the night here again. Early today Brn. Nathl. Byhan and Gottl. Clauder left here in our small stage for a visit to Salem. Br. Byhan will take care of the school during Br. Nathl. Byhan's absence as far as time allows him to do so.

[M 414-4-18: Translated by Julie Tomberlin Weber. Addressed to: Revd. Theodor Shulz, Salem, Stokes County, North Carolina. No postmark. Received Sept. 11.]

Springplace, Aug. 27, 1829

My dear Br. Shulz,

Last Monday, the 24th of this month, Br. Clauder arrived at our place from Tekoah completely unexpected with Sr. A. M. Gambold. Br. G. Clauder came with sack and pack, ready for the journey to Salem because his circumstances, or those in Tekoah, were such that he believed the journey could no longer be postponed. He will be able to give you better information about this. I believe I have already informed you in previous letters that our Nathl. has decided to visit Salem with Br. Clauder. They are planning to begin their journey tomorrow or the day after tomorrow.

On this occasion I am sending the Spring Place Diary, as far as I have been able to manage, as well as the account or the income and expenditures, from Oct. 18, 1827, until June 30, 1929.[1] I would like to have specified all the little details if I had had more time, because I had to copy my entire journal, and I decided that was not necessary. However, if it is requested, I will do it when I can. So I have included only the money income and expenditures. Many posts are very high, but everything here in this country is much more expensive than where you are, and I can say in good conscience that I have not spent anything unnecessarily. When I get time, I will write to you again with the next mail and note various things about the account, which will go through Oct. 1.

---

[1] Br. Byhan's account for Springplace from Oct. 18, 1827, to June 30, 1829, is filed at M 419-B-6-b, Moravian Archives, Winston-Salem, North Carolina.

Otherwise, we want to commend our Nathanael to you dear Brn. in the best manner. We are happy that he can visit with you on this occasion. He will also be able to tell you how he is planning to serve the mission further. He told us that he will return to Spring Place this fall in any case to continue helping with the mission work here. In his absence I will take care of the school as well as I can. Perhaps our Rachel will assist me with this. Admittedly I will sometimes not have time for it, and so I really hope that Nathl. does not stay gone for too long. I do not even need to say that we all hope that Br. G. Clauder will come back. I also wanted to mention that Nathl. said that if the Cherokees must move west, he would not be opposed to going with them under certain conditions.

Now may the Lord guide these two Brn. there and back, so that they can help carry out the mission work with renewed courage in the future, because the harvest is great and the laborers are few.

Now I would also like to ask you to send the following articles on this occasion:

1 or 2 pairs of shoes for G. Byhan
1 pair for Mother Byhan
2 pairs for Rachel Byhan
1 pair bombazine overalls for G. Byhan
1 pair bombazine overalls for Nathl. Byhan
1 overcoat for Nathl. Byhan
Some summer vests for Nathl. Byhan
And 1 or 2 summer vests for G. Byhan
Sour drops from Doct. Kühln for Mother Byhan
Stouton's bitters
Some Glauber salt
Opium
A hat for G. Byhan, if they can pack it
A German ABC book, Ebersdorfer, from Br. Benzien
A German Bible from Br. Benzien
Slate pencils
3 or 4 thimbles, thread, primarily blue
Some shirt linen for us Brn.
Snuff ? — if there is room.

I would also like to ask you if our Sophia should come to you for payment for some Haubes she is making for our Sr. Delila McNair, please pay her and let me know the price, so that I can get the payment here from Sr. McNair. We must do all we can for our McNairs, because they serve and help us in any way they possibly can. They show that they are our friends through their actions.

We are currently reasonably healthy. Mother Byhan is somewhat better rather than worse since my last letter to you, although she is still very weak.

With today's mail we received your dear letter from Aug. 12th, along with *Wöchent.* and *Monatl. Nachr.*, for which we thank you sincerely. We are certainly very touched by dear father Abr. Steiner's loss, and we sincerely wish him comfort from above, which he can receive from the One who can comfort those who are troubled and who look to Him. We gladly grant Mother Steiner the great happiness of resting at Jesus' feet after so many hours of suffering. Please greet dear father Steiner very warmly from us. We were touched to hear that poor Jacob Blum departed so beautifully and sweetly. He could have shared in no greater happiness, although it is very hard for the family remaining behind.

The 28th. Since the Brn. are leaving here this morning, I will close this letter. They will also be able to explain the situation and circumstances in which we currently live better than I can write about them. We greet you all most sincerely and you, dear Br., accept the warmest greeting from your upright, loving, poor Br.,

Gottlieb Byhan

I gave Nathanael $10 travel money, although I currently have little or nothing in the account, and this left me only about $4 in it.

G. B.

# Periodical Accounts, *1829*

[*Periodical Accounts*, London, 11 (1829-31), 468-71.]

MISSION AMONG THE NORTH AMERICAN INDIANS.

*Extract of the Report of the Directors of the Brethren's Society for Propagating the Gospel among the Heathen, established at Bethlehem, in Pennsylvania.*
Communicated at the Annual Meeting of the Society in August 1829.

THE following concise statement of the critical circumstances in which the Cherokee nation, and the mission established among them, are placed by the course of political events, will doubtless be received with interest and sympathy by the members and friends of the Society.

It is generally known, that, at a time when former experience did not warrant the idea that an Indian nation was likely to abandon a hunting life, and in consequence was presumed to be nearly indifferent to its place of residence, provided it afforded plenty of game, and under views of the political rights of such nations, which, whatever may be thought of their justice, were too generally adopted at the time — the Government of the United States concluded a contract with the State of Georgia, agreeably to which that state ceded to the United States a large portion of its chartered territory, therefrom to form new states (Alabama, for instance), and to dispose of the lands thereof as the United States should think best.

By way of consideration for this ample cession, the United States engaged, at their own expense, to extinguish the Indian claims within the remaining territory of Georgia, as soon as this could be effected, upon reasonable and peaceable terms. This contract the United States have been endeavouring to fulfil, and several millions of dollars have been expended for the purpose.

In the meantime, the humane plan of civilizing the Indians, and rendering them an agricultural people, was steadily kept in view by the federal government, probably without adverting to the bearing which an alteration in their mode of life would have on the disposition of the Indians to accede to a final removal. The endeavours of all who strove to make the Indians acquainted with Christianity, were greatly favoured and encouraged. As regards the numerous nation of the Cherokees, whose principal residence is within the limits of Georgia, an unexpected degree of success has attended these plans. A large proportion of the nation appear to have already abandoned the chace, and to have become agricultural, at the same time adopting, in a great measure, the way of life of their white neighbours; and it is well known, that the gospel has made very considerable progress among them, both through the endeavours of the Brethren, and of other zealous missionaries.

For a long time the State of Georgia witnessed the progress of this alteration in silence. At length, however, it began to appear, from the failure of the repeated attempts of the government to induce the Cherokees to sell more and more of the lands occupied by them within the limits of Georgia, that the nation, having become in a measure an agricultural one, and therefore no longer indifferent to the place where they located, had determined to sell no more of the soil, which they considered their paternal inheritance. Georgia, nevertheless, insisted upon the fulfillment of the contract; and the government of the United States in vain endeavoured to act accordingly, the Cherokees declining absolutely to listen to any proposals of removal.

In addition to these difficulties, the nation came to the resolution of forming for itself a written constitution, on the model of the constitutions of other states, without abandoning their national independence, and thus establishing an independent community and government within the state of Georgia. This measure necessarily brought on a crisis; the endeavours of the government to urge forbearance on the part of the state of Georgia, and the necessity of removal upon the Cherokees, have had but little success, and it remains to be seen in what manner an event will be brought about, which there is too much reason to consider unavoidable.

The Indians have been informed by the government, that they will have to choose between the following alternatives, either to abandon their independent nationality, and, retaining their actual possessions, to become subject to the laws of Georgia, (to which they have a natural repugnance, greatly augmented by the circumstance, that the laws of that state, as they now stand, deprive them of certain civil and political rights which they consider essential), or to accept of a permanent residence, to be guaranteed to them by the United States, beyond the Mississippi, and to remove thither; in which case they are to be duly indemnified for their present improvements.

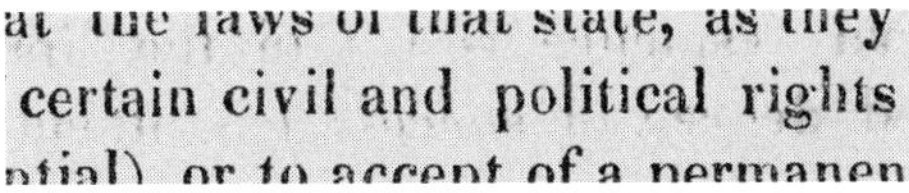
certain civil and political rights

To this latter alternative, those among them who have made the greatest advances in civilization, and those also who have become true Christians, are strongly opposed, because they regard it as a step toward a certain relapse into barbarism; and in fact there is no small danger in this respect, because the civilized part of the nation would then again come into contact with that portion of their countrymen who have already emigrated on account of their adverse disposition. It is easy to conceive, that the election which the poor Indians are called upon to make, is a most distressing one, and they scarcely know what to resolve upon.

The circumstance, that several of the Indians belonging to the missions of the Brethren are among those to whom both their countrymen and the government look up for an influential decision, renders the case peculiarly delicate for our missionaries, contradictory things being likely to be required from them; on which account they strive to abstain from any interference. As yet there is no reason to fear, that the Cherokees will be induced to make an appeal to arms, which would inevitably bring on their destruction, and that of the missions among them.

On the part of the Brethren, there is no doubt that every thing possible will be done not to abandon their little flock, even if obliged to emigrate. Let us pray that these severe trials may be sanctified to the believers and ultimately tend to the spiritual benefit of the whole nation, however little we can understand the means by which the Lord is pleased to effect this purpose. Every member of the Society will feel how powerfully this state of' things claims his faithful intercession, and remember at the same time, that the work of the Lord can never be really endangered by human power.

# 1829, part 6

[Springplace (M 407-1) and Oochgeelogy (M 409-1) Diaries. Translated by Julie Tomberlin Weber. Handwritings are Henry G. Clauder's[1] (Ooch.) and Gottlieb Byhan's (Spg.).]

*Aug. 29.* [Spg.] Mr. Dav. Vann today stopped in at our place on his way to Capt. Dav. McNair's. We had already heard in recent days that the Governor of Tennessee had visited with the Chiefs to find out if they would be willing to negotiate with him. Accordingly the Chiefs had held a private Council with him and told the Governor that they are always willing and prepared to hear what he or the Government had to say to them. However, concerning ceding the land or a part of it, they had to tell them that they had no more land to give away. And with this the Governor returned home. People supposedly heard him say that he did not expect, and would not have imagined, that the Cherokees were so advanced in civilisation, and he had imagined a bunch of wild people, which only, so to say, live in the bush in miserable cabins, and that he had gotten a completely different understanding of the Indians.

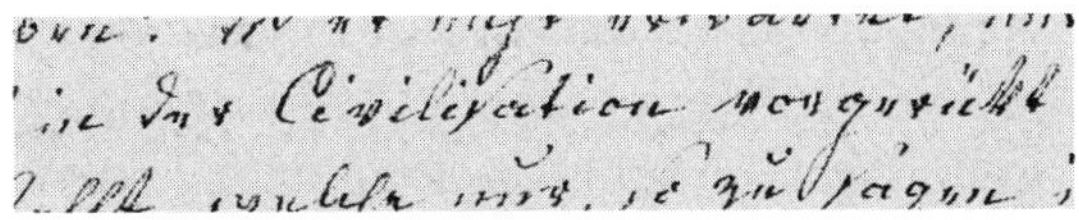

*Sun., Aug. 30.* [Ooch.] We prayed the Church Litany and then read some passages from the *Idea Fidei Fratrum* instead of having

[1] Evidently Br. Clauder relied on Br. Franz Eder's notes when copying the Oochgeelogy Diary for the period he was away to Salem.

a sermon for the few who were here, and thus we concluded our worship service.

*Sun., Aug. 30.* [Spg.] Since the Methodists had already been holding a camp meeting not far from Mr. McNair's since day before yesterday, and most of our Brn. and Srs. were attending this today, only a few of our closest neighbors were here for our Sunday services today.

*Sept. 2.* [Spg.] Mr. Rodgers, who is married to Mr. McNair's daughter Polly, and his brother, a missionary among the Creeks, came to our place and spent the night here. This Mr. Rodgers told us that the Creek Indians had decided not to move across the Mississippi, but to stay where they are now.

*Sept. 3.* [Spg.] The visitors traveled on to New Echota. Toward evening we had another visit from Mr. Blount with his wife and child from Brainerd. They also spent the night here, and on

*Sept. 4* [Spg.] they traveled on to Brainerd.

[M 414-4-19: Translated by Julie Tomberlin Weber. Addressed to: Revd. Theod. Shulz, Salem, Stokes County, North Carolina. Postmark: Springplace, C.N., Sept 3. Free. Gottlieb Byhan, P.M. Handwriting is Gottlieb Byhan's.]

Springplace, Sept. 3, 1829

Dear Br.,

Since I have about a quarter hour before the post comes, I want to use it to write you a couple of words. On Aug. 27th I received your letter dated Aug. 12 along with *Wöchent.* and *Monatl. Nachr.*, and I thank you sincerely for this. Enclosed is a receipt from H. Clayton for the $20 recently received from Mart. Hauser. Please send it to him when you get a chance. When this reaches you, the two Brn., G. Clauder and Nathl. Byhan, will probably already be with you, because they set out from Spring Place on Aug. 28.

Otherwise, everything is in its usual routine here. Everyone is healthy except for Mother Byhan, who continues to be very weak. Sometimes we allow ourselves to have troubled thoughts about her, because at times she is so weak that she almost cannot get up. May God grant her recovery soon.

The Cherokees are very quiet in their current troubled circumstances. Last week the Governor of Tennessee, Mr. Carroll, visited the Chiefs in this nation to ask them if they would listen if he perhaps wanted to enter into negotiations with them in the future. As far as I know, they were not told what he wanted to negotiate. Some Chiefs then gathered and held a private Council and gave Gov. Carroll this answer: That they will always be willing to listen whenever and to whatever the government of the United States has to say to them. However, they were in agreement concerning the cession of the land, or a part of it, that they could not give away any more of it. As we hear, Mr. Carroll returned home very satisfied. He is also supposed to have said that the affairs of this nation, that is, regarding the civilisation of it, have exceeded his expectations.

Along with sincere greetings to all of you, we remain your poor Br. and Sr.,

G. and Dor. Byhan

[Springplace (M 407-1) and Oochgeelogy (M 409-1) Diaries.]

*Sept. 6.* [Ooch.] Not a single soul came to our service because of a Methodist camp meeting held close to our place. And so there was no service. In the evening the honorable Doctor Bean delighted us with a visit. We heard from him, as well as from many others who had been at the camp meeting, that a large number of people of color were present. More than 20 people were baptized in one service, and most of them were adult Cherokees. As pleasing as this is on one hand, we can't deny that it is also somewhat demoralizing for us, since nothing is going on here. Certainly it is true that the Methodists' plan here among this Nation, where people live so scattered and isolated, is much more suitable and far more appropriate than ours! They do not have particular stations or large farms, but they have schoolhouses at various sites where they hold school for a while, and after a while move to another place so that the somewhat more distant ones can also enjoy it. Furthermore, they move to the so-called native circuit riders, which are under the jurisdiction of the closest conference. In this way the poor Cherokees (the entire country is divided into circuits) are visited again from time to time, and indeed by Cherokees who can speak with them; only in this way are their efforts crowned with success. We, on the other hand, sit here with our hands and minds occupied only with external business and naturally also without success. There is a great work taking place in this Nation, and this can surely find direction among heathen peoples who live together in towns and allow themselves to be civilized in order to make a living. However, this is not the case among this Nation.

*Sun., Sept. 6.* [Spg.] The Sunday services were held as usual. First was the Litany, and then the sermon, then Bible reading.

[M 414-4-20: Translated by Julie Tomberlin Weber. Addressed to: Revd. Theod. Shulz, Salem, Stokes County, North Carolina. Postmark: Springplace, C.N., Sept. 10. Free. Gottlieb Byhan, P.M.]

Springplace, Sept. 10, 1829

My dear Br. Shulz,

Along with sincere greetings, I wanted to inform you in just a few lines that my dear wife is somewhat better since my last letter to you and that we are otherwise healthy, praise God.

From a note I received from Br. Shaaf last Thursday, we saw that the Brn. of the Helf. Conf. are not happy that our Nathl. Byhan is paying you a visit. We personally cannot see why he cannot pay a visit to you as well as Br. Clauder can, and we want to ask you, dear Br., not to let our Nathl. know that you would have preferred that he did not come. We hope that this visit might serve to encourage him. In addition to that, he was told two years ago that if he did not like things here he could come back for a while. Since this is not the case, but he is planning to continue here, as he said to us he will tell you personally in what capacity, so we believed it is good if he can talk to you personally and explain things. Otherwise we hope that he might return as soon as possible with Br. Clauder, because I cannot manage the school and my other work. And since I am not a school man, you can easily imagine that holding school is very difficult for me.

I would also be very glad if I could once personally talk to you about the progress of the mission here, because it cannot be done well in writing and would also be very incomplete.

Now we want to lay the entire work on the faithful heart of the Lord. He will arrange everything for the best. Since my last letter, nothing else has happened regarding the moving away of the nation. Your faithfully obliged Br.,

Gottlieb Byhan

I want to share with you here the Creditors and Debtors as they appear in my book on June 30, 1829:

| Debtors | |
|---|---|
| Polly Vann | $0.25 |
| McNair | 3.30¼ |
| Boudinott | 4.37½ |
| Wm. Coody | 3.00 |
| Densby | 6.00 |
| Tekoah | 338.07 |
| Cash | 66.06¾ |
| Expenses | 1,512.80¾ |
| Bal. | 63.92¼ |
| | $1,997.79½ |

| Creditors | |
|---|---|
| Joseph Vann | $22.89 |
| Nicls. Ignatius | 0.18¾ |
| John Adams | 50.66¾ |
| Post Office | 1.46 |
| Diacony of Missions | 1,779.00 |
| Nathl. Byhan | 7.41¼ |
| John Hollars | 7.93¾ |
| Anna Marg. Becker | 10.65 |
| Gen. Post Office | 20.41½ |
| Freshour | 0.87½ |
| Allen Brock | 63.75 |
| John Crumly | 32.55 |
| | $1,997.79½ |

P.S. Our Rachel was probably planning a visit now with the Brn. in Salem. Only once has she, so to speak in fun, said that she would like to go along too, but she was never serious about it, and she will not come to Salem until we come ourselves. Presumably I or Nathl. wrote what she told our Sophia — I cannot remember if I wrote it or not. If I did, there is no harm done and it doesn't mean anything. In my opinion, it was never her intention to go now. Please greet our Sophia from us.

G. Byhan

[B 61-3: Provinzial Helfer Conferenz, meeting in Salem. Translated by C. Daniel Crews.]

*Tues., Sept. 8.* On 27 Aug. we received letters from the U.A.C. from Br. Hüffel and Br. S. C. Reichel in answer to the letters we sent in May concerning the request of Br. Eder. He is called by the U.A.C. to service in the Danish West Indies Islands. On the other hand, our Br. G. Clauder, with the confirmation of our dear Lord in the Lot *, has received appointment to be an actual missionary among the Cherokees. In case he accepts this, it is dependent on his marriage. Also included from Br. Hüffel with this was a written ordination for him as a deacon of the Brethren's Church.

Since we are expecting our Br. Clauder any time now, we decided to hold the letters for him and for Br. Eder until then. We will share Br. Clauder's with him soon after his arrival, and if he — as we hope — indicates courage and joy to accept this important appointment, we will carry out the rest of the things relating to him, and we will send the letter to Br. Eder along with him, so that he can make preparations for his departure. Our tentative plans, which we think will answer best for the journey of Br. and Sr. Eder to the Danish West Indies Islands, call for them to sail from Wilmington. Also since after Br. Clauder's marriage a wagon must be sent to the Cherokee Land, it can bring Br. and Sr. Eder back here, and if a ship from Wilmington can be found for them in Nov. or Dec. (we will find out about that by writing), then Br. and Sr. Eder can go by land to Fayetteville and from there to Wilmington by water.

The name Tekoa, given by our Brethren to the mission place

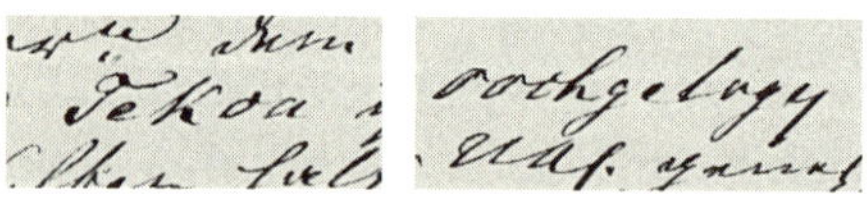


at Oochgelogy was not accepted by the U.A.C. However, it declined to decide on another. The best thing would be to wait and see how things fall out about the Cherokees' staying there.

It was a comfort to us to learn from our Brn. Anders and v. Schweinitz in the name of the Pennsylvania P.H.C. that in case of the removal of the Cherokee Nation to the Arkansas we can count on their co-operation so that they [the Cherokees] will not be abandoned by our missionaries, but accompanied by them. However, since this may be put off for a long time, we decided for now that we are not able to make use of their aforementioned suggestions, for we ourselves do not yet know which of our missionaries there will be inclined to move with them.

The Brethren mentioned above also referred to a society or association originating in New York whose members are working in favor of the goal of the General Government in Washington for the best possible method to induce the Indians to move to the West, since in the end it must come to that. Their [the Pennsylvania P.H.C.] thought, that it might be recommended to our missionaries that they be of assistance to that society in making the Cherokee so inclined [to move to the West], is not comprehensible to us, because our Brn. and Srs. could get into considerable trouble by doing that. The advice, which has often been given them from our side, not to meddle in the political conditions of the Cherokee Nation, has held well up to now and will be recommended to them again. This should be repeated in the present time especially with the guarantee, that if they should ask for it, if they indeed must migrate to the West, they would not be abandoned by us, but where possible they would be accompanied by their teachers.

[*Records: N.C.*, 8:3873: Salem Diary.]

*Sept. 11.* The Single Brn. Heinrich Gottlieb Clauder and Nathanael Byhan came from the Cherokee land on a visit.

[B 61-3: Provinzial Helfer Conferenz, meeting in Salem.]

*Sat., Sept. 12.* We had a detailed conversation with our single Br. H. G. Clauder, who arrived for a visit here yesterday from the Cherokee Land. This included the situation and circumstances of the Cherokee Nation in general as well as the Mission in Oochgelogy in particular, which this Brother has been serving faithfully as assistant. The school for girls there consists of 13 children who live with them, and also the 13 communicant Brn. and Srs. who belong to the congregation there who attend the Sunday services faithfully. He attested that through their Christian conduct and behavior they are showing themselves to be faithful followers of Jesus and give Him and the Brethren's Church glory and joy.

We asked him whether he would be inclined to devote himself further for this important service in which he has been engaged up to now, and follow them even if the Cherokees were compelled to move to the Arkansas. This is in the light of the decision of the P.H.C. that on the part of the Brethren's Church — which sent the first missionaries into the Cherokee Land — they are will not be abandoned. He answered that he has a heartfelt love for the Indians, and if it is the Lord's will, then he feels bound by bonds of thanks for the grace he himself has experienced in his heart, even with all his shortcomings and weakness, to sacrifice himself for them, and if the members of their congregation move to the West, he would like to follow them.

Upon this, the President [of Helf. Conf.] handed him the appointment as a missionary among the Cherokees which was contained in Br. Hüffel's letter in the name of the U.A.C., in which he would learn our dear Lord's will and intent for him. After he had read this himself, and humbly declared that he was willing to accept this important call, we spoke with him about the changed state which this entailed. Upon being asked, he named the single Sr. Elisabeth (Betsy) Ruede of this place in whom he believed he would find a suitable helpmeet for his service. He could accept her with the conviction of his heart without use of the Lot * as from the hand of the Lord. The Sister, of course, is free to pose the question in the Lot * if she so desires. We then talked more about his return journey, which is

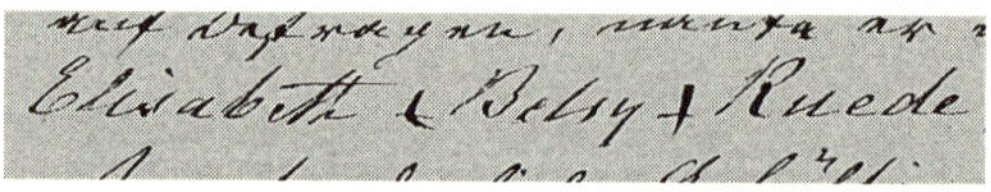
Elisabeth (Betsy) Ruede

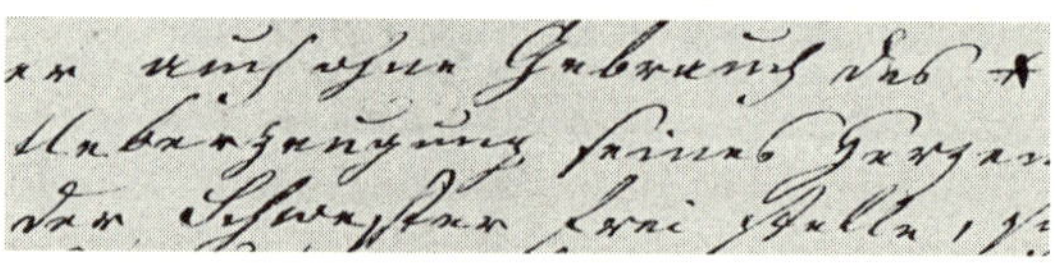

to be in two weeks if possible so that Br. and Sr. Eder, in accord with the wish of the U.A.C., can arrive as assistants in the Danish West Indies Islands as soon as possible. Br. Clauder also expressed his agreement to this.

After Br. Clauder left we considered if there was any objection on the part of the P.H.C. to the Sr. named above, and whether we had other suitable suggestions? And since the answer to both questions was No, we decided in reference to the remarks on this subject made in Br. Hüffel's letter, to have the above proposal made to Sister Elisabeth Ruede, with the proviso that the Aelt. Confz. be given notice of this this afternoon.

Br. Schulz was appointed to have a conversation with Br. Nathaniel Byhan from Springplace, who came along on the visit, concerning his service there up to now and about the state of his heart.

[Springplace (M 407-1) and Oochgeelogy (M 409-1) Diaries.]

*Sept. 12.* [Spg.] Toward evening the Indian Br. and Sr. Samuel and Br. Israel with his 7 year-old son came to our place and spent the night here. This was the first time Br. Samuel visited us since he had the misfortune of falling from his horse when he sprained his arm, which had remained stiff as a result. And he himself now looks very pitiful. Br. Israel brought his son here to the school.

*Sun., Sept. 13.* [Ooch.] The sermon was on Matt. 25:31-46. Afterward Br. Eder, through an interpreter, had a sincere talk with a Cherokee [Watie] whose wife has already been associated with our community for a number of years. His words were reassuring and pleasing. When asked if he wouldn't soon follow the good example of his wife and give his whole heart to the Savior, who won his life and salvation through His meritorious life, sufferings, and bloodshed, he answered that he had been considering this for a number of years; he had been very uneasy for some time and this occupied his mind day and night. I [Br. Eder] told him that I was happy about this and that this was the surest sign of the Spirit of God's work of grace in his heart. I asked him not to waste this time of grace and to surrender his whole heart and will to the Savior. Then he would enjoy more calm, peace, and blessings in his soul. We sincerely wished this for him and all lost souls. He went home very satisfied about this after he promised to visit us again next Sunday.

*Sun., Sept. 13.* [Spg.] In the morning was the sermon and after this was the baptism of the baby girl born to our neighbor Jos. Vann and Polly Vann, with the name Sally. Afterward was Bible reading. After this there was singing in Cherokee, and Br. Samuel gave an address to the Brn. and Srs. Also today we were asked for the first time by Br. Samuel what we would do if the Indians had to move west. We answered him that we would not leave them, but our Directors would take care that teachers would go with them. They seemed to be very satisfied with this. Further, he asked us what we then actually thought about the whole matter. We told him that we really did not know what to think about it. Admittedly we clearly see that the Cherokees currently are in a besieged and difficult situation, and we can do nothing more or better than commend them to the Lord of all in our prayers, because He has the hearts of humans in His hand and can guide them to the best ways for the poor Indians. At this he said that He indeed does this. When he had sat deep in thought

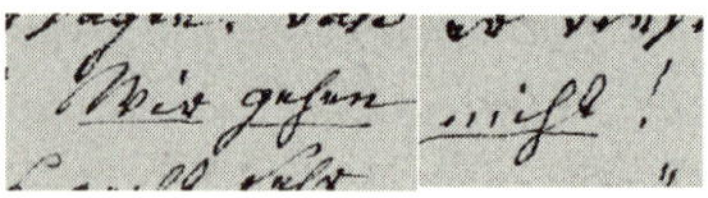

for a little while, he said: We are not going! And this ended the discussion. Afterward everyone went home quite satisfied, which we could clearly see from their looks.

[M 414-4-21: Translated by Julie Tomberlin Weber. Addressed to: Revd. Theodor Shulz, Salem, Stokes County, North Carolina. Postmark: Springplace, C.N., Sept. 17. Free. Gottlieb Byhan, P.M. Received Oct. 1.]

Springplace, Sept. 16, 1829

My dear Br. Shulz,

On the 10th of this month I received your dear letter of Aug. 27th, with the enclosed note for Nathl.

The H.C.f.G.'s wish for Brn. Nathl. and G. Clauder's journey to visit Salem, that Br. Clauder should not make his trip until Oct. and that Nathl. should stay here, could not be followed. You wrote to me Aug. 27th of your desire, and they left here on the 28th.

Now concerning Br. Clauder's haste about the visit, he originally planned not to leave here until Sept. 7th, and to our amazement and complete surprise he arrived here in Spring Place on Aug. 24th ready to travel. He will also be able to explain this and the reasons better than I can.

Now concerning Nathl.'s visit, he was partly encouraged to this by Br. Clauder, since in the beginning he had no desire or inclination to go. And we cannot deny that we also approved that he make a visit so he could finally tell you in person of his plan and decisions, and especially since he was explicitly told two years ago that if he did not like it he could come back for a while. Since this is not the case, but his plan is rather to stay and continue to serve the mission as far as he is able, for our part we cannot see what is unreasonable about this visit of his with an opportunity like this.

But if the cost of the journey is too high for the Brethren of the Heathen Society for the Oct. 1st [meeting], or if they should say that they were unnecessary expenses, then that is fine, and they can deduct it from my account and repay the Heathen Society or the Mission Diacony. Since I cannot imagine what kind of gossip Nathl.'s visit might actually cause, about which you express concern in your dear letter, we can only think that it might be the expenses. Here among our Brn. and Srs. and among the Indians there is nothing of this kind to worry about. I believe we can assure you of this.

We were very happy to see from your letter that the Helf. Conf. both in Salem and in Bethlehem have made preliminary considerations of what should be done if it really happens that our Indians must move, and to have the assurance that if our Brn. and Srs. go we will not let them go without teachers. Last Sunday I had the first opportunity to tell our Brethren and Sisters this, because Br. Samuel asked if we would go with them if they moved west. I was then able to answer this directly from your letter, and Br. Samuel seemed to be very satisfied with this. After he was silent for a while as if deep in thought, he said: We are not going! Br. Samuel asked us then what we thought about this. We told him that we hardly know what we should think about the entire matter. We could do nothing but commend this matter and the Cherokees to the Lord, Who is Lord of all lords and has the hearts of humans in His hand, and what He has decided about a people or a nation is always the best for them. To this he replied that is true, and thus the talk about this matter ended. Otherwise, it is quiet here in the nation. Each person continues in his usual way, at least around us, and if we did not get newspapers here we would not notice or know that they are supposed to move west.

My dear wife is still very weak and cannot continue as she has been accustomed. Rachel also suffers a lot from headaches. Otherwise, praise God, we are all healthy. Last Sunday we again received a new scholar and indeed our Br. Israel's son [Jesse], about 7 years old. Currently there are 7 scholars here, and I hold school for them as well as my strength and circumstances allow.

The last 3 weeks we have had very dry weather, so that we successfully brought in our corn feed, and we finished this the day before yesterday. We thank the dear heavenly Father sincerely for this. This year we also expect a plentiful Indian corn harvest, since it has grown very nicely at our place and in our entire neighborhood.

Since Monday I have had a carpenter again, who is working on my house. His name is King, a nephew of the well-known Samuel King in Iredell County. Today he finished the bedroom, so that we now have one room in our new house finished. He works for $1 a day. If my account could be fattened somewhat I would be very happy. Now concerning the *Western Carol.* I already asked your dear son Aug. Heinrich when he was visiting here to tell you that I do not want to receive it anymore. Please be good enough and cancel it. I suppose, however, that it must already have been canceled, because I have not received any more for a long time now. Br. Clauder will be able to give you a more thorough report about the situation concerning the Tracts. It seems you have had warmer weather in Salem this summer than we have here. Only once this summer was it 101°, and at your place it was up to 104 degrees.

Please greet everyone most sincerely, and you, dear Br., accept the warmest greeting from your loving, humble Br.,

Gottlieb Byhan

P.S. As soon as I hear anything new about the Cherokees moving away that I have not seen from the newspapers, especially during the Council, I will report it immediately.

G. B.

[*Records: N.C.*, 8:3873: Salem Diary.]

*Sept 17.* The single Br. Heinrich Gottlieb Clauder was married to the single Sr. Charlotte Elisabeth Rude.

[Springplace (M 407-1) and Oochgeelogy (M 409-1) Diaries.]

*Sept. 17.* [Spg.] Today Doct. Buttler, missionary at Turnip Mountain, came to our place with his wife who is very ill and 3 children and an Indian girl, and spent the night, and on

*Sept. 18* [Spg.] they went on to Brainerd.

*Sept. 19.* [Spg.] Today we finished making our hay and corn-feed. Our barn this year was completely filled with such feed, and we had to erect another hay floor and one for oats in the barn. Thanks be to the heavenly Father for these rich blessings!

*Sun., Sept. 20.* [Ooch.] Only a few people came here for the service, and instead of having a sermon we considered the Story of the Son of Man. It seemed to be a blessing for hearts. Then we refreshed our needy hearts in the most sacred enjoyment of the body and blood of Jesus in Holy Communion. This was a blessing for us. Today we heard from numerous people that many in our neighborhood were currently sick with a bad fever; we had previously heard this as well.

*Sun., Sept. 20.* [Spg.] Mr. Richard Taylor and another Indian

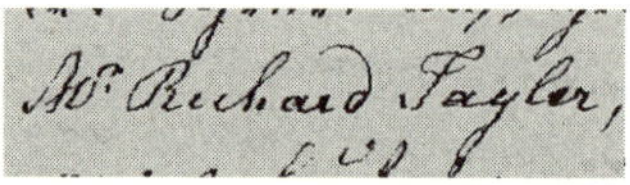


came over from Mr. Vann's to attend our services, after the bell had been rung for services the first time. In the first service was the Litany and sermon and in the second a Bible reading. After this Mr. Taylor gave a long address to the Brn. and Srs., as did another Indian who was with him. Mr. Taylor said that it was very regrettable that we had no interpreter here, and said if talks which were held for them in the English language were interpreted into Indian, they would have made a deep impression on their hearts. The message of the sermon was that of true faith in Jesus. The Savior could be felt in our midst in the services today. Upon leaving, Mr. Taylor offered to serve us sometime as interpreter. Mr. Taylor and the Indian who accompanied him returned from a Council which the Chiefs had held in the mountains toward Georgia. We could not learn what was actually agreed there. Toward evening Br. and Sr. Byhan visited at Jos. Vann's, because they thought they would find our Sr., old Mother Vann, who had visited there today, still there. But she had already gone home. Today some Indians who live close by brought us some fish.

*Sept. 23.* [Ooch.] Br. Eder visited an Indian woman who is ill. She is completely heathen, and he made her aware through an interpreter of the salvation of her immortal soul and how quickly she could be called out of this world during this fever and where she would end up without having a Savior or believing in Him. He could not feel very peaceful about her in this respect because for many years she has had such a good opportunity to hear about God's word and the good news of a Savior for sinners. Until now she had closed her ears, etc. She replied that she was always prepared to die, because she knew that she would go to a good place. I then had her told not to comfort herself with this false, unfounded idea. We poor people were by nature inclined to think better of ourselves than we really are. If we were enlightened by God's Spirit, then we saw and felt our sins and helplessness and that we would be completely lost without a Savior. She seemed very grateful for the visit and talk, and promised to attend our services regularly again, as she had done earlier, when she had recovered.

[B 61-3: Provinzial Helfer Conferenz, meeting in Salem.]

*Tues., Sept. 22.* Next Saturday the 26th at 9 A.M. has been set for the formal delivery to Br. G. H. Clauder, in the presence of the Aelt. Confz., of the written ordination prepared by Br. Hüffel. At the same time, Sr. Charl. Elisabeth Clauder and Br. Nathl. Byhan will be received as Acoluths. The latter has declared not only his entire agreement for service in the Cherokee Mission, but also to move with them to the West. Also on this occasion this company will be formally sent off by the P.H.C. to their future service.

*Sat., Sept. 26.* After the things decided in the last minutes were carried out in a solemn manner in the near presence of God our Lord, we had a thorough discussion in the P.H.C. with Br. and Sr. Clauder and the single Br. Nathl. Byhan concerning their future important service before their journey next Monday the 28th into the Cherokee Land, laid them on our hearts, and blessed them cordially in their important call, and wished them Jesus' grace and His future presence, wisdom, and support, and that of His Spirit with the assurance of our tender loving union with them and our faithful remembrance in intercession for them.

[*Records: N.C.*, 8:3873: Salem Diary.]

*Sun., Sept. 27.* Fervent prayers were offered for Br. and Sr. Clauder and Br. Byhan who will leave tomorrow for the Cherokee Mission. . . .

[*Records: N.C.*, 8:3884: Bethabara Diary.]

*Sept. 28.* Today Br. and Sr. Clauder and the young single Br. Byhan passed through enroute to the Cherokee Mission. On the 17th Br. Clauder was married to the single Sr. Elisabeth Ruede.

[Springplace (M 407-1) and Oochgeelogy (M 409-1) Diaries.]

*Sun., Sept. 27.* [Ooch.] We were troubled to hear that there is another ballplay in our neighborhood. Usually old and young participate in these, so not many people were here again today. We were happy to see that the old Cherokee Watee, whom we have already mentioned, was among the few people here. Br. Eder read them a little tract about the Savior's love for sinners, which seemed to make a special impression. At the end of a conversation we had with him, we experienced the joy of hearing this old heathen ask for holy baptism. We were all as happy as children about this. In the meantime, we asked him to be patient and immediately told him he should continue to visit us regularly so we could give him the preliminary instruction for holy baptism. He promised to do so.

*Sun., Sept. 27.* [Spg.] In the morning was the sermon on Isa. 53:4,5. Afterward was Bible reading. Today we also spoke with our single [*sic*] Sr. Sally who had already arrived here yesterday evening with another communicant Sr., and who is a candidate for Holy Communion. She expressed herself very contritely about her spiritual condition and indicated her honest intention to become Jesus' property and to remain so. In recent days various Indians came past here, and some of them came expressly to get apples from us, which we also let them have.

*Sept. 28.* [Spg.] We began driving home the bricks which Mr. Jos. Vann had burned for our chimney, and on

*Sept. 29* [Spg.] we began driving home chalk, which we burned about 1½ miles from here, and finished this on Sept. 30th.

*Oct. 2.* [Ooch.] Br. G. Byhan from Spring Place delighted us with a brief but very pleasant visit, and he pleased Br. and Sr.

Eder with some letters from the U.A.C. in Berthelsdorf, as well as from our Br. Theo. Shulz in Salem. From this we learned that Br. and Sr. Eder had received a call to serve the mission on the Danish West Indian Islands, which they joyfully accepted, and Br. and Sr. Heinrich G. Clauder have been called here.

*Oct. 2.* [Spg.] Br. Byhan went to Oochgelogy on business today, and returned from there on

*Oct. 3.* [Spg.] This evening a number of Brn. and Srs. had already gathered here for tomorrow's services.

*Sun., Oct. 4.* [Ooch.] Because of the impending opening of the Council, only a few people were here for the service. We encouraged ourselves with some passages from *Idea Fidei Fratrum.* Most of our scholars went home today, as they always do when the Council is in session.

*Sun., Oct. 4.* [Spg.] In the morning was the sermon on 1 Pet. 1:18,19. In the second service was the confirmation of Br. Israel and Sr. Rosina in their baptismal covenants, for their first enjoyment of Holy Communion. During this the married Br. Israel and the married Sr. Rosina joined in the enjoyment of this for the first time. The married Sr. Sally watched during this as a candidate for the first time.

[M 414-4-22: Translated by Julie Tomberlin Weber. No address; no postmark. Handwriting is Franz Eder's.]

O____gy, Oct. 5, 1829

My dear Brother Schulz!

Last Friday on the 2nd of this month we had the pleasure of seeing our dear Br. G. Byhan at our place on a short but very pleasant visit. Through him I also received your kind letter and those from Brn. Hueffel, Schneider, and Plitt. We were both delighted and humbled to learn from these of our Lord's merciful condescension in our call to the Danish West Indies, which we both accepted with agreement and great joy. I will skip over everything else for now, my dear Br., and mention briefly just this much: I would like to speed our departure from Salem as much as possible to your satisfaction and that of the Brn. and Srs. on the said islands, who are perhaps already waiting for us. However, my dear wife's previously mentioned pregnancy is an obstacle. Praise be to the Savior, she is healthy, but we will be happy and grateful when we have our return journey to Salem behind us, especially since we do not think we can depart until the 18th or 19th of this month. In addition, there is the fact that my dear wife is not so sure of her calculations, which often tends to happen the first time, as Sr. Gambold told her, and so her delivery could take place as early as Dec. rather than Jan. Then it would be even more awkward to undertake another land journey with her and even more so a journey by sea.

Furthermore, it is common knowledge that one cannot always go to sea right away, and if that would be the case, I am afraid the seasickness that few are spared could have very disadvantageous consequences for her. I cannot deny that secretly I have already had many worries about her on the journey to Salem. Still our dear Lord will help us mercifully.

Therefore, if we receive the approval of the P.H.C., which we herewith sincerely request, and also if our dear parents would let us move into their only little room and their main room for a short time so that my dear wife could have her delivery in the parents' house, it would be very comforting for us and for the parents, I believe especially for the poor blind mother. In this way we could really be at home with them until our next departure, and it would not cost the Mission Diacony as much as if it should happen on the way.

Therefore, I want to implore you, my dear Brother Schulz! to decide the matter according to your best judgment and to help bear or at least lighten the heavy worry and pain for me, a poor man for whom this is the first time this is associated with the blessed feeling of a father's joy. Please give the enclosed letter to our dear parents. It contains the question of whether they will give us or let us use the little room for a brief time.

Nothing special has happened during the absence of dear Br. G. H. Clauder. Thanks be to the Savior, all the work has continued as usual. A certain Watie, the father of E. Budinot in New

Echota, has already visited. Br. Clauder will already have told you he has been attending our services regularly for a long time, and on these occasions we have always spoken seriously with him. He has been here almost every Sunday since Br. Clauder's departure, and after I had spoken with him again through our Br. A. Wm. Hicks, I had the joy of hearing him request holy baptism. We are even happier about this, because his wife, our Sr. Watie, has already belonged to our congregation for years and has led a life consistent with the Gospel.

Since the Council begins next week, all but three of our children have scattered to their homes. Sr. Gambold, who commends herself to your love, was not very well several days last week, so we were very worried about her because of the fever that has been spreading here and with which some people are really suffering. Praise God, she is better again now. We send the sincerest greetings, and we commend ourselves to your compassionate love, requests, prayer, and intercession from our dear Savior. Your faithfully obliged Brother and Sister,

Franz and Carolina Eder

[Springplace (M 407-1) and Oochgeelogy (M 409-1) Diaries.]

*Oct. 6.* [Spg.] Today we began building the chimney of our new house. Mr. Jos. Vann and Mr. James Brown also visited us. In the evening Mrs. Bean, Capt. David McNair's daughter, came to our place on a visit and spent the night here.

*Oct. 8.* [Spg.] We heard that Mrs. Bean, who returned home from here yesterday, had the misfortune about 4 miles from here of falling from the horse with her child, and that she had really injured herself, so that she had to be carried home.

*Oct. 10.* [Spg.] Mr. Dav. Steiner Tazizi came to our place on business and spent the day here the following Sunday.

*Sun., Oct. 11.* [Ooch.] After a long drought, it began to rain this morning and continued pretty heavily almost all morning, so that we could not expect anyone to come to the service. Only a couple of children from our neighborhood came. We read them a little tract. Right at the end, our baptismal candidate Watee came. We sincerely regretted that we had no one to help us speak with him.

*Sun., Oct. 11.* [Spg.] Since it rained heavily this morning and the whole early part of the day, no one came to the services today. Yesterday evening the Indian Deer in the Water, who has two children in the school, had arrived here and spent the night. We took this opportunity to speak thoroughly with him about the behavior and actions of his children here. We have not been able to be satisfied with them for some time now. Mr. D. St. Tazizi was our interpreter. The General Council will begin in New Echota tomorrow, and the Deer in the Water was going to New Echota after breakfast this morning, since he is a member of the National Committee.

*Oct. 12.* [Spg.] This evening was the wedding of Mr. James Sanders and Miss Dorcas Fields. They will live in the area of Fortville, where our Sr. Felicitas Hicks lives.

*Oct. 13.* [Ooch.] In the evening we received a pleasant visit from Mr. David McNair, his wife and her sister, along with her husband Nicholson. They stayed until the 14th.

[M 414-4-23: Translated by Julie Tomberlin Weber. Addressed to: Revd. Theodor Shulz, Salem, Stokes County, North Carolina. Postmark: Spring Place, C.N., Oct. 15. Free. Gottlieb Byhan, P.M. Received Oct. 29.]

Springplace, Oct. 13, 1829

My dear Br. Schulz,

Your kind letter of Aug. 27 reached my hands on Sept. 10, and the one from Sept. 21 did so on Oct. 8. Accept my best gratitude for both.

The advice of the P.H. Conf. that our son Nathanael should <u>not</u> make the visit to or in Salem arrived here too late to cancel his visit, because your letter was written on Aug. 27, and they left here on Aug. 28. And so nothing could be done, and we could not do anything about how he would be received in Salem. And we cannot deny that the thought he would not be well accepted worried us somewhat at first. We believed a visit in Salem would certainly be an encouragement for him, and he could then explain things to you personally about what he has decided to do. From your kind letter of Sept. 21, we saw that the latter was indeed the case, and we were very glad to hear that he has offered to serve and wants to be used where the Savior wants to have him. May the Savior preserve his intention and equip him with gifts and strength!

It was certainly not by accident that both Brn. had to leave here so early, when you consider how things went for both Brn., and especially with Br. Clauder. Then you cannot fail to recognize the Lord's hand in the entire matter. We learned the first news about Br. Clauder's marriage and our Nathl.'s acceptance as an acolyte from a note Br. Shaaf sent to us, which reached our place after a journey of 10 days. Your kind letter of Sept. 13th had also arrived here already on the 24th.

Since I believed that Br. and Sr. Eder also received letters with the post on the 25th informing them of their call away and their assignment, I did not hurry to share with them the contents of your letter to me, but postponed my visit in Ochgoloogy 8 more days. When I went through New Echota, I asked in the Post Office there if there might be any letters for Br. Eder, and I received the answer that two letters had been lying there for 9 days already. I took them with me and gave them to Br. Eder, one from you and the enclosure from the U.A. Conf., which had also made the journey from Salem to N. Echota in 10 days. Br. and Sr. Eder seemed to be happy about their call away and their assignment, and they want to prepare for their departure. Sr. Gambold was not well at that time, but since then I have heard that she has recovered again. I visited there on Oct. 3.

Oct. 14. Now concerning Sr. Gambold's return, I would prefer not to have anything to do with this, and we think the best thing is to leave it entirely up to her whether she wants to return or not. On one hand, it would perhaps be good if she got away from there, which there is no room to explain here and must be done in person. We believe any other person, if she were in <u>that same</u> situation that she is in and had to hear as much about herself as <u>she</u> has had to hear, would not endure a single week longer there but would leave and the sooner the better. However, if I can express myself thus, the reason is nothing but her <u>extreme loyalty</u> through which she brings unpleasant things upon herself, because people <u>here</u> hardly know what the word <u>loyalty</u> actually means. Enough of this for now.

On the other hand, it would also be good if she stayed for a while longer to introduce Sr. Clauder appropriately to the external economy. But if Br. and Sr. Copeland arrive in Ochgelogy about the same time as Br. and Sr. Clauder, it might perhaps work without Sr. Gambold. But if this is not the case it would be good if the latter held out there a little longer. Thus we do not know what to advise Sr. Gambold, especially since Br. Clauder himself wishes that she would stay there. On my last visit, she said that she would leave it up to the Brethren of the H. Conf. whether she should return or stay. She would be willing to do either. But she had to say that she was more inclined to go than to stay. Time will tell what she will decide after receiving your letter.

We are expecting our dear travelers any day now. Without a doubt we will hear from them tomorrow, that is, if they really left Salem on Sept. 28th.

Praise God, we are currently all healthy. Mother is recovering a little as well, although it is going very slowly. Her great weakness has at least subsided somewhat so that she can get around again, thanks be to God.

But, dear Br., things with our old Pleasant really cannot continue anymore. She does more harm than good to the work here. She is a godless person; she says the most blasphemous things to us, about us, and about the mission work here, and in the presence of other people. It would be too much to report all her behavior here. We will assign Sr. Eder the job of reporting to you in person about her behavior. And so we have wondered if we should not send her to Salem with Br. Phil. Blum's wagon. You could perhaps lodge her at your Quarter. Since she would like to return to Salem, sending her away would not cause any difficulty. <u>We</u> cannot possibly keep her here any longer and be bothered by her. Everything would continue then. But believe us that she is the greatest harm to the mission work here with her godless talk.

Day before yesterday the Council gathered in New Echota. We will hear in time what they will decide now. Otherwise, everything in the nation is quiet for now. Last Sunday Dav. Steiner Tazize was here visiting us. He told us that in the area around Ridge's about 200 Indians are moving west. There are also some in our neighborhood who want to move. This is admittedly a great encouragement for Georgia.

On my last visit in Ochgoloogy Br. and Sr. Eder told me that Sr. Eder's condition will not allow her to make a journey by sea this winter. As far as I can tell at this time, Br. and Sr. Eder's departure will not cause any unpleasantries. They are happy that Br. Clauder will return married.

Oct 15. I have just received Br. Schaaf's letter of Sept. 28. Please report this to him and give him my sincere greetings. All of you accept the most sincere greetings from all of us, and you accept a special greeting from your loving Br.,

Gottlieb Byhan

[Springplace (M 407-1) and Oochgeelogy (M 409-1) Diaries.]

*Oct. 15.* [Spg.] Capt. Dav. McNair and his wife, our Sr. Delila, returned from a trip to visit with their daughters. They stopped in at our place and spent the night. Also Mr. Thomson and his wife from Hightower stopped in at our place and spent the night.

*Oct. 16.* [Spg.] The entire company traveled on.

*Oct. 17.* [Spg.] We had the joy of seeing dear Br. and Sr. Clauder, Br. Nathl. Byhan, Br. Phill. Blum and the boy Sanford Shulz arrive here safe and sound from Salem. We joined them in thanking our dear Lord for keeping them healthy and well on their journey here from Salem and protecting them from harm and misfortune.

*Sun., Oct. 18.* [Ooch.] Many of our Brn. and Srs. and friends came to say goodbye to Br. and Sr. Eder. Considering our brief presence here, we feel humbled by the love and friendship we have enjoyed from so many for some time already. With gratitude we blushed with shame and bowed before our dear Lord. After we prayed the Church Litany, we encouraged ourselves by reading the 5th, 6th, and 7th chapters of the Gospel of Matthew. Then Br. Eder spoke privately with our Brn. and Srs. and admonished them all to remain with the Savior, so that one day we will see each other again before the Savior's throne. This seemed to touch them deeply, and thus we lovingly said farewell to them.

*Sun., Oct. 18.* [Spg.] In the morning Br. Clauder gave the sermon here in Spring Place and Br. Byhan led the Bible reading. Because of the Council, which is now going to be held in New Echota, not many Brn. and Sr. were able to come for the services.

*Oct. 19.* [Spg.] The above-mentioned company traveled on to their destination at Ochgeloogy, accompanied by our best wishes for blessings. Sr. Rachel Byhan and Anna Marg. Becker went with them to visit there.

[Br. Clauder leaves a blank space where his copying the Ooch-geelogy Diary from Br. Eder's notes ends and his keeping the Diary begins.]

*Oct. 19.* [Ooch.] At eight o'clock in the evening Br. and Sr. H. G. Clauder, who have been called to serve the mission here, arrived full of praise and gratitude to our dear Lord for His merciful guidance and protection which they experienced on their 21-day journey here from Salem.

# *1829, part 7*

[M 414-4-24: Translated by Julie Tomberlin Weber. Addressed to: Revd. Theod. Shulz, Salem, Stokes County, North Carolina. Postmark: Springplace, C.N., Oct 22. Free. Gottlieb Byhan, P.M. Received Nov. 11.]

Springplace, Oct. 20, 1829

My dear Br. Theod. Schulz,

Last Saturday, the 17th of this month, we had the joy of seeing Br. and Sr. Clauder, Nathl. Byhan, Phil. Blum, and his helper Sanford Shulz arrive at our place in Spring Place. We joined them in thanking our dear Lord for leading them safely here and for keeping them all healthy. With them I received your dear letter of Sept. 27th along with *Nachrichten*, and through Nathanael $200, which I really needed. Accept my very sincere gratitude for everything.

After Br. Clauder delivered the sermon here on the 18th, he and his dear wife traveled on to Ochgelogy yesterday the 19th. Since various things on the small stage wagon were broken, he had to take our one-span wagon. Br. Phil. Blum also followed him there yesterday with his large wagon. Sr. Rachel Byhan and Nancy Becker went with him for a visit. The latter had never been in Ochgelogy before. Since the wagon has to camp, they will arrive in Ochgelogy today if everything went well. In the meantime, Br. Phil. Blum planned to begin his return journey from here on Saturday the 24th or Monday the 26th.

But we must send our old Pleasant back with them, because we cannot endure it with her any longer. She is a godless person and is damaging to the mission work here through her godless, blasphemous talk. We have done everything we could and asked her to consider the salvation of her soul. But she seems to have a distaste for God's word and doesn't want to hear anything like this. She never comes to services, and she discourages those Negroes who sometimes want to come, so that they do not come either. And the damage that she causes among our children is indescribable. She has often been told and asked to think about the salvation of her soul and not to serve the devil so willfully, as she really does through her talk and lies. But words were useless and do not have any effect on her. She even says, as she has actually said, that she would not die yet because the devil

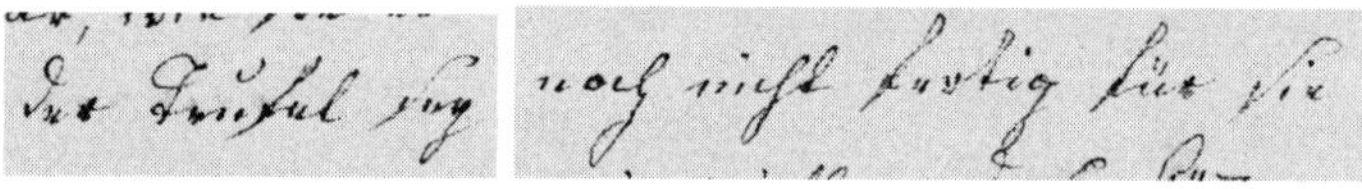
der Teufel sey noch nicht fertig für sie

was not ready for her, not to mention many other godless things.

Thus we cannot do anything but send her away. Br. and Sr. Eder will also be able to tell you more about her. We can answer before God for trying to send her away.

The rapid departure of Br. and Sr. Eder from Ochgelogy will not cause any unpleasantness.

Currently it almost seems as if the Indians will move gradually, because we continue to hear about more who are planning to move west. Still we cannot say anything with certainly. I have not heard anything new from the Council yet. Day after tomorrow the Message of the Chief — John Ross — to the Council will appear in print; it is supposed to be included in the *Phönix* of Oct. 21st.

We were sorry that we did not learn earlier that a 4-span wagon would come out here, which could have brought us all kinds of small items. I would especially like to have had various articles for our new house which cannot be gotten here or are much more expensive than in Salem. I am sorry that once again no hat could be brought along for me, and in Knoxville the dear Brn. forgot to buy one for me. But we sincerely thank you, and all of you, for the items you actually did send. I would really like to have had a Clark's *Commentary*, but since I heard that it is too expensive, I will be glad to do without this, although it could have been of great use to me.

Our new house construction is going slowly, but this week one chimney will be finished and next week the other should be started. I have a good mason, but he is very slow, and the work is not easy for him. Still he is diligent when he works.

The 21st. Today we had the first frost here. I have just heard at 4 o'clock in the afternoon that Br. and Sr. Eder were already on their way here this morning, and it seems everything is being done very quickly.

The 22nd. Yesterday evening Br. and Sr. Eder arrived here in Springplace healthy and well on their journey to Salem. We are expecting the large wagon here tomorrow, and then they are planning to continue their farther journey on the 24th.

Praise God, we are currently all tolerably healthy. Mother Byhan is gradually recovering, although it is going very slowly. Our Nathl. has begun his work and service with new heart. May the Savior preserve him in his intention of daring his life and limb in His service!

Along with sincere greetings from all of us to all of you, I remain your faithfully obliged Br.,

Gottlieb Byhan

[M 414-4-25: Translated by Julie Tomberlin Weber. Addressed to: Revd. Theodore Shulz, Salem, North Carolina. No postmark. Received Nov. 16.]

Oogillogy, Oct. 21, 1829

Dear Brethren,

I received your 2 dear letters. Their contents were important to me, because I learned from them that the Brethren of the PHC consider it appropriate to let me decide whether to use this opportunity to return to Salem with Br. Blum because of my sickliness and increasing weakness from old age. As much as I would like to have used it, and as much as I would like to have fulfilled the earnest wishes of my dear children, I cannot be inwardly joyful about returning at this time in any case. I feel much more joy in sacrificing my weak services and the rest of my strength a little longer in the service among the dear Cherokees, which is so important to me. My health is admittedly not what I wish it were. However, the small bouts of weakness are of little significance. Since the matter was given to me as a choice, I can do nothing but follow my feelings and stay here longer. Accept the most sincere gratitude for the compassion you have shown me, and be assured of my continued good will for the good of this mission.

Your most humble Sister,
Anna Maria Gambold

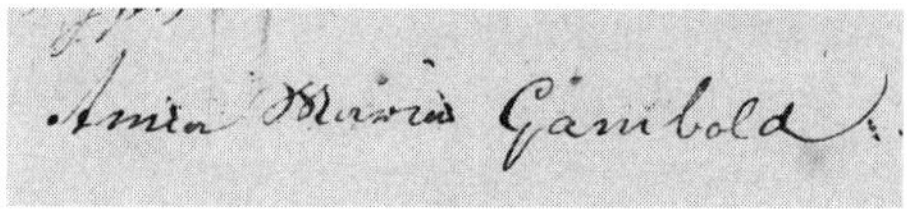

[Springplace (M 407-1) and Oochgeelogy (M 409-1) Diaries. Translated by Julie Tomberlin Weber. Handwritings are Henry G. Clauder's (Ooch.) and Gottlieb Byhan's (Spg.).]

*Oct. 21.* [Ooch.] Early in the day we sincerely bid farewell to our Br. and Sr. Eder, who left here today in accordance with their call to serve in the Danish West Indies. They were planning to spend a few more days in Spring Place. Our best wishes for blessings accompanied this dear Br. and Sr. on their long pilgrimage to their destination.

*Oct. 22.* [Spg.] Br. and Sr. Eder, who have received the call from the U.A.C. to go to the West Indies, arrived here today with Br. Phil. Blum's wagon from Oochgeloogy, on their way to Salem. Sr. Rachel Byhan and Anna Marg. Becker also returned from their visit.

This week one of the chimneys in our new house was also finished, and we began building the other one. We were sorry that the bricklayer is going home Oct. 24, and the work will have to be stopped again. Still he promised to return next week without fail.

*Oct. 24.* [Ooch.] Br. and Sr. Clauder visited our neighbor Austin Copeland, a white man whose wife belongs to our Gemeinlein. They received us most lovingly, and our visit was beneficial to everyone.

*Sun., Oct. 25.* [Ooch.] Among the visitors at our worship service today were some members of the Council, who were extremely friendly toward us. One of them, Major Waters, who was raised in England and seemed to be familiar with the Brethren's mission work, especially commented on the quiet and simplicity with which the Brethren carry out their work among the heathen, unlike some other confessions that showed a great concern for acquainting the entire world with it. In the sermon on Matt. 11:28 these gentlemen were attentive listeners; after this another man, Richard Taylor, who belongs to the mission in Brainerd, held a talk for the Cherokees who were here in their language.

*Sun., Oct. 25.* [Spg.] In the morning was the sermon on the words: The Son of man is come to seek and to save that which was lost [Luke 19:10]. Afterward was the baptism of the baby girl born to Michael, our Negro woman Pleasant's son, and his wife Hannah, with the name Rosana. Finally, Br. Nathl. Byhan led the Bible reading. Afterward our Indian Brn. and Srs. sang some hymns in their language. The single Br. Solomon was lead singer. A sweet feeling of the presence of our dear Lord could be felt in all of our services. In the evening during the evening meal Mr. and Mrs. Gold, the parents of Mrs. Boudinott in New Echota, came to our place to visit their children in New Echota. They are planning to stay here in the country for approximately one year. They spent the night here. Before we went to bed we had one more service, in honor of the planned departure tomorrow of Br. and Sr. Eder and company to Salem.

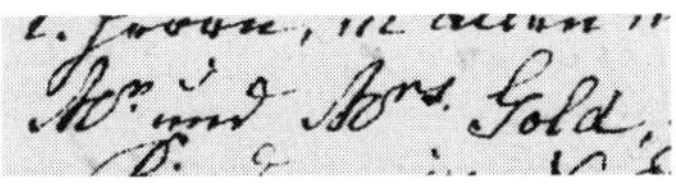
Mr. und Mrs. Gold,

[M 414-4-26: Translated by Julie Tomberlin Weber. No address. No postmark. Received Nov. 11.]

My dear Brother Schulz!

Monday the 19th of this month we had the pleasure of welcoming our dear Brother and Sister G. H. Clauder safe and sound among us. We joined them in thanking the Savior for His special love, mercy, and faithfulness, which they received from Him during their two-week journey here, just as if He had held them by His faithful and strong hand and brought them to their appointed place.

The large wagon arrived on the afternoon of Tuesday the 20th and we immediately unloaded it and put the rest of our things in the box of Br. and Sr. Clauder, so that there was no need to stay on our account. After I had given Br. Clauder, who we all know knows about the entire matter, what was mentioned in your dear letter, we had a German service in the evening, and I thanked our dear Savior in a sincere prayer on my knees for the mercy, faithfulness, and assistance shown to us in these years; I commended the work here, those who serve it, and most especially the newly arrived Br. and Sr. to Him for the special merciful guidance of his spirit, so that He might equip them with grace, strength, and steadfast courage to witness, and might make them worthy to gather many, many souls from the Nation here as a reward for His sufferings.

With this and similar feelings we said farewell on Wednesday the 21st, accompanied by the singing of some verses from dear Br. and Sr. Clauder and Sr. Gambold in the most loving way and went with a small wagon to Springplace where we arrived safe and sound in the evening and were warmly accepted by dear Br. and Sr. Byhan.

Sunday the 18th many of our Brn. and Srs. came to say farewell to us again, including Sr. Ridge and her husband old Ridge and also his brother, our baptismal candidate Waitie and his wife, and I spoke privately with them after the service and admonished them to remain here with our dear Savior to whom they would doubtless one day go with body and soul, and at every temptation to sin or to fall away from Him to flee to Him immediately in prayer. He will not leave them, but will always, even now, help them in their great trials with victory and blessing. How great, inexpressibly great, our joy will be one day, when we all see each other before the Savior's throne, etc. The emotions of saying farewell prevailed, and everyone melted in tears, and the comments of the Brethren and Sisters really touched me. Old Ridge spoke especially comfortingly, expressing his hope that in the end he would also find himself among the gathering of the faithful. Naturally I encouraged him further to do so. He was especially moved.

My dear wife tolerated the driving quite well on the first day, which was a great relief to me. According to dear Mother Byhan, it is not supposed to be as bumpy in a large wagon as in a small one. Br. Blum, who is very compassionate, I am pleased to say, says the same, and he is doing all he can to make things easy for her. Sr. Gambold could not yet decide to go back to Salem. Br. and Sr. A. Copeland were not yet there when we left, and we did not yet know for sure when they will come, since he could not yet sell his things.

People are talking about the move of the poor, troubled Cherokees more than they did a while back, but perhaps this is just meaningless talk once again.

Because of Br. Blum's horses, we had to postpone our departure until Monday the 26th of this month, so that in the end we probably not will be able to celebrate Nov. 13th with the Gemeine in Salem. At your instruction, my dear Br. Schulz, Br. Clauder provided me with $60.81 travel money; hopefully we will not need all of it.

Please greet our dear parents in advance for us. We wish and hope that they that they will be able to let us use the little room above their living room for a brief time. We are also planning, if you do not have anything against it, my dear Br., to get off at their place.

Please accept the sincerest greetings for you and yours, along with your dear colleagues, the Brn. of the P.H.C., from your faithfully obliged Brother and Sister,

Franz Eder

Springplace, Oct. 25, 1829

P.S. We will go halfway like Br. and Sr. Clauder, and perhaps if things go well, as we are pleading from our dear Savior, as they did yesterday, we can be in Salem in three weeks. Unfortunately, dear Br. and Sr. Byhan sent their old, almost inept Negro woman along with us. Br. Byhan has surely written you already to explain the reason. Br. Blum really does not want to do this, but for their sake he is willing to take her along.

[Springplace (M 407-1) and Oochgeelogy (M 409-1) Diaries.]

*Oct. 26.* [Spg.] This company then left Spring Place for Salem, accompanied by our best wishes for blessings. Mr. and Mrs. Gold also left here afterward to go on to their children in New Echota. This week we had an unusual number of visits from travelers who were coming from and going to the Council. Mr. Dav. Steiner Tazizi also stayed in our neighborhood the entire week and at our place. The most unpleasant thing about these visitors is always that their horses have to be fed, and since it is always residents of this country, one cannot ask them for anything in return for this. This sometimes seems somewhat hard to us, if we have to feed 24 horses overnight in one week, which was the case this week. Then we have to think: The ways of the country!

*Oct. 28.* [Ooch.] Br. and Sr. Clauder visited in New Echota. Our acquaintance John Fields, who has been requesting holy baptism for years and was finally accepted as a baptismal candidate, was seriously reminded to listen to the faithful voice of Jesus the Shepherd and surrender his entire heart to be His property and to put aside his service to Satan. He seemed to have slipped and generally fallen into an apathetic spiritual state before he was able to participate in this high good. He appeared to take everything seriously and showed some remorse over his previous living habits.

*Sun., Nov. 1.* [Ooch.] The sermon today was on 1 Pet. 4:8: Above all things have fervent charity among yourselves, etc. Once again a good number of listeners were present including some Councilors. In the evening our little house congregation sang a liturgy on the Church Triumphant and joined in spirit with our dear Brn. and Srs. in the Unity.

*Sun., Nov. 1.* [Spg.] In the first Sunday service, which Br. Byhan, Sr., led, he read for the few Indians who had gathered today something out of the American Tracts, interpreted by Mr. Tazizi. In the second service, which Br. Nathl. Byhan led, was Bible reading. After a chapter had been read in the English language, the single Indian Br. Ignatius interpreted it into the Cherokee language. Since the Gospel of Matthew had recently appeared in print in the Cherokee language, we decided to have one chapter read aloud in the last service every Sunday, especially since we have noticed that the Brn. and Srs. like to listen when something is read in their own language, or sung. The latter happens most Sundays.

*Nov. 2.* [Ooch.] Br. Clauder and Sr. Gambold visited our Brn. and Srs. and friends in New Echota. Many of the former are currently there to take care of the people, and so they cannot attend our services as everyone would wish while the Council is in session.

*Nov. 2.* [Spg.] Today Mr. Tazizi returned to New Echota.

*Nov. 3.* [Ooch.] My wife and I visited our Sr. Sussan Charity Wa-tee 8 miles from here. Since they cannot speak or understand English, we took one of our scholars to interpret for us. Our Sister was all alone at home with her young child, and she expressed her gratitude for our visit. When asked if she did not feel very lonely and abandoned while her husband and their children, who are in Echota, were gone, she answered that at such times she especially liked to talk with the Friend of her Soul, our Savior, and she felt so blessed by His presence that she could not possibly complain about loneliness. Her words about her spiritual state were very pleasing. May she continue to submit herself completely to the Holy Spirit's guidance; then she will not lack any blessings.

*Nov. 4.* [Ooch.] Br. Samuel from Spring Place brought 3 of his young girls to the school here.

*Nov. 4.* [Spg.] Today Br. and Sr. Alexander Copeland stopped in at our place on their way to Ochgeloogy. Br. Alex. Copeland will primarily take on the external work. And Sr. Copeland will, as far as her time and circumstances allow it, help with the school. After they had eaten lunch with the driver, Mr. Samuel Henry, they went on, so they could cross the Holley Creek about 8 miles from here this evening and then camp in the bush.

*Nov. 5.* [Ooch.] We were happy to see our Br. and Sr. Alexander Copeland arrive here. They lived in the neighboring state of Tennessee for about one year, but they had to live completely without the fellowship of Brethren. They were very happy to receive a request to move here and take care of the economy as well as to assist in the school, and they followed this gladly and willingly. We are even happier about this, since they are already familiar with all the work here, because they previously lived here for some time.

*Nov. 5.* [Spg.] With the mail today we received a pamphlet from the Secty. of War, the Honorable John H. Eaton, containing the *Proceedings of the Indian Board* in the City of New York, with Col. McKenny and his address to them. It seems that a great change awaits this Nation, that it either must move or surrender itself to the laws of the State of Georgia. Now time will tell which of the two they will do. It seems that the Cherokees in their Council this year took little or no notice of this matter. We can do nothing except commend this poor Nation in our prayers to the One who has human hearts in His hands, that the outcome of this matter might be for their best interests.

*Sun., Nov. 8.* [Ooch.] The sermon was on the words of Psalm 107:8,9. During this we most gratefully remembered the countless blessings from God which we daily experience externally as well as internally. After the sermon we had another conversation with the previously mentioned baptismal candidate, Wa-tee. At the end of this he replied that he had often felt the Holy Spirit's guidance to convert, but he had not paid it any attention. However, he could not possibly resist the Spirit's very strong voice any longer. He was very sorry he had not followed the good advice of blessed Br. Gambold a long time ago and surrendered himself as the Savior's property. That was his intention now, a decision made in God's power, and he hopes he can remain faithful to this.

*Sun., Nov. 8.* [Spg.] In the morning was the sermon on the Gospel story of the wedding garment. Afterward was Bible reading, which Br. Nathl. Byhan led. After the reading in the English language, the same was repeated in the Cherokee language.

*Nov. 9 and 10.* [Ooch.] My wife and I visited our Sisters Ridge and Leslie 20 miles from here. The latter lives 35 miles from here, but she is currently staying at the house of one of her relatives, near the Ridges' farm. Because of the great distance, these Sisters can rarely come to our services, and so they were very happy we visited them. Sr. Leslie has been suffering from physical weakness for a long time, which is why we visited her. We used this opportunity to remind her of her completion. She said that this matter often occupies her thoughts, and she longs for eternal rest. Still she feared she was not completely prepared. We tried to comfort her and admonished her to remain faithful to the Savior and for now and eternity to put her trust only in Him, the Friend of Sinners. He will comfort her and strengthen her in her trials, and He will not leave her.

*Nov. 12.* [Ooch.] A certain Mr. Gold and his wife, who are currently visiting here, came to see us. They live in the state of Connecticutt.

[M 414-4-27: Translated by Julie Tomberlin Weber. Addressed to: Revd. Theodor Shulz, Salem, Stokes County, North Carolina. Postmark: Springplace, C.N., Nov. 12. Free. Gottlieb Byhan, P.M. Received Nov. 26.]

Springplace, Nov. 10, 1829

My dear Br. Shulz,

Your kind letter of Oct. 13 and the enclosure from Br. Grunewald reached my hand on Nov. 5th. We thank you very sincerely for this. It is a shame that we cannot get the printed *Gem. Nichr.*

and the written *Nachrichten* by post, because, as you note, with the current strict management of the postal system, the delivery would be very slow if they actually went at all. The strict postmaster in Salem will surely know best.

When this reaches you, our dear travelers will have been with you for a long time already.

On the last mail day, the 5th of this month, I was astonished to receive a printed pamphlet from the Sect. of War entitled *Documents and Proceedings relating to the Formation and Progress of a Board in the City of New York, for the Emigration, Preservation, and Improvement of the Aborigines of America,*[1] July 22, 1829. This pamphlet is interesting to read. The entire Indian matter is clearly examined in it, and one can see the Government's attitude toward the Indians.

I do not know <u>why</u> he sent a document like this to me and to us. We do not like to get involved in this matter, and we will take care as far as we can and it is possible for us to do, because as soon as the Indians find out that we would also be in favor of their moving west, they would be more than a little distrustful of us. Things are beginning to get somewhat critical here now, so that we must be extremely careful not to arouse suspicion toward ourselves, and I might almost wish nothing like this had been sent to us. It is not our place to tell the Indians that moving is the best thing for them, as the pamphlet asks of everyone who wants to seek the best for the Indians.

Otherwise, it is still peaceful in the Nation, but one hears them say more and more: We must move in the end. ([Margin note:] Many Indians are quietly moving to the west.) The Council is still in session, but as far as we know nothing has come up so far in the Council about moving away. We think that the Council will break up today. We have heard incidentally that our neighbor Jos. Vann and Mr. Richard Fields will go to Washington this winter, but we do not have this news from the accurate source.

<u>The 11th</u>. I think today is finally the day that the mason will

---

1 On the Internet at https://archive.org/details/documentsandpro00amergoog.

finish the chimney on our new house, and since there are currently two carpenters here working on it, there is a possibility that we might be able to move into it at the beginning of Dec. And how happy we will be to be free of this construction! I personally will not attempt constructing another house in this country.

But dear Br., have there been initial considerations about what will be done with this site if the Indians actually move west? Blessed Br. Benzien said about 25 years ago — at a time when people were saying the Indians should move away — that the Brn. Unität should take a quantity of acreage here, because a congregation of white people could perhaps gather here someday — those were his views at that time.[1]

Judging from the relationship the Indians currently have with the government, I do not believe that we should expect any more assistance for the school. Still we will find out this winter. The last support from there was for the first half of the year 1828. I personally expect nothing more. About 3 months ago Col. Montgomery, the Agent, sent word to me through Mr. McNair — he had spent the night at his place — that the money he had received from the General Government for the schools here was not sufficient to give any to our school for now. I have not heard any more about it since then. I do not understand much about the matter. I know this much: In Sept. the school in Brainerd had not yet received anything either. Thus the support seems to be very slow, and it seems to me that it will stop completely.

You will be surprised that we are sending old Pleasant to Salem with Blum's wagon. However, we can assure you that we could do nothing else, and as I have already informed you, she was more harm than benefit to the work here. This could not continue any longer. Either she had to give in or we did. She is a godless human! Now everything here in the kitchen proceeds quietly in a peaceful and loving manner, and without arguments.

I will send you a copy [of the report] to the Secretary of War, which I sent some time ago. Perhaps this is the last report that will be sent from here, because one can clearly tell that the

---

[1] See *Records: Cherokees*, 2:729.

Cherokees' stay here will not last much longer, and as long as they are here, they cannot expect — as it has been expressed somewhere — any more help and support from the General Government, and thus neither can we.

8 o'clock in the evening. I have just heard that the Council broke up this afternoon. Among other things it was decided that 6 Delegates will go to Washington this winter: the Assistant Chief

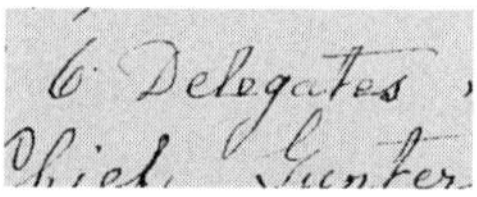
6 Delegates,
Chief Gunter

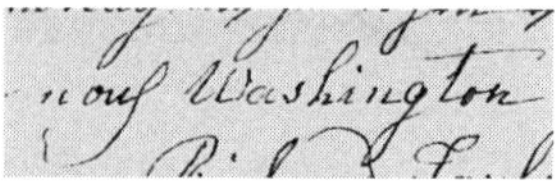
Washington

Gunter, Joseph Vann, Richard Taylor, Wilm. S. Coody, Wilm. Abr. Hicks, and Lewis Ross. It is said they will go to Nashville first and from there continue by water. They will set out from here on Dec. 1. Dav. Vann and John Ridge are going to Washington on Creek business, and they want to set out from here next week. I just saw a *Phönix* which was printed in New Echota today; it contains a letter from Col. McKenney to Mr. Boudinott and latter's answer, or his remarks about it. Both are very sharp. God alone knows what else will happen and how things will turn out. We will commend the matter to Him. The said pamphlet also appeared in New Echota and stirred up the Indians.

Praise God, we are currently all healthy, and we greet everyone most sincerely. Last week Br. and Sr. Alex. Copeland moved to Ochgeloogy. Sr. Copeland was not well, however, but it was nothing significant. Still she will not be able to do much for now, until her condition has changed somewhat, which we hear will happen at the end of next month or the beginning of January.

The 12th, morning. I want to wait until the mails for today have arrived before I close this letter to see if perhaps something comes from you dear ones in Salem, and then I can inform you of this right away.

Since it seems we did not receive anything from Salem today, I will close this letter and commend us to your further remembrance and prayer before our dear Lord. I send sincere greetings and remain your faithfully obliged Br.,

Gottlieb Byhan

[Springplace (M 407-1) and Oochgeelogy (M 409-1) Diaries.]

*Nov. 11.* [Spg.] Today we finally finished building the second chimney in our new house, so that the bricklayer could leave us on the 12th. We were very happy and grateful for this.

*Nov. 14.* [Ooch.] I visited with many of our neighbors in New Echota. I used the opportunity to speak with one of them, Austin Copeland, about his spiritual condition. He is a regular visitor at our services. He seemed to enjoy this, and it was clear from his words that the Holy Spirit is working in this man's heart. May the faithful Shepherd of our souls make him a participant, as a reward for His bloodshed and death.

*Nov. 14.* [Spg.] Mr. Jos. Vann visited us on business. He was named with 5 others in the last Council to appear as Delegates of the Cherokee Nation this winter during the session of the Congress of the United States in Washington in matters concerning this land. They are planning to travel from here at the end of this month or the beginning of next month.

*Sun., Nov. 15.* [Ooch.] Quite a good number of listeners came for the service in which the Gospel lesson for today, Matt. 18:21-35, served as the basis for our reflection. The session of the Council ended some days ago, and our Brn. and Srs. who had to be there on business have now returned to their homes, so today we experienced the joy of seeing a good number of them here at our place. After the sermon our scholars sang many Cherokee hymns and then small books sent by the scholars at the female Sunday school in Salem were distributed among them as a gift. Our deepest thanks go to these young friends for all their interest in the well-being of the youth here.

*Nov. 15.* [Spg.] In the first service was the litany and sermon, and in the second was Bible reading. Br. Nathl. Byhan led the latter. As is usual, what was read was afterward repeated in the Cherokee language, and this time by our single Indian Br. Solomon. After this some more hymns were sung in the Cherokee language.

*Nov. 16.* [Spg.] Mr. John Schneider, Sr. Byhan's brother, came to our place from Tennessee for a visit.

[M 414-4-28: Translated by Julie Tomberlin Weber. No address; no postmark.]

Ooichgillogy, Nov. 17, 1829

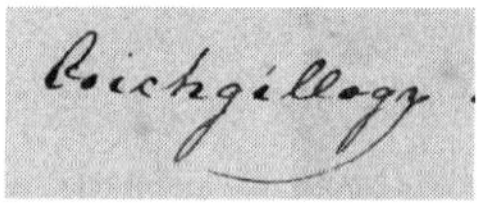


Dearly beloved Brother,

For the first time since my return here I take up my quill to inform you how we are all doing. May the Lord be praised and exalted for His goodness and mercy, through daily trust in His merciful assistance we are all happy and content, each in the work of his calling.

Last week the Cherokee Council ended after a brief session of 4 weeks. The most important thing was the appointment of a very honorable and respected Delegation to the next Congress of the United States with the following important assignments. First, to present to them a memorial concerning their rights to this land. 2nd, to appear before the Committee of Indian Affairs and to insist on a hearing for their concerns in which they could clearly and plainly explain these. And 3rd, in the last and most extreme case to turn to the Supreme Court of the U.S. and in this Tribunal to investigate the constitutionality of the Georgians' actions and of the Cabinet of the United States. The hope of this poor people depends on this. May the just Ruler of the universe grant that they are not deceived and that they receive justice. This company includes our dear old William A. Hicks and Joseph Vann, the friend of the Spring Place Mission.

On the 5th of this month we were delighted to welcome our dear Br. and Sr. Copeland here at our place. Saml. Henry, our Tennessee trader, brought them here with their things, and we had to give him $25 for this. They could hardly have been transported less expensively.

Sr. Copeland is busy in the school, which was opened yesterday with 11 scholars. Br. Copeland is taking care of the external economy, so we let our previous hired hand go.

We want to present the following matter to you and get your answer as soon as possible. Since Br. and Sr. Copeland are now in the mission service, do they have the right to attend our Conferences, even if only as listeners? It would perhaps be advisable to set aside all distinctions. Copeland brought along a lot of his belongings, some of which will be used in the house and fieldwork. Should this be purchased from him? What we do not use is and remains his, and he can use it as he wants. Further, until what date did Br. Eder send the Diary from here? I presume no further than my departure from here last August. ([Br. Schulz pencils in:] yes, Aug. 16.)

You will have joined us in rejoicing that the Holy Spirit has finally led another baptismal candidate to us, our old well-known Watee. He continues to attend our services and gives clear signs of the sincerity of his desire to surrender himself as the property of the Savior, the Friend of Sinners. In this way, one person after another finds his way to the true Shepherd like a lost sheep, despite all appearances that there is no one else here to win for Him.

We are very hopeful about winning for the Savior soon our neighbor Copeland, a brother of our [Copeland]. On a visit I recently made there, Sr. Copeland suggested a conversation with her husband about his spiritual condition, which then took place at the first opportunity. He seems to reflect seriously upon himself and expressed the desire to join us, but there still seems to be something in his way, which is still unclear to him. May the Lord have mercy on him and illuminate his soul with the luster of His glory. Then everything that is still darkness will be destroyed.

The enclosed $5 is not accepted here, so I am sending it back along with the attached bill. We are finally completely out of debt. The last significant debt we paid was to the smith, Copeland, for work during the last 2 years. Henry, the man who purchased the Negro woman, has almost completely paid his debt here and in Spring Place. The rest of the debt to Alexander Copeland for work including the debt to Doctor Fore, which Copeland paid from his money and which should be paid back to him now, adds up to $218.36½, and he should be sent a bond for this. Perhaps it would be fitting to allow him the interest for this debt for one year and to add this to the capital above. But Br. Copeland will accept your judgment in this.

Greet my dear parents and all the friends of the mission. We commend ourselves to your continued prayer, your love and compassion, and we remain your faithfully obliged fellow participants in the salvation of the Lamb until the gentle rest at His wounds,

Henry Clauder

Revd. Th. Shulz, Salem, N.C.

[M 419-B-7a: Transcribed by Richard W. Starbuck. Addressed to: Revd. Theodore Shulz, Salem, North Carolina. Postmark: Springplace, C.N., Nov. 26, 18¾. Received Dec. 10.]

Account Current of Cash receipts & expenditures at Ooichgillogy from May 5th to Nov. 17th, 1829

| 1829 | Received | |
|---|---|---|
| May 5 | Balance on hand | 32.24¾ |
| | recd. for lead sold 12½; recd. of Br. Byhan $25 | 25.12½ |
| | amt. of specie left by Br. Zevely in April | 6.50 |
| July 28 | recd. of Br. Byhan at Spr. Place | 88.00 |
| Aug. | recd. for butter, lard, corn & oats sold | 2.75 |
| Oct. | recd. of Br. Shulz at Salem | 200.00 |
| | ([Br. Schulz writes:] only $100) | |
| | recd. for sundries sold | 0.62½ |
| | recd. of Samuel Henry in change | 1.70 |
| | recd. of George A. Hicks on acct | 10.00 |
| | recd. for tea cups sold | 0.25 |
| | | $359.19¾ |
| 1829 | Expended | |
| June | Pd. Br. Clauder traveling expenses to Tennessee & for sundries | 6.18¾ |
| June 20 | Pd. Oliver Gann for work 26.62½; postage 0.50 | 27.12½ |
| June 26 | Pd. George Hicks on a loan | 21.00 |
| | Pd. John Hollers for work 0.56¼; to an Indian for work 1.75 | 2.31¼ |
| Aug. 11 | Pd. A. Copeland premium in a horse swap | 25.00 |
| | For venison 0.18¾; ferriage 0.25; J. Hollers for 6 mos. work $60.64½ | 61.08¼ |
| Oct. | Pd. expenses on Br. Clauder's journey from Salem hither | 46.00 |
| | Pd. to Br. Eder for his journey to Salem | 60.81¼ |
| | ([for these two items Br. Schulz writes:] $100 ded.) | |

| | | |
|---|---|---|
| | Pd. George Roach for work on the farm | 22.75 |
| Sept. | Pd. an Indian for work \$1.50; ferriage of Br. Clauder & Sr. Gambold 1.12½ | 2.62½ |
| | 30 lbs. fish, etc. 0.75; to Saml. Henry \$45.00 on acct. | 45.75 |
| Nov. | cups & saucers 0.62½; ribbon 0.75; comb 0.50 (at Council) | 1.87½ |
| | Pd. Joseph Copeland for blacksmith work for 2 years | 17.00 |
| | sundries purchased at Council \$1.00; for Cerokee books \$1.00 | 2.00 |
| | pair of buckskin moccasins | 0.25 |
| | postage of letters | 0.37½ |
| | for a [curry] comb | 0.25 |
| | Balance on hand | 16.80¼ |
| | | \$359.19¾ |

[Springplace (M 407-1) and Oochgeelogy (M 409-1) Diaries.]

*Nov. 16.* [Ooch.] The school began again after a break of several weeks; there were 11 scholars.

*Nov. 19 and 20.* [Ooch.] We visited our Brn. and Srs. who live nearby. At Br. and Sr. Wm. Ab. Hicks's we learned that on the latter morning a number of Cherokee emigrants, more than one hundred persons, had passed by there on their way to the Arkansaw territory west of the Mississippi River. These poor people, who lived close to the Georgia border, had to emigrate to avoid the oppression of the white people, which they carried out to an extreme. The sight of such a large company of people who have been driven, so to speak, from their rightful property must have made an extremely discouraging impression on those remaining behind. The only wise Ruler will certainly know how to use this seeming evil for the best. May He find us completely surrendered to His will.

*Nov. 21.* [Spg.] This evening about 90 Cherokees camped beneath our spring on the Georgia road. They lived in the area of the Coosa River, about 60 miles from here and were traveling west. There were various relatives of Mr. Jos. Vann among them. They are going to the Agency on the Highwassee here by land, and from there by water to Arkansas. Mr. Jos. Vann and one of his wives, Jane, today paid us a cordial visit. Today we also finished harvesting our welsh corn, which produced plentifully this year. We are sincerely grateful to the heavenly Father for this.

*Sun., Nov. 22.* [Ooch.] We were happy and encouraged to see a good number of attentive listeners at our service once again. In a second service just for the communicants we had a preparatory talk for the coming enjoyment of Holy Communion, in which the Friend of Souls revealed himself.

*Sun., Nov. 22.* [Spg.] The Sunday services were held as usual. Early today a young Indian named Archibald, from the area of Coosaywatee, visited us. He knows English well enough that we could talk with him. He told us he was planning to move to our Br. Joshua's, so that he could attend our Sunday services. We gave him the Gospel of Matthew in the Cherokee language, which he read while he was walking and standing. He seemed uneasy and concerned about himself, and as he said, wished to be saved. We told him that we have a Savior who accepts all poor sinners, if we turn to Him with our poverty and misery, etc., and encouraged him to come to our services often. As he was going home he said: Next Sunday I'll come back, still holding the Gospel of Matthew open in his hand. In the evening we had a strong storm with heavy downpours of rain, so that we were worried about our old roofs on our old houses. But praise God, the storm passed without doing significant damage. At 9 o'clock the storm stopped all of a sudden, and it became very quiet. Today we also heard that various people from our neighborhood are planning to move to the Arkansas.

*Nov. 23 and 24.* [Ooch.] I went to Spring Place on business. On my return journey on the 24th, I almost had an accident crossing the Cooswatee River on horse. It was very swollen because of recent rains. The horse had to swim, and it was very difficult to hold on to it. However, He who guides his poor ones through the depths also remembered the poorest of the poor, and I reached the other side safely. After half an hour, I reached our Sr. Gann's house where I dried my partially wet clothing and was given food and drink.

*Nov. 23.* [Spg.] Today Br. Clauder came to our place from Ochgeloogy on business. He returned there on Nov. 24th.

*Nov. 28.* [Spg.] Already in the evening some of our Brn. and Srs. had arrived here for tomorrow's Sunday services. Our Br. Israel's brother was also here and indicated his desire to belong to our congregation. This led us to talk with him about Jesus' love for sinners, and to tell him that God had sent his only begotten Son into the world to redeem us, and that if we turn to Him in our sinfulness, He forgives our sins for the sake of His shed blood, and makes us His children and the heirs of eternal salvation, etc. This seemed to be something new to him. When asked if he had already joined the Methodists or any other confession, he said he had been with the Methodists, but had not yet been baptized, and had not yet spoken a word with any Methodist, and also not with the Methodist preacher Turtlefields, although he had attended his sermons. But he had never heard what he heard from us about Jesus Christ. We advised him to consider it well, and to think about what he had heard about Jesus Christ our Savior, the redeemer of our sins. He promised to do so and to visit us often. His name is Feather.

*Sun., Nov. 29.* [Ooch.] It was the first of Advent and we prayed the Litany of the Life, Sufferings, and Death of our incarnate Savior Jesus Christ as we entered this time of rich blessing. Then there was a talk on the Doctrinal Text for today: The true light now shineth, 1 John 2:8. During this we proclaimed to the many attentive listeners that Jesus Christ came into the world to redeem us from the power of darkness and the shadow of death and to make us the happy children of light. In a second service, we joined our dear Cherokee communicants in Holy Communion, which provided nourishment for all our souls. We could feel the sweet presence of our crucified Savior so strongly that all eyes shed tears of gratitude, and everyone surrendered himself anew to be His preciously earned property. What most impressed us in this blessed service was that our dear Br. Wm. Abr. Hicks, who is ready to begin his journey to Washington City on National business, was still present. In a fervent prayer we commended him to the guidance, protection, and faithful care of the Savior. After he had delivered a sincere exhortation to the Brn. and Srs. and had commended himself to their prayer as well as ours, we concluded by singing him a fitting farewell hymn, which was very emotional. Then he shook all of our hands and immediately began his journey.

*Sun., Nov. 29.* [Spg.] First Sunday in Advent. In the morning we prayed the Litany of the Life, Sufferings, and Death of our Lord Jesus Christ. Afterward was the sermon on the Doctrinal Text for today: The true light now shineth. After this Br. Samuel gave a talk to the Brn. and Srs. In the afternoon, with the feeling of our dear Lord's presence, we had the enjoyment of the body and blood of Jesus in Holy Communion, during which the married Sr. Sally watched for the last time as a confirmand. After this we had a thorough talk with our Br. Samuel's mother's sister, who expressed her desire today to become the property of Jesus and to belong to our congregation. She was clearly told what it depends on, and what is involved in belonging to the Savior, and how one can attain grace and the forgiveness of sins from Him, etc. Then she expressed herself in such a way that we could really tell that God's Spirit is working in her heart. She was asked to be patient and to visit us often, and told that we would be prepared at all times to acquaint her with God's council for our salvation.

*Nov. 30.* [Spg.] Today our neighbor Mr. Jos. Vann left from here as a member of a Delegation from the Cherokees, which is being sent to the government. He promised to write us now and again from Washington and to report on their negotiations there.

*Dec. 1.* [Ooch.] My wife and I visited our Sr. Catherine Gann, 10 miles from here. She and her husband, a white man who does not belong to any religious confession, were very friendly and appreciative for our visit.

*Dec. 1.* [Spg.] Today when our school children were busy playing, it happened that one of them kicked another in the nose so that it bled. When the smallest and youngest of them saw this he said: That makes me remember that the Savior shed all drops of blood. The child's words seemed to say a lot to us, and from this we could conclude that God's Spirit is also working in the hearts of the children, revealing Jesus Christ the crucified to them.

## *1829, part 8*

[M 414-4-29: Translated by Julie Tomberlin Weber. Addressed to: Revd. Theodor Schulz, Salem, Stokes County, North Carolina. Postmark: Springplace, C.N., Dec. 3. Free. Gottlieb Byhan, P.M. Received Dec. 23.]

Springplace, Dec. 1, 1829

My dear Br. Shulz,

From one post day to the next, we look for a letter from you, but nothing arrives. So I will now begin again. On the last post day, the 26th of last month, I received Br. Shaaf's lines, dated the 16th, for which I ask you to thank him and give him our greetings.

Praise God, we are all healthy at this time. About 2 weeks ago Mother was seriously ill, but she is quite energetic again.

This is the first letter I have written you from our new house. We have not moved in yet, but there is a little room ready in the rafters where I now have my writing materials. I am also planning to bring the Spring Place archives here, since the space under the baement stairs in the church is too small, as you presumably know. I have also brought the Post Office, or the postal system, here, since it was also in the church, which was very difficult especially in the winter. Next to my little room upstairs, a small room with a nice fireplace is set up for our Rachel and Nancy, and they can hardly wait until they can move into it. The down-stairs rooms are ready except for a cabinet in each room where we can put things away, because until now our things have mostly lain around on boards or shelves, accessible to people and dust.

The kitchen still lags behind somewhat. The stove and a small baking oven next to it are ready, but the ceiling and the floor have not yet been laid. I am planning to line the ceiling with old boards which we used for scaffolding and the floor with bricks, which will be the cheapest in the long run. We are still missing 28 light window frames, but they are being made right now. We are planning to move in completely before Christmas. I cannot describe to you how happy we will be when we are finally finished with construction and have moved out of our houses, which are really very dilapidated, because I will not undertake any more construction here. Building in the Gemeine is nothing compared to what it is here. The worry, troubles, and irritations, and what has to be endured here when you have to have strange people. Praise God! It will soon be over! But dear Br., will you think of me and my account again? Because the $200 I last received has been spent now for the construction and the household, and I have nothing more on hand.

From Br. Shaaf's note we learned that Br. and Sr. Eder and the wretched Pleasant arrived in Salem on Nov. 15th. We thank God and are happy that we are free of the latter and do not have to worry about her godless talk anymore. We are much better off now; everything is peaceful and loving. On this occasion I would like to add that as soon as there is transportation between Spring Place and Salem, our Rachel would like to return with it and that she should be remembered even if it were already next spring.

Now concerning our mission work here, we are continuing quietly as usual. Our Brn. and Srs. attend the services as often as one can expect, considering the distance most of them live from here, and one can say that most of them intend to remain faithful to the Savior and the Gemeine. As far as we can tell and know, Brotherly love prevails among them, which is always to be seen as a fruit and sign of Jesus' followers.

Day before yesterday, the 1st Sunday in Advent, we had a blessed enjoyment of the body and blood of Jesus in Holy Communion, during which the married Indian Sr. Sally watched as a confirmand for the last time. We also rejoiced that 2 people asked to be accepted into the congregation and explained their intention to become Jesus' property and to live for Him alone in this world. The 1st was the brother of the Indian Br. Israel. His name is Feather. He had already come to us last Saturday to explain his desire, as he said. We then had a thorough conversation with him concerning our spiritual salvation and that out of love for us poor humans, God sent his Son Jesus Christ into this world to redeem us fallen humans through His bitter sufferings and death, since He himself had taken on the punishment which we earned from our sins before God, etc. He answered that he really belonged to the Methodists, but his preacher — Turtlefields — had never told him anything like this. He had also never had a private word with his preacher. We asked him to visit us often and especially our services. He promised to do this, but he kept repeating that he wanted to belong to our church.

The 2nd person is our Br. Samuel's mother's sister, Tuka by name. She seems to be very concerned about her spiritual salvation and would like to be cleansed of her sins through Jesus' blood in holy baptism and to be accepted as a child of God. We explained to her clearly what the most important thing is to be counted among the faithful and to become an heir to eternal salvation. She seemed to be very moved and promised to visit us again.

Br. Samuel also told us 14 days ago that another one of his relatives would like to join our church. He actually lives close to the Brainerd mission, but prefers to belong to our church. Br. Samuel told us that he would visit us very soon, and then we could talk personally with him.

In Ochgeloogy next Sunday the 6th is the baptism of the Indian Owetee, Mr. Boudinott's father, whom I have known well for 25 years. Br. Clauder asked me to go there and perform the baptism, if the wind and weather allow it, I believe because he has never attended the baptism of an adult heathen. All of this is very encouraging for all of us, since for a while it has seemed as if we were working in vain. But the Savior knows His time. He himself must touch the hearts of humans, and His spirit must reveal the crucified One himself, and He alone knows the best time and hour for this.

Day before yesterday our neighbor Jos. Vann began his journey to Washington. He promised to write me from time to time and to inform us of his, or their, negotiations in Washington. Everything in the Nation is quiet, which is to say that there is no arguing or fighting among them. Anyone who wants to go west goes, and anyone who wants to remain, remains; everything is done calmly. They do not think badly of each other for going or staying.

Last Saturday plus 8 days ago, about 100 Cherokees camped at our Spring Branch on their way to the west. They had 11 wagons along, which were transporting their things as far as the Agency. The drivers were from Tennessee. From the Agency they are traveling by water down the Highwassee, etc.

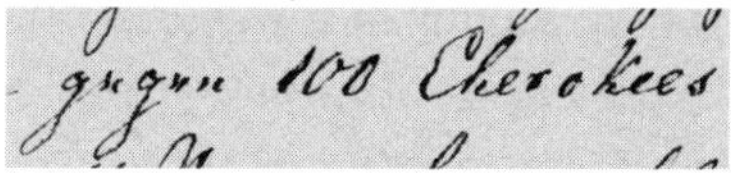
100 Cherokees

All souls are anxious to see what will happen and how the decision of this most important matter concerning the Cherokees will turn out this winter, and we are no less anxious. It is cause for gratitude that there is no bitterness or contentious language to be heard when the Cherokees discuss this matter among themselves, and we are very happy about this. Usually it is discussed as if it were someone else's business, and who knows whose. As you can easily imagine, our feelings in these circumstances are of a special kind. It now seems like a sudden calm in the middle of a storm, and we are anxiously awaiting the gusts of wind that will follow, because more dark storm clouds can clearly be seen from afar. Still the Lord is sitting on His throne and guides everything well! Why should we be afraid?

From your letters we saw that printed and written *Gem. Nachr.* for us are lying in Salem again. If only we had them here! Please extend our greetings to Brn. and Srs. Bechler, Shaaf, Reichel, Benzien, Eder, Father Steiner, and also our Sophia. And you, accept the most sincere greetings from your upright loving Br.,

Gottlieb Byhan

[Springplace (M 407-1) and Oochgeelogy (M 409-1) Diaries.]

Dec. 5. [Spg.] Br. Byhan, Sr., went to Oochgeloogy today on the invitation of Br. G. Clauder to attend the baptism of the Indian Owety.

*Sun., Dec. 6.* [Ooch.] We enjoyed a true day of blessing that the Lord made. The weather was extremely beautiful, and a pretty good number of listeners were at our services. The sermon, delivered by Br. G. Byhan, who had just arrived from Spring Place yesterday, began at 12; it was on John 3:16-18. After this, Br. Samuel from Spring Place held a talk in their language for the Cherokees who had gathered. He fervently and warmly explained to them the need for a true conversion of the heart. In the second service the frequently mentioned Indian Oa-tee was baptized into Jesus' death with a heartrending awareness of Jesus' presence. He received the name Christian David. The baptized one's brother, the well-known Major Ridge, was also present, but he showed no particular emotion during this sacred event. Still he gratefully received the sincere admonition to consider his spiritual salvation, and he promised to pay more attention to his eternal well-being in the future. Nothing is impossible for God; even the shortcomings of this world can be made into a humble child of God through the Spirit's power.

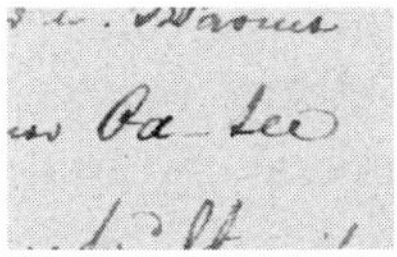

*Sun., Dec. 6.* [Spg.] Br. Nathl. Byhan today took care of the Sunday services.

*Dec. 7.* [Spg.] Br. Byhan, Sr., returned from his visit in Ochgeloogy. This afternoon we heard that the wife of Mr. Nicolson, Mr. Vann's overseer, had died. They live about two miles from here at Mr. Vann's old place. She had already been sick for a long time and was, as everyone believed, now recovering. But completely unexpectedly a stroke overcame her which brought her end. She was raised by the Presbyterians, and since she has lived close to us she has often attended our services. Mr. Nicolson asked for a little place for her on our God's Acre, and we could not turn him down.

*Dec. 8.* [Spg.] Early today we heard that our Negro Br. Christian Jacob was dying. Br. and Sr. Byhan went immediately to visit him, and in fact found him dying. After singing some verses, Br. Byhan blessed him and offered a prayer for his homegoing, and 10 minutes later he departed. He had been healthy 3 days earlier and on Dec. 4 had done his daily work as usual. In the evening of the mentioned day, he complained of pain in his neck. The pain soon moved to his chest and ended his life.

Our blessed Br. Christian Jacob was born in the Tjimba Nation in Africa and came to this land as an adult. About three years ago he became concerned about his salvation and wanted to be cleansed of his sins through Jesus' blood in holy baptism. He then received this grace on July 29, 1827. On July 20, 1828, he attained the enjoyment of Holy Communion for the first time with the congregation here in Spring Place, which was a very important grace to him. Since he was a widow and had to raise several children, his household was often difficult for him, and sometimes he had to be directed in his distress to the Helper who never leaves anyone who remains with Him and pleads for help. To this he usually replied: "I hold closely to Him; I do not leave him." Since he had not really mastered the English language, he could not express himself as he wished. But we could clearly see in him that he had sought and found grace with the Savior. Accordingly we could do nothing but confidently believe that the dear Savior has taken him to Himself in His heavenly kingdom as a pardoned sinner.

Br. and Sr. Byhan today visited at Mr. Nicolson's, since Sr. Byhan had been asked to come there to help the women there in word and deed with the body of Mrs. Nicolson. Br. Byhan returned home immediately. Sr. Byhan, however, stayed there until toward evening, and since it rained heavily was brought home in our small stage wagon.

*Dec. 9.* [Spg.] At 12 o'clock noon the above-mentioned two corpses were brought here and set down in front of our church. Then we went into the church, and after Ps. 39:4,5 was read, we accompanied them to God's

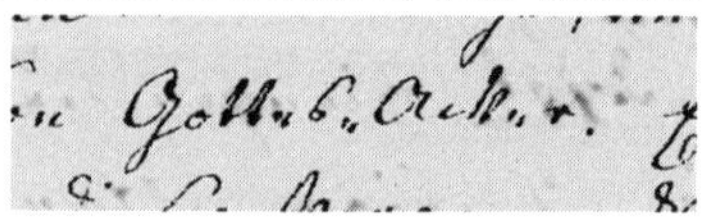

Acre. A crowd of people had gathered, especially many Negroes. This occasion, that two bodies were buried at one time, seemed to make a deep impression on everyone present.

[M 414-4-30: Translated by Julie Tomberlin Weber. Addressed to: Revd. Theodor Schulz, Salem, Stokes County, North Carolina. Postmark: Springplace, C.N., Dec. 10. Free. Gottl. Byhan, P.M. Received Dec. 23.]

Spring Place, Dec. 9, 1829

My dear Br. Shulz,

Eight days ago I wrote you a letter which without a doubt was very pleasing to you dear ones just as the contents of it are very pleasing and encouraging for us, so this week I must write you a couple of lines to inform you of the unexpected and rapid homegoing of our Negro Br. Christian Jacob, which took place yesterday. Last Friday he was still going about his usual business. In the evening of that day, he complained about pain in his neck. The pains moved to his chest and robbed him of his ability to reason, and yesterday morning he died.

I returned from Ochgeloogy on Monday evening, where I had gone on the 5th of this month to baptize the Indian Owety. This took place on Sunday the 6th and was accompanied by a sweet feeling of our dear Lord's presence. When I arrived in Spring Place I also heard immediately that the wife of a certain Nicolson, Jos. Vann's overseer, who lives about two miles from here and who had already been sick for a long time but seemed to be recovering, suddenly on the 7th died from lung disease.

Early on the 8th, yesterday morning, we learned that our Negro Brother was dying. Mother and I went there immediately, and when we arrived he was indeed dying. I blessed him then for his journey home, and 10 minutes later he died. Today was the burial. Mr. Nicolson, whose wife had died, as mentioned above, asked us to give his wife a place on our God's Acre. We could not refuse his request, although we were unsure and did not know what to do in such a case. We did not see how we could have refused this without causing great displeasure. We thus began a new journey with her.

We ask you to let us know your thoughts about this, whether we acted correctly or not, and how we should behave in similar situations in the future, so that if the same thing should happen again in the future, it would be one way of proceeding. They were both buried at the same time, and provided a view which truly encouraged us to hold even more firmly to Him who is Lord over death and life, and not to waste any time, and to let our election to grace be secured, through grace.

On the 3rd of this month we received your dear letter of Nov. [blank], along with German Daily Texts and written *Gem. Nachr.* We thank you very sincerely for everything. Praise God, we are all healthy at this time. Mother Byhan is quite well again. God maintain her thus! We send you all our most sincere greetings. Next week we are planning to move into our new house. Accept the most sincere greetings from your humble, loving Br.,

Gottl. Byhan

[Springplace (M 407-1) and Oochgeelogy (M 409-1) Diaries.]

*Dec. 10.* [Ooch.] We had a brief visit from Mr. Chamberlain, a missionary in Will's Valley in this Nation, 60 miles from here.

*Dec. 11.* [Spg.] Toward evening the following 7 persons on a journey to the Agency came to our place and spent the night here: the first Chief, Mr. John Ross, Major Ridge, John Ridge, and an Indian, Standing Turkey.

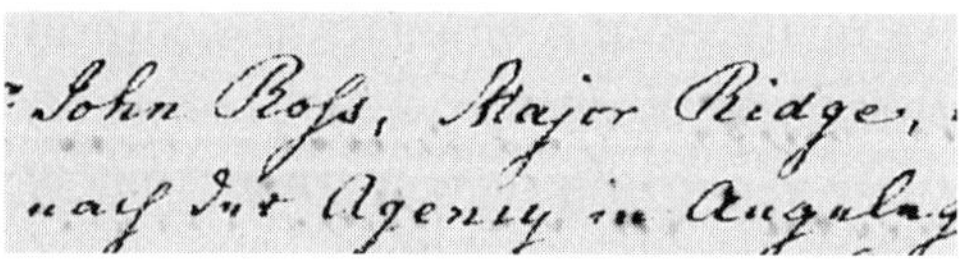


They went to the Agency on business concerning a certain border between the Cherokee and Creek land, which the Governor of Georgia recently had run. Further, Mr. Chamberlane and Mr. Dav. Steiner Tazizi, who were going to Brainerd, and Mr. Furnell, who was traveling from Brainerd to Carmel. Since the living room in our new house was finished, we were able to lodge all of these guests there. If this had not been the case, it would have caused us more than a little difficulty to lodge them in our small dwellings. We spent an exceptionally happy evening with this dear company. The Chief Mr. John Ross was especially talkative and very happy.

*Dec. 12.* [Spg.] Early in the day the whole company traveled on.

[B 61-3: Provinzial Helfer Conferenz, meeting in Salem.]

*Sat., Dec. 12.* Reviewed the minutes of 8, 12, 22, and 26 Sept.

Br. and Sr. Clauder and Br. Nathl. Byhan arrived well in Springplace on 17 Oct., and the former arrived at Oochgelogy on the 19th. After they had taken heartfelt leave with Br. and Sr. Eder on the 21st, the latter began their return journey to us. They left Springplace on 26 Oct., and arrived here safely on Sunday evening 15 Nov. Since there was the prospect of a ship sailing from Wilmington, N.C., to St. Thomas they planned to begin their farther journey on 23 Nov. by way of Fayetteville, to which place their things had been sent on the 20th. However, circumstances with Sr. Eder on the 21st made it clear that her confinement in childbirth would come soon — as she expected— and so this made their farther travel impossible before the first of the year.

In his last letter Br. G. H. Clauder laid several questions before the P.H.C. for answering, which we took up, and which Br. Schulz will answer in the name of the Conferenz.

a. The P.H.C. is not in favor of Br. and Sr. Alexander Copeland's attending their Mission Conference there, since Br. and Sr. Clauder and the widowed Sr. Gambold already make up a small Conference there, and besides an agreement has already been reached with Br. Gottlieb Byhan that the Brn. and Srs. in Springplace will hold a monthly Conference with the missionaries of Oochgelogy, alternating from place to place, where this is possible or advisable. This is for them to share advice on details of the mission work and to encourage and lend a hand to one another. This will continue. Since Br. Copeland is now to assist in material and monetary matters, and Sr. Copeland, m.n. Gambold, is employed in the Girls School, the Conferenz recommends holding Congregation and House Conferences to discuss and agree upon all matters of housekeeping and related matters, and in this the Copelands can participate.

b. In case the house and kitchen equipment, which Br. and Sr. Copeland wish to sell, can be of use in the housekeeping there, the Conferenz allows them to take this and put it on the Mission expense account. However, Br. Clauder is to take note of their current uncertain situation and not overload himself with too much household gear which may afterward turn into a burden.

[Springplace (M 407-1) and Oochgeelogy (M 409-1) Diaries.]

*Dec. 13.* [Ooch.] In the first service, after we sang some hymns and offered a prayer, we read Psalm 107 and had a talk on the words of verse 20, from which the Daily Text for today was taken. In the 2nd service, mission reports from Greenland and South Africa were read.

*Sun., Dec. 13.* [Spg.] Since today only a few Br. and Srs. came here, we prayed the Church Litany in the first service, and then there was a talk on the Daily Text [Ps. 107:20 & 1 John 4:2] for today. In the second service, which Br. Nathl. Byhan led, there was Bible reading, which was repeated in the Cherokee language by the single Indian Br. Nicl. Ignatius. The Indian Feather, who was mentioned on Nov. 28th, visited us again today. However, since we had no interpreter, we could not speak with him much today. Besides what we discussed with him through our Flea, one of our school children who has also not mastered the English language, which we regretted, he promised to visit us again at Christmas. Since Br. and Sr. Clement Vann have now moved close to us, to Mr. Jos. Vann's, they will be able to attend our services more often than previously, as today they were both present in our services.

*Dec. 15.* [Spg.] The day finally came when we were able to move into our newly built house, with praise and thanksgiving to our dear Lord. This new house has two living rooms and two chambers, so that 2 families can live comfortably together in it. Between these 2 living rooms and the 2 chambers is an 8-foot-wide hall that goes through the house. Above is a room for 1 or 2 people with a small fireplace, and next to this a small room for the archives, since this will now hold the Post Office. The kitchen, which is built onto the north gable end of the house, is not yet completely finished. But we hope to be finished with it by the beginning of Jan. We cannot be grateful enough to our dear Lord for protecting us and all those who worked on it from harm and misfortunate during the construction.

Since this construction has slowed us some, indeed very much in the last 2 years from our real calling, we are looking forward to the future, when we will be able to pursue this more and undisturbed, and especially visits with our Brn. and Srs., most of which has been neglected due to this construction.

*Dec. 16.* [Spg.] Today Br. Byhan went to Coosawaytee on business to speak with Judge Martin, but he did not find him at home and returned home in the afternoon without accomplishing his business.

*Dec. 17.* [Spg.] Mr. Dav. McNair and Mr. John Ridge returned to our place on their way to the Forks of Coosa, and spent the night here.

*Dec. 18.* [Spg.] In the morning they went on. Today Mr. John Ross, head Chief of the Cherokees, Major Ridge, Chulioa, Standing Turkey, and Br. Clement Vann also came by here on their way to the Forks of Coosa. They greeted us cordially and continued on their journey.

*Dec. 19.* [Spg.] Mr. Dav. Steiner Tazizi came to our place with his brother to spend Sunday with us tomorrow.

*Sun., Dec. 20.* [Ooch.] The sermon was on Deut. 32:29 and carelessness over the final end. Since most of those attending the service were youth, they were particularly and urgently reminded to have an eye on their final end and not to allow themselves to be caught up in the sin of inattention, through which their souls would entirely lose salvation in Christ. After the service we had a good conversation with the recently baptized Christian David, during which we reminded him of the need for vigilance.

*Sun., Dec. 20.* [Spg.] There were only a few Brn. and Srs. in our services here, which is quite common here when there are holy days next week. We still wished that many had come, because Mr. Tazizi could have served as interpreter. Mr. Tazizi promised in the meantime to come to our place for Christmas, and to interpret for us. Br. Byhan, Sr., led the morning reading service, and afterward Br. Nathl. Byhan led the Singstunde.

*Dec. 21.* [Spg.] Mr. Tazizi went into the bush today with his brother to look for some of his cattle which are staying close to our place. He found them and came back to our place this evening with his brother to spend the night here.

Today we heard that 7 boatloads of Cherokees recently left from the Agency down the Highwassee going to Arkansas. In each boat were 20 people. According to this 140 Cherokees moved west at one time. Many are still getting ready to go and are busy diligently building boats. It almost seems as if the Cherokees are really going to move to the West, because there are so many who are planning to go, that those who are not giving up the land and want to stay are almost giving up courage and consider everything lost. It is impossible to see in advance how everything will turn out. But we are leaving it up to Him, who has human hearts in His hands. All will turn out for the best. He can arrange it as it pleases Him. It is certainly intended for the best interest of this poor Nation, because we believe that He has thoughts of peace for the residents of this country and that He will still gather for Himself a rich reward for His pain from among this Nation, whether it is here now or where they will live in the future.

[M 414-4-31: Translated by Julie Tomberlin Weber. Addressed to: Revd. Theodore Schulz, Salem, Stokes County, North Carolina. Postmark: Spring Place, C.N., Dec. 24. Free. Gottl. Byhan, P.M. Received Jan. 7, 1830.]

Spring Place, Dec. 22, 1829

Dearly beloved Br. Shulz,

Although I do not have anything particular to report, I cannot let this post day go by without writing you a couple of lines and informing you of how we all are doing.

We finally moved into our new house on the 15th of this month, full of praise and thanksgiving to our dear Lord, who has helped us thus far and who has mercifully protected us from all harm and misfortune during this construction. Now *we*, and the Brn. and Srs. who will live and work here after us, will have a house where they can nourish themselves and live pleasantly or "comfortable," as one says in English. But the kitchen has not yet been occupied, because various details are still missing there.

But at this point one might ask for *whom* was this house built? This question occupies us a great deal, because it almost seems now that the Cherokees will give in ultimately, or *must* give in, because we hear almost every day of Indians or residents who are "enrolling," as it is called, to move west. Last week 140 persons traveled down the Highwassee to Arkansas, and more of them are going or want to go. We hear that the Head Chief, John Ross, allegedly said that things are over for the nation, because so many are moving west, but we do not whether this is true or not.

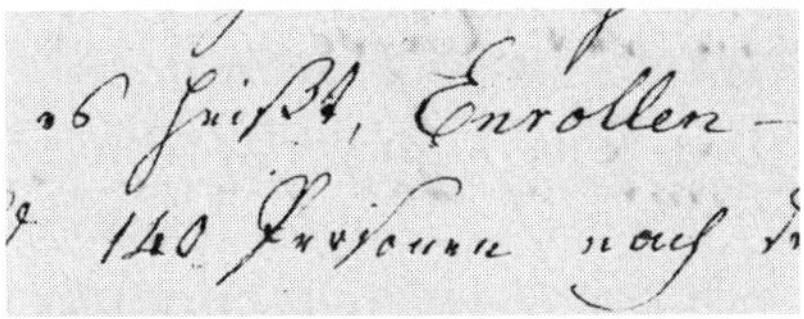


Last week we had a pleasant visit from the Chief John Ross, Major Ridge, John Ridge, Standing Turky, Mr. Chamberlane, and Mr. Furnel from Brainerd, and Mr. Dav. Steiner Tazizi. They all were here on one and the same evening, so we really did not know how to lodge them all at one time. They all were very friendly toward us, especially the Chief, Mr. John Ross. We were happy that we finally an opportunity to have the latter in our house as a guest.

We cannot describe how we feel in the current situation in which we find ourselves and the Cherokees. But at this time we cannot do anything but commend ourselves and them to the faithful Eye and Protector of Israel and ask Him to take them and us into His protection. He knows what is best and what is good for us, and we trust that He will arrange things for the best and will certainly end everything in glory.

With the last mail on the 17th of this month I received 10 English Daily Texts from Bethlehem which Br. Seidel sent. Please tell him this when you get a chance and thank him for this and greet him for me. Earlier I received the 2 German Daily Texts which you had sent me and which I surely reported to you. We would really appreciate it if you could send me one more German almanac. Presumably I have also already informed you that the first delivery of written *Gem. Nachr.* has arrived here.

But my dear Br., I do not have a cent of money in my cash box. The creditors almost run into my house, and I cannot satisfy them. I implore you to please send me some money immediately when you receive this letter, if some is not already on the way for me. Nothing is harder for me than having to ask for money. I hope we will not need so much anymore in the future, since I am pretty much finished with our construction. Don't think badly of me for begging. I am forced to do so.

Our school work is currently very weak. No new scholars are coming, which is really not very surprising when one considers the current situation of the Indians. And those who were here are being taken home, so that we currently have only 4 children at our place who need to be fed. Just today 2 more were taken home for 2 or 3 weeks, as they say, to have clothes made for them. But they usually stay gone for 3 or 4 months until they have forgotten almost everything they had learned and have become wild again. Then we must start at the beginning again with them.

We have Christmas ahead of us again, and it is our request that this might be blessed anew during the reflection on our Lord Jesus Christ's incarnation, for us and especially for our dear Cherokee Brethren and Sisters. We expect a pretty good number of visitors this year, since we have heard from far and wide of those who want to visit in Spring Place. Oh, may this visit provide a blessing to everyone who should come!

We have not heard anything from our Brn. and Srs. in Ochgelogy for 2 weeks now, and so we do not know how they are doing now.

The 24th. Before the post leaves I want to quickly end this letter and send it, primarily for the sake of my cash. Br. and Sr. Clayten are here with us. They are planning to go to Indiana in a couple of weeks. Their youngest child is supposed to be baptized tomorrow. We are all pretty well, except that Mother is complaining a little today, which comes with all the work and preparation for the holy days. We hope that they will be a blessing for us, for our Brn. and Srs., and for you dear ones. We greet all of you. Accept special greetings from your familiar and loving Br.,

Gottl. Byhan

Once again no letter or money from Salem.

[Springplace (M 407-1) and Oochgeelogy (M 409-1) Diaries.]

*Dec. 23.* [Spg.] Br. and Sr. Clayten came to our place from Columbus in Tenn. with their two children for a visit with us and to spend the Christmas fest with us.

*Dec. 24.* [Ooch.] About 80 persons came for the Christmas Eve celebration at our place. All of them were very attentive and behaved very orderly. As happy as we were about this, we also had reason to regret the great impenitance and blindness of those who consciously chose to attend a heathen dance which was taking place during the night some miles from here instead of a worship service. Oh, may the power and clarity of the divine light illuminate these poor servants of Satan and transform them into happy children of the light whose joy is in the Savior, the One who rescues them from eternal death and eternal darkness.

*Dec. 24.* [Spg.] In the afternoon Mr. Dav. McNair and Mr. Dav. Vann with his wife came to us to spend Christmas Eve and Christmas Day with us, and toward evening a crowd of people of all colors gathered here. In the evening we gathered at half past 6 in our church, which was completely filled, and brought our incarnate God thanks and adoration for his inexpressible love, which drove Him to us in this world to redeem us through suffering and death. During the lovefeast we worshipped the baby Jesus in the manger with hymns, and a loving feeling of our dear Lord's presence prevailed.

*Dec. 25.* [Ooch.] Because of the heavy and constant rain, only a few listeners came for the holy day service. This service began with all our scholars singing an appropriate hymn they had memorized. Then we offered our humble gratitude to the newborn Savior of humanity for His love and mercy in which He allowed us poor and lost humans to participate. Our friend Elias Boudinott was a willing assistant today, as he was yesterday evening. He provided us a valuable service by translating into the local language. In the evening we concluded this festal day with a pleasant service of praise in our house congregation.

A strong storm with thunder and lightning passed over us this evening and led us to assume that the weather, which had been warm until now, would become cold. However, this did not happen and the spring-like weather continued, so that in some places young green grass is appearing.

*Dec. 25.* [Spg.] Christmas Day. In the first service was the festal sermon on the love of Jesus for us fallen humans, which moved Him to become human to redeem us from the rule of sin through His sufferings and death, and that if we now believe in Him He forgives our sins and makes us heirs of eternal salvation. In the second service was the baptism of the baby girl born Sept. 25th to Br. and Sr. Clayton with the name Margareth Elisabeth. Since it had rained very heavily last night and especially this morning, the visitors left for home very happy but in a hurry after the services to get across the streams before they are too flooded. We hope that what the visitors heard in our services might have made an impression on their hearts. We had another thorough conversation with the above-named Indian Feather, and our Br. Samuel's mother's sister. Both of them expressed themselves in such a way about their spiritual condition that we had the joy of considering them baptismal candidates.

*Dec. 26.* [Spg.] We heard that the streams had risen to an extraordinary height. And so on

*Sun., Dec. 27,* [Spg.] only our closest neighbors and some Negroes could come to the services. An Indian, Archy Sheet, who had already attended our services often and understands a little English and can also speak it, had come today to attend our services. To our amazement he stayed here until toward evening, despite the fact that all the visitors had left. And since Mr. Dav. Steiner Tazizi was here, he asked to speak with us in the evening through the latter. With tears he then explained to us his intention and his desire to become Jesus' property, and that he believed that he must be lost in the condition which he was in, etc. With joy we directed him to the best Friend of Sinners, who does not turn away anyone who considers Him the redeemer of our sins in faith, etc. In the long conversation we had, we could clearly tell that God's Spirit had come into his heart, so that he is convinced that he must be lost if he is not assured of the forgiveness of his sins through the merit of Jesus. In brief, his expressions were of such a nature that we also had the joy of considering him as a baptismal candidate.

*Sun., Dec. 27.* [Ooch.] Almost 50 listeners came for the sermon, which we combined with praying the Litany. The words of Luke 2:13,14 served as the basis of our reflection.

*Dec. 31.* [Ooch.] For the last time this year we gathered for our usual evening devotions and remembered the many proofs of mercy our Lord and Savior has so lovingly shown us this year and allowed us to participate in. We offered Him our thanks and dedicated our poor hearts to Him anew, to belong completely to Him. We praised Him for His mercy which endures forever, and promised Him new faithfulness and action, as much as our weak ability allows. With the invigorating feeling of His dear presence we concluded the year 1829 with the prayer that He would not abandon us, His poor children, but would continue to guide us, protect us, and keep us, and that He would strengthen our weak hands to carry out His work here for the salvation of many Cherokee souls. At the end of 1829, our Gemeinlein consists of 13 Cherokee communicants, 1 baptized person who is not a communicant, 20 children under 12 of Brn. and Srs., along with 12 scholars who are now in our care; all together 46 people. We commend them and ourselves to the prayer and intercession of all friends of our Lord Jesus Christ,

Br. and Sr. Heinrich G. Clauder and the widowed Sr. Anna Maria Gambold

*Dec. 31.* [Spg.] In the evening we remembered the many good deeds and proofs of grace which we enjoyed from our faithful and dear Lord in this year now ending, confessed ourselves great debtors before him in what we should have been to Him, and especially in the calling given to us to help gather in His reward for pain among this Nation. But He let us feel His dear presence and His great forgiveness in a comforting way. We especially brought our dear Lord sincere thanks for His merciful assistance during the construction of our new house, during which He protected us and everyone who worked on it from harm and misfortune. We had the pleasure of being able to move into it on Dec. 15. Now the Brn. and Srs. who live here and who will be assigned here in the future have a spacious house compared to the one which now will be left, which in fact was too small, uncomfortable, and dilapidated. But whether the little gathering of souls from this Nation which has joined the Gemeine of believers will be able to maintain itself, and whether this newly built house can now be occupied for a time yet by our missionaries among the Cherokees, can certainly not be known in advance, since things look more and more as if the poor Indians will have to give in after all in the end. However, we do not want to worry about this but leave it up to the One who has human hearts in His hands, and who guides them as He sees fit.

At the end of the year 1829, the Gemeinlein in Spring Place consists of:

29 adult baptized Brn. and Srs., 27 of whom are communicants
27 baptized and unbaptized children
3 baptismal candidates
Total: 59 people, 4 more than at the close of last year.
In addition are the missionaries and their family:
5 persons
Total: 64 persons

[*Records: N.C.*, 8:3868: Salem Memorabilia of 1829. Translated by Douglas L. Rights.]

Br. and Sr. Eder, who were installed in the service of the mission to the Cherokees last year, have received a call from the U.A.C. to the Mission in the Danish West Indies. In the place of Br. Eder the Lord has called our dear Br. Heinrich Gottlieb Clauder, *a child of this congregation*, who has been serving there as assistant. With this in view he came hither; on September 17 he entered into the holy estate of matrimony with the single Sr. Charlotte Elisabeth Rüde; and September 29th, in a solemn service, the written ordination as a deacon of the Unity was handed him — it was sent by Br. Gottlieb Hüffel of the U.E.C. Their companion, Br. Nathanael Byhan, *a child of the Cherokee mission*, and Sr. Charlotte Elisabeth Clauder were received as Akoluthes, for encouragement in their service in the Cherokee mission.

Br. Philip Blum, who accompanied the above named pilgrims to Springplace and Ooyugillogee with his wagon, returned on Nov. 15, bringing Br. and Sr. Eder from there. They would gladly have continued their journey to the West Indies at once, but have been detained by family circumstances, so they are still with us but hope, God willing, to reach their destination next spring.

# *1830, part 1*

[Springplace (M 407-2) and Oochgeelogy (M 409-1) Diaries. Translated by Julie Tomberlin Weber. Handwritings are Henry G. Clauder's (Ooch.) and Gottlieb Byhan's (Spg.).]

[*Jan. 1.* Ooch.] The believers among this people observed the first day of this year as a day of fasting and prayer because of the current difficult situation facing the Nation. We also gathered with some of our Brn. and Srs., and after we considered the purpose of our gathering, we bowed before the Lord, the almighty ruler of all things, and pleaded with Him to guide us mercifully in this trial and to protect us from the disorderly things in this world, to give us patience and faith to submit completely to His holy will, and to make His ways clear to us. We thus spent the day in quiet reverence before the Lord with the blessed awareness of His dear presence.

*Jan. 1.* [Spg.] We entered into the year 1830 with pleas, prayer, and intercession for ourselves and all people, and especially for our poor Cherokee Nation, that our dear Lord might look upon them with grace and help them this year out of the desperate situation in which they currently find themselves, and especially that He might still received more from this Nation as a reward for his pain. This day was designated by the Chiefs of this Nation as a day of repentance and prayer, on which all religious confessions were asked to send their prayers for the well-being of this Nation to the One who is Lord of lords and King of kings to stand by this Nation in her desperate situation. Accordingly in the first service the sermon was on Ps. 62:5-8.[1] In the second service we read another sermon on the words: The very hairs of your head are all numbered [Luke 12:7]. We closed with a prayer on our knees.

*Sun., Jan. 3.* [Ooch.] Two very wild Indians came here and asked for gunpowder. We told them that this was a day of peace, on which those who believe in Jesus Christ do not participate in trade and work. We also admonished them to give up their rough and heathen ways and turn to God. One of them answered that he has heard that those who believe in God must die right away; since he didn't want to die, he could not become a believer! We tried to free this poor man of these superstitious ideas and give him a better understanding of God, the creator and sustainer of all creatures, by telling him that those who were faithful would receive eternal life and after this life would be transported to a better one. In our Sunday service we read a talk about the progress of grace in people's hearts, along with a chapter from the Gospel of John and a brief talk. Since the Methodists had services close to us yesterday and today, only a few listeners were present here.

*Sun., Jan. 3.* [Spg.] Since no one except two Negroes came to our place today, the services had to be canceled.

*Jan. 6.* [Spg.] It now seems as if we are going to get some cold weather, though it has been very warm until now, so today 9 of our pigs were slaughtered.

*Sun., Jan. 10.* [Ooch.] Despite the heavy rain, more than 20 people gathered for worship. Epiphany was celebrated at other mission sites on the 6th, and in honor of that the sermon on Isa. 52:15 reflected on the means God is using in this time of rich blessings to spread the Gospel of Jesus' incarnation and death among so many heathen peoples, and how the power of this is being seen in so many souls, making them holy and beautiful.

*Sun., Jan. 10.* [Spg.] The services were held in the usual order.

*Jan. 11.* [Spg.] In the evening Mr. Dav. Steiner Tazizi came to our place and spent the night here, and on the 12th went

[1] Verse 6 states: I shall not be moved.

home. He told us he wanted to come to our place on New Year's Day to serve as interpreter as he had promised, but he had been at Brainerd two days earlier, and they would not allow him to come here, because they reminded him that he belongs to their church. Accordingly he must assist them with interpreting, and they hoped that he might visit them more often. To this he answered them that he would not visit them anymore at all if he did not belong to their church.

[M 414-5-1: Translated by Julie Tomberlin Weber. Addressed to: Revd. T. Shulz, Salem. No postmark. Handwriting is Henry G. Clauder's.]

Oochgillogy, Jan. 13, 1830

Dear Br. Schulz,

In opening our correspondence for this year, I would like to wish you and yours and the Brn. of the P.H.C. a happy new year, during which we all might receive from on high the comfort we need in our various situations and trials, so that we can pursue faithfully our various undertakings. On the 2nd of this month I received your kind letter of Dec. 14, and some weeks ago the German Daily Texts came. These delighted and encouraged us. Your dear letters are always very encouraging to us, so I ask you to delight us more frequently with these than in the past.

Praise God, we are all healthy and able to pursue our work, except our Sr. Copeland, who gave birth to an lively baby boy on the 8th of this month. Mother and child are well, although her delivery was extremely difficult and the midwives present here were not very hopeful. And so we have our hands full in every respect.

The school currently consists of 15 scholars. Sometimes they make good progress in their studies, and generally they bring us more joy than sorrow. Still one must pray daily for sufficient patience to overcome their often inopportune apathy and negligence. For example, every morning you must tell them to light a fire in their schoolhouse, although they have already been told a hundred times. It still is not done until they are told again to do so, and you stand there until they have done it. Otherwise, you really cannot expect anything, because from the time they are young they do not learn anything about orderliness until perhaps they have the opportunity to attend a mission school and then learn something about it.

The children are left more to themselves on Sundays than I would like, because we are completely busy with visitors, so I think it is essential that we open a Sunday school for them as soon as possible, in the same way the Sunday schools in Salem are carried out. I would have good — and I believe reliable — assistants in both Hickses, in Br. Copeland, and in some or at least one of my current older girl students, so that I could manage it despite my other responsibilities. Still this matter must be postponed until the return of Wm. Ab. Hicks. Then without a doubt he will agree to help with this matter. In the meantime I will write to one of the members of the Stokes County S.S. Union to ask for their working assistance.

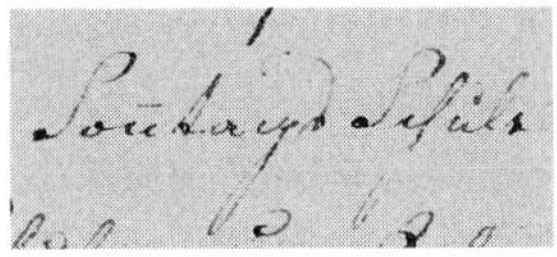

I thought I had informed you in my last letter that Copeland is planning to take the usual percentage on his bill of $218.36½. But since I did not do this, I do this herewith in Copeland's name. He wants to know that his money is safe, even if he gets only 3 percent. He would like to receive payment of the amount of interest for one year, which you offered to add to it. Concerning the household equipment they brought along, after investigating this there is nothing more to note.

I have not yet reported anything about the baptism of Oa-tee on the 6th of last Dec., presuming that Br. Byhan, who led the proceeding, had already done this. So I must ask you to excuse me. Otherwise, I would gladly have sent you the news about it a long time ago. Since then the baptized man brings us much joy in his walk of grace. All else you will see from my enclosed Diary, which goes until the close of the old year and which I commend to your patience and good will because of the many mistakes and imperfections in it.

It will not be unpleasant for you to hear more about our economy and establishments. Sr. Gambold, whose help is of great value, continues in her busy manner taking care of the domestic work and especially with the livestock, some of the older children helping her with this. Sr. Clauder with Sr. Gambold takes care of the kitchen and the laundry and everything related to that. I myself take care of the school completely alone now, although Sr. Copeland will now continue helping my wife every afternoon after school as much as she is able. There is never a shortage of work, and it is often midnight before we can lie down to rest. But we always have cause to praise and thank the One who gives us courage and strength for this.

The quantity of corn which was planted here last year is estimated by many to be about 500 bushels, which will feed our large family along with the horses and pigs this year. We need 2 bushels each week just to supply our table and our children's table with bread. A number of pigs, which we have not yet slaughtered, need almost as much daily, but this will not last much longer. Thirty odd horn cattle belong to this list as well. These are admittedly matters which do not really belong here, but perhaps it will not be unpleasant for you to hear things of this nature as well. Br. Steiner, Sr., sent a note of hand for Major Ridge, which was payable a long time ago, but which has not yet been paid here. The situation of the debtor is supposed to be quite intricate. John Ridge is currently with the Creek Delegation in Washington as their clerk.

In conclusion, I must still mention the quiet and blessed walk of our Cherokee Gemeinlein, which fills us with praise and thanksgiving toward the good Shepherd of souls, who knows His little sheep and leads them to green pastures and protects them and guards them from wolves in this world. From the enclosed Diary, dear Br., you will see that my dear and faithful helpmeet and I have visited many of our Brethren and Sisters, especially the most distant ones, and I must confess it has been a great blessing for our own hearts as well as a blessing and encouragement for the Brn. and Srs. As soon as circumstances allow, we are planning to continue with this, and the Lord who has always done great things through weak means will also mercifully reveal Himself in our desire to serve Him.

In the meantime, accept our deepest gratitude for your love and compassion which you show us. We commend ourselves to your continued prayer and intercession, and we remain until the end your loving,

Heinrich G. and Elisab. Clauder

[M 414-5-2: Translated by Julie Tomberlin Weber. No address; no postmark.]

Springplace, Jan. 13, 1830

My dear Br. Schulz,

My hand is somewhat shaky for writing today, because I am not feeling very well, but I cannot neglect to express my gratitude and ours for your kind letter of Dec. 15 of last year and *Wöch. Nachr.* along with the minutes of the Society for the Heathen's meeting, all of which reached my hands on Dec. 31. In this new year we wish much grace and many blessings from the bounty of Jesus' blessings for you and for all of us.

Without a doubt this year will be a remarkable one for our Cherokee Indians and our mission among them. However, we want to look to Him, who can arrange everything for the best and who has numbered every hair on our heads, so that not a single one falls to the earth without His will.

We celebrated a blessed and happy Christmastide and New Year. On New Year's Day we experienced another joy when a young Indian came to us and tearfully declared that he sincerely wished to become Jesus' property, because he believes that in his current condition he must be lost. We directed him to the best Friend of Sinners, who does not turn anyone away who comes to Him as a truly repentant sinner, because He himself has taken on the punishment for our sins, etc. Now we have two baptismal candidates, and we joyfully laid them before the Savior in our last Conference concerning baptism. But He did not give His approval for this <u>at this time</u>.

We really wanted to try to follow the wishes of the H.C.f.G. and we ourselves wish we could have Mission Conferences more often when we all, from both sites, could be present. Since it is hardly possible to get from one site to the other, especially in the winter, this was never done. However, in the future we want to try to arrange to have joint Conferences now and then, even if it cannot be every month. On this occasion I want to ask the question of whether the H.C. has anything against it if we take our Nathl. into our Conference? We think he belongs in it, since he has submitted himself for service and since late last year we have also accepted him into it.

I think I have already informed you that I received the English Daily Texts which Br. Seidel sent. Day before yesterday I received a letter from Br. Clauder, in which he reports that on Jan. 8 after a very difficult delivery Sr. Copeland was delighted by the birth of a healthy baby boy. Br. Clauder is planning to visit in Spring Place soon.

We moved completely into our new house on Dec. 15. As I already mentioned, we moved in, and on Jan. 2 we moved the kitchen, so now we are completely at home. The cooks are especially grateful because things are much more comfortable for them now that they no longer have to go outside of the house when they want to go into the kitchen.

But, dear Br. Schulz, now I come to the matter of money. I think I already informed you in my previous letters and indicated that my cashbox is empty, but until now this has not helped. Now, however, I must ask you for God's sake to help me out of the distress in which I currently find myself. I had to let the workers go without being able to pay them, and now I am overrun every day, which brings me one order after the other to satisfy my creditors, and I do not have a single cent of money. And so I ask you to send me money immediately and help me out of my trouble, which is not insignificant. After all, it is the last time I will ask for money for the house construction. I will not do anything more on it now until we know how things will turn out with the Cherokees. The sum I currently owe various people for the house construction and hourly workers amounts to about $250-260. Please help me from this distress as soon as possible. We hope not so much money will be required in the future.

Now I would like to commend one more matter to the consideration of the P.H.C. Dear Br., you will remember that in Sept. 1827, when we received the assignment of serving the mission among the Cherokees, we accepted the assignment with one condition: As soon as a more suitable Br. and Sr. were found, we would return. I do not know if the P.H.C. has been concerned about getting a Br. and Sr. to take our place, but we really wish that such a couple who are willing to relieve us might be found by late next year, because we want to return to the Gemeine by then.

Since writing is difficult for me today, I ask you to be satisfied with these few lines for now. Perhaps more next time. The rest of our little house family are healthy and greet everyone. And you, accept a special greeting from your loving friend and Br.,

Gottlieb Byhan

[Springplace (M 407-2) and Oochgeelogy (M 409-1) Diaries.]

*Jan. 14.* [Spg.] Toward evening the Indian Conondoah came to our place with his wife, our Sr. Hannah, and spent the night.

*Jan. 15.* [Spg.] The Indian Conondoah is the first Indian who asked us what we knew about the relationship between Georgia and the Cherokee Indians. Br. Byhan told him that we knew nothing except what we saw in the newspapers from time to time. Then we read aloud for him a letter from the Governor of Georgia to the legislators of Georgia from the newspaper, which satisfied him for the most part. He also asked what would happen with the land when the Georgians had introduced their laws in this country. Br. Byhan told him that we knew nothing about these matters and so could not give him any information about it. He finally said that the Indians would surely not move west, because God had given them this land, and so they also wanted to end their brief lives here. Br. Byhan told him that we had to commend this matter to God, who would arrange for everything to work out for the best, and that He had perhaps allowed these circumstances to happen to them, so that they would hold all the more closely to Him, and to pull them closer to Himself through these circumstances, so that His name would be glorified more and more through them, etc., to which he agreed. This Indian belongs to the Methodists, and as we hear, he has already been baptized by them twice. In the evening the Indian Deer in the Water came to bring his two children back to the school. They have been at home about 4 weeks.

*Jan. 16.* [Spg.] Toward evening the Choctaw Chief Greenwood Leflore came with his wife, whom he recently married here in this country. He spent the night here. He said that he was planning to visit all the mission sites in this country and in general to see how far the Cherokee Indians have progressed in religion and civilisation, so he would be able to tell his people, the Choctaw Indians. We spent a pleasant evening with him. We talked mostly about religious matters. Our schoolchildren had to be called into our house, so he could hear from them themselves how far they have come in learning. He then gave them another admonition to be very diligent in learning, so that his children, that is, those children in the Choctaw Nation, would not get ahead of them in learning, etc. Otherwise, he regreted very much that he saw that the Cherokee Indians are not united among themselves about their land, as many of them are moving to the west. This really strengthens the white people in their belief that they wanted to surrender their land with no further circumstances and leave. For our part, we must be very careful on such occasions that our words do not make us appear dissatisfied with one party or the other. We must ask for grace from our dear Lord for this.

*Sun., Jan. 17.* [Spg.] This Chief traveled on to Goosawaytee to Judge Martin's, because he had already told him to come there yesterday, so he had to be there today, despite the fact that it is the Sabbath, as he said. By the way, he can speak English very well, although somewhat brokenly. He is a very upstanding, pleasant man by nature, and dealing with him is very genial.

The Sunday services were held as usual today. After the second service, which was Bible reading, Br. Samuel gave another talk to the Brn. and Srs. in the Cherokee language. Afterward we spoke individually with our single Br. Solomon, who is a candidate for Holy Communion, about his spiritual walk, as well as with the young Indian Iskittihee, who came and expressed his desire to become the property of Jesus and to belong to our congregation. Both of them expressed themselves in such a way that we believe they are serious about wanting to live in this world only for the Savior. Today the boy Alexander Sanders, who had been at home with his parents for some months, also returned to the school.

*Sun., Jan. 17.* [Ooch.] The sermon was on Num. 14:24, about faithful obedience to the Lord, without which the promised heavenly Canaan can never be reached, and how the spirit of this world, a spirit of skepticism and unbelief, is completely repugnant to these faithful followers of the Lord, while another spirit, the spirit of God, His voice and instruction are necessary for this and for all who have faithful intentions and listen to and follow it daily. A heathen Indian named Wolf was present; he has often shown himself to be a bitter enemy of the Gospel and opposed it with word and deed. He has never been here before, but today he listened attentively to the interpreter's words.

[M 414-5-3: Translated by Julie Tomberlin Weber. Addressed to: Revd. Theodor Shulz, Salem, Stokes County, North Carolina. Postmark: Springplace, C.N., Jan. 21. Free. Gottl. Byhan, P.M. Received Feb. 4.]

Spring Place, Jan. 19, 1830

My dear Br. Schulz,

On the 16th of the month after a long wait we once again had the pleasure of receiving letters from you, of Dec. 29th and Jan. 5th, along with written *Gem. Nachrichten* and $130 mammon, for which I had waited anxiously for a long time, so I could pay off my workers completely. Although what was sent is not enough, at least I can pay some of it. From my last letter to you,

you will have seen how much I needed at the time to get out of debt. Be good enough and help me out this time, because I am overrun daily to pay.

Sincere thanks for everything sent this time. The printed *Gem. Nachrichten* which you mentioned sending in your kind letter of Jan. 5th have not yet arrived. Hopefully they will come later this week. One must be patient, because the mails and posts have also suffered a change here. Previously all four mails came here together on Thursday. Now, however, after Jan. 1, the Georgia and New Echota mails come on Thursdays, the Knoxville on Saturday evening, and the Western, or Nashville, mail, comes Sundays. One can indeed say new lords, new laws. I would like to have no mail on Sunday, but this can't be changed.

Last Saturday evening the Choctaw Chief Greenwood Leflord and his Lady, daughter of Mr. Jos. Coody in Rossville, whom he recently married, arrived at our place completely unexpectedly, and they spent the night here. He is a pleasant man and can speak English well. He said he wanted to see all the mission sites among the Cherokees before he returned home, and in general to learn how far the Cherokees are in Religion and Civilisation, whether they were further in this respect than the Choctaws, or whether they were behind them. Since he was in a hurry to attend a meeting set by Judge Martin — 14 miles from here — he continued on his way Sunday morning, the 17th.

We have not yet heard anything from the Delegates in Washington. However, as soon as we hear anything from them we will gladly let you know. How will things turn out with the Indian matter, and what will the end be? Everyone here is waiting for the decision in Congress, and the people are very anxious, but everyone is quiet.

Praise God, we are currently all healthy. If I am correct, I have already informed you that we have been living in the new house since Dec. 15, and we are happy!

<u>Jan. 21</u>. We are expecting someone from Ochgoloogy any day, but no one has come. Owetee received the name Christian David in holy baptism. It is no surprise that old Pleasant is causing you much trouble; she troubled us for 9 years. We could

not endure things with her any longer. She is a miserable creature! Be satisfied with these few lines for now. I mostly wanted to inform you that the written *Nachr.* and the money arrived safely. Was the offer of Mr. Smith in Beufort in Georgia not acceptable? I would almost want to go there, if only it were not on the coast. A sincere greeting from all of us and especially from your humble Br.,

Gottlieb Byhan

[Springplace (M 407-2) and Oochgeelogy (M 409-1) Diaries.]

*Jan. 21.* [Ooch.] I went to Spring Place for a brief visit, and I returned from there the next day. We were delighted to receive letters and *Gemein Nachrichten*, which encouraged us.

*Jan. 21.* [Spg.] Today we received a pleasant visit from Br. H. G. Clauder from Ochgeloogy. We had various conversations with him about both of our mission sites. We were happy about the grace which is prevailing among our Brn. and Srs., but also had cause to humble ourselves before our dear Lord and ask Him to remove the things about us and our Indian Brn. and Srs. which are displeasing to Him, and to let us all grow and increase more and more in love for Him and among ourselves, so that through word and deed we may show that we are children of the Spirit. We also decided that we want to plan to establish a Sunday school here in Spring Place as well as in Ochgeloogy in order to provide our youth around us here with opportunity to learn and read the Word of God. Everyone, old and young, white, brown, and black, can come here in the hope that the Lord will lay His blessing on our weak efforts.

*Jan. 22.* [Spg.] Br. G. Clauder returned to his post at Ochgeloogy.

*Jan. 23.* [Spg.] Br. Byhan today rode on business to Mr. Nicolson at Vann's old place, and to Mr. Froshour's, about 4 miles from here. At both places he announced that we would establish a Sunday school in Spring Place. They expressed their joy at this and promised to send their children without fail.

*Jan. 23.* [Ooch.] We visited at our Br. and Sr. George Augustus Hicks. Unfortunately they had completely separated and it was our intention to talk with them about this. Our intention to address them about this was partly thwarted by the husband's absence, but we tried to explain to her (the wife) that she needed to humble herself before God and to win her husband again through love and gentleness. After a number of days, we were fortunate enough to find everything going well with these two otherwise dear people. Both expressed their sincere remorse over their unchristian and unsavory behavior, and hoped they had learned more about their hearts through this situation.

*Sun., Jan. 24.* [Spg.] In the morning was the sermon on Rom. 3:23-25. Then there was the baptism of the baby daughter, born on the 1st of this month to Mr. Charles Buttler and our Sr. Anna Johanna, with the name Anna Rosina. In the 3rd service we had a blessed enjoyment of the body and blood of Jesus in Holy Communion. The married Sr. Sally joined us for the first time as a participant after her preceding confirmation. Since the weather was beautiful, most of our communicants came today. Martha Vann, daughter of our neighbor Capt. Dav. McNair, was present as a guest at our Holy Communion today. She requested this, and since in her church at the Methodists she had already participated in Holy Communion, we could not turn down her request.

*Sun., Jan. 24.* [Ooch.] The sermon was on 1 Tim. 6:12, and a pretty good number of listeners were present for it, especially women. But we had no translator, so they could understand little or none of it.

*Jan. 30.* [Ooch.] Samuel Ka-na-qui-awk, who belongs to Spring Place visited us and stayed until the next day. In our evening devotions he held a serious talk for all the scholars and sang and prayed with them in Cherokee, which we were very happy about although we understood little or none of it.

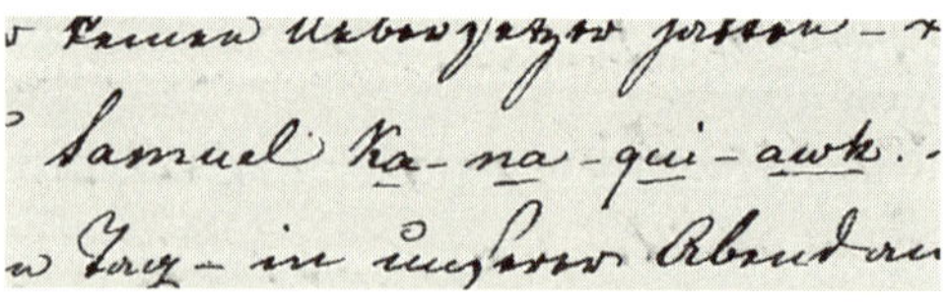
Samuel Ka-na-qui-awk.

# *1830, part 2*

[M 414-5-4: Translated by Julie Tomberlin Weber. Addressed to: Revd. Theodor Schulz, Salem, Stokes County, North Carolina. Postmark: Spring Place, C.N., Jan. 28. Free. Gottlieb Byhan, P.M. Received Feb. 10.]

Springplace, Jan. 25, 1830

My dear Br. Schulz,

On the 21st of this month we were delighted to receive the 5th issue of the printed 1828 *Gem. Nachr.* by mail, and on the 23rd your dear note of the 12th of this month along with the German calender. We thank you sincerely for everything.

From your kind letter we learned that we can expect another visit from Salem, Brn. Proske and Theoph. Vierling. If they have marched well we can expect them at the end of this week. It seems Br. Proske still has affection for the Cherokees, because he wants to see them again before they move. But I do not think they will move so soon. Everything in the nation is quiet, although the

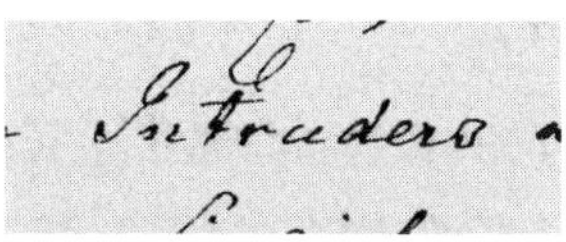


Intruders are causing the Cherokees lots of problems on the Georgia border. They just move in without any notice. Sometimes they also steal from the Cherokees, and if they cannot do this during the night then they do it in the light of day completely in the open. Since the Indians do not want to have any arguments or fights with them, they tolerate things as much as they can. Certainly the Indians put up with a lot of things from the white people, so that they are not blamed for anything like treating the white people badly, and in their current situation they are exercising great patience. Last week Mrs. Vann received a letter from Mr. Jos. Vann in Washington, but it does not include anything interesting. They arrived in Washington on Jan. 2nd, and the letter was sent from Washington on the 5th. Willm. Coody, one of the Delegates, had to stay behind in Pittsburg because of illness. Two of them stayed with him, but Br. Wilm. Abr. Hicks was with Mr. Jos. Vann in Washington. How are things going to turn out in Congress regarding the Indians?? We are <u>really</u> anxious to hear! Just as <u>everyone</u> in this Nation is curious to hear what their fate will be.

Last week Br. Clauder was visiting us in Spring Place. On this occasion we held a joint Conference. It was decided during this that we would hold Sunday school at both sites and set them up as soon as possible. Perhaps this will bring a blessing among the youth here, who will then have an influence on others throughout their lives. Our Nathl. is very willing to do everything to get this going. He has also made himself pretty well known in the neighborhood, and all show great willingness to send their children. Br. Clauder will also set up a school like this in Ochgeloogy. Our Rachel and Nancy Becker are also willing to help. May the Lord lay His blessing on this weak effort of ours so that it contributes to the furthering of His kingdom!

Here I must mention an unpleasant circumstance which Br. Clauder shared with us when he was here. I would like to ask you, if Br. Clauder does not say anything to you about this in his letters to you, do not let him know that I wrote you about it. We had always believed that our Br. George Hicks, who belongs to the congregation in Ochgeloogy, was a thoroughly converted person, and during my conversations with him, which <u>I</u> had with him, I often wished and regretted that we here in Spring Place did not have such a supporter in the congregation, who leads the rest of the Brn. and Srs. with word and deed.

Recently however, Sr. Hicks, his wife, went to Br. and Sr. Clauder and told them in tears that her husband, Br. George Hicks, had beat her horribly and chased her away, and she wanted Br. and Sr. Clauder to tell her what she should do. Naturally Br. and Sr. Clauder advised her to return home and reconcile with her husband, as is the custom of children of God. Br. Clauder also heard that her husband, Br. George Hicks, was very sorry that he had treated his wife thus. He himself had not yet talked with him when Br. Clauder was in Spring Place. We all thought it was good, despite the fact that he expressed remorse, to announce through Br. Clauder that both of them should abstain from Holy Communion this time, because they had created more than a slight offense against the rest of the Brn. and Srs.

Br. Clauder tells us the discord and fighting stems from his occasional accusations that she has been unfaithful in their marriage, which she has endured calmly for a long time. When she got tired of this, she also began objecting to this, which led to this troubled scene. This circumstance, as you can imagine, is in fact very discouraging for us and makes us sigh to the Savior that He might ground the hearts of our Br. and Sr. more and more in Himself and in His blood and death, so that they might also show through word and deed what spiritual children they are.

I ask you once again if Br. Clauder should not mention this matter to you do not let him know that I did so, although I believe that he should do this and perhaps will indeed do so.

Last Sunday, yesterday, we had a blessed enjoyment of the body and blood of Jesus in Holy Communion. The Indian Sr. Sally first received the confirmation blessing and then enjoyed this highest good for the first time with the Gemeine.

By the way, I am now very happy that there is hope I will be able to pay off my house debts soon. However, I still owe Willm. Henry Clayton, who has now moved to Indiana, $40, because he worked here on the house some, and then we received flour, shoes, some horse equipment, and horse collars from him, all of which we needed. I had to give him a note of hand, six month after date, dated Jan. 1, 1830, if I am not mistaken. He told me he still has a few things in Salem, I don't know with whom, so we thought it might work if he received the payment from you, because, as he said, without a doubt someone from Indiana will visit in Salem next summer to take care of his things. I also used the $90 which Br. Alex. Copeland gave me to keep, which Br. Clauder had already paid him last year, so that this $90 must be considered as if sent from the Mission Diacony to me, so it should be debited from Spring Place and credited to Br. Alex. Copeland in your books, and now he hopes to draw interest. I think all of this has already been arranged by Br. Clauder.

Eight days ago we had a visit from the Choctaw Chief Greenwood Leflord. He and his wife, whom he married recently in this country, spent the night with us. He told us that he is traveling around in this country primarily to see how far the Cherokees have progressed in religion and civilisation — although since then we heard of other reasons he left his nation. He is a pleasant man. One hardly notices that he is an Indian. He also speaks English well.

It seems that our post run is going well, both through Georgia and through Knoxville, and especially now through the last place, because your dear letter of the 12th of this month had already arrived here by the 23rd, as I have already noted. The newspapers which Br. Schaaf always sends me usually arrive here in 10 or 11 days. And so I am inclined to send most of the letters through Knoxville. In general it is good in the current circumstances with Georgia if one changes regularly. I will send this letter through Georgia, because otherwise it has to lie around here too long.

Praise God, we are all quite healthy right now. Accept the most sincere greetings from all of us, and you, dear Br., accept another special greeting from your loving but poor Br.,

Gottlieb Byhan

[Br. Schulz writes:] Concerning Clayton: Note of $40 dated 1 Jan. 1830 — six mo. after date to be paid by Indiana N[ote]
$90 of Alex. Copeland for Springplace

[Springplace (M 407-2) and Oochgeelogy (M 409-1) Diaries. Translated by Julie Tomberlin Weber. Handwritings are Henry G. Clauder's (Ooch.) and Gottlieb Byhan's (Spg.).]

*Jan. 27.* [Spg.] Toward evening the bush fire, which has been threatening to come close to us for several days already, finally came so close to us that Mr. Vann's overseer, Mr. King, asked us to help him extinguish the fire, which then took place with a great deal of effort.

*Jan. 29.* [Spg.] Br. Byhan went to Judge Martin's in Goosawaytee on business. Rachel Byhan went along for a visit. Toward evening they returned here. Today we also had the pleasure of welcoming the two single Brn. George Proske and Theophilus Vierling from Salem here on a visit. With them we received a packet of written *Gem. Nachrichten*, for which we were very thankful.

*Jan. 30.* [Spg.] In the evening a certain Mr. Dale came to our place and spent the night here. This Dale had been in the college in Marysville in Tenn. some time ago in preparation to be a preacher. But it seemed he is of a very simple and naive nature, and, as he himself told us, he was told that he would never be able to preach because of his pronunciation, so he was let go from the college. Now he is traveling through Cherokee country and visiting all the mission sites in it. In the summer or fall he is planning to return to Massachusetts, where he was born.

[M 414-5-5: Translated by Julie Tomberlin Weber. Addressed to: Revd. Theod. Schulz, Salem, Stokes County, North Carolina. Postmark: Springplace, C.N., Jan. 30. Free. Gottlieb Byhan, P.M. Received Feb. 15.]

Springplace, Jan. 30, 1830

My dear Br. Schulz,

Here I am beginning to send the Diary, and I will send a half sheet every week, if nothing important intervenes. I am sending it by way of Knoxville, because I almost believe it goes quicker.

Yesterday toward evening on the 29th Brn. Proske and Vierling safely arrived here in Spring Place. With them we received the hand-written *Gem. Nachr.* you sent along with $71 of Georgia money. Very sincere thanks for everything. This time I did not receive a letter and for now must do without.

Praise God, we are all well. Everything in the Nation is still quiet. God knows how long it will remain thus. The Indians are becoming increasingly anxious to know how their matter will turn out in Congress. In the last *Intel.* there was already something about the thoughts of some in Congress concerning the Cherokees. The reason was they had seen the Memorial from New York. May God see that things are done fairly!

Nothing else for now. Accept the most sincere greetings from all of us. And you, accept another special greeting from me, your humble Br.,

Gottl. Byhan

P.S. Please greet our Sophia from us and tell her that her letter to us of Jan. 10 arrived here on the 28th.

G. B.

[Springplace (M 407-2) and Oochgeelogy (M 409-1) Diaries.]

*Sun., Jan. 31.* [Spg.] Since the weather today was very cold and unfriendly, only our closest neighbors came to the services. At 11 o'clock we prayed the Church Litany, and afterward the sermon was on Matt. 7:21. Since in our last Mission Conference it was decided that a Sunday school would be established here and in Ochgeloogy to give the children in our neighborhood who do not attend the weekday school a chance to learn, this was organized today by Br. Nathl. Byhan and established. Today children from the neighborhood came for the first time. We hope that this plan will not be without blessing!

*Sun., Jan. 31.* [Ooch.] The service was quite well attended again, and afterward we went on a brief visit to our Sr. Lydia, who lives close to us and is not well. However, we found her quite active and in good hope of recovering completely within a few days.

In the first days of February many able-bodied Indians marched out of our neighborhood at the order of their head Chief toward the Georgia border in order to drive back the white people who have forced their way into Cherokee country and are set on robbing. One of our people was among them. Previously, the Indians' ownership of their land and property was protected by the government of the United States, which by the way was only fulfilling one of the frequently repeated promises ([inserted:] in the most solemn treaties) that the government had made. Unfortunately for the Cherokees, this was not being done any more, and the white people were showing more and more hostility to them every day, so the Cherokees felt justified in using force against further offenses.

*Feb. 1.* [Spg.] Mr. Dale, who spent Sunday with us yesterday and attended the first school session today, went on to Brainerd without taking leave from us.

*Feb. 4.* [Spg.] We slaughtered our last pigs for this winter, and Brn. Proske and Vierling lent a helping hand with this.

*Feb. 4.* [Ooch.] I visited our Br. and Sr. Christian David Oatee. Full of sorrow, they reflected on the misfortune threatening this Nation and the general misery associated with having to leave their dear fatherland, in which the bones of their ancestors rest, to use their words, or to submit themselves to intolerable oppression. I tried to comfort them and encouraged them to put their faith in God alone, the omniscient ruler. From there I went to the parents of one of our scholars; they are still blind and wild heathens. A number of Indians were there. Some were lying and sleeping drunken, and others sat by the fire and talked. I did not understand anything they said, but since I was familiar to them they were very cordial. Although I could not completely achieve the purpose of my visit because there was no interpreter, I saw something of their miserable life, and I was also brought again to the realization that it is necessary and extremely desirable to have a thorough knowledge of their language.

*Feb. 6.* [Spg.] Despite the unfriendly and cold weather we had here today, where it rained, snowed, and sleeted the entire day and all the streams froze to ice, our Br. Boas, who lives 10 miles from here, still arrived here already by evening for tomorrow's Sunday services.

[M 414-5-6: Translated by Julie Tomberlin Weber. Addressed to: Revd. Theod. Schulz, Salem, Stokes County, North Carolina. Postmark: Springplace, C.N., Feb. 7. Free. Gottlieb Byhan, P.M. Received Feb. 22.]

Springplace, Feb. 6, 1830

My dear Br. Shulz,

On Jan. 31st your kind letter of Jan. 19th and some handwritten *Nachrichten* arrived here safely. We sincerely thank you for this.

In my previous letter, dated Jan. 30, I already informed you that Brn. Proske and Vierling arrived here on the 30th. They have been with us for one week now and have helped us in various ways, especially slaughtering pigs, which we had planned to do this week. Next Monday they are planning to go to Ochgeloogy if the wind and weather allow it. But it doesn't look today as if they can travel, because it is very cold and raining, hailing, and snowing, so they will surely not be able to go.

I think I have already informed you that we decided in our Conference to set up a Sunday school both here and in Ochgeloogy. We began this at our place last Sunday. We had 15 scholars gathered. We hope that this arrangement will not remain without blessing.

Praise God, we are currently healthy except for Mother Byhan, who was bothered this week with toothaches and headaches, and otherwise, as it seems, is generally not healthy. We have not heard anything from Ochgeloogy for 2 weeks now. Recently a letter from Br. Clauder to me took 8 days, while a letter from Salem to Spring Place sometimes arrives in only 10 days. With these lines I am again sending you some of the Spring Place Diary, until the end of Nov. of last year. More next week.

Accept the most sincere greetings from all of us, and you, accept another special greeting from your familiar, poor Br.,

Gottlieb Byhan

(Please greet our Sophia from us.)

[Springplace (M 407-2) and Oochgeelogy (M 409-1) Diaries.]

*Feb. 6.* [Ooch.] We had the coldest and most unpleasant day of this winter, as it rained and immediately froze the entire day. Since the weather was not yet clear, the next day, Sunday the 8th, only a few of the closest neighbors came to our place for the service. After a brief talk, our Br. and Sr. Copeland's baby boy, born Jan. 8, was baptized into Jesus death with the name John Gambold.

*Sun., Feb. 7.* [Spg.] Although the weather today was still very unfriendly, a number of Brn. and Srs. who live from 12 to 14 miles from here came for the services. Since it was extremely cold in our church, only one service was held, in which a sermon and a chapter from the Bible in the Cherokee language were read by our single Br. Nicl. Ignatius. Also a nice number of children from the neighborhood came for Sunday school, among whom were also some Negro children. Toward evening our baptismal candidate Archy Sheet stopped in at our place and asked for some paper so he could copy some hymns in the Cherokee language. We gave this to him. When we asked how things were going with his heart, he said, I often pray to the Savior, and then I feel well. Since it was already late in the evening and he lives 4 or 5 miles from here, he really hurried so that he could get home this evening.

*Feb. 8.* [Spg.] Br. Nathanael Byhan today went with Brn. Proske and Vierling to Oochgelogy on a visit.

*Feb. 8.* [Ooch.] We were informed that some of the Indians who on the 3rd went to face the so-called white intruders have returned. They achieved their purpose by burning the houses and fences of that mob. Even so, this matter did not end without bloodshed. A Cherokee was murdered in an inhumane manner by the enraged white people, and 3 were captured and taken to Georgia. Eventually they all got away from there. The Indians did not spill a single drop of their white enemies' blood, although they had them completely in their power. But since they made the most horrible threats of taking revenge and the Cherokees were expecting a hostile attack, several hundred of them stayed on that side of the stream to defend themselves if necessary. As upsetting as this news was for us, we could still delight in putting our firm assurance in Him, the strongest of the strong, without whose knowledge and consent no hair falls from our head. This same evening we had the unexpected pleasure of seeing both of the single Brn. George Proske and Theophilus Vierling from Salem arrive here. They were accompanied by Br. Nath. Byhan from Spring Place.

[M 414-5-7: Translated by Julie Tomberlin Weber. Addressed to: Revd. Theodore Shulz, Salem, Stokes County, North Carolina. Postmark: Springplace, C.N., Feb. 11, paid 18¾. Received Feb. 24.]

Ochgillogy, Feb. 8, 1830

Dear Brother,

You will already know that the Agent of this Nation has repeatedly received orders from the War Secretary to drive out the intruding Georgians, but this has not been done. This delay provoked the Cherokees to take the matter into their own hands in their last Council, and men were designated and given the responsibility of gathering the people of this nation, or a sufficient number of them, to drive out the white people. Last week the work was begun, following orders of the head Chiefs. I have just heard through reliable channels that the Indians forced 15 white families to move back by burning their houses and fences, etc., and they also burned many unoccupied houses. During this an Indian was shot by the white people and 4 were arrested and taken to Georgia. One escaped from there, though. There are supposed to be about 300 armed Indians at Ridge's and Ross's ready to oppose the expected attack by the Georgians. This news disturbs us more than a little; it has finally come to open hostilities, which God knows will never end. I have written this letter very hastily, and before it is sent I will try to get more news and add it later.

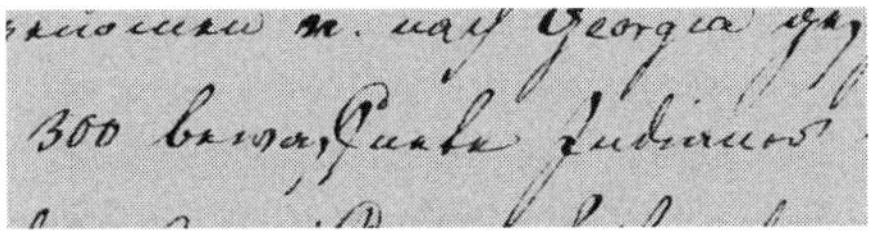

Several weeks ago we had a small disturbance in our little congregation; I believe it has calmed down through God's help and assistance. Our Br. and Sr. George Augustus Hicks unfortunately had a disagreement, made shameful accusations against each other, and the result was that the husband really mistreated his wife. Then she and 2 of her children came to us and complained about her problems. We clarified her responsibilities as well as we could from the Holy Scriptures and admonished her not to leave her husband under any circumstances, as is the custom here, but to reconcile with him in a Christian manner. We were also able to assist with this a couple of days later on the occasion of a visit. Both expressed their great remorse at the offense they had caused themselves and others and with tears promised to be more watchful of their sinful hearts, to humble themselves before the Savior, and to look to him more firmly and unwaveringly.

It is really an unpleasant matter to negotiate between husband and wife, but every duty becomes easy through love and faithful intentions for the good of preciously purchased souls. In a case like this, the Holy Scripture is the only guide, isn't it? For this and other reasons, we postponed Holy Communion until next Sunday, when we are planning to enjoy this high good if it is the Lord's will. Since both the Br. and Sr. mentioned expressed their remorse and contrition and promised to live together as well as possible, we could hardly refuse them this enjoyment, which they themselves desired.

Be so good, dear Br., and let me know what you think about

this situation. With my youth and inexperience, I gladly seek instruction.

Yesterday, the 7th, I had the great joy and grace of imparting the bath of holy baptism to the young Copeland child, and he received the name John Gambold. Since her delivery, Sr. Copeland has been suffering a great deal from fits, but she has recovered somewhat and is active.

The number of scholars is currently 17, of whom 15 live here completely and bring us joy as well as sorrow sometimes, as must be expected with children.

The 9th. Yesterday evening we had the unexpected pleasure of seeing our familiar Theo. Vierling arrive here, accompanied by Nathl. Byhan. Br. Proske is supposed to be in the neighborhood and without a doubt will visit us in the next few days. We sincerely welcome them. We were delighted that they brought us letters and handwritten *Nachr.*, which encouraged us. I also received your dear letter of Jan. 19 at the same time.

Now to touch on the matter of hostilities again, we have learned the following. The fleeing white people sent a threatening letter to Major Ridge, as well as to Ross, in which they promised to destroy their houses and farms with fire and sword. An express messenger was sent to the Agent Montgomery but has not yet returned. This news will perhaps upset you. I will write to you again next week if possible.

Yesterday I was brought a fake $10 Augusta note by J. Crutchfield, which he said he had gotten from Br. Smith. Since the entire matter seemed so extremely unlikely, I naturally did not accept it. Perhaps Br. Smith still knows what kind of money he paid Crutchfield. But the entire matter seems so suspicious to me that I firmly believe it is an attempt to deceive us, because Smith received his money from you, and I cannot believe that you sent such obviously counterfeit money to him.

I will try to answer your inquiry about the Cherokee characters as well as I can. Attempts to learn the language are going slowly with so much other business. But praise God, I am far enough that I can read intelligibly to the Cherokees.

Otherwise, we are all healthy and happy and firm in our faith in the One who knows the number of hairs on our heads. Br. and Sr. Copeland, Sr. Gambold, and Sr. Cl. greet you and your loved ones sincerely, as well as the dear Brn. of the PHC. But most especially I commend myself to your prayer and your intercession, your faithfully obliged friend and Brother,

H. G. Clauder

On Jan. 14 [13] I wrote that the Diary to the end of 1829 was sent to you.

[M 407-2: Springplace Diary.]

*Feb. 9.* [Spg.] Today Miss Sally Ridge, her sister and brother, and Mr. Gold from New Echota stopped in at our place and asked for young apple, pear, cherry, china, and other flower trees, which we gladly gave them. They really hurried home, because they had heard that the Georgia Intruders had killed an Indian in their neighborhood who had belonged to a group of Cherokees who tried to drive a number of Intruders out of Cherokee country, and that the Georgians had taken 2 or 3 of the Indians with them to Georgia, and had them imprisoned there. Two of them ran away from them again, and so they actually had taken only one along and put into prison. Everyone really regretted that the Indian had drunk too much brandy wine. May God prevent more serious incidents between the Georgians and the Cherokees! It is regrettable how the white people treat the poor Cherokees when they push into the country and take house and home away from the Indians and drive the residents from their homes with force. They now have also threatened to burn the houses of Major Ridge and some others who live in the area there. May the Lord look into this and bring about some justice for the Cherokees!

Since the road through the bottom land between Spring Place and our neighbor Jos. Vann's was hardly passable anymore, Mr. Vann's overseer sent us notice today that he was planning to improve this road with his Negroes, and he would be happy if we would help him with this work. Accordingly we sent one of our workers to help him. The road was then improved so that one can go from one house to the other now with dry feet.

*Feb. 10.* [Spg.] Today Br. Nathl. Byhan returned here from his visit in Ochgeloogy.

[M 414-5-8: Translated by Julie Tomberlin Weber. Addressed to: Revd. Theod. Schulz, Salem, Stokes County, North Carolina. Postmark: Springplace, C.N., Feb. 11. Free. Gottlieb Byhan, P.M. Received Feb. 24.]

Springplace, Feb. 11, 1830

My dear Br. Schulz,

I want to inform you right away — although Br. Clauder will also have done so — that it appears the peace we have enjoyed till now will finally be disrupted between Georgia and the Cherokees. The Georgians, or Intruders, murdered an Indian, because the latter, the Indians, could no longer endure things and so — as we heard — were sent by Chief Mr. John Ross to drive the intruders back. They took the white people's things from their houses — N.B. which they, the whites, had taken by force from the Indians and occupied — and then burned them. This outraged the Georgians, so that they gathered and moved against the Indians and killed one and took 2 or 3 with them to Georgia and imprisoned them. Br. Clauder, who lives closer to the place where this occurred, will also be able to write you more details about this. God alone knows what the consequences of this situation will be. The matter seems to be somewhat unclear to us, and we keep wondering if the Indians were not a little too hasty in this matter, which might easily harm them and their just cause.

But we can see and conclude from everything that we must especially commend ourselves to Him who said not a hair from our head would fall to the earth without His knowledge. Continue to remember us in your prayers before our dear Lord. It seems the time of trial is here, and so we want to hold firmly to Him. He will not abandon His poor children.

Day before yesterday Mr. Williams, the Subagent for the Cherokees, passed by here to investigate the matter at the scene. Mr. Ross, the Chief, had asked the Agent himself, Mr. Montgomery, to come, but it appears he sent his Subagent in this important matter. If I hear any more about this matter before next Sunday I will write you again by way of Knoxville.

Praise God, we are all pretty well and greet you all most sincerely. I send you my sincerest greetings and remain your loving but humble Br.

Gottl. Byhan

Last Sunday, the 7th of this month, I received 2 more packets of printed *Gem. Nachr.* from Knoxville. Many thanks for this! I believe I have already informed you that we have started a Sunday school here. Last Sunday 30 people, old and young, were present for this. Nathl. is very busy and diligent in this. Srs. Rachel and Nancy are also a help with this.

[Springplace (M 407-2) and Oochgeelogy (M 409-1) Diaries.]

*Feb. 12.* [Spg.] Mr. Dav. St. Tazizi came to our place with his brother and spent the night here.

*Feb. 13.* [Spg.] He went to Goosawaytee to get some salt, and he returned here in the evening to celebrate Sunday with us.

*Feb. 13.* [Ooch.] Early in the morning one of our scholars suffered the misfortune of stepping too close to the fire, and her clothing immediately caught on fire. Before the general screaming of the other children got our attention and we could rush over, the poor child was already engulfed in flames from head to foot. I was still fortunate enough to rescue her from a terrible death, and while doing this I burned my right hand badly enough that I could not do anything with it for a week. The poor child was really burned all over her body, so that in the first days we didn't know if she would recover. However, the Lord blessed the treatments so that we had some hope that she might recover. We were even more grateful toward our heavenly Helper, because her parents, who belong to the Turnip Mountain mission, have only this one daughter and they love her tenderly.

*Sun., Feb. 14.* [Spg.] Mr. Tazizi was our interpreter in our Sunday services today, which always pleases our Brn. and Srs. There came 45 scholars to our Sunday school today. Finally, after the usual Sunday services, we spoke with the Indian Feather, who expressed his desire to belong to our congregation and to become the property of Jesus. We told him what the most important thing was, to belong to a living congregation of Jesus. He once again expressed himself very contritely and said that he really wants to become Jesus' property. He was encouraged to turn in faithful confidence with all of his misery to the One who Himself paid for all of our sins and redeemed us from the rule of sin, through bitter suffering and death and made us heirs of eternal salvation.

*Feb. 15.* [Spg.] Today the Indian Br. Israel came to us thinking that today was Sunday. When he heard that yesterday had been Sunday, he was very embarrassed and could hardly finish excusing himself for having missed Sunday. We had trouble convincing him and reassuring him that we did not hold this against him since it did not happen intentionally. We told him that we can pray to the Savior and talk with him every day, at which he said that he did this every morning and evening. Since the weather recently has been very good for boiling sugar, many of our Brn. and Srs. are now busy with this work. Thus it also happened that on Sunday, yesterday, only a small number of them had come to our services.

[M 414-5-9: Translated by Julie Tomberlin Weber. Addressed to: Revd. Theodore Shultz, Salem, Stokes County, North Carolina. Post stamped: New Echota, Cher. Na., Feb. 18, 25. Received March 7.]

Oochgillogy, Feb. 15, 1830

Dear Br. Schultz,

As I promised, I am writing again today to tell you more about the recent unrest. I am actually using my dear wife's hand for this for the following unfortunate reason. Several days ago one of our female scholars caught on fire in a horrible manner, out of carelessness with her clothing, and she would probably have died in this horrible manner if I had not torn her flaming clothes from her body with my bare hands. The poor child is still alive but badly burned, and we alternate between fear and hope for her recovery. Her parents, who live 15 to 20 miles from here, were immediately brought here, and they will probably stay here one or two weeks. My right hand and some fingers on the other one are badly burned, and I will probably not be able to do anything with my own hand for several weeks. Because of this unfortunate event, we could not celebrate our dear Lord's memorial meal yesterday, and I was barely able to hold one talk. We are in a bad situation, but despite all the misery we are well and full of trust in the One who will remove this at the appropriate time.

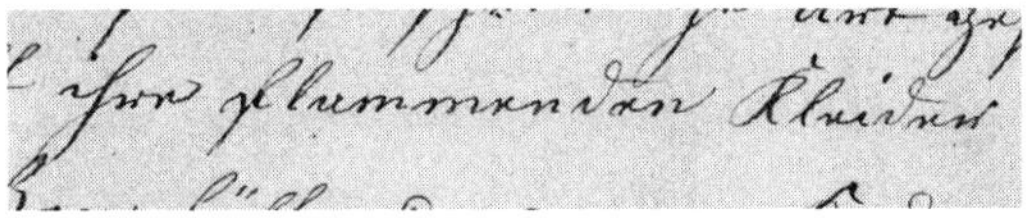

We know nothing more about the recent unrest except that a number of Indians are still staying with Ridge and Ross. The Indians are very alarmed, and since we cannot hold school in our current situation anyway, most of the children have gone home.

As soon as my hand has healed I will let you know, dear Br., how we are doing. Be good enough to share the contents of these few lines with our parents. We all commend ourselves to your prayer. Special greetings from your faithfully obliged Brother,

Henry Gottlieb Clauder

[M 414-5-10: Translated by Julie Tomberlin Weber. Addressed to: Revd. Theod. Shulz, Salem, Stokes County, North Carolina. Postmark: Springplace, C.N., Feb. 18. Free. Gottlieb Byhan, P.M. Received March 3.]

Springplace, Feb. 17, 1830

My dear Br. Schulz,

Your brief but kind letter of Feb. 2, along with the *Missy. Intel.* and $30 of Georgia money arrived safely here on the 14th. We sincerely thank you for everything! Since I do not have anything particular to report at this time, I want to ask you to accept these few lines.

Things are currently very still and quiet concerning the Indians' move. However, everyone is very anxious to hear what Congress says about what will happen, and God alone knows what will happen when the latter has made its statement. When you receive this, you will also know about events at Ridge's. As far as we know, no one here is saying much about this anymore. There will certainly be consequences, even if they do not happen immediately.

Brn. Proske and Vierling have already been in Ochgeloogy for 2 weeks and are expected back in Spring Place next Sunday or Monday.

Our Sunday school is being well attended. Last Sunday 45 scholars were here. Nathl. is very committed to this. Rachel and Nancy Becker are also helping with it.

Concerning our release from the post here, the intention was not to be released before we know how things will actually turn out with the Cherokee land, which we hope and desire will become clear this summer. The situation in which the Cherokees currently are living cannot continue, because they would not be able to tolerate it for long. And so it would be good if their issues were resolved this summer and the matter cleared up. Certainly it would be unnecessary to send a Br. and Sr. to take our place now in this uncertainty. We only want the promise made to us when we accepted this post to be remembered.

Did Br. Eder not receive the letter I wrote him on Jan. 21 before his departure? I am very sorry about that. Except for Mother Byhan, who occasionally is overcome with her weakness, we are all healthy. We greet everyone most sincerely. Please accept the sincerest greetings from your loving, humble Br.,

Gottlieb Byhan

[Springplace (M 407-2) and Oochgeelogy (M 409-1) Diaries.]

*Feb. 18.* [Spg.] With regret we learned from a letter from Ooyugelogy that one of their scholars recently had the misfortune when she was standing too close to the fireplace of having her dress catch on fire. She burned her whole body so badly and Br. Clauder had also burned his hand when he was trying to rip the clothes from her body, so that he cannot do any work.

*Feb. 20.* [Spg.] This evening Brn. Samuel and Israel came here to celebrate Sunday with us tomorrow. We had a long and pleasant conversation with Br. Samuel about spiritual matters, as well as about the current situation of the poor Cherokees. If more such events should take place like the ones that are mentioned on the 9th of this month, it would be feared that the Indians would not watch patiently, but it might lead to more serious things. May the Lord look into this and allow justice for the injured party, and to this whole Nation!

*Feb. 20.* [Ooch.] In the morning Brn. Proske and Vierling left us after staying here 12 days. This was pleasant and encouraging for us as well as for them.

*Sun., Feb. 21.* [Spg.] For the beginning of Lent, we prayed the Litany of the Life, Sufferings, and Death of our Lord Jesus Christ in the morning. Afterward was the sermon on the Doctrinal Text for today, John 12:23. Despite the fact that it looked like rainy weather would start today, about forty scholars came for Sunday school.

*Sun., Feb. 21.* [Ooch.] The sermon was on Psalm 103[?]:7, and then a Cherokee believer who belongs to the Turnip Mountain mission held a talk and prayer in Cherokee. As far as we could learn about this, he spoke fervently, and warmly extolled to his heathen countrymen the saving faith in Christ. In a second service everyone in our little communicant congregation was invited to join us next Sunday in the memorial meal of the sufferings and death of our Redeemer.

[M 414-5-11: Translated by Julie Tomberlin Weber. Addressed to: Revd. Theod. Schulz, Salem, Stokes County, North Carolina. Postmark: Springplace, C.N., Feb. 21. Free. Gottlieb Byhan, P.M.]

Springplace, Feb. 21, 1830

My dear Br. Schulz,

I am writing you a few lines to send with the Knoville mail to inform you of an unhappy circumstance that occurred eight days ago yesterday, the 13th of this month, in Ochgeloogy at our Br. and Sr. Clauder's, since Br. Clauder is currently not able to write.

One of the scholars there got too close to the fire and her clothes caught on fire. She went running out of the house and was soon engulfed in flames. Br. and Sr. Clauder were just having breakfast. When Br. Clauder heard the screaming he ran out to see what was wrong and saw the child in flames there. Br. Clauder ran to help her and tore the burning clothes from her body. In the process he burned his hands so that they were one big blister. The child is apparently badly burned, but there is hope she will recover. Yesterday evening when Brn. Proske and Vierling returned to Spring Place from there, they told us that Br. Clauder's hands are starting to heal. I will visit them this week if I possibly can. Otherwise, everyone there is apparently completely healthy, as are we here in Spring Place, praise God!

Yesterday evening Brn. Samuel and Israel came to our place to spend this Sunday with us. We had a long conversation with Br. Samuel yesterday evening, about both spiritual matters and the current situation of the Cherokees.

One comment he made made an impression on me. He said that the Cherokees would rather fight and die on their own land than move west. We admonished him to commend the matter to the Savior, who is Lord of all lords and holds the rule of humans in His hands. We just had to remain calm and diligently lay the matter before His faithful heart in our prayers; He will make everything work out for our good. He promised to do this. Our situation is critical in this respect, and sometimes we are in a real predicament trying not to arouse suspicion on either side. And so we have special cause to plead diligently with the Savior for the necessary wisdom and cleverness in this matter, so as not to cause offense on either side. Without a doubt you also remember us diligently in your prayers before the dear Lord in this respect as well.

Concerning the last event on the Coosa River, when the Intruders killed an Indian — which you will have heard about — everyone is currently relatively calm and wants to wait calmly to see what the government will say about this.

Nathl. just rang the bell for Sunday school, and since I am supposed to give a talk to those present afterward, I must close. All of you, accept the sincerest greetings from all of us. And you, dear Br., accept a special greeting from your loving friend and Br.,

Gottl. Byhan

[Springplace (M 407-2) and Oochgeelogy (M 409-1) Diaries.]

*Sun., Feb. 28.* [Spg.] Our small church was pretty full of listeners. In the first service was the sermon on Jesus' sufferings on the Mount of Olives in response to today's Doctrinal Text [Matt. 26:37,38]. In the second was the baptism of the baby daughter, born to our Indian Br. and Sr. James and Rosanna on the 7th of this month, with the name Catharina. Sunday school was held before and after the services, as is usual every Sunday. Today an unusually large number had come for this.

*Sun., Feb. 28.* [Ooch.] Today we joined our dear Cherokee congregation in the memorial meal of our Redeemer, who died for us on the cross; this was a great blessing for us. He revealed Himself during this, which was evident in the tears that our dear brown ones shed. In a general conversation after this, one Sr. said: "I always try to hold closer to Jesus, and in everything I do I try to have him before my eyes. He always helps me through." Another one said with tears: "I often feel badly toward my Savior, but He awakens me over and over. I seek nothing but to follow Him and to grow in His grace." We realized a long time ago it would be beneficial to open a Sunday school here, partly to keep the children who live here at our place productively occupied and partly to provide those who cannot attend school during the week an opportunity to learn how to read. We discussed this matter with our dear colleagues in Spring Place and agreed it would be good to open a Sunday school there as well as here. This has already been accomplished in Spring Place, and it has not been done here sooner than today because of several circumstances. And so we gathered in our Saal early in the day and sang, and then knelt and prayed to the Friend of Children and the Humble to bless, protect, and guide this undertaking. Thus we started a Sunday school here with 12 scholars. May the Lord, who does not despise small things, mercifully reveal Himself in our endeavor.

*Mar. 4.* [Ooch.] Major Ridge visited us. His brother Oa-tee was recently baptized here. He said: "My brother and my friend William Hicks both belong to the church. They are good people now. However, I am still the same old bad human!" We pointed out to him how essentially depraved the human heart is and that perhaps its pride and stubbornness are keeping him from becoming like his brother and his friend; as soon as he is ready to repent and humbly seek his true salvation with Jesus, he will also receive the power to renounce all evil. He left us with the promise that he would visit us again next Sunday.

*Mar. 6.* [Spg.] In the evening several of our communicant Brn. and Srs. arrived here for tomorrow's services. Among others was Br. Samuel, with whom we had a pleasant conversation about things related to our spiritual salvation. He asked among other things how often and how many times a member of the congregation who has gone astray and been excluded from the congregation can be taken in again and his misdeeds forgiven. The appropriate information about this was given him. He further said the Savior had said that if a Br. or a member of the congregation does something to hurt another someone else, we should forgive him many times. This was also explained to him and clarified, and he showed his satisfaction with this. This conversation led us in general to the only thing needful, that we hold firmly to Him who loved us until death, and shed His blood for us, and bore the punishment for our sins. If we believe in Him and turn to Him daily, indeed hourly, with our contrition and poverty, He will forgive our sins and make us children of God and heirs to eternal salvation.

*Sun., Mar. 7.* [Spg.] Today most of our Brn. and Srs. came here. At 11 o'clock we gathered for the praying of the Church Litany. Afterward was the sermon on today's Doctrinal Text, Matt. 26:63,64. At the conclusion Br. Samuel led another long talk for the Brn. and Srs. in Cherokee. Afterward we had a blessed enjoyment of the body and blood of Jesus in Holy Communion, during which we were aware of the Savior's presence in our midst in a comforting manner. Then we talked with two of our baptismal candidates, who expressed their deep desire to become Jesus' property and to be cleansed of their sins in Jesus' blood in holy baptism. We also found it necessary to talk lovingly and seriously with the single Indian Br. Solomon, who is a candidate for Holy Communion, and to call his attention to what he promised the Savior in holy baptism. This seemed to make a healthy impression on him. We can honestly say that today was a day of true blessing for our Brn. and Srs. and us, which served as a great encouragement to us.

*Sun., Mar. 7.* [Ooch.] One of the few visitors who came here to our service today despite the rain was the above-named Indian Ridge. Instead of having a sermon, we read an instructive text and concluded with an appropriate talk and a prayer. Ridge spent the night at our place and we used this opportunity to discuss various things with him about his eternal well-being. We also read him some chapters from the Gospel of Matthew which has recently been translated into Cherokee. Among other things he said: "I was still a young man when the first missionaries (Brn. Steiner and Schweinitz in the year 1799-1800) came to us. Now they are all gone and some of them in the earth. However, I am still here. I am now old, my hair is getting gray, and I cannot live many more years. Many of my countrymen are now Christian. They no longer drink alcohol and are better people than they used to be. I am grateful that I am still here, and now I also want to seek what is good." We explained to him that he would not be able to keep his good intentions through his own power, but that he, as a poor sinner, would have to turn to Christ and seek His forgiveness for his sins and the power to follow goodness. Upon leaving the next morning, he said: "Now I will think about everything you told me and read to me."

[M 414-5-12: Translated by Julie Tomberlin Weber. Addressed to: Revd. Theodor Shulz, Salem, Stokes County, North Carolina. Postmark: Spring Place, C.N., March 7. Free. G. Byhan, P.M. Received March 22.]

Spring Place, C.N., March 5, 1830

My dear Br. Shulz,

A quarter of an hour ago Brn. Proske and Vierling left here to return to Salem and are planning to arrive back in Salem in about 16 days. They intend to take the shortest route over the mountains, to look around the mountain area, and then to cross the Shallowford on the Yadkin to get home.

Although we have received nothing from Salem for several post days and are really anxious to hear something from there, I will send you a couple of lines with the next Sunday mail and let you know how we are doing.

We are still living in quiet and peace regarding the Cherokee matter. Things have remained peaceful so far since the last event with the Georgians and Cherokees on the border, but we still sometimes hear that the Georgians are stealing horses, cattle, and such from the Indians.

When our Br. Boas came to our place last Saturday evening, he told us that he had met an Indian who told him that he was on his way to see the Agent to complain to him about his trouble, since they almost cannot endure things with the Georgians on the border any longer, because they could not get any more horses or cattle from them. Unfortunately the Indians have little faith in their Agent anymore — he is after all from ______, and is afraid to do for the Indians what he is actually supposed to do. Things might indeed be difficult for the poor man, because no one can serve two masters, and neither can the Agent. He is sitting just as the saying goes, between two stools. It would be good if matters concerning the Cherokees were dealt with soon in Congress, so that things would be clarified. Mr. John Ridge, as you will surely have seen from the *Phönix*, had a strange reception in Washington. We are surprised that we have not yet heard anything of consequence from our Delegates.

Sunday the 7th. I just received a matter about which I would like to know the thoughts of the P.H. Conf. Yesterday evening our baptismal candidate, the Indian named Feather, his wife, and two children came to our place to spend this Sunday with us. This morning he shared his desire to have his youngest child, who is about one year old, baptized. I must admit, this request concerned me since the parents do not yet belong to a church of any denomination, although we consider the father a candidate for holy baptism. I comforted the father by suggesting we postpone the child's baptism a little in order, as I thought to myself, to win some time to present the matter to the Conf. in Salem and get instructions on how to act in such cases, whether we should baptize children whose parents do not yet belong to any church. I ask you to inform me of your thoughts about this, and as quickly as possible. We once considered the father of this child — Feather — for baptism in our Conference, but the Savior has not yet approved him.

Today we have the enjoyment of the body and blood of Jesus in Holy Communion before us. May the Savior allow this to strengthen our faith and reliance on Him anew.

Sincerest greeting from all of us to all of you. And you, accept a special separate greeting from your poor, loving Br.,

Gottl. Byhan

P.S. We are really eager to hear something from you dear ones in Salem again. Several post days have passed without anything from you. What's wrong?

I just received printed *Gem. Nachr.* along with 2 kind letters from Feb. 16 and 23. Many thanks to you! But I can't read them now, because the first bell for the sermon has already rung.

G. B.

[M 414-5-13: Translated by Julie Tomberlin Weber. Addressed to: Revd. Theodore Schulz, Salem, Stokes County, North Carolina. Post stamped: New Echota, Cher. Na., Mar. 11, 50. Received March 25.]

Ooyugillogy, March 8, 1830

Dear Br. Schulz,

On Jan. 14 I sent you a packet containing the Diary of this mission until the end of this last year, but I still have no news about whether you received it or not. You will have seen from our last letter with what a sad event the Lord has tested us, when one of our scholars was dangerously burned. While saving the child I injured my own hand, so that I could not use it for a while. Praise God, the child has almost recovered and without a doubt is out of danger, if her parents are not in too much of a hurry to take her home, which might cause her to get a cold. The parents of this child have been here three weeks already, and we have shown them all possible friendship and have provided the child with all imaginable care. We thought we would win their affection in this way, since they both belong to the Presbyterians and want to be Christians. However, we were unfortunately deceived, as we discovered in the following painful manner.

The child's father went home last week and sent one of his sons, a boy of about 15 years, to help take care of the child. This young person was in the school in Brainerd for 6 years, and we thought we would find him to be a somewhat well-mannered person, but instead he proved to be extremely wild and offensive. When I let him know he could not possibly remain here if he behaved this way, he promised to improve, and he stayed here another day and behaved pretty well. After two days he left complaining. and then we could only expect that we would have to deal with his aspersions and just swallow them patiently, since it is the Indians' manner to blindly believe everything from their children and to hate anyone who says anything bad about them. Our unpleasant expectations were fulfilled. Late in the evening last Saturday, the old man came and commanded me to appear before him. He began his complaints as follows:

1. He had sent his son here, but I had chased him away. 2. His son had been given something to eat only once in two days. 3. His sick child had not had anything to eat for 2 days, etc. I tried to clarify all of this for the old man and turned to his wife, who had been here the entire time. But she evaded the question, so she would not have to testify against her son. I also pointed out that he himself could see the unfounded nature of these accusations because he had been here for 2 weeks and had seen how we live during this time. But all this was in vain. His son had complained about us, and we, as white people, could not defend ourselves.

Yesterday was holy Sunday (especially holy among the Presbyterians), and we naturally did not get a friendly glance, and our attempts to win them through friendship and love remained fruitless. But the sacredness of Sunday must have softened his obstinance and his anger. When he was getting ready to leave with sack and pack with the child, who could neither stand nor walk, we tried to persuade him to be patient for a few more days, since the child would certainly get a cold after all efforts thus far to save her, and that could cause her death. Finally after many of our neighbors who were here, as well as Major Ridge, protested so strongly against this, they agreed and became a little more friendly.

This morning the man returned home without leaving us particularly good feelings. The child and her mother, the cause of all of this unpleasantness, are still here.

These are facts, I am making no comments, since I am not inclined to complain.

In general the current time is a time of trial for us, which the Lord has allowed to come upon us for our own good, and we share in the most blessed experience which all true believers from time immemorial have had and will have as long as the world continues, that the greater the external trouble is, the more powerfully one feels the divine comfort and rejoices in the knowledge that all trials are not only intended for the best, but that they also are appropriate to our strength, and have their measure and purpose.

As great as the unpleasantness of this is on the one hand, we still find encouragement here and there. For example, through two visits which Major Ridge, whom you know, made here several days ago, and during which he commented on many things concerning his inner situation, we took new hope that this man is not far from God's kingdom, because from his words we could conclude that he is concerned about something better than this world. Yesterday he was here in the service and remained here until this morning. Upon leaving he promised of his own accord that he would really reflect on everything we had said to him here. But perhaps I am too hasty in my expectations. Last week he was here and paid $50 toward the note he had given Br. Reichel through his son John for the education of his daughter. Br. Abraham Steiner, Sr., gave me the note last fall when I was in Salem. Since I am completely out of money, I paid this $50 into the mission account. If I am not wrong, the agreement was that you pay Br. Reichel what Major Ridge paid here toward his note.

Since there is a lot of work this time of year, for example repairing fences, planting, and sowing, we found it necessary a month ago to engage a hired hand for a while. We will let him go again as soon as possible. Greet your dear family, my dear parents, and also the dear Brn. of the P.H.C. from all of us. We commend ourselves to your further compassion and intercession. Your obliged friend and Br.,

Henry G. Clauder

Dear Br. Schulz,

I am using this opportunity to explain the following situation. Some years ago my eldest daughter Gertraut received a Com-

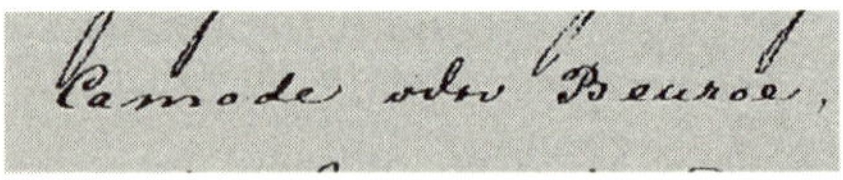

ode or Beuroe, which Br. Samuel Schulz bought for her with the stipulation that my brother in Bethania should pay him back. But now this has not yet been done. And so I would like to ask you to pay this amount to Br. Saml. Schulz. If you have interest on hand which could be given given to my daughter Gertraut, perhaps the debt could be paid out of this. If not, you can take some from my own. It is my desire that Br. Saml. Schulz should be paid as soon as possible. Greet your dear family from me. I remain yours,

Anna Maria Gambold

[Springplace (M 407-2) and Oochgeelogy (M 409-1) Diaries.]

*Mar. 12.* [Spg.] Br. Byhan, Sr., today went to Ochgeloogy on business. Today we also heard that the Delegates who were sent to Washington by the Creek Nation had come back and had spent the night at our neighbor Mr. Jos. Vann. Among them was also Mr. John Ridge, who acted as secretary for them in Washington. We heard that they had given their Memorial to Congress and that they had no further instructions to do anything further for the Creeks there. The Creeks had also not set aside any appropriation for them, so they had to come back home, and now they want to wait peacefully to see what more the government will do for them.

*Mar. 12.* [Ooch.] We received a brief visit from our dear Br. Byhan in Spring Place, which was encouraging to everyone.

*Mar. 13.* [Ooch.] He returned in the morning. Through him we received a letter from Br. Th. Schulz in Salem, as well as some handwritten and printed *Gem. Nachr.* Through these we were transported spiritually from this remote region into the midst of our dear Gemeine. In recent days the leaves in the bush around our establishment were set on fire and burned in order to improve the pasture for livestock. This method is common here in this country.

*Mar. 13.* [Spg.] Br. Byhan today returned from Oochgeloogy.

*Sun., Mar. 14.* [Spg.] The sermon was on the Doctrinal Text for today, Luke 22:61,62. Sunday school today was well attended again, before and after the sermon. Afterward we spoke with one of our baptismal candidates, who expressed himself very contritely and satisfactorily. Today the western post rider also brought us the official news that the mission place

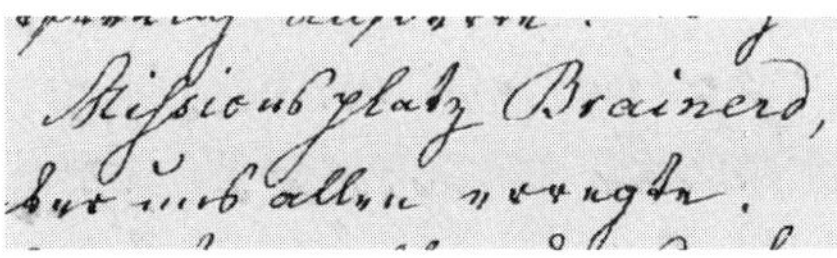
Missionsplatz Brainerd,

Brainerd was almost completely burned down last Friday, which aroused deep compassion in us all.

*Sun., Mar. 14.* [Ooch.] After a very rainy night, we had a beautiful spring day today. Some new scholars visited our Sunday school for the first time. We were also very happy to see that many of the young girls are trying to study and memorize Bible passages and hymn verses. One of them who had enjoyed a minimal education here had memorized Matthew 5 and two whole hymns from Watts's *Hymns*, containing 16 verses, and recited all of this publicly today. This brought us great joy and encouraged us. In the sermon on the Doctrinal Text for today (Luke 22:61[,62]), we explained the danger followers of Christ experience when they begin trusting in their own strength and works. Through this they, like Peter, deny their Lord and Master and sooner or later experience a sorrowful fall and thus recognize their inability in a painful but saving manner.

*Mar. 15.* [Spg.] Finally we were able to begin sowing oats, because we had been lacking help on the farm until then. Throughout this week, however, rainy weather prevented us from continuing with this.

*Mar. 16.* [Ooch.] We were delighted by a brief visit by Mr. Worcester, the preacher in New Echota, accompanied by a traveling preacher from Boston named Greenwood. They were taken into the school and observed the work of the scholars. They expressed their interest in this and in the entire mission work of the Brethren, and they hoped the Lord would continue to bless and support this service to Him. In the evening we had a strong storm that soaked the ground so thoroughly we could not work in the fields for several days.

*Mar. 17.* [Ooch.] Very early in the day an Indian came here with his wife to beg. For this purpose he showed a so-called begging letter. The best gift we could give him was a sincere admonition to be diligent and to work hard, which, however, seemed to make little impression on him.

*Mar. 17.* [Spg.] We had an especially heavy downpour with stormy weather, such as we have not had for a long time.

[M 414-5-14: Translated by Julie Tomberlin Weber. Addressed to: Revd. Theodor Shulz, Salem, Stokes County, North Carolina. Postmark: Spring Place, C.N., March 18. Free. G. Byhan, P.M. Received Apr. 1.]

Spring Place, March 17, 1830

My dear Br. Schulz,

On the 7th of this month your two kind letters of the 16th and 23rd and my private account of Feb. 10th arrived at our place, as well as issue No. 1 of the printed *Gem. Nachr.* from 1829. On the 14th of this month I received your letter of March 2, along with issue No. 2 of the printed *Gem. Nachr.* from 1829. Accept our deepest gratitude for all of this. It seems that there are no more handwritten *Gem. Nachr.* for us in Salem?

On this occasion I want to inquire why it is that the *Missionary Intel.* comes so irregularly and indeed mixed up? Since Mr. Buttrick in Hightower also receives a copy, he always relies on me to send it to him. Now it has happened that the *Intelligencers* for Mr. Buttrick were addressed to him, but in my care or to forward, which I then send him when an opportunity arises. I do not know who takes care of sending it from Philadelphia, but this much is certain: They should either all be addressed to me or those for Mr. Buttrick should be directed straight to Hightower P.O., Cherokee Nation. The latter would be the best, since he then would pay the postage, which from the beginning has been paid by our mission and has not yet been repaid, because he has gotten used to it. Please take care of this matter.

I already informed you in my previous letter dated the 7th of this month that the single Brn. Proske and Vierling left Spring Place on the 5th of this month to return to Salem, and they will probably already be back in Salem when this letter arrives.

Our Sunday school is going well. Nathl. completely takes care of this. Srs. Rachel B. and Nancy B. help him faithfully. I myself cannot do this, because I must see to the visitors on Sunday. Otherwise, I must take care of two miserable posts on Sundays, and since these come before the service, I really do not welcome them. In addition I fear that the other two will also arrive on Sunday in a while.

We were happy to hear the thoughts you shared with us in your letters dated Feb. 16th. Concerning the assistance for the Sunday school here in Spring Place, we can take care of things ourselves, because Nathl. has Rachel and Nancy to help him if necessary. We also have Br. Samuel's son Flea, who is in our week-school and, I must say, can read well. If we really needed him he could also pitch in, so that at least in this respect there is no need here at this time. And since Nathl. is very keen in this, and looks after it completely, I can take care of the visitors without being disturbed, so that the main work does not suffer at all from this. Since the Sunday school has been going, our services are better attended than ever. And finally it can hardly be thought it could or might perhaps lead to feeding the many visitors, which had been partially stopped, because those who live far away bring their own food with them. It is also clear to see that people do not expect at all that they all receive something to eat here. More about this matter another time in person.

I believe that in Ochgeloogy there might be more difficulties because of the school, because Br. Clauder is alone, so to speak. Sr. Copeland is surely there to help, but it is not the same as it is at our place here in Spring Place. Also not nearly as many come to their Sunday school as to ours. Br. Clauder will be able to report the circumstances there better than I can. I was there for a brief visit last week and found the Brn. and Srs. all well. Br. Clauder's hands are almost healed. However, the poor child whose clothing burned is indeed pitiful to look at. I have never seen such a sight in my life as I when I saw this child. Br. Clauder will probably also have informed you in detail of this situation.

On this occasion I also want to add that last Sunday the western post rider brought us the extremely sad news that the mission site Brainerd was completely burned down in the night from the 12th to the 13th of this month. We have not heard anything else particular from there since then. If this is really true it will surely appear in the *Phönix* here.

Last Saturday our friend Mr. Boudinott told me that our Church Litany has now been set in type and will very soon be printed. Since Br. Clauder lives closer to New Echota, he will take care of trimming the booklets, etc. The Nation is currently very quiet and is waiting with anxiety for things that should or will come — and we have to admit we also.

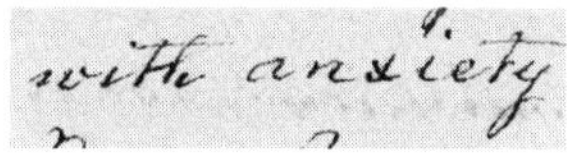
with anxiety

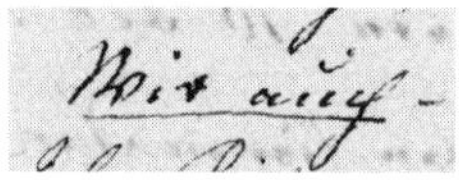

Last week the Creek Delegates came by here on their way back from Washington, and Mr. John Ridge was with them. They had submitted their Memorial to Congress and now want to wait out the course of events quietly at home, because they had orders from the Chiefs of the Creek Nation that they should come home as soon as they handed out their Memorial. Mr. Jos. Vann did not write home on this occasion but sent word through Mr.

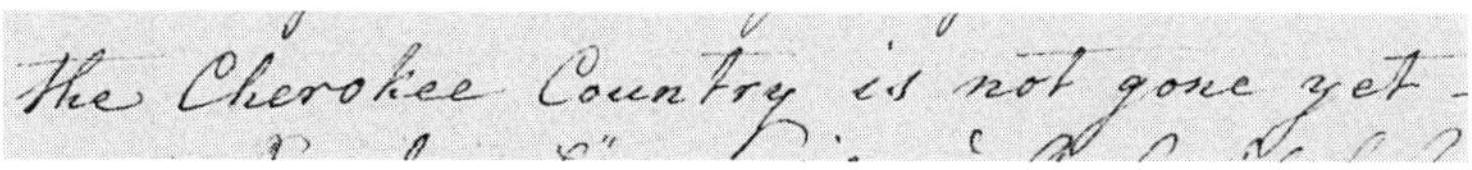
the Cherokee Country is not gone yet.

John Ridge that we should just remain calm and: "The Cherokee Country is not gone yet."

We have just heard that it has been confirmed that the mission site Brainerd has indeed been burned down. Three large houses are burned. Since the smith and their mill stood a good distance away they kept these houses. The missionaries are currently living in the smith shop. They saved very few of their belongings and apparently lost several thousand dollars worth. It is horrible! May God protect us and everyone from such misfortune!

You reported to me that our Diary till the end of Nov. reached you. I think the one from Dec. till the close of the year should have reached your hands as well by now.

On Palm Sunday, Apr. 4th, we have the baptism of an adult Indian before us, our Br. Israel's natural brother named Feather. He had shared his desire often and let us know his intention to become the property of Jesus, and during our conversations with him it was clear to see that he is very serious about belonging to the One who suffered and died to achieve our eternal salvation and did so for his sake as well, and [he] deeply desires to be cleansed of his sins and purified in holy baptism through Jesus' blood. About 14 days ago his wife was here with him. She also expressed her intention to become Jesus' property. She was told about contrite love, and this seemed to make an impression on her.

We currently have 2 more baptismal candidates besides Feather and his wife. An Indian woman not far from Charles R. Hicks's place sent word through our Sr. Felicitas Hicks that she wants to join our community and become the property of Jesus. We are planning to visit her as soon as possible if the weather and streams will still allow it. In general, we are trying to visit all our Brn. and Srs. in a round.

Everyone here greets all of you sincerely. Remember us diligently in your prayer before our dear Lord. Accept also the most sincere greetings from your lowly but loving friend and Br.,

G. Byhan

[Springplace (M 407-2) and Oochgeelogy (M 409-1) Diaries.]

*Mar. 19.* [Ooch.] We learned from a letter from our dear Br. Byhan in Spring Place and from the Cherokee newspaper that the mission station in Brainerd in the northern part of this country had been completely lost to flames, including all the possessions of the missionaries. As a result, the flourishing mission school there was completely disrupted for now. The fire broke out at midnight and had spread extensively before it was discovered.

*Mar. 20.* [Spg.] Mr. Dav. Vann came to our place with his wife and child on their way home. They had already stayed for a long time at Capt. Dav. McNair's. They spent the night here. In the evening, despite the fact it was very rainy, various of our Brn. and Srs. arrived at our place for tomorrow's Sunday services.

*Sun., Mar. 21.* [Spg.] Mr. and Mrs. Vann continued on early today in order to cross Holly Creek, which is 8 miles from here, early before it got too high from the rain which has been falling. In the first Sunday service a sermon was read on Jesus' sufferings. Afterward was Bible reading. Br. Nathl. Byhan led this. Then the single Br. Niclaus Ignatius repeated in the Cherokee language what had been read. Afterward was a speaking with 3 of our baptismal candidates. We had the joy of informing one of them, the Indian Feather, that two weeks from today he would be able to participate, and he was very happy about this and assured us that he believes he is saved solely through the sufficient merit of Jesus. Today our Br. Boas's wife also told us of her desire to become Jesus' property and to belong to our congregation. She was clearly told what was the most needful thing when a person wants to become a living member of Jesus Christ's body and a member of our congregation, that one turn with all his misery and with all his sinfulness to the Savior, who does not turn anyone away who comes to Him as a remorseful sinner. He is always prepared to forgive the sins of such a person for the sake of His merit and to accept him as His child. This person had already said two years ago that she wanted to belong to us. Accordingly, we had her called so we could speak with her confidentially and sincerely, in her husband's presence. However, she did not come. Since then she has visited us from time to time with her husband, our Br. Boas, who regularly attends our services. And when we asked Br. Boas if his wife was not willing to give her heart to the Savior and to convert, his answer was usually: She is preparing herself for this. And so we made it clear to her today that we must come to the Savior just as we are, even if we feel so bad and sinful. Those who feel themselves to be the most wretched and sinful are dearest to him, because we ourselves cannot help ourselves. Our own efforts and our own preparation to become pleasing to Him do not help us at all. Through His grace alone and through the workings of His Holy Spirit we can be improved and made into children of God, etc. It seemed that this brought her to deep reflection about herself, and she left us quite happily.

*Sun., Mar. 21.* [Ooch.] We had a really good number of scholars and listeners in the school and in the service. Both of our interpreters, the Brn. Hickses, are currently away from home. And so many of our Brn. and Srs. do not find what we sincerely desire for them, since they do not understand English. Even so, this is just the case with 5 of them. We are pleased that under such circumstances they try to instruct each other. In recent days we have been busy planting corn and our children helped us with this.

[*Records: N.C.*, 8:3915: Salem Diary. Translated by Douglas L. Rights.]

*March 22.* The Single Brethren Georg Proske and Theophilus Vierling returned from their visit to the land of the Cherokees and we rejoiced at the reports from our Brn. and Srs. there.

[Springplace (M 407-2) and Oochgeelogy (M 409-1) Diaries.]

*Mar. 27.* [Spg.] In the evening various of our Brn. and Srs. and also some who do not belong to us arrived here for the celebration of Sunday tomorrow.

*Sun., Mar. 28.* [Spg.] In the morning was the sermon on today's Sunday Epistle lesson, Heb. 9:11-15, before a large gathering. Afterward Br. Nathl. Byhan led the Bible reading, which was repeated in the Cherokee language by our Indian Br. Solomon, and we closed with the singing of some hymns in the Cherokee language.

*Sun., Mar. 28.* [Ooch.] Since the Methodists held a large service close to our place, only a few visitors were here. We could feel the truth of our Lord's comforting promise [Matt. 18:20]: "Where two or three are gathered together in my name, there am I in the midst of them." And when we considered the story of the thief on the cross (Luke 23:42,43) our hearts felt the merciful presence of the One who promised heavenly paradise to those who are humble and poor in heart. The parents of the unfortunate child who was burned with her clothes in the fire about six weeks ago, left with her in the afternoon. Although she was severely burned, she had healed enough that they could take her with them.

# *1830, part 3*

[M 414-5-15: Translated by Julie Tomberlin Weber. Addressed to: Revd. Theodore Schulz, Salem, Stokes County, North Carolina. Postmark: Springplace, C.N., Apr. 1, paid 18¾. Received Apr. 24. Penciled in: About sundry books for S. School at O___y.]

Ooyugillogy, March 29, 1830

Dear Br. Schulz,

Your dear letters of the 16th of last month and the 9th of this one, the first with Br. Copeland's note, arrived safely in our hands, which delighted us. On the 10th I sent a letter to you which you will surely have received by now. Praise God, we are all healthy, and although overwhelmed with work in the fields and gardens, we have gotten far enough along with this that we will get by. The [oats] were sown long ago and the corn has been partially planted.

In a letter I received yesterday from Br. Byhan, I saw your request to receive a specific account of expenses from here for last year. In letters dated May 5 and Nov. 5 [17], 1829, I sent the requested accounts, which you received. From these accounts you can see which articles were purchased with cash expenditures, and our dear Brn. of the U.A.C. will be in a position to judge how economically things here are managed.

A single case which serves as future instruction for me is that I loaned a sum of money to one of our Cherokees, which, however, has been partially repaid. In this case, by the way, I followed the example of the blessed Father Gambold, who did the same in many cases.

Certainly it is the responsibility of all who are supported and fed by the mission accounts to observe the strictest thriftiness, not only because they must be accountable to humans, but because they must answer for everything to the Lord of all on the day of general judgment about how they used the talents given to them [Matt. 25:14-30]. This is a much stronger reason that missionaries should be economical and that so many should observe the blessing word: Temperence above all and in all, which, however, is not the case in all places. Since we sold a Negro woman a year ago, as you know, for such articles as are necessary here and in Spring Place, and therefore everything accepted on this condition did not appear in the cash account, so I will add a very specific copy of everything received here. Br. Byhan will surely report what was received in Spring Place.

It encourages us to learn that the P.H.C. is willing to provide support for our Sunday school. The schools here and in Spring Place are in a blessed routine; we just lack the necessary books in the appropriate number. And so we sincerely hope that the Lord might soon provide an opportunity through which we might receive the following articles, which can be found in the Depository of S.S. books: 100 blue and 500 red tickets, 2 dozen ABC cards. Hymn books. Testaments. Class Sheets. 2 dozen spelling books. Reward books. 2 dozen S. School primers. Meanwhile, we must manage as well as we can, and if God is with and for us we will not lack any blessing, which is, after all, above any action and discovery of humans.

Thank you for the comments which you made in your first kind letter of Feb. 16th regarding the Sunday school. In answer to this same letter I will add the following. It is certainly true that we are extremely busy on days when most of our Brn. and Srs. are here. But this is not the case every Sunday. In such cases, I can always get the opportunity to speak with them when an interpreter is available. It is highly unlikely that the small meal service, which was done away with long ago but still continued in a small way, might be renewed through this, because since the school lasts until 3 in the afternoon and the last and final meal of the day is eaten at 4 o'clock, all the visitors are at home or on the way, and those who come to school from the neighborhood return home immediately after it ends, so that we now have fewer guests to feed than otherwise. Still one cannot judge by individual cases since hospitality is a well-known tradition in this area.

The poor suffering child is still here. Her parents still do not seem to be reconciled. They are planning to move in a few days when the weather is favorable. It has been six weeks today since the misfortune occurred. During the entire time we had the child's mother here, and often her father and brother. Praise and thanks to the Lord for the gracious assistance which He granted us in this trial. It was a very difficult but also a blessed school for us, which we hope will serve to everyone's improvement.

We greet all of you sincerely and commend ourselves and our work to your prayer and remembrance.

H. G. Clauder

Copy of the articles in account received from Samuel Henry ([penciled in:] for Negro sale).

| 1829 | | |
|---|---|---|
| Mar. | 31 lb. iron at $0.16: $3.10; 78 lb. flour $2.53½; 17 yds. tow linen $4.25 | $9.88½ |
| Apr. | 2 bbls flour at $7.00: $14.00; powder and lead $5.50 | $19.50 |
| | 5½ yds. linen $1.37½; horse collar $1.75; 10 gals. whisky for vinegar $5.00 | $8.12½ |
| Aug. | 3 bbls flower at $6.50: $19.50; 129 lbs. coffee at $0.25: $32.25 | $51.75 |
| | 8½ yds. cotton cloth $1.70; 6 yds. tow cloth $1.50; curry comb $0.25 | $3.45 |
| | 1 gallon cherry bounce $0.50; 4 lbs. sheet iron $2.00 | $2.50 |
| Sept. | 39 lbs. sugar $6.50; 1 gallon wine for communion $3.00 | $9.50 |
| | 1 gal. rum $2.75; 61 yds. tow cloth for beds $15.25 | $18.00 |
| | 18½ yds. cotton mix for towels, table cloth, etc. at $0.33 1/3[?] | $6.25 |
| | 7 yds. flax cloth at $0.37 for shirts: $2.62½; 1 bbl. flour $6.50 | $9.12½ |
| | 2 bbls. salt $26.50 | $26.50 |
| Oct. 27 | 174½ lbs. flour $5.65; dried apples $0.87½ | $6.52½ |
| Nov. 5 | for moving Mr. Copeland from Tennessee, all expenses included | $25.00 |
| | | $196.11 |

I will try to send an exact account of all debtors and creditors in my next letter. Against the above account S. Henry received corn, provender, hides, etc., valued at $20.

P.S. The dear Sisters request a German almanac for this year. Could you send it to us with the mail?

[Springplace (M 407-1) and Oochgeelogy (M 409-1) Diaries. Translated by Julie Tomberlin Weber. Handwritings are Henry G. Clauder's (Ooch.) and Gottlieb Byhan's (Spg.).]

*Mar. 29.* [Spg.] Br. and Sr. Byhan and their daughter Rachel visited in the area of the Chickamaga to see and speak with our Brethren and Sisters who live in the area there. About 3 miles from Spring Place they passed the Conossauga River which was somewhat swollen. And so riding through it was somewhat dangerous, as the water came up to their saddles. But they passed safely through and about 2 o'clock in the afternoon arrived at Mr. Nathan Hicks, a son of the blessed Br. Charles Renatus Hicks, 22 miles from Spring Place. After they had eaten lunch there they traveled on, accompanied by our former scholar Charles Hicks, son of Nathan Hicks, who was willing to serve them as interpreter. Toward evening they arrived at Fortville, where our Sr. Felicitas Hicks lives. But they did not find her at home. They spent the night there, although this visit was not very welcome to the son and daughter of our Sr. Hicks. Since in the previous night there had been a dance in this area, they either did not find people at home or they were lying down and sleeping.

*Mar. 30.* [Spg.] After eating breakfast they traveled on and toward 10 o'clock arrived in the area called Dogwood Settlement, where our baptismal candidate Tuka and one old Indian woman named Caty live. The latter, who may be in her 80's, had expressed her wish to become the property of Jesus and said she would like to be baptized. Since both of these Indian women live together, Jesus' love for sinners was extolled to both of them, and they were told that through faith in Jesus' sufficient merit we can be justified and saved. They promised to visit in Spring Place soon. Since it seemed as if rainy weather was coming, Br. and Sr. Byhan hurried back to Fortville, where they arrived at noon. Our Sr. Felicitas had not yet come home, so after a brief stay there they rode on to visit Br. and Sr. Samuel. First they came to Br. and Sr. Israel's farm. But their house was locked and no one was at home. Now Br. and Sr. Byhan knew no better than their interpreter which way to go to find Br. and Sr. Samuel's farm, since the interpreter could not get any appropriate information about the area, so they rode around lost in the bush for a long time, through hill and vale, and finally arrived at Br. and Sr. Israel's again. But they still were not at home. Now they sent the interpreter alone to another area to look for Br. and Sr. Samuel's farm. Br. and Sr. Byhan endured a strong rainstorm during this time, in which they tried to protect themselves in a little house as well as they could. In half an hour the interpreter finally returned with the happy news that he had found Br. and Sr. Samuel. They then set out once again on the way and finally, after an indescribably bad road for half a mile through mountains and swamps and a creek, they arrived at Br. and Sr. Samuel's, where we were cordially taken in. We spent the evening there in pleasant conversations and felt at home.

*Mar. 30.* [Ooch.] In the afternoon a bad storm cloud moved over us, accompanied by almost unbelievably large hail. It broke about 12 window panes on the south side of the mission house. This terrible weather drove our herd of cattle to come home and seek shelter. Usually they do not come home without being fetched.

*Mar. 31.* [Spg.] In the morning after breakfast, after they had let go the boy Charles Hicks, who had served as their interpreter until then, and now had taken our scholar Flea, Samuel's son, as further escort and guide, they traveled on and arrived at our communicant Sr. Hannah's toward noon. Farther 1½ miles, they stopped at the the communicant Sr. Sarah Deborah's. From there the way went across the Conossauga River at Br. and Sr. Joshua's, where they crossed the river in a boat, and the horses were swum through. To their sorrow they did not find Br. and

Sr. Joshua at home, so they did not stay there long and in the afternoon returned healthy and well back here at Spring Place. Three hours after the arrival of Br. and Sr. Byhan, we had the pleasure of seeing dear Br. and Sr. Clauder from Ochgeloogy arrive at our place for a visit. In the evening we had a Singstunde at the piano. During the absence of Br. and Sr. Byhan, Mr. Dav. Steiner Tazizi had stopped in on his way home from Carmel and promised Br. Nathl. Byhan that he would serve us as interpreter in our services for the coming Easter holy days.

*Mar. 31.* [Ooch.] Despite yesterday's rainy weather, this morning was beautiful and pleasant. This allowed me to fulfill my wish and travel to Spring Place for a visit, accompanied by my dear wife. When we arrived at the Cooswaytee River, we found it pretty swollen and rapid, and our crossing in a ferry boat, guided by 2 Indian women, was more than a little dangerous. Since the road was unusually bad and we had gotten stuck in the mud with our wagon several times, we gave up hope of reaching Spring Place today, especially since there was still another significant creek to cross, and it quickly becomes impassable when there is heavy rain. Still when we got there we found that yesterday's storm had not reached that far and contrary to our expectation we could cross the creek after all, which we safely did. We reached Spring Place after sunset in the evening, happy and grateful for the assistance our dear Lord had shown.

*Apr. 2.* [Spg.] Br. and Sr. Clauder today traveled back to their post in Ochgeloogy.

*Apr. 2.* [Ooch.] We began our return journey, which was less difficult than the previous one. After we had enjoyed hospitality while lodging with our dear friends Boudinots in Echota, we returned to our dear ones in Oochgillogy on the 3rd, healthy and encouraged.

*Apr. 3.* [Spg.] Last night we had a heavy frost which did some damage to field and garden crops.

*Apr. 4.* [Spg.] Palm Sunday. Almost all of our Brn. and Srs. and a large number of neighbors came to our Sunday services. Br. George Hicks from Ochgeloogy arrived at our place this morning to serve us today as interpreter. He set out from his house at 2 o'clock this morning to get here in time for our services. In the first service we prayed the Litany of the Life, Sufferings, and Death of our Lord Jesus Christ, and then there was the sermon on the Doctrinal Text for today [Matt. 27:45, etc.]. In the second service was the baptism of the Indian Feather, with the name Emmanuel, during which we were deeply aware of the close presence of our dear Lord. In the third service was the baptism of the little daughter born to the just-baptized Indian Br. and his wife Waky with the name Jane. In the fourth service we began reading the Passion story of our dear Lord with the request to Him that He might let the consideration of His bitter suffering and death be blessed anew to our hearts, and that many more might be awakened from their sleep of sin by the hearing of this and be brought to self awareness through His Spirit so that they might also surrender their hearts as a reward for His bitter pains. Mr. Jos. Vann's two wives were also present in all the services today. One of them, Jane, is supposed to have said that she had never had such a feeling as today, especially during the baptism of Br. Emanuel. By the way, she attends our services most Sundays, and how happy we would be if she one day wanted to completely surrender herself to the Savior with body and soul, to be His property, and through His grace wanted to rid herself from the things of this world in which she currently takes great pleasure.

*Sun., Apr. 4.* [Ooch.] In our first service, we entered into Passion Week by bringing our Intercessor and Redeemer the most sincere thanks for all He has done for us through His sufferings and His bitter death, and we pleaded with Him to be near us in these days of His suffering and also to let those who still are in the darkness and in the shadow of death feel the necessity of participating in His meritorious sufferings and death. Since our interpreter Br. George Hicks had gone to Spring Place to serve in a baptism there, we were fortunate to have Elias Boudinott fill his place.

*Apr. 5.* [Spg.] Br. George Hicks today returned to Ochgeloogy. In the afternoon Mr. Buttrick arrived at our place from Hightower on his way to Brainerd and spent the night here.

*Apr. 8.* [Spg.] Toward evening Mr. and Mrs. McNair came to our place to celebrate Easter with us. At our invitation Mr. Steiner Tazizi also came to our place late this evening to serve as interpreter during the Easter holy days.

*Maundy Thurs., Apr. 8.* [Ooch.] We had a happy and blessed lovefeast in the afternoon hour and then partook of Holy Communion with our small flock of Cherokee communicants. During this we also thought lovingly of our Brother Wm. Abr. Hicks, who has been absent for 4 months. He is with the Cherokee Delegation in Washington, and we pleaded for a blessing from above for him. The Lord made the next day, as well as the first day of Easter, true days of blessing. On the latter day we prayed the Easter Morning Litany in our little Saal with a significant number of listeners. Then there was a sermon on Acts 13:32-33.

*Apr. 9.* [Spg.] On Good Friday we considered and read the sufferings and death of our dear Lord in three services, which were interpreted word for word. And we hope that the consideration this time of what our dear Lord endured for our sake might have made a deep impression on our Brn. and Srs. and others present. We were aware of the dear presence of the Savior in a very comforting manner in all of our services.

*Apr. 11.* [Spg.] Easter Sunday. We prayed the Easter Litany in the first service. In the second was the sermon on the resurrection of our dear Lord. In the third service we had a blessed enjoyment of the body and blood of Jesus in Holy Communion. The single Indian Br. Solomon watched as a confirmand during this. Mr. Dav. Steiner Tazizi and Mrs. Elis. Bean were also present as guests during this Holy Communion, at their request. Our Brn. and Srs. then went happily home, and without a doubt some of them received a new impression about our Savior's love for sinners which drove Him to distress and death to win eternal life and eternal salvation for us, and they took this home with them.

[M 414-5-16: Translated by Julie Tomberlin Weber. Addressed to: Revd. Theodor Schulz, Salem, Stokes County, North Carolina. Postmark: Springplace, C.N., Apr. 18. Free. Gottl. Byhan, P.M. Received May 3.]

Springplace, Apr. 16, 1830

Dear Br. Schulz,

Finally I take up my quill once again to inform you of the receipt of your kind letter of March 23, which I received on the 4th of this month along with issue No. 3 of the published *Gem. Nachr.* I also want to answer it immediately. In a letter dated March 9, you informed me that last year's accounts of the Cherokee Mission seemed unusually high to you and to the U.A.C. This news weighed me down greatly, and we hope that you will readily believe that we have not spent anything unnecessarily except for the $15 for a cow, an ox, and a calf, which you will have noticed in the expenditures. <u>All</u> else was necessary and had to be acquired.

Certainly the house construction cost a lot. It would have been possible to build a house like that in Salem for half the price, and if we had known that the Cherokees would get into a situation as they are currently in, we could have stopped the building in the process. Since the situation and circumstances here in Spring Place require that we have two hired workers, the construction costs a lot annually, $240. However, there is no other way. At least I do not see any other way for the time being, and as long as circumstances here remain the same, <u>one</u> worker cannot manage the work to be done on the construction, although we have discussed concentrating the work so it is closer together than it currently is, so that it would not require spending so much money, but we do not see any possibilities for changing things.

When we think about whether <u>one thing</u> or <u>another</u> could be changed, we realize that this would cause a problem in another area, where we would then have to spend more money again and perhaps even more than what we currently do. Last summer, Br. Clauder in Ochgeloogy could not grasp why each mission site has to have 2 workers, because he certainly believed that <u>one</u> hired worker would be sufficient for <u>one</u> site, and thus could save money spent for one. Now, however, he too agrees that he cannot manage with one; he also had to hire one in addition to Br. Copeland. Admittedly it does not cost him as much, because he has to pay only one, while we have to pay 2.

As long as the mission here is in this situation and in its current circumstances, it will always be an expensive mission. And what is actually to be regretted is that the dear Brn. of the H.C.f.G. have never yet been adequately informed about the actual situation, circumstances, and relationships of the Cherokee Mission — I mean the external ones. If the Brn. of the H.C.f.G. found it good to send dear Br. Schulz to visit Spring Place now, he would surely obtain clearer insights into the entire matter than 5 or 6 years ago. Not the least things would be withheld from him, and in my opinion the dear Brn. should be thoroughly acquainted with all concerning the Cherokee posts.

One cannot write everything, and not everything can even be written. I have always said and I still claim that of all the heathen posts the Brethren's Unity has, the missions among the Cherokees are the most difficult heathen posts for the missionaries posted there and for those who will be posted there in the future, primarily because of their location, character, circumstances, and situation, which no other mission has. Therefore, it cannot help but be expensive. I cannot analyze and explain everything with the quill. It needs to be done in person, and I hope this can be done next fall. Otherwise, I will make a copy of my journal and ledger and send it to the end of May, so it will be sent at the beginning of June. Admittedly it will require a lot of writing, so I must use the evenings and nights, but I will be glad to do it.

The answer to the question about whether it is correct for us to baptize children of unbaptized parents arrived on the 4th of this month, one hour before the baptism of the adult Indian Feather, who received the name Emanuel during baptism. Afterward his youngest child was also baptized with the name Jane. Overall, Palm Sunday was a day of blessing for the Spring Place congregation. The Savior could be powerfully felt in all our services. Br. George Hicks from Ochgeloogy had come from Ochgeloogy expressly to serve as our interpreter.

The week [March 29-31] before Easter we, my dear wife and Rachel and I, visited our Brn. and Srs. across the Conossauga River in the western area. We first went to see Mr. Nathan Hicks, then to our Sr. Felicitas Hicks. Then we visited our baptismal candidate Fields, where we spoke with an old Indian who is concerned about her salvation and asked for holy baptism. We directed her to the Savior of Sinners and comforted her. She promised to visit us soon. Then we stopped in to see our Sr. Hannah, as well as our Sr. Sarah Deborah, and then also at Br. and Sr. Josua's, and we returned home on Wednesday evening. Charles Hicks, son of Nathan Hicks, went with us as interpreter.

That same day, March 31, Br. and Sr. Clauder arrived at our place for a visit and stayed with us for one day. We had a joint Conference with them, and 2 points were recommended, among other things, if the H. Conf. in Salem agrees: First that we, for now, will not pray the Easter Litany on God's Acre as in the Gemeinen, but in our church, because it is currently associated with many unpleasantries here in Cherokee country which I cannot discuss here, and it also has caused all kinds of disorder, and also because many people mock it, etc., and we cannot appropriately explain to our Indians what the purpose actually is for praying the Easter Litany on God's Acre. Our Sr. Delila McNair also says that it has not been explained to them in the Cherokee language, and the appropriate meaning and the whole idea cannot be explained as in English.

Here and in Ochgeloogy also, as in the Gemeinen, we have had a lovefeast on Christmas Eve in which we celebrate the newborn baby Jesus, and we are sorry to find it necessary to suggest changes for this lovefeast as well. For this lovefeast, everyone in the entire neighborhood comes: young and old, including those who have not come to the services the entire year, all the Negroes from Vann's, and also all the Negroes from other places, in brief, anyone who could possibly come. Since everyone knows now that there is cake and coffee in the church, everyone crowds in here and runs past each other and fills the places where our Brn. and Srs. should actually sit. But they stand back, so they themselves do not get a seat in the church. This could still be changed if we took serious measures, although this also has some dangers associated with it, because one is hardly allowed to use seriousness here, because they are not used to it and it is strange to them. In short, what happens is that our Brn. and Srs. have to stand back and not share in the lovefeast, when it seems to me it is primarily for them.

Now imagine the trouble and the unrest of the mission Brn. and Srs. on such an evening. With so many people there is no thought of anyone helping them. Everything has to be done by them. It is almost intolerable. The Srs. dread Christmas Eve the entire year, and it is no wonder! Furthermore, the crowd mocks the entire thing. We have heard comments about lovefeast, cake, and coffee which I would not want to put on paper. But they are responsible for it!

Imagine the crowd of horses all these people bring along with them. All of them have to be fed. Otherwise, it would not be appropriate in this country. Corn, hay, feed, etc., must be provided, which costs more than a little. Then we must give our Brn. and Srs. something to eat. If the others see this, then they also come, and one cannot turn them away, and there is no thought of much rest for the mission Brn. and Srs. on this night.

Now instead of having a lovefeast on Christmas Eve, we thought about postponing it until January 6th to celebrate with our baptized Brn. and Srs., since this day is a festival day for the heathen Gemeinen anyway. Then we could celebrate it with just our Gemeine. Since we could postpone the lovefeast to this day, this festival of the heathen would never be rescheduled, but would always have to be celebrated on Jan. 6, no matter what day it falls on.

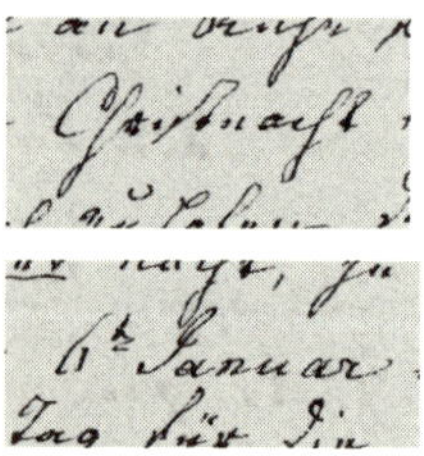
Christnacht
6t Januar

We ask you to let us know your thoughts about these two matters.

Apr. 17. We had a very happy and blessed Easter. In the 3rd service on Easter Sunday, we had a blessed enjoyment of the body and blood of Jesus in Holy Communion, during which the blessed Indian Br. Solomon observed as a confirmand for the last time. Doct. Bean's wife, our Sr. Delila McNair's daughter, and our friend Dav. Steiner Tazizi, who served us as interpreter during these holy days, were present as guests.

Along with everyone here, we are now anxiously waiting to see what will happen on the border of Georgia. You will already know that a large number of white people have entered this country from Georgia to dig for gold, and as we hear they are finding a lot. Now the Agent, Col. Montgomery, was appointed to drive these gold diggers back and to order them out of the Cherokees' territory. However, most of them do not listen to him. Some of them came back across the border. Col. Montgomery wanted to force them back with the law, but the Judges and higher authorities were not willing to listen. Individuals in the neighboring counties in Georgia had to leave without accomplishing their business. Since he has left, those who crossed the border in his presence have come back again and a large number more with them, so that people say thousands of them are there. It is supposed they live a very godless life. There are also supposed to be Baptist preachers among them who preach for them on Sundays, as we hear, but they are commonly interrupted during their sermons by the screaming and chaos of the people and prevented from continuing. Now the military from Fort Mitchel has been ordered out to drive these people back across the border, and this is expected to happen in a couple of weeks. God alone knows what the end of this will be. We are afraid this is the beginning of horrible events. Meanwhile, God will look upon this. We want to trust in Him. He is the Helper in all distress. He will not abandon us.

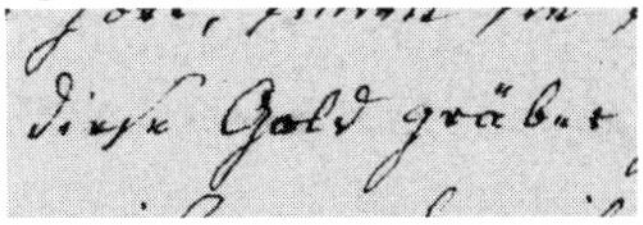

I had planned to visit the Agent, Col. Montgomery, as soon as possible to discuss the assistance of the Government for our school, because we not only have not received any for a long time, but also no longer hear why we do not receive anymore. I also wanted to discuss the expenses of our new house, since this construction was undertaken with the foreknowledge of the Government. However, I must postpone this visit for a while, because we hear that he must go to the Georgia border when the military arrives, and it is probable that he will stop in at our place, and I can talk with him about the above matters.

We hear nothing from our Delegates. Hopefully the debates in Congress about the Cherokees will soon begin. We are very eager to hear what the result will be. Our Sunday school is continuing as usual, and we hope that our efforts will not remain without blessing. We are currently having very dry weather. Yesterday we had a little rain, but it soon cleared up from the north, with a cold wind. Even so, nothing froze last night, but we fear that tonight will be much colder, so that the fruit might well suffer.

Praise God, we are currently nice and healthy, except for my dear wife who occasionally is unwell. This happened to her last Easter Sunday when we were sitting in the living room after the services and talking with some of our Brn. and Srs. She suddenly said: Carry me to bed, I'm going to fall over. She was immediately taken to her bed, and she soon recovered, praise God!

Now, dear Brn., remember us before our dear Lord in your prayers, that He will not leave us, His poor servants, in the critical situation in which we currently find ourselves and that He does not allow us to lose our confidence in <u>Him</u> in <u>all</u> circumstances. <u>All</u> greet you sincerely, and I especially greet you, your familiar friend and lowly Br.,

Gottl. Byhan

P.S. Please give our Sophia our best greetings and tell her that we received her letter on her birthday, the 4th of this month, which really pleased us. I will answer it very soon.

On Apr. 4 I received a letter from H. Clayton from Indiana State, in which he writes that he really likes things there. Among other things he writes: "I have concluded to make an improvement on Congress land. I have contracted with a man to build me a house & clear some land, & I expect to work on it myself. Now I want you to order Br. Shults to send me them forty Dollars you owe me, in U. States or Specie by some safe opportunity as quick as possible, for after I have done some work on the piece of Land, some person might enter it, & I would loose all my labour. The place we live is about 44 miles from the Ohio River, & about the same from White River, 90 miles from Lewisville, Ky., & 100 from Cincinaty." It is a question whether you will be able to send him this money just as he wants it. He is a critical man. G. B.

[Springplace (M 407-2) and Oochgeelogy (M 409-1) Diaries.]

*Sun., Apr. 18.* [Spg.] Since almost no one came here for the services today, the Church Litany was prayed in our services and a sermon was read. Sunday school was held again today, since it had to be canceled on Palm Sunday and Easter Sunday.

*Sun., Apr. 18.* [Ooch.] The sermon was on Zach 12:10, and dealt with what leads to gospel repentance and true spiritual conversion. The work of God's Spirit leads to self-awareness and repentance, and further shows us the One who bled to death on Golgotha and attained our salvation and bliss. Today we learned that many of our Brn. and Srs. are planning to go to the recently discovered gold mines in the northern part of this nation for a while, and try to escape their poverty by collecting this metal. These gold mines are supposed to be very rich and are worked by several thousand white people. A number of U. States troops from Fort Mitchell have been posted there to drive away these robbers and to protect this shining property of the Cherokees.

*Apr. 19.* [Spg.] Mr. Boudinott from New Echota came to our place on business and spent the night here. He told us that our Church Litany was now printed in the Cherokee language. Br. Clauder will help take care of cutting this, etc.

*Apr. 19.* [Ooch.] We received the Litany of the Brethren's Church translated into the Cherokee language and printed by our honorable friend Elias Boudinott. This will now be used in our worship services. This is the third booklet that has appeared in the Cherokee language. The first two, a hymnal and the Gospel of Matthew, were published at the cost of the American ([inserted:] another) Missions Society. ([Br. Schulz pencils in:] There is no <u>American Missions</u> Society.)

*Apr. 20.* [Spg.] Today Mrs. Bean from Sumak brought her 7-year-old son, David McNair, to our school.

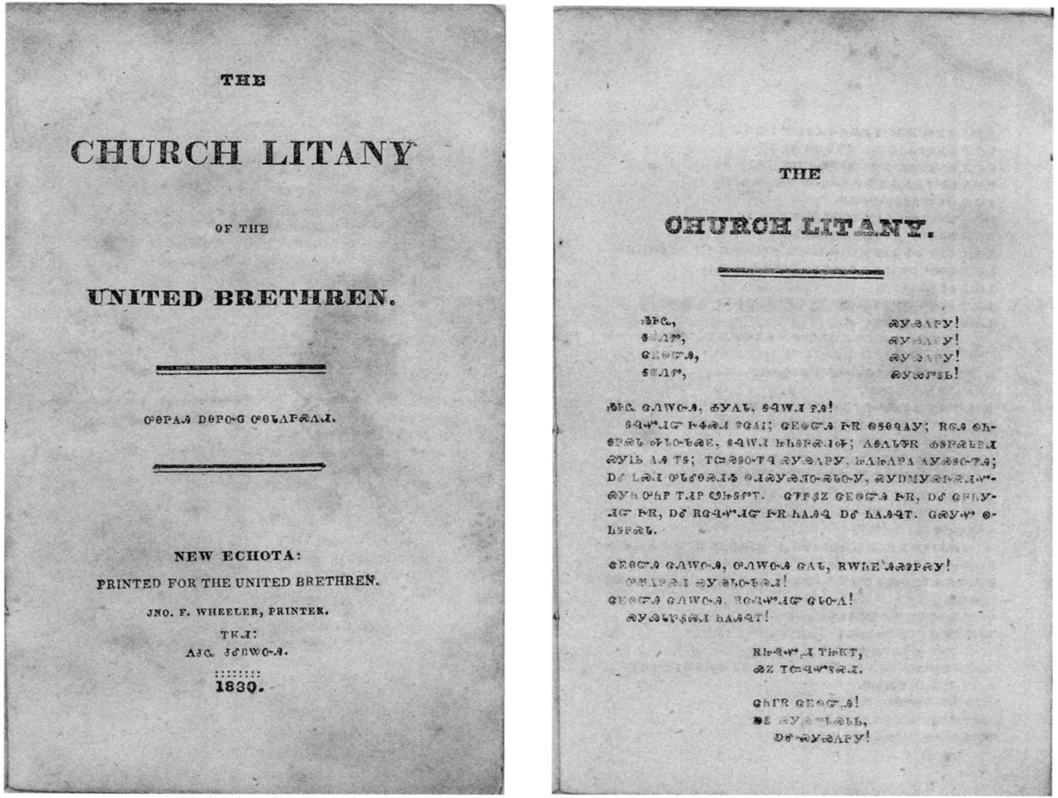


*M 421-A-1: The title page and first page of the Moravian Church Litany, printed at New Echota in 1830 in the Cherokee language (actual size 6½ x 4 inches, 12 pages; includes the Doxology and Luke 2:1-20)*

*Apr. 21.* [Spg.] It has been so extremely dry recently that we could only take care of our field and garden cultivation with trouble. The ground is now so dry that our workers today said that they could no longer plow and that if they would continue to plow they would ruin the land, since it would break up in such large clods. And in fact the ground is currently so dry that when plowing, some clods measure two feet square. Never since we have been living here have we had such dry weather for so long. Everything seems to want to die, because there is not the least bit of fruitfulness left in the ground. We really wish and ask our heavenly Father for a merciful rain.

*Apr. 23.* [Ooch.] After a long drought, the thirsty ground and plants were refreshed by a gentle rain. Our peach trees are already bowing under the weight of fruit that is still very small.

*Apr. 24.* [Ooch.] Sr. Clauder, accompanied by our Sr. Lydia, visited Sr. Maria Rosina, who lives about 7 miles from here, and some other friends who live in that area.

*Sun., Apr. 25.* [Spg.] In the morning was the sermon. In the second service Br. Samuel gave a talk to the Brn. and Srs. and a prayer on his knees, during which the Brn. and Srs. were very touched. Toward evening our dear heavenly Father gave us a refreshing rain after a long and great drought, for which we were sincerely grateful to Him.

*Sun., Apr. 25.* [Ooch.] We had extremely rainy weather, so many of our Brn. and Srs. and friends could not come to the service. Among the few who came, some of them completely soaked, was a heathen with her daughter, whom she wanted to leave with us to educate. But since our school is completely full and we do not have room to enlarge it, we found it necessary to turn her away.

From all sides we hear of the plight of the poor Cherokees because of the white people. For example, our Sr. Hicks received a letter from her brother in the northern part of the Nation in which he complains that white people from Tennessee tried to drive him and his family, along with many Cherokees who live in his neighborhood, out of their homes, and they were extremely hostile toward them. The Cherokees' only hope now is the protection promised by the government of the U. States.

*Apr. 30.* [Spg.] Mr. Proctor from Carmel came to our place today and spent the night here.

*May 1.* [Ooch.] It was our Sr. Sarah Hicks's birthday, which was celebrated festively. We spent the day at her house and everyone enjoyed it. On the following day,

*Sun., May 2,* [Ooch.] it rained so hard that the number of visitors was very small. We did not have an interpreter, so we were happy that a Cherokee believer from Turnip Mountain who was present gave an instructive talk and then, as we learned, spoke with a serious voice against the drinking and dancing that has been going on in our neighborhood for a number of days. Two of these miserable people were ashamed listeners during this. We also had problems with a drunken Indian a number of days ago, but he was carefully watched, and his weapon was taken away from him as soon as he arrived, so he could not do us any further harm. When he regained his wits the next morning he wanted to leave, and we used the opportunity to explain to him the viciousness and great sin of drunkenness. He replied with visible apathy that he would inform me when he was no longer given to drinking.

*May 5.* [Spg.] Br. Byhan presided at the wedding of Mr. Joshua Roach and Miss Almira Harlin, daughter of Mr. George Harlin. Toward evening Mr. Dav. Steiner Tazizi also came to our place and spent the night. Today we also finished planting corn.

*May 8.* [Spg.] Early at dawn we had an unusually heavy storm, but with little rain.

[M 414-5-17: Translated by Julie Tomberlin Weber. Addressed to: Revd. Theodor Shulz, Salem, Stokes County, North Carolina. Postmark: Springplace, C.N., May 9. Free. Gottl. Byhan, P.M. Received May 24.]

Springplace, May 8, 1830

My dear Br. Schulz,

On Apr. 25 I received your kind letter of Apr. 13 along with *Wöchentl. Nachr.* and also a copy of James Hall's shoe bill. I have nothing more to say to the letter except that it bothers me that he had made a pair of shoes for our blessed Rebecca in June 1827, when she died in May 1824. Since I find nothing in my old accounts that can prove that I paid him, so the matter is closed. I also received the 2 bonds for me and Nancy Becker. On May 2nd your kind letter of Apr. 20th and 4 issues of the written *Gem. Nachr.* also reached me. We thank you sincerely for all of this. Reading the news gives us a very happy hour, which usually takes place in the evening, and they are a real pasture for us.

My last letter to you was from the 16th and 17th of Apr., and they will now probably have reached your hands, and I expect an answer to it soon. Did my letter to Br. Eder, dated Jan. 21st, arrive in Salem? Or did it arrive too late for Br. E. Perhaps it was sent after him; I really hope that this might have been done. Let me know if you know anything about this.

Eight days ago another *Missionary Intel.* for Mr. Butrick arrived at my place, directed to Spring Place. I wish you could arrange for his *Intel.* to be directed to Head of Coosa. I do not know who is sending them. Otherwise, concerning the subscription money, he previously paid it to the missionaries here, and as long as I have been here he has paid me, which you will find in my income. I do not know when this began and how it was set up. Perhaps Br. Smith knows more about this matter.

You ask how the fire in Brainerd was started. This is not known for sure, because when they were awakened by the smoke from the fire the roof in the kitchen was already completely in flames. So it must have broken out in the kitchen, but they cannot tell how. They will not build again until they know what will happen with the poor Cherokees. And we all sincerely hope that the matter might soon be decided!

Please greet the dear Brn. of the U.A.C. sincerely from us. Poor Br. Micke, it seems as if he will lose his dear wife early and become a widow. When this reaches you Br. G. Benj. Reichel and his wife will probably be in your midst. Please greet both of them very sincerely for us and tell him that we rejoice with him that he has been provided with a helpmeet again, and we wish him all the best from our dear Lord. Please greet Br. and Sr.

Bechler and Br. and Sr. Shaaf most sincerely for us. The notations of the latter arrive at my place regularly, for which I ask you to thank him sincerely, until I can do so in person. Please greet our dear elderly Br. Abr. Steiner very sincerely for us and tell him: Old love does not rust!

I do not have anything noteworthy to report from here this time. We try to fill our calling as well as the Lord provides opportunity and grace. Since Easter our Brn. and Srs. have not visited us as regularly as usually. The reason right now is that it is a very busy time for taking care of their fields.

We have information to share about their matter in Congress. Most of our Brn. and Sr. who come here want to know how far their matters in Congress have gone, and I really cannot tell them anything more than what we read from week to week in the newspapers. Nothing encourages them more than when we tell them that they have many friends in Congress and that one of them spoke 6 hours in their favor. The poor Indians, they are truly to be pitied! The Georgians continue to dig for gold on Cherokee land, and we hear they are finding a good bit. Some time ago we heard that the regular troops from Fort Mitchel were ordered to drive out these gold diggers, but it seems they never arrived. In general the Indians are surprised that this riffraff is not driven out of the country, and they do not know what they should think about this.

We have not heard anything from our dear Brn. and Srs. in Ochgeloogy for a long time since current time and circumstances do not allow us to visit them. My planned visit with the Agent has not yet been possible, because circumstances have not yet allowed, and I have continued to live in the hope that he, Col. Montgomery, would perhaps come by here when he went to the gold mines and I could discuss the necessary matters with him then. However, he has not yet come. Next week we are planning to visit our Brn. and Srs. up the Canaussaga, and if I can learn for certain that he will not come into this area, then it might be possible that I would go visit him right away at the Agency.

On the 5th of this month we had a wedding here, a certain Joshua Roach from Tennessee with Miss Almira Harlin, daughter of our neighbor George Harlin. I officiated.

Otherwise, praise God, we are all pretty healthy here except my dear wife, who is often afflicted with weakness, so that she sometimes cannot continue as she would like. Our Rachel is often bothered by headaches and wishes to return to Salem, and we cannot deny that we also wish this.

After a long and intense drought, we are now having nice fruitful weather, although it is a little cool. Our peach trees are now so full of peaches that they are already breaking. We have already fetched 2 wagons full of stakes from the bush and staked them, but it does not help. The trees are still breaking here and there. There are not so many apples, and not many pears. There will be an overabundance of cherries.

Now, dear Br., accept this tangle for now. If I can, I will do things better next time. Apropos — my cashbox is literally empty! Please! At the end of this month the requested accounts will follow. All here greet you most sincerely, and I especially greet you,

Gottl. Byhan

[Springplace (M 407-2) and Oochgeelogy (M 409-1) Diaries.]

*Sun., May 9.* [Spg.] The services were held as usual, first the Litany, and then the sermon on the Sunday Epistle lesson. Afterward we spoke with our baptismal candidate Skitihee, who really wishes to participate in grace and be cleansed of his sins in holy baptism through Jesus' blood. He said he always prays to God, and then he feels happy. He is also convinced that he is a bad person and has an evil heart. And so he often asks the Savior to forgive his sins and make a child of God out of him.

*Sun., May 9.* [Ooch.] Only a few listeners were present at our service. Paul's words from Phil. 2:5 provided us with instructional material. Recently we were overjoyed to receive one of our older female scholars as a candidate for holy baptism. She is the daughter of our Br. and Sr. William Abr. and Sarah Hicks and has been here in the school for a long time, since she became a cripple as a child due to the so-called white swelling. There have often been signs of the Holy Spirit's work in her heart. This has been particularly true since the last Easter holy days. She was often seen with tearful eyes; once she said she was too great a sinner to be allowed to hope in God's mercy. The story of our Intercessor and Redeemer's suffering and death made a powerful and blessed impression on her troubled heart, and then she came to us and said that her only desire was to live for Jesus and to become His property. She also expressed her desire to join the visible church soon through holy baptism. After a thorough conversation about her spiritual condition, during which she was very emotional, we were completely overjoyed to accept her as a candidate for this grace, and we joined her in thanking the good Savior of our souls for the mercy she is able to participate in.

*May 10.* [Spg.] Today an Indian brought us a fish which weighed 24 pounds after it was cleaned.

*May 11.* [Spg.] A certain Mr. Müller, who lives in Major Ridge's area and has a son in the school here, came to our place to visit him. His wife, who lives in Capt. Dav. McNair's area, had brought him here to the school. Since Mr. Müller has left his wife, he was planning to take this child away with him, which the wife, or the child's mother, did not agree to. Thus she also came here today to prevent him from taking the child away with him. They both spent the night here.

*May 11.* [Ooch.] We were delighted and encouraged by letters and *Gemein Nachrichten* that a messenger brought us from Spring Place.

*May 12.* [Spg.] In the morning Mr. Müller went back to his home and his wife to hers, and the child stayed here in the school. This Müller is a white man from Kentuky and married here in this country, and otherwise does not have the best character.

*May 14.* [Ooch.] I visited our neighbor Austin Copeland and found an opportunity to have a thorough talk with him about his spiritual condition. On this day, as well as on the two following days, the Methodists in our neighborhood had a quarterly service which was very well attended. So on

*Sun., May 16,* [Ooch.] only a small number of listeners were here. We read and explained some statements about <u>salvation</u>

from the *Idea Fidei Fratrum.* Since many of our Brn. and Srs. have already been gone to the gold mines for a long time, we have very sparse attendance at church. Recently the *Nachrichten* from the Brüder Gemein have provided us with spiritual nourishment and instruction and encouragement.

*Sun., May 16.* [Spg.] In the first service was the sermon on Isa. 1:18. In the second service we prayed the Church Litany, and since this has now appeared in print in the Cherokee language, it was repeated by our Indian Br. Solomon. Everyone seemed to be very attentive to it. Throughout this week we had very beautiful weather so that our Indian corn fields could be plowed over one time.

*May 19.* [Ooch.] I visited with our Br. Christian David. The friendship with which he received me was encouraging. Laying his hand on his heart he said in Indian: "I feel very well here," and his eyes also showed this.

*May 21 & 22.* [Ooch.] I visited the Hickses and the Ridges 20 miles from here. On this short journey I passed through an important Indian village called Springtown, where the Methodists preach from time to time.

[M 414-5-18: Translated by Julie Tomberlin Weber. Addressed to: Revd. Theodor Shulz, Salem, Stokes County, North Carolina. Postmark: Springplace, C.N., May 23. Free. Gottl. Byhan, P.M. Received June 7.]

Springplace, May 22, 1830

My dear Br. Schulz,

Your kind letter dated the 4th of this month and some sheets of handwritten *Gem. Nachr.* arrived here on the 10th, and we thank you sincerely for these. We hope that you have recovered from your illness by now. How would it be if you paid us another visit? Do you think this would agree with your health?

Anyway, it seems we are getting deeper into a situation with the Indian work that probably requires more face-to-face advice from you than we are able to write about. It is true that we have a Lord who does not abandon us and who can protect His poor children, but in my opinion it would certainly be very good if one of you could be present here to consider together the entire current situation of the mission here, as well as the likely impending situation it will face, and to help advise us. This thought follows me recently, and I must admit that I feel too poor and unable, if the worst should happen between Georgia and the poor Cherokees, to guide the entire mission work here and all that belongs to it. I am not in a position to acquaint you sufficiently, dear Brn., with the current situation and circumstances of this mission in letters. If the Cherokees really must leave, then we would most especially need your advice to make a decision and carry on in a well-advised manner.

However, we do not know what might happen first, before things get that far. Very recently things have seemed very dark in the Nation. Everyone believes that something large and difficult lies ahead of the Nation. And judging from the state of things for a short while, it also seems that events are coming which are not good and will have a great influence on the mission work here. We want to commend the mission work here and all of our dear Brn. and Srs. here to Him who has counted every hair on our heads, so that none falls to the earth without His will.

Please do not think badly of me for sharing my thoughts with you here. I tell you once again, the future is very, very dark, and I must frankly admit that if the Cherokees end up staying here after all, a change and improvement in the external situation and circumstances of the mission here should be undertaken. More about this point another time. It is not yet the time for that.

Yesterday we heard that the regular soldiers are only about one day's journey from the gold mines in this country. They were ordered from Fort Mitchel to persuade the gold diggers to go back to Georgia or to drive them out. They stopped to learn from Agent Col. Montgomery what else should be done. To that end 2 expresses passed here yesterday going to the Agency. People say that between 6-7,000 Georgians are at the gold mines and that only 90 soldiers are coming to drive these thousands away. God alone knows how this will turn out!

We also heard yesterday that notes or bonds were presented to Mr. John Ross, Chief, Major Ridge, Dav. Vann, Judge Martin in Coosawatee, and many others, in which they apparently undersigned for thousands, who do not know anything about this, as people are saying. If this is really true, then it is indeed horrible, because the Georgians know that the oath of the Cherokees counts for *nothing* [in court]. But the matter seems too godless to me to *fully* believe it, although the southeastern neighbors are capable of acting in this manner with the Cherokees. Most of those affected had stores, and it might be that they are somewhat in debt to those from whom they get their goods — and what storekeeper is not generally somewhat in debt? — which they now want to have paid. We will hear how the matter turns out.

Yesterday we also heard that the Choctaw Indians killed their new Chief, Mr. Greenwood Leflore, after they had turned their land over to the U.S., and that they are also after the life of the second Chief — it can not be said for sure what his name is — so that he had to be guarded by his party. Time will tell whether this news will be confirmed.

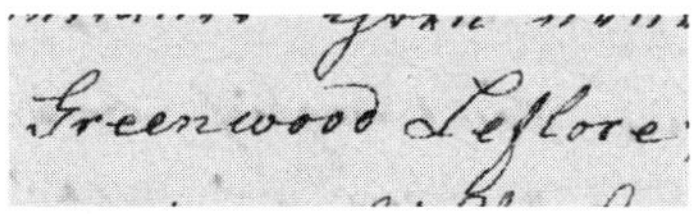


We are eagerly awaiting the mail tomorrow to see and hear what else has happened in Congress concerning the Cherokees. What should we think about our Congress? Otherwise things are still quiet in the Nation, but everyone is waiting for the things that should come. We cannot imagine at all how things will be on the first of June regarding the Georgia Law in this country. Most everyone says that they do not want to be under it.

Our Church Litany has now been printed and delivered to Br. Clauder for binding, etc.; 300 have been printed. The price for translating, printing, etc., is $20. Now there is the question of what to do with these pamphlets to distribute them among the Brn. and Srs. Should we accept payment for them or give them away free? We join Br. Clauder in asking you to give us information about this question as soon as possible. It will be difficult to get anything for them from *our* Indians, and yet it seems to us it is not quite right if they get them for nothing, since the mission here costs so much anyway, and the Brn. and

Srs. here are favored anyway. If I can express myself thus, I must say they have been spoiled from the beginning, concerning being helpful to the missionaries and paying for anything. And so we ask you to let us know what you think.

Our Indian Brn. and Srs. and we can currently rejoice in a pretty good health. Our Sunday schools are continuing in their usual manner, although they are no longer quite as well attended as in the beginning. Since many Negroes attended them, things have not been as they will be after June 1st when the Georgia law is supposed to be put into effect, because it is forbidden on threat of serious and horrible punishment to provide Negroes with instruction in reading and writing. We must wait for this time and see how things go.

Our week school is currently very small as well. Most of them have been taken home to help with the fieldwork. Children are often brought to sign up, and although they say they will bring them back in a couple of days or in a week, they never, or seldom, come back, that is, those parents and children who do not belong to us.

Now, dear Br., accept these few lines for this time since I also need to write Br. Clauder today and my time today has therefore run out. But, dear Br., I am expecting some money from you, because as you will see from the accounts which I will send on June 6th at the latest — once again deep in debt.

Accept the most sincere greetings from all of us, and especially from me, your loving, humble Br.,

Gottlieb Byhan

[Springplace (M 407-2) and Oochgeelogy (M 409-1) Diaries.]

*Sun., May 23.* [Spg.] Despite the fact there was rainy weather today, a nice number of listeners still came for the services. Since we were not able to celebrate the festival of Ascension last Thursday, we celebrated it today. Accordingly this was remembered in our first service, and the story of the Ascension of our dear Lord was read, and after a prayer on our knees was the sermon on the Ascension story, primarily about the blessing of our dear Lord which He laid on this world, on His disciples and apostles, upon His departure, and that He commanded them to go into all the world to proclaim the Gospel, and that whoever believes and is baptized will be saved and that this word, this Gospel, echoes also in this country. The listeners were asked to accept this.

*Sun., May 23.* [Ooch.] In our service we considered story of our resurrected Redeemer's Ascension, and then we used the opportunity to discuss His return and the end time. As usual, only a few visitors were here. From the gold mines we hear that our Brn. and Srs. are healthy and are enjoying pretty good success in their work. They plan to return home in a few weeks.

*May 24.* [Spg.] From 4 o'clock in the morning until noon we had heavy and uninterrupted rain, and during this it was so cool that we could stand a good fire in the fireplace. The streams around us are so swollen from this that most of them have overflowed their banks.

*May 24.* [Ooch.] During a visit to New Echota, I had opportunity to see the school there. There were about 20 scholars, most of them female, and some of whom were busy spelling. Some of the older ones were being tested in American geography. The younger ones recited some of the Ten Commandments. At the close of school I took the opportunity to give the scholars a sincere admonition to be diligent and obedient, as well as to surrender themselves now, in their tender childhood years, to the faithful care of the best Friend of Children who would give them power and wisdom, and to use their school time well.

*Sun., May 30.* [Spg.] Pentecost. Br. Nathl. Byhan led the first holy day service. Afterward was the baptism into Jesus' death of the baby daughter, born Apr. 15th to our Br. and Sr. Israel and Esther, with the name Susanna. In the third service we had a blessed enjoyment of the body and blood of Jesus in Holy Communion. After the preceding confirmation of the single Indian Br. Niclaus Salomon, he joined us for the first time as a participant in this high good. Br. Byhan, Sr., led the two last services although he was very weak, because he not been very well for a whole week already and stayed in bed for the most part.

*Sun., May 30.* [Ooch.] It was holy Pentecost, and we took the opportunity during the sermon to talk about the wonderful outpouring of the Holy Spirit during the first Christian Pentecost in Jerusalem. In the afternoon I visited with my wife our sick Sr.

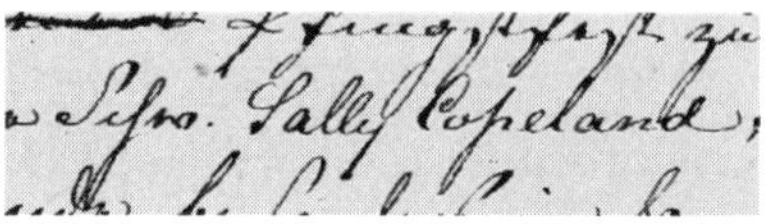

Sally Copeland, who has been suffering from consumption for some time. In answer to the question about how she was doing, especially in her heart, she said: "Oh, my soul is very blessed. I cannot thank my Redeemer enough for the grace He has given me here on my sick bed. I cannot do anything but cry tears of gratitude." In answer to the question about whether she did not wish to get well soon, she said: "As the Lord wills. If I lie here a long time, He will strengthen me. Still I would be grateful if he gave me my health." This is just a little of what she said. Remorse about her shortcomings, gratitude for the grace the Lord has already shown her, and complete surrender to His will — these were the matters that filled her heart. At her request, we sang some verses at her bedside, during which she also joined in. We thanked the dear Savior of Souls for the comfort this sick woman has enjoyed until now, and we pleaded with Him to continue to remain very, very close to her, so she can feel it.

In conclusion, we commend ourselves and the work here to the loving remembrance and the faithful intercession of all friends of our Lord Jesus Christ and His work on earth.

Br. and Sr. Clauder
and the widowed Sr. Anna Maria Gambold

## *1830, part 4*

[M 414-5-19: Translated by Julie Tomberlin Weber. Addressed to: Revd. Theodore Schulz, Salem, Stokes County, North Carolina. Post stamped: New Echota, Cher. Na., June 12, 75. Received June 28.]

Ooyugillogy, Ch. Nat., June 2, 1830

Dear Br. Schulz,

I received your kind letter of Apr. 20 enclosed in an almanac. We thank you sincerely for this, although it is against the postal law to send any written communication with printed pamphlets and the charges made for those. By the way, this small deviation from the law was discovered by the Post Master in New Echota, but as a favor he did not require letter postage. However, it is doubtful that he would do this a second time.

On the other side you will see our debts along with our income and expenditures for the past half year. I am also planning to enclose the Diary for here, which I commend to your best forbearance. In this as in so many other regards I must learn through experience.

Our Church Prayer and Litany has appeared in the Cherokee language, thanks to the kindness of our honorable friends Elias Boudinott and Worcester. At my request the latter provided me with an English literal retranslation of the Cherokee for you and the rest of the Brn. of the P.H.C., through which you can become acquainted with the actual meaning of the phrases that come closest to the Cherokee sentences. I will send you this manuscript and a copy of Reverend Worcester's letter about this through Br. Byhan at the next opportunity.[1]

Praise God, we are all healthy and continue in peace and harmony, although the Methodists continue proselytizing in this area frequently and with much bluster. Our adult scholar's request for holy baptism as well as her overall walk served as a great encouragement for us. She is the daughter of our Br. and Sr. Wm. A. Hicks. You will be able to learn the rest from our Diary.

Only the One who knows hearts knows what will become of our neighbor Austin Copeland. After some sincere conversations, which have already taken place between us, I find reason to believe that he is also not far. Obviously there has been a significant change for the better within one year in this man who previously scorned religion.

The poor Indians are now anxiously awaiting their fate. They are still united now and are resolved to stay here and die under the Georgia government. The private Agents who are expected here will also not do much of anything, because the bloody example which the Choctaws recently provided when they murdered one of their Chiefs who became a traitor is a sharp warning to those in this Nation not to do the same. There are already rumors circulating about what and how the head people should respond after the laws have extended to this country.

Currently we are in a trying situation because this small congregation is scattered, and secondly, we have experienced some bitterness from the Methodists, who have done all sorts of things through deception and other falsity to oppose our effectiveness. We are protecting ourselves as much as possible from entering into contention with them, because it seems as if they try to have this conflict with other confessions almost everywhere to win a name for themselves.

I must also note that I made a successful attempt at getting the books which were brought into our school from Augusta. I received them here for the same price as we would get them in Salem. Our school currently has 14 scholars, and since we have

---

[1] See this volume's frontispiece and M 411-1-30, page 4248.

been pretty successful preventing all visits from the children's homes, we are finding much joy in the progress which they are making in their studies. I also made a small beginning with those who can read to have them learn the questions and answers in the small instruction booklets. They are publicly examined in the Sunday school.

Since I wrote the above, our Sr. Sarah, Austin Copeland's wife, delivered a baby about three weeks ago. She had been suffering from consumption for a long time, and she showed signs of her approaching release due to the consumption. We took turns staying with her throughout the entire week and found her in an extremely blessed spiritual state, except when thoughts of her little one troubled her motherly heart. On the 4th of this month, the small newborn boy became seriously ill, and it was uncertain whether he would live more than a few hours as a result of the neglect he had experienced in bad hands. At the request of the parents, he was baptized into Jesus' death on this day (the 4th) with the name William Hicks. In accordance with the wishes of the mother, who will probably not be here below many more days, and considering the indescribable misery which prevails in that house during the illness of the house-mother, we found various reasons to take this baby into our care for now. Sr. Clauder will try to serve in the mother's place until his mother has either recovered or another place has eventually been found for him. Otherwise, he is in good health again now.

Since the 1st of this month there have been many rumors about the Georgia laws. The regrettable consequences of this usurpation can already be seen here and there, and more can be expected. When I reflect on the course of events not only here but in the entire country, I might say in the entire world, it seems to me that the time is pregnant with trials for God's people, through which a sifting, a cleansing will take place. May the Lord give us grace to remain faithful to Him and to follow Him until the day of our Lord Jesus Christ.

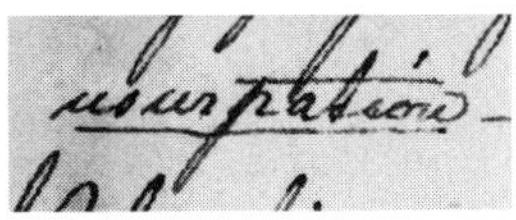

Br. Copeland greets you most especially — he seems to be very content and happy here, and in his special area, the field-work, he is the man who is needed here. May the Lord keep us all together in love and peace as previously. We greet [page torn] everyone — your dear family and everyone interested in the well-being of this mission, and commend ourselves to your prayer and loving remembrance. Your faithfully obliged friend and Brother,

Henry G. Clauder

The 10th. P.S. At 9 o'clock this morning our Sr. Sarah Copeland was completed, gently and blissfully. She will be buried here in our God's Acre tomorrow as a first-fruit of our Cherokee congregation.

H. G. C.

Balances & Accounts due to and from the Mission at Ooyugillogy C.N., May 5, 1830

| Debtors | | |
|---|---|---|
| Austin Copeland, balance | | $13.20 |
| * Saml. Henry, sale | | 44.68¾ |
| sale to Spg | 30.35½ | |
| & | 24.39½ | |
| John Hollers, bal. | | 0.50 |
| Towers, acct. | | 0.50 |
| George A. Hicks, sale | | 38.87½ |
| Elias Boudinott, balance | | 7.81 |
| Andrew Agnew | | 1.37½ |
| John Fields | | 0.50 |
| Alexander McCoy, balance | | 11.77½ |
| Walter S. Adair | | 3.50 |
| Evan Nicholson | | 1.00 |
| Lydia Chisholm | | 1.75 |
| Wm A. Hicks | | 10.37½ |
| Major Ridge | | 12.50 |
| | | $148.34¾ |

| Creditors | |
|---|---|
| Spring Place for cash recd. last year | $155.87½ |

[Br. Schulz calculates in Salem:]

The bal. due to Springplace is, according to G. B. ledger May 1, 1830, $345.06

* Note Saml. Henry paid off to G. B. in favor of O—y more than he seems to be indebted here, of which Br. Hy. Clauder should have been informed as well as for the other items put to his credit in Springplace ledger to prevent any mistake between his credit and his debts.

Cash acct. of receipts & expenditures
from Nov. 5. 1829, to May 5, 1830

Receipts

| | |
|---|---|
| 1829 | |
| Nov. 17 amt. cash in hand | 16.80¼ |
| Dec. 2 E. Boudinott on acct. | *3.25 |
| " 2 Lead sold | *0.25 |
| " 2 Butter | 1.50 |
| Jan 21 ditto | 0.68¾ |
| Mar. 1 potatoes | *0.25 |
| 1 b. oats | *0.50 |
| Mar 22 D. Vann 15 b. oats | *7.50 |
| Ridge for Br Reichel | *50.00 |
| Mar 27 Potatoes | 0.31¼ |
| | 81.05¼ |

[Br. Schulz calculates in Salem:]

| | |
|---|---|
| On acct. | 3.25 |
| Lead | 0.25 |
| Butter | 2.18¾ |
| Potatoes | 0.25 |
| Oats | 0.50 |
| ditto | 7.50 |
| potatoes | 0.31¼ |
| | 10.75 |

Expenses

| | | |
|---|---|---|
| Nov. 17 | Bank bill returned to Salem | $ 5.00 |
| | George Roach in full for work | 5.00 |
| | 30 lbs sugar $5.00 ferriage 1.00 | 6.00 |
| Jan | S. Hicks midwifery | 1.00 |
| | ferriage & postage | 0.37½ |
| Jan 25 | A. Miller one day work | 0.50 |
| | postage sundry times | 1.15½ |
| | washerwoman 2 days | 1.00 |
| | ferriage 0.25; brick 1.50 | 1.75 |
| Apr. | ferriage with a waggon | 0.87½ |
| | 200 feet plank | 2.00 |
| | Jesse Copeland 2 mo. wages Feb. & Mar. | 20.00 |
| 31 | knife with a horse fleam | 1.50 |
| | Jos. Copeland smithing | 7.00 |
| | Ruth Hicks washing last fall | 1.00 |
| | Jesse Copeland 1 mo. wages (Apr.) | 10.00 |
| | Cash in hand | 16.90 |
| | | 81.05½ |

[Br. Schulz calculates in Salem:]

N.B.
16.90 cash on hand
add 21.00 lent to G. A. Hicks June 26, 1829; omitted in acct. for U.V.C.
37.90 as cash in hand May 1st 1830
Stated in my extract for U. Miss. C.,
Te. Sz. [Theodor Schulz]

[M 414-5-20: Translated by Julie Tomberlin Weber. Addressed to: Revd. Theod. Shulz, Salem, Stokes County, North Carolina. Postmark: Springplace, C.N., June 6. Free. G. Byhan, P.M. Received June 21.]

Springplace, June 3, 1830

Dearly beloved Br. Shulz,

Although I am still feeling quite unwell, I will try to write you a few lines once again. Since we had a very rainy day last Monday, May 24, I have suffered a lot physically. Because I got wet on the said day, I caught such a bad cold that pain in my back and legs has left me no peace night or day. I also lost my appetite, and I became very lethargic and weak; I still have not gotten it back. Since the pain had not let up despite all the measures taken, we decided to apply Spanish fly plasters to both calves. This lessened the pain in my back between my shoulders and in my lower back, but the pain in my right leg on which <u>one</u> fly plaster was laid does not want to heal now, and the tendons and sinews in that leg were so affected that I can hardly stand on it, and it takes great effort and much pain to cross the yard once a day with a crutch, and when I sit I hardly know <u>how</u> or where to lie. I also tried to be bled, but after our Doct. Bean tried twice to let the blood it had to be given up. It seemed to me as if we were asking too much of him to undertake <u>such</u> an operation.

<u>June 4th</u>. On the 30th I received your kind letter of May 18 along with 2 festival odes. Many thanks for both. I see the Prov. Helf. Conf. has given its approval of the two suggestions from our Mission Conference to reschedule the Christmas Eve lovefeasts to Jan. 6th and then only with our Brn. and Srs., and that <u>for now</u> the Easter Litany will be prayed inside the church and not on God's Acre. We do not doubt that this change will be agreeable to our Brn. and Srs.

In answer to the question whether the children of the blessed Charl. Ren. Hicks visit our place regularly, I must answer no. They never let us see them. If you remember, a long time ago I reported a comment by Elijah Hicks in New Echota which was <u>not</u> in favour of missions here in the country. And most all of them are like this. His brothers, however, do not express themselves like the very pompous Elijah Hicks.

Mrs. Bean is a full member of the Methodist Church, and so when she was here at our place with her mother, we could not very well refuse her request to receive Holy Communion with us as a guest, and it also would have really offended her mother, our Sr. Delila McNair, if we had refused her request.

Concerning the note for $40 I gave Clayton on Jan. 1, 1830, I have really forgotten how I gave it to him and wrote it. I think it specified 6 months after date, but I do not want to and I cannot claim that it was written that way. Before I wrote it, we discussed various things about how it would be repaid, and I think he was finally willing to have it written as note 6 months after date — or five months — if he could receive the money promptly from you by then. I also assured him that you would certainly repay him when you had the opportunity to do so. Otherwise, we were very happy here when he moved away, because he is pretty twisted in his dealings. The mistaken idea that the Missions Diacony has no foundation and therefore it as well as the missionaries inflated things and I might say fleeced them, was pretty deeply ingrained in his thoughts. While he lived at Columbus, Tenn., he was up to any trader and peddler in dealing with us poor missionaries; he had no compassion with his Brethren, as he calls them.[1]

Now concerning the $90 Br. Alexander Copeland asked me to make good last year, whether it was included in the note for $218 or not I cannot tell you with certainty now, because my illness has prevented me from discussing this with Br. Clauder. I think, however, that it was included in the $218, because I can hardly imagine that his credit in Ochgeloogy would have been $308. This is what happened with the $90 I received in my hands from Br. Copeland: Br. and Sr. Copeland moved to Tennessee in the fall of 1828 when the mission in Ochgeloogy was quite in debt to him for work there; how much was unknown to me. In the spring of 1829 Br. Clauder gave me $50 to send to Br. Copeland in Tennessee. I wrote to Br. Copeland and asked

[1] This sentence is in English in the original German manuscript.

him if I should send him this money or not. He wrote me that I should not send it to him, but I should keep it for him. In the meantime, Br. Clauder gave me another $40 for Br. Copeland. I then kept this $90 for him and kept it separate from my other money. However, to get money so I could pay the workers, I took it and opened an account for Alexander Copeland in my books, as you will soon see in my ledger. I have told Br. Clauder all this, and therefore I believe that this $90 is included in the $218.

June 5th. I had promised to send you my accounts tomorrow, the 6th, but I have not been able to complete them because of my illness, and so I cannot send them before the 13th of this month. I hope it will work out to send them on with your other accounts. I hear Br. Clauder will send his from Ochgeloogy with the mail tomorrow.

What should I report about the Cherokees now? I hardly know anything. Since last Tuesday we have been under the Georgia laws, but I have not yet heard anything about this and everyone around us is calm. Time will tell how things turn out. It seems that everyone is waiting for the conclusion of their issues in Congress and for the return of the Delegates. We are very eager to hear the government's statement on the matter in general. But judging by the thoughts and comments of the Cherokees, it seems probable that things could perhaps become less peaceful in the Nation, because the Georgians are really trying to provoke unrest, arguments, and disagreements among them. Recently we heard that those Indians who are now living in the mountains on the border of North Carolina and up in the mountains not far from the South Carolina border are laying all the blame on the preachers among them, and a certain Turtlefields, who has often preached to the Indians in our area, recently had to leave in haste to escape being mistreated by them. We also heard that the gold seekers on the Georgia line are actually starting to disperse. We cannot yet say whether this is out of fear of the regulars, who have apparently finally arrived there, or whether they will return with unified power when the regulars have left again. We also heard recently that a certain Blair from Tennessee will greet Mr.

Jos. Vann with a bill from his father James Vann for $6,000. These are presumably some fruits of the law which is now supposed to be carried out in Cherokee Country. How will things continue? And what else will we experience here? May God remain with us and help us, and keep us in His protection!

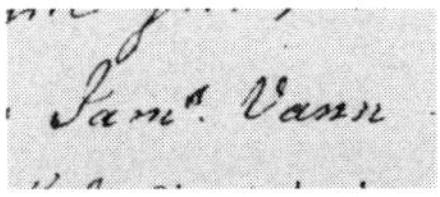

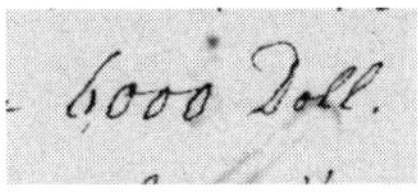


Otherwise the house family is pretty well, except that Mother Byhan is very bothered by some kind of rash on her hands and face which disturbs her at night. Hopefully I will be able to report in my next letter that I am also completely recovered, since I seem to be improving.

Just this moment we have heard that the gold seekers, 4-5,000 of them, are paying no attention at all to the 80 regulars who have come to oppose them, but are continuing to do as they please.

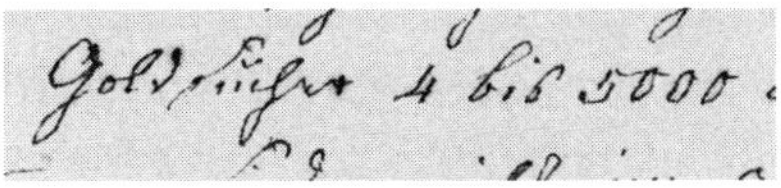

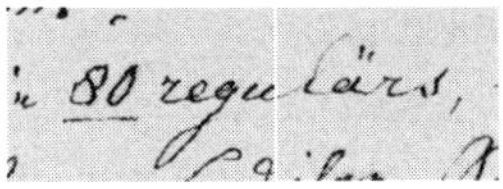


Everyone greets you most sincerely and you, dear Br., accept a special greeting from your friend and Br.,

Gottl. Byhan

[Springplace (M 407-1) and Oochgeelogy (M 409-1) Diaries. Translated by Julie Tomberlin Weber. Handwritings are Henry G. Clauder's (Ooch.) and Gottlieb Byhan's (Spg.).]

*June 4.* [Ooch.] In the afternoon we visited our Sr. Copeland again. She has not been well, and we found her little 3-week old baby boy apparently in the last throes of his brief life. At the request of his parents, he was immediately baptized into Jesus' death with the name William Hicks. The measures we used to help him recover were blessed for now. His mother could no longer take care of him, and she asked us to take him into our care for now. We had no choice but to grant her wish.

*Sun., June 6.* [Spg.] Few of our Brn. and Srs. came for the Sunday services. But since Mr. Dav. Steiner Tazizi came to our place yesterday, we read some in the first service from the *Idea Fidei Fratrum* and this was interpreted sentence for sentence into Indian by Mr. Tazizi. Afterward we spoke with our Br. Boas's wife, who some time ago expressed her wish and intention to become Jesus' property and to belong to our congregation. She once again expressed herself very contritely and expressed her deep desire to be cleansed of her sins through Jesus' blood in holy baptism. And so we had the joy of accepting her into the class of baptismal candidates. Today we had a heavy downpour of rain again, as we have had almost every day in the last week, so that the work in field and garden could not be done as needed. But everything is up and growing very nicely, but the weeds are really taking over, because they cannot be weeded because of the rainy weather.

*Sun., June 6.* [Ooch.] Once again we had a good number of listeners at our worship service. Because of the heavy rain they could not return home immediately after the service, and so we had an opportunity to have uplifting conversations with many of them.

*June 9.* [Spg.] Mr. Tazizi once again came to our place and told us that a couple of days ago a hurricane-like storm had raged on the [Little] Tennessee and Highwassee rivers. It had taken the roofs off of most of the houses in its path and had blown down all the fences, and also some people had been injured. We also had felt such gusts of wind in the night here, but no further damage except that our very heavily laden peach trees suffered a lot when many branches were broken off them.

*June 11.* [Ooch.] The burial of blessed Sr. Copeland, who died on the 10th, took place at 4 in the afternoon. Many visitors came to this, so our Saal was very full. There was a sincere talk admonishing them to follow Isa. 55:6 and seek the Lord while He can be found and not to postpone their conversion from year to year and thus miss their day of grace for all eternity. An emotional event happened on God's Acre. We were just getting ready to lower the coffin into the grave when Br. Clauder was asked to wait just a little, since the deceased woman's sister, who lives 70 miles from here, was on the way and should be very close. She wanted to see her deceased sister one last time if at all possible. This was agreed upon without making particular arrangements. The waiting time was spent singing appropriate verses, and a Methodist preacher who was present also helped us. When asked, he held a very evangelical talk for those gathered. In the meantime, the coffin was opened at the wish of the woman who had just arrived. She looked at the body of her blessed sister and thus said farewell to her. Then we continued praying the burial litany without any further disturbance or disorder resulting from this unusual circumstance.

[M 414-5-21: Translated by Julie Tomberlin Weber. No address; no postmark. Received June 28.]

Springplace, June 11, 1830

My dear Br. Schulz,

I have just finished writing out the accounts from July 1, 1829, until May 31, 1830, the journal and ledger, if one can call them that. It was a pleasure for me to copy them out of my books[1] because you will be able to see somewhat from them <u>how</u> I keep my accounts here, because it also seems impossible, at least <u>to me</u>, to note all expenditures and income there without seeing the books themselves. I have often really wished that you could see my books yourself, which is also the main reason I have copied them word for word. I will send the journal first with the next post on the 13th of this month, and 8 days later the ledger, because it would be too large a package to send all at once. Also since there is some space left at the end of the ledger, I will add more comments about the accounts. I hope they will arrive in good time so that you can send them on with yours

---

[1] Br. Byhan's neatly kept journal book, 1828-36, and ledger book, 1828-34, are filed at M 419-B-1 and M 419-B-2, Moravian Archives, Winston-Salem, North Carolina. The copies Br. Byhan made for July 1, 1829, to May 31, 1830, are filed at M 419-B-6-d.

to the Missions Department. Illness prevented me from sending them sooner.

Praise God, I have pretty much recovered. I still feel somewhat weak, and I still must walk with a limp, because my legs have not healed completely from the miserable fly plaster. Praise God, Mother Byhan has been able to continue her business pretty well lately, although she is still weak. Otherwise, everyone here is healthy.

On the 6th of this month I received your kind letter of May 25th and 3 enclosures of written *Gem. Nachrichten* and $100 Georgia notes. Accept my most sincere gratitude for these. The *Nachr.* are a real pasture for us; we are always happy to receive them.

What should I report to you now about our poor Indians? There would be much to write about how they are currently deceived and oppressed by the neighbors now. We hear all sorts of rumors about the Goldminers, some true, some not true. Meanwhile, the desire and the curiosity to learn how things concerning their land will turn out in Congress continues to grow.

Our idea is that everyone will remain peaceful until the Delegates return from Washington, which is expected to happen in a couple of weeks. But then a new period will begin in this country. They are now tolerating all that they must endure from the neighbors with amazing patience, even when their mills and such are warranted by the Agent, as happened to our Sr. Felicitas Hicks. In brief, things are currently happening here in this country to bother the Indians, which you cannot make sense of and can hardly believe that a person can do such godless things, even those who are supposed to be respectable people. We hope God will look upon this and bring justice!

I have heard nothing from our Brn. and Srs. in Ogeloogy for several [weeks]. Some time ago Br. Clauder invited us to a conference, but my circumstances and other obstacles have not allowed us to visit there yet. After having damp and cool weather for a while, we are now having beautiful, warm, and fruitful weather.

On May 30th we had the blessed enjoyment of the body and blood of Jesus in Holy Communion, during which the single

Indian Br. Niclaus Solomon was confirmed to partake in this for the first time. We also had the baptism of the baby girl, named Susanna, born Apr. 15th to our Br. and Sr. Israel.

Heartfelt greetings to you all. Don't forget to greet Br. and Sr. Shaaf, Br. and Sr. Bechler, Br. and Sr. Reichel, Father Steiner, Sr., Br. and Sr. Benzien. And you, dear Br., accept a special greeting from your constantly loving friend and humble Br.,

Gottlieb Byhan

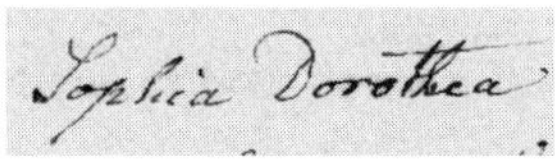


P.S. From the last news, we see that our dear daughter Sophia Dorothea was married to the single Br. Evan Boner yesterday, for which she has our parental blessing. In one of her last letters she asked me to give her our wall clock which is at your place, so she can have it in her living room until our return. Dear Br., if you do not have anything against this, be good enough to let them have it.

G. Byhan

[Springplace (M 407-2) and Oochgeelogy (M 409-1) Diaries.]

*June 12.* [Spg.] Mr. Chamberlane from Brainerd stopped in at our place for a brief time to rest a little. Since he will preach about 14 miles from here tomorrow, he went on after he had eaten lunch with us.

*Sun., June 13.* [Spg.] The sermon was on Rom. 10:9,10. Afterward was Bible reading, which was repeated in the Cherokee language by the Indian Br. Nicl. Ignatius.

*Sun., June 13.* [Ooch.] Among the visitors today was the elderly Sr. Anna Felicitas, the surviving widow of blessed Charles Renatus Hicks. When she left we spoke some words of comfort to her, since she has suffered much worry and sorrow because of her children. We took the words of 1 Pet. 4:19 to heart for our Sunday service: Those that suffer according to the will of God commit the keeping of their souls to him in well doing, as unto a faithful Creator. And from this we tried to draw comfort for the troubled Cherokees in their current situation.

*June 16.* [Spg.] In the evening our neighbor Mr. Jos. Vann, who had spent the winter in Washington as one of the Delegates of the Cherokee Nation during the session of Congress, returned home. On the morning of

*June 17* [Spg.] Brn. Byhan, Sr., and Nathl. Byhan went there to welcome him. However, since a lot of visitors were there, there was no opportunity to talk with him about what he and his colleagues had done in Washington. He said this much, however:

The land was not yet gone. We should just be of good courage, and now it would depend a great deal on the Cherokees themselves to keep their land for a while yet if they behaved peacefully and did not move west. The more Cherokee families who move west now, the more families of white people will come into the country. Concerning the Georgia law now being intro-duced into Cherokee country, this will be felt little by the common people and will primarily affect those who have much contact with the white people. Thus if they behave peacefully, the Indians can still keep their land for a long time.

*June 18.* [Ooch.] Br. Clauder, accompanied by Sr. Gambold, went to Springplace for a brief visit.

*June 18.* [Spg.] We had a pleasant visit from Br. Clauder and Sr. A. M. Gambold. We had various pleasant conversations with them about our mission here and about our Brn. and Srs.

*June 19.* [Spg.] They returned to Oochgelogy.

*June 19.* [Ooch.] They returned from there in the evening. Since the oppressive laws of Georgia have gone into legal force in this country, we have heard with compassion and regret about the injustices and atrocities many white people have carried out against the poor Cherokees. Recently one of these miserable people was attacked in his house by a troop of white people and robbed. When he tried to defend himself, he was knocked to the ground with a weapon and was stabbed in his torso by another of these robbers. Then he had to watch sorrowfully as his few possessions, his horse and cattle, were driven away. It is known that no Cherokee will receive a hearing from the authorities in Georgia, no testimony of any native ([margin note:] against a citizen of Georgia) will be heard in those courts.

[M 414-5-22: Translated by Julie Tomberlin Weber. No address; no postmark.]

Springplace, June 19, 1830

Dearly beloved Br. Schulz,

Yesterday we were delighted to have dear Br. Clauder and Sr. A. M. Gambold for a visit with us. They left the rest of the Brn. and Srs. in Ochgeloogy healthy.

Br. Clauder brought me the literal translation of our Church Litany into English to send to you, so at this time I cannot send you all of my ledger for the journal I had sent. Otherwise, the packet would be too large. But I will send the rest of it with the next mail. Praise God, we are currently all well here in Spring Place, except for Mother Byhan who is suffering a lot from bouts of weakness. I have recovered my usual health.

On Wednesday evening the 16th our neighbor Mr. Jos. Vann came home from Washington. Nathl. and I visited him early on the 17th to welcome him home. Otherwise, he was not able to tell us anything new about the removal of the Cherokees than what we had already seen in the newspapers 4 days earlier. Since things have reached a conclusion regarding the Cherokees for now, we would really like to know the thoughts of the Pr. Helf. Conf. about the Cherokee mission. As things stand now, we personally see new difficulties ahead, but we can do nothing but rely on the only Helper in all distress.

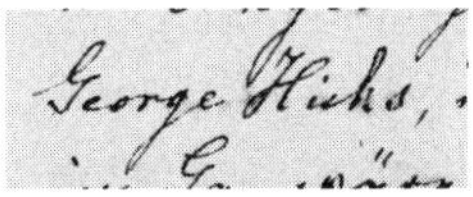

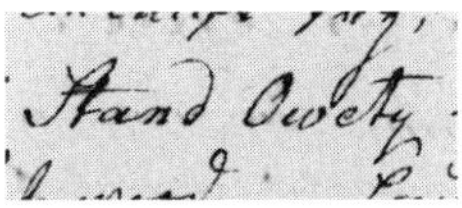

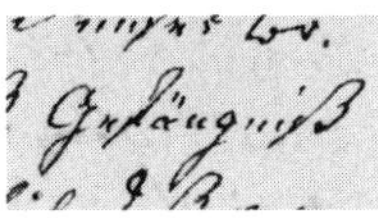


Br. Clauder told me that there is a rumor going around in Ochgeloogy that our Br. George Hicks and Mr. Stand Owety were taken to prison in Georgia, primarily because they had been active in driving the Intruders out of the country, and they were there when the houses, which the Emigrants had left behind and into which the Intruders had moved, since the houses and improvements were seen as Government property, were burned down. This happened when the one Indian lost his life. God alone knows how things will continue! He will help us through.

The above news concerning G. Hicks and Stand Owety must be confirmed, however, before we can accept it as certain.

We want to see what the Lord will do. In order to keep our courage from sinking He provides us and grants us and His small gathering here days of encouragement, which we remember as comfort in our services on Sundays, especially when occasionally a soul comes who is tired of serving sin and is concerned about salvation and we have the joy of baptizing such a soul into Jesus' death and being able to deliver it to its Redeemer through this. We have this before us again on July 11, when 2 people from among the heathen will be baptized: our Br. Boas' wife and a certain Fields, named Duka, who lives in the area near our Sr. Felicitas Hicks. This provides us courage again and encourages us to do all we can to extend His kingdom.

All here send their best greetings, and you, accept a special greeting from your upstanding friend and Br.,

Gottlieb Byhan

[Springplace (M 407-2) and Oochgeelogy (M 409-1) Diaries.]

*Sun., June 20.* [Spg.] The Methodists had services yesterday and today on this side of Mr. McNair's and in the neighborhood of our Brn. and Srs. who live there, so only a few of our Brn. and Srs. came here to the services. In the first service a sermon on the Sunday Gospel for today was read. In the second one Br. Samuel gave a talk for our Brn. and Srs. with a prayer on his knees. Recently our scholar Flea, son of our Br. Samuel who was here in the school a number of years, was baptized by the Methodists and then joined their community. He made a lot of trouble for us recently because of his contrary and proud nature and behavior. When we complained to his father about this, he seemed to be very surprised and said we should have punished him, because he had always been punished here and otherwise took no notice of it. He took him home to help in the fieldwork, which is also very good for him since his inclination to lethargy is very great. He would never have learned to work from us, because when we told him to do something he said that he came here to go to school and not to work.

*June 22.* [Spg.] We had a cordial visit from our neighbor Jos. Vann, and then had an opportunity to talk with him about the current situation and circumstances of the Cherokees. Judging from current circumstances, the Cherokees will not move to the west so soon. According to the decision of Congress, it would now depend a great deal on the Cherokees themselves whether they want to move or not, since the treaties which the United States have made with the Cherokees should not be changed. He also told us that as soon as the rest of the Delegates had come back, a Council will probably be held to consider what else should be done in this matter.

*June 22.* [Ooch.] Br. and Sr. Clauder visited with our Sr. Lucy Hicks, who returned from the gold mines several days ago. From the bottom of our hearts, we were grateful to our dear Lord, who so mercifully protected this Sr. and her husband George Augustus from all physical and spiritual danger in this godless pit. She could not find words to describe the bad behavior of the crowds there. During her stay there she held morning and evening devotions in her tent daily, and other Indian women often came to this. On Sundays Br. Hicks also held services in both languages, despite the mocking and scorn he had to endure because of this.

[M 414-5-23: Translated by Julie Tomberlin Weber. Addressed to: Revd. Theodor Schulz, Salem, Stokes County, North Carolina. Postmark: Springplace, C.N., June 27. Free. Gottl. Byhan, P.M. Received July 12.]

Springplace, June 25, 1830

My dear Br. Schulz,

On the 20th of this month your kind letter of June 8, in response to my letter to you dated May 22nd, arrived here, and I want to reply to this briefly now. In my previous letter I had already informed you that Mr. Jos. Vann returned from Washington last week. This week he paid a friendly visit at our place, and we had the opportunity to discuss various issues concerning the Cherokee Nation and to ask him about many things. Admittedly, he could not tell us much besides what we had already seen in the newspapers concerning the decision of Congress. I will not neglect to grant your request to acquaint you in detail with everything I hear. Concerning the current situation of the Nation, all is quiet, and we hear nothing about disturbances, so that we live in uninterrupted peace and in safety. Our Brn. and Srs. do not say much about their situation either, at least they have not done so until now. In my conversation with Br. Samuel, which took place here last Saturday, to hear about the conclusion of Congress, he said the Cherokees would not move, but would also not submit to the Georgia Law. This was all he told me.

The good Indians really imagine too great and horrible things when they hear that the Georgia laws will extend over the Cherokees. Sometimes one might almost believe that that these laws were so horribly described to them by white people with bad intentions who live in the country and who want the Indians just to move. These are only my thoughts. Otherwise, we have not yet noticed or experienced anything about the Georgia laws in our neighborhood. But this can still happen. I am only writing about the current circumstances of the Nation and what is known to me.

However, I believe, and Mr. Jos. Vann said the same, and many reasonable people in the Nation, that the Cherokees will remain here a number of years longer if they are not driven away by force. Mr. Vann believes that a Council will be held as soon as the rest of the Delegates come home, and after this it will become easier to learn the thoughts of the Cherokees. I will try to attend this if at all possible. In brief, there is currently no thought of moving away.

In a letter to you, I informed you that our Sr. Felicitas Hicks's mill and the miller's house were lost, with the consent of the Agent. This is true. She not only lost her mill and all that goes with it, but also her house and the rest of the improvements. This is how it happened. One of her sons, I think his name is

Leonard, let the Agent sign him up last year as an Emigrant to Arkansas. But he did not go, and he was paid by the Agent for all these improvements, as we hear, without the knowledge of his mother, our Sr. Felicitas. Now according to the current laws, this improvement belongs to the Government, and the Agent can let anyone he wants move into it. This is how this all happened. From the outset it seemed strange to us that the Georgians would drive out the old mother so that they could move in.

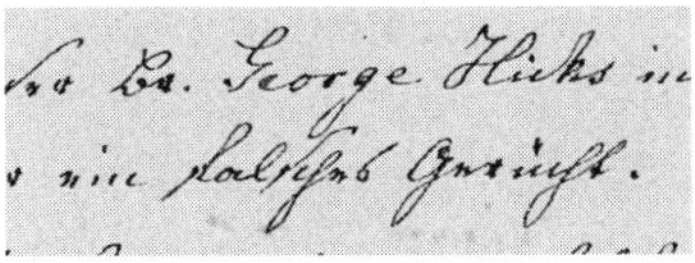
Br. George Hicks in
falsches Gerücht.

It was not confirmed that our Br. George Hicks was in prison in Georgia; this was a false rumor.

However, if it actually comes to the point that the Indians move west, which is currently extremely improbable, we want to faithfully try to meet the wishes you expressed about this in your dear letter regarding our dear Brn. and Srs. We are also very happy now that we can speak openly and freely with our Brn. and Srs. about their situation if an opportunity arises, since previously we hardly knew how and what we should say to them in order to avoid any offense on either side, and have tried to avoid conversations about this.

Now concerning the hope you express in your letter — that you especially hope Br. and Sr. Clauder might move west with our Brn. and Srs., it is not my place to respond. We have discussed together sometimes that he would move with them under certain conditions, but I will let him speak for himself. You also ask what our Nathl. thinks about this. I posed this question to him and received the answer that the Indians are not yet moving. And so it was not yet time to give a definite answer about this. A person could change his mind if he made a statement about this matter too far in advance.

From the above, dear Brn., you will see that the removal of the Indians and our Brn. and Srs. to the west will not happen so soon, and it might perhaps be years before it gets to this, so we ask the dear Brn. of the Prov. Helf. Conf. once again to consider our recall by this coming fall. The dear Brn. will not think badly of me if I name three reasons which lead us to ask for our recall.

First, I think it will be easy to find another Br. who is more able, who can work among this Nation with more blessing, and who is also more gifted in the English language than I. And on this occasion I must honestly assure you that I am convinced in my heart that I am too inadequate and powerless for that which I think I should be for the Savior in His work here, and I often reproach myself inwardly that I cannot do that for Him and I must say cannot do that which I actually should. I am no friend of making something look good when it is in fact not so. Therefore, I am convinced that it is necessary for a more active and energetic and more gifted person, and one who can speak English well, to replace me to work in the Lord's vineyard here. The field here is ripe for the harvest, and there is much to do here.

Second, my wife's illness and weakness is also a reason we wish to be recalled. In fact, as things appear, she can no longer endure things in this large household. She is often so worn out that she can hardly go on, and yet the household circumstances require her to crawl around. The only comfort she has and that keeps up going is this: She is doing it for the sake of the Savior and His work. Otherwise, she would surely already have collapsed under the burden.

Third, the promise which we were made upon our departure in 1827, which I do not want to repeat again here, requires that we be replaced, and we accepted the call here based on this promise, as Br. Theod. Schulz will still remember, because we and the dear Brn. of the Prov. Helf. Conf. were convinced that we could not tolerate things here very long.

I overlooked a question in your dear letter, which I will make up now: What will happen with Br. and Sr. Copeland if the Indians should move west? I believe and am convinced that they will move with them. He, Br. Copeland, is always an upstanding and very useful person who does all he can, so to speak, and would be very useful to them in setting up there.

I will diligently write you, dear Br. Schulz, about what is going on from time to time in the Nation and what new things I have heard, but I always believe that Br. Clauder is better situated than I to learn about news and events in the Nation, because he is closer to New Echota where everything, so to speak, is centered, and also because he lives closer to the Chief, Mr. John Ross, and to Br. Wm. Abr. Hicks, where he can learn a lot concerning the Nation much sooner than we here in Spring Place.

Now may the faithful Savior be our Comfort, Advisor, and Helper in our current situation. We want to trust in Him alone. He will arrange everything for the best.

We saw in a note dated June 7 from dear Br. Shaaf that our daughter Sophia Dorothea was engaged to the single Br. Evan Boner for holy marriage. They both have our parental blessing for their plan. Greet both of them for us.

All of you accept the most sincere greetings from us, with no exception. And you, my dear Br. Schulz, accept another special one from your dear, loving friend and Br.,

Gottl. Byhan

Herewith you receive the last part of my ledger[1] along with comments.

[Springplace (M 407-2) and Oochgeelogy (M 409-1) Diaries.]

*Sun., June 27.* [Spg.] A pretty large number of our Brn. and Srs. came for the services. In the first service was a sermon on 1 Tim. 2:4-6. In the second was the baptism of the little son born on Apr. 8th to our neighbor Jos. Vann with the name Joseph Webster. Afterward we had a conversation with our Brn. and Srs., which we were led to as a result of all sorts of rumors which are currently going around in the country to stir up the Indians. We advised them lovingly to show themselves children of God in their current certainly critical situation and to remember what the Savior promised them in holy baptism so that their countrymen could see what children of the Spirit they are and to whom they belong, etc. In recent days we heard, even from our Br. Samuel, that things might get stirred up in that district, Chatuga, where some of our Brn. and Srs. live. They are gathering and

[1] See footnote, page 4229 above.

deciding among themselves not to move west and also not to be subject to the laws of Georgia. As far as we could tell from our Br. Samuel's talk, they had decided to protect themselves with force against the Georgians. This news certainly excited unrest in us, especially since Br. Samuel told us that the Indians were also gathering in his house to discuss these matters. Even Br. Samuel himself told us that they were ready for the Georgians!

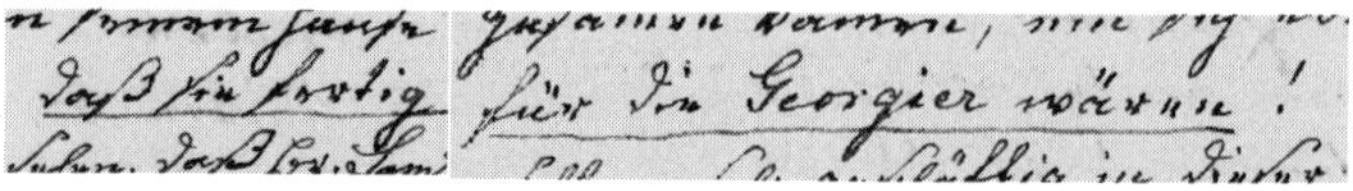
daß sie fertig für die Georgier wären!

It hurts us and makes us worry more than a little to see Br. Samuel himself so very active in this matter, since we would have least expected from him that he would get involved in such things. May the Savior give us wisdom to meet this matter so that His work will not be diminished by our Brn. and Srs. May He stand with us! Today we also heard that a Council is supposed to be held in New Echota 15 days from now when the rest of the Delegates have returned.

*Sun., June 27.* [Ooch.] Many of our Sunday school scholars have distinguished themselves by studying diligently, and they received small hymnals as a reward today, since singing verses is such a pleasant activity for them and naturally provides us with joy and encouragement. They were delighted to receive them. We cannot help but express gratitude toward our Lord that our scholars generally bring us so much joy. Here and there the good fruits of beneficial admonitions are also visible.

*June 28.* [Spg.] After pretty dry weather, today we had a nice refreshing rain for which we were sincerely grateful to our dear heavenly Father.

*June 29.* [Spg.] Br. and Sr. Byhan went with their daughter Rachel to visit the Indian Brn. and Srs. in Sumack, Mr. McNair's, and down the Connassauga River. They found most of the Brn. and Srs. at home, and they were very happy about the visit. They were taken in very cordially everywhere.

*June 30.* [Spg.] We had a strong rain shower, the likes of which we have not had for a long time. The storm knocked down much of our Indian corn, and the water streamed through our field like a creek. In our springhouse it rose about two feet. But the Indian corn stood back up again in the following days.

*July 1.* [Spg.] Br. and Sr. Byhan returned home with their daughter from the above-mentioned visit. Since the heat in recent days has been very great, this trip really affected and exhausted Sr. Byhan, so that she could hardly reach Spring Place. She recovered, though, in a few days.

*Sun., July 4.* [Spg.] Only a few of our Brn. and Srs. came to our place, and so today we had only one service, in which the Church Litany was prayed and a sermon was read on the words: When I am lifted up from the earth, I will draw all people unto me, John 12:32.

*Sun., July 4.* [Ooch.] First we had the sermon and then the baptism of our Sr. Sussannah Fields's baby boy. Since most of most of our communicants were gathered here today, we celebrated our Redeemer and Savior's sacred meal. In the evening our scholars delighted us with their singing. The Lord truly brought praise from the mouths of the youthful Cherokees; may they also live and grow completely to His honor.

[M 414-5-24: Translated by Julie Tomberlin Weber. Addressed to: Revd. Theodore Schulz, Salem, Stokes County, North Carolina. Postmark: Springplace, C.N., July 11, paid 18¾. Received July 26.]

Ooyugillogy, Ch. Nat., July 1, 1830

Dear Br. Schulz,

We received your kind letter of June 8th some days ago, and it was a delight and encouragement to us, since we had spent almost 2 lonely months without any communication from our friends in Salem. This led me to pay a visit to Spring Place some weeks ago accompanied by Sr. Gambold. There we were very interested to learn a number of things about you all in the Gemeine through letters which Br. Byhan had received.

Concerning your dear letter of June 8th in which you discuss various things about the impending emigration of the Indians and our missions among this people, I will make some comments that might be helpful to you and the Brethren of the P.H.C. in your considerations, as you requested. I do not know what Br. Byhan's views about our entire situation might be, and I find it difficult myself to decipher the signs of the time. It appears there are one or more obvious ambiguities in the decisions of Congress regarding the Indians. How should the treaties be observed, although the Government is failing to provide the protection promised in the treaties against tyrannical states. Without a doubt it will be clear to you that on our side the strictest caution in actions and speech is necessary, and we do not like to talk about this matter even with our Brn. and Srs. If we spoke happily and with nice words about emigrating, they might immediately suspect we were connected with the New Yorker Indian Board, to which one Brother belongs, because although this society, as far as I know, was never active and now perhaps does not exist anymore, many among this people know that a society with the well-known purpose of assisting the Indians to move and to persuade them to do so was formed, and that a Moravian also belonged to it, because of which a sharp eye is kept on us, even if secretly.

On the other hand, we bring suspicion upon ourselves if we encourage them to wait. However, this is the decision of the Cherokees thus far, as you can see in the *Phönix* even though unjust measures are poured out on this country and hundreds of the poor Indians as a result suffer in the prisons of Georgia. The Indians with their inborn pride would prefer to let themselves be irritated by the oppressions than to weaken. This is the language of the *Phönix* and the people, as you yourself can see.

It is admittedly true that now and then they talk about moving, and Br. Byhan told me many of the Brn. and Srs. there had talked about this, but absolutely not with any certainty, and their questions about whether we would go with them can be attributed more to their curiosity. I do not believe that a single soul among our people has seriously thought about emigrating, and so we must remain patient and wait for the conclusion of this entire difficult matter.

However, I will now consider the possibility that a general emigration could take place. My view about this would be that it would be better to follow our little congregation afterward rather than move with them, because where do they want to move? They do not want to remain under the protection of the United States, as one can easily understand. So some of them will go to Mexico and some of them to the other regions in the west, until they are completely destroyed by wars with other nations and poverty.

If, however, this were not the case and they would settle in the region intended for them, and if our people would agree to move together and settle in one area (which, however, is not to be expected for various reasons), would it not be good for a couple of experienced, well-informed Brethren first to make an exploratory journey there? Before a Brother and Sister make the long and difficult journey there in uncertainty? I must admit I have several concerns about going there in this manner.

I am well aware of the beautiful and glorious examples which have been left to us by our predecessors in missionary service, by Zeisberger, Mack, Sensemann, and others, which provide me great encouragement. But there are other circumstances here that were not the case for them, like my youth and lack of experience. Oh, if I were more firmly grounded in faith and in the very necessary experience which is so unavoidably necessary in establishing a new mission.

Things with our Brn. and Srs. here are also completely different than with those who made the pilgrimage from one place to another. They had lived for years with their teachers in orderly congregation towns, had daily instruction in the truths of salvation and showed their gratitude toward their teachers in such a way that they really had no choice but to remain with them. But here the situation is different. Our Brn. and Srs. live scattered around. Some come to services just once in 3 or 4 weeks. Sometimes it is months before they come to visit. If one is lucky enough to have an interpreter here (which, however, is often not the case) they can be given only a little instruction, because there is too little time. Without first thinking about the lameness of this method it will certainly be clear that not much can be done in this way.

Another problem that discourages the mission work is the great ingratitude of the people and unfortunately many of those who have been baptized and the youth who were raised in our mission schools. This is not only my testimony, but all the Brn. and Srs. who have served here will agree with me that this is the truth. Every rose has thorns, so also here.

Despite all the difficulties and trials, many show the fruits of a blessed growing faith in Jesus Christ, and this binds hearts in love together. Even though many are ungrateful and go their way in proud independence, there is still a small number of those who know in whom they believe and through whose assistance they were introduced to Jesus.

As often as I reflect on this entire matter, and my soul becomes filled with dark and troubling worries, I come to the conclusion in quiet submission to let the only wise Ruler of the world do what He has decided in His incomprehensible council. He who makes a path for the clouds, air, and winds will also find a path for a weak person like me.

But now to get back to the subject. My view is this: we wait patiently until we see what our Brn. and Srs. will do. We cannot rely on talk. By being too hasty we will bring suspicion upon ourselves, and it is well known that this is a great problem among the Indians. By acting this way we would naturally have to suffer a lot from the Georgians when they see that the Indians with the missionaries really do not like to give in, but if we wanted to stay with the Indians and enjoy their trust, we must show our loyalty during suffering and oppression.

On the 12th of this month a Council is supposed to begin in New Echota. It will become clear what the Cherokees are planning to do during this. Contrary to expectations, our Br. Wm. Abr. Hicks has not yet returned home, although the rest of the Delegates returned home 3 weeks ago. They left him in Washington, since he was planning to return with a private conveyance. You will already have read about the most recent events in the Nation in the *Phönix*.

Everyone here is healthy except the small little boy left behind to us by our blessed Sr. Copeland. He has been seriously ill for a number of days now. He was weak and frail since his birth, and it would be best for him if he soon followed his mother. Since the death of the mother, extreme distress and misery have prevailed in the house of our neighbor Copeland.

The 5th. Yesterday we once again had the joy of nourishing and instructing our needy souls and sharing with most of our communicants in Holy Communion. The Lord revealed Himself to us in love. This was the first Holy Communion since last Maundy Thursday when our Brn. and Srs. were scattered like sheep and in part still are. Sr. Ridge and Susannah Fields were also here, the latter with her little 5-week-old baby boy who was baptized into Jesus' death on this occasion. I shared the greetings from your last letter to those here and assured them of your concern for them and that of the Gemeine in their current troubled circumstances, and they expressed their sincere gratitude for this.

Concerning our baptismal candidate Peggy Hicks, nothing more has been decided by our dear Lord. The question has already been answered negatively twice in *. Now the One who knows all hearts knows everything best. The time of waiting is often a special time of grace. The number of candidates has not yet increased here, so we are all the more interested in the grace [torn page]. Spring Place, in which two adults are supposed to receive the bath of holy baptism next Sunday and during which I am also planning to be present at Br. Byhan's invitation.

In our area here everyone is becoming Methodist — hardly a day goes by that there is not preaching somewhere in the neighborhood. Despite this, the ruinous ballplays, dances, and horse-racing still continue. Last week there was supposed to be a large ballplay very close to us — because of some circumstance one of the parties did not come, so the spectacle was avoided. I have a suspicion that the purpose of this was just to aggravate me since I spoke publicly against such entertainment on one occasion. Let it be so! I would speak against it every time.

Greet my dear parents sincerely for us, as well as the rest of the Brn. of the P.H.C. Br. and Sr. Copeland and Sr. Gambold send sincere greetings. We all commend ourselves to your continued care and prayer. Most especially, your obliged Br.,

Henry G. Clauder

You will have received the Diary along with the accounts by now.

Our cash box is almost empty. I do not have enough money to pay our hired worker, who is supposed to be dismissed next week. Before my next letter I will try to find out the cost of the improvements here and then report them.

P.S. The 8th. This evening at 8 o'clock the small child we had in our care for approximately 5 weeks died after 5 days of almost indescribable suffering from an internal infection. Br. Wm. Hicks finally returned home safely yesterday the 7th.

H. G. C.

[M 414-5-25: Translated by Julie Tomberlin Weber. Addressed to: Revd. Theod. Schulz, Salem, Stokes County, North Carolina. Postmark: Springplace, C.N., July 4. Free. Gottl. Byhan, P.M. Received July 19.]

Springplace, July 3, 1830

My dear Br. Schulz,

Your kind letter of June 15, along with three enclosures of written *Gem. Nachr.* and an enclosure of $122, arrived here safely on June 27. Thanks, very sincere thanks for all! Today I am sending you a copy of Revd. S. A. Worcester's letter concerning the Church Litany, which Br. Clauder sent me to send on to you. We were very interested in all you reported to us in your last note and delighted by it. According to this, Br. and Sr. Eder had a happy and speedy journey to the West Indies. I can imagine his great joy at being away from America; may it remain so. But everywhere in this vale of tears has its problems, and there will surely be something in the West Indies as well. When you write to him, give them our greetings.

Nothing else has happened here since my last letter to you dated June 25, that is, between Georgia and the Cherokees. I can report the following to you from, or about, our area. Last

Saturday evening our Br. Samuel came here with his son Flea and one of his wives, Sr. Rachel. I immediately assumed that he either had something to ask or to tell, and this was indeed the case. First, he asked if we had heard anything new about the Georgians. We replied that we had heard nothing new recently. Then he told us that the Indians in Chatuka, or in his neighborhood, were restless again and were holding meetings to consider what they would do if the Georgians did not leave them in peace, or came to their place, and that tomorrow evening, June 27, another one of these meetings would be held in his house. He added that they were ready for the Georgians if they came.

This frightened me, and I immediately took the opportunity to tell him that we hoped our Brn. and Srs. might keep themselves out of such things and behave as children of God in the current circumstances. And since I noticed that he himself, Br. Samuel, was quite intensely involved in this matter, I reminded him among other things of the promise he and the other Brn. and Srs. had made to the Savior in holy baptism: to live for Him alone in this world and to prove themselves as children of God before the world, so that the world would see what spiritual children they are, etc. But this conversation did not reassure us. We considered it our responsibility on Sunday to discuss this matter with all the Brn. and Srs. who were present in a separate service. We lovingly admonished them to remain calm in their current situation and to show themselves to be children of God and to hold firmly to the One to whom they surrendered upon their baptism, to live in this world for Him alone, so that they would not dishonor Him or the Gemeine, etc. They seemed to accept the admonition in love. We noticed that the discouragement on their faces before the conversation vanished, and we hope that it might have been beneficial.

We hear that a Council will be held in New Echota on the 12th of this month, and a large crowd of Indians will gather for it. If it is possible, I will also attend this. Now may the Savior have mercy on this Nation and bless those who hold to Him! It is not possible to include here all the news and rumors which are currently circulating — true and untrue. You will read the most important things in the *Phönix*, and the true things. Among other things, we hear that the Governor of Ga. in a proclamation has forbidden the white people as well as the Cherokees from mining for gold until further orders from the President. We also hear now that the President will come to Tennessee soon, and that he has invited the Chiefs to come to Nashville to have a discussion with them about their land. I cannot say whether the latter is the truth.

Last Sunday the baby boy born to our neighbor Jos. Vann on Apr. 8th was baptized with the name Joseph Webster. The Delegates have not all arrived home yet as far as we know; Br. Wm. Abr. Hicks at least is not yet home. This week Mother Byhan and Rachel and I paid a very pleasant visit to our Brn. and Srs. in Sumack, the McNairs, and down both sides of the Conossauga River. We found all the Brn. and Srs. healthy and unusually happy about this visit with them. Everyone is well except for Mother Byhan, who returned home from the mentioned visit quite weak but has now recovered somewhat, praise God! Everyone sends greetings! And you, dear Br., accept a special greeting from your sincerely loving friend and Br.,

Gottlieb Byhan

[M 411-1-30: Transcribed by Grace S. Robinson. Handwriting is Henry G. Clauder's. Penciled in: The Litany 1830. See the frontispiece of this volume.]

Copy of Revd. S. A. Worcester letter

New Echota, May 25, 1830

Revd & dear Sir

A literal translation from English, into Cherokee, or from Cherokee into English, is impossible, on account of the widely different construction of the two languages. In these translations of the Litany from Cherokee into English, I have endeavoured to be faithful in giving the real import of the Cherokee, and to be as nearly literal as I could without rendering my English awkward and obscure.

In translating we did not think it necessary to follow the English as closely as in translating scripture, but aimed at giving substantially the same sentiment. How nearly we have approached, the retranslation will show. Some few errors we did not perceive till they were brought to view by retranslating, after the work had been printed. I am happy in the belief that none of these errors conveys a sentiment materially incorrect. The only inaccuracy in sentiment so occasioned, is where the Cherokee reads Let us, as far as we are able, be peaceably disposed & e. It is impossible that there should not be some ambiquities, arising from the fact that on a subject which is new to a people, as the Christian religion is to the Cherokees, it is necessary to make new applications of words, with new shades of signification with which it requires time for them to become familiar.

If ever a second edition should be called for I might be improved, but I hope that this, as it is, will prove to be for the edification of your people. I intended to remark that, in the translation of the poetry the sentiment has been of necessity abridged, to bring the words within the measure.

With hearty wishes for the prosperity of your churches,

I am your Br. in the labor of the Gospel.

S. A. Worcester

Revd. H. G. Clauder

[Springplace (M 407-2) and Oochgeelogy (M 409-1) Diaries.]

*July 6.* [Spg.] Early in the day we had the joy of welcoming our Br. Wm. Abr. Hicks on his return journey from Washington, where he had been sent with four others in Dec. 1829 as a Delegate for the Cherokees. Although the time was short, we had very pleasant conversations with him. After he had had breakfast with us he traveled on, so that he could still get home today if possible, although he was very tired. He showed us a letter from President

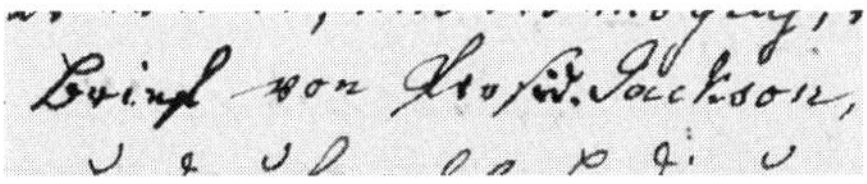


Jackson concerning the Cherokees, in which the former expresses

his whole mind to the latter, and on what conditions they can be protected by him in the future. If they stay where they currently are, they must live under the laws of the State of Georgia and they do this at their own risk and cannot put their confidence in him, because he has no power or right to get mixed up in the laws of individual states. However, he wants to stop those white people who have no right from settling in their country. On the other hand he assured them that if they move west, they will be under his protection or that of the United States. And that the President and the Secty. of War will make a journey to Tenn., so the former invites the Chiefs of this Nation to come to Nashville to speak with him about their concerns. At the same time he tells them that if they do not want to come or cannot come with power to negotiate the sale of their land, it would not be necessary for them to come. Mr. Tazizi had spent the night with us, and he also went home this morning. Also this evening James McNair came to our place and spent the night.

*July 7.* [Spg.] After breakfast he went on. In recent days we heard that next Saturday, the 10th of this month, there would be horse race in Mr. Vann's field right behind our God's Acre. These are always extremely unpleasant times for us, since on such occasions it gets very rowdy, because the Indians usually bring along brandy wine, and such gatherings always end with arguing if not with actual fighting.

*July 7.* [Ooch.] Br. Clauder visited our elderly Br. William Abraham Hicks, who returned home today after being gone for seven months. Br. Hicks was part of the Cherokees' legation to the United States Congress, which did not achieve its purpose as is generally known. Although they defended their concerns powerfully and persuasively there, nothing was accomplished to benefit the Cherokees in the end. Br. H. seems to have surrendered completely to the guidance of the Almighty.

*July 9.* [Ooch.] Today was the burial of our blessed Sarah Copeland's deceased baby boy; he died after a painful pilgrimage of 8 weeks. During the last 5 days he suffered constantly from the results of an internal infection.

*July 10.* [Ooch.] Br. Clauder went to Spring Place, where there was a blessed baptismal proceeding on the 11th. On the 12th he returned.

*July 10.* [Spg.] To our joy Br. G. Clauder came to our place from Ochgeloogy for a visit and to spend Sunday with us tomorrow. Toward evening was the above-mentioned horse race in Jos. Vann's field. Hundreds of people, men, women, and children had gathered for this. It was not a peaceful time for us, since we are bothered more than a little by them, especially by the women when the latter push into the houses and go into the living rooms and bedrooms and discuss everything and pick it up in their hands so that we really have to watch out that this or that is not stolen. On this occasion our apple trees were pretty much bared when throngs of people went into the orchards and got apples, as many as they could carry away. Throughout the night it was very loud at our north spring, which is closest to our houses, since the Indians had a lot of brandy wine. We were happy and grateful that some of our Indian Brn. and Srs., among others Br. Samuel, were already here this evening so that we were not alone on the place. Otherwise, we would not have been able to talk with them if the drunken Indians had disturbed us. Thus we spent the night pretty peacefully. Mr. Tazzizi had also come to serve tomorrow as our interpreter.

*Sun., July 11.* [Spg.] In the morning we were disturbed by some drunken Indians. Our Br. Samuel and Mr. Tazizi, however, controlled them so that they went away pretty soon, and from then on we were not troubled by them anymore. At 11 o'clock Br. Clauder gave the sermon to a large crowd of listeners on the words [Heb. 12:2]: Look to Jesus, the author and finisher of our faith. At 1 o'clock Br. Byhan presided at the baptism of the Indian woman Betsy, our Br. Boas's wife. She received the name Lydia Elisabeth. In the evening there was a Singstunde, which Br. Nathl. Byhan led. The presence of our dear Lord could be felt in our services today in a comforting manner. We could see in all of our Brn. and Srs. that they took home a blessing from what they enjoyed in the services today, because they were extremely happy and loving upon saying farewell. Mr. Tazizi, who interpreted for us today, also left for home today although he lives 16 miles from here.

*July 12.* [Ooch.] Today the Council of the Nation gathered to receive the message the President of the United States sent this Nation through the recently returned legation, along with other important communications. Mr. Worcester, missionary in New Echota, opened this meeting with a Christian prayer.

[M 414-5-26: Translated by Julie Tomberlin Weber. Addressed to: Revd. Theod. Schulz, Salem, Stokes County, North Carolina. Postmark: Springplace, C.N., July 11. Free. Gottl. Byhan, P.M. Received July 26.]

Springplace, July 7, 1830

My dear Br. Schulz,

Since my last letter on the 3rd of this month, nothing else noteworthy has taken place in the Nation. However, it seems that important things will happen soon which will show us how the matter with the poor Cherokees will finally turn out. They have now been summoned to the President to declare whether they will stay here and submit to the laws of Georgia, in which case they should not expect any further protection from him. If they would move west, they would be protected by the Government. They were ordered to make their statement by fall or next spring. I received a copy of this letter from Br. Wm. Abr. Hicks, who arrived here on the 5th of this month and had breakfast with us yesterday morning. If I did not believe that this letter would appear in the next *Phönix*, which you also receive, I would copy it. However, if it does not appear in the *Phönix*, I will copy it for you, word for word.

Next week a Council will be held in New Echota, which will probably take up this letter, and the points contained therein will be discussed. According to this, it has not been decided that the Cherokees are now completely under the authority of the Georgia, which, as can be presumed, will not deal with them very fairly if they have the slightest reason for this. Surely there would also be a lot to say on the other side, but this would be too much to include here and to analyze. Sometimes we do not know why God allows certain things to happen to a country or people. He always has His wise purposes for allowing these things, and so we must lay our hands on our mouths and then say: What God does is well done. His will is just. Without His knowledge not a hair falls from our heads.

Things concerning the Cherokees' staying here look pretty uncertain. Perhaps we can learn more at the Council, which the Indians will presumably attend very well. Some say they do not want to move west, but they also do not want to be under the jurisdiction of Georgia. One can surely guess which middle way they want to take, which would naturally bring their ruin.

May the Lord who arranges everything provide us with grace, wisdom, and courage, especially now in these complicated times. We commend ourselves to your loving remembrance and prayer before our dear Lord. Day after tomorrow we expect dear Br. Clauder here in Spring Place to support 2 adult Indian women in holy baptism on Sunday, the 11th of this month. Mr. Dav. St. Tazizi, who was here the last few days, promised to interpret for us on those days.

Sunday, the 11th. Yesterday the Indians had a horse race behind our God's Acre in Jos. Vann's fields. About 100 Indians, men, women, and children, had gathered for this, which led to a very restless night because of drunken Indians. Our apple trees were pretty well stripped, which we had to watch with patience. Many pushed into our house and had to be fed. The stalls and our lots were also full of horses which also had to be cared for. These are trying times! People in the Gemeine cannot imagine this. Yesterday Br. Clauder came from Ochgeloogy to our place for a visit to help me today with half the services. Be satisfied with these few lines for now, because there is not enough time to write more. Everyone sends sincere greetings. Praise God, we are all pretty well just now. I remain your loving Br.,

Gottlieb Byhan

[Springplace (M 407-2) and Oochgeelogy (M 409-1) Diaries.]

*July 12.* [Spg.] Br. Clauder set out on his return journey to Ochgeloogy today.

*July 14.* [Spg.] Today Br. Byhan went to Ochgeloogy and New Echota on a visit to attend the Council which will be held in the latter place this week, and he returned from there on the 16$^{th}$. At this Council the Indians decided not to move west and to patiently bear everything the white people, or much more the Georgians, would do with them. They also want to start legal proceedings over their matter in the U. St. ([inserted:] Supreme) Court where they believe they will receive justice.

*July 14 and 15.* [Ooch.] Brn. Byhan and Clauder attended the Council. The events of these days included reading the above mentioned communications, in which this Nation is once again urgently called upon to emigrate to the west and given the firm promise of the great benefit they will receive through this. At the conclusion of the proceedings on July 15 the speaker of

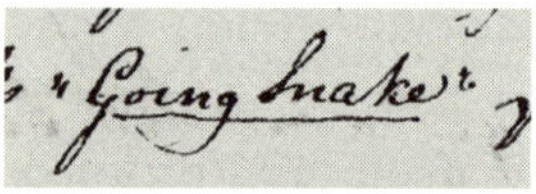


the Council, Going Snake, addressed the people, as did Major Ridge on the following day. During this he publicly explained his views about this matter as well as his advice.

*July 17.* [Spg.] In the evening our baptismal candidate Tuka Fields, who was supposed to have been baptized last Sunday but was prevented from coming here by illness in the family, came to our place. We had let her know through a letter that she would be baptized last Sunday. She had received the letter, but she did not have anyone who could read it to her until it was too late for her to come here last Sunday. So she was very sorry that she had missed it.

[M 414-5-27: Translated by Julie Tomberlin Weber. Addressed to: Revd. Theodor Schulz, Salem, Stokes County, North Carolina. Postmark: Springplace, C.N., July 18. Free. Gottl. Byhan, P.M. Received Aug. 2.]

Springplace, July 17, 1830

My dear Br. Schulz,

First, I just wanted to inform you that your dear letter of June 22nd along with written *Gem. Nachr.* arrived here on the 11th of this month, and we thank you sincerely for these. I have only the following to reply to this.

Praise God, we here are all quite healthy except my dear wife, who is suffering from an ulcer on her leg. The $90 I borrowed from Br. Alex Copeland last year and spent is included, as Br. Clauder tells me, in his note, which you gave him. I cannot see the Agent Col. Hugh Montgomery. I will not see him either, unless I make a special trip to the Agency. I have already asked him several times through Capt. McNair if he would stop in at our place on his way to the goldmines, but he says he has always been in too big a hurry to come by our place, because it is about 2 or 3 miles out of the way. I would like to talk with him once about our mission and the annual contribution to our school from the Genl. Government, although I believe that we cannot count on this any longer.

From your letter, I see that you receive the *Phönix* only every now and again, which we were not happy to hear. Since the newspaper passes through my hands, I will send it by way of Knoxville, etc., in the future, instead of by way of Georgia as usual. At least we will see if it arrives regularly then; I will begin doing this tomorrow.

Now I come to the Cherokee matter; I can give you some news about how things in the Nation are looking now. Last Monday the Indians gathered in New Echota for a Council. Most of the Delegates were present, that is, those who were in Washington last winter, to consider and discuss how they should behave and what is the best thing to do in their current situation and circumstances. Last Wednesday I went there also, and yesterday evening

I returned home. I was worried that I might perhaps miss something at the beginning of the week, but I found that nothing significant had happened in the first days except that they had been busy reading and translating letters. There was an incredible number of these on hand, from the Delegates from Washington to the Chief of the Cherokee Nation and from him back to them, from Jackson to the Delegates and from the latter to the former. In brief, what occupied the Council until Thursday noon was sharing letters from all the people in Washington who had anything to say about the Cherokee matter, which was interesting to hear.

The letters and the answers to these were read publicly. Then a respected Indian named Goingsnake held a talk. I did not learn what the message of this was. And with this the day's session was closed.

Now when the Council gathered again on Friday, yesterday, Major Ridge opened it with an extremely long address to the Indians in which he first explained the current situation of the Cherokees and how they were being oppressed and pressured by the Georgians, and that no help could be expected from the Government; they were now left to themselves, but even so they had not been abandoned because a God who would not abandon them lives in heaven. Among other things, he also said that there were many good people (Cherokees) among them; they also had good white people (missionaries) in their country. There were also many good people in the United States, all of whom would pray to God for them. And that they have now decided not to emigrate, but to stay in this country, which they had received from their ancestors. They had now decided to remain calm and let everything happen and bear everything with patience. He, Major Ridge, also said that they were even willing to be imprisoned by the Georgians and that he himself was willing to spend 7 years in the penitentiary and that if the laws did not help him out of this, then God in heaven would do this.

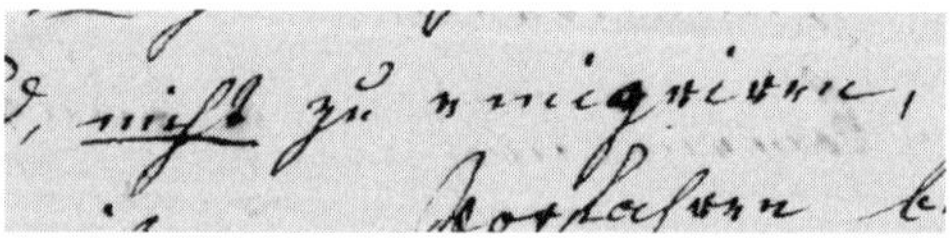

This is what Mr. John Ridge and Elias Boudinott shared with us from the address. Revd. Worcester, Jones, missionary in the Valley Towns, and I asked Ridge and Boudinott to allow the address to appear in the *Phönix*. We will see if this happens.

([Margin note:] The Cherokees are planning to appeal their matter to the Supreme Court of the United States. A certain Wirt will oversee the matter for them.)

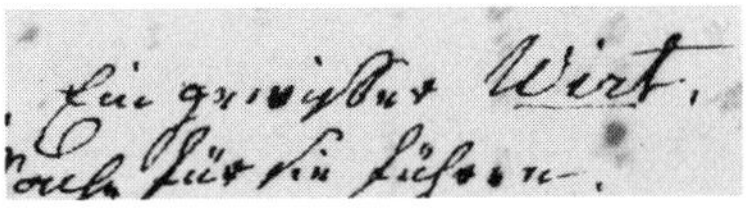

I have already attended a number of Councils among the Cherokees, but I must admit not a single one was like this one, where one sees the poor Indians so discouraged, so quiet and serious, and at the same time so composed. When you speak with them they act so loving toward us that we feel deep compassion and regret their current situation. This visit at an Indian Council will always remain in my memory, and the emotions I felt during it actually pressed tears and sighs from me: Dear Savior, have mercy on these poor lost sheep and care for them mercifully!

How can it help but arouse compassion when one sees the Indians, who are in distress and cannot expect any more assistance from humans, trusting in God. That says a lot.

From the above you dear Brn. will now see that the Indians are no longer thinking of moving to the West. The entire 3 days I was there I did not hear a single word about this. People believe the Council will not adjourn until the 21st of this month. If I hear anything in the next eight days, or if I hear something new by the next mail day, I will report it to you. Otherwise, the Indians were very happy when they saw that various missionaries had come to their Council, and they loudly expressed their pleasure at this. When the Chief, Mr. John Ross, saw me sitting among the Indians, he immediately came through the rows and cordially gave me his hand. To give you an impression of the Chief, just think about a man like Br. Benade in Litiz, the same stature, physiognomy, walk, and everything.

Now I have informed you of the most important events here since my last letter to you, and for this time nothing remains but to report the following not very happy circumstance, at Br.

Clauder's request. It concerns our Br. W. Abr. Hicks, who as I reported returned home from Washington about 10 days ago. Since he has been home now, he has been very discouraged, he hardly leaves the house, and he speaks very little. When he came home he apparently told his wife he had not acted correctly, and he also has not been as friendly to her anymore as he used to be. She tearfully complained about this to Br. Clauder, but he does not say what he did that was not right. We do not know what to make of this matter or what to think about it. Recently, Br. Clauder gave the burial address for the child of his neighbor, Copeland, and he was present. When he went home he apparently said that he would not come back to Ochgeloogy, where Br. and Sr. Clauder live, anytime soon. We learned this much: While he was in Washington he was very involved with a certain Walker, from Arkansas, who is supposed to be a bad man.

This is also the only reason we have learned so far that might be the cause of his discouragement. We also heard that he could not get along well with 2 of the Delegates. In brief, we do not know the cause, and it will perhaps become clear with time. It is disturbing and causes us and especially Br. and Sr. Clauder much worry. He also did not come to the Council, which they held against him.

Sr. Clauder is suffering from sore feet and legs, so that she cannot get around much. Sr. Copeland has frequent bouts of her illness, mostly at night, but not very bad. This really bothers her head; her memory is particularly suffering. The others are well and send sincere greetings. Last Sunday was a day of true blessing here in Spring Place. Br. Clauder was here from Ochgeloogy, and he delivered the sermon. Afterward, the wife of our Indian Br. Boas was baptized into Jesus' death with the name Lidia Elisabeth. We could sense the Savior in our midst.

You, dear Brn., will now see from the above that the Indians are not moving west for now. And so we ask you once again to consider our recall, because it is essential due to circumstances too extensive to describe here. My letter of June 25 should now be in your hands?

Sunday morning the 18th. Late yesterday evening our baptismal candidate Tuka Fields came, who was supposed to be baptized with Br. Boas' wife last Sunday. Illness prevented her from coming here last Sunday, and now she will be baptized next Sunday the 25th. In this way a lost sheep finds the Savior now and again, to be counted among His flock! My wife was quite weak this morning. Sincerest greetings from all of us, and especially from me, your loving but poor Br.,

Gottl. Byhan

[Springplace (M 407-2) and Oochgeelogy (M 409-1) Diaries.]

*Sun., July 18.* [Spg.] Because of the Council in New Echota, only a few of our Brn. and Srs. came to our place today. And so we read a sermon on the words of our Savior on the Cross [Luke 23:43]: Today shalt thou be with me in paradise. Afterward we talked thoroughly with our baptismal candidate, Tuka Fields, through our Sr. Maria Vann, regarding her baptism which was set for next Sunday. She expressed herself very contritely and was uncommonly happy that she should now have the grace of being cleansed from her sins through Jesus' blood in holy baptism.

*Sun., July 18.* [Ooch.] We had only a small number of listeners for our service, which consisted of a prayer, the Litany, and a talk. We were sorry that we did not have an interpreter, so the few who were present and could not understand English could not enjoy anything really essential.

*July 21.* [Ooch.] Br. and Sr. Clauder visited in the area.

*July 23.* [Ooch.] Br. Clauder visited at William Ab. Hicks. This man was baptized 10 years ago and was previously a very ardent supporter of the Lord's work in this country. It is very painful for us that he has ended up in an unblessed, worldly spiritual state as a result of his stay in a city [inserted: Washington], and now exhibits a lamentable apathy. May the Lord awaken him anew in a powerful manner and bless our attempts to set him straight. On the occasion of my visit with him today, he told me openly and tearfully about his sorrowful, crooked situation, and he immediately submitted himself to the necessary church consequence: exclusion from Holy Communion. He accepted gratefully the admonitions given to him to turn again to the only faithful Friend of Sinners and to seek forgiveness and help from Him, with his best promises.

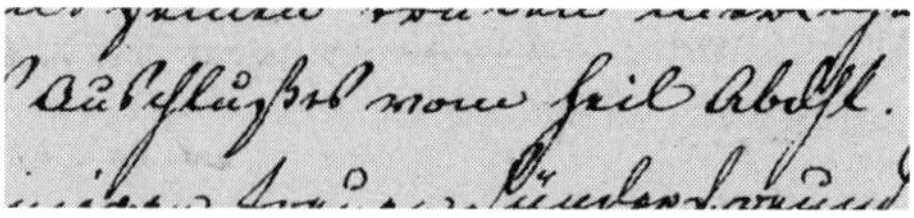

*July 24.* [Ooch.] Our neighbr Austin Copeland, the surviving widower of our blessed Sr. Sarah, visited us. During a conversation with him, he shared his desire to join the number of believers through the bath of holy baptism. Since he has been one of our most diligent church participants for years already, and he otherwise exhibits a very changed and acceptable way of life, we gratefully and joyfully accepted him as a candidate for baptism.

*Sun., July 25.* [Ooch.] Once again we had a nice number of listeners in our services, during which our friend Boudinott served as interpreter. In the sermon we spoke on the comforting words of Isa. 49:14-16. All present were sincerely encouraged to put their trust only in the more-than-motherly faithfulness of God during the current time of trials. He will not forget His people, much less leave them.

*Sun., July 25.* [Spg.] Many people gathered here. At 11 o'clock there was the first service, in which the words of our dear Lord were discussed: Go into all the world. Teach the heathen and baptize them in the name of the Father, and the Son, and the Holy Spirit [Matt. 28:19]. Afterward was the baptism of the Indian woman Tuka Fields. She received the name Sophia Carolina. The presence of our dear Lord was powerfully felt during this baptismal proceeding. In the second service we enjoyed the body and blood of Jesus with our communicants in Holy Communion. Mr. Tazizi came to our place on a visit today, as he said, to attend the baptismal proceeding. But unfortunately he arrived here too late, since he had not left home until this morning. He stayed here overnight, as did Sr. Delila McNair.

*July 26.* [Spg.] In the morning both of them went home.

*July 29.* [Spg.] After a great drought, today we received a nice rainstorm, which for the most part refreshed the field and garden crops, since everything had seemed as if it wanted to die. This week we began drying apples. We had built a new little drying house for this, since the old one could no longer be used, because it was pretty much fallen in.

*July 29.* [Ooch.] Br. and Sr. Clauder visited our neighbors and friends 4-5 miles from here. Most of them belong to the Methodist faith. They were accepted cordially and lovingly everywhere.

*July 30.* [Spg.] Since Mr. Vann's mill cannot work anymore because of a lack of water, we had to send one of our day workers with Br. Nathl. Byhan to Mr. George Harlen's mill, 11 or 12 miles from here, to get corn milled.

*July 31.* [Spg.] They returned home, but were able to get only half of the corn they had taken with them milled, because there was also too little water to mill.

[B 61-3: Provinzial Helfer Conferenz, meeting in Salem. Translated by C. Daniel Crews.]

*Fri., July 30.* Since the Congress of the United States at the end of May legally decided, and gave the President power to

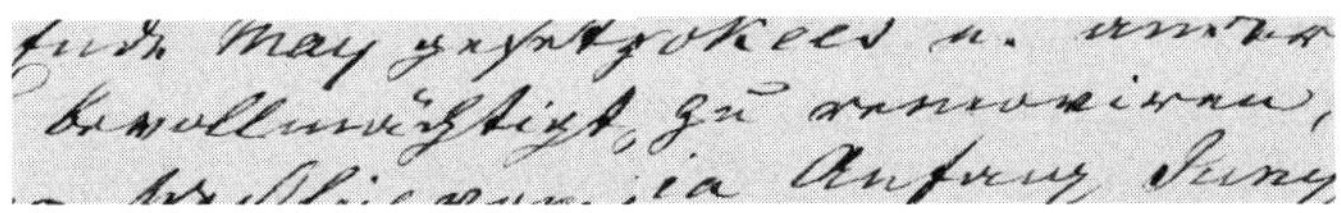

remove the Cherokees and other Indian Tribes to the west of the Mississippi, and soon thereafter the Governor in Georgia at the beginning of June through a public proclamation extended the jurisdiction of this state over the Land of the Cherokees, in accord with the law made by the Assembly there in Dec. of last year, it fell to us not only to inform our dear missionaries of this but also to recommend to them the requisite wisdom and prudence not to meddle in political affairs in the slightest and to refrain from everything contrary to the Georgia laws, e.g., those about teaching Negroes to read in the Sunday schools, etc., with the request to keep us informed about all developments in the Cherokee Nation which have a bearing on any change in their situation.

We also recommended to them that in case of a genuine decision of the Nation for Removal they should prepare themselves, and in regard to the movable and unmovable property of the mission, to draw attention to the compensation we would expect for that and to seek to find out their prospects for that.

Not only that, but we often spoke urgently at this time about the situation of this work of the Lord itself which is ongoing among this Nation, about this and its missionaries also, and in several services the entire Congregation was encouraged to share in concern and sympathy with them.

Added to this is the fact that recently the Government Agent in the Cherokee Nation, H. Montgomery, forwarded a letter of the War Secretary to the Chief, Mr. John Ross, for public announcement in which a definite answer was demanded from the Cherokees as to whether they wanted to remain under the jurisdiction of Georgia or move to the West. In the first case, they were not to count further on the protection of the President or the G[enera]l Government, but they must expect to be treated according to the laws of Georgia. In the latter case [removal] they would be assured of the further protection of the Government, and they could learn more from the President in Nashville, who finds himself there at present.

Of this the last letters received from Brn. G. Byhan and Clauder, dated the 11th and the 8th, gave us a report, with the addition that the Cherokee Nation on the 12th of July was called together to a General Council for deliberation and drafting the required decision. At the same time they stated that their situation with that of the whole nation was precarious, unfortunate, and dark for the future. What the Nation would decide, they [the missionaries] did not know. According to some expressions they do not want to come under Georgia's laws, but neither do they want to migrate, and would rather let themselves be destroyed. They seemed also to want to get the thoughts of the United States Supreme Court concerning the validity of the various treaties which they have had up to now with the General Government, which have all been ratified and paid heed to in the Senate of the United States and by the Presidents up to the present. And if then they must go, they do not want to remain under the protection of the United States Government but to go somewhere else.

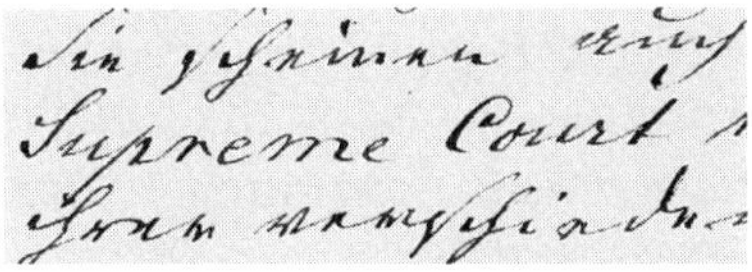


In this dilemma our dear Missionaries feel very much in need of counsel, but trust in a childlike way in the further support of the Lord.

As gladly as we would come to their assistance with advice, for the present we can do nothing more than what has been done up to now and what has been reported about them so far, until the Cherokee Nation comes to a further decision. Should our baptized members, who belong to the civilized part of the Nation, still remain under Georgia jurisdiction, it would then be determined whether one of the missionaries can remain among them. And if they should decide to move to the Arkansas, then our Brn. and Srs. would be advised to keep together as much as possible, and in our view the best thing would be if they were accompanied by our missionaries. If their migration, which is not expected, is to Mexico or outside the United States where the Catholic Religion is predominant, the continuation of the mission would hardly be feasible.

In any case, our dear missionaries must persevere patiently there, and if they are asked, they should neither advise the Cherokees either to this or to that course, but rather leave all to their conviction and to the leading of God. They should encourage their baptized members to faithful trust in the Lord and to childlike prayer and to continue as before in the recommended cautious way of proceeding. It still seemed advisable to us to request them to consult some of the more insightful Cherokees who have come to their notice about one of our preachers becoming a member of the New York society which has come together to encourage the Indians to migrate to the West. It should be explained that this would not be from any hostile point of view, but rather would be looking out for what is best for them, in that another of our preachers, on the contrary, is a member of the other society there which is working to support the opposite course for the Indian Nations.

Br. Gb. Byhan, who on several grounds, and especially on account of his wife's illness, has requested a leave of absence until the end of next year, is to be encouraged in the name of the Conferenz to hold out in Springplace until a fuller resolution of the current crisis has been reached. To our joy and their encouragement, they are planning on the 11th to hold the baptism of two adults, and Br. Clauder from Oochgelogy is also planning to attend.

# *Glossary-Index*

For the most part, sources for this glossary-index are:

*Records of the Moravians among the Cherokees* (*Records: Cherokees*), volumes 1-8;

*Records of the Moravians in North Carolina* (*Records: N.C.*), translated and edited by Adelaide L. Fries and Douglas LeTell Rights (Raleigh: State Department of Archives and History, 1954, v. 8 (1823-1837), https://archive.org/search.php?query=moravians%20north%20carolina;

"Catalogue of Scholars at Springplace, Cherokee Country, 1804-1842," unpublished ms., Moravian Archives, Bethlehem, Pa., box 197, folder 5;

*Dienerblätter*, multivolume set containing brief biographical sketches of every known servant of the Moravian Church; compiled by the Unity Archives in Herrnhut, Saxony;

*Periodical Accounts Relating to the Missions of the Church of the United Brethren* (London: Brethren's Society for the Furtherance of the Gospel among the Heathen) v. XI, 1829-1831, https://catalog.hathitrust.org/Record/100432371;

McClinton, Rowena, *The Moravian Springplace Mission to the Cherokees* (Lincoln, Neb., and London: University of Nebraska Press: 2007);

Phillips, Joyce B. and Paul Gary Phillips, *The Brainerd Journal, a Mission to the Cherokees, 1817-1823* (Lincoln, Neb., and London: University of Nebraska Press, 1998);

Moulton, Gary E., ed., *The Papers of Chief John Ross* (Norman, Okla.: University of Oklahoma Press, 1985);

Schultze, Augustus, *Guide to the Old Moravian Cemetery of Bethlehem, Pa., 1742-1910* (Lancaster, Pa., 1912);

Kluge, Edw. T., "The Moravian Graveyards at Nazareth, Pa., 1744-1904," *Transactions of the Moravian Historical Society*, 7:3 (Bethlehem, Pa.: Times Publishing Co., 1904);

Beck, Abraham Reinke, "The Moravian Graveyards of Lititz, Pa., 1744-1905," *Transactions of the Moravian Historical Society*, 7:4 (Bethlehem, Pa.: Times Publishing Co., 1905);
Levering, Joseph Mortimer, A History of Bethlehem, Pennsylvania, 1741-*1892* (Bethlehem, Pa.: Times Publishing Co., 1903).

Many thanks to Jack D. Baker and David Hampton of the Cherokee Nation for their assistance in sorting out Cherokee relationships. Any errors in this glossary-index are strictly my own.

Richard W. Starbuck
January 6, 2018

**— A —**

## — C —

## — D —

— E —

— H —

**— I —**

— **M** —

**— Q —**



**— R —**

— S —

## — T —

**— U —**



**— V —**

**— W —**

— Y —



— Z —



*Records of the Moravians among the Cherokees* was compiled and edited on Microsoft Word computer program. Printed and bound by Thomson-Shore, Inc., Dexter, Michigan.